# SUBMARINES

# SUBMARINES

## AN ILLUSTRATED HISTORY
## OF THEIR IMPACT

Paul E. Fontenoy

A B C ❖ C L I O

Santa Barbara, California • Denver, Colorado • Oxford, England

Copyright 2007 by ABC-CLIO

Library of Congress Cataloging-in-Publication Data

Fontenoy, Paul E.
Submarines : an illustrated history of their impact / Paul E. Fontenoy.
p.    cm. — (Encyclopedias of weapons and warfare series)
Includes bibliographical references and index.
ISBN-13: 978-1-85109-563-6 (hard cover : alk. paper)
ISBN-13: 978-1-85109-568-1 (ebook)
1. Submarines (Ships)—History.    I. Title.

V857.F65 2007
359.9'3—dc22
                                        2006039316


11  10  09  08  07  /  10  9  8  7  6  5  4  3  2  1

This book is also available on the World Wide Web as an eBook.
Visit abc-clio.com for details.

ABC-CLIO, Inc.
130 Cremona Drive, P.O. Box 1911
Santa Barbara, California 93116-1911

Senior Production Editor, Cami Cacciatore
Editorial Assistant, Sara Springer
Production Manager, Don Schmidt
Media Manager, Caroline Price
Media Editor, J. R. Withers
File Management Coordinator, Paula Gerard

This book is printed on acid-free paper. ∞
Manufactured in the United States of America

# CONTENTS

# INTRODUCTION TO
# WEAPONS AND WARFARE SERIES

WEAPONS BOTH FASCINATE AND REPEL. They are used to kill and maim individuals and to destroy states and societies, and occasionally whole civilizations, and with these the greatest of man's cultural and artistic accomplishments. Throughout history tools of war have been the instruments of conquest, invasion, and enslavement, but they have also been used to check evil and to maintain peace.

Weapons have evolved over time to become both more lethal and more complex. For the greater part of human existence, combat was fought at the length of an arm or at such short range as to represent no real difference; battle was fought within line of sight and seldom lasted more than the hours of daylight of a single day. Thus individual weapons that began with the rock and the club proceeded through the sling and boomerang, bow and arrow, sword and axe, to gunpowder weapons of the rifle and machine gun of the late nineteenth century. Study of the evolution of these weapons tells us much about human ingenuity, the technology of the time, and the societies that produced them. The greater part of technological development of weaponry has taken part in the last two centuries, especially the twentieth century. In this process, plowshares have been beaten into swords; the tank, for example, evolved from the agricultural caterpillar tractor. Occasionally, the process is reversed and military technology has impacted society in a positive way. Thus modern civilian medicine has greatly benefited from advances to save soldiers' lives, and weapons technology has impacted such areas as civilian transportation or atomic power.

Weapons can have a profound impact on society. Gunpowder weapons, for example, were an important factor in ending the era of the armed knight and the Feudal Age. They installed a kind of rough democracy on the battlefield, making "all men alike tall." We can only wonder what effect weapons of mass destruction (WMD) might have on our own time and civilization.

This series will trace the evolution of a variety of key weapons systems, describe the major changes that occurred in each, and illustrate and identify the key types. Each volume begins with a description of the particular weapons system and traces its evolution, while discussing its historical, social, and political contexts. This is followed by a heavily illustrated section that is arranged more or less along chronological lines that provides more precise information on at least eighty key variants of that particular weapons system. Each volume contains a glossary of terms, a bibliography of leading books on that particular subject, and an index.

Individual volumes in the series, each written by a specialist in that particular area of expertise, are as follows:

Aircraft Carriers
Ancient Weapons
Artillery
Ballistic Missiles
Battleships
Cruisers and Battle Cruisers
Destroyers
Helicopters
Machine Guns
Medieval Weapons
Military Aircraft, Origins to 1918
Military Aircraft, 1919–1945
Military Aircraft in the Jet Age
Pistols
Rifles
Submarines
Tanks

We hope that this series will be of wide interest to specialists, researchers, and even general readers.

*Spencer C. Tucker*
Series Editor

# PREFACE

FROM THE ADVENT OF THE EARLIEST of the type, submarine design has always pressed against the outer limits of the contemporary technological envelope. Inventors and engineers have, of necessity, incorporated new and untested machinery and equipment into their craft in order to meet their goals of creating effective undersea vessels. The underwater environment, moreover, is unforgiving; errors in operation or failures of equipment have very dangerous and even fatal consequences. Success in submarine design, therefore, has come to those naval architects who have combined innovation and experimentation with substantial direct, prior experience or knowledge.

The obvious potential military advantages of the stealthy and lethal capabilities of successful submarines soon attracted the attention of admiralties around the world. Early designers of practical craft found a relatively ready market for their wares, either through export or license construction by their customers. Designs by the German Wilhelm Bauer were constructed in Germany and Russia, while George Garrett's boats, built by the Swedish industrialist Thorsten Nordenfeldt in Sweden and Britain, were marketed to Greece, Turkey, and Russia. Beginning in the years around 1900, boats by Maxime Laubeuf in France, the Italian Cesare Laurenti, and above all, John P. Holland in the United States, found ready markets in navies around the world in the years before World War I.

The maturation of submarines as a result of operations during World War I expanded the global demand for the type. Design teams with successful records dominated this worldwide arms market. Firms from Britain, France, Germany, Italy, and the United States prevailed in this trade in submarines. In the German case, since indigenous submarine design and construction had been prohibited by the Versailles Treaty, the design teams established themselves across the border in the Netherlands and contracted out construction to yards in other European countries. A similar situation pertained after World War II, although Italian designs, no longer on the cutting edge, faded from the export market, while the emphasis on nuclear propulsion in the United States led that nation to withdraw from overseas sales to avoid the distribution of sensitive technologies. Its place was taken by substantial export of both vessels and designs by the Soviet Union, the resurgence of the German submarine industry, and the maturing of Swedish design and construction.

To more accurately reflect the sources of the global distribution of submarines, I have chosen to organize the reference sections by the national origins of the various designs rather than by the navies that operated them (national operators are indicated thus: [Norway]). This focus on the design origins overrides consideration of construction location; for example, submarine construction began in both the Netherlands and Sweden before World War I but neither nation produced many truly indigenous designs until well after the war's end. This approach allows readers more readily to comprehend both the extent of design distribution to the various operators and the evolution of submarine designs within specific national contexts.

# CHAPTER ONE

# Early Submarines

EARLY SUBMARINES, IN GENERAL, were the products of individual innovators who pursued their obsessions with creating practical underwater craft independent of governments or navies. Their designs usually came to fruition despite the lack of any perceived need for their development—indeed, quite often it was in the face of opposition that these craft saw the light of day. This phenomenon contrasts dramatically with the developmental story of the aircraft carrier, that other most revolutionary warship of the twentieth century, whose features and evolution invariably reflected official concepts and requirements. Furthermore, the influence of individual designers' innovative ideas on submarine development was to persist strongly throughout much of the type's history.

While suggestions for various "diving boats" had been put forward on occasion from the time of Alexander the Great, the first designer to produce a vessel that successfully traveled underwater seems to have been Cornelius Drebbel, a Dutchman serving as court inventor to King James I. His boat, propelled by twelve oarsmen, made a submerged voyage along the River Thames at London in 1623. Unfortunately, while eyewitnesses described the event, they gave no indication of how Drebbel's boat functioned.

During the eighteenth and nineteenth centuries, designers in Russia were prolific in projecting submarine boats, although quite a few of the proposals from that period were conceptual rather than actual. Czar Peter I supported Yefim Nikonov's proposal for a submarine armed with rocket missiles, leading to the completion of a prototype in June 1720. Its trials were sufficiently successful to support orders for further boats, but problems with their leaking, and the death of Peter in January 1725, led to the project's abandonment.

The next Russian project came to fruition over a century later, when Engineer-General Karl Andreyevich Shilder's iron submersible was completed by Ivan Fedorovich Aleksandrovskiy's yard at St. Petersburg in May 1834. After trials, a larger version was constructed that Shilder used to destroy a target vessel with a towed mine in July 1838. Trials continued until the fall of 1841, when Shilder was ordered to terminate the project.

Wilhelm Bauer, a former noncommissioned officer in the Bavarian Army, was one of the archetypical submarine designers of the latter half of the nineteenth century. Between 1850 and his death in 1875, Bauer generated several submarine designs that he attempted to sell to governments in Germany, France, the United Kingdom, Russia, Austria, and the United States. His prototype was constructed at August Howaldt's Kiel shipyard. The *Brandtaucher* was deployed briefly during the First Schleswig War and caused the Danish Fleet blockading Kiel to move farther off shore; however, when Bauer demonstrated it to the public on 1 February 1851, it sank in the harbor, without loss of life. The wreck was recovered in 1887 and is now exhibited in the Deutsches Armeemuseum at Potsdam. Bauer produced an enlarged and improved design that he promoted, unsuccessfully, to the Bavarian, Austrian, and British governments. Eventually, however, largely because of the outbreak of the Crimean War, he attracted the support of the Russian Grand Duke Konstantin Nikolaevich, leading to the construction of his design by the Leuchtemburg Works at St. Petersburg and its acceptance by the Russian Admiralty as the *Diable Marin* on 2 November 1855. His submarine, driven by a single propeller powered by a crew working treadmills geared to the shaft, was remarkably successful. It made 134 dives between May and October of 1856, including one four-hour mission on 6 September for the coronation festivities of the new czar, Aleksandr II, during which a four-piece brass ensemble played while underwater, being clearly audible on the surface. Nevertheless, although Bauer continued to receive support from the grand duke for designing an even larger boat, the Admiralty was less enthusiastic, leading him to leave Russia in frustration during the spring of 1858. He returned to Germany and continued promoting his designs, without success, until his death on 20 June 1875.

The Crimean War also stimulated the development of indigenous submarine projects in Russia. Several naval officers put forward suggestions for submarines to be deployed in defense of Sevastopol, though there is no evidence that any were built. Major General Konstantin Borisov Gern also proposed a series of submarine designs for boats to defend Russian Baltic ports and managed to interest the war ministry in constructing at least three different craft between 1855 and 1871. His final design was steam powered and carried a self-propelled torpedo, but, after initially successful trials, the ministry lost interest. Aleksandrovskiy, whose shipyard had built Shilder's boat in 1834, also designed a large 355-ton submarine that was completed by the Baltic Works at St. Petersburg in May 1866. Powered by two 70-horsepower compressed-air engines, it also used compressed air to evacuate the ballast tank and incorporated an airlock through which divers could exit to place its mine armament against its targets. It ran extensive trials until 1871, when a 100-foot dive exceeded its crush limits and the hull collapsed. Aleksandrovskiy proposed at least two further designs, although no construction ensued.

Grand Duke Konstantin also gave his support to the Polish-born engineer Stefan K. Drzewiecki's submarine projects. Again, conflict provided the immediate impetus, in this instance the outbreak of the Russo-Turkish War of 1877. Drzewiecki built and tested two successive designs for small, man-powered submersibles that led to the construction of a series of 50 production units for the war ministry by the Nevskiy Shipbuilding and Machinery Works at St. Petersburg between 1879 and 1881. The army deployed these craft in the defense of Kronshtadt and Sevastopol until they were transferred to the navy in 1885, whereupon they were discarded as ineffective. Drzewiecki himself moved to France in 1887, where he proposed several semisubmersible designs for the French Fleet, none of which were built, and also developed his very successful drop-collar torpedo launch system that saw extensive use on both French and Russian submarines into the 1920s.

Russian interest in submarines revived in the 1890s, leading to the establishment of a special submarine committee on 19 December 1900, headed by Ivan Grigorevich Bubnov. It evaluated both foreign and native designs and by June 1901 had produced an indigenous design that was constructed as the *Delfin*. Bubnov went on to design a series of submarines for the Imperial Russian Navy, culminating with the *Bars* class, laid down immediately before World War I.

U.S. inventors also were prolific producers of submarine proposals. David Bushnell's *Turtle* made the first (abortive) attack on a surface ship, when Sergeant Ezra Lee of the Continental Army used it in an attempt to attach an explosive charge to the British 64-gun ship *Eagle* in New York harbor on 7 September 1776. Robert Fulton, famous later for his success with steam-propelled vessels, built a submarine, the *Nautilus,* at Paris in 1800 that he successfully demonstrated to the French government. He hoped to sell the boat—copper skinned over iron frames and driven by a hand-cranked propeller while submerged—but was rebuffed and sold the craft for scrap. Two other U.S. submarines apparently were on occasion operated during the War of 1812. Among other submarines proposed or built subsequently were two by the Indiana shoemaker Lodner D. Phillips, the second of which succeeded in diving to 100 feet in 1852. Phillips offered his boat to the U.S. Navy but was rejected; he was turned down again when he offered to build another submarine at the outbreak of the Civil War in 1861.

Nevertheless, the Civil War stimulated unofficial interest in submarines in both the Union and the Confederacy. At least three Northern projects saw fruition. The first, the *Alligator,* was the brainchild of Brutus de Villeroi, a French immigrant inventor who, in 1859, had built a submarine for a Philadelphia treasure-hunting consortium. (Before coming to the United States, de Villeroi had taught mathematics in France. His students, it seems, included Jules Verne, whose 1870 novel *Twenty Thousand Leagues under the Sea* greatly popularized the notion of submarines.) De Villeroi's earlier project still was extant in 1861 when war came and he staged a dramatic demonstration in Philadelphia harbor—during which he and the submarine were arrested—to promote his concepts.

The *Alligator* was built for the U.S. Navy by the Philadelphia Navy Yard and commissioned in May 1862. After ineffective service on the James and Appomattox rivers (the waters there were too shallow), the boat was refitted at Washington Navy Yard and dispatched to engage in operations off Charleston, South Carolina. While under tow to the war zone, the *Alligator* foundered in a storm off the North Carolina Outer Banks on 2 April 1863; its wreck is currently the subject of a major search.

Also vying for a navy contract was Julius Kroehl, a German immigrant engineer who had considerable experience working with diving bells. Kroehl built his design as a private venture after de Villeroi won the official contract, but his boat was still incomplete at the end of the war. He succeeded, however, in selling both his *Sub Marine Explorer* and his own expertise to the Pacific Pearl Company in 1866 as a platform for exploiting the prolific pearl oyster beds off the Panamanian Pacific coast, where it operated for three years. The abandoned craft was found close inshore in 2000 and currently is under active archaeological investigation.

The third Northern boat, the *Intelligent Whale,* was built by the American Submarine Company, a group of speculators who planned to use it as a privateer. When that plan failed and the U.S. Navy declined to accept the boat, construction slowed and it was not completed until 1866. In 1872 the navy eventually agreed to undertake trials of the *Intelligent Whale,* which it failed, and the submarine was abandoned. It still survives, however, and is on exhibit at the National Guard Militia Museum of New Jersey at Sea Girt.

Inventors in the Confederacy also produced several submarines, the best known being James R. McClintock's series of boats, initially built as private venture privateers. The first, the *Pioneer,* was built for Horace L. Hunley's New Orleans privateering consortium but was scuttled before becoming operational when the city fell to the Union in April 1862. McClintock then built the *Pioneer II* at Mobile. Efforts to make first an electric motor and then a steam plant functional both failed, and McClintock had to revert to a hand-cranked propeller to drive his boat. The *Pioneer II* was not a great success, and it sank while being towed to attack the Union Fleet off Fort Monroe. The expanded consortium constructed a third boat, the *H.L. Hunley,* whose trials proved more successful; its transfer in July of 1863 to Charleston, South Carolina, led to its proposed use to break the Union blockade by General P. G. T. Beauregard, the local commander. The Confederate Navy, reluctant to trust the abilities or enthusiasm of the boat's civilian crew, seized it and manned it with naval personnel. An accident drowned five of its crew on 30 August, and another on 15 October drowned the entire replacement crew, including Hunley himself. The boat finally went into action on the night of 17 February 1864, sinking the steam sloop *Housatonic,* but it failed to return. The novelist Clive Cussler funded an expedition that located the wreck of the *H.L. Hunley* in May 1995. It was raised in August 2000 and is currently undergoing conservation in Charleston.

In addition to a series of semisubmersible spar torpedo boats, known as Davids, for the Confederate Navy, the South produced several other submarines. Little is known about the origins of a boat built at New Orleans in June 1861, although it is most probably the vessel that was found during dredging operations there in 1879; it is now on exhibit at the Louisiana State Museum in the city. The Tredegar Ironworks at Richmond, Virginia, built at least one boat to a design by William Cheeney. After successful trials on the James River in October 1861, it was sunk while attacking a Union ship in Hampton Roads the following month. John Halligan designed a submarine, the *St. Patrick,* which was built at the Selma Navy Yard for the Confederate Navy and commissioned in January 1865. It made an abortive attack on the gunboat *Octorara* on 27 January and most probably was scuttled in April when the war came to an end.

The U.S. Navy, especially after its unhappy experiences with first the *Alligator* and then the *Intelligent Whale,* expressed no interest in submarines, but that did not deter private inventors. The most successful and influential of them was John P. Holland, an Irish immigrant who single-mindedly pursued the creation of a practical submarine for 40 years from 1874, submitting in that year a design for a one-man submarine to the navy. It was rejected, but Holland found financial backing from the Fenian Brotherhood, an organization working for Irish independence that saw the potential for submarines in overturning the Royal Navy's supremacy and forcing Britain to give up its rule of Ireland. He built a gasoline-engine-powered prototype (*Holland I*) in 1878, followed by the larger *Fenian Ram* in 1881. After two years of meticulous trials in New York Harbor, the Fenian Brotherhood, frustrated by Holland's perfectionism, seized the boat and moved it to New Haven, Connecticut. It eventually was exhibited in Holland's hometown of Paterson, New Jersey, where it remains today. Holland, meanwhile, formed a new partnership, the Nautilus Submarine Boat Company, with a group led by Edmund L. Zalinsky, a U.S. Army artillery officer. Using additional data gleaned from a half-size boat (*Holland III*) he had built while the *Fenian Ram* was undergoing trials, Holland developed a new submarine armed with Zalinsky's dynamite gun (*Holland IV*). A botched launching on 4 September 1885 sank the new boat, but it was raised, repaired, and tested. The partnership was unable to find a purchaser for its submarine, however, and the company folded by the winter of 1886.

An open U.S. Navy competition for submarine designs in 1888 revived Holland's hopes. His design was judged the best, but his sponsoring shipbuilder—the William Cramp and Sons Ship and Engine Building Company at Philadelphia—declined to guarantee its performance and the contract was canceled. He won a second competition the following year, only to see that contract also canceled, when President Benjamin Harrison's new secretary of the navy, Benjamin F. Tracy, transferred the funds to surface ship projects. Congress again funded a submarine in 1893 and Holland's design once more won the competition, but it was not until 1895 that the John P.

Holland Torpedo Boat Company received a contract to build the *Plunger* for the U.S. Navy. Official requirements included steam propulsion and a triple screw arrangement, both of which Holland correctly anticipated would cause problems.

While the *Plunger* was still being built, the company began construction of a private venture boat, the *Holland VI*, that more accurately reflected Holland's concept of a submarine to meet the navy's needs. This boat proved itself one of the most successful submarines yet built; it attracted much foreign attention and eventually was purchased by the U.S. Navy on 11 April 1900 and commissioned as the *Holland*. The costs of testing and perfecting it, however, forced Holland to seek additional capital, leading to the incorporation of his firm in 1899 into the Electric Boat Company as a subsidiary. He became the company's general manager but soon was demoted to chief engineer and learned that ownership of his patents, both U.S. and international, had passed to the Electric Boat Company. He resigned from the firm on 28 March 1904, even as his improved Holland VII design became a spectacular success: 24 examples served with the U.S., British, Russian, Japanese, and Dutch fleets, and provided the starting point for further major development in those countries and Austria-Hungary. Only two further boats designed by Holland himself were constructed, for Japan, before he died on 12 August 1914. The Electric Boat Company, in the meantime, went on to dominate the design of submarines for the U.S. Navy until after the end of World War I and continued as a major exporter of both vessels and designs.

Holland was not without rivals for submarine work. In 1885, Josiah H. L. Tuck constructed a submarine that used caustic soda to generate heat for a boiler that provided steam to its engine. The *Peacemaker* had a submerged endurance of five hours and participated in the U.S. Navy's 1888 and 1889 competitions. Tuck's family, fearing that he had squandered most of his fortune on his experiments, had him committed to an insane asylum soon afterward. Holland also faced competition from George C. Baker in 1893. Not only did Baker have a full-size submarine to demonstrate (Holland was quite complimentary about its use of swiveling propellers amidships and the incorporation of a clutch that allowed the steam engine to charge the batteries while running on the surface) but he also was well connected in Washington, which accounted for a good part of the delay in awarding the contract to Holland.

Holland's most serious competitor, however, was Simon Lake, who adopted a very different approach to submarine operation.

Holland designed his submarines to operate underwater with a small net positive buoyancy and to dive, maintain depth, and surface using the dynamic forces generated by the motion of water over the stern diving planes. His main ballast tanks filled completely upon submerging to achieve stability by eliminating free-surface motion and maintaining a fixed center of gravity amidships. This formula made his boats safe and maneuverable underwater but also made them slow to dive. Lake relied on a combination of ballast adjustment to control buoyancy—using several tanks and pumps—and multiple diving planes to control depth. His submarines dived and rose on a level keel. Lake's formula made his submarines potentially less safe and less hydrodynamically efficient than Holland's, but also much faster divers. Lake's early submarines (*Argonaut I* and *II*) also incorporated diver's airlocks and wheels for movement on the seabed, largely because he initially conceived his craft for salvage operations. They were not successful at first in attracting interest from the U.S. Navy but were exported to Russia and Austria-Hungary. His designs, in the absence of adequate patent protection, were also thoroughly exploited by Krupp's Germania shipyard and its submarine designer, Raimondo Lorenzo D'Equevilley-Montjustin, in producing its first boats, supplied to the Russian, German, Austro-Hungarian, and Norwegian fleets. Lake obtained his first domestic contract in 1909 and continued to build a relatively small number of boats for the U.S. Navy until his firm went out of business in 1924.

The French Navy was the most enthusiastic advocate of submarines prior to 1900. Its first boat, the *Plongeur,* was designed by Charles Brun and Siméon Bourgeois, entering service in 1867. It used an 80-horsepower compressed-air engine for propulsion and relied on small stern diving planes and an elaborate water transfer system, also compressed-air operated, to maintain position. This system proved ineffective, and the *Plongeur* soon was set aside. Electric propulsion underwater seemed a superior solution and was demonstrated by Claude Goubet in two small private venture boats that otherwise were unsuccessful. The French Navy's return to submarine construction was also all-electric. The *Gymnôte,* designed by Gustave Zédé, entered service in 1888 and was followed by Gaston Romazzotti's *Gustave Zédé* five years later. Both boats were largely experimental, relied wholly on batteries without onboard recharge equipment to power their electric motors (severely restricting their range), and required many modifications, especially to their diving plane arrangements, to become effective.

In 1898 the French Navy announced an open international submarine design competition. Maxime Laubeuf's design, the *Narval*, was the winner, and, although many of the boat's features were short-lived, it established the essential characteristics of the vast majority of the world's naval submarines until the end of World War II. Laubeuf designed the *Narval* as a double-hulled craft; the inner hull was strongly constructed to resist water pressure, while the outer hull was lightly built and optimized for surface performance. The space between the hulls accommodated ballast and trim tanks. The *Narval*, like almost all submarines for the next 50 years, was essentially a surface torpedo boat that could submerge to attack and make its escape. Like many French submarines of the next 25 years, it was steam powered: the French Navy was uncomfortable with using gasoline engines in submarines because of the explosion hazard. In 1904 the *Aigrette* became the first submarine to be fitted with a diesel engine, and with few exceptions all later French submarines used either diesel or steam plants. Steam engines remained attractive because France did not have access to sufficiently powerful diesel engines for its large boats.

The Royal Navy came late to submarine operation, and much of its early design development built upon experience with Holland's boats. There had, however, been an earlier native effort in submarine design. In 1878, George W. Garrett built a small submarine (*Resurgam*) driven by a hand-cranked propeller, and he followed it the next year with a larger steam-powered craft. The *Resurgam II* relied on the retained superheated steam in its boiler to power its engine while submerged. Garrett had not fully solved his boat's longitudinal stability problems, but it nevertheless attracted the attention of the Swedish industrialist Thorsten Nordenfelt, who contracted with AB Palmcrants and Company in Stockholm to build an enlarged version of the *Resurgam*. Known as the *Nordenfelt I*, it was purchased by the Greek Navy in 1886 at a time of considerable tension over the status of Macedonia. In response the Turkish government ordered two larger boats of similar type that were delivered in 1887, one of which, the *Abdul Hamid*, was the first submarine to launch a self-propelled torpedo while submerged. The final Garrett-designed boat, the *Nordenfelt IV*, was built for Russia in 1887 at the Barrow-in-Furness yard, which would later become the most prolific producer of submarines in the United Kingdom. *Nordenfelt IV* ran aground off the Danish coast while on its delivery voyage and was lost.

British submarine design took a decisive turn away from Holland's concepts with the development of the D class, which entered service in 1908. These much larger boats introduced saddle tanks for ballast and marked the British shift to long-range craft optimized for surface operation and seaworthiness. They set the pattern for subsequent British development that was broken only by the R class, built as antisubmarine platforms and optimized for underwater performance, which entered service very late in World War I. The only other deviation was the manifestation of a fixation for "fleet submarines"—boats fast enough to accompany the battlefleet while on the surface and operate as stealth torpedo boats upon contacting the enemy. The J class was essentially a normal British type fitted with greatly increased engine power. The K class used steam turbines to generate the speed required, but it proved appallingly dangerous and difficult to operate.

Despite Bauer's early work and the considerable effort expended on submarines in both Russia and France in the later nineteenth century, there was little German interest in the type until the dawn of the twentieth century. The Krupp industrial conglomerate, however, saw the potential for a new market and began working aggressively to stimulate it. It began by building a small boat designed by a Spanish engineer, Raimondo Lorenzo D'Equevilley-Montjustin, whose ideas owed much to Nordenfelt's submarines. His *Forelle* proved moderately successful but did not attract German naval attention. Fortunately for Krupp, lack of U.S. Navy interest in his designs led Simon Lake to turn to Europe as a market for his boats. He attempted to negotiate a license arrangement with Krupp, in the process transferring much of his design information to the firm as an inducement. The deal fell through, but Krupp retained the data; D'Equevilley exploited this knowledge to produce a very competent design that found buyers in Russia, Norway, Austria-Hungary, and Germany. This activity stimulated official interest, leading the Torpedo Department of the Imperial German Navy to set up the Unterseebootkonstruktionsbüro in 1904, led by Gustave Berling; it developed its own somewhat similar submarine design, which went into production in 1907.

The departure of the non-German D'Equevilley and his replacement by Hans Techel on 1 July 1907, opened the way for cooperation between Krupp and the navy and rapid design development in the years before World War I. The result was technical improvement and growth in size and capabilities, although it is notable that the navy was slow to adopt diesel engines in place of gasoline or oil engines.

During World War I the Imperial German Navy accepted some 100 new boats of the Mobilization type, a largely standardized design subject to continual improvements culminating in the Mittel-U type, which proved very capable. These standard submarines were supplemented by mass-produced coastal boats particularly suited to the geographic advantage of operating from Flanders against enemy shipping from 1915. The UB series of conventional submarines evolved, from very small UB-I boats of 127 tons with 14-man crews, to the 516-ton UB-III boats that were essentially diminutives of the Mittel-U type. The parallel UC series of coastal minelaying submarines followed a similar evolutionary path. In addition, the navy also commissioned a few full-size minelayers and a series of very large, long-range boats, the U-cruisers.

Both Italy and Sweden began indigenous submarine design and construction virtually contemporaneously with similar developments in Germany. Italian submarine development was dominated by the concepts of Cesare Laurenti, whose designs conformed to the submersible torpedo boat school propounded by Laubeuf. The Swedish Navy sent one of its designers, Carl Richson, on a mission to study overseas submarine design and construction. Upon his return he began development of his own boats, drawing heavily on Holland principles at first but soon trending more toward submersible-type craft.

## ALLIED SUBMARINE OPERATIONS DURING WORLD WAR I

At the outbreak of World War I, the British and French navies were by far the two largest operators of submarines in the world, each possessing more than twice as many as the German Fleet. The Russian Fleet had a relatively long tradition of submarine operation, but its force was small and divided between the Baltic and Black seas. Like all the world's navies, they had no clear doctrines for the use of their submarine forces, nor any real appreciation of the directions that wartime operations would take.

The main British submarine force was deployed as the 8th (Overseas) Submarine Flotilla, with the most modern, long-range boats at Harwich. Its primary role was offensive patrol and reconnaissance off the German coast. The older, short-range vessels were deployed to Grimsby, Dover, and Portsmouth, to provide coastal defense patrols along the eastern and southern coasts. French submarines were deployed in the Channel and, initially, in a defensive barrier to cover the movement of troops from North Africa to Metropolitan France.

The British overseas submarines undertook patrols in the Helgoland Bight from the outset, bringing back useful information about the German Fleet's movements. Several attempts were made to employ submarines in conjunction with surface units during sweeps intended to trap and destroy elements of the High Seas Fleet, but none were very successful. Patrol lines intended to ambush German Fleet units became a regular feature of British North Sea submarine operation throughout the war. They had some successes and caused the Germans to exercise caution in their operations, but overall they were relatively unproductive.

Russia had eight active submarines in the Baltic, of which only one was capable of more than short-range operation. The Admiralty decided to send submarines to the Baltic to support Russian operations and to attack the ore traffic from Sweden to Germany. In October 1914, two submarines, the E-1 and the E-9, passed through the Danish Straits and arrived at Lapvik to commence operations. German antisubmarine activity forced a third submarine to return. They undertook several patrols in conjunction with Russian submarines before the onset of winter ended operations.

Baltic submarine operations resumed in late April. The E-9, commanded by Lieutenant-Commander Max Horton, gained the first success by sinking the collier Dora Hugo Stennes and severely damaging the destroyer S-148 on 5 June 1915. The British sent four additional submarines to the Baltic in August, one of which ran aground off Copenhagen and was destroyed; the others successfully joined operations. The E-1, commanded by Lieutenant-Commander Noel Laurence, damaged the battlecruiser Von der Tann on 19 August; the E-8 destroyed the armored cruiser Prinz Adalbert on 23 October; and the E-19 sank the light cruiser Undine on 7 November. In addition, British and Russian submarines sank or captured 17 freighters and caused 4 more to strand. These operations, especially against German warships, caused considerable disruption of German operations in the Baltic during the year and prompted the Swedish Navy to begin convoying its shipping.

In response to the depredations of Allied submarines in 1915, the German commander-in-chief, Grossadmiral Prinz Heinrich von Preussen, introduced escorted convoy of shipping between Sweden and Germany. That proved very successful: only five freighters were lost, despite intensive Allied submarine activity, while one British submarine sank after hitting a mine. The British sent another four small submarines to the Baltic in August via Arkhangel'sk, but they were not operational until early October; they undertook only one patrol before ice ended operations.

During 1917, Allied submarines were heavily engaged in an attempt to hinder German advances into the Gulf of Riga, in which they were largely unsuccessful. Only a single freighter was sunk during that year, while one British and three Russian submarines were lost. In addition, German advances led to the scuttling of four Russian and seven British submarines to prevent them from falling into enemy hands.

The Anglo-French assault on the Dardanelles in April 1915 prompted both navies to send submarines into the Sea of Marmora to attack Turkish shipping and warships supporting the defenders. A total of 13 submarines attempted the passage, but only five succeeded in reaching their goal, four from each navy being lost. The submarines sank the battleship *Barbarossa,* the coast defense ship *Messudiyeh,* 6 smaller warships, 55 merchant ships, and 148 sailing vessels, although some of those subsequently were salved. Russian submarines also operated against Turkish shipping in the Black Sea with some success. The submarine *Nerpa* was particularly successful: on 5 September, operating with two destroyers, it wiped out a Turkish convoy of five ships by driving them ashore where the destroyers shelled them to destruction.

Russian operations continued against Turkish and German shipping in the Black Sea throughout 1916 and 1917, right up to the time of the Russian Revolution. Although the number of vessels they sank was relatively small, their operations caused considerable disruption of vital traffic, especially coal deliveries. By the end of 1916, the shortage of coal was such that the Turkish Fleet at Istanbul had been essentially immobilized. The Russians never deployed more than ten submarines in the Black Sea: they carried out well over 250 patrols during 1916 and 1917, with the loss of only one boat.

France deployed submarines to the Adriatic in 1914, losing the *Curie* on 8 December in an attempt to penetrate the Austrian base at Pola. After Italy entered the war, 6 French submarines joined some 20 Italian boats in operations in the Adriatic. Both sides in the Adriatic conducted a campaign of hit-and-run raids and ambushes throughout much of the war. Allied submarines played a major role in these operations, but overall their successes were very limited: a half-dozen small warships and fewer than 50 merchant vessels, for the loss of 12 of their own number.

Allied submarines also took part in the antisubmarine campaign. Between May and October 1915, the British deployed submarines towed behind decoy trawlers, the two vessels communicating via telephone lines. When a U-boat approached the trawler, the towed submarine would be cast off and would maneuver to attack it. The program had two successes but was abandoned once the British learned that the Germans had become aware of its existence. Anti-submarine warfare became the primary mission of the British submarine force during the final two years of the war, and they were joined by U.S. Navy boats in March of 1918. The Admiralty divided the waters around the British Isles into patrol areas in which individual submarines operated for eight-day periods, submerging by day and surfacing at night. The campaign succeeded in sinking 13 out of 390 sighted U-boats. The low ratio of sightings to sinkings was primarily a consequence of the low speed of submerged submarines. That led to the development of the specialized "R" class boats, whose underwater speed was almost twice that of their surfaced speed; however, these submarines entered service too late to have an impact on the war.

## CENTRAL POWERS SUBMARINE OPERATIONS DURING WORLD WAR I

When war began in 1914, both Germany and Austria-Hungary had small but relatively up-to-date fleets of submarines (there were 31 operational U-boats in the German Navy and 5 in the Austro-Hungarian). Like the Allies, they had no clear doctrines concerning their use. Furthermore, the prewar plans of neither fleet long survived contact with the realities of the war. The Royal Navy adopted a strategy of distant blockade rather than the close blockade that the German Navy had anticipated, while Italy declined to join its allies in the Triple Alliance and chose to remain neutral, upsetting Austrian expectations of the situation in the Adriatic.

Germany adopted a strategy of *kleinkrieg*, seeking to draw out elements of the Grand Fleet into disadvantageous positions, both geographically and numerically, and whittling away at British naval strength with mines and submarines. During 1914, German U-boats, demonstrating much greater operational capabilities than prewar exercises had suggested, scored considerable successes. The most spectacular was on 22 September, when Kapitänleutnant Otto Weddigen, commanding the *U-9*, torpedoed and sank three British armored cruisers—the *Aboukir*, the *Cressy*, and the *Hogue*—within little more than an hour off the Dutch coast. The Royal Navy very quickly came to regard the menace of German submarines as the greatest single threat to its naval superiority.

Despite this success, by early 1915 it was clear that the strategy of *kleinkrieg* was not working. The British distant blockade was proving all too effective in cutting off Germany's access to most foreign trade, while the Grand Fleet, far from allowing detached elements to fall into German traps, was succeeding in cutting off detachments of the High Seas Fleet and inflicting serious damage upon them. The threat of an intensified British mining campaign and the expansion of the terms of the blockade were tightening the screw.

German submarines had not conducted any coordinated campaign against Allied merchant shipping: the transport of the British Expeditionary Force to France and its subsequent supply had been conducted virtually without any interference from the German Fleet. But German submarines had demonstrated that U-boats could be effective in that role, even under the limitations of the Prize Regulations of the Declaration of London of 1909, which required warships either to take merchant crews and passengers on board or provide for their safety prior to sinking their ships. A growing number of officers within the navy, as well as influential politicians and businessmen, began to see a "counterblockade" of Britain as the solution to Germany's dilemma, using submarines to attack and sink without warning all British shipping and neutral vessels trading with the United Kingdom. The government was well aware of the potential for serious repercussions from neutral nations, especially the United States, but it decided that the gains were worth the risk. Therefore, on 4 February 1915, the waters around Great Britain and Ireland, including the whole of the English Channel and the western portion of the North Sea, were declared to be a war zone within which any merchant ship, British or neutral, would be destroyed, without necessarily being possible to ensure the safety of crew or passengers.

The German Navy began this first unrestricted submarine campaign against merchant shipping with very limited resources. Typically there were no more than about 25 operational U-boats available, of which only about one-third were deployed on station at any one time (the remainder being either in transit or refitting). The campaign began on 28 February, and, despite the small number of active U-boats, did well. In all, 29 vessels totaling some 89,500 gross tons were sunk in March; 33 ships totaling 38,600 tons in April; 53 vessels totaling 126,900 tons in May; 114 ships totaling 115,291 tons in June; 86 ships totaling 98,005 tons in July; 107 vessels totaling

182,772 tons in August; and 58 ships totaling 136,048 tons in September. British antisubmarine measures accounted for 15 U-boats, but the German Navy commissioned 25 new boats during the period.

The German announcement of 4 February had almost immediate diplomatic repercussions, especially the U.S. government's note warning Germany that it would be held strictly accountable for any loss of U.S. ships or lives. Consequently, the German government compromised on its initial declaration, placing some restrictions on attacks against vessels flying neutral flags. That was much to the chagrin of officers in the fleet, who had envisaged the unrestricted campaign so terrorizing neutral shippers that they would cease to trade with Great Britain. A number of attacks on Dutch, Greek, Norwegian, and Swedish vessels, including some inside areas declared safe, provoked outraged diplomatic responses from those neutrals and led to the German government offering compensation in several instances and prohibiting attacks against neutral vessels.

The major blow, however, to the unrestricted campaign was the sinking of the transatlantic liner *Lusitania* without warning off the western coast of Ireland on 7 May 1915, by Kapitänleutnant Walter Schwieger, commanding the *U-20*. Among the 1,201 passengers and crew who lost their lives were 128 U.S. citizens, causing a major diplomatic furor between the United States and Germany that was heightened by the torpedoing of the U.S. ship *Nebraskan* without warning on 25 May. Chancellor Bethmann Hollweg, despite strong opposition from the fleet, forbade attacks on large passenger liners, whatever flag they flew, and his efforts succeeded in mollifying President Wilson's government—although Germany still suffered from a sharp drop in the U.S. public's estimation.

As the sinking record shows, these greater restrictions did not substantially affect the success of the campaign against merchant shipping. Nevertheless, there remained the threat of further incidents that might force Germany to terminate the campaign. Kapitänleutnant Schwieger, who had sunk the *Lusitania,* succeeded in providing two such incidents by sinking the British liner *Arabic* without warning on 19 August and the U.S. liner *Hesperian* later in the month. Those two events provoked a further crisis between the United States and Germany and exacerbated the concerns of the German Army's general staff about increased complications with neutral nations in light of an impending shortage of troops. The government, over the protests of senior naval officers, forced a prohibition of attacks against any liners and a withdrawal of all U-boats from operations in the western approaches to the English Channel.

Admiral Henning von Holtzendorff became head of the naval staff, and, on 18 September, after deciding that the submarine campaign had failed, he terminated most U-boat operations against shipping. He also bound all continued action to conform with the Prize Regulations, thus ending the unrestricted campaign.

The British merchant marine had lost 1,294,000 tons of shipping from all causes up to the end of September 1915. New construction totaled 1,233,00 tons, and captured enemy shipping added a further 682,000 tons. Nevertheless, losses were outstripping replacements, while the sinkings in August and September were a serious concern and an omen for the future potential of a submarine campaign.

Holtzendorff continued the restricted campaign against merchant shipping. From October 1915 to February 1916, U-boats sank 209 ships totaling 506,026 gross tons (about 75 percent of those sinkings were in the Mediterranean). The campaign sharpened after attacks without warning were permitted against armed merchant vessels, beginning on 29 February. During the next two months the U-boats sank 143 ships totaling 347,843 tons, but again an incident involving U.S. citizens precipitated a further diplomatic crisis. On 24 March, Oberleutnant zur See Pustkuchen, commanding the *UB-29*, torpedoed the French cross-Channel steamer *Sussex* without warning off Dieppe, killing some 50 passengers and crew including 25 Americans. President Wilson reacted by warning Germany that any further incident would lead to the United States severing diplomatic relations. On 24 April, Holtzendorff reinstated his order requiring submarines to operate within the Prize Regulations, causing Admiral Scheer angrily to order all submarines to cease operation. British losses fell immediately, to 64,000 tons in May and only 37,000 tons in June. Nevertheless, British shipping losses for the first half of 1916 approached a half-million tons, well over twice the rate of new construction.

For the next few months the High Seas Fleet boats operated primarily in support of fleet operations on the North Sea, leaving attacks on merchant shipping to the Flanders boats and U-boats in the Mediterranean. The pace of the restricted campaign picked up in September, when 172 ships totaling 231,573 tons were sunk. Between October 1916 and January 1917 a further 757 ships totaling 1,304,290 tons were sunk in all theaters. This increase reflected the larger number of operational U-boats, which reached a total of 103 submarines in January 1917.

Despite this advance, the navy was convinced that the restricted campaign was doomed to failure in bringing Britain to terms. When combined with the Allied rejection of German peace proposals and successes on the Eastern Front that released additional troops, the consensus among the high command and in government tipped toward renewal of the unrestricted campaign. Holtzendorff, relying on calculations of available British shipping and requirements, and assuming that neutrals would be terrorized into ceasing to trade with Britain, determined that an unrestricted campaign sinking 600,000 tons of shipping per month would reduce traffic to and from the United Kingdom by close to 40 percent within five months and force a peace settlement. There was a very real risk that such a campaign would bring the United States into the war against Germany, but it was thought that U.S. shipping and troops could not participate in time to influence the outcome. On 9 January 1917, the government decided that an unrestricted campaign would begin on 1 February.

The predicted diplomatic consequence of launching the new unrestricted campaign was not long in coming. On 3 February 1917, President Wilson severed diplomatic relations with Germany. The Zimmerman Telegram—containing a proposal for a German-Mexican and even a German-Japanese alliance against the United States—surfaced and exacerbated the tension between the two nations. A series of almost inevitable sinkings of U.S. ships or vessels carrying U.S. citizens as passengers hastened matters, and on 6 April the United States declared war on Germany.

The campaign commenced on schedule, with some 120 U-boats deployed. Shipping losses rose dramatically to 520,412 tons in February; 564,497 tons in March; and 860,334 tons in April, at the cost of only nine U-boats. From that peak, losses dropped to 616,316 tons in May and 696,725 tons in June. As the British gradually expanded the scope of convoy from mid-May, losses declined still further to 555,514 tons in July; 472,372 tons in August; 353,602 tons in September; 466,542 tons in October; 302,599 tons in November; and 411,766 tons in December. Forty-three U-boats were sunk in the same six-month period, more than three times the number lost in the first six months of the year. During the first six months of 1918, U-boats sank 1,864,440 tons of shipping and a further 889,442 tons up to the Armistice on 11 November. German losses were high—more than 120 U-boats were sunk. Furthermore, as the U-boats sought out weak links—areas in which ships sailed without the benefit of convoy—the Allies extended the scope of the system until the vast majority of shipping was covered. The German unrestricted submarine campaign against shipping had failed.

The small number of Austrian submarines in operational service at the beginning of the war and their limited range effectively confined their use to the Adriatic. After France declared war on 13 August 1914, elements of its Mediterranean Fleet commenced operations there, making sweeps with heavy ships and undertaking minor landings—all in the hope of influencing Italy to join the Allies. Austrian submarines always were a threat, one that became a reality on 21 December, when the *U-12* torpedoed the French flagship, the dreadnought *Jean Bart*, without, however, sinking the battleship. This incident convinced the French to give up offensive operations in the Adriatic and focus instead on a distant blockade of the Straits of Otranto.

In the run-up to the entry of Italy into the war on the side of the Allies, the French moved their blockading squadron further north into the Adriatic. Linienschiffsleutnant Georg Ritter von Trapp (better known as the Baron in the *Sound of Music*), commanding the *U-5*, succeeded in torpedoing and sinking the armored cruiser *Leon Gambetta*, with heavy loss of life, on the night of 26 April 1915— demonstrating once again the vulnerability of surface vessels in these confined waters. After Italy entered the war, the situation remained much the same. In the face of the threat posed by submarines, heavy ships could not operate effectively in the Adriatic, and operations became largely a quasi-guerrilla war in which the Austrian submarines, reinforced by small German U-boats transferred overland, played a major role.

Germany began transferring submarines to the Mediterranean theater in May 1915, when it became clear that the limited Austrian submarine force could do little to affect operations in the area, despite their effectiveness in the Adriatic. They scored some considerable successes on arrival. Kapitänleutnant Otto Hersing, commanding the *U-21*, torpedoed and sank the British pre-dreadnought battleship *Triumph* at the Dardanelles on 25 May and another, the *Majestic*, two days later. Two smaller submarines, however, proved very much less effective, and subsequent German submarine operations during the Dardanelles campaign proved largely inconsequential.

The German Navy continued to send U-boats to the Mediterranean, sending the smaller boats overland by rail for assembly at Pola and passing the larger boats through the Straits of Gibraltar. One early arrival, the *UB-15*, commanded by Oberleutnant zur See von Heimburg, sank the Italian submarine *Medusa* in the Adriatic on

1 June 1915. Von Heimburg, now commanding the *UB-14,* then sank the Italian armored cruiser *Amalfi* on 7 July, before sailing into the Mediterranean.

The Mediterranean theater was attractive because there were clearly defined focal points through which much traffic had to pass. It obviously was crucial for French and Italian traffic, and much British shipping sailed through the sea. The weather would permit operations during the fall and winter, when it could hamper Atlantic operations, and it also was much less probable that problems would arise with the United States, since few U.S. ships or passengers sailed through.

The German submarine campaign in the Mediterranean began in earnest in October 1915. The submarines used Austrian bases at Pola and Cattaro for their operations. During that month five large U-boats sank 63,848 tons of shipping—more than three-quarters of all merchant vessel sinkings in all theaters. More large and small boats reinforced the Mediterranean flotilla, with merchant shipping losses reaching 152,882 tons in November and 76,693 tons in December.

During 1916 the U-boat campaign in the Mediterranean continued its successes. The first quarter of the year saw losses decline as the U-boats underwent refits, contended with winter weather, and were subject to restrictions on attacking passenger liners. Nevertheless, losses were high enough to lead the Allies to strengthen their patrol systems and divert as much shipping as possible from sailing through the Mediterranean, even though that extended voyages and tied up vessel capacity. New boats arriving from Germany and existing boats returning to service pushed merchant shipping losses in the Mediterranean for the second quarter of 1916 to 192,225 tons, about half of all losses in all theaters. These successes continued into the summer and fall, as German U-boats sank 321,542 tons of shipping between July and September. Nor was there any real relief in the fall and early winter, since a further 427,999 tons of shipping went down by the end of the year. In aggregate, German U-boats sank well over a million tons of shipping during 1916, while losing only two submarines, one of which sank after running into one of its own mines.

The beginning of 1917 brought the illusion of calm, as most of the German U-boats were refitted. Losses fell to 78,541 tons in January, before rising again to 105,670 tons in February and then dropping to 61,917 tons in March. The Germans reinforced their Mediterranean flotilla, and new Austrian boats, based on the German UB-II class, joined the German submarines in operations in the central Mediterranean. Together they sank 277,948 tons of shipping in April. The Allies were forced to reappraise their system of trade protection and began introducing convoy of merchant shipping in late May. Losses fell to 180,896 tons in May and 170,473 tons in June. Even though the Germans increased their U-boat force by more than 25 percent, losses continued to decline in July and August, to 107,303 tons and 118,372 tons, respectively. An unprofitable diversion of U-boats in the fall to support operations in Syria against the Allied offensive netted a few small warships but relieved the pressure on merchant shipping. Success returned, however, as the U-boats re-entered the campaign against merchant shipping in December, at which time losses rose to 148,331 tons. Once again, Germany's total U-boat loss for the year was two boats, while the German and Austrian submarines sank well over 1.25 million tons of shipping.

Finally in 1918, Allied efforts to protect trade bore fruit. During the first six months of the year, German and Austrian submarines sank about 600,000 tons of shipping, but their losses rose to ten boats, twice their total losses for the previous three years. The submarines' success rate fell dramatically in the months before the Armistice: they sank less than 250,000 tons of shipping and lost an additional four boats in the process. Moreover, these diminished accomplishments came about despite the fact that almost twice as many submarines were operational as in 1917.

Between 1915 and 1917, the German Navy operated a small number of submarines in the Black Sea. The first boats arrived in May 1915 as part of Germany's support for Turkey during the Dardanelles campaign. Most of the boats deployed were small UB- or UC-type coastal submarines; their successes were very limited, although their operations did cause the Russians to deploy their own hunting squadrons of destroyers. The few larger submarines dispatched to the Black Sea had no greater success. In all, Germany sent three large and about a dozen small submarines to the Black Sea, losing almost half of them, mostly to mines.

In summation, then, the most important campaign in which the submarines of the Central Powers engaged—their operations against merchant shipping—came close to total success in April 1917, only to fail completely to overcome the effectiveness of the convoy system. In the process, however, they permanently redefined the role of the submarine in warfare.

# CHAPTER TWO

# A War-Winning Weapon?

THE NAVIES OF THE WORLD now moved to focus their attention on developing boats to serve in the roles of reconnaissance, offensive patrols against enemy warships, and cooperation with the battle-fleet—all missions that had been envisaged prior to the outbreak of World War I. They were motivated in particular by the accomplishments of the Imperial German Navy's submarine arm; the success of Allied countermeasures in the later stages of the conflict and the impending emergence of superior detection equipment; and a general revulsion against the very idea of unrestricted submarine warfare against merchant shipping. Navies in general sought to produce faster, stronger, more powerfully armed, and longer-range boats to fulfill these tasks. The improved submarine types shared many features. Functionally they were submersibles, rather than true submarines; their designs were optimized for operation on the surface, with only limited capabilities submerged. Underwater, they relied for propulsion on electric motors fed by large storage batteries; on the surface, they used diesel engines for propulsion and to recharge the batteries. While they incorporated substantial batteries of torpedo tubes and reload torpedoes, they also carried guns for use against surface or aerial targets. Their operational range was a function of their bunkerage for diesel fuel, while their submerged radius of action was limited by battery cell capacity. Maximum submerged speed usually was not much more than half of their surface speed, and maintaining high submerged speeds was impossible for any length of time without totally draining the batteries and forcing the submarine to the surface. Consequently, most navies conceived of operating their submarines primarily as stealthy surface vessels with the ability to submerge for evasion or escape prior to or after an attack.

German submarine designs exerted a major influence, either directly or indirectly, on most of the world's submarine development in the years between the two world wars—except in Britain and, to a lesser extent, the Soviet Union. All the major navies of the victorious Allies—Britain, France, Italy, Japan, and the United States—received examples of the latest German U-boats under the terms of the Armistice and the Treaty of Versailles. They intently examined and analyzed these German craft to determine the applicability and suitability of their features for incorporation into their own types and, in several instances, commissioned former German submarines into their own services to acquire operational experience in their use. Both Italian and French designers were very much influenced by studying and operating examples of the later Mittel-U and UB-III types prior to developing their first new postwar boats. The big U-cruisers had even more impact. The first French oceangoing submarines, the *Requin* class, benefited substantially from their designers' study of U-cruisers. The big U.S. Navy fleet boats owed a great debt to the German boats (including even their diesel engines, in some cases), and German engineers were intimately involved in the development of the early Japanese *kaidai* and *junsen* types.

German design influence spread to lesser fleets too, largely through the activities of the Ingenieurskantoor voor Scheepsbouw (IvS). The IvS was established in July 1922 at Den Haag in The Netherlands by a consortium of the Krupp and Vulcan shipbuilding yards to circumvent the Versailles Treaty's prohibition on submarine design and construction. The engineering staff was led by Hans Techel, who had headed Krupp's submarine design team since 1907, and the firm also received clandestine financial support from the German Navy, which was desirous of maintaining German submarine design expertise despite the treaty. IvS engineers produced submarine designs that were constructed for Turkey, Finland, the Soviet Union, Spain, and Sweden, and also served as prototypes for the German Navy's Type IIA coastal, Type IA long-range, and Type VII oceangoing U-boats.

During the period between the two world wars, the world's major navies constructed small series of submarines that served the dual purpose of meeting immediate operational needs and also providing data for the development of improved vessels. By the mid-1930s most of these navies had evolved one or two basic types apiece that were well matched to their operational requirements, had attained substantial design maturity, and were suited to large-scale series production. In general, and with very few exceptions, the vast majority of the submarines that served during World War II were of these standardized types, modified in the light of operational experience, rather than radically new designs.

The U.S. Navy took the process of type standardization the furthest, entering World War II with a single basic design that was improved but never replaced during the course of the conflict. These "fleet boats" emerged through the crystallization and synthesis of a series of designs produced to meet requirements for fleet submarines to accompany the battlefleet, cruiser submarines for long-distance raiding, and patrol submarines for offensive operations in the Pacific. Nine vessels, essentially experimental prototypes, in five classes were produced between 1921 and 1934, ranging in size from 1,100 to 2,700 tons standard (defined by the Washington Treaty as fully-equipped except for crew and fuel) on the surface. Overall these submarines were not very successful, suffering problems with their diesel machinery, diving ability, and general reliability, but they provided valuable experience and data for an improved design.

The new series that began with the *Porpoise* class of 1934 were of 1,310 to 1,475 tons standard on the surface. They introduced diesel-electric reduction drive, which proved vastly more reliable than previous arrangements. Surface cruising range was 11,000 miles at 10 knots, and they had a patrol endurance of 75 days. They could operate for up to 48 hours submerged at 2 knots and had a safe operating depth limit of 250 feet. A battery of 6 to 8 torpedo tubes with 16 to 24 torpedoes was fitted, along with a light deck gun. Between 1934 and 1940, 38 submarines of this group were constructed, and they formed the backbone of the U.S. submarine force when the United States entered World War II.

The *Gato* class that followed became the first mass-produced wartime class. Displacement rose to 1,526 tons, the torpedo tube battery increased to 10 tubes, and safe depth increased to 300 feet. They were followed by the very similar *Balao* class, which featured a deeper safe operating depth of 400 feet, accomplished by substituting high-tensile steel for the mild steel used in earlier boats. The *Tench* class introduced diesel-electric direct drive that brought about a very significant reduction in noise and internal machinery space, leading to the addition of four reload torpedoes to the outfit. A total of 221 submarines from these three classes were completed during or immediately after World War II. Significant wartime modifications included reducing superstructure, adding radar, and enhancing the gun armament by fitting 4- or 5-inch deck guns and adding multiple light antiaircraft weapons.

Japan also constructed very large submarines, intended to operate primarily as integral components of the battlefleet. The *kaidai* type design was based on a large German cruiser submarine from World War I; the type evolved into a series of 24 boats in five classes, constructed between 1921 and 1935. These vessels displaced between 1,390 and 1,635 tons standard, had operating ranges of between 10,000 and 14,000 miles at 10 knots, carried a battery of 6 to 8 tubes with 14 to 16 torpedoes, could operate submerged for 36 hours at 2 knots, and had a safe operating depth of between 200 and 250 feet. Japan, with considerable assistance from German engineers, also developed very large cruiser submarines of the *junsen* type between 1924 and 1938. These eight huge vessels had standard displacements of between 1,970 and 2,231 tons and an operational range of 24,000 miles at 10 knots; they could dive safely to 300 feet.

In 1939, Japan essentially standardized its large submarine type with a vessel design displacing about 2,100 tons capable of cruising for 14,000 miles at 16 knots, or 24,000 miles at 10 knots, and diving to 330 feet. Three models were produced: a headquarters type emphasizing communications and command facilities, an attack type emphasizing torpedo armament, and a scouting type that added hangar space and a catapult for a small reconnaissance floatplane. Some 46 of these large submarines were constructed, as well as three others that brought together the facilities of all three types into the *sen-toku* type, a single monster hull displacing 3,530 tons standard. Japan also constructed 10 final examples of the *kaidai* type early in World War II.

Unlike the United States, Japan also developed and constructed a series of medium submarines intended for coastal work. In addition, considerable effort was expended on midget submarines—small boats with two-man crews intended for stealthy attacks on ports and roadsteads after they had been transported close to the scene of operation by larger submarines. Finally, late in World War II, Japan was developing submarines with high underwater performance, but these never entered service.

German submarines were developed clandestinely, inasmuch as the Versailles Treaty prohibited them in the German Navy. Design work, both at IvS and by the Blohm und Voss firm, continued for foreign navies with production undertaken in the customer's yards under German supervision. These boats also served as prototypes for domestic production, which made it possible for the first new German submarine, the *U-1*, to be completed on 29 June 1935, only five weeks after the repudiation of the Versailles Treaty.

The overwhelming majority of the 1,150 U-boats commissioned between 1935 and 1945 belonged to two groups: the so-called 500-ton Type VII medium boats, and the 740-ton Type IX long-range submarines. The Type VIIC actually displaced between 760 and 1,000 tons on the surface, had a cruising range of 6,500 to 10,000 miles at 12 knots on the surface and 80 miles at 4 knots submerged. They had a battery of 5 torpedo tubes with 14 torpedoes, an 88mm deck gun, and ever-increasing numbers of light antiaircraft weapons. Almost 700 of these boats in all of their variants entered service during World War II. The Type XIC actually displaced 1,120 tons; it had a cruising range of 11,000 miles at 12 knots on the surface and 63 miles at 4 knots submerged. They had a battery of 6 torpedo tubes with 22 torpedoes, a 105mm deck gun, and ever-increasing numbers of light antiaircraft weapons. Almost 200 of this type and its variants were commissioned.

Germany also commissioned a number of other important types during World War II. Among the most important were the Type X minelayers and the Type XIV supply boats. Both types operated as resuppliers for the operational boats during the Battle of the Atlantic, providing fuel, provisions, medical supplies, reload torpedoes, and even medical care and replacement crew members. Consequently they became prime targets for Allied antisubmarine forces, and few survived. The other major vessels were the radical Type XXI and Type XXIII boats, designed for high submerged speed and extended underwater operation. Revolutionary streamlined hull shapes, greatly increased battery space, and the installation of snorkels allowed these boats to operate at submerged speeds that made them very difficult targets for Allied antisubmarine forces. Confused production priorities, however, and the general shortage of materials late in the war prevented more than a very few from putting to sea operationally.

British submarine development also was influenced by the cruiser and fleet submarine concepts, though the manifestation of those ideas was almost entirely through evolution from designs existing at the end of World War I. The main thrust of early evolution between the wars centered on the overseas patrol type, displacing 1,475 tons on the surface, with a range of 10,900 miles at 8 knots, a submerged endurance of 36 hours at 2 knots, and a diving depth of 500 feet. Armament included a battery of 8 torpedo tubes with

14 torpedoes and a 4-inch deck gun. A group of minelaying submarines of similar size also were built, as well as a small series of very fast large submarines for work with the fleet. Both of those developments, however, proved very costly and of limited operational utility.

In the early 1930s a fresh start was made with the *Swordfish* class, designed for offensive patrols in narrow waters. These boats displaced 640 tons standard, had a cruising range of 3,800 miles at 9 knots on the surface and 36 hours at 3 knots submerged, and could dive to 300 feet. Armament was 6 torpedo tubes with 12 torpedoes and a 3-inch gun. A larger overseas patrol type, the *Triton* class, appeared in 1937. These displaced 1,090 tons standard, had a cruising range of 4,500 miles at 11 knots on the surface and 55 hours at 3 knots submerged, and could dive to 300 feet. Armament was 10 torpedo tubes with 16 torpedoes and a 4-inch gun. Britain concentrated its production of submarines during World War II on these two types, producing a total of 62 of the "S" type and 53 of the "T" type.

Just before World War II the Royal Navy developed a small submarine for training not only crews and new commanding officers but also antisubmarine vessels. When war came the design was quickly adapted for operational use and proved particularly useful in confined waters such as the North Sea and Mediterranean. The U class displaced between 540 and 646 tons on the surface. It had a range of 3,600 miles at 10 knots on the surface, a submerged endurance of 60 hours at 2 knots, and a diving depth of 200 feet. Armament included a battery of 6 torpedo tubes with 10 torpedoes and a 3-inch deck gun. A total of 71 boats were constructed of this class and its slightly improved successors of the V class. While they were useful boats in the early part of the war, later examples diverted resources from the construction of more effective vessels. Britain also constructed some 36 midget submarines, with four-man crews, for attacks on shipping at anchor in harbor.

Italian submarines were of four basic types: very large oceangoing cruiser submarines, large minelayers, large long-range patrol boats, and medium-size vessels. The cruisers, few in number, proved rather unsuccessful, especially as they were slow to dive; they saw little operational service. The minelayers, however, were much more successful. They displaced between 1,054 and 1,305 tons standard on the surface, with a range of 8,500 miles at 9 knots on the surface, a submerged endurance of 60 hours at 2 knots, and a diving depth of 330 feet. Armament included a battery of 6 to

8 torpedo tubes with 8 to 14 torpedoes, 36 mines, and one or two 3-inch deck guns.

The two series of patrol submarines emerged as essentially standard designs immediately before World War II began. The larger group displaced between 920 and 1,000 tons standard on the surface, with a range of 9,000 miles at 8 knots on the surface, a submerged endurance of 60 hours at 2 knots, and a diving depth of 330 feet. Armament included a battery of 8 torpedo tubes with 12 torpedoes and one 4-inch deck gun. The smaller group displaced between 650 and 680 tons standard on the surface, with a range of 5,000 miles at 8 knots on the surface, a submerged endurance of 60 hours at 2 knots, and a diving depth of 330 feet. Armament included a battery of 6 torpedo tubes with 12 torpedoes and one 4-inch deck gun. These smaller patrol submarines were very successful boats, performing well in the shallow, clear waters of the Mediterranean; the larger boats performed quite effectively in the Atlantic.

France constructed three series of submarines in the period between the wars: large, oceangoing, long-range vessels for worldwide service and for operation with the fleet; smaller boats for offensive patrols in European waters; and a successful group of minelayers. The 31 large submarines of the *Redoutable* class were generally regarded as very effective boats. They displaced 1,384 tons standard on the surface, with a maximum range of 10,000 miles at 10 knots on the surface and a submerged endurance of 60 hours at 2 knots. They had a battery of 11 torpedo tubes (seven of them in two remote-controlled, trainable external mounts), with a total of 13 torpedoes and a single 3.9-inch deck gun. The series of smaller patrol submarines began with 12 boats of the "600-tonne" type, followed by 30 of an improved "630-tonne" model, several of which were still incomplete when France fell in June of 1940. They had a range of 4,000 to 5,600 miles at 10 knots on the surface, an underwater endurance of 48 hours at 2 knots, and a safe operating depth of 330 feet. The torpedo battery comprised 9 tubes (three in an external, remote-controlled trainable mount) with a total of 9 torpedoes, plus a single 3.9-inch deck gun. The minelayers displaced 761 tons, could cruise for 7,000 miles at 10 knots on the surface, had a submerged endurance of 48 hours at 2 knots, and could safely operate to a depth of 250 feet. They carried 5 torpedo tubes (three in a trainable external mount) with 7 torpedoes, 32 mines, and a single 3-inch deck gun.

The French Navy also operated the largest submarine in the world between the two world wars. The *Surcouf* was designed for long-range commerce war and displaced 2,880 tons standard on the surface, had a range of 10,000 miles at 10 knots on the surface and 60 hours at 2 knots submerged, and could operate safely at 250 feet. The *Surcouf*'s battery included no fewer than 12 tubes (eight in external mounts) with 22 torpedoes, two 8-inch guns in a special turret mounting, and a seaplane stowed in a hangar and launched with a catapult. The *Surcouf* was also equipped with a special compartment to accommodate prisoners taken from intercepted vessels and a small motor launch to transport boarding parties. The submarine proved to be successful in peacetime but never operated as designed during combat because of the fall of France and the boat's subsequent loss in a collision.

Soviet production of new submarines began in 1927. Clandestine cooperation with Germany gave Soviet engineers access to design data for German types from late World War I: minelayers, Type UB-III, and Mittel-U. The Soviets salved and recommissioned the sunken British submarine *L-55*, which gave them access to late-war British design information. Soviet designers also gained considerable data from rehabilitating the later czarist-era Bubnov-designed boats and the final examples of the ubiquitous Holland H-type submarines. Synthesizing this information permitted the Soviets to produce a wide variety of submarines on a large scale. There were two basic series of "M"-type coastal submarines, two basic medium submarine series—the "Shch" or Pike type of indigenous origin (though strongly influenced by British practice), and the later "S"-type derived from the same basic design as the German Type VII, minelayers of the "L"-type developed from the *L-55*, and long-range boats of the "K"-type. At the outbreak of World War II in September 1939, the Soviet Union deployed the world's largest submarine force, with 168 boats in service.

The final "M"-type displaced 283 tons surfaced, had a range of 4,500 miles at 8 knots on the surface or 36 hours at 3 knots submerged, could dive to 295 feet, and had a battery of 2 torpedo tubes with 4 torpedoes and a 45mm antiaircraft gun. The developed "S"-type displaced 856 tons surfaced, had a range of 9,500 miles at 9 knots on the surface or 45 hours at 3 knots submerged, could dive to 330 feet, and had a battery of 6 torpedo tubes with 12 torpedoes and a 4-inch deck gun. Their indigenous rivals displaced 587 tons, had a range of 3,650 miles at 7 knots or 50 hours at 2.5 knots submerged, could dive to 295 feet, and carried 6 torpedo tubes with 10 torpedoes. The minelayers displaced 1,108 tons, had a range of 10,000 miles at 8.6 knots or 60 hours at 2.5 knots submerged, could dive to 330 feet, and carried 8 torpedo tubes with 14 torpedoes and 20 mines. The "K"-type were very popular with their crews and were regarded as the best Soviet submarines of World War II. They displaced 1,480 tons, had a range of 15,000 miles at 9 knots or 50 hours at 2.5 knots submerged, could dive to 330 feet, and carried 10 torpedo tubes with 24 torpedoes. Despite this variety, the Soviet Union's yards produced large numbers of submarines during World War II, completing some 200 boats during the course of the conflict.

## ALLIED SUBMARINE OPERATIONS IN WORLD WAR II

In most navies prior to World War II, the principal missions of submarines were offensive operations against enemy warships and reconnaissance. Britain, France, The Netherlands, and the United States, in particular, deployed many of their long-range boats in the Far East as counters to the powerful Imperial Japanese Navy concentrated there. A secondary task was campaigning against enemy merchant shipping, within the limits permitted by the Prize Regulations of the 1909 Declaration of London, which required ensuring the safety of ships' crews.

For the first year of the war, Allied submarines operated predominantly in their primary prewar roles, undertaking patrols in the North Sea, Atlantic, and Mediterranean to find and attack enemy warships, with generally limited success. They also undertook a campaign against the German merchant fleet's attempt to return to its homeland, with mixed results. In September 1940, however, the Admiralty lifted almost all restrictions on submarine operations against enemy merchant shipping, setting the stage for a sustained campaign against German and Italian trade.

Norwegian and Swedish ore traffic formed Germany's most important European trade, and their protection became the principal focus of the navy's trade protection efforts throughout the war. After the successful German invasion of Norway, the *Kriegsmarine* began convoying merchant shipping along the Norwegian coast from late in 1940. Convoys generally were small—three to six ships—escorted by a few torpedo boats, trawlers, and light craft. British submarines maintained a continuous effort against this trade for the remainder of the war, both by attacking convoys with torpedoes and by laying extensive minefields along the various routes they followed. After the German assault on the Soviet Union, Soviet Northern Fleet submarines initiated attacks on German shipping in northern Norway, and they were soon joined by British submarines operating from Kola Bay. Joint operations continued until 1944, when the British crews were brought home and the submarines were passed to the Soviet Navy. This assault against the northern Norwegian convoys cost the Germans some 500,000 tons of shipping, a relatively negligible amount, considering that annual traffic was well in excess of 6 million tons.

Soviet submarines also threatened the Swedish ore traffic. This shipping was encouraged to keep within Swedish territorial waters as far as possible, and was escorted for the final leg behind the protection of defensive minefields and net barriers. During 1942 and 1943, Soviet submarines succeeded in sinking only about twenty ships, totaling some 40,000 tons, out of more than 1,900 vessels in convoy representing well over 5.6 million tons of shipping. During 1944 the Soviet army's advances and the defeat of Finland meant that aircraft played a greater role in antishipping operations, but, even so, German losses remained relatively light. The collapse of German positions on the Baltic coast early in 1945 required the evacuation by sea of more than 2 million troops and refugees. Despite some spectacular successes—the sinking of the liners *Wilhelm Gustloff* (with some 9,300 casualties), *General Steuben* (when only 300 survived of the 4,000 passengers embarked), and *Goya* (with but 183 survivors from among the more than 7,000 passengers and crew)—Soviet attacks were remarkably ineffective, the Germans losing only about thirty ships totaling some 100,000 tons. Overall, the Allied submarine campaign against German shipping was both relatively ineffective and costly (sixteen Allied and more than forty Soviet submarines were lost): it faced strong and effective countermeasures, especially very efficient radio direction finding and relatively powerful convoy escorts, and it was conducted in confined coastal waters that eased the defender's task.

When Italy entered the war in June 1940, British submarines, in conjunction with surface warships and aircraft, commenced an interdiction campaign against convoy traffic carrying supplies to Italian forces in Libya almost immediately. Italian convoys generally were small—three to six merchant vessels—with two or three escorting destroyers or torpedo boats. As British surface forces operating from Malta began attacking Libya-bound shipping, the Italian Navy had to deploy heavier covering forces, often including cruisers, to support particularly valuable convoys. In this struggle over shipping, the British possessed two great advantages: radar, which vastly enhanced the night-attack capabilities of its aircraft and surface ships; and signals intelligence, which consistently gave them advance convoy routing information. Axis fortunes in this campaign fluctuated greatly. From mid-1941, Axis forces in North Africa required approximately 100,000 tons of supplies each month. In March 1942, for example, only 47,588 tons got through, whereas in April, 150,389 tons arrived. Overall, the Italian and German navies succeeded in bringing about 80 percent of all convoyed shipping in the Mediterranean through to its destination, losing two cruisers and seven destroyers to submarines in the process, while Axis antisubmarine forces and mines destroyed more than forty-five Allied submarines during the course of the campaign.

By far the most successful Allied submarine campaign during World War II was that of the U.S. Navy's boats in the Pacific against Japanese merchant shipping and warships. The effort got off to a mediocre start, not least because the early loss of the Philippines forced U.S. submarines to traverse long distances from either Hawai'ian or Australian bases to reach their targets. In addition, Australian bases initially lacked adequate facilities, U.S. torpedoes were highly unreliable and required major attention to correct their deficiencies, and fleet doctrine required submarines to prioritize their efforts against Japan's major warships. It took time to fix these problems: bases in Australia were not adequately equipped until the fall of 1942; it was June 1943 before destroying Japan's merchant fleet became a doctrinal priority; and the torpedo problem was not corrected until October of 1943. During this time, however, the Pacific Fleet was able to commission modern boats, upgrade existing vessels, and substantially improve the quality of its submarine commanders.

Japan began the Pacific War with 6,150,000 tons of merchant shipping. New construction and captures added 832,000 tons during 1942. U.S. (and small numbers of British and Dutch) submarines sank 620,600 tons of Japan's total merchant shipping losses of 1,065,000 tons during that year. During 1943, Japan added 878,000 tons of new merchant shipping to its fleet, but U.S. submarines alone sank 1,340,000 tons; another 441,000 tons were lost to other factors (air and surface attack and maritime hazards).

Despite its direct experience of successful convoy operations by its destroyers in the Mediterranean during World War I, the Imperial Japanese Navy was very slow to introduce convoying of merchant shipping after the Pacific War began. The navy possessed very few suitable escort vessels at the outbreak of the war, but that simply reflected the overwhelming emphasis it placed on planning for the decisive fleet action that was the centerpiece of its operational strategy. Japan's response to the burgeoning unrestricted submarine campaign by the United States against its shipping was to increase aggressive surface and air patrols and to continue to eschew defensive convoy of its traffic. Not until the end of 1943, when its merchant fleet was being devastated by U.S. submarines, did the navy begin convoying shipping on a limited scale—especially the crucial tankers bringing fuel from the Dutch East Indies.

The Pacific Fleet responded by introducing the wolf-pack tactics that had served German U-boats so well in the Atlantic. In particular, coordinated night attacks by surfaced submarines relying on guidance from sophisticated radar proved devastating. As a result, 1944 was a catastrophic year for Japan's merchant fleet. Even though Japanese shipbuilders launched 1,735,000 tons of new merchant shipping, U.S. submarines sank 2,430,000 tons, and Japan lost a further 1,550,000 tons to other causes. Shortage of targets and a highly successful aerial mining campaign in Japanese home waters cut the successes of U.S. submarines during 1945 to 400,000 tons of shipping, but the net outcome of the campaign was to all but paralyze Japan's maritime transportation system.

Overall, U.S. submarines accounted for two-thirds of all of Japan's losses of merchant ships, some 4.8 million tons, as well as one-third of its warship casualties. The price of this success was high. Despite the generally low level of effectiveness of Japanese antisubmarine measures, fifty submarines and 3,500 crewmen were lost during the campaign, a little more than one-fifth of all that undertook operational missions.

## AXIS SUBMARINE OPERATIONS
## IN WORLD WAR II

The outbreak of World War II found the German submarine arm well trained but deficient in numbers. From the moment of its reestablishment, the submarine force had concentrated much of its effort on validating Kommodore Karl Dönitz's concepts for an all-out assault on enemy trade using concentrated groups of submarines under central shore-based control to locate and destroy convoyed shipping, primarily through surfaced night attacks (wolf-pack tactics). Dönitz was promoted Konteradmiral in October 1939, but shortages of U-boats, Adolf Hitler's initial insistence on Germany's adherence to the Prize Regulations, and demands on the submarine force for its support of surface naval operations prevented him from exploiting the potential of the wolf-pack tactics for most of the first nine months of the conflict. On average only six boats were at sea at any one time during this period, forcing them to attack individually, although some attempts were made to mount combined attacks whenever possible.

As a result of its World War I experience after 1917, Britain was quick to begin the convoying of merchant vessels. There was some initial hesitation because of the feared detrimental effect that convoys could have on the efficient employment of shipping, but when the liner *Athena* was torpedoed and sunk without warning on 3 September 1939, Britain took this to indicate that Germany had commenced an unrestricted campaign of submarine warfare against merchant vessels. Regular east coast convoys between the Firth of Forth and the River Thames started on 6 September and outbound transatlantic convoys from Liverpool two days later.

The conquest of Norway and the collapse of France in June 1940 brought substantial changes to the U-boat war against trade. From French bases, German reconnaissance and long-range bomber aircraft operated far into the Atlantic, while the operational range of the U-boats sailing from Norway and French Biscay ports increased dramatically. Italy's simultaneous entry into the war terminated all commercial traffic in the Mediterranean except for very heavily escorted operational convoys bringing supplies into Malta. It also substantially increased the number of submarines available for the Atlantic campaign against shipping, inasmuch as Italian submarines began operating from Biscay ports, effectively doubling the total Axis force at sea. This situation allowed Dönitz to introduce his wolf-pack tactic on a large scale into the Atlantic shipping campaign, just as the British faced an alarming shortage of oceanic convoy escorts because of the neutralization of the French Fleet and their decision to retain destroyers in home waters to guard against a German invasion. The results vindicated Dönitz's belief in the effectiveness of wolf packs. In the first nine months of the war, German U-boats sank a little more than 1 million tons of shipping, whereas they and the Italians together destroyed more than 2.3 million tons between June 1940 and February 1941. However, the release of destroyers from their guard duties, the addition of new escorts, and the transfer of fifty obsolete destroyers from the U.S. Navy improved the situation. The dispersal point for westbound transatlantic convoys and the pickup point for escort groups meeting eastbound shipping gradually moved westward as the range of the escorts was increased. This pushed the main arena of Axis submarine operations more toward the mid-Atlantic zone, which reduced the time that boats could spend on station. In mid-1941 the United States imposed its so-called Neutrality Zone on the western Atlantic and began escorting British convoys in conjunction with Royal Canadian Navy escorts, operating from Argentia in Newfoundland. North Atlantic convoys now were escorted throughout by antisubmarine vessels. Nevertheless, these additions to the escort force had only a limited impact on losses, since German and Italian submarines succeeded in sinking a further 1.8 million tons in the following nine months prior to the U.S. entry into the war.

The German declaration of war on the United States on 10 December 1941 brought a major westward expansion of U-boat operations against shipping. A disastrous period followed, while the U.S. Navy struggled with the problems of finding the escorts and crews required to convoy the enormous volume of merchant traffic along the East Coast of the United States, and with the very concept of convoy itself. Axis submarines sank more than 3 million tons of Allied shipping between December 1941 and June 1942, well over 75 percent of it along the East Coast of the United States and Canada. Nevertheless, by mid-1942 an elaborate and comprehensive system of interlocking convoy routes and sailings was established for the East Coast of North America and the Caribbean.

As Dönitz became aware of the extension of convoy along the Atlantic East Coast, he shifted U-boat operations back to the mid-Atlantic. His all-out assault on the North Atlantic convoy systems inflicted heavy losses: between July 1942 and March 1943, Axis (almost entirely German) submarines destroyed more than 4.5 millions tons of Allied shipping, over 633,000 tons in March alone. Nevertheless, new Allied countermeasures became available at this crucial moment, and U-boat successes fell to 287,137 tons in April, 237,182 tons in May, and only 76,090 tons in June. Dönitz's reaction was to deploy his U-boats in areas where Allied antisubmarine forces were weak, anticipating that this would compensate for the lack of success in the North Atlantic. Initially this plan to some extent met his expectations, since sinkings rose to 237,777 tons in July, but the success of the Allied assault on U-boats in transit to their patrol stations rendered the German accomplishment transitory; merchant ship sinkings dropped to 92,443 tons in August, never to surpass 100,000 tons per month at any subsequent time during the war.

The collapse of the U-boat offensive in mid-1943 resulted from the Allies' concurrent deployment of a series of new countermeasures and technologies that reached maturity almost simultaneously: centrimetric radar aboard both ships and aircraft, efficient shipborne high-frequency direction finding, ahead-throwing weapons that permitted ships to fire antisubmarine bombs forward and thus retain sonar contact, very-long-range shorebased antisubmarine aircraft, escort carriers and escort support groups, and advances in decryption of German communications codes. The U-boat arm attempted to defeat these countermeasures by deploying its own new weaponry, the most important elements of which were radar warning receivers, heavy antiaircraft batteries, and acoustic torpedoes designed to hunt antisubmarines vessels. Not only did these fail to stem the tide of Allied success against the U-boats, but new convoy communications codes also defeated German cryptographers, rendering locating targets much more difficult. Then, in 1944, Allied military successes in France began to force German U-boats to make more extended passages to their patrol areas as their home ports moved farther from the Atlantic; German air bases also ceased to give aircraft quick access to British coastal waters.

During the final year of this conflict, U-boats equipped with snorkels entered service. The production of new, fast *elektroboote* (the radical new Type XXI submarines with high underwater speed) allowed the first examples to become operational, but their numbers were far too few to make any difference. Also, there were insufficient experienced crews available to exploit their potential. Such was the success of Allied antisubmarine measures during this period that full-scale convoying became unnecessary in some areas, and much of the focus of their escorts turned to hunting U-boats rather than directly protecting merchant shipping. The full measure of the defeat of the U-boats is indicated by the fact that more than two-thirds of the 650 German submarines lost during World War II were sunk in the last two years of the war.

Italian submarines were active in the North Atlantic and the Mediterranean during World War II. In the North Atlantic they were quite successful, sinking more than 500,000 tons of shipping during about 180 patrols out of Bordeaux between mid-June 1940 and the end of 1942. In the Mediterranean, however, their successes were few and their losses high: they sank about 200,000 tons of shipping during the course of more than 1,500 wartime patrols. That was largely because of the Italian Fleet's tactical doctrine, which envisaged using its submarines for daylight submerged attacks rather than nighttime operations on the surface, as was the German practice.

The Imperial Japanese Navy saw submarines as an essential component of its basic strategy for a Pacific war, the *yogeki zengen sakusen* (ambush-attrition operation). The purpose of all Japanese auxiliary forces (originally all warships other than battleships, although aircraft carriers later were given capital rank) was to wear down an advancing U.S. Fleet as it crossed the Pacific, so that it would be reduced in numbers and strength to a point that the main, untouched Japanese Fleet could crush it in a decisive battle. Submarines, therefore, operated almost exclusively as scouts and raiders against warships of the U.S. Navy and rarely against even the fleet train, let alone merchant shipping. While some boats achieved spectacular successes—such as the *I-19*'s salvo of four torpedoes on 15 September 1942, which sank the carrier *Wasp*, damaged the destroyer *O'Brien* so severely that it later sank, and forced the new battleship *North Carolina* to proceed to Pearl Harbor for repairs—most operations were unproductive. Overall, the Japanese submarine force was responsible for sinking about twenty warships and a little more than 100 merchant vessels during World War II; it suffered devastating losses itself.

Technology played a major part in determining the effectiveness of submarines. Most navies encountered problems with their torpedoes early on, especially those submarine arms that relied on magnetic rather than contact pistols. Radar development conferred a special advantage on Allied submarines in particular, offsetting the edge in optical quality possessed by German and Japanese vessels. U.S. submarines were almost unsurpassed in their level of habitability—they were almost the only boats that featured full air-conditioning and adequate space for their crews to sleep. Sonar developed rapidly, as did countermeasures, while some navies put much effort into stealth and self-defense measures by emphasizing the use of wakeless electric torpedoes and special antiescort homing torpedoes. The course of the submarine war demonstrated that those forces that fell behind in the technological battle suffered disproportionately heavily in combat.

# CHAPTER THREE

# The Advent of True Submarines

DURING WORLD WAR II the submarine's principal roles were commerce destruction and hunting enemy surface warships. The antisubmarine forces of the United States and the British Commonwealth comprehensively defeated the submarine campaigns of both Germany and Japan against both merchant shipping and naval forces with a combination of superior tactics and technologies. Nevertheless, it was clear that new submarine technologies could potentially negate this superiority. In particular, the advent of the German Type XXI submarines, the *elektroboote,* was especially worrying. They combined high underwater speed, rapid maneuverability, substantial submerged endurance, deep diving, and long range without needing to surface. These attributes resulted from the installation of greatly enlarged batteries and more powerful electric motors in a shorter, deeper, stronger, streamlined hull, and the use of snorkels to operate the main diesel engines underwater. While the Type XXI did not represent a mature technology, its potential was clear, and its design features powerfully influenced submarine development after World War II, especially in the United States and the Soviet Union.

The advent of the Cold War forced a thorough reappraisal of the role of submarines in the fleets of the United States and its allies. Maintenance of maritime commerce, the movement of troops, munitions, and equipment across the oceans to Europe and the Far East, and the forward deployment of powerful naval surface forces, centered mainly on aircraft carriers, all were vital components of the

West's strategy for containing the Soviet Union and for conducting operations should a war break out. The deployment of mature submarines with the capabilities of the *elektroboote* potentially could jeopardize the West's ability to undertake all three. One part of the solution to countering fast, true submarines was the deployment of fast, effective surface and aerial antisubmarine assets, but that addressed only containing and defeating submarines once they had reached the open ocean. The other, and potentially more efficient, option was to deploy the West's own submarines to hunt and kill enemy submarines before they could reach the oceans, and that therefore became one of the submarine's primary missions.

The Soviet Union also had to re-evaluate the purpose of its submarine force. One primary role quickly emerged: defending the nation's coast and ports against attack through offensive operations against the West's surface maritime assets—especially carrier forces and oceanic lines of communications—and defensive operations against submarines attempting to prevent the egress of Soviet boats. Both sides in the Cold War quickly came to view enemy submarines as the primary target of their own boats, especially as both began deploying submarines as platforms for strategic missile attack against the other's homeland; in addition, the Soviet Union also placed great emphasis on offensive missions against the West's carrier groups.

At the beginning of the Cold War, all operational submarines used diesel-electric drive. This required submarines either to surface frequently to recharge their batteries, or that they be equipped with a snorkel breathing device. The initial primary focus of submarine development, especially in the United States and the Soviet Union, was the integration of experience from analyzing and operating the German *elektroboote* into their fleets.

The U.S. Navy took a three-track approach to this task. The first, longer-term approach was to explore new propulsion technologies that would free submarines from the limitations of diesel-electric drive; this led to the introduction of nuclear-powered boats. The second was to develop new designs that embodied the principles of the Type XXI boats within the framework of U.S. requirements. New long-range submarines of the *Tang* class and short-range hunter-killer types emerged, but their numbers fell far short of the fleet's requirements. To a great extent, however, budgetary constraints forced the U.S. Navy to pursue most vigorously the least attractive option: modifying, through the GUPPY program, as much as possible of the large existing fleet of new but obsolete submarines built during World War II for greater speed and underwater endurance. Large numbers of almost new *Gato, Balao,* and *Tench* class fleet submarines received more streamlined casings and sails, enlarged batteries, snorkels, and improved sensors to suit them for submerged operation for more extended periods.

The United States also undertook research on improved hull forms for extended high-speed submerged operation, leading to the construction of the experimental *Albacore* by the Portsmouth Naval Shipyard in 1952–1953.

The *Albacore* was revolutionary: the hull was a teardrop shape, optimized for underwater operation; there was a single propeller; and the installation of a massive battery permitted very high submerged speed, albeit for only short periods. The new hull form demonstrated great maneuverability, and exploiting it led to substantial improvements in subsequent submarine control systems, making them more akin to flying an aircraft than operating a boat. The *Albacore* also was subject to many modifications, especially to the stern, which eventually received an X-tail that increased overall length to 210′6″; several different types of propeller and rudder arrangements were tried, and the boat also tested new configurations for sonar installations.

The new shape demonstrated by the *Albacore* quickly found its way into operational submarine service, both for diesel boats and for nuclear-powered submarines, in the United States and elsewhere. Its wide adoption marked the completion of the process of transformation from submersible surface craft to full submarines. In the United States it found its principal application in the development of nuclear-powered boats; only the three diesel-electric submarines of the *Barbel* class took advantage of its characteristics.

The Soviet Union followed a somewhat different course in developing its new submarine fleet. In many ways it was far more conservative, from a design standpoint. Essentially, it chose to integrate the principles of the *elektroboote* into the design of updated iterations of the existing three basic types: coastal, medium-range, and long-range boats. Unlike the United States, the Soviet Union put these new designs into mass production, building 32 coastal Project 615 (NATO-designated Quebec) boats, more than 200 Project 613 (NATO-designated Whiskey) medium submarines, and 22 of the long-range Project 611 (NATO-designated Zulu) type.

The Soviet Union also explored new submarine propulsion technologies and adopted nuclear power some four years after the United States. Unlike the United States, however, the Soviet Union did not end production of conventionally powered submarines,

Large numbers of new diesel-electric Project 633 (NATO-designated Romeo) and Project 641 (NATO-designated Foxtrot) boats, again of relatively conservative design, were built to supplement the earlier Project 613 and Project 611 types. Both types nevertheless were successfully exported to countries within the Soviet sphere of influence and laid the basis for conventional submarine production in both China and North Korea.

The Soviets in addition saw a role for conventionally powered submarines in the anticarrier mission, manifested in the production of the Project 651 (NATO-designated Juliett) and Project 641BUKI (NATO-designated Tango) boats in the 1960s and 1970s, whose principal weapons were antiship cruise missiles. The earlier type saw operational characteristics on the surface take pride of place, inasmuch as it had to surface to launch its missiles and needed stability for that purpose. The missiles of the later boats were launched while it was submerged, and consequently a modified form of the earlier Project 641 attack submarine hull was found satisfactory.

The Royal Navy took a somewhat different approach to new submarine production immediately after World War II. Alone among Allied navies, it had direct experience in creating submarines with high underwater speed during the war, having converted several S class boats into high-speed targets for antisubmarine forces. It used that experience, plus additional information derived from study of the German *elektroboote,* to generate its own conversion program to build up a force of fast boats from recently completed T and A class submarines, while working to make more radical propulsion technologies reach production maturity.

The Admiralty looked into nuclear propulsion but decided to exploit the German Walther close-cycle turbine system for its non–air breathing submarines, because it seemed less expensive and closer to being ready for service. Unfortunately, British experts were under the impression that German technicians who had tested this system in a small number of experimental platforms were much closer to solving all of its problems than was really the case. The Royal Navy built two special experimental boats, the *Explorer* and the *Excalibur,* as platforms to bring the Walther system to production status; in the meantime, they built new conventional submarines that, while very reliable and generally quite effective, did not represent much of an advance on the conversions of wartime boats or the German *elektroboote.* The failure of the work in developing a mature Walther system left the Royal Navy no alternative but to turn to the United States for nuclear power technology when the time came for it to build its own submarines that would be free from the limitations of diesel-electric propulsion.

In the early 1980s the Soviet Fleet introduced a new conventionally powered attack submarine, in large part because it was easier to create a quiet diesel-electric boat. The Project 877 (NATO-designated Kilo) type was specifically designed for antisubmarine warfare and combined a teardrop hull form with a powerful sensor suite and stringent measures to reduce acoustic and magnetic signatures. These relatively large, conventionally powered boats proved very successful. They were among the quietest boats of their era and also became a considerable export success, both in their original form and as the upgraded Project 636 (also designated Kilo by NATO).

For most other nations the leap to nuclear power for submarines was out of the question, because of the absence of the necessary industrial and scientific infrastructure, its great expense, and, in some instances, political obstacles. Instead, they exploited the *elektroboote* technologies to produce a new first generation of Western, conventionally powered fast submarines.

The second generation of postwar diesel-electric boats represented a substantial advance on the earlier types. Three elements combined to create these new boats: great strides in battery technology, new hull forms inspired by the *Albacore* design, and advances in reducing acoustic and magnetic signatures. New battery designs not only generated more power for the same space and weight but also recharged much faster, enabling submarines to operate fully submerged for longer periods and use their snorkel on a much more limited scale. New hull forms, and advances in metallurgy, endowed these boats with higher speed, greater maneuverability, and deeper diving capabilities. Reduced magnetism came from using nonmagnetic, high-tensile steel or active demagnetizing. The biggest asset, however, that these later-generation diesel-electric boats possessed was quietness and, therefore, stealth. Rafted machinery, slow-speed motors, advanced propeller designs, sophisticated streamlining, and anechoic hull coatings all dramatically reduced their acoustic signatures. When combined with their small size, especially relative to nuclear-powered submarines, and thus an ability to operate in confined waters, this stealth made later diesel-electric boats very difficult targets for aerial, surface, and subsurface antisubmarine forces.

Several producers of advanced conventional boats were able to turn these assets into lucrative export production. Beginning in the 1970s, France, Sweden, and above all Germany began to dominate the market for advanced conventionally powered submarines worldwide. The most successful by far is the family of German Type 209 submarines, of which almost 60 have been delivered or are on order for 15 nations. Moreover, since many of these export boats were ordered by fleets without solid experience of modern submarine operations, lucrative training and support contracts often accompany the orders for the hardware, and contribute to the spread of a remarkably uniform ethos of operation.

## AIR-INDEPENDENT PROPULSION

From the very early days of modern submarine development in the late 1800s, designers have been interested in developing means whereby submarines could operate for extended periods without having to return to the surface, relying instead on propulsion systems that simultaneously could operate independent of an air supply and were functional for an extended period of time. There were a number of experiments with operating internal-combustion engines from an onboard oxygen supply in the Italian and Russian fleets around 1900, but none were very successful and all encountered substantial safety issues.

In the late 1930s, Helmuth Walter, an engineer with the Germania submarine construction firm, began exploring a variety of options for closed-cycle machinery aboard submarines. His initial idea contemplated using diesel engines running on oxygen created by breaking down high-test hydrogen peroxide, but he moved from that concept to exploiting the production of steam from the same source to drive a turbine. In his process, hydrogen peroxide was broken down in a catalyzer into steam and oxygen. They both passed into a combustion chamber, were mixed with water and diesel fuel, and were ignited to produce steam at a very high temperature and pressure to drive a turbine. The exhaust went to a condenser where the water was condensed and passed back into the system and the waste gases were expelled overboard. This lightweight plant was demonstrated in a series of experimental prototypes that ran trials between 1940 and 1944 and led to the production of a very small number of potentially operational boats using the same type of machinery.

Only three boats of Type XVII were completed, and they were scuttled at the end of World War II. Two were recovered, however, going to the United States and Britain for trials. The United States did not foresee a service application for Walter's system, but the Royal Navy, which commissioned its boat as the *Meteorite,* saw the hydrogen peroxide turbine as a less expensive alternative to nuclear power that also had the potential to enter fleet service more quickly. In that expectation it was to be disillusioned, since the Walter turbine system was far from ready for operational use; the Royal Navy's many troubles with its experimental prototypes, the *Explorer* and the *Excalibur,* seriously set back work on developing air-independent propulsion systems.

Interest in such powerplants lingered, and it revived significantly in the 1980s, when very effective stealthy diesel-electric boats became a significant part of the world's submarine fleet. The first such successful system was developed by the Swedish Kockums company, and, like all modern AIP plants, it is an add-on system: a module that can be inserted into an existing submarine design. The Kockums AIP system uses a Stirling engine that burns oxygen and diesel fuel in a pressurized combustion chamber. Oxygen is carried in liquefied form in tanks. It is mixed in the chamber with diesel fuel from the boat's bunkers, and exhaust gases are mixed with seawater and discharged overboard. The engine drives a generator that is used to power the main electric motors and also to recharge the submarine's batteries. This system adds about 25 feet to the submarine's length. It is very quiet and almost vibration free, has a very low infrared signature, and enables the boat to operate for 14 to 18 days without having to use its snorkel to recharge its batteries.

France developed its MESMA (Module d'Energie Sous-Marin Autonome) system using a Rankine-cycle turbo-alternator running on steam produced by the combustion of ethanol and oxygen. Liquid oxygen and ethanol are combined in a combustion chamber at a pressure of 60 psi; the steam is passed through the turbine, and the exhaust is expelled overboard. Operating the system does not increase the submarine's acoustic signature. It has a low infrared signature, and it is potentially more powerful than the Stirling engine system, but less efficient in its fuel consumption.

A third AIP system uses a closed-cycle diesel engine. When switched to the closed-cycle mode, the engine operates using an artificial atmosphere synthesized from oxygen, an inert gas such as argon, and recycled exhaust products. The exhaust passes through coolers and scrubbers that separate out the argon and a small part of the other gases and mixes the rest with seawater for discharge overboard. Although this is potentially the simplest system to install, it has been tested in only one boat and has yet to be used in an operational submarine.

The final AIP system currently employed uses fuel cells. Both Howaldtswerke-Deutsche Werft and Fincantieri are offering such systems, which essentially insert modular banks of fuel cells into the submarine to generate the power for its electric motors. This installation adds about 20 feet to the length of the boat. It has the advantage of generating no waste products for discharge overboard, and its modularity makes it attractive because the cells can be installed shoreside without requiring special handling.

Air-independent propulsion is still largely in its infancy in diesel-electric submarines. No system's power output is yet sufficient to allow it to become the primary powerplant for a submarine, so all operate as supplements to the standard installation, permitting the boat to operate for two to four weeks without requiring an external air source but not bestowing the unlimited submerged operation of a nuclear plant.

## NUCLEAR PROPULSION

At the beginning of the Cold War, all operational submarines used diesel-electric drive. This required submarines either to surface frequently to recharge their batteries or that they be equipped with a snorkel breathing device to operate their diesel engines while under water. New approaches to the design of conventional submarines—such as the German Type XXI *elektroboote,* which greatly increased submerged range and speed mainly by tripling the size of the battery—were clearly only temporary substitutes for finding power plants that were not dependent on an external air supply for continuous operation. The Walter turbine, powered through the breakdown of hydrogen peroxide, had potential, but it too suffered from limitations. Its operation was hazardous, the technology was immature, and it had a voracious appetite for fuel, severely limiting the duration of a submarine deploying the plant.

The physicist George Pegram, at a specially convened meeting on 17 March 1939, suggested to the U.S. Navy that a suitable nuclear fission chamber could be used to generate steam for a submarine power plant; three days later, the Naval Research Laboratory was granted $1,500 to begin research into its feasibility. The outbreak of war and the concentration of the nation's nuclear physicists on the creation of an atomic bomb sidelined further work until late in 1944, when it resumed. Serious research into nuclear power for submarines, which promised essentially unlimited high-speed submerged operation, began immediately after World War II, leading to the establishment of the Nuclear Power Branch, headed by Captain Hyman G. Rickover, within the Bureau of Ships in August of 1948. A Division of Reactor Development, also headed by Rickover, in the Atomic Energy Commission, was inaugurated the following February.

The U.S. Navy followed two tracks simultaneously in developing reactors for use in submarines, developing units using either pressurized water or liquid sodium to transfer heat to the steam generators. Its first submarine with a nuclear power plant was the *Nautilus*, commissioned on 30 September 1954, although it was not underway under nuclear power until 17 January 1955. The *Nautilus* used a pressurized water reactor, identical to a unit tested on land prior to the installation of its power plant. It was a resounding technical success, although it suffered from extraordinarily high noise levels that made its deployment as an operational boat in wartime problematic. The *Nautilus* was followed by the *Seawolf*, powered by a liquid sodium reactor, which commissioned on 30 March 1957. The navy found that the liquid sodium reactor required detailed attention to maintaining precise and limited operational parameters, and it decided against further investment in its development. Instead, all resources went into production and improvement of pressurized water units.

The Soviet Union began research work on nuclear power plants for submarines in 1946, but very little progress was made because of the need to concentrate resources in the field of nuclear energy on the production of bombs, to break the U.S. monopoly on such weapons. Consequently, it was not until 1952 that significant effort was devoted to the project, leading to the testing of a land-based prototype beginning in March 1956. Construction of the Soviet Union's first nuclear-powered submarine began with the laying of the keel for the *K-3* at the Molotovsk yard in September 1955. The boat was launched on 9 August 1957 and commissioned on 7 January 1958. Unlike the American *Nautilus*, the *K-3* was the first of a class of 13 boats of the Project 627 (NATO-designated November) type, which also differed from U.S. practice in using two reactors for its power plant. Their greater power output endowed them with higher performance than their U.S. counterparts, but, like American nuclear boats, they were very noisy.

The Soviet Union also explored the use of other media for transferring heat to the steam generators, in this instance, liquid lead-bismuth. Its first submarine powered by such a plant was the *K-27*, built to Project 645, using the same hull design as the Project 627 boats lengthened to accommodate the bulkier reactors. The liquid metal, although less dangerous in the event of an accident than the sodium of the *Seawolf's* plant, was somewhat less efficient as a heat exchanger and also required constant heat to keep it from solidifying, leading to a requirement to either run the reactor continuously or provide en external heat supply while the boat was in port. Although initial trials were satisfactory, the *K-27* subsequently suffered a series of mechanical problems that led to its early decommissioning; the experience, however, was not sufficient to induce the Soviets to abandon lead-bismuth reactors immediately.

With the advent of ballistic missile submarines, both the United States and the Soviet Union sought to protect themselves from a first strike at the hands of the other by developing fast, stealthy submarines to intercept the ballistic missile boats, while simultaneously endeavoring to preserve their own strike capability through defeating the interceptors. Very quickly the principal target of attack submarines became enemy submarines, and the demand for high speed, maneuverability, and quiet operation led to the rapid adoption of the hull form pioneered by the *Albacore:* the teardrop, or body-of-revolution, shape. The Soviet Fleet introduced the remarkable titanium-hulled, highly automated Project 705 (NATO-designated Alfa) type into limited service. Powered by a single, very powerful lead-bismuth reactor, these boats could safely dive as deep as 2,000 feet and attain submerged speeds well in excess of 40 knots. The complexity of their reactors, however, caused problems in service and rendered them anomalies among the second-generation of attack boats: the Soviet Fleet's Project 671 (NATO-designated Victor) and the U.S. Navy's *Thresher* and *Sturgeon* classes became the most numerous and characteristic nuclear-powered attack submarines of the Cold War.

The Soviet Fleet also established a second requirement for its nuclear submarines, leading to the production of a series of specialized boats equipped with cruise missiles with the dedicated mission of tracking and, in the event of war, destroying the fast carriers of the U.S. Navy. Initially these cruise missiles had to be launched from the surface, so their platforms, the Project 675 (NATO-designated Echo-II) type, were optimized for stability on the surface. It was not until the Project 670 class (NATO-designated Charlie-I) nuclear-powered cruise-missile submarines that the Soviets developed the capability to launch cruise missiles while submerged.

The third generation of attack and cruise-missile submarines were the U.S. *Los Angeles* class and the Soviet Type 971 boats (NATO-designated Akula). Both embody considerable advances in reducing acoustic, magnetic, and infrared signatures, as well as greater operational flexibility compared with their precursors. The end of the Cold War, however, has curtailed their construction or operational deployment substantially.

Britain, France, and China all have deployed nuclear-powered attack submarines, while India is working toward deploying such boats in the not-too-distant future. Britain launched its first nuclear-powered submarine, the attack-type Dreadnought on 21 October 1960. It used a U.S. nuclear power plant, enabling the British to save both considerable time and money. Later British boats were fitted with British-built power plants, though these derived substantially from U.S. prototypes. Under President Charles de Gaulle, the French also built up a nuclear submarine force during the Cold War. The French took a different path than the Americans, British, and Soviets, however, in that they first built nuclear-powered ballistic missile submarines rather than nuclear-powered attack submarines. The country's first attack boats used power plants similar to those of its ballistic missile submarines. The low ebb of relations between France and the United States at the time meant that French designers could not draw on U.S. assistance or expertise in developing their nuclear reactors or submarine propulsion systems. Consequently, French submarine reactors were heavier than their U.S. and British counterparts. Their propulsion system also was very different, since French designers elected to use turbo-electric drive rather than steam turbines, and that preference has continued with the design for the next generation of attack submarines for the fleet, the Barracuda class, scheduled to begin deploying in 2010.

## Cold War Submarine Operations by the West

Three circumstances radically changed the paradigm of Western submarine operators immediately after World War II: the Allies' overwhelming victory in that conflict, the transformation of the Soviet Union from an ally into the West's preeminent opponent, and the advent of true submarines—epitomized by the German Type XXI boats, whose technology was readily accessible to all the erstwhile allies. Countering the potential major threat fast submarines could present to transatlantic and transpacific lines of communications and to the free operation of Western surface task forces permeated naval planning. Consequently, antisubmarine warfare, both defensive and offensive, became the central focus of Western submarine operations.

The limitations of existing boats, even after major modifications such as the GUPPY program in the U.S. Navy, and the constraints of current propulsion technologies at first entailed concentration on interception. Submarines were deployed forward, ideally in close proximity to Soviet naval bases or, if that was impractical, at "choke points," relatively tightly defined passages through which Soviet boats would have to travel to reach their targets. Early hunter-killer tactics relied on slow, stealthy boats using passive sonar and fire-control equipment, but actual operations quickly demonstrated the limited effectiveness of both the boats and their electronics.

The advent of nuclear-powered boats quickly changed the anti-submarine warfare situation for Western submarines forces from the 1960s. Their greater size provided space for very powerful sonar outfits whose capabilities finally came close to fulfilling the needs of stealthy hunter-killer operations. Their vastly enhanced submerged endurance made prolonged ambush deployments off Soviet bases or at choke points a realistic option. Powerful sonar, speed, and endurance also opened up the possibility of maintaining continuous submerged surveillance of Soviet submarines; an urgent requirement in the Cold War situation once the Soviet Union began deploying strategic missiles aboard dedicated submarine platforms. Furthermore, the submerged speed and endurance of nuclear boats at last made feasible the long-running concept of fleet submarines. They, however, did not take on the role of ambushers of enemy surface forces (the original fleet submarine concept) but rather operated as effective wide-ranging, stealthy escorts for important fast surface task forces, especially those centered on carriers which had become the principal targets of Soviet submarines. The operations of British nuclear boats as distant escorts for the task force operating against the Falklands/Malvinas in 1982 vividly illustrated this role; the sinking of the Argentinian cruiser *General Belgrano* on 2 May by HMS *Conqueror* and the subsequent self-blockade of Argentina's carrier *Veinticinco de Mayo* in port thereafter clearly demonstrated how effectively submarines could perform task force escort missions.

Two developments further expanded the mission portfolio of Western submarines: the use of submarine-launched cruise missiles and the growth of the Soviet surface fleet. The addition of cruise-missile launch capability to attack submarines enabled them to perform land attack missions with great precision against narrowly-defined targets. During the 1990s submarine-launched punitive Tomahawk cruise missile strikes against facilities of specific importance became the means of choice whereby the United States attempted to reinforce its foreign policy decisions and retaliate against regimes and organizations for attacks on U.S. citizens and assets. For example, on 20 August 1998 the United States launched Tomahawk missiles against six terrorist bases in Afghanistan and a factory in Sudan suspected of producing nerve gas in retaliation for the bombings of U.S. embassies in Kenya and Tanzania on 7 August. The commissioning of aircraft carriers into the Soviet Fleet also promptly revitalized the submarine mission of surface warship attack, so that Western nuclear boats took on the role of shadowing Soviet carrier forces that long had been an important function of Soviet submarines.

## Cold War Submarine Operations by the Soviet Bloc

At the end of World War II the Soviet Union had the largest submarine force in the world, although it was far from being the most effective either in the quality of its equipment or its operators. The onset of tensions with its erstwhile allies in Western Europe and North America that led to the Cold War made containing the threat of the West's overwhelming naval preponderance, and especially its carrier forces, a major Soviet military goal. Consequently, using as a basis the captured German *elektroboote* technology, the Soviet Union rapidly built up a very large force of modern submarines whose primary missions were intercepting and shadowing Western carrier forces and, should a conflict occur, attacking the transatlantic shipping bridge that carried reinforcements and supplies from North America to Europe.

A second mission quickly developed: countering Western submarines that had adopted antisubmarine warfare as their primary task. A dangerous cat-and-mouse game ensued that persisted throughout the Cold War between Soviet and Western submariners, primarily in the waters of the Arctic, North Atlantic, and Northwestern Pacific oceans, and the Mediterranean Sea. The boats, their equipment, their weapons, and their operators became ever more sophisticated but the objective remained the same: to secretly intercept an opponent and maintain stealthy contact thereafter.

The deployment of Western ballistic missile submarines quickly led the Soviet Navy to react in the same way as Western forces by deploying its attack submarines for operations to locate and shadow the missile boats from their departure from port throughout their missions. Stealth, endurance, and sophisticated sonar and fire control were crucial to the success of such operations, which persisted throughout the Cold War and beyond to the present.

Anticarrier operations received a substantial boost in effectiveness with the advent of fast nuclear boats armed with long-range anti-shipping missiles. This development closely coincided with the deployment of Soviet strategic missile submarines, whose survival in the open waters of the Atlantic and Pacific depended heavily on the ability of Soviet attack boats to neutralize Western carriers and submarines. This became even more important with the advent of long-range ballistic missiles capable of targeting North America without their launch platforms having to leave the relative safety of the Arctic Ocean. The Soviet Navy developed the concept of "bastion defense" in which its attack submarines and strong surface antisubmarine forces would neutralize Western efforts to penetrate this zone of safety with their boats while the Soviet anticarrier force prevented U.S. carrier task forces from supporting penetration operations or initiating their own attacks on the strategic missile submarines.

Throughout the Cold War attack submarines operated by all the protagonists played a vital role. They were in the forefront of both defensive and offensive operations, operating right off their opponent's bases, trailing both surface and submerged opposition assets, and protecting their own forces from interception and possible attack.

# CHAPTER FOUR

# Strategic Missile Submarines

THE ADVENT OF ATOMIC and nuclear weapons, the physical distance between the two principal protagonists in the Cold War, the range limitations of existing and imminent missile technologies, and concerns about the vulnerability of bomber aircraft led to the investigation of the potential of submarines as launch platforms for missiles. As the United States and the Soviet Union explored the possibilities of this new submarine mission, the craft's added attractions—stealth, mobility, and relative invulnerability—became more apparent, and it eventually came to occupy a position of at least parity with land-based strategic missiles and clear superiority over conventional bombers.

Because Germany was the first nation to deploy strategic missiles, its experience and concepts played a noticeable role in the development of U.S. and Soviet concepts. When Allied forces landed in Normandy and advanced into northern France and Belgium, they over-ran the launching sites for Germany's V-2 ballistic missiles. The range limitations of the V-2 missile (approximately 185 miles) had placed most targets in the United Kingdom beyond its strike capabilities, and attacks against the United States had clearly been far beyond the bounds of possibility. Such considerations had led the missile development staff at Peenemünde to study options for launching ballistic missiles at sea. The solution they chose was a self-contained canister, incorporating a launching platform, control space, and propellant stowage, that could be towed by a submarine to its firing position and water-ballasted upright for launch. Successful shoreside testing of this system was completed in late 1944, and construction of operational units had commenced; none, however, were completed before the war ended.

The United States and the Soviet Union each took possession of both the technology and the engineers from the V-2 missile at the end of World War II. This knowledge laid the foundations for both nations' subsequent development of strategic ballistic missiles for the delivery of atomic and nuclear warheads. Similarly, they used the knowledge acquired from the German V-1 program as the basis for developing their own land-attack cruise missiles that, initially, were more attractive than ballistic missiles because it was easier to endow them with longer reach. Both navies quickly appreciated the advantage of deploying land-attack missiles aboard submarines, since it offered the potential for launching weapons against their opponent's homeland from a stealthy platform.

The U.S. Navy initially concentrated its efforts in exploiting cruise missile technology for land-attack missions. It conducted test firings of Loon missiles (the U.S. production version of the V-1) from the submarines *Cusk* and *Carbonero* in early 1947, using radio-command guidance to improve their accuracy. Both boats served as guidance ships for later trials of the Regulus near-supersonic nuclear-armed cruise missile, fired from surface ships. Two other fleet submarines, the *Tunny* and the *Barbero*, received full conversions for front-line operation of Regulus missiles, entering service in 1953 and 1955, respectively. They soon were joined by the two purpose-built boats of the *Grayback* class and, in 1959, by the nuclear-powered *Halibut*. A large force of more elaborate nuclear-powered cruise missile submarines was proposed to supplement the *Halibut*. All boats were to carry the supersonic Regulus II, but, after limited testing, that missile was canceled in December 1958 as redundant to requirements (and to concentrate funding and effort on the Polaris ballistic missile); thus the submarines were reordered as nuclear-powered torpedo-attack craft.

The Soviet Navy exploited the concepts of the German V-2 missile launch canisters to develop a design for a very large submarine capable of firing both ballistic and cruise missiles against land targets. In the 1949 preliminary design the 5,400-ton (surfaced) Project P-2 boat could carry twelve R-1 ballistic missiles (the Soviet production version of the V-2) and additional cruise missiles, but its engineers were unable to solve a host of development problems, leading to the project's termination. The same design bureau began work the following year on Project 624, a 2,650-ton (submerged) cruise missile submarine powered by a closed-cycle Walter steam turbine based on the plant designed for the German Type XXVI boat. When that, too, was halted, work began on Project 628, a cruise missile–armed development of the wartime Series XIV design, but the Soviet Navy's rejection of its missile terminated efforts in 1953.

Thereafter, the Soviet Navy simultaneously pursued the development and deployment of both cruise and ballistic missile submarines. The diesel-electric Project 611A class (NATO-designated Zulu-IV) submarine B-62, with a single launch tube, was the first to fire an R-11 ballistic missile (NATO-designated Scud) on 16 September 1955. The succeeding Project 611AB class (NATO-designated Zulu-V) were the first operational ballistic missile submarines, the first boat (the B-67) commissioning on 30 June 1956. These six boats could launch their two R-11FM missiles from vertical tubes in the sail and retained the torpedo capabilities of their conventionally armed sisters. They were followed by 22 Project 629 class (NATO-designated Golf) boats armed with three improved R-13 missiles and 9 similarly armed nuclear-powered boats of the Project 658 class (NATO-designated Hotel).

Meanwhile, after trials with two boats between 1955 and 1959—a Project 611 (NATO-designated Zulu) and a Project 613 (NATO-designated Whiskey)—two series of operational conversions based on the Whiskey design entered service from 1960, as the six Project 644 class (NATO-designated Whiskey Twin Cylinder) and the six Project 665 class (NATO-designated Whiskey Long Bin). Soviet designers also pursued development of nuclear-powered cruise missile submarines, initially exploring a modified version of the fleet's first nuclear-powered attack boat as Project 627A and then a much larger 7,140-ton (submerged) type as Project 653, both optimized for submerged operation. But problems with the P-20 missiles for those vessels halted development. Instead, a new nuclear-powered design, Project 659 (NATO-designated Echo I), which featured a conventional hull form to maximize stability while launching missiles on the surface, entered service from 1961. On 14 December 1959, however, the new Strategic Rocket Forces were established. That arm of service took control of all land-based strategic missiles, downgrading the importance of the navy's cruise missile boats and leading to the decision to concentrate efforts on sea-based ballistic missiles and focus cruise missile efforts on antiship warfare.

Soviet ballistic missile submarines were initially very vulnerable during launch, because they had to surface to fire their missiles. On

10 September 1960, the *B-62* of the Project 611AB class successfully fired a ballistic missile while submerged. The new D-4 launch system it tested replaced the earlier D-2 system originally fitted in the Project 629 and Project 658 classes of ballistic missile submarines that began entering service in 1960. The upgraded Project 629A and Project 658M boats carried three liquid-fueled R-21 (NATO-designated Sark) missiles with a range of 870 miles (twice that of the earlier R-13 weapons) in vertical tubes and recommissioned beginning in February 1962.

In 1955, the United States began work on a submarine-launched ballistic missile that would ultimately become the Polaris. Designers also began working on options for launching ballistic missiles from submarines. Initially their designs were conceived to accommodate modified versions of the U.S. Army's liquid-fueled Jupiter missile and emerged as similar to the *Skipjack* class attack boats, with much enlarged sails incorporating the necessary launch tubes. The urgent development of the solid-fueled Polaris, however, made a more efficient arrangement possible. The first U.S. ballistic missile submarines used a modification of the *Skipjack* class attack boat design, lengthening the hull by 130 feet to accommodate 16 launch tubes in two rows of eight, additional auxiliary machinery, and special navigation and missile-control equipment. The navy was able to accelerate production by reordering a nuclear attack boat, the *Scorpion,* as a ballistic missile submarine and incorporating its machinery and structural material into its construction. The first U.S. Navy ballistic missile submarine, the *George Washington,* commissioned on 30 December 1959. The *George Washington* test-fired two Polaris missiles while submerged on 20 July 1960 in the Atlantic and departed on its first operational patrol on 15 November 1960.

The Polaris missile was upgraded over time, its range increasing with each iteration. The fourth upgrade produced a new missile, the Poseidon, which featured Multiple Independently Targeted Re-entry Vehicles (MIRVs). Each missile could carry 10–14 independently targeted nuclear warheads. It was relatively straightforward to upgrade existing ballistic missile submarines to launch successive versions of Polaris/Poseidon missiles, since it was not necessary to enlarge their launch tubes to accommodate them. The first boat to take Poseidon missiles to sea, the *James Madison,* departed on patrol on 30 March 1971, while the final war patrol by any of the 41 submarines armed with these missiles was not completed until 1994.

The Soviet Union was slower than the United States in developing ballistic missile submarines capable of carrying heavy loads of these weapons. In part this was attributable to an attraction toward deploying cruise missile boats, since cruise missiles seemed to offer greater and less complex development potential than ballistic weapons and the submarines would be capable of undertaking a broader range of missions. The emergence of a politically powerful rival for funding in the form of the Strategic Rocket Forces also inhibited development of boats matching the weapons capabilities of U.S. strategic submarines. The disappointing results of efforts to field long-range, heavily armed cruise missiles and the success in overcoming difficulties in developing solid-fueled ballistic weapons led the Soviet Fleet to develop and deploy a large force of powerfully armed strategic missile submarines: 34 of the Project 667A class (NATO-designated Yankee) followed by 43 of the various versions of the Project 667B type (NATO-designated Delta), which entered service between late 1967 and early 1986.

Both the United States and the Soviet Union continued to develop longer-range, more powerful ballistic missiles, which therefore were larger, and the bigger submarines required to accommodate them. For the United States the new missile was the Trident—substantially larger than the Poseidon—which led to the design of the *Ohio*-class submarines, the largest in the world at that time. They embarked 24 of the new weapons, an arrangement regarded as a considerably more efficient use of submarine platforms. The first of 18 boats, the *Ohio*, commissioned on 11 November 1981. All remain in service, although four are being converted to launch up to 154 cruise missiles via 22 vertical tubes, rather than ballistic missiles, with more possibly converting in the future. The Soviet Union countered with its Project 941 class ballistic missile submarines (NATO-designated Typhoon), the first, the *TK-208*, commissioning on 12 December 1981. They use an unusual double pressure hull form, are even larger than the *Ohio* class, and thus are the world's largest submarines, although they carried only 20 R-39 ballistic missiles (NATO-designated Sturgeon) in vertical tubes. The six boats of the class remain in service.

Britain, France, and China also operate strategic missile submarines. The British turned to the United States for their missiles, purchasing Polaris A-3 missiles, launch tubes, and control systems but developing their own warheads. The design process for the four boats of the *Resolution* class took a path similar to that of the first U.S. ballistic missile submarines. The British essentially used the design for their own *Valiant* class attack submarines and inserted the missile launching section from contemporary U.S. vessels abaft the sail to create the final design for their own boats. The first of the class, the *Resolution,* departed on its first operational patrol on 15 June 1968. When the United States developed the more powerful Trident missile, Britain negotiated an amendment to the original Polaris agreement in 1982 to acquire the new weapon and the necessary systems for its operation. The four boats of the *Vanguard* class used a greatly enlarged version of the *Resolution* class design. Unlike their U.S. equivalents, the British boats carry only 16 missiles. They began operational patrols in December 1994.

Largely at the instigation of President Charles de Gaulle, the French also created a submarine nuclear deterrent force. The French took a wholly independent route, developing their own indigenous M1 strategic ballistic missile system. The six submarines of the *Rédoutable* class also were the first French nuclear-powered boats, and they began operational patrols in 1971. After 1985 these boats were upgraded to launch the M4 missile with MIRV capability. As in the United States, the Soviet Union, and Britain, advances in missile design necessitated the development of larger submarines to accommodate the more powerful weapons. The four French boats of the *Triomphant* class carry 16 M45 ballistic missiles capable of launching up to 6 MIRV warheads to a distance of 3,750 miles. These large boats are unusual in using a nuclear-powered turbo-electric propulsion system. They are scheduled to receive upgrades to launch new M51 weapons, with a range of 5,000 miles, beginning in 2010.

After China joined the "nuclear club," it too inclined toward developing submarines to launch strategic missiles. In the absence of indigenous capability to realize that ambition, it turned to its then ally for assistance. The Soviet Union fabricated hull sections for two Project 629 class (NATO-designated Golf) ballistic missile submarines at Komsomolsk and transferred them, together with machinery and launch systems, to China in the early 1960s. The Chinese assembled one boat at Darien in the mid-1960s and commissioned it as its Type 035. The other boat, however, was never assembled. The completed submarine was deployed for testing: first of Soviet R-11F weapons and later of indigenously derived missiles. In 1981, China launched a single example of its Type 092 ballistic missile submarine (NATO-designated Xia). This was an enlarged version of China's first nuclear-powered attack submarine design, the Type 091 class (NATO-designated Han), lengthened to accommodate launch tubes for twelve JL-1 solid-propellant ballistic missiles with a range of 1,100 miles carrying a 200- to 300-kiloton warhead. That single boat became operational in 1983, although it was not until 1988 that the Chinese satisfactorily resolved launch control problems. Between 1995 and 1998 it was upgraded to deploy improved JL-2 weapons equipped with up to four MIRV warheads and with a maximum range of 5,000 miles. China is reported to be developing a new class of four nuclear-powered ballistic missile submarines (Type 094), but little reliable information on their characteristics is available.

## STRATEGIC MISSILE SUBMARINE OPERATIONS

The U.S. Navy began operating its Regulus-armed submarines on strategic deterrent patrols in September 1958. Exactly one year later, these boats initiated the continuous deployment of one or more cruise missile submarines in the North Pacific, targeting sites in the Soviet Far East for attack in the event of war. These patrols continued until July 1964, when the boats terminated their deterrent mission. Conventional Soviet cruise missile boats, on the other hand, undertook only relatively short-range missions in the Baltic Sea and Arctic Ocean until they were withdrawn from front-line service in the late 1960s, although they no longer operated land attack missiles after 1965. Their nuclear-powered cohorts of the Project 659 class (NATO-designated Echo I), however, were very active in the North Atlantic and the Pacific. One boat, the *K-122*, was seriously damaged internally by a battery fire on 21 August 1980 while operating off Okinawa; the fire killed nine crewmen and left the ship without power. Soviet ships had to tow the submarine to its base at Vladivostok.

U.S. ballistic missile submarines began deterrent patrols in the Atlantic in November 1960 and in the Pacific in December 1964. To maximize sea time, the U.S. Navy introduced a new system for operating its strategic missile submarines. Each boat was assigned two complete crews (differentiated as the Blue and Gold crews, the navy colors). While one crew took the boat on a 60-day deterrent patrol, the other was training, resting, or on leave. Upon the boat's return to port, the active crew oversaw replenishment and repairs, then exchanged with the alternate crew, which took the boat on patrol again. This crewing system has been maintained continuously to date; it allows the navy to maintain up to two-thirds of its active ballistic missile submarine fleet at sea at any moment.

The early Soviet conventional Project 611AB class (NATO-designated Zulu-V) operated exclusively in European waters as theater threat weapons. The later conventional Project 629 class (NATO-designated Golf) and nuclear-powered boats of the Project 658 class (NATO-designated Hotel) operated extensively with the Northern, Baltic, and Pacific fleets from 1962 until 1989. During those operations the *K-129* of the Project 629 class was lost on patrol in the North Pacific after an internal explosion on 8 March 1968. The Central Intelligence Agency undertook a clandestine salvage operation in 1974 using the purpose-built salvage vessel *Glomar Explorer* to recover the Soviet submarine. During the lifting of the wreck the hull broke apart, and only the forward section was recovered for examination and subsequent disposal. The Project 658 class was plagued with problems, largely a consequence of poor workmanship and inadequate quality control. A coolant pipe burst aboard the lead member of the class, the *K-19*, while it was operating submerged near Greenland on 4 July 1961, exposing the entire crew of 139 officers and men, of whom 14 died, to excessive radiation. After repairs the *K-19* returned to operations but collided with the U.S. nuclear-powered attack submarine *Gato* on 15 November 1969, damaging both boats. Then, on 24 February 1972, while on patrol 800 miles northeast of Newfoundland, the *K-19* suffered a catastrophic failure in its cooling system, resulting in the deaths of 28 of its crew. The powerless submarine was towed back to its base on the Kola Peninsular, repaired, returned to service on 5 November 1972, and not decommissioned until 1990. Other members of the class also suffered major power plant problems, often requiring tows back to port, and leading to a major reappraisal of inspection procedures during construction and repair.

The Soviet Union began deploying the large strategic missile submarines of the Project 667A class (NATO-designated Yankee) on deterrent patrols off the Atlantic coast of the United States from June 1969 and off the Pacific coast from October 1970. Thereafter, the Soviet Navy maintained two to four of the class off the Atlantic coast and at least one off the Pacific coast. After these submarines had been supplemented by the larger boats of the Project 667B type (NATO-designated Delta), the Soviets kept 10 to 14 vessels at sea on deterrent patrols, with about three-quarters of all its ballistic missile submarines ready for almost immediate service. It also developed systems enabling submarines to launch missiles while alongside in their homeports to maximize their ability to intervene in a conflict at short notice. This disposition of forces exploited the range advantage of the Soviet liquid-fueled missiles, which enabled their submarines to operate within "bastions," oceanic areas protected by the Soviet Fleet's own antisubmarine and antiship forces from attack by NATO antisubmarine and strike operations. That capability became even more effective when the huge Project 941 class ballistic missile submarines (NATO-designated Typhoon) became operational in late 1981; the range of their weapons was sufficient for them to operate in the Arctic Ocean, where they were virtually immune from attack.

Both the British and French ballistic missile submarine forces adopted a crewing system similar to that devised by the U.S. Navy, using two crews to maximize operational deployments. The two forces have consistently maintained about three-quarters of their submarines in operational status, with the other quarter undergoing major refits. However, the smaller number of submarines each navy possessed meant that few boats were at sea. During the Cold War up to half of the total forces were deployed on deterrent patrols at any one time, but both navies now operate at a reduced tempo. Each fleet is currently reduced to four submarines, usually with only one on patrol at any given time. China, with a single boat, does not maintain standing patrols. Its single Type 092 submarine has rarely ventured outside Chinese territorial waters.

# SUBMARINES OF THE WORLD

# Pioneers

| | |
|---|---|
| Netherlands | Drebbel's submarine (1620) |
| United States | *Turtle* (1776) |
| | *Nautilus* (1800) |
| Germany | *Brandtaucher* (1850) |
| United States | Phillips's submarines (1852) |
| Germany | *Diable Marin* (1855) |
| Spain | *Ictineo* (1859) |
| United States | *Pioneer* (1862) |
| | *Pioneer II* (1862) |
| | *Alligator* (1862) |
| | *H.L. Hunley* (1863) |
| France | *Plongeur* (1863) |
| United States | *Sub Marine Explorer* (1866) |
| Russia | Aleksandrovski's submarine (1866) |
| United States | *Intelligent Whale* (1868) |
| Russia | Drzewiecki Type I (1877) |
| | Drzewiecki Type II (1878) |
| | Drzewiecki Type III (1878) |
| United States | *Holland I* (1878) |
| United Kingdom | *Resurgam I* (1878) |
| | *Resurgam II* (1879) |
| United States | *Fenian Ram* (1881) |
| | *Holland III* (1883) |
| | *Peacemaker* (1884) |
| | *Holland IV* (1885) |
| United States | Baker's submarine (1892) |
| United States | *Plunger* (1895) |
| | *Argonaut I* (1897) |
| | *Argonaut II* (1899) |

# Submarine Builders

SUBMARINE CONSTRUCTION, as many navies have learned to their cost, is and always has been a complex and technically challenging task. Consequently, many of the yards currently involved in building submarines are complexes with long histories of constructing this type of boat. In several instances, these shipyards have built submarines for a hundred years or more. Over that stretch of time, however, they have altered greatly, adding new equipment and capabilities, and, very often, passing through multiple changes of ownership and business designation. In an attempt to convey this continuity, the reference section shows only one name for each yard. The full list of business names over time follows.

**61 Kommuna**: 61 Kommuna Yard No. 445, Nikolayev.

**Admiralty**: Admiralty Shipyard, St. Petersburg. It became the Marti Yard No. 194, Leningrad, in 1922; the Leningrad Admiralty Association in 1972; and the United Admiralty Association, St. Petersburg, in 1999.

**A.G.-Weser**: *see* **Bremen**.

**Ansaldo**: S. A. Ansaldo, Sestri Ponente-Genoa.

**Armstrong**: Sir W. G. Armstrong, Whitworth and Company, Newcastle-upon-Tyne. It became Vickers-Armstrong, Ltd. in 1927.

**ASC**: Australian Submarine Corporation, Adelaide.

**Atlas**: Atlas Werke, Bremen.

**BAE Systems Marine**: *see* **Barrow**.

**Baltic**: Baltic Works, St. Petersburg. It became the Ordzhonikidze Yard No. 189, Leningrad, in 1922, and the Baltic Shipyard in 1999.

**Baltic Yard**: Baltic Yard, Nikolayev. This yard was a subsidiary of the Baltic Works in St. Petersburg.

**Barrow**: Barrow Ship Building Company, Barrow-in-Furness. It became the Naval Construction and Armaments Company in 1888; Vickers, Sons and Maxim, Ltd. in 1897; Vickers, Ltd. in 1911; Vickers-Armstrong, Ltd. in 1927; Vickers-Armstrong Shipbuilders in 1955; Vickers, Ltd. Shipbuilding Group in 1968; British Shipbuilders in 1977; Vickers Shipbuilding and Engineering, Ltd. in 1986; Marconi Marine in 1995; and BAE Systems Marine in 1999.

**Beardmore**: William Beardmore and Company, Glasgow.

**Bergsund**s: Bergsunds Verkstad, Stockholm.

**Bethlehem Shipbuilding Corporation**: *see* **Quincy**.

**Blohm und Voss**: Schiffswerft und Maschinenfabrik Blohm und Voss, Hamburg. It became Blohm und Voss A.G. in 1955 and was acquired by Thyssen Industrie A.G. in 1996.

**Bong Dao Bo**: Bong Dao Bo Shipyard, Singpo.

**Boston**: Boston Navy Yard, Charlestown, Massachusetts.

**Bremen**: A.G.-Weser, Bremen. It became the principal component of the Deutsche Schiff- und Maschinenbau Aktiengesellschaft (Deschimag) in 1926.

**Brest**: Arsenal de Brest.

**British Pacific**: British Pacific Construction and Engineering Company, Vancouver, British Columbia.

**British Shipbuilders**: *see* **Barrow** *and* **Cammell Laird**.

**California**: California Shipbuilding Company, Long Beach, California.

**Cammell Laird**: Cammell Laird, Birkenhead. It became British Shipbuilders in 1977, and Vickers Shipbuilding and Engineering, Ltd. in 1986.

**Canadian Vickers**: Canadian Vickers, Ltd. Montreal.

**Cantieri Navali del Quarnaro (CNQ)**: *see* **Fiume**.

**Cantiere Navale Triestino (CNT)**: *see* **Monfalcone**.

**Cantieri Riuniti dell'Adriatico (CRDA)**: *see* **Monfalcone**.

**Carraca**: Arsenal de la Carraca, Cadiz.

**Cartagen**a: Sociedad Española de Construcion Naval, Cartagena Dockyard. It became the Empresa Nacional Bazan de Construciones Navales Militaries S. A. in 1947; Izar Construciones Navales S. A. in 2001; and Navantia S. A. in 2005.

**CDT**: Cantieri del Tirreno, Riva Trigoso.

**Chatham**: Chatham Dockyard.

**Chernomorskiy Yard No. 444**: *see* **Nikolayev.**

**Cherbourg**: Arsenal de Cherbourg. Redesignated Direction des Constructions Navales (DCN) in 1998.

**CNF**: Chantiers Navals Français, Caen.

**Copenhagen**: Orlogsværftet (Copenhagen Navy Yard).

**Cramp**: William Cramp and Sons Ship and Engine Building Company, Philadelphia, Pennsylvania.

**Crescent**: Crescent Shipyard, Elizabethport, New Jersey.

**Crichton**: Crichton Yard, St. Petersburg.

**Crichton-Vulcan**: Crichton-Vulcan, Aabo.

**Daewoo**: Daewoo Shipyard, Okpo.

**Dalzavod**: Dalzavod Yard No. 202, Vladivostok.

**Danubius Shipyard**: *see* **Fiume.**

**Danzig**: Kaiserliche Werft (Imperial Dock Yard) Danzig.

**Danziger**: Danziger Werft, Danzig.

**Denny**: William Denny and Brothers, Dumbarton.

**De Schelde**: Koninklijke Maatschappij De Schelde (De Schelde Royal Dock Yard), Vlissingen.

**Deutsche Schiff- und Maschinenbau Aktiengesellschaft (Deschimag)**: *see Bremen and Seebeckwerft.*

**Deutschewerft**: Deutsche Werft A.G., Hamburg. It merged with Howaldtswπerke in 1968 to become Howaldtswerke-Deutsche-Werft A.G. with yards in Kiel and Hamburg.

**Deutsche Werke**: *see Kiel.*

**Devonport**: Devonport Dockyard.

**Direction des Constructions Navales (DCN)**: *see Cherbourg.*

**Dubigeon**: Anciens Chantiers Dubigeon, Nantes.

**Echevarrieta y Larrinaga**: Astillero Echevarrieta y Larrinaga, Cadiz.

**Ekensberg**: Ekensberg A.B., Stockholm.

**Electric Boat**: Electric Boat Company, Groton, Connecticut. It became the Electric Boat Division of General Dynamics Corporation in 1952.

**Empresa Nacional Bazan de Construciones Navales Militaries S. A.**: *see Cartagena.*

**Fairfield**: Fairfield Shipbuilding and Engineering Company, Govan.

**FIAT**: Societa FIAT-San Giorgio de Spezza, La Spezia.

**Fijenoord**: Maatschappij voor Scheeps-en Werktuigbouw Fijenoord, Schiedam. It became N.V. Dok- en Werfmaatschappij Wilton-Fijenoord in 1929.

**Fincantieri**: *see Monfalcone and Muggiano.*

**Fiume**: Danubius Shipyard and Machine Works Company, Fiume. It became the Ganz Machine, Wagon, and Shipyard Company in 1911 and the Cantieri Navali del Quarnaro (CNQ) in 1920 after Fiume became part of Italy.

**Flenderwerke**: Flenderwerke, Lübeck.

**Flensburger**: Flensburger Schiffaht-Gesselschaft, Flensburg.

**Fore River Ship and Engine Company**: *see Quincy.*

**Galati**: Santieri Galati, Galata.

**Ganz Machine, Wagon, and Shipyard Company**: *see Fiume.*

**General Dynamics Corporation**: *see Electric Boat and Quincy.*

**Germania**: Norddeutsche Schiffbau A.G., Kiel. It became the Friedrich Krupp Germania-Werft A.G. in 1883 and merged with Howaldtswerke, Kiel, in 1945.

**Gironde**: Forges and Chantiers de la Gironde, Bordeaux.

**Golcük**: Golcük Naval Shipyard, Izmir.

**Gorkiy**: Sormovski Yard, Nizhniy Novgorod. In 1922 it became the Krasnoye Sormovo Yard No.112, Nizhniy Novgorod (renamed Gorkiy in 1932).

**Guangdong**: Kiang Chou Ship Yard, Guangdong.

**Hamburg**: Stettiner Maschinenbau A.G. Vulcan, Hamburg. It became Howaldtswerke Hamburg A.G. in 1930, and it merged with Deutsche

Werft in 1968 to become Howaldtswerke-Deutsche-Werft A.G., with yards in Kiel and Hamburg. The Hamburg yard was sold to Blohm und Voss in 1986.

**Hellenic**: Hellenic Shipyard, Skaramanga.

**Horten**: Horten Navy Yard.

**Howaldtswerke-Deutsche-Werft A.G.**: *see Deutschewerft, Hamburg, and HWK*.

**Howaldtswerke Hamburg A.G.**: *see Hamburg*.

**Howaldtswerke, Kiel**: *see HWK*.

**HSK**: Hietalahden Sulkutelakka ja Konepaja, Helsinki.

**Huludao**: Bohai Shipbuilding Heavy Industrial Company, Huludao.

**HWK**: Howaldtswerke, Kiel. It was sold to the Kriegsmarine in 1939; reverted to Howaldtswerke in 1943; and merged with Deutsche Werft in 1968 to become Howaldtswerke-Deutsche-Werft A.G., with yards in Kiel and Hamburg.

**Hyundai**: Hyundai Heavy Industries, Ulsan.

**Ingalls**: Ingalls Shipbuilding Corporation, Pascagoula, Mississippi. It became Litton Industries Ingalls Shipbuilding Corporation in 1961, and Northrop Grumman Ship Systems Ingalls Operations in 2001.

**Istanbul**: Pendik Naval Shipyard, Istanbul.

**Italcantieri**: *see Monfalcone and Muggiano*.

**Izar Construciones Navales S. A.**: *see Cartagena*.

**Jiangnan**: Jiangnan Shipyard, Shanghai.

**John Brown**: John Brown and Company, Clydebank.

**Karachi**: Karachi Shipyard.

**Karlskrona**: Karlskrona Örlogsvarvet (Navy Yard).

**Kawasaki**: Kawasaki Shipbuilding, Kobe.

**Kawasaki Shipbuilding, Tanagawa**: *see Tanagawa*.

**Kiel**: Kaiserliche Werft (Imperial Dock Yard), Kiel. It became the Reichswerf in 1919; privatized as Deutsche Werke in 1925; merged with Howaldtswerke Kiel in 1937; was sold to the Kriegsmarine in 1939 and became the Kriegsmarine Werft Kiel in 1943; and it reverted to Howaldtswerke in 1945.

**Kockums**: Kockums Mekaniska Verkstad, Malmö.

**Komsomolsk**: Leninsky Komsomol Yard No.199, Komsomolsk-on-Amur.

**Kriegsmarine Werft Kiel**: *see Kiel*.

**Krupp Germania-Werft A.G.**: *see Germania*.

**Kure**: Kure Navy Yard.

**La Ciotat**: Chantiers Navale La Ciotat, Le Trait.

**Lake**: Lake Torpedo Boat Company, Bridgeport, Connecticut.

**La Seyne**: Forges et Chantiers de la Méditeranée, La Seyne.

**La Spezia**: Arsenale Militare Marittimo della Spezia.

**Leningrad Admiralty Association**: *see Admiralty and Sudomekh*.

**Litton Industries Ingalls Shipbuilding Corporation**: *see Ingalls*.

**Loire**: Ateliers et Chantiers de la Loire, Nantes.

**Lorient**: Arsenal de Lorient.

**Manitowoc**: Manitowoc Shipbuilding Company, Manitowoc, Wisconsin.

**Marconi Marine**: *see Barrow.*

**Mare Island**: Mare Island Navy Yard, Vallejo, California.

**Marti Yard No. 194**: *see Admiralty.*

**Marti Yard No. 444**: *see Nikolayev.*

**Mayang Do**: Mayang Do Ship Yard.

**Mazagon**: Mazagon Dock, Ltd. Mumbai.

**Metal Works**: Metal Works, St. Petersburg.

**Mitsubishi**: Mitsubishi Shipbuilding and Engineering Company, Kobe.

**Mitsui**: Mitsui Shipbuilding and Engineering Company, Tamano.

**Molotovsk Yard No. 402**: *see Severodvinsk.*

**Monfalcone**: Cantiere Navale Triestino (CNT), Monfalcone. It became the Cantieri Riuniti dell'Adriatico (CRDA) in 1920, after Trieste became part of Italy; it was nationalized as part of Italcantieri in 1969, and reorganized as Fincantieri in 1984.

**Moran Brothers Company**: *see Seattle.*

**Motala**: Motala Verkstad.

**Muggiano**: S. A. Cantieri Navali del Muggiano, Muggiano-La Spezia. It became part of the Odero-Terni-Orlando (OTO) conglomerate in 1923, nationalized as part of Italcantieri in 1969, and reorganized as Fincantieri in 1984.

**Nagasaki**: Kawasaki Shipbuilding, Nagasaki.

**Naval Construction and Armaments Company**: *see Barrow.*

**Naval Yard**: *see Nikolayev.*

**Navantia S. A.**: *see Cartagena.*

**Nederlandsche**: Nederlandsche Dok en Scheepsbouw, Amsterdam.

**Neptun**: Neptun Schiffswerft und Maschinenfabrik A.G., Rostock.

**Nevskiy**: Nevskiy Shipbuilding and Machine Works, St. Petersburg.

**Nevskiy Nikolayev**: Nevskyi Yard, Nikolayev. This yard was a subsidiary of the Nevskiy Shipbuilding and Machine Works, St. Petersburg.

**Newport News**: Newport News Shipbuilding and Drydock Company, Newport News, VA. It became Northrop Grumman Newport News in 2001.

**New York**: New York Ship Building Corporation, Camden, New Jersey.

**Nikolayev**: Nikolayev Shipbuilding, Mechanical, and Iron Works, Nikolayev. It became the Naval Yard in 1917; the Marti Yard No. 444 in 1922; the Nosenko Yard No. 444 in 1956; and the Chernomorskiy Yard No. 444 in 1964.

**Nobel and Lessner**: Nobel and Lessner Yard, Reval.

**Nordseewerke**: Rheinstahl-Nordseewerke A.G., Emden. It became ThyssenKrupp Marine Systems Nordseewerke in 1991.

**Normand**: Ateliers et Chantiers Augustin-Normand, Le Havre.

**Northern Shipyard**: *see Zhdanov.*

**Northrop Grumman Newport News**: *see Newport News.*

**Northrop Grumman Ship Systems Ingalls Operations**: *see Ingalls.*

**Nosenko Yard No. 444**: *see Nikolayev.*

**Odero**: Cantiere Odero, Sestri Ponente-Genoa.

**Odero-Terni-Orlando (OTO)**: *see Muggiano.*

**Ordzhonikidze Yard No. 189**: *see Baltic.*

**Orlando**: Cantiere Navale Luigi Orlando, Livorno.

**Palmer**: Palmer's Shipbuilding and Iron Company, Jarrow.

**Pembroke**: Pembroke Dockyard.

**Pola**: Kaiserliche Werft (Imperial Dock Yard), Pola.

**Portsmouth**: Portsmouth Naval Shipyard, Seavey Island, Maine.

**Portsmouth DY**: Portsmouth Dockyard.

**Puget Sound**: Puget Sound Naval Shipyard, Bremerton, Washington.

**Pula**: Uljanik Yard, Pula.

**Putilov Works**: *see Zhdanov.*

**Quincy**: Fore River Ship and Engine Company, Quincy, Massachusetts. It became Bethlehem Shipbuilding Corporation in 1913, and the Quincy Shipbuilding Division of General Dynamics Corporation in 1964.

**Reichswerf**: *see Kiel.*

**Reihersteigwerft**: Reihersteigwerft, Hamburg.

**Rio de Janeiro**: Arsenal de Marinha, Rio de Janeiro.

**Rochefort**: Arsenal de Rochefort.

**Rotterdamse**: Rotterdamse Droogdok Maatschappij, Rotterdam.

**Sasebo**: Sasebo Navy Yard.

**Schichau**: F. Schichau GmbH., Danzig.

**Schneider**: Ateliers et Chantiers Schneider-Creusot, Chalon-sur-Saône.

**Scott**: Scott's Shipbuilding and Engineering, Greenock. It became Scott-Lithgow, Ltd. in 1970.

**Scott-Lithgow, Ltd.**: *see Scott.*

**Seattle**: Moran Brothers Company, Seattle, Washington. It became the Seattle Construction and Drydock Company in 1911, and the Todd Dry Dock and Construction Company in 1916.

**Seebeckwerft**: Seebeckwerft, Bremerhaven. It became a component of the Deutsche Schiff- und Maschinenbau Aktiengesellschaft (Deschimag-Seebeckwerft) in 1926.

**Seine-Maritime**: Ateliers et Chantiers de la Seine-Maritime, Le Trait.

**Severnoye Mashinostroitelnoye Predpriyatie (Sevmash) Yard**: *see Severodvinsk.*

**Severodvinsk**: Molotovsk Yard No. 402, Severodvinsk. It became the Severnoye Mashinostroitelnoye Predpriyatie (Sevmash) Yard No. 402 in 1957.

**Sevmash**: *see Severodvinsk.*

**Shanghai**: Kiangman Yard, Shanghai.

**Sormovo Yard No.112**: *see Gorkiy.*

**Split**: Split Shipyard.

**St. Nazaire**: Ateliers et Chantiers de St. Nazaire-Penhoët.

**Stockholm**: Stockholm Örlogsvarvet (Navy Yard).

**Stülcken**: Stülcken und Sohn, Hamburg.

**Sudomekh**: Sudomekh Yard No. 196, Leningrad. It merged with the Marti Yard No. 194 in 1972 to become the Leningrad Admiralty Association, which became the United Admiralty Association, St. Petersburg, in 1999.

**Sverdlovsk**: Ural Machine Works, Sverdlovsk.

**Swan Hunter**: Swan Hunter and Wigham Richardson, Newcastle-on Tyne.

**Tanagawa**: Kawasaki Shipbuilding, Tanagawa.

**Thornycroft**: John I. Thornycroft and Company, Woolston.

**Thyssen Industrie A.G.**: *see Blohm und Voss.*

**ThyssenKrupp Marine Systems Nordseewerke**: *see Nordseewerke.*

**Todd Dry Dock and Construction Company**: *see Seattle.*

**Tosi**: Cantieri Tosi S. A., Taranto.

**Toulon**: Arsenal de Toulon.

**UBAG**: Ungarische Unterseebootsbau A.G., Fiume.

**Union Iron Works**: Union Iron Works, San Francisco, California.

**United Admiralty Association**: *see Admiralty and Sudomekh.*

**Vegesack**: Bremer Vulkan A.G., Vegesack.

**Venezia**: Regia Arsenale di Venezia.

**Vickers-Armstrong, Ltd.**: *see Armstrong and Barrow.*

**Vickers-Armstrong Shipbuilders**: *see Barrow.*

**Vickers, Ltd.**: *see Barrow.*

**Vickers, Ltd. Shipbuilding Group**: *see Barrow.*

**Vickers Shipbuilding and Engineering, Ltd.**: *see Barrow and Cammell Laird.*

**Vickers, Sons and Maxim, Ltd.**: *see Barrow.*

**Vulcan**: Stettiner Maschinenbau A.G. Vulcan, Stettin. It was reincorporated as Stettiner Vulcan A.G. in 1930.

**White**: J. Samuel White and Company, Cowes.

**Whitehead**: Whitehead and Company Torpedo and Machine Works, Fiume.

**Wilhelmshaven**: Kriegsmarine Werft (Naval Dock Yard), Wilhelmshaven.

**Wilton-Fijenoord**: *see Fijenoord.*

**Wuchang Shipbuilding Industry Company**: *see Wuhan.*

**Wuhan**: Wuchang Shipyard. It became the Wuchang Shipbuilding Industry Company in 2004.

**Yarrow**: Yarrow and Company, Scotstoun.

**Yokohama**: Yokohama Navy Yard.

**Yokosuka**: Yokosuka Navy Yard.

**Zhdanov**: Putilov Marine Engine Works, St. Petersburg. It became the Putilov Works, Petrograd, in 1912; the Northern Shipyard, Leningrad in 1923; the Zhdanov Yard No.190 in 1934; and the Northern Shipyard in 1989.

# DATA TABLES EXPLANATORY NOTE

**DATES:** vessel launch dates are in parentheses after name.

**DISPLACEMENT:** tables show tonnage for submarines in both surfaced and submerged mode. Unless otherwise indicated, this figure is for "standard" tonnage/displacement with a full crew and all munitions and stores but without fuel.

**DIMENSIONS:** overall length, beam, and draft while surfaced.

**ENDURANCE:** nuclear powered submarines essentially have unlimited range until their reactors require refueling. Their period of continuous operation instead is limited by their supplies of provisions, water, and crew necessities.

**MACHINERY:** since many submarines have used separate plants for propulsion on the surface and while submerged, power outputs are given for each set of machinery.

**BUNKERAGE AND RANGE:** where known, this shows fuel capacity in tons and range at economical cruising speed in nautical miles (6,080 feet rather than 5,280 feet).

**ARMAMENT:** torpedo tubes expel torpedoes, usually using compressed air. Torpedoes exit "swim-out" tubes under their own power. Drop collars are devices that carry suspended torpedoes and swing outboard to launch them.

**NATIONALITY:** the tables list submarines by the national origin of their designs rather than by the nation which operated them. National operators are indicated by enclosing the name of the country in square brackets before the list of the vessels' names; e.g. [Norway].

# Early Submarines

## FRANCE
### *GYMNÔTE* (24 SEPTEMBER 1888)

BUILDER: La Seyne

DISPLACEMENT: 30 tons (surfaced), 31 tons (submerged)

DIMENSIONS: 58'5" x 5'11" x 5'6"

MACHINERY: 1 Krebs electric motor, 1 shaft. 51 shp = 7.25/4.25 knots

RANGE: 65 nm at 5 knots surfaced, 25 nm at 4.25 knots submerged

ARMAMENT: 2 x 356mm torpedoes (2 Tissier drop-collars)

COMPLEMENT: 6

NOTES: The *Gymnôte*, a single-hulled steel vessel designed by Gustave Zédé, was the first submarine to demonstrate satisfactory submerged depth control. Initially it relied on two horizontal and two vertical hydroplanes at the extreme stern for directional control. Additional pairs of hydroplanes on each side amidships and aft were added in 1893 and 1895, respectively. From 1889 it used a Maugin periscope for observation while submerged. Its principal operational deficiency was a very short range that resulted from total reliance on all-electric propulsion, which drew on a 564-cell battery. Nevertheless, the experimental *Gymnôte* proved very successful and laid the foundation for subsequent French submarine development.

In 1894 the *Gymnôte* received an improved 204-cell battery. It was lengthened by 2 feet in 1898, fitted with a new 108-cell battery, a 90-shp Sautter-Harlé electric motor, a large casing and conning tower, and an improved retractable Daveluy et Violette periscope, increasing surface displacement to 33 tons.

The *Gymnôte* operated from Toulon until it accidentally sank at dockside on 19 June 1907. It was refloated but stricken from service on 22 May 1908 because of excessive repair costs.

### *GUSTAVE ZÉDÉ* (1 JUNE 1893)

BUILDER: La Seyne

DISPLACEMENT: 266 tons (surfaced), 272 tons (submerged)

DIMENSIONS: 159'1" x 10'6" x 10'7"

MACHINERY: 2 Sautter-Harlé electric motors, 1 shaft. 720 shp = 9.25/6.5 knots

RANGE: 220 nm at 5.5 knots surfaced, 105 nm at 4.5 knots submerged

ARMAMENT: 1 x 450mm torpedo tube, total 3 torpedoes

COMPLEMENT: 19

NOTES: The single-hull submarine *Gustave Zédé* was designed by Gaston Romazotti, who had supervised the *Gymnôte*'s construction; it was built of Roma metal (a type of bronze) to limit corrosion. Its original 720-cell battery exploded while being charged and was replaced by a 360-cell unit that cut performance from the designed 15/8 knots. The evolution of its directional control surfaces followed the same pattern as that of the *Gymnôte* and proved equally successful. In 1900 the *Gustave Zédé* received a new battery and an enlarged superstructure that supported a lookout platform.

The *Gustave Zédé* operated out of Toulon until stricken on 8 September 1909, when it was sold for scrap.

## *MORSE* CLASS (1899)

*Morse* (4 July 1899), *Français* (29 January 1901), *Algerien* (25 April 1901)

BUILDER: Cherbourg

DISPLACEMENT: 147 (*Morse:* 143) tons (surfaced), 160 (*Morse:* 149) tons (submerged)

DIMENSIONS: 120'5" (*Morse:* 119'8") x 9'0" x 9'3"

MACHINERY: 1 (*Morse:* 2) Sautter-Harlé electric motor(s), 1 shaft. 307 (*Morse:* 284) shp = 10/8.25 knots (*Morse:* 7.25/5.5 knots)

RANGE: 135 nm at 6 knots surfaced, (*Morse:* 90 nm at 4.5 knots) surfaced, 97 (*Morse:* 25) nm at 4.5 knots submerged

ARMAMENT: 1 x 450mm torpedo tube (bow), 2 x 450mm torpedoes (external cradles), total 4 torpedoes (*Morse:* 1 x 450mm torpedo tube, total 3 torpedoes)

COMPLEMENT: 13

NOTES: The *Morse* class was another single-hull design by Romazotti. The *Morse* was constructed of Roma metal, while the later boats were of steel. The design was intermediate in size between its two precursors and brought together their best features. A national subscription organized by the newspaper *Le Matin* generated the funding for constructing the two later vessels.

The class operated in the English Channel. The *Morse* was stricken from service on 14 September 1908, and the *Français* and the *Algerien* on 26 March and 1 January 1914, respectively.

## *NARVAL* (21 OCTOBER 1899)

BUILDER: Cherbourg

DISPLACEMENT: 117 tons (surfaced), 202 tons (submerged)

DIMENSIONS: 111'7" x 12'6" x 6'1"

MACHINERY: 1 Brule triple expansion steam engine, 1 Adolphe-Seigle tubular boiler, 2 Hillairet-Huguet electric motors, 1 shaft. 225 ihp/86 shp = 9.75/5.25 knots

RANGE: 345 nm at 8.75 knots surfaced, 58 nm at 2.75 knots submerged

ARMAMENT: 4 x 450mm torpedoes (Drzewiecki drop-collars)

COMPLEMENT: 13

NOTES: Maxime Laubeuf's design for the *Narval,* a surface torpedo boat that could submerge to make a stealthy attack, was revolutionary. It was a double-hulled vessel with a strong pressure-resistant inner hull, containing the crew and machinery, surrounded by a seaworthy buoyant outer shell that incorporated the ballast tanks. The oil-fired steam plant made diving a leisurely process, because it took 12 minutes to cool the boiler and vent excess steam before submerging. Nevertheless,

the *Narval* was very successful and set the pattern for submarine development worldwide up until late in World War II.

The *Narval* operated mainly in the English Channel and North Atlantic until stricken on 3 September 1909, though the hulk was used for experiments and not sold until 6 February 1920.

## *SIRÈNE* CLASS (1901)

*Sirène* (4 April 1901), *Triton* (13 July 1901), *Espadon* (7 September 1901), *Silure* (29 October 1901)
BUILDER: Cherbourg
DISPLACEMENT: 157 tons (surfaced), 213 tons (submerged)
DIMENSIONS: 99'3" x 12'10" x 8'2"
MACHINERY: 1 Brule triple expansion engine, 1 du Temple boiler, 1 Hillairet-Huguet electric motor, 1 shaft. 275 ihp/100 shp = 9.75/5.75 knots
RANGE: 600 nm at 8 knots surfaced, 55 nm at 3.75 knots submerged

ARMAMENT: 4 x 450mm torpedoes (Drzewiecki drop-collars)
COMPLEMENT: 13
NOTES: This class used a developed *Narval* design. Improved power plant arrangements reduced time required to dive to as little as 6 minutes.

The class operated out of Cherbourg in the English Channel and Atlantic until sold on 12 November 1920.

## *FARFADET* CLASS (1901)

*Farfadet* (17 May 1901), *Korrigan* (25 January 1902), *Gnôme* (24 July 1902), *Lutin* (12 February 1903)
BUILDER: Rochefort
DISPLACEMENT: 185 tons (surfaced), 202 tons (submerged)
DIMENSIONS: 135'6" x 9'6" x 8'9"
MACHINERY: 2 Hillairet-Huguet electric motors, 1 shaft. 183 shp = 6/5.25 knots
RANGE: 115 nm at 5.25 knots surfaced, 28 nm at 4.25 knots submerged
ARMAMENT: 4 x 450mm torpedoes (external cradles)
COMPLEMENT: 16
NOTES: This class used a single-hull design

by Gabriel-Émile-Marie Maugas that owed much to earlier Romazotti types.

The class operated in the Mediterranean. The *Farfadet* sank in an accident at Bizerta on 5 July 1905 with the loss of fourteen crew, was salved, and returned to service as the *Follet*. It was stricken on 22 November 1913. The *Lutin* also sank accidentally, with the loss of the entire crew, near Sidi-Abdallah on 16 October 1906. It was salved but stricken on 9 June 1907. The *Korrigan* and the *Gnôme* were disarmed on 10 March 1910 and sold.

## *NAÏADE* CLASS (1903)

*Ludion* (18 March 1903), *Souffleur* (20 April 1903), *Perle* (1 November 1903), *Dorade* (5 November 1903), *Esturgeon* (8 January 1904), *Bonite* (6 February 1904), *Thon* (18 March 1904), *Grondin* (15 July 1904), *Anguille* (8 August 1904), *Alose* (12 October 1904), *Truite* (14 April 1905)

BUILDER: Toulon

*Loutre* (25 August 1903), *Castor* (5 November 1903), *Phoque* (16 March 1904), *Otarie* (16 April 1904), *Méduse* (15 June 1904), *Oursin* (26 September 1904)

BUILDER: Rochefort

*Protée* (8 October 1903), *Lynx* (24 November 1903), *Naïade* (20 February 1904)

BUILDER: Cherbourg

DISPLACEMENT: 70.5 tons (surfaced), 73.5 tons (submerged)

DIMENSIONS: 77′11″ x 7′5″ x 8′6″

MACHINERY: 1 Panhard and Levasseur gasoline engine, 1 SEE electric motor, 1 shaft. 57 bhp/95 shp = 7.25/6 knots

RANGE: 200 nm at 5.5 knots surfaced, 30 nm at 4 knots submerged

ARMAMENT: 2 x 450mm torpedoes (external cradles)

COMPLEMENT: 12

NOTES: Romazotti's single-hull design for this class introduced internal combustion engines into French submarines. The short range of these boats was a major deficiency.

All the class operated in the Mediterranean, apart from the three boats built at Cherbourg, which served in the English Channel. The *Esturgeon* was stricken on 7 June 1912, the *Grondin* on 8 May 1913, and the remainder on 21 May 1914.

## *X* (15 NOVEMBER 1904)

BUILDER: Cherbourg

DISPLACEMENT: 168 tons (surfaced), 179 tons (submerged)

DIMENSIONS: 123′8″ x 10′2″ x 8′1″

MACHINERY: 2 Panhard et Levasseur gasoline engines, 2 Sautter-Harlé electric motors, 2 shafts. 260 bhp/230 shp = 8.5/6 knots

RANGE: 170 nm at 8.25 knots surfaced, 60 nm at 4.5 knots submerged

ARMAMENT: 1 x 450mm torpedo tube (bow), 3 x 450mm torpedoes (2 x Drzewiecki drop-collars, 1 x external cradle), total 6 torpedoes

COMPLEMENT: 15

NOTES: Romazotti modified Maugas's design for the *Farfadet* to create an experimental submarine that was the first to use two shafts.

Renamed the *Dauphin* on 13 February 1911, this submarine served in the English Channel until stricken on 21 May 1914.

## Z (28 MARCH 1904)

BUILDER: Rochefort
DISPLACEMENT: 202 tons (surfaced), 222 tons (submerged)
DIMENSIONS: 135'6" x 9'10" x 9'2"
MACHINERY: 1 Sautter-Harlé diesel engine, 1 Sautter-Harlé electric motor, 1 shaft. 190 bhp/180 shp = 9/7 knots
RANGE: 500 nm at 5 knots surfaced, 45 nm at 4 knots submerged
ARMAMENT: 2 x 450mm torpedo tubes (bow)
COMPLEMENT: 16
NOTES: Maugas modified his *Farfadet* design by adding a diesel engine for surface propulsion to create this experimental submarine.

The Z operated in the Mediterranean until it was stricken on 9 March 1910.

## AIGRETTE CLASS (1904)

*Aigrette* (23 January 1904), *Cicogne* (11 November 1904)
BUILDER: Toulon
DISPLACEMENT: 178 tons (surfaced), 253 tons (submerged)
DIMENSIONS: 117'7" x 13'3" x 8'7"
MACHINERY: 1 diesel engine, 1 electric motor, 1 shaft. 150 bhp/139 shp = 9.25/6.25 knots
RANGE: 1300 nm at 8 knots surfaced, 65 nm at 3.75 knots submerged
ARMAMENT: 4 x 450mm torpedoes (2 x Drzewiecki drop-collars, 2 x external cradles)
COMPLEMENT: 14
NOTES: These boats were essentially diesel-engined versions of Laubeuf's *Sirène* class submarines. Planned construction of eleven additional boats was canceled in September 1902.

Both submarines served in the Mediterranean until stricken on 12 November 1919.

## Y (24 JULY 1904)

BUILDER: Toulon
DISPLACEMENT: 178 tons (surfaced), 253 tons (submerged)
DIMENSIONS: 117'7" x 13'3" x 8'7"
MACHINERY: 1 diesel engine, 1 shaft. 250 bhp = 10/6 knots
ARMAMENT: 2 x 450mm torpedo tubes (bow), 3 x 450mm torpedoes (2 x Drzewiecki drop-collars, 1 x external cradle aft)
COMPLEMENT: 15
NOTES: Émile Bertin designed this experimental, single-hull submarine that used a diesel engine for both surfaced and submerged propulsion. A plan to fit an electric motor and batteries to drive it while submerged was abandoned.

The Y remained in trials status throughout its career. It was disarmed and stricken on 1 March 1909.

## *OMEGA* (28 NOVEMBER 1905)

BUILDER: Toulon
DISPLACEMENT: 306 tons (surfaced), 409 tons (submerged)
DIMENSIONS: 160'5" x 13'9" x 9'3"
MACHINERY: 1 du Temple triple expansion engine, 1 du Temple boiler, 1 Nancy electric motor, 1 shaft. 350 ihp/234 shp = 10.25/6 knots
RANGE: 1076 nm at 8 knots surfaced, 45 nm at 5 knots submerged
ARMAMENT: 2 x 450mm torpedo tubes (bow), 4 x 450mm torpedoes (2 x Drzewiecki drop-collars, 2 x external cradles aft), total 6 torpedoes
COMPLEMENT: 22
NOTES: An experimental double-hull submarine designed by Émile Bertin and Emmanuel Petithomme that used half the machinery arrangements of the later *Pluviôse* class boats.

The *Omega* was renamed the *Argonaute* on 27 September 1910. It operated in the Mediterranean until stricken on 20 May 1919.

## *ÉMERAUDE* CLASS (1906)

*Émeraude* (6 August 1906), *Opale* (20 November 1906), *Rubis* (26 June 1907)
BUILDER: Cherbourg
*Saphir* (6 February 1908), *Topase* (2 July 1908), *Turquoise* (3 August 1908)
BUILDER: Toulon
DISPLACEMENT: 392 tons (surfaced), 425 tons (submerged)
DIMENSIONS: 147'4" x 12'10" x 12'0"
MACHINERY: 2 Sautter-Harlé diesel engines, 2 Sautter-Harlé electric motors, 2 shafts. 600 bhp/450 shp = 11.5/9.25 knots
RANGE: 2000 nm at 7.25 knots surfaced, 100 nm at 5 knots submerged
ARMAMENT: 6 x 450mm torpedo tubes (4 bow, 2 stern), total 6 torpedoes
COMPLEMENT: 21
NOTES: These single-hull boats designed by Maugas were based on his earlier design for the *Farfadet* class, modified for two-shaft propulsion. They lacked an adequate reserve of buoyancy and also initially had problems with their diesel engines. The *Topase* and the *Turquoise* were fitted with single 37mm deck guns in August 1915.

These boats operated primarily in the Mediterranean. The *Saphir* was mined and sunk in the Sea of Marmara on 15 January 1915. The *Turquoise* was beached as a result of damage from Turkish guns in the Sea of Marmara on 30 October 1915 and taken into the Turkish Fleet as the *Mustadieh Ombashi* but saw no further service. After its return to French control, it was stricken with its sisters on 12 November 1919.

## *CIRCÉ* CLASS (1907)

*Circé* (13 September 1907), *Calypso* (22 October 1907)
BUILDER: Toulon
DISPLACEMENT: 392 tons (surfaced), 425 tons (submerged)
DIMENSIONS: 147′4″ x 12′10″ x 12′0″
MACHINERY: 2 MAN diesel engines, 2 Hillairet-Huguet electric motors, 2 shafts. 630 bhp/460 shp = 12/7.75 knots
RANGE: 2160 nm at 8 knots surfaced, 98 nm at 3.5 knots submerged
ARMAMENT: 6 x 450mm torpedoes (2 x Drzewiecki drop-collars, 4 x external cradles), 1 x 47mm gun
COMPLEMENT: 22
NOTES: Laubeuf developed this design as an enlarged two-shaft version of his earlier boats to produce a high-seas submarine type.

Both boats operated in the Mediterranean before World War I. The *Calypso* sank after the *Circé* collided with it on 7 July 1914 off Toulon. The *Circé* operated in the Adriatic during the war, sinking the German submarine *UC-24* on 25 May 1917 and itself succumbing to a torpedo attack by the German *U-47* on 20 September 1918.

## *PLUVIÔSE* CLASS (1907)

*Pluviôse* (27 May 1907), *Vendémiaire* (7 July 1907), *Ventôse* (15 September 1907), *Germinal* (7 December 1907), *Floréal* (18 April 1908), *Prairial* (26 September 1908), *Messidor* (24 December 1908), *Thermidor* (3 July 1909), *Fructidor* (13 November 1909)
BUILDER: Cherbourg
*Papin* (4 January 1908), *Fresnel* (16 June 1908), *Berthelot* (19 May 1909), *Watt* (18 June 1909), *Cugnot* (14 October 1909), *Giffard* (10 February 1910)
BUILDER: Rochefort
*Monge* (31 December 1908), *Ampère* (30 October 1909), *Gay-Lussac* (17 March 1910)
BUILDER: Toulon
DISPLACEMENT: 398 tons (surfaced), 550 tons (submerged)
DIMENSIONS: 167′4″ x 16′4″ x 16′3″
MACHINERY: 2 triple expansion engines, 2 du Temple boilers, 2 electric motors, 2 shafts. 700 ihp/450 shp = 12/8 knots
RANGE: 1500 nm at 9 knots surfaced, 50 nm at 5 knots submerged
ARMAMENT: 1 x 450mm torpedo tube (bow), 6 x 450mm torpedoes (2 x Drzewiecki drop-collars, 2 x external cradles forward, 2 x external cradles aft), total 8 torpedoes
COMPLEMENT: 24
NOTES: Laubeuf reverted to steam surface propulsion for this large class of high-seas submarines, which proved very successful in service despite their slow diving time. In May 1910 the *Ventôse* cruised 1000 nautical miles in six days without replenishment. The internal bow torpedo tube was removed from all boats except the *Floréal*, the *Germinal*, the *Monge*, and the *Ventôse* prior to World War I as a result of an operational accident aboard the *Fresnel* on 5 October 1908 that flooded the boat.

These boats saw extensive service in the English Channel and the Mediterranean before World War I. The *Pluviôse* was rammed and sunk near Calais by the cross-channel steamer *Pas-de-Calais* on 26 May 1910 with the loss of the entire crew, but it was salved and returned to service. During World War I these boats operated extensively in the Adriatic. Austro-Hungarian aircraft and surface ships surprised the *Fresnel* off Cattaro on 5 December 1915, driving it ashore. The destroyer *Warasdiner* destroyed it with gunfire. While attacking the Austro-Hungarian cruiser *Helgoland* and five destroyers as they sortied from Cattaro on 29 December 1915, the *Monge* itself was rammed by the cruiser, forced to the surface, and sunk by gunfire. Only one crewmember survived when the *Vendémiaire* was rammed and sunk by the battleship *Saint-Louis* in the English Channel on 8 June 1912. The *Prairial* sank after colliding with the British steamer *Tropic* off Le Havre on 29 April 1918. The British armed boarding ship *Hazel* accidentally rammed and sank the *Floréal* off Mudros on 2 August 1918. The surviving boats were stricken in November and December 1919.

## *ARCHIMÈDE* (4 AUGUST 1909)

BUILDER: Cherbourg

DISPLACEMENT: 598 tons (surfaced), 810 tons (submerged)

DIMENSIONS: 197'0" x 18'5" x 13'7"

MACHINERY: 2 triple expansion engines, 2 du Temple boilers, 2 electric motors, 2 shafts. 1700 ihp/1230 shp = 15/11 knots

RANGE: 1160 nm at 10 knots surfaced, 100 nm at 4.5 knots submerged

ARMAMENT: 1 x 450mm torpedo tube (bow), 6 x 450mm torpedoes (4 x Drzewiecki drop-collars, 2 x external cradles), total 8 torpedoes

COMPLEMENT: 26

NOTES: Julien Hutter was responsible for this boat's design as an expanded version of Laubeuf's successful submarines of the *Pluviôse* class.

Before World War I, the *Archimède* operated in the English Channel and Atlantic. It then operated with British submarines based at Harwich until mid-1915. The *Archimède* transferred to the Adriatic for the remainder of the war, where it sank four Austro-Hungarian transports. It was stricken on 12 November 1919.

## *CHARLES BRUN* (14 SEPTEMBER 1910)

BUILDER: Toulon

DISPLACEMENT: 356 tons (surfaced), 450 tons (submerged)

DIMENSIONS: 144'4" x 13'1" x 10'10"

MACHINERY: 2 Indret steam engines, 2 Schneider accumulators and alternators, 2 shafts. 1300/200 shp = 13.5/7.25 knots

ARMAMENT: 2 x 450mm torpedo tube (bow), 4 x 450mm torpedoes (2 x Drzewiecki drop-collars, 2 x external cradles aft), total 8 torpedoes

COMPLEMENT: 24

NOTES: Maurice Just designed this boat with its experimental power plant. Problems with the *Charles Brun*'s power plant kept it from active service. It was stricken on 7 June 1920.

## *BRUMAIRE* CLASS (1911)

*Brumaire* (29 April 1911), *Frimaire* (26 August 1911), *Nivôse* (6 January 1912), *Foucault* (15 June 1912), *Euler* (12 October 1912), *Franklin* (22 March 1912)
BUILDER: Cherbourg
*Bernouilli* (1 June 1911), *Joule* (7 September 1911), *Coulomb* (13 June 1912), *Arago* (29 June 1912), *Curie* (18 July 1912), *Le Verrier* (31 October 1912)
BUILDER: Toulon
*Faraday* (27 June 1911), *Volta* (23 September 1911), *Newton* (20 should 1912), *Montgolfier* (18 April 1912)
BUILDER: Rochefort
[United Kingdom]—*W-1* (19 November 1914), *W-2* (15 February 1915), *W-3* (1 April 1915), *W-4* (25 November 1915)
BUILDER: Armstrong
DISPLACEMENT: 397 (*W-3* and *W-4*: 321) tons (surfaced), 551 (*W-3* and *W-4*: 479) tons (submerged)
DIMENSIONS: 170'11" x 17'9" x 10'2." (*W-3* and *W-4*: 149'11" x 17'10" x 9'4")
MACHINERY: 2 MAN diesel engines, 2 electric motors, 2 shafts. 840 bhp/660 shp = 13/9 knots
RANGE: 1700 nm at 10 knots surfaced, 84 nm at 5 knots submerged
ARMAMENT: 1 x 450mm torpedo tube (bow), 6 x 450mm torpedoes (4 x Drzewiecki drop-collars, 2 x external cradles), total 8 torpedoes (*W-1* and *W-2*: 2 x 18" torpedo tubes [bow], 4 x 18" torpedoes [4 x Drzewiecki drop-collars], total 6 torpedoes; *W-3* and *W-4*: 2 x 18" torpedo tubes [bow], total 4 torpedoes)
COMPLEMENT: 29
NOTES: Laubeuf produced this class as a diesel-engined version of his earlier steam-powered *Pluviôse* class boats. The engines were MAN diesels built by French manufacturers under license and much more reliable than earlier units.

The later pair of British boats used a design modified by Laubeuf himself. Most French boats received a single 47mm or 75mm deck gun during 1916. The later pair of British boats added single 3" AA guns on completion, and the earlier pair received single 3" AA guns when they transferred to Italian service.

All the French boats served in the Mediterranean prior to World War I and were very active in the Dardanelles and Adriatic thereafter. The *Curie* succeeded in entering Pola on 20 December 1914 but was trapped in the net barrage, forced to surface in the harbor, and captured. Lieutenant Georg von Trapp commissioned the submarine into the Austro-Hungarian Navy as the *U-14* on 1 June 1915. Already successful, he went on to become the leading Austro-Hungarian submarine ace. The French repossessed their submarine and put it back into service at the end of World War I. The *Joule* struck a Turkish mine in the Dardanelles on 1 May 1915 and was lost with all hands. Austro-Hungarian flying boats bombed the *Foucault* off Cattaro on 15 September 1915, forcing it to the surface, where it was abandoned and scuttled, the first aircraft victory over a submarine. The *Bernouilli* torpedoed the Austro-Hungarian destroyer *Csepel* in Cattaro harbor on 4 April 1916 without sinking it. It was lost to a mine off Durazzo on 13 February 1918. The surviving boats were stricken in the 1920s.

The British boats operated only briefly in the Royal Navy and were sold to Italy in July 1916. In Italian service they operated extensively in the Adriatic, the *W-4* being lost, probably to a mine, off Cape Rodoni between 4 and 6 August 1917.

## *DELFIN* CLASS (1911)

[Greece]—*Delfin* (1911), *Xifias* (1912), [Peru]—- *Ferre* (1912), *Palacios* (1913)
BUILDER: Schneider
DISPLACEMENT: 310 tons (surfaced), 460 tons (submerged)
DIMENSIONS: 164′0″ x 15′5″ x 9′0″
MACHINERY: 2 Schneider-Carels diesel engines, 2 Schneider electric motors, 2 shafts. 720 bhp/460 shp = 13/8.5 knots
ARMAMENT: 1 x 450mm torpedo tube (bow), 4 x 450mm torpedoes (Drzewiecki drop-collars), total 6 torpedoes
COMPLEMENT: 24

NOTES: These were Laubeuf boats for export. Peru's boats saw little operational service because of shortages of batteries and spare parts, and they were stricken in 1919. The Greek boats were in action during the Balkan War, during which the *Delfin* made an unsuccessful attack on 9 December 1912 against the Turkish cruiser *Medjidieh* outside the Dardanelles. They served under French command in 1917–1918, returned to Greek control, and were stricken in 1920.

## *MARIOTTE* (2 FEBRUARY 1911)

BUILDER: Cherbourg
DISPLACEMENT: 531 tons (surfaced), 627 tons (submerged)
DIMENSIONS: 210′3″ x 14′1″ x 12′6″
MACHINERY: 2 Sautter-Harlé diesel engines, 2 Breguet electric motors, 2 shafts. 1400 bhp/1000 shp = 14.25/11.5 knots
RANGE: 1050 nm at 10 knots surfaced, 100 nm at 5 knots submerged
ARMAMENT: 4 x 450mm torpedo tubes (bow), 2 x 450mm torpedoes (Drzewiecki drop-collars), total 8 torpedoes

COMPLEMENT: 29
NOTES: This large single-hull submarine, designed by Charles Radiguet, was similar to the earlier *Émeraude* class but featured a large forward casing to improve sea-keeping.

The *Mariotte* transferred from the English Channel to the Mediterranean late in 1914 and operated in the Dardanelles until it was caught in Turkish net defenses on 27 July 1915, forced to surface, and sunk by shore artillery.

## *AMIRAL BOURGEOIS* (25 NOVEMBER 1912)

BUILDER: Rochefort
DISPLACEMENT: 556 tons (surfaced), 735 tons (submerged)
DIMENSIONS: 184′5″ x 18′1″ x 12′0″
MACHINERY: 2 Schneider diesel engines, 2 SEE electric motors, 2 shafts. 1400 bhp/1000 shp = 13.75/8.5 knots
RANGE: 2500 nm at 10 knots surfaced, 100 nm at 5 knots submerged
ARMAMENT: 4 x 450mm torpedo tube (2 bow, 2 stern), total 8 torpedoes

COMPLEMENT: 25
NOTES: A large, long-range, double-hull submarine designed by Bourdelle. Problems with the diesel engines caused considerable delays in its entry into service. A 65mm deck gun was fitted in August 1917. The *Amiral Bourgeois* operated in the English Channel throughout its career and was stricken on 12 November 1919.

## *CLORINDE* CLASS (1913)

*Clorinde* (2 October 1913), *Cornélie* (29 October 1913)
BUILDER: Rochefort
DISPLACEMENT: 413 tons (surfaced), 567 tons (submerged)
DIMENSIONS: 176'10" x 16'9" x 11'2"
MACHINERY: 2 MAN-Loire diesel engines, 2 Nancy electric motors, 2 shafts. 800 bhp/700 shp = 13/9 knots
RANGE: 1300 nm at 10 knots surfaced, 100 nm at 5 knots submerged
ARMAMENT: 8 x 450mm torpedoes (6 x Drzewiecki drop-collars, 2 external cradles)
COMPLEMENT: 29
NOTES: These boats were essentially Hutter's enlargement of Laubeuf's *Brumaire* design. Single 75mm deck guns were fitted when these boats entered service in 1916.

The boats operated in the Atlantic and English Channel until they were stricken on 20 December 1926.

## *GUSTAVE ZÉDÉ* (20 MAY 1913)

BUILDER: Cherbourg
DISPLACEMENT: 849 tons (surfaced), 1098 tons (submerged)
DIMENSIONS: 242'9" x 19'8" x 12'2"
MACHINERY: 2 Delaunay-Belleville triple expansion engines, 2 du Temple boilers, 2 Schneider electric motors, 2 shafts. 3500 ihp/1640 shp = 17.5/11.5 knots
RANGE: 1400 nm at 10 knots surfaced, 135 nm at 5 knots submerged
ARMAMENT: 6 x 450mm torpedo tube (4 forward, 1 twin trainable external mount aft), 2 x 450mm torpedoes (external Simonot cradles), total 10 torpedoes, 1 x 75mm gun, 1 x 47mm gun
COMPLEMENT: 47
NOTES: Jean Simonot designed this long-range, high-seas submarine for diesel engines but recast it for a steam plant because the diesels proved less powerful than anticipated. The *Gustave Zédé* was reconstructed in 1921 to 1922. Two MAN 1200-bhp diesel engines from the surrendered German *U-165* replaced the steam plant, a large new bridge and conning tower were fitted, and two ballast tanks were converted to fuel bunkers.

The *Gustave Zédé* operated in the Adriatic during World War I and in the Atlantic after the war. It was stricken on 26 April 1937.

## *ARMIDE* CLASS (1913)

*Armide* (11 November 1913), [Japan]—*No. 15* (7 April 1916)
BUILDER: Schneider
*Amazone* (August 1916), *Antigone* (October 1916)
BUILDER: Gironde
[Japan]—*No. 14* (28 March 1918)
BUILDER: Kure
DISPLACEMENT: 457 tons (surfaced), 670 tons (submerged)
DIMENSIONS: 184'5" x 17'1" x 9'10"
MACHINERY: 2 Schneider-Carels diesel engines, 2 Schneider electric motors, 2 shafts. 2200 bhp/900 shp = 17.5/11 knots
RANGE: 2600 nm at 11 knots surfaced, 160 nm at 5 knots submerged
ARMAMENT: 4 x 450mm (Japanese boats: 18") torpedo tubes (2 bow, 2 stern), (*No. 14*: 2 x 18" torpedoes [external cradles] in addition), total 6/8 torpedoes. (*Armide*: 6 x 450mm torpedo tubes [2 bow, 4 trainable external mounts], total 8 torpedoes)
COMPLEMENT: 31
NOTES: These were Laubeuf export boats ordered from Schneider for Japan and Greece. The *Armide* was requisitioned on 3 June 1915, the two others on 30 May 1917.

All three French boats operated in the Mediterranean throughout their careers. The *Antigone* was stricken on 31 August 1927 and the two others on 27 August 1935. The Japanese boats were stricken on 1 December 1928.

## *NÉRÉIDE* (9 MAY 1914)

BUILDER: Cherbourg
DISPLACEMENT: 849 tons (surfaced), 1098 tons (submerged)
DIMENSIONS: 242'9" x 19'8" x 12'2"
MACHINERY: 2 Schneider-Carels diesel engines, 2 Schneider electric motors, 2 shafts. 2400 bhp/1640 shp = 17.25/10.5 knots
RANGE: 3120 nm at 10 knots surfaced, 90 nm at 4 knots submerged
ARMAMENT: 6 x 450mm torpedo tube (4 forward, 1 twin trainable external mount aft), 2 x 450mm torpedoes (external Simonot cradles), total 10 torpedoes, 1 x 75mm gun, 1 x 47mm gun
COMPLEMENT: 47
NOTES: The *Néréide* was completed to Simonot's original design for a long-range, high-seas submarine. The *Néréide* received a large new bridge and conning tower, similar to the *Gustave Zédé*'s, in 1921–1922.

The *Néréide* operated in the Atlantic throughout its career until it was stricken on 27 August 1935.

## *AMPHITRITE* CLASS (1914)

*Amphitrite* (9 June 1914), *Astrée* (6 December 1915)
BUILDER: Rochefort
*Ariane* (5 September 1914), *Andromaque* (13 February 1915)
BUILDER: Cherbourg
*Atalante* (14 April 1915), *Artémis* (14 October 1915), *Amarante* (11 November 1915), *Aréthuse* (20 April 1916)
BUILDER: Toulon
DISPLACEMENT: 414 tons (surfaced), 609 tons (submerged)
DIMENSIONS: 176'10" x 17'9" x 10'10"
MACHINERY: 2 MAN diesel engines, 2 Nancy electric motors, 2 shafts. 800 bhp/700 shp = 13/9.5 knots
RANGE: 1300 nm at 10 knots surfaced, 100 nm at 5 knots submerged
ARMAMENT: 8 x 450mm torpedoes (6 x Drzewiecki drop-collars, 2 external cradles)
COMPLEMENT: 29
NOTES: This was Hutter's modestly improved version of his *Clorinde* design, powered by French license-built MAN diesel engines. The *Amarante* and the *Astrée* were modified after launching as minelayers with ten Normand-Fenaux system vertical tubes in their ballast tanks amidships, increasing their displacement to 440 tons surfaced and 610 tons submerged. All the other boats entered service fitted with single 47mm deck guns, replaced in 1916 by 75mm weapons.

All this class served in the Mediterranean and Adriatic. The *Ariane* was torpedoed and sunk by the German *UC-22* off Cape Bon on 19 June 1917. The surviving boats were stricken in the late 1920s and early 1930s.

## *BELLONE* CLASS (1914)

*Bellone* (8 July 1914)
BUILDER: Rochefort
*Gorgone* (23 December 1915), *Hermione* (15 March 1917)
BUILDER: Toulon
DISPLACEMENT: 523 tons (surfaced), 788 tons (submerged)
DIMENSIONS: 216'6" x 17'9" x 11'6"
MACHINERY: 2 St.-Etienne diesel engines, 2 electric motors, 2 shafts. 1640 bhp/800 shp = 14.75/9 knots
RANGE: 2300 nm at 10 knots surfaced, 100 nm at 5 knots submerged
ARMAMENT: 8 x 450mm torpedo tubes (2 bow, 2 stern, 4 trainable external mounts), total 8 torpedoes, 1 x 75mm gun
COMPLEMENT: 38
NOTES: Hutter enlarged and improved his *Clorinde* design for this class. Postwar, these boats received upgraded periscopes and new 1200-bhp Sulzer diesel engines and other equipment changes that led to faster diving times.

The *Gorgone* and the *Hermione* operated in the Adriatic during World War I, while the *Bellone* served in the Atlantic. They then were in the Mediterranean Fleet until stricken on 27 August 1935.

## *DUPUY DE LÔME* CLASS (1915)

*Dupuy de Lôme* (9 September 1915), *Sané* (27 January 1916)

BUILDER: Toulon

DISPLACEMENT: 849 tons (surfaced), 1098 tons (submerged)

DIMENSIONS: 246'1" x 21'0" x 11'10"

MACHINERY: 2 triple expansion engines, 2 du Temple boilers, 2 Belfort electric motors, 2 shafts. 3500 ihp/1640 shp = 17/11 knots

RANGE: 2350 nm at 10 knots surfaced, 120 nm at 5 knots submerged

ARMAMENT: 8 x 450mm torpedo tubes (4 forward, 2 aft, 2 trainable external mounts), total 8 torpedoes, 1 x 75mm gun, 1 x 65mm gun

COMPLEMENT: 43

NOTES: Hutter substantially enlarged his *Archimède* design and powered it with the *Gustave Zédé*'s steam plant to create this class. In the early 1920s these boats received new, enlarged bridges and conning towers. Two 1200-bhp diesel engines and four Siemens 664-shp electric motors from former German U-boats replaced their original power plants.

Both boats were based at Gibraltar during World War I. Postwar, they operated mainly in the Atlantic until they were stricken on 27 August 1935.

## *DIANE* CLASS (1915)

*Daphné* (20 October 1915), *Diane* (30 September 1916)

BUILDER: Cherbourg

DISPLACEMENT: 633 tons (surfaced), 891 tons (submerged)

DIMENSIONS: 223'1" x 18'1" x 12'2"

MACHINERY: 2 diesel engines, 2 Sabathé electric motors, 2 shafts. 1800 bhp/1400 shp = 17/11.5 knots

RANGE: 2500 nm at 10 knots surfaced, 130 nm at 5 knots submerged

ARMAMENT: 6 x 450mm torpedo tubes (4 forward, 2 aft) 4 x 450mm torpedoes (external Simonot cradles), total 12 torpedoes, 1 x 75mm gun

COMPLEMENT: 43

NOTES: This was a diminutive version of Simonot's *Néréide* design. Both boats operated in the Atlantic. The *Diane* was lost to an internal explosion off La Pallice on 11 February 1918. The *Daphné* was stricken on 27 August 1935.

## *JOESSEL* CLASS (1917)

*Joessel* (21 July 1917), *Fulton* (1 April 1919)

BUILDER: Cherbourg

DISPLACEMENT: 870 tons (surfaced), 1247 tons (submerged)

DIMENSIONS: 242'9" x 21'0" x 11'10"

MACHINERY: 2 Schneider-Carels diesel engines, 2 Nancy electric motors, 2 shafts. 2700 bhp/1640 shp = 16.5/11 knots

RANGE: 4300 nm at 10 knots surfaced, 125 nm at 5 knots submerged

ARMAMENT: 8 x 450mm torpedo tubes (4 forward, 2 aft, 2 trainable external mounts), total 10 torpedoes, 2 x 75mm guns

COMPLEMENT: 47

NOTES: These boats were originally designed by Simonot as slightly enlarged versions of his *Néréide*, powered by two 2000-shp Parsons geared steam turbines but recast with diesel engines. Six additional planned boats were canceled. They were fitted with enlarged bridges and conning towers plus upgraded periscopes in the 1920s.

Both boats operated in the Atlantic until the early 1930s, when they transferred to Indo-China. They were stricken in May 1936.

## *LAGRANGE* CLASS (1917)

*Lagrange* (31 May 1917), *Romazotti* (31 March 1918), *Regnault* (25 June 1924)
BUILDER: Toulon
*Laplace* (12 August 1919)
BUILDER: Rochefort
DISPLACEMENT: 920 tons (surfaced), 1318 tons (submerged)
DIMENSIONS: 246'9" x 20'8" x 11'10"
MACHINERY: 2 Sulzer diesel engines, 2 Belfort electric motors, 2 shafts. 2600 bhp/1640 shp = 16.5/11 knots
RANGE: 4300 nm at 10 knots surfaced, 125 nm at 5 knots submerged
ARMAMENT: 8 x 450mm torpedo tubes (4 forward, 2 aft, 2 trainable external mounts), total 10 torpedoes, 2 x 75mm guns
COMPLEMENT: 47
NOTES: Originally designed by Hutter as slightly enlarged versions of his *Dupuy de Lôme* powered by two 2000-shp Parsons geared steam turbines but recast with diesel engines. They were fitted with enlarged bridges and conning towers plus upgraded periscopes in the 1920s.

These boats operated in the Mediterranean throughout their careers. They were stricken between 1937 and 1939.

## *O'BYRNE* CLASS (1919)

*O'Byrne* (22 May 1919), *Henri Fournier* (30 September 1919), *Louis Dupetit-Thouars* (12 May 1920)
BUILDER: Gironde
DISPLACEMENT: 342 tons (surfaced), 513 tons (submerged)
DIMENSIONS: 172'0" x 15'5" x 8'6"
MACHINERY: 2 Schneider-Carels diesel engines, 2 Schneider electric motors, 2 shafts. 1020 bhp/400 shp = 14/8 knots
RANGE: 1850 nm at 10 knots surfaced, 55 nm at 5 knots submerged
ARMAMENT: 4 x 450mm torpedo tubes (forward), total 6 torpedoes, 1 x 47mm gun
COMPLEMENT: 25
NOTES: These Laubeuf export boats were ordered by Romania from Schneider and requisitioned in 1917. They were completed with enlarged bridges and conning towers.

All three boats served in the Mediterranean throughout their careers. The *Louis Dupetit-Thouars* was stricken on 9 November 1928, the other two in August 1935.

# GERMANY
## [RUSSIA]—*FORELLE* (8 JUNE 1903)

BUILDER: Germania

DISPLACEMENT: 16 tons (surfaced), 17 tons (submerged)

DIMENSIONS: 43′0″ x 7′0″ x 7′0″

MACHINERY: 1 electric motor, 1 shaft. 60 shp = 5.5 knots

RANGE: 25 nm at 4 knots submerged

ARMAMENT: 2 x 450mm torpedo tubes, total 2 torpedoes

COMPLEMENT: N/A

NOTES: Raimondo Lorenzo D'Equevilley-Montjustin designed this single-hull boat as an experimental craft. It featured internal ballast and compensating tanks, fixed angled aft planes, and movable forward units for dive control. The torpedo tubes were external and launched torpedoes using compressed air. This submarine was designed to be carried into action aboard a surface ship and launched close to its target; hence the absence of a separate surface propulsion system. The Imperial Russian Navy purchased the boat in April 1904 for service in the war against Japan. It operated out of Vladivostok from August 1904 until it sank in an accident in 1910.

## *KARP* CLASS (1905)

[Russia]—*Karp* (30 August 1905), *Karas* (12 June 1906), *Kambala* (16 March 1907), [Norway]—*Kobben* (5 May 1909)

BUILDER: Germania

DISPLACEMENT: 207 tons (surfaced), 235 tons (submerged)

DIMENSIONS: 130′0″ x 9′0″ x 8′8″

MACHINERY: 2 Körting kerosene (*Kobben*-Körting diesel) engines, 2 electric motors, 2 shafts. 400 bhp/200 (*Kobben*: 450 bhp/250) shp = 10/8.5 knots

RANGE: 1250 nm at 9 knots surfaced, 50 nm at 6.5 knots submerged

ARMAMENT: Russian boats: 1 x 450mm torpedo tube, 2 x 450mm torpedoes (Drzewiecki drop-collars), total 3 torpedoes. *Kobben*: 3 x 18″ torpedo tubes (2 bow, 1 stern). Total 4 torpedoes

COMPLEMENT: 28

NOTES: D'Equevilley-Montjustin also designed this class of double-hull boats whose form was optimized for surface cruising. The design represented a radical departure from the experimental *Forelle* and owed much to data that Krupp received during abortive license negotiations with Simon Lake. They had internal saddle ballast tanks, compensating tanks at each end, and diving planes fore and aft. The *Kobben* was an improved version of the original type for Russia.

The Russian boats were transferred by rail to Odessa on the Black Sea in 1908. The battleship *Panteleimon* accidentally rammed and sank the *Kambala* on 30 May 1909. The two other boats were hulked at Sevastopol in May 1917 and scuttled there on 26 April 1919.

The *Kobben* became the *A-1* in 1913. After serving primarily as a training vessel, it was sold for scrap in 1933.

## *U-1* CLASS (1906)

*U-1* (4 August 1906), [Austria-Hungary]—
*U-3* (20 August 1908), *U-4* (20 November 1908)

BUILDER: Germania

DISPLACEMENT: 238 tons (surfaced), 283 tons (submerged)

DIMENSIONS: 138'9" x 12'6" x 10'6"

MACHINERY: 2 Körting kerosene engines, 2 electric motors, 2 shafts. 400 bhp/400 shp = 10.75/8.75 knots (Austrian boats: 600 bhp/320 shp = 12/8.5 knots)

RANGE: 1500 nm at 10 knots surfaced, 50 nm at 5 knots submerged (Austrian boats: 40 nm at 3 knots submerged)

ARMAMENT: 1 (Austrian boats: 2) x 450mm torpedo tube(s), total 3 torpedoes

COMPLEMENT: 18

NOTES: This class was a modest enlargement of D'Equevilley-Montjustin's previous double-hull design. The *U-1* operated primarily as a trials and training vessel. It was stricken in 1919, purchased by Krupp, and donated to the Deutsches Museum in Munich for exhibit. The Austro-Hungarian boats were modified with fixed aft planes and no planes at the bow. They served extensively during World War I. The *U-3* was sunk by the French destroyer *Bisson* on 13 August 1915 after an abortive attack on the Italian armed merchant cruiser *Citta di Catania*. The *U-4* sank the Italian armored cruiser *Giuseppe Garibaldi* on 18 July 1915. It was ceded to France at the end of the war and scrapped in 1920.

## *U-2* (18 JUNE 1908)

BUILDER: Kiel

DISPLACEMENT: 341 tons (surfaced), 430 tons (submerged)

DIMENSIONS: 148'11" x 18'0" x 10'2"

MACHINERY: 2 Daimler kerosene engines, 2 electric motors, 2 shafts. 600 bhp/630 shp = 13.25/9 knots

RANGE: 1600 nm at 13 knots surfaced, 50 nm at 5 knots submerged

ARMAMENT: 4 x 450mm torpedo tubes (2 bow, 2 stern), total 6 torpedoes

COMPLEMENT: 22

NOTES: Gustave Berling, of the Imperial German Navy's Unterseebootkonstruktionsbüro, designed this double-hull boat with saddle ballast tanks. It was optimized for high surface speed and also featured a much heavier torpedo armament than the earlier Germania design. The *U-2* operated primarily as a trials and training vessel, survived World War I, and was sold for scrap in 1919.

## *U-3* CLASS (1909)

*U-3* (27 March 1909), *U-4* (18 May 1909)
BUILDER: Danzig
DISPLACEMENT: 421 tons (surfaced), 510 tons (submerged)
DIMENSIONS: 168′4″ x 18′4″ x 10′2″
MACHINERY: 2 Körting kerosene engines, 2 electric motors, 2 shafts. 600 bhp/1030 shp = 11.75/9.5 knots
RANGE: 1800 nm at 12 knots surfaced, 55 nm at 4.5 knots submerged
ARMAMENT: 4 x 450mm torpedo tubes (2 bow, 2 stern), total 6 torpedoes
COMPLEMENT: 22
NOTES: These boats were an enlarged version of Berling's earlier design and also served primarily in trials and training roles. The *U-3* sank in the North Sea on 1 December 1918 while sailing to internment in Britain, and the *U-4* was sold for scrap in 1919.

## *U-5* CLASS (1910)

*U-5* (8 January 1910), *U-6* (18 May 1910), *U-7* (28 June 1910), *U-8* (14 March 1911)
BUILDER: Germania
DISPLACEMENT: 505 tons (surfaced), 636 tons (submerged)
DIMENSIONS: 188′0″ x 18′4″ x 11′10″
MACHINERY: 4 Körting kerosene engines, 2 electric motors, 2 shafts. 900 bhp/1040 shp = 13.5/10.25 knots
RANGE: 1900 nm at 13 knots surfaced, 80 nm at 5 knots submerged
ARMAMENT: 4 x 450mm torpedo tubes (2 bow, 2 stern), total 6 torpedoes
COMPLEMENT: 29
NOTES: Hans Techel designed this class, bringing together the best features of earlier Germania and Unterseebootkonstruktionsbüro boats. Apart from the continued use of kerosene engines for surface propulsion, they were the equals of, or superior to, their foreign contemporaries, and were in front-line service at the outbreak of World War I. The *U-5* was mined off Zeebrugge on 18 December 1914. The *U-22* torpedoed and sank the *U-7* in error on 21 January 1915; the British destroyers *Ghurka* and *Maori* sank the *U-8* near Dover on 4 March 1915; and the British submarine *E-16* torpedoed and sank the *U-6* off Stavanger on 15 September 1915.

## GERMANY: *U-9* CLASS (1910)
*(Courtesy of Art-Tech)*

*U-9* (22 February 1910), *U-11* (2 April 1910), *U-12* (6 May 1910), *U-10* (24 January 1911)

BUILDER: Danzig

DISPLACEMENT: 493 tons (surfaced), 611 tons (submerged)

DIMENSIONS: 188'4" x 19'8" x 10'2"

MACHINERY: 4 Körting kerosene engines, 2 electric motors, 2 shafts. 1050 bhp/1160 shp = 14.25/8 knots

RANGE: 1800 nm at 14 knots surfaced, 80 nm at 4.5 knots submerged

ARMAMENT: 4 x 450mm torpedo tubes (2 bow, 2 stern), total 6 torpedoes

COMPLEMENT: 29

NOTES: Berling's design for this class represented the Unterseebootkonstruktionsbüro's response to the same requirements as the *U-5* class. They, too, were in frontline service upon the outbreak of war. The *U-9* sank three British armored cruisers, the *Aboukir,* the *Cressy,* and the *Hogue,* on 22 September 1914 and survived the war to be scrapped in 1919. The *U-11* was mined off Zeebrugge on 9 December 1914; the British destroyers *Ariel* and *Attack* sank the *U-12* off the Scottish coast on 10 March 1915; and the *U-10* probably was mined in the Gulf of Finland in June 1916.

## U-13 CLASS (1910)

U-13 (16 December 1910), U-14 (11 June
   1911), U-15 (18 September 1911)
BUILDER: Danzig
DISPLACEMENT: 516 tons (surfaced), 644
   tons (submerged)
DIMENSIONS: 189'11" x 19'8" x 11'2"
MACHINERY: 4 Körting kerosene engines, 2
   electric motors, 2 shafts. 1200 bhp/1200
   shp = 14.75/10.75 knots
RANGE: 2000 nm at 14 knots surfaced, 90
   nm at 5 knots submerged
ARMAMENT: 4 x 450mm torpedo tubes (2
   bow, 2 stern), total 6 torpedoes

COMPLEMENT: 29
NOTES: This class was a modest improvement of Berling's previous design. The
   British cruiser Birmingham rammed and
   sank the U-15 off Fair Isle on 9 August
   1914; the U-13 was probably mined in
   the Heligoland Bight on 12 August 1914;
   the U-14 was rammed and sunk by the
   armed trawler Hawk near Peterhead on
   1 June 1915.

## U-16 (23 AUGUST 1911)

BUILDER: Germania
DISPLACEMENT: 489 tons (surfaced), 627
   tons (submerged)
DIMENSIONS: 189'8" x 19'8" x 11'2"
MACHINERY: 4 Körting kerosene engines, 2
   electric motors, 2 shafts. 1200 bhp/1200
   shp = 15.5/10.75 knots
RANGE: 2100 nm at 15 knots surfaced, 90
   nm at 5 knots submerged

ARMAMENT: 4 x 450mm torpedo tubes (2
   bow, 2 stern), total 6 torpedoes
COMPLEMENT: 29
NOTES: The Germania equivalent of the U-
   13 class, this boat survived the war and
   sank in the North Sea on 8 February
   1919 while under tow to Britain.

## [ITALY]—ATROPO (22 MARCH 1912)

BUILDER: Germania
DISPLACEMENT: 231 tons (surfaced), 320
   tons (submerged)
DIMENSIONS: 146'0" x 14'5" x 8'10"
MACHINERY: 2 Germania diesel engines, 2
   AEG electric motors, 2 shafts. 700
   bhp/200 shp = 14.75/8 knots
RANGE: 1440 nm at 8 knots surfaced, 70
   nm at 4 knots

ARMAMENT: 2 x 450mm torpedo tubes
   (bow), total 4 torpedoes
COMPLEMENT: 14
NOTES: The Atropo was a diminutive of
   Techel's designs for the German Fleet. It
   operated extensively in the Adriatic during World War I and was scrapped in
   1919.

## *U-17* CLASS (1912)

*U-17* (16 April 1912), *U-18* (25 April 1912)
BUILDER: Danzig
DISPLACEMENT: 564 tons (surfaced), 691 tons (submerged)
DIMENSIONS: 204′9″ x 19′8″ x 11′2″
MACHINERY: 4 Körting kerosene engines, 2 electric motors, 2 shafts. 1400 bhp/1120 shp = 14.75/9.5 knots
RANGE: 6700 nm at 8 knots surfaced, 75 nm at 5 knots submerged
ARMAMENT: 4 x 450mm torpedo tubes (2 bow, 2 stern), total 6 torpedoes

COMPLEMENT: 29
NOTES: These boats were further enlargements of Berling's Unterseebootkonstruktionsbüro design. The *U-18* was sunk in the Pentland Firth by the trawler *Dorothy Gray* and the destroyer *Garry* on 23 November 1914. The *U-17* was used for training from 1916 and was scrapped in 1919.

## GERMANY: *U-19* CLASS (1912), *U-21* (1913)
*(Courtesy of Art-Tech)*

*U-19* (10 October 1912), *U-20* (18 December 1912), *U-21* (8 February 1913), *U-22* (6 March 1913)
BUILDER: Danzig
DISPLACEMENT: 650 tons (surfaced), 837 tons (submerged)
DIMENSIONS: 210′8″ x 20′0″ x 11′10″
MACHINERY: 2 MAN diesel engines, 2 electric motors, 2 shafts. 1700 bhp/1200 shp = 15.5/9.5 knots
RANGE: 7600 nm at 8 knots surfaced, 80 nm at 5 knots submerged
ARMAMENT: 4 x 500mm torpedo tubes (2 bow, 2 stern), total 6 torpedoes, 1 x 88mm gun

COMPLEMENT: 35
NOTES: This was the first German class powered by diesel engines and was an enlargement of the previous design for that purpose. These boats also introduced deck guns into the German submarine fleet. The *U-19* stranded on Jutland on 4 November 1916. The other boats survived the war and were scrapped in 1919–1920, apart from the *U-21*, which sank while under tow in the North Sea on 22 February 1919.

## [NORWAY]—*A-2* CLASS (1913)

*A-2* (1913), *A-3* (1913), *A-4* (1913), *A-5* (9 May 1914)

BUILDER: Germania

DISPLACEMENT: 268 tons (surfaced), 355 tons (submerged)

DIMENSIONS: 152'7" x 15'9" x 8'10"

MACHINERY: 2 Germania diesel engines, 2 electric motors, 2 shafts. 700 bhp/380 shp = 14.5/9 knots

RANGE: 900 nm at 10 knots surfaced, 76 nm at 3.25 knots submerged

ARMAMENT: 3 x 18" torpedo tubes (2 bow, 1 stern), total 5 torpedoes

COMPLEMENT: 17

NOTES: These submarines were diminutives of contemporary Germania boats for the German Fleet. The *A-5* was undelivered when World War I began and was taken over as the German *UA*. It was used for training from 1916 and was scrapped in 1919. The *A-2* was scrapped in 1940, and the two other boats were scuttled on 16 April of the same year.

## *U-23* CLASS (1913)

*U-23* (12 April 1913), *U-24* (24 May 1913), *U-25* (12 July 1913), *U-26* (16 October 1913)

BUILDER: Germania

DISPLACEMENT: 669 tons (surfaced), 864 tons (submerged)

DIMENSIONS: 212'3" x 20'8" x 11'6"

MACHINERY: 2 Germania diesel engines, 2 electric motors, 2 shafts. 1800 bhp/1200 shp = 16.75/10.25 knots

RANGE: 7620 nm at 8 knots surfaced, 85 nm at 5 knots submerged

ARMAMENT: 4 x 500mm torpedo tubes (2 bow, 2 stern), total 6 torpedoes, 1 x 88mm gun

COMPLEMENT: 35

NOTES: This class was an enlargement of the earlier Germania type with diesel engines and a deck gun. The British submarine *C-27* torpedoed and sank the *U-23* off Fair Isle on 20 July 1915, and the *U-26* probably was mined in the Gulf of Finland in September 1915. The two other submarines were surrendered to Britain and scrapped in 1921–1922.

## *U-27* CLASS (1913)

*U-27* (14 June 1913), *U-28* (30 August 1913), *U-29* (11 October 1913), *U-30* (15 November 1913)

BUILDER: Danzig

DISPLACEMENT: 675 tons (surfaced), 867 tons (submerged)

DIMENSIONS: 210'8" x 20'0" x 11'10"

MACHINERY: 2 MAN diesel engines, 2 electric motors, 2 shafts. 2000 bhp/1200 shp = 16.75/9.75 knots

RANGE: 7900 nm at 8 knots surfaced, 85 nm at 5 knots submerged

ARMAMENT: 4 x 500mm torpedo tubes (2 bow, 2 stern), total 6 torpedoes, 1 x 88mm gun

COMPLEMENT: 35

NOTES: With this design, derived from his earlier types, Berling began to emphasize short diving time, which was reduced to 80 seconds. Later in the war, boats carried two 88mm deck guns and could stow up to ten torpedoes. The battleship *Dreadnought* rammed and sank the *U-29* in the Pentland Firth on 18 March 1915; the Q-ship *Baralong* sank the *U-27* off the Scilly Isles on 19 August 1915; the

*U-28* was sunk by the explosion of its target, the ammunition ship *Olive Branch*, off the North Cape on 2 September 1917. The *U-30* surrendered and was scrapped in 1919.

## GERMANY: *U-31* CLASS (1914)
*(Courtesy of Art-Tech)*

*U-31* (7 January 1914), *U-32* (28 January 1914), *U-34* (9 May 1914), *U-33* (19 May 1914), *U-35* (18 April 1914), *U-36* (6 June 1914), *U-37* (25 August 1914), *U-38* (9 September 1914), *U-39* (26 September 1914), *U-41* (10 October 1914), *U-40* (22 October 1914)

BUILDER: Germania

DISPLACEMENT: 685 tons (surfaced), 878 tons (submerged)

DIMENSIONS: 212′3″ x 20′8″ x 11′10″

MACHINERY: 2 Germania diesel engines, 2 electric motors, 2 shafts. 1850 bhp/1200 shp = 16.5/9.75 knots

RANGE: 7800 nm at 8 knots surfaced, 80 nm at 5 knots submerged

ARMAMENT: 4 x 500mm torpedo tubes (2 bow, 2 stern), total 6 torpedoes, 1 x 88mm gun

COMPLEMENT: 35

NOTES: This class was the Germania equivalent of the *U-27* type and could dive in 100 seconds. From mid-1915 they carried two 88mm guns, replaced in the surviving boats by a single 105mm gun from mid-1916. In 1915 the *U-31* probably was mined of the east coast of Britain in January; the British trawler *Ste. Jemanne* rammed and sank the *U-37* near Fécamp on 30 March; the *U-40* was torpedoed and sunk by the British submarine *C-24* off Aberdeen on 23 June; the Q-ship *Prince Charles* sank the *U-36* in the Hebrides on 24 July; the Q-ship *Wyandra* sank the *U-41* near the Scilly Isles on 24 September. In 1918 the British sloop

*Wallflower* sank the *U-32* near Malta on 8 May; the *U-35* (the most successful single U-boat in either world war, which sank 224 ships totaling 535,900 gross tons) and the *U-39* were interned in Spain after action damage and subsequently scrapped; the *U-34* was sunk by the sloop *Privet* on 9 November.

## *U-43* CLASS (1914)

*U-43* (26 September 1914), *U-44* (15 October 1914), *U-45* (15 April 1915), *U-46* (18 May 1915), *U-47* (16 August 1915), *U-48* (3 October 1915), *U-49* (26 November 1915), *U-50* (31 December 1915)

BUILDER: Danzig

DISPLACEMENT: 725 tons (surfaced), 940 tons (submerged)

DIMENSIONS: 213'3" x 20'4" x 12'2"

MACHINERY: 2 MAN diesel engines, 2 electric motors, 2 shafts. 2000 bhp/1200 shp = 15.25/9.75 knots

RANGE: 8100 nm at 8 knots surfaced, 51 nm at 5 knots submerged

ARMAMENT: 4 x 500mm torpedo tubes (2 bow, 2 stern), total 6 torpedoes, 2 x 88mm gun

COMPLEMENT: 36

NOTES: This class was the first of the largely standardized Unterseebootkonstruktionsbüro war mobilization types.

From mid-1916 they were fitted with a single 105mm gun, and the *U-43* and the *U-44* were modified as minelayers. In 1917 the British destroyer *Oracle* rammed and sank the *U-44* off the Norwegian coast on 12 August; the *U-50* was mined near Terschelling on 5 September; the steamer *British Transport* rammed and sank the *U-49* in the Bay of Biscay on 11 September; the *U-45* was torpedoed and sunk by the British submarine *D-7* in the Shetlands on 12 September; the *U-48* was driven ashore on the Goodwin Shoals by British trawlers and blown up by its crew on 24 November. The *U-47* was scuttled off Pola on 28 October 1918. The *U-43* and the *U-46* were surrendered after the war, the latter becoming the Japanese *O-2*, and were scrapped in 1922.

## GERMANY: TYPE UB-I, *UB-1* (1915)

*(Courtesy of Art-Tech)*

*UB-1* (19 January 1915), *UB-2* (18 February 1915), *UB-3* (5 March 1915), *UB-4* (March 1915), *UB-5* (March 1915), *UB-6* (March 1915), *UB-7* (April 1915), *UB-8* (April 1915)

BUILDER: Germania

*UB-9* (6 February 1915), *UB-10* (20 February 1915), *UB-11* (2 March 1915), *UB-12* (2 March 1915), *UB-13* (8 March 1915), *UB-14* (25 March 1915), *UB-15* (March 1915), *UB-17* (21 April 1915), *UB-16* (26 April 1915), [Austria-Hungary] – *U-15* (21 August 1915), *U-16* (28 August 1915), *U-17* (3 September 1915)

BUILDER: Bremen

DISPLACEMENT: 127 tons (surfaced), 142 tons (submerged)

DIMENSIONS: 92'2" x 10'6" x 9'10"

MACHINERY: 1 diesel engine, 1 electric motor, 1 shaft. 60 bhp/120 shp = 6.5/5.5 knots

RANGE: 1500 nm at 5 knots surfaced, 45 nm at 4 knots submerged

ARMAMENT: 2 x 450mm torpedo tubes (bow), total 2 torpedoes, 1 x 8mm machine gun

COMPLEMENT: 14

NOTES: These small coastal boats were designed for very rapid construction to operate around the British Isles from bases in Flanders. They featured a single hull optimized for surface operation, internal ballast and compensation tanks, diesel drive using a small Körting engine already in mass production for use in motor launches, no compartmentation, and two torpedo tubes forward arranged side by side. The hull sections were designed for easy rail transportation on only three rail cars. The design of the ballast tanks endowed them with a diving time of only 22 seconds. Production actually exceeded expectations: the intent was for boats to take four months to build, but the first examples were delivered in only seventy-five days.

In 1915 the *UB-3* was lost in May in the Gulf of Smyrna, and the Q-ship *Inverlyon* sank the *UB-4* off Yarmouth on 15 August. During 1916 the British destroyer *Afridi* and the drifter *Gleaner* probably sank the *UB-13* off Zeebrugge on 25 April, and the *UB-7* failed to return from a mission in the Black Sea in September. The *UB-6* ran aground on the Dutch coast on 23 February 1917 and was interned (it was scrapped postwar). In 1918 the *UB-17* probably was sunk by the British *CMB-20* off the coast of Flan-

ders on 18 March; the British submarine *E-34* torpedoed and sank the *UB-16* off Harwich on 10 May; the *UB-13* failed to return from a mission in the English Channel in August; the *UB-10* was scuttled at Zeebrugge on 5 October. The surviving boats were surrendered at war's end and scrapped in 1920.

The *UB-1* and the *UB-15* were transferred to Austria-Hungary soon after completion, becoming its *U-10* and *U-11*. The *U-16* sank the Italian destroyer *Nembo* on 17 October 1916 but then was rammed and sunk by the steamer *Borminda*, which the destroyer was escorting. The other Austro-Hungarian boats were surrendered at war's end and scrapped in 1920.

The *UB-8* was transferred to Bulgaria on 25 May 1916 and became its *U-18*. It escaped to Bizerta in 1919 and was scrapped there in 1921.

## TYPE UC-I (1915)

*UC-11* (11 April 1915), *UC-12* (29 April 1915), *UC-13* (May 1915), *UC-14* (13 May 1915), *UC-15* (19 May 1915)

BUILDER: Bremen

*UC-1* (26 April 1915), *UC-2* (12 May 1915), *UC-3* (28 May 1915), *UC-4* (6 June 1915), *UC-5* (13 June 1915), *UC-6* (20 June 1915), *UC-7* (6 July 1915), *UC-8* (6 July 1915), *UC-9* (11 July 1915), *UC-10* (15 July 1915)

BUILDER: Hamburg

DISPLACEMENT: 168 tons (surfaced), 183 tons (submerged)

DIMENSIONS: 111'6" x 10'4" x 10'0"

MACHINERY: 1 diesel engine, 1 electric motor, 1 shaft. 90 bhp/175 shp = 6.25/5.25 knots

RANGE: 780 nm at 5 knots surfaced, 50 nm at 4 knots submerged

ARMAMENT: 6 x 100cm mine tubes, total 120 mines

COMPLEMENT: 14

NOTES: Dr. Werner of the Torpedo Inspectorate was responsible for the design of these small minelayers. They were based on the UB-I type with inclined minelaying tubes installed in a revised bow section and uprated engines to compensate for the greater weight and less streamlined lines. They were built very quickly but suffered from problems with their minelaying system, which could cause the mines to arm before leaving the tubes and explode prematurely.

During 1915 the steamer *Cottingham* rammed and sank the *UC-2* off Yarmouth on 2 July; the *UC-9* blew up on its own mines in the North Sea on 21 October;

the *UC-8* grounded on the Dutch coast on 14 November and was interned (it became the Dutch *M-1* and was scrapped in 1932); the *UC-13* wrecked in the Black Sea on 29 November. The following year the *UC-12*'s own mines sank it off Taranto on 16 March (Italy salved and rebuilt it as the *X-1*, scrapped in 1919); the *UC-5* wrecked in the Thames estuary on 27 April; the *UC-3* and the *UC-7* were mined off Zeebrugge on 27 May and 5 July, respectively; the British submarine

*E-54* torpedoed and sank the *UC-10* off the Dutch coast on 21 August; the *UC-15* failed to return from a Black Sea patrol in November. In 1917 the *UC-1* was mined off Nieuport on 19 July; the *UC-6* was destroyed by British aircraft in the Thames estuary on 27 September; the *UC-14* was mined off Zeebrugge on 3 October. The *UC-11* was mined in the English Channel on 16 June 1918, and the *UC-4* was blown up at Zeebrugge on 5 October.

## *U-66* CLASS (1915)

*U-66* (22 April 1915), *U-67* (15 May 1915), *U-68* (1 June 1915), *U-69* (24 June 1915), *U-70* (20 June 1915)

BUILDER: Germania

DISPLACEMENT: 791 tons (surfaced), 933 tons (submerged)

DIMENSIONS: 228'0" x 20'8" x 12'6"

MACHINERY: 2 Germania diesel engines, 2 electric motors, 2 shafts. 2300 bhp/1260 shp = 16.75/10.25 knots

RANGE: 6500 nm at 8 knots surfaced, 115 nm at 5 knots submerged

ARMAMENT: 5 x 450mm torpedo tubes (4 bow, 1 stern), total 12 torpedoes, 1 x 88mm gun

COMPLEMENT: 36

NOTES: The Austro-Hungarian Navy ordered these boats prior to the war, but they were taken over by Germany in 1915. The Q-ship *Farnborough* sank the *U-68* off the Irish coast on 2 March 1916. In 1917 the *U-69* probably was sunk by the British destroyer *Patriot* in the same area on 12 July, and the *U-66* probably was mined on the Dogger Bank on 3 September. The two surviving boats were surrendered after the war and scrapped in 1920–1921.

## *U-71* CLASS (1915)

*U-73* (16 June 1915), *U-74* (10 August 1915)
BUILDER: Danzig
*U-71* (31 October 1915), *U-72* (31 October
    1915), *U-75* (31 January 1916), *U-76*
    (12 March 1916), *U-77* (9 January
    1916), *U-78* (27 February 1916), *U-79* (9
    April 1916), *U-80* (22 April 1916)
BUILDER: Hamburg
DISPLACEMENT: 755 tons (surfaced), 832
    tons (submerged)
DIMENSIONS: 186′4″ x 19′4″ x 16′10″
MACHINERY: 2 diesel engines, 2 electric
    motors, 2 shafts. 900 bhp/800 shp =
    10.5/8 knots
RANGE: 5800 nm at 7 knots surfaced, 83
    nm at 4 knots submerged
ARMAMENT: 2 x 500mm torpedo tubes (1
    bow, 1 stern), total 4 torpedoes, 2 x
    100cm stern mine tubes, total 34 mines,
    1 x 88mm gun
COMPLEMENT: 32
NOTES: These single-hull saddle ballast
    tank–type minelayers represented a de-
    parture from the usual Unterseebootkon-
    struktionsbüro double-hull design. They
were designed by Dr. Werner (also responsible for the Type UC-I coastal
minelayers) as simple, long-range craft.
Their arrangement, with the minelaying
tubes aft, caused considerable longitudinal stability problems, and their engine
power was inadequate. Nevertheless,
they were quite successful boats.

   In 1916, British antisubmarine
trawlers sank the *U-74* off Peterhead on
27 May, and the *U-77* vanished in the
North Sea in July, possibly after striking
one of its own mines. The *U-76*
foundered in heavy weather after action
damage off the North Cape on 22 January 1917; the *U-75* was mined off Terschelling on 10 December; the *U-78* was
torpedoed and sunk by the British submarine *G-2* in the Skagerrak on 28 October 1918. The *U-72* and the *U-73* were
scuttled off Pola on 30 October 1918,
and the two other boats were surrendered
after the war and scrapped.

## TYPE UB-II (1915)

### GROUP I

*UB-18* (21 August 1915), *UB-19* (2 Septem-
    ber 1915), *UB-20* (26 September 1915),
    *UB-21* (26 September 1915), *UB-22* (9
    October 1915), *UB-23* (9 October 1915)
BUILDER: Blohm und Voss
*UB-24* (18 October 1915), *UB-25* (22 No-
    vember 1915), *UB-26* (14 December
    1915), *UB-28* (28 December 1915), *UB-
    29* (31 December 1915), UB-27 (10 Feb-
    ruary 1916)
BUILDER: Bremen

### GROUP II

*UB-30* (16 November 1915), *UB-31* (16
    November 1915), *UB-32* (4 December
    1915), *UB-33* (4 December 1915), *UB-
    34* (28 December 1915), *UB-35* (28 De-
    cember 1915), *UB-37* (28 December
    1915), *UB-39* (29 December 1915), *UB-
    36* (15 January 1916), *UB-38* (1 April
    1916), *UB-40* (25 April 1916), *UB-41*
    (6 May 1916)
BUILDER: Blohm und Voss

*UB-42* (4 March 1916), *UB-43* (8 April 1916), *UB-44* (20 April 1916), *UB-45* (12 May 1916), *UB-46* (31 May 1916), *UB-47* (17 June 1916)

BUILDER: Bremen

[Austria-Hungary]—*U-27* (19 Oct 1916), *U-28* (8 Jan 1917), *U-40* (21 Apr 1917), *U-41* (11 Nov 1917)

BUILDER: Pola

[Austria-Hungary]—*U-29* (21 October 1916), *U-30* (27 December 1916), *U-31* (20 March 1917) *U-32* (11 May 1917)

BUILDER: Fiume

DISPLACEMENT: Group I: 263 tons (surfaced), 292 tons (submerged), Group II: 279 tons (surfaced), 305 tons (submerged)

DIMENSIONS: Group I: 118'5," Group II: 121'0" x 14'5" x 12'2"

MACHINERY: 2 diesel engines, 2 electric motors, 2 shafts. Group I: 270 bhp/280 shp, Group II: 284 bhp/280 shp = 9/5.75 knots

RANGE: Group I: 6650 nm at 5 knots surfaced, Group II: 8150 nm at 5 knots surfaced, 45 nm at 4 knots

ARMAMENT: 2 x 500mm torpedo tubes (bow), total 6 (Group I and Austrian boats: 4) torpedoes, 1 x 50mm gun (Austrian boats: 1 x 75mm gun, 1 x 8mm machine gun)

COMPLEMENT: 22

NOTES: These boats were enlarged to accommodate two-shaft machinery for greater reliability and range, and the single-hull design also featured saddle ballast tanks to increase internal space and forward diving planes to improve control. Their greater size made them more difficult to transport by rail.

During 1916 the French destroyer *Trombe* sank the *UB-26* off Le Havre on 5 April; the *UB-44* failed to return from a patrol in the Aegean in August; the *UB-45* was mined in the Black Sea on 6 November; the Q-ship *Penhurst* sank the *UB-19* in the English Channel on 30 November; the British destroyer *Landrail* sank the *UB-29* off Bishop's Rock on 15 December. The *Penhurst* sank the *UB-37* in the English Channel on 14 January 1917; the *UB-39* was mined off Dover on 15 May; the *UB-36* was sunk off Ushant on 20 May; the *UB-20* was mined off Zeebrugge on 28 July; a British antisubmarine vessel sank the *UB-27* in the North Sea on 29 July; the *UB-23* was interned at La Coruna after serious action damage on the same day; British aircraft bombed and sank the *UB-32* in the Thames estuary on 22 September; the *UB-41* was mined off Scarborough on 5 October; the British trawler *Ben Lawer* rammed and sank the *UB-18* in the English Channel on 9 December. The *UB-22* was mined in the North Sea on 19 January 1918; the British destroyer *Leven* sank the *UB-35* near Calais on 26 January; the *UB-38*, the *UB-33*, and the *UB-31* were mined off Dover on 8 February, 11 April, and 2 May, respectively; British trawlers sank the *UB-30* off Whitby on 13 August. The surviving boats were surrendered at war's end and scrapped postwar.

The Austro-Hungarian *U-30* was lost to unknown causes in the Straits of Otranto in April 1917, and the other boats were ceded to France and Italy and scrapped after World War I.

## *U-51* CLASS (1915)

*U-51* (25 November 1915), *U-52* (8 December 1915), *U-53* (1 February 1916), *U-54* (22 February 1916), *U-55* (18 March 1916), *U-56* (18 April 1916)

BUILDER: Germania

DISPLACEMENT: 715 tons (surfaced), 902 tons (submerged)

DIMENSIONS: 213'11" x 21'0" x 11'10"

MACHINERY: 2 MAN diesel engines, 2 electric motors, 2 shafts. 2400 bhp/1200 shp = 17/9 knots

RANGE: 9000 nm at 8 knots surfaced, 55 nm at 5 knots submerged

ARMAMENT: 4 x 500mm torpedo tubes (2 bow, 2 stern), total 8 torpedoes, 2 x 88mm gun

COMPLEMENT: 35

NOTES: This class was the first of the largely standardized Germania war mobilization types. From mid-1916 they were fitted with a single 105mm gun. In 1916 the British submarine *H-5* torpedoed and sank the *U-51* in the Ems estuary on 14 July, and the *U-56* disappeared off Lapland after suffering damage from Russian antisubmarine vessels on 2 November. The surviving boats were surrendered at war's end (the *U-55* becoming the Japanese *O-3*) and were scrapped in 1922.

## GERMANY: TYPE UC-II (1916), *UC-48* (1916)
*(Courtesy of Art-Tech)*

*UC-16* (1 February 1916), *UC-22* (1 February 1916), *UC-17* (19 February 1916), *UC-23* (19 February 1916), *UC-18* (4 March 1916), *UC-24* (4 March 1916), *UC-19* (15 March 1916), *UC-20* (1 April 1916), *UC-21* (1 April 1916), *UC-34* (6 May 1916), *UC-35* (6 May 1916), *UC-37* (5 June 1916), *UC-38* (5 June 1916), *UC-36* (25 June 1916), *UC-39* (26 June 1916), *UC-65* (8 July 1916), *UC-66* (15 July 1916), *UC-67* (6 August 1916), *UC-69* (7 August 1916), *UC-70* (7 August 1916), *UC-68* (12 August 1916), *UC-71* (12 August 1916), *UC-72* (12 August 1916), *UC-73* (26 August 1916)

BUILDER: Blohm und Voss

*UC-25* (10 June 1916), *UC-26* (22 June 1916), *UC-27* (28 June 1916), *UC-28* (8 July 1916), *UC-29* (15 July 1916), *UC-30* (27 July 1916), *UC-31* (7 August 1916),

*UC-32* (12 August 1916), *UC-33* (26 August 1916), *UC-40* (5 September 1916), *UC-41* (13 September 1916), *UC-42* (21 September 1916), *UC-43* (5 October 1916), *UC-44* (10 October 1916), *UC-74* (19 October 1916), *UC-45* (20 October 1916), *UC-75* (6 November 1916), *UC-76* (25 November 1916), *UC-77* (2 December 1916), *UC-78* (8 December 1916), *UC-79* (19 December 1916)

BUILDER: Hamburg

*UC-46* (15 July 1916), *UC-47* (30 August 1916), *UC-48* (27 September 1916), *UC-61* (11 November 1916), *UC-62* (9 December 1916), *UC-63* (6 January 1917), *UC-64* (27 January 1917)

BUILDER: Bremen

*UC-55* (2 August 1916), *UC-56* (26 August 1916), *UC-57* (7 September 1916), *UC-59* (28 September 1916), *UC-58*

(21 October 1916), *UC-60* (8 November 1916)

BUILDER: Danzig

*UC-49* (7 November 1916), *UC-50* (23 November 1916), *UC-51* (5 December 1916), *UC-52* (23 January 1917), *UC-53* (27 February 1917), *UC-54* (20 March 1917)

BUILDER: Germania

DISPLACEMENT: 417 tons (surfaced), 480 tons (submerged)

DIMENSIONS: 162′0″ x 17′2″ x 12′2″

MACHINERY: 2 diesel engines, 2 electric motors, 2 shafts. 500 bhp/460 shp = 11.5/7 knots

RANGE: 7280–10,108 nm at 7 knots surfaced, 54 nm at 4 knots submerged

ARMAMENT: 3 x 500mm torpedo tubes (2 bow, 1 stern), total 7 torpedoes, 6 x 100cm mine tubes, total 18 mines, 1 x 88mm gun

COMPLEMENT: 26

NOTES: The design for the second series of coastal minelayers paralleled that of the UB-II type. It was enlarged to accommodate two-shaft machinery, a torpedo battery, and much greater range, allowing all requirements for easy rail transportation to be deleted. In service the problems with the minelaying system proved not to be wholly resolved.

The destroyer *Ariel* sank the *UC-19* southwest of Ireland on 6 December 1916. The destroyer *Liberty* rammed and sank the *UC-46* in the English Channel on 8 February 1917; the destroyer *Thrasher* sank the *UC-39* in the North Sea the same day; the Q-ship *Lady Olive* sank the *UC-18* in the English Channel on 19 February (and itself sank from torpedo damage); their own mines sank the *UC-32*, the *UC-36*, the *UC-44*, and the *UC-42* on 23 February, 19 May, 4 August, and 10 September, respectively; the British submarine *G-3* torpedoed the *UC-43* in the Atlantic on 10 March; the British submarine *C-7* sank the *UC-68* off the Dutch coast on 5 April; the *UC-30* was mined near Horns Reef on 21 April; the destroyer *Milne* rammed and sank the *UC-26* in the Thames estuary on 8 May; the French submarine *Circé* sank the *UC-24* off Cattaro on 24 May; the Q-ship *Pargust* sank the *UC-29* off the Irish coast on 7 June; the trawler *Sea King* sank the *UC-66* in the English Channel on 12 June; the *UC-61* ran aground and was destroyed by its crew on 26 July; the Q-ship *Acton* sank the *UC-72* in the Bay of Biscay on 20 August; British trawlers sank the *UC-41* in the Tay estuary the following day; the patrol boat *PC-61* rammed and sank the *UC-33* in St. George's Channel on 26 September; the *UC-21*, the *UC-16*, and the *UC-62* were mined in the English Channel in October; the submarine *E-52* torpedoed the *UC-63* and the submarine *C-15* torpedoed the *UC-65* in the English Channel on 1 November and 3 November; the *UC-51* was mined in the English Channel on 17 November; the patrol boat *P-57* rammed and sank the *UC-47* in the English Channel on 18 November; the *UC-57* was mined in the Gulf of Finland in November; the *UC-69* sank after a collision on 6 December; and the French destroyers *Lansquenet* and *Mameluck* sank the *UC-38* in the Gulf of Corinth on 14 December. During 1918 the destroyer *Nubian* sank the *UC-50* in the Straits of Dover on 4 February; the destroyer *Loyal* badly damaged the *UC-48*, which interned itself at Ferrol on 23 March; the *UC-79*, the *UC-78*, and the *UC-64* were mined near Dover on 19

April, and 2 May, and 20 June, respectively; the French patrol boat *Ailly* sank the *UC-35* near Sardinia on 17 May; the destroyer *Fairy* rammed and sank the *UC-75* in the North Sea on 31 May (itself sinking because of the damage it suffered); British drifters sank the *UC-77* in the Straits of Dover on 10 July; the destroyer *Opossum* sank the *UC-49* off Berry Head on 8 August; the destroyer *Ouse* sank the *UC-70* off Whitby on 28 August. The *UC-25*, the *UC-34*, the *UC-53*, and the *UC-54* were scuttled in the Adriatic on 28 October 1918. The surviving boats were surrendered and scrapped postwar.

## *U-63* CLASS (1916)

*U-63* (8 February 1916), *U-64* (29 February 1916), *U-65* (21 March 1916)
BUILDER: Germania
DISPLACEMENT: 810 tons (surfaced), 927 tons (submerged)
DIMENSIONS: 224′5″ x 20′8″ x 13′2″
MACHINERY: 2 Germania diesel engines, 2 electric motors, 2 shafts. 2200 bhp/1200 shp = 16.5/9 knots
RANGE: 8100 nm at 8 knots surfaced, 60 nm at 5 knots submerged
ARMAMENT: 4 x 500mm torpedo tubes (2 bow, 2 stern), total 8 torpedoes, 2 x 88mm gun
COMPLEMENT: 35
NOTES: These Germania war mobilization boats could dive in 50 seconds. They received a single 105mm deck gun in 1917. British antisubmarine vessels sank the *U-64* off Cape Bon on 17 June 1918; the *U-65* was scuttled at Pola on 28 October; the *U-63* was surrendered and scrapped.

## *U-57* CLASS (1916)

*U-57* (19 April 1916), *U-58* (31 May 1916), *U-59* (20 June 1916), *U-60* (5 June 1916), *U-61* (22 June 1916), *U-62* (2 August 1916), *U-99* (27 January 1917), *U-100* (25 February 1917), *U-101* (1 April 1917), *U-102* (12 May 1917), *U-103* (9 June 1917), *U-104* (3 June 1917)
BUILDER: Bremen
DISPLACEMENT: 786 tons (surfaced), 902 tons (submerged)
DIMENSIONS: 213′11″ x 20′8″ x 12′6″
MACHINERY: 2 MAN diesel engines, 2 electric motors, 2 shafts. 1800 bhp/1200 shp = 14.75/8.5 knots
RANGE: 7730 nm at 8 knots surfaced, 55 nm at 5 knots submerged
ARMAMENT: 4 x 500mm torpedo tubes (2 bow, 2 stern), total 8 torpedoes, 2 x 88mm gun
COMPLEMENT: 35
NOTES: These war mobilization boats were built to a Germania design and could dive in 50 seconds. The later boats were refitted with single 105mm guns. The *U-59* was mined off Horns Reef on 14 May 1917; the Cunard liner *Valeria* rammed and sank the *U-99* southwest of Ireland on 20 June; the U.S. destroyer *Fanning* sank the *U-58* off Milford Haven on 17 November. The British patrol boat *P-51* sank the *U-61* in St. George's Channel on 26 March 1918; the sloop *Jessamine* sank the *U-104* in the same location on 25 April; the liner *Olympic* rammed and sank the *U-103* in the English Channel on 11 May; the *U-102* failed to return from a North Sea patrol in September. The surviving boats were surrendered at war's end and scrapped in 1920.

## *U-87* CLASS (1916)

*U-87* (22 May 1916), *U-88* (22 June 1916), *U-89* (6 October 1916), *U-90* (12 January 1917), *U-91* (14 April 1917), *U-92* (12 May 1917)

BUILDER: Danzig

DISPLACEMENT: 757 tons (surfaced), 998 tons (submerged)

DIMENSIONS: 224'9" x 20'4" x 12'9"

MACHINERY: 2 MAN diesel engines, 2 electric motors, 2 shafts. 2400 bhp/1200 shp = 15.5/8.5 knots

RANGE: 8000 nm at 8 knots surfaced, 56 nm at 5 knots submerged

ARMAMENT: 6 x 500mm torpedo tubes (4 bow, 2 stern), total 12 torpedoes, 1 x 105mm gun

COMPLEMENT: 36

NOTES: These submarines represented an important advance on previous Unterseebootkonstruktionsbüro double-hull war mobilization boats, featuring a heavier torpedo armament and improved bow for better sea-keeping. The U-88 was mined off Terschelling on 5 September 1917, and the sloop *Buttercup* rammed and sank the U-87 in the Irish Sea on 25 December. The cruiser *Roxborough* rammed and sank the U-89 off Malin Head on 12 February 1918, and the U-92 failed to return from a Bay of Biscay patrol in September. The two surviving boats were surrendered and scrapped.

## *U-81* CLASS (1916)

*U-81* (24 June 1916), *U-82* (1 June 1916), *U-83* (13 June 1916), *U-84* (22 June 1916), *U-85* (22 August 1916), *U-86* (7 November 1916)

BUILDER: Germania

DISPLACEMENT: 808 tons (surfaced), 946 tons (submerged)

DIMENSIONS: 230'0" x 20'8" x 13'2"

MACHINERY: 2 MAN diesel engines, 2 electric motors, 2 shafts. 2400 bhp/1200 shp = 16.75/9 knots

RANGE: 8100 nm at 8 knots surfaced, 56 nm at 5 knots submerged

ARMAMENT: 4 x 500mm torpedo tubes (2 bow, 2 stern), total 8 torpedoes, 2 x 88mm gun

COMPLEMENT: 35

NOTES: These boats were a further improvement on the previous Germania design. The Q-ship *Farnborough* sank the U-83 southwest of Ireland on 17 February 1917; the British sloop *Privet* sank the U-85 off Start Point on 12 March; the British submarine E-54 torpedoed and sank the U-81 off the Irish coast on 1 May; the patrol boat PC-62 rammed and sank the U-84 in St. George's Channel on 26 January 1918. The two surviving boats were surrendered and scrapped.

## *U-93* CLASS (1916)

*U*-93 (15 December 1916), *U-94* (5 January 1917), *U-95* (20 January 1917), *U-96* (15 February 1917), *U-97* (4 April 1917), *U-98* (28 February 1917), *U-105* (16 May 1917), *U-106* (12 June 1917), *U-107* (28 June 1917), *U-108* (11 October 1917), *U-109* (25 September 1917), *U-110* (28 June 1917), *U-111* (5 September 1917), *U-112* (26 October 1917), *U-113* (29 September 1917), *U-114* (27 November 1917)

BUILDER: Germania

*U-160* (27 February 1918), *U-161* (23 March 1918), *U-162* (20 April 1918), *U-163* (1 June 1918), *U-164* (7 August 1918), *U-165* (21 August 1918), *U-166* (6 Sep1918), *U-167* (28 September 1918), *U-168* (19 October 1918)

BUILDER: Vegesack

DISPLACEMENT: 838 tons (surfaced), 1000 tons (submerged)

DIMENSIONS: 234′11″ x 20′8″ x 12′9″

MACHINERY: 2 MAN diesel engines, 2 electric motors, 2 shafts. 2400 bhp/1200 shp = 16.75/8.5 knots

RANGE: 8300 nm at 8 knots surfaced, 50 nm at 5 knots submerged

ARMAMENT: 6 x 500mm torpedo tubes (4 bow, 2 stern), total 12 torpedoes, 1 x 105mm gun

COMPLEMENT: 36

NOTES: This Germania design paralleled the advances of the *U-87* class. The *U-169–U-172* and the *U-201–U-209* were broken up incomplete after the war, while the *U-210–U-212* were ordered but never commenced construction.

The *U-106* was mined in Heligoland Bight on 7 October 1917. The steamer *Braeniel* rammed and sank the *U-93* near Lizard Point on 7 January 1918; the *U-95* and the *U-109* were mined in the Straits of Dover on 19 January and 24 January, respectively; the destroyer *Michael* sank the *U-110* near Malin Head on 15 March. The surviving boats were surrendered at war's end and scrapped with the exception of the *U-105*, the *U-108*, the *U-162*, and the *U-166*, which entered French service as the *Jean Autric*, the *Léon Mignot*, the *Pierre Marrest*, and the *Jean Roulier* and were discarded in 1937.

## GERMANY: TYPE UB-III (1917), *UB-64* (1917)
*(Courtesy of Art-Tech)*

*UB-48* (6 January 1917), *UB-49* (6 January 1917), *UB-50* (6 January 1917), *UB-51* (8 March 1917), *UB-52* (8 March 1917), *UB-53* (9 March 1917), *UB-75* (5 May 1917), *UB-76* (5 May 1917), *UB-77* (5 May 1917), *UB-78* (2 June 1917), *UB-79* (3 June 1917), *UB-104* (1 July 1917), *UB-103* (7 July 1917), *UB-105* (7 July 1917), *UB-109* (7 July 1917), *UB-106* (21 July 1917), *UB-107* (21 July 1917), *UB-108* (21 July 1917), *UB-110* (1 September 1917), *UB-111* (1 September 1917), *UB-112* (15 September 1917), *UB-113* (23 September 1917), *UB-114* (23 September 1917), *UB-115* (4 November 1917), *UB-116* (November 1917), *UB-117* (21 November 1917)

BUILDER: Blohm und Voss

*UB-60* (14 April 1917), *UB-61* (28 April 1917), *UB-62* (11 May 1917), *UB-63* (26 May 1917), *UB-64* (9 June 1917), *UB-65* (26 June 1917), *UB-72* (30 July 1917), *UB-73* (11 August 1917), *UB-74* (12 September 1917), *UB-88* (11 December 1917), *UB-89* (22 December 1917), *UB-90* (12 February 1918), *UB-91* (6 March 1918), *UB-92* (25 March 1918), UB-93 (12 April 1918), *UB-94* (26 April 1918),

*UB-95* (10 May 1918), *UB-96* (31 May 1918), *UB-97* (13 June 1918), *UB-98* (1 July 1918), *UB-99* (29 July 1918), *UB-100* (13 August 1918), *UB-101* (27 August 1918), *UB-102* (13 September 1918), *UB-154* (7 October 1918), *UB-155* (26 October 1918)

BUILDER: Hamburg

*UB-54* (18 April 1917), *UB-55* (9 May 1917), *UB-56* (6 June 1917), *UB-57* (21 June 1917), *UB-58* (5 July 1917), *UB-59* (21 July 1917), *UB-80* (4 August 1917), *UB-81* (18 August 1917), *UB-82* (1 September 1917), *UB-83* (15 September 1917), *UB-84* (3 October 1917), *UB-86* (10 October 1917), *UB-85* (26 October 1917), *UB-87* (10 November 1917), *UB-118* (13 December 1917), *UB-119* (13 December 1917), *UB-121* (6 January 1918), *UB-122* (2 February 1918), *UB-120* (23 February 1918), *UB-123* (2 March 1918), *UB-126* (12 March 1918), *UB-124* (19 March 1918), *UB-128* (10 April 1918), *UB-125* (16 April 1918), *UB-127* (27 April 1918), *UB-129* (11 May 1918), *UB-130* (27 May 1918), *UB-131* (4 June 1918), *UB-132* (22 June 1918), *UB-142* (23 July 1918), *UB-148*

(7 August 1918), *UB-143* (21 August 1918), *UB-149* (19 September 1918), *UB-144* (5 October 1918), *UB-150* (19 October 1918), *UB-145* (November 1918), *UB-146* (November 1918), *UB-147* (November 1918), *UB-151* (November 1918), *UB-152* (November 1918), *UB-153* (November 1918)

BUILDER: Bremen

*UB-66* (31 May 1917), *UB-67* (16 June 1917), *UB-68* (4 July 1917), *UB-71* (12 July 1917), *UB-69* (7 August 1917), *UB-70* (17 August 1917), *UB-133* (27 September 1918), *UB-136* (27 September 1918), *UB-137* (2 November 1918), *UB-138* (2 November 1918), *UB-139* (2 November 1918), *UB-140* (2 November 1918), *UB-141* (2 November 1918), *UB-134* (November 1918), *UB-135* (November 1918)

BUILDER: Germania

DISPLACEMENT: 516 tons (surfaced), 651 tons (submerged)

DIMENSIONS: 181′5″–183′3″ x 19′0″ x 12′2″–12′6″

MACHINERY: 2 diesel engines, 2 electric motors, 2 shafts. 1100 bhp/788 shp = 13.5/7.5 knots

RANGE: 7200–9040 nm at 6 knots surfaced, 40 nm at 4.5 knots submerged

ARMAMENT: 5 x 500mm torpedo tubes (4 bow, 1 stern), total 10 torpedoes, 1 x 88mm (105mm from *UB-88*) gun

COMPLEMENT: 36

NOTES: The design for this third group of coastal submarines broke away from the earlier pattern of simple single-hull vessels with external saddle ballast tanks. Instead, the new boats essentially were diminutives of contemporary war mobilization submarines. An additional ninety-eight boats were ordered but not completed and were broken up on the building ways after the war's end.

The *UB-61* was mined off the Dutch coast on 29 November 1917, and the *UB-56*, the *UB-75*, and the *UB-81* were mined in the English Channel in December. The sloop *Cyclamen* sank the *UB-69* near Bizerta on 9 January 1918; the sloop *Campanula* sank the *UB-66* off Cape Bon on 18 January; the *UB-63* failed to return from a patrol in the Irish Sea in February; the *UB-54* and the *UB-58* were mined in the Straits of Dover in March; British drifters sank the *UB-82* in the Irish Sea on 17 April; the motor launch *ML-413* sank the *UB-71* in the Straits of Gibraltar on 21 April; the *UB-55* was mined in the Straits of Dover on 22 April; the drifter *Coreopsis* sank the *UB-85* off Belfast Lough on 30 April; the *UB-70* failed to return from an Adriatic mission in April; the *UB-119* was missing in the Irish Sea during May; the steamer *Queen Alexandria* rammed and sank the *UB-78* in the English Channel on 9 May; the submarine *D-4* torpedoed the *UB-72* in the English Channel on 12 May; the submarine *H-4* torpedoed the *UB-52* off Cattaro on 25 May; the armed yacht *Lorna* sank the *UB-74* in Lyme Bay on 26 May; the *UB-108* was lost in the English Channel during July; the *UB-65* sank off the Irish coast after an internal explosion on 10 July; the destroyer *Garry* sank the *UB-110* off Hartlepool on 19 July; the destroyers *Marne* and *Milbrook* sank the *UB-124* in the Irish Sea on 20 July; the destroyer *Vanessa* and the drifter *Calvia* sank the *UB-107* off Scarborough on 27 July; the *UB-53* was caught in the Otranto mine barrage on 3 August and scuttled by its crew; the *UB-57* and the *UB-109* were mined in the Straits of Dover in August; the *UB-103* and the *UB-127* failed to return in September from patrols and probably were mined in the Northern Barrage, as were the *UB-156* on 25 September and the *UB-123* on 19 October; the destroyer *Ophelia* sank the *UB-83* in the Pentland Firth on 10 September; the destroyers *Ouse* and *Star* sank the *UB-115* off Sunderland on 29 September; the steamer *Queensland* sank the *UB-68* (commanded by Karl Dönitz) near Malta on 4 October; the *UB-113* probably was mined off Boulogne on 9 October; the submarine *L-12* torpedoed the *UB-90* off the Norwegian coast on 16 October; the *UB-116* was mined off the Orkneys on 28 October. The *UB-59* was scuttled at Zeebrugge on 5 October 1918, and the *UB-89* sank after a collision with the German cruiser *Frankfurt* on 21 October. The surviving boats were surrendered at war's end and scrapped in 1921–1922 (the *UB-125* served briefly as the Japanese O-7), with the exception of the *UB-99*, which became the French *Carissan* and was not discarded until 1935.

## GERMANY: *U-151* CLASS (1917)
*(Courtesy of Art-Tech)*

*U-155* (28 March 1916), *U-151* (4 April 1917)
BUILDER: Flensburger
*U-156* (17 April 1917)
BUILDER: Atlas
*U-152* (20 May 1917), *U-153* (19 June 1917), *U-154* (10 September 1917)
BUILDER: Reihersteigwerft
*U-157* (23 May 1917)
BUILDER: Stülken
DISPLACEMENT: 1512 tons (surfaced), 1875 tons (submerged)
DIMENSIONS: 213′3″ x 29′2″ x 17′4″
MACHINERY: 2 Germania diesel engines, supplemental diesel generator, 2 electric motors, 2 shafts. 800 bhp/800 shp = 12.5/5.25 knots
RANGE: 25,000 nm at 5.5 knots surfaced, 65 nm at 3 knots submerged
ARMAMENT: 2 x 500mm torpedo tubes (bow), total 18 torpedoes, 2 x 150mm guns, 2 x 88mm guns
COMPLEMENT: 56
NOTES: Three boats of this class were designed and laid down as merchant submarines intended to break the British blockade and establish a service between Germany and the United States. The *Deutschland* (later the *U-155*) made two round-trip voyages to the United States in 1916 that were both commercial and propaganda successes. Its sister, the *Bremen,* was sunk on its maiden voyage to the United States in October 1916, probably by a mine. The third boat, the *Oldenburg,* was taken over by the navy before completion, converted, and commissioned as the *U-151.*

Five additional examples were ordered as U-cruisers from the outset. Although their origins endowed them with very great range, they were too slow and too weakly armed to operate effectively as warships. The submarine *E-35* torpedoed the *U-154* in the Atlantic west of Cape Saint Vincent on 11 May 1918, and the *U-156* was mined in the Northern Barrage on 25 September. The surviving boats were surrendered at war's end and scrapped between 1921 and 1922.

## *U-127* CLASS (1917)

*U-135* (8 September 1917), *U-136* (7 November 1917), *U-137* (8 January 1918), *U-138* (26 March 1918)
BUILDER: Danzig
DISPLACEMENT: 1175 tons (surfaced), 1534 tons (submerged)
DIMENSIONS: 273′11″ x 24′7″ x 14′0″
MACHINERY: 2 diesel engines, 2 supplemental diesel generators, 2 electric motors, 2 shafts. 3500 bhp plus 900 shp/1690 shp = 17/8 knots
RANGE: 10,000 nm at 8 knots surfaced, 50 nm at 4 knots submerged
ARMAMENT: 6 x 500mm torpedo tubes (4 bow, 2 stern), total 14 torpedoes, 2 x 150mm guns
COMPLEMENT: 46
NOTES: The design for this class was the first for a very long range submarine, termed a U-cruiser. The larger size increased bunkerage and range, and a 150mm deck gun was fitted for use against merchant vessels to supplement the torpedo armament. The supplemental diesel generators provided dash speed on the surface. A total of twelve boats were ordered, four each from Germania (the *U-127–U-130*), A.G. Weser (the *U-131–U-134*), and the Kaiserliche Werft Danzig. Only the last four were launched before the war's end, the others being scrapped on the building ways, together with the *U-137* and the *U-138*, which were not completed. The other two boats were surrendered and scrapped in 1921.

## [SWEDEN]—*HAJEN* CLASS (1917)

*Hajen* (8 November 1917), *Sälen* (31 January 1918), *Valrossen* (16 April 1918), *Bävern* (5 March 1921)
BUILDER: Kockums
*Illern* (30 June 1921), *Uttern* (25 June 1921)
BUILDER: Karlskrona
DISPLACEMENT: 422 (last three: 472) tons (surfaced), 600 (last three: 650) tons (submerged)
DIMENSIONS: 177′2″ (last three: 187′0″) x 17′1″ (last three: 19′0″) x 11′6″
MACHINERY: 2 diesel engines, 2 electric motors, 2 shafts. 2000 bhp/700 shp = 15.5/9 knots
ARMAMENT: 4 x 18″ torpedo tubes (bow), total 8 torpedoes, 1 x 75mm gun
COMPLEMENT: 30
NOTES: A.G. Weser supplied Kockums with the design for the first group of this class. It was a modification of the UB-III design that eliminated the stern tube and thus shortened the boat. The same design was very slightly enlarged to build the second group. The *Sälen* was stricken on 24 July 1942, the *Hajen* and the *Valrossen* on 19 March 1943, and the *Bävern* and *Uttern* on 6 October 1944 and scrapped. The *Illern* was sunk in a collision in Kalmar Sound on 12 August 1943, salved, and scrapped.

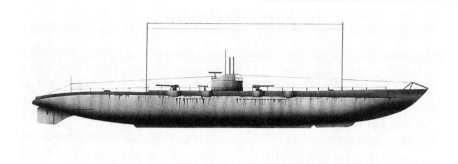

# GERMANY: *U-139* CLASS, *U-140* (1917)

*(Courtesy of Art-Tech)*

*U-139* (3 December 1917), *U-140* (4 November 1917), *U-141* (9 January 1918)

BUILDER: Germania

DISPLACEMENT: 1930 tons (surfaced), 2483 tons (submerged)

DIMENSIONS: 301'10" x 29'10" x 17'4"

MACHINERY: 2 MAN diesel engines, supplemental diesel generator, 2 electric motors, 2 shafts. 3300 bhp plus 450 shp/1690 shp = 15.25/7.5 knots

RANGE: 17,750 nm at 8 knots surfaced, 53 nm at 4.5 knots submerged

ARMAMENT: 6 x 500mm torpedo tubes (4 bow, 2 stern), total 19 torpedoes, 2 x 150mm guns

COMPLEMENT: 66

NOTES: This Germania design for a U-cruiser was the largest type of submarine to enter service with the German Fleet during World War I. The supplemental diesel generator provided dash speed on the surface. Twenty-seven larger versions of this type were ordered, but none had been completed before the end of the war; all were scrapped in 1919–1920. The very long range of these boats and their fine performance, particularly on the surface, was very influential on postwar submarine design, especially in Japan and the United States. All three boats survived the war. The *U-129* went to France and served as the *Halbronn* until stricken in 1935; the *U-140* went to the United States and was sunk as a target in 1921; and the *U-141* went to Britain and was scrapped in 1923.

## U-117 CLASS (1917)

U-122 (9 December 1917), U-123 (26 January 1918), U-124 (28 March 1918), U-125 (26 May 1918), U-126 (16 June 1918)

BUILDER: Blohm und Voss

U-117 (10 December 1917), U-118 (23 February 1918), U-119 (4 April 1918), U-120 (20 June 1918), U-121 (20 September 1918)

BUILDER: Hamburg

DISPLACEMENT: 1164 tons (surfaced), 1512 tons (submerged)

DIMENSIONS: 267'4" x 24'3" x 13'8"

MACHINERY: 2 diesel engines, 2 electric motors, 2 shafts. 2400 bhp/1200 shp = 14.75/7 knots

RANGE: 9400 nm at 7 knots surfaced, 35 nm at 4.5 knots submerged

ARMAMENT: 6 x 500mm torpedo tubes (4 bow, 2 stern), total 12 torpedoes, 2 x 100cm stern mine tubes, total 42 mines, 1 x 88mm gun

COMPLEMENT: 40

NOTES: This class was a greatly enlarged version of the previous design for an ocean-going minelayer with much more powerful machinery, a heavier battery, reduced mine load, and very long range. It retained the single-hull form with large saddle ballast tanks and added an improved bow form for better sea-keeping. All boats were surrendered at war's end and scrapped in 1921–1922 except the U-119, which became the French René Audry and was retained until 1937 (the U-125 briefly served as the Japanese O-1).

## TYPE UC-III (1918)

UC-90 (19 January 1918), UC-91 (19 January 1918), UC-92 (19 January 1918), UC-93 (19 February 1918), UC-94 (19 February 1918), UC-95 (19 February 1918), UC-96 (17 March 1918), UC-97 (17 March 1918), UC-98 (17 March 1918), UC-99 (17 March 1918), UC-100 (14 April 1918), UC-101 (14 April 1918), UC-102 (17 April 1918), UC-103 (14 April 1918), UC-104 (25 May 1918), UC-105 (25 May 1918), UC-106 (25 May 1918), UC-107 (2 June 1918), UC-108 (2 June 1918), UC-109 (2 June 1918), UC-110 (6 July 1918), UC-111 (6 July 1918), UC-112 (6 July 1918), UC-113 (6 July 1918), UC-114 (11 August 1918), UC-115 (11 August 1918), UC-116 (11 August 1918), UC-117 (11 August 1918), UC-118 (11 August 1918), UC-119 (September 1918), UC-120 (September 1918), UC-121 (September 1918), UC-122 (1 October 1918), UC-123 (1 October 1918), UC-124 (1 October 1918)

BUILDER: Blohm und Voss

DISPLACEMENT: 491 tons (surfaced), 471 tons (submerged)

DIMENSIONS: 214'10" x 18'0" x 12'6"

MACHINERY: 2 MAN diesel engines, 2 electric motors, 2 shafts. 600 bhp/770 shp = 11.5/6.5 knots

RANGE: 9850 nm at 7 knots surfaced, 40 nm at 4.5 knots submerged

ARMAMENT: 3 x 500mm torpedo tubes (2 bow, 1 stern), total 7 torpedoes, 6 x 100cm mine tubes, total 14 mines, 1 x 105mm gun

COMPLEMENT: 32

NOTES: The design for the third group of coastal minelayers was a modestly enlarged development of the previous type. The principal differences were an improved bow section for better seakeeping, heavier pressure hull plating to increase the diving depth, and a bigger deck gun. An additional 88 boats were ordered, of which 34 were laid down and scrapped incomplete in 1919 and the remainder canceled at war's end. All the class survived the war and were surrendered. The *UC-90* and the *UC-99* commissioned in the Imperial Japanese Navy as the *O-4* and the *O-5* and were scrapped in 1921. The other boats were broken up between 1919 and 1922.

**NOTE:** *U-115, U-116, U-142–U-150, U-158, U-159, U-173–U-200, UB-156–UB-249,* and *UC-125–UC-192* were broken up on the slip incomplete at the end of World War I or cancelled prior to construction.

# ITALY
## *DELFINO* (1892)

BUILDER: La Spezia

DISPLACEMENT: 98 tons (surfaced), 108 tons (submerged)

DIMENSIONS: 80′9″ x 9′5″ x 5′3″

MACHINERY: 1 electric motor, 1 shaft. 65 shp = 6/5 knots

RANGE: 24 nm at 2 knots surfaced or submerged

ARMAMENT: 1 x 405mm torpedo tube (bow)

COMPLEMENT: 11

NOTES: The *Delfino*, designed by Giacinto Pullino, was a single-hull type with main ballast tanks amidships and trim tanks at bow and stern. In addition to a pair of planes forward there were two vertical screws driven by the single electric motor to assist in diving and maintaining depth. Between 1902 and 1904 the *Delfino* was reconstructed. A large forward deck casing and a substantial conning tower were fitted, a 130 bhp gasoline engine was installed for surface navigation, a fixed periscope was added, and a 450mm torpedo tube replaced the original unit. The rebuilt *Delfino* displaced 102 tons surfaced, 113 tons submerged, and had a surface range of 165 nautical miles at 2 knots. After serving as a training vessel during World War I, the *Delfino* was stricken on 16 January 1919.

## *GLAUCO* CLASS (1905)

*Glauco* (9 June 1905), *Squalo* (10 June 1906), *Narvalo* (21 October 1906), *Otaria* (25 March 1908), *Tricheco* (6 June 1909)

BUILDER: Venezia

DISPLACEMENT: 161 tons (surfaced), 244 tons (submerged)

DIMENSIONS: 120'9" x 14'1" x 8'8"

MACHINERY: 2 Fiat (*Otaria* and *Tricheco*: Thornycroft) gasoline engines, 2 Savigliano electric motors, 2 shafts. 600 bhp/170 shp = 14/6 knots

RANGE: 900 nm at 8 knots surfaced, 40 nm at 5 knots submerged

ARMAMENT: 2 (*Glauco*: 3) x 450mm torpedo tubes (bow), total 4 torpedoes

COMPLEMENT: 15

NOTES: Cesare Laurenti's design for this class established a pattern followed in the construction of the majority of Italian submarines until the end of World War I. It featured a partial double hull containing the midship main ballast tanks, with trim tanks in the single-hull sections fore and aft. The hull shape was optimized for surface navigation with a broad, flat stern, a wide upper surface that served as a deck, and a pronounced bow overhang projecting forward of the muzzles of the torpedo tubes. Planes at bow and stern were employed for diving and depth control. These boats were deployed for harbor defense at Brindisi and Venice during World War I and were stricken in early 1918.

## *FOCA* CLASS (1908)

*Foca* (8 September 1908), [Sweden]— *Hvalen* (16 February 1909)

BUILDER: Fiat

DISPLACEMENT: 185 tons (surfaced), 280 tons (submerged)

DIMENSIONS: 139'5" x 14'0" x 5'3"

MACHINERY: 2 Fiat gasoline engines, 2 Siemens electric motors, 2 shafts. 600 bhp/160 shp = 16/6 knots

RANGE: 875 nm at 8 knots surfaced, 40 nm at 4 knots submerged

ARMAMENT: 2 x 450mm torpedo tubes (bow), total 4 torpedoes

COMPLEMENT: 17

NOTES: This class was an improved Laurenti type with a larger conning tower. The *Foca* originally had three engines (a total of 800 bhp) and three shafts. It was scuttled at Naples after a gasoline explosion on 26 April 1909, salved, and refitted with the center engine and shaft deleted. The *Foca* served in the Adriatic during World War I and was stricken in November 1918. The *Hvalen* caused a sensation at the time by making the 4,000-mile voyage from La Spezia to Stockholm under its own power and without any escort. It was stricken in 1919 and sunk as a target.

## [DENMARK]—*DYKKEREN* (18 JUNE 1909)

BUILDER: Fiat

DISPLACEMENT: 105 tons (surfaced), 130 tons (submerged)

DIMENSIONS: 113'10" x 10'10" x 7'3"

MACHINERY: 2 Fiat gasoline engines, 2 Siemens electric motors, 2 shafts. 400 bhp/210 shp = 12/7.5 knots

RANGE: 100 nm at 8 knots surfaced, 40 nm at 4 knots submerged

ARMAMENT: 2 x 18" torpedo tubes (bow)

COMPLEMENT: 9

NOTES: This boat was a smaller version of the previous Laurenti design. The Norwegian steamer *Vesle* accidentally rammed and sank it on 9 October 1916.

## *MEDUSA* CLASS (1911)

*Velella* (25 May 1911), *Medusa* (30 June 1911), *Argo* (14 January 1912), *Jalea* (3 August 1912), [Portugal]—*Espadarte* (5 October 1912)

BUILDER: Fiat

*Fisalia* (25 February 1912), *Zoea* (2 March 1913)

BUILDER: Orlando

*Salpa* (14 May 1912), *Jantina* (20 November 1912)

BUILDER: Muggiano

DISPLACEMENT: 248 tons (surfaced), 305 tons (submerged)

DIMENSIONS: 147'8" x 13'9" x 9'6"

MACHINERY: 2 Fiat (*Velella*: MAN) diesel engines, 2 Savigliano (*Velella*: Siemens) electric motors, 2 shafts. 650 bhp/300 shp = 12/8 knots

RANGE: 1200 nm at 8 knots surfaced, 54 nm at 6 knots submerged

ARMAMENT: 2 x 450mm (Portuguese boat: 18") torpedo tubes (bow), total 4 torpedoes

COMPLEMENT: 21

NOTES: This class was a further development of the Laurenti type. The most important advance was the installation of diesel engines. The boats were considered very stable and maneuverable while submerged. The Italian boats served extensively in the Adriatic. The German *UB-15* torpedoed the *Medusa* in the northern Adriatic on 10 June 1915, and the *Jalea* was mined in the Gulf of Trieste on 17 August. The surviving boats were stricken in 1918. The Portuguese *Espadarte* served operationally until 1931.

## [UNITED STATES]—*THRESHER* (15 AUGUST 1912)

BUILDER: Cramp
DISPLACEMENT: 360 tons (surfaced), 470 tons (submerged)
DIMENSIONS: 157'6" x 17'6" x 10'11"
MACHINERY: 2 gasoline engines, 2 electric motors, 2 shafts. 1000 bhp/440 shp = 14/9.5 knots
RANGE: 2500 nm at 8 knots surfaced, 70 nm at 5 knots submerged
ARMAMENT: 4 x 18" torpedo tubes (bow), total 4 torpedoes
COMPLEMENT: 24

NOTES: The design for this boat was essentially an enlarged version of Laurenti's *Foca* with a heavier torpedo battery and more extensive conning tower. Its focus on superior operational qualities on the surface was a marked contrast with contemporary U.S. submarines of the Holland type that emphasized submerged performance. The *Thresher* was renamed the *G-4* before it was launched. It operated from New London during World War I and was stricken on 5 September 1919.

## *NAUTILUS* CLASS (1913)

*Nautilus* (25 April 1913), *Nereide* (12 June 1913)
BUILDER: Venezia
DISPLACEMENT: 225 tons (surfaced), 320 tons (submerged)
DIMENSIONS: 134'4" x 14'1" x 9'4"
MACHINERY: 2 Sulzer diesel engines, 2 Ansaldo electric motors, 2 shafts. 600 bhp/320 shp = 13.25/8 knots
RANGE: 1000 nm at 10 knots surfaced, 64 nm at 3 knots submerged
ARMAMENT: 2 x 450mm torpedo tubes (bow), total 4 torpedoes
COMPLEMENT: 19

NOTES: Curio Bernadis was responsible for this single-hull design with a large midship main ballast tank and fore and aft diving tanks. It was unusual in using only forward diving planes. The boats served in the Adriatic during World War I. The Austrian submarine *U-5* torpedoed the *Nereide* near Pelagosa Island on 5 August 1915, and the *Nautilus* was stricken in 1919.

## *PULLINO* CLASS (1913)

*Giacinto Pullino* (21 June 1913), *Galileo Ferraris* (9 November 1913)
BUILDER: La Spezia
DISPLACEMENT: 345 tons (surfaced), 405 tons (submerged)
DIMENSIONS: 138'5" x 13'5" x 12'4"
MACHINERY: 2 Fiat diesel engines, 2 Savigliano electric motors, 2 shafts. 1460 bhp/520 shp = 14/9 knots
RANGE: 1690 nm at 8 knots surfaced, 170 nm at 2.5 knots submerged
ARMAMENT: 4 x 450mm torpedo tubes (2 bow, 2 stern), 2 x 450mm torpedoes (external racks), total 8 torpedoes, 1 x 57mm gun, 1 x 37mm gun
COMPLEMENT: 21

NOTES: Virginio Cavallini designed these double-hull submarines. They were the first Italian boats to carry deck guns and also had the heaviest torpedo armament of the fleet's prewar submarines. The *Giacinto Pullino* ran aground on Galioli Island on 31 July 1917, was captured by Austrian forces, and sank while under tow to Pola. The *Galileo Ferraris* was stricken in 1919.

## F CLASS (1913)

[Brazil]—*F-1* (11 June 1913), *F-3* (9 November 1913), *F-5* (1913), [Italy]—*F-1* (2 April 1916), *F-2* (4 June 1916), *F-3* (6 June 1916), *F-5* (12 August 1916), *F-7* (23 December 1916), *F-8* (13 November 1916), *F-9* 24 September 1916), *F-10* (19 October 1916), *F-11* (17 September 1916), *F-12* (30 November 1916), *F-19* (10 March 1918), *F-20* (17 March 1918), *F-21* (19 May 1918), [Portugal]—*Foca* (18 April 1917), *Golfinho* (1917), *Hidra* (9 August 1917), [Spain]—*Narciso Monturiol* (1917), *Cosme Garcia* (1917), *A 3* (1917)

BUILDER: Fiat

*F-4* (12 August 1916), *F-6* (4 March 1917), *F-13* (20 May 1917), *F-15* (27 May 1917), *F-17* (3 June 1917)

BUILDER: Orlando

*F-14* (23 January 1917), *F-16* (19 March 1917), *F-18* (15 May 1917)

BUILDER: Odero

DISPLACEMENT: 262 tons (surfaced), 319 tons (submerged)

DIMENSIONS: 149'7" x 13'9" x 10'2"

MACHINERY: 2 Fiat diesel engines, 2 Savigliano electric motors, 2 shafts. 670 bhp/500 shp = 12.5/8.25 knots

RANGE: 1300 nm at 9 knots surfaced, 120 nm at 2.5 knots submerged

ARMAMENT: 2 x 450mm (Brazilian, Portuguese and Spanish boats: 18") torpedo tubes (bow), total 4 torpedoes, 1 x 3" AA (Italian boats)

COMPLEMENT: 26

NOTES: These boats, designed by Laurenti, were improved versions of the earlier *Medusa* with upgraded equipment, enlarged conning towers, and arrangements to dive faster. The Italian boats also had two periscopes and a deck gun. The type originally was developed for export to Brazil but was put into production for the Italian Fleet when Italy entered World War I.

The Italian Fleet considered these craft its best coastal submarines of World War I, and all survived the war. The *F-2*, the *F-4*, the *F-8*, and the *F-11* were stricken in 1919; the *F-14* was rammed accidentally by the destroyer *Giuseppe Missori* off Pola on 6 August 1928 and sunk; and the other boats were stricken between 1929 and 1935.

The export boats also had very long service lives. The Brazilian boats were stricken in 1933, the Portuguese submarines in 1934–1935, and the Spanish examples in 1936.

## *ARGONAUTA* CLASS (1914)

*Argonauta* (5 June 1914), [Russia]—*Svyatoy Giorgiy* (1916)

BUILDER: Fiat

[Sweden]—*Svärdfisken* (30 August 1914), *Tumlaren* (14 October 1914)

BUILDER: Kockums

[United Kingdom]—*S-1* (15 September 1915), S-2 (20 September 1915), S-3 (26 September 1915)

BUILDER: Scott

DISPLACEMENT: 255 tons (surfaced), 306 tons (submerged)

DIMENSIONS: 148'0" x 13'9" x 9'10"

MACHINERY: 2 diesel engines, 2 electric motors, 2 shafts. 700 (Swedish boats: 1000) bhp/450 shp = 13.5 (Swedish boats: 14.25)/8 knots

RANGE: 1600 nm at 9 knots surfaced, 120 nm at 3 knots submerged

ARMAMENT: 2 x 450mm (British boats: 18") torpedo tubes (bow), total 4 torpedoes

COMPLEMENT: 24

NOTES: Laurenti designed this class for export. The *Argonauta* was ordered by Russia as the *Svyatoy Giorgiy* but was taken over when Italy entered World War I. The Swedish boats had more powerful engines and carried a 37mm deck gun. The first two British boats served briefly with the Royal Navy but were sold to Italy along with the S-3, still completing, on 1 November 1915. The *Svyatoy Giorgiy* was ordered to replace the original boat and differed in carrying a 75mm deck gun.

The Italian boats served in the Adriatic. The formerly British submarines were stricken in 1919, but the *Argonauta* remained in service until 1928. The Swedish boats received 57mm guns in place of their 37mm weapons in the 1920s and were stricken in 1936. The *Svyatoy Giorgiy* joined the Arctic Fleet in September 1917, was taken over by the Bolsheviks and renamed the *Kommunar*, and was stricken in July 1924.

## *BALILLA* CLASS (1915)

*Balilla* (4 August 1915), *Pacinotti* (13 March 1916), *Guglielmotti* (4 June 1916)

BUILDER: Fiat

[Japan]—*No. 18* (28 June 1919), *No. 21* (22 November 1919), *No. 31* (10 March 1921), *No. 32* (22 June 1921), *No. 33* (17 September 1921)

BUILDER: Nagasaki

DISPLACEMENT: 728 tons (surfaced), 875 tons (submerged)

DIMENSIONS: 213'3" x 19'8" x 13'5"

MACHINERY: 2 diesel engines, 2 electric motors, 2 shafts. 2600 bhp/900 shp = 14/9 knots

RANGE: 3500 nm at 10 knots surfaced, 75 nm at 4 knots submerged

ARMAMENT: 5 (*Balilla*: 4) x 450mm (Japanese boats: 18") torpedo tubes (2/3 bow, 2 stern), total 6/8 torpedoes, 2 x 3" guns (Italian boats)

COMPLEMENT: 38

NOTES: Germany ordered a large submarine from Fiat in 1913 as the *U-42*, built to a single-hull design (with a prominent raised bow casing) developed by the firm from earlier Laurenti types. It was incomplete when Italy entered World War I and was taken over as the *Balilla*. Its two very similar sister ships carried an extra bow torpedo tube and reverted to a flush deck. The Japanese boats used a design very similar to that of the *Pacinotti*. They were designated the F1 and the F2 classes, and were the Imperial Japanese Navy's first long-range submarines.

The Austro-Hungarian torpedo boats *Tb.65F* and *Tb.66F* sank the *Balilla* near Lissa on 14 July 1916; the British sloop *Cyclamen* mistakenly attacked and sank the *Guglielmotti* off Capraia on 10 March 1917; the *Pacinotti* was stricken in 1921. The Japanese boats were redesignated the *RO-1* through *RO-5* in 1924 and stricken 1930–1932.

## *X-2* CLASS (1917)

*X-2* (25 April 1917), *X-3* (29 December 1917)

BUILDER: Ansaldo

DISPLACEMENT: 403 tons (surfaced), 468 tons (submerged)

DIMENSIONS: 139'9" x 18'1" x 10'2"

MACHINERY: 2 Sulzer diesel engines, 2 Ansaldo electric motors, 2 shafts. 650 bhp/325 shp = 8.25/6.25 knots

RANGE: 1200 nm at 8 knots surfaced, 70 nm at 3 knots submerged

ARMAMENT: 9 x mine tubes, total 18 mines, 1 x 3" AA gun

COMPLEMENT: 23

NOTES: Bernadis undertook the reconstruction as the Italian *X-1* of the German coastal minelayer *UC-12* after its recovery. He adopted the German minelaying system using inclined tubes when he came to design his own coastal minelayers. The design used a single-hull with saddle main ballast tanks and minelaying tubes in the after section of the hull. These submarines operated briefly during World War I but saw very little postwar service, though they were not discarded until September 1940.

## *MICCA* CLASS (1917)

*Pietro Micca* (3 June 1917), *Luigi Galvani* (26 January 1918), *Torricelli* (16 June 1918), *Lorenzo Marcello* (29 September 1918), *Angelo Emo* (23 February 1919), *Lazzaro Mocenigo* (26 June 1919)

BUILDER: La Spezia

DISPLACEMENT: 842 tons (surfaced), 1244 tons (submerged)

DIMENSIONS: 207'63" x 20'4" x 14'0"

MACHINERY: 2 diesel engines, 2 electric motors, 2 shafts. 2600 bhp/1300 shp = 11/11 knots

RANGE: 2100 nm at 10 knots surfaced, 180 nm at 3 knots submerged

ARMAMENT: 6 x 450mm torpedo tubes (4 bow, 2 stern), total 8 torpedoes, 2 x 3" guns

COMPLEMENT: 40

NOTES: The design for these large double-hull submarines was completed before World War I by the Comitato Progetti Navi (Ship Projects Committee) in conjunction with Cavallini. As designed they were to carry a twin rotating torpedo tube mount on deck in addition to the internal tubes. Three boats, the *Lorenzo Marcello,* the *Angelo Emo,* and the *Lazzaro Mocenigo,* were ordered from the Regia Arsenale Venezia in 1914, but construction was halted in 1915, the hulls dismantled, and they were reordered from La Spezia. None of the class were completed until after World War I. Their machinery was unreliable and their maneuverability poor, so they were partially reconstructed beginning in 1923 with larger deck casings and conning towers. The *Lorenzo Marcello* was stricken in 1928, the *Pietro Micca,* the *Angelo Emo,* and the *Torricelli* in 1930, and the other two boats between 1937 and 1938.

## N CLASS (1917)

*N-1* (6 September 1917), *N-2* (26 January 1918), *N-3* (27 April 1918), *N-4* (6 October 1918)

BUILDER: Ansaldo

*N-5* (18 November 1917), *N-6* (20 September 1918)

BUILDER: Tosi

DISPLACEMENT: 277 tons (surfaced), 363 tons (submerged)

DIMENSIONS: 150'6" x 14'0" x 10'2"

MACHINERY: 2 diesel engines, 2 electric motors, 2 shafts. 700 bhp/400 shp = 12.5/7.5 knots

RANGE: 1300 nm at 8 knots surfaced, 45 nm at 2 knots submerged

ARMAMENT: 2 x 450mm torpedo tubes (bow), total 4 torpedoes

COMPLEMENT: 23

NOTES: Bernardis updated his *Nautilus* design for this class with improved machinery and a deck gun, and continued his preference for bow diving planes only. Their construction was prolonged by material shortages during World War I. They were active postwar until stricken between 1929 and 1935.

## *BARBERIGO* CLASS (1917)

*Agostino Barbarigo* (18 November 1917), *Andrea Provana* (27 January 1918), *Sebastiano Veniero* (7 June 1918), *Giacomo Nani* (8 September 1918)

BUILDER: Fiat

DISPLACEMENT: 762 tons (surfaced), 924 tons (submerged)

DIMENSIONS: 219'10" x 19'4" x 12'6"

MACHINERY: 2 Fiat diesel engines, 2 Ansaldo electric motors, 2 shafts. 2600 bhp/1400 shp = 16/9.75 knots

RANGE: 2070 nm at 11 knots surfaced, 100 nm at 4.5 knots submerged

ARMAMENT: 6 x 450mm torpedo tubes (4 bow, 2 stern), total 8 torpedoes, 2 x 3" guns

COMPLEMENT: 40

NOTES: Laurenti and Cavallini jointly designed these large, partially double hull submarines. This class introduced a full-length deck (from the after end of the torpedo compartment to the stern) above the batteries, which were contained in four separate watertight compartments. These boats were both fast and maneuverable, and they were very popular with their operators. The steamer *Capena* sank the *Sebastiano Veniero* in a collision off Cape Passero on 6 August 1925; the *Agostino Barbarigo* and the *Andrea Provana* were stricken in 1928; the *Giacomo Nani* was stricken in 1935.

# JAPAN
## TYPES K1 (1917), K2 (1919), K3 (1920), AND K4 (1921)

*No. 19* (15 October 1917), *No. 20* (1 December 1917), *No. 22* (31 March 1919), *No. 23* (26 August 1919), *No. 24* (14 October 1920), *No. 34* (24 February 1921), *No. 35* (25 March 1921), *No. 36* (28 December 1920), *No. 37* (22 April 1920)

BUILDER: Kure

*No. 38* (26 October 1920), *No. 39* (26 October 1920), *No. 40* (15 October 1921), *No. 41* (25 October 1921), *No. 58* (22 June 1922)

BUILDER: Yokosuka

*No. 42* (8 December 1919), *No. 43* (17 February 1920), *No. 45* (18 October 1921), *No. 62* (13 April 1922)

BUILDER: Sasebo

DISPLACEMENT: 735–770 tons (surfaced), 1030–1080 tons (submerged)

DIMENSIONS: 227'0" (Type K2 and K3: 230'0", Type K4: 243'0") x 20'10" x 12'0"

MACHINERY: 2 Sulzer diesel engines, 2 electric motors, 2 shafts. 2600 bhp/1200 shp = 18/9 knots

RANGE: 4000–6000 nm at 10 knots surfaced, 85 nm at 4 knots submerged

ARMAMENT: 4 x 18" (Nos.45, 58, 62: 21") torpedo tubes (bow), 2 x 18" (Nos. 45, 58, 62: 21") torpedoes (external cradles), total 10 torpedoes, 1 x 3" AA gun.

COMPLEMENT: 45

NOTES: Japanese naval constructors derived the design for these boats, built in four series, from earlier Schneider-Laubeuf submarines for the fleet. They conformed well to Japanese requirements for long range and heavy firepower. The last group introduced 21-inch torpedoes into Japan's submarine force.

These boats were redesignated the *RO-11* through the *RO-28* in 1924. All except the *RO-17* through the *RO-19* and the *RO-26* through the *RO-28* were stricken in 1931–1932. The *RO-17* through the *RO-19* were stricken in 1936, and the last three boats were discarded in 1940.

# RUSSIA
## *DELFIN* (1903)

BUILDER: Baltic

DISPLACEMENT: 113 tons (surfaced), 124 tons (submerged)

DIMENSIONS: 64′3″ x 11′0″ x 9′6″

MACHINERY: 2 gasoline engines, 1 electric motor, 1 shaft. 300 bhp/120 shp = 9/4.5 knots

RANGE: 243 nm at 8 knots surfaced, 285 nm at 2.5 knots submerged

ARMAMENT: 2 x 450mm torpedoes (Drzewiecki drop collars)

COMPLEMENT: 22

NOTES: Designed by Ivan Grigorevich Bubnov, Mikhail Nikolaevich Beklemishev, and Igor Stanislavovich Goryunov, who together formed the Imperial Russian Navy's Construction Commission for Submarines. The *Delfin* had a single hull with saddle tanks located toward the stern (a Bubnov characteristic). The hull was sheathed with teak planking to prevent damage should it ground while diving. It sank on trials in June 1904 but was raised, refitted, and transferred to Vladivostok for service in the war with Japan. In February 1916 the *Delfin* moved to the Arctic, but it was stricken in August 1917.

## *KASATKA* CLASS (1904)

*Kasatka, Makrel, Nalin, Okun, Skat, Feldmarshal Graf Sheremetev*

BUILDER: Baltic

DISPLACEMENT: 140 tons (surfaced), 177 tons (submerged)

DIMENSIONS: 116′6″ x 11′0″ x 11′3″

MACHINERY: 1 kerosene engine, 1 electric motor, 1 shaft. 200 bhp/100 shp = 8.5/5.5 knots

RANGE: 700 nm at 8 knots surfaced, 50 nm at 3 knots submerged

ARMAMENT: 4 x 450mm torpedoes (Drzewiecki drop collars)

COMPLEMENT: 24

NOTES: These boats were enlarged versions of the *Delfin*. Larger conning towers were fitted to all boats after the Russo-Japanese War, and the *Makrel* and the *Okun* received 120-horsepower diesel engines in 1906. All but the *Makrel* and the *Okun* (deployed in the Baltic) initially served in the Far East. The *Nalim* and the *Skat* transferred to the Black Sea in 1914, decommissioned in May 1917, and were scuttled at Sevastopol on 26 April 1919. The *Kasatka* and the *Feldmarshal Graf Sheremetev* went to the Arctic in 1915 and to the Baltic in 1917. The *Kasatka*, the *Makrel*, and the *Okun* transferred to the Caspian in 1918, were decommissioned on 21 November 1925, and scrapped. The *Feldmarshal Graf Sheremetev* was renamed the *Keta* on 4 August 1917, sank accidentally at Petrograd in 1922, and was salved and scrapped in 1924.

## *POCHTOVY* (1908)

BUILDER: Metal Works

DISPLACEMENT: 134 tons (surfaced), 146 tons (submerged)

DIMENSIONS: 118'1" x 10'6" x 8'10"

MACHINERY: 2 gasoline engines, 1 diesel-electric generator, 1 shaft. 260 bhp/130 shp = 11.5/6.5 knots

RANGE: 350 nm at 10 knots surfaced, 28 nm at 2.5 knots submerged

ARMAMENT: 4 x 450mm torpedoes (Drzewiecki drop collars),

COMPLEMENT: 22

NOTES: Stefan K. Drzewiecki designed this submarine, which originally was to use a single diesel-electric generator. An internal oxygen supply made possible operation of the gasoline engines while the boat was submerged, the exhaust gases being expelled by a compressor through a perforated pipe below the keel. This system functioned reliably but caused heavy internal condensation from steam generated by submerged engine operation, while the exhaust left a very visible wake of bubbles. Drzewiecki also experimented briefly with using a liquid oxygen closed-cycle system. The *Pochtovy* served in the Baltic and was stricken in 1913.

## *MINOGA* (11 OCTOBER 1908)

BUILDER: Baltic

DISPLACEMENT: 117 tons (surfaced), 142 tons (submerged)

DIMENSIONS: 105'7" x 9'2" x 8'3"

MACHINERY: 2 Nobel diesel engines, 1 Volta electric motor, 1 shaft. 240 bhp/140 shp = 11/5 knots

RANGE: 600 nm at 10 knots surfaced, 70 nm at 3.5 knots submerged

ARMAMENT: 2 x 450mm torpedo tubes (bow), 1 x 37mm AA gun

COMPLEMENT: 22

NOTES: This Bubnov-designed boat was the first Russian submarine fitted with diesels. It also introduced a variable-pitch propeller. The *Minoga* served in the Baltic, was transferred to the Caspian in November 1918, and was stricken on 21 November 1925 and scrapped.

## *AKULA* (22 AUGUST 1909)

BUILDER: Baltic

DISPLACEMENT: 370 tons (surfaced), 475 tons (submerged)

DIMENSIONS: 184'0" x 12'0" x 11'0"

MACHINERY: 2 Nobel diesel engines, 1 electric motor, 3 shafts. 900 bhp/300 shp = 10.5/6.5 knots

RANGE: 1900 nm at 8 knots surfaced, 38 nm at 5 knots submerged

ARMAMENT: 4 x 450mm torpedo tubes (2 bow, 2 stern), 4 x 450mm torpedoes (Drzewiecki drop collars), total 8 torpedoes, 4 mines, 1 x 47mm gun

COMPLEMENT: 24

NOTES: Bubnov also designed this boat, in which the diesel engines and the electric motor drove separate shafts were each fitted with variable-pitch propellers. After some initial mechanical problems it proved very successful. The *Akula* served in the Baltic and was mined and sunk off Windau on 28 November 1915.

## *KRAB* (19 AUGUST 1912)

BUILDER: Nikolayev

DISPLACEMENT: 560 tons (surfaced), 740 tons (submerged)

DIMENSIONS: 173'3" x 14'3" x 12'9"

MACHINERY: 4 Curtiss gasoline engines, 2 electric motors, 2 shafts. 1200 bhp/400 shp = 11.75/7 knots

RANGE: 1700 nm at 8.5 knots surfaced, 82 nm at 4 knots submerged

ARMAMENT: 2 x 450mm torpedo tubes (bow), 2 x 450mm torpedoes (Drzewiecki drop collars), total 4 torpedoes, 60 mines, 1 x 75mm gun

COMPLEMENT: 50

NOTES: The world's first minelaying submarine was designed by Mikhail N. Naletov. It had a single hull with saddle tanks. The mines were carried in two longitudinal tubes within the hull casing, along which they were transported by an electrically driven chain conveyor and launched through stern doors. The *Krab* served very actively in the Black Sea on minelaying operations during World War I. It was seized by German forces in May 1918, surrendered to the British in November, and scuttled at Sevastopol on 26 April 1919.

## *MORZH* CLASS (1913)

*Morzh* (28 September 1913), *Nerpa* (19 October 1913), *Tyulen* (19 October 1913)

BUILDER: Baltic Yard

DISPLACEMENT: 630 tons (surfaced), 760 tons (submerged)

DIMENSIONS: 220'0" x 15'0" x 13'0"

MACHINERY: 2 diesel engines, 2 electric motors, 2 shafts. 500 bhp/800 shp = 10.75/8.5 knots

RANGE: 2500 nm at 7 knots surfaced, 120 nm at 4 knots submerged

ARMAMENT: 4 x 450mm torpedo tubes (2 bow, 2 stern), 8 x 450mm torpedoes (Drzewiecki drop collars), total 12 torpedoes, 1 x 75mm gun, 1 x 37mm (*Tyulen*: 47mm) AA gun

COMPLEMENT: 47

NOTES: Bubnov designed this class as a development of the *Akula* design. Originally they were to use two 1140 bhp Krupp diesel engines, but the outbreak of war halted delivery. They operated in the Black Sea, where the *Morzh* was lost in May 1917, probably on a mine. The *Tyulen* was seized by German forces in May 1918, surrendered to the British in November, and scuttled at Sevastopol on 26 April 1919. The *Nerpa* was taken over by the Soviet Navy and recommissioned on 3 June 1922 as the *Politbuk*. It was redesignated *No. 11* in 1923, decommissioned on 30 December 1930, and scrapped.

## *BARS* CLASS (1915)

*Bars* (2 June 1915), *Gepard* (2 June 1915), *Vepr* (August 1915), *Volk* (1915), *Edinorog* (1916), *Zmeya* (1916)

BUILDER: Baltic

*Tigr* (18 September 1915), *Lvitsa* (23 October 1915), *Pantera* (26 April 1916), *Forel* (1916), *Kuguar* (1916), *Leopard* (1916), *Rys* (1916), *Tur* (1916), *Ugor* (1916), *Yaguar* (1916), *Ersh* (1917), *Yaz* (1917)

BUILDER: Nobel and Lessner

*Burevestnik* (7 October 1916), *Orlan* (1916), *Lebed* (September 1917), *Pelikan* (September 1917)

BUILDER: Nikolayev

*Gagara* (24 September 1916), *Utka* (1916)

BUILDER: Baltic Yard

DISPLACEMENT: 650 tons (surfaced), 786 tons (submerged)

DIMENSIONS: 223'0" x 15'0" x 13'0"

MACHINERY: 2 diesel engines, 2 electric motors, 2 shafts. 2640 bhp/900 shp = 18/10 knots

RANGE: 400 nm at 17 knots surfaced, 25 nm at 9 knots submerged

ARMAMENT: 4 x 450mm torpedo tubes (2 bow, 2 stern), 8 x 450mm torpedoes (Drzewiecki drop collars), total 12 torpedoes, 1 x 57mm gun, 1 x 37mm AA gun

COMPLEMENT: 33

NOTES: Bubnov designed this class as enlarged and improved versions of the earlier *Morzh* class. Most received much lower powered diesel engines from Vickers or NLSECO because the designed Nobel engines were not available. Armament also varied. The *Ersh* and the *Forel* were armed with only two 450mm tubes in the bow, carried only four torpedoes, and were fitted with two minelaying tubes with forty-two mines, similar to the arrangements aboard the *Krab*. The *Bars*, the *Vepr*, and the *Volk* had two 63mm guns; the *Gagara*, the *Pantera*, the *Rys*, the *Tigr*, and the *Utka* had two 75mm guns and deleted the antiaircraft weapon, while the *Burevestnik* and the *Orlan* had one 75mm gun in place of the 57mm weapon. All the class probably used variable-pitch propellers, and the *Kuguar* was fitted with a telescoping tube to supply air to operate the diesels while submerged, a forerunner of the snorkel.

The Black Sea boats saw only limited service. The *Lebed* and the *Pelikan* still were incomplete when the British scuttled them at Odessa in February 1920. The others were seized by German forces in May 1918, surrendered to the British in November, and scuttled at Sevastopol on 26 April 1919.

The Baltic boats saw considerably more use. The *Bars* was sunk by German warships off Norrkoping on 28 May 1917. The *Lvitsa* was lost on 11 June 1917, and the *Gepard* was sunk on 28 October 1917 near Luzerort—both, most probably, by mines. The *Edinorog* sank while under tow in the Gulf of Finland on 25 February 1918. Three boats still incomplete after the end of World War I (the *Forel*, the *Ugor*, and the *Yaz*) were scrapped by the Soviets. The *Vepr* was used as a Soviet stationary training vessel and scrapped in 1925. The others were taken over by the Soviet Navy and designated *No. 1* (*Tigr*), *No. 2* (*Volk*), *No. 3* (*Tur*), *No. 4* (*Leopard*), *No. 5* (*Pantera*), *No. 6* (*Zmeya*), *No. 7* (*Rys*), *No. 8* (*Yaguar*), *No. 9* (*Ersh*), and *No. 10* (*Kuguar*). They were renamed the *Kommunar*, the *Batrak*, the *Tovaritsch*, the *Krasnoarmeyets*, the *Komissar*, the

*Proletariy*, the *Bolshevik*, the *Krasnoflotets*, the *Rabochiy*, and the *Bednyak* on 17 January 1923. The *Bednyak* was stricken on 4 October, 1926, and the *Rabochiy* was lost in an accident on 22 May 1931 in the Gulf of Finland. The surviving boats became the *B-1*, the *B-5*, the *B-8*, the *B-7*, the *B-2*, the *B-6*, the *B-3*, and the *B-4* respectively. All were taken out of service between 1934 and 1936.

## SPAIN
## *PERAL* (8 SEPTEMBER 1888)

BUILDER: Carraca
DISPLACEMENT: 77 tons (surfaced), 85 tons (submerged)
DIMENSIONS: 70′0″ x 8′6″ x 8′0″
MACHINERY: 2 electric motors, 2 shafts. 60 shp = 7.75/3 knots
RANGE: 396 nm at 3 knots surfaced
ARMAMENT: 1 x 356mm torpedo tube (bow), total 3 torpedoes
COMPLEMENT: 10
NOTES: Teniente de Navio Isaac Peral y Caballero, at that time a professor at the Academia de Ampliacion de la Armada, designed his submarine in 1887. It used ballast tanks and vertical screws for diving and depth control and carried two Schwarzkopf spar torpedoes, in addition to the weapon in its single tube. Although extensive trials proved successful, the boat saw little service and was discarded in 1909.

## SWEDEN
## *HAJEN* (16 JUNE 1904)

BUILDER: Stockholm
DISPLACEMENT: 107 tons (surfaced), 127 tons (submerged)
DIMENSIONS: 70′10″ x 11′10″ x 9′10″
MACHINERY: 1 Avance paraffin oil engine, 1 Luth and Rosén electric motor, 1 shaft. 200 bhp/70 shp = 9.5/7 knots
ARMAMENT: 1 x 450mm torpedo tube (bow), total 3 torpedoes
COMPLEMENT: 11
NOTES: The Swedish Navy sent Carl Richson to the United States in 1900 to study submarine design and construction. On his return he began designing a boat for the navy. Its design owed much to contemporary Holland single-hull types. In 1916 a 135-bhp diesel engine replaced the paraffin oil engine, and the casing was substantially enlarged. The *Hajen* was stricken in 1922 and is preserved as a museum exhibit.

## *UNDERVATTENSBÅTEN NO. 2* CLASS (1909)

*Undervattensbåten No. 2* (25 February 1909), *Undervattensbåten No. 3* (14 April 1909), *Undervattensbåten No. 4* (16 October 1909)
BUILDER: Motala
DISPLACEMENT: 138 tons (surfaced), 230 tons (submerged)
DIMENSIONS: 87'8" x 11'10" x 9'10"
MACHINERY: 1 Polar diesel engine, 1 Luth and Rosén electric motor, 1 shaft. 420 bhp/200 shp = 8.75/6.5 knots

ARMAMENT: 1 x 450mm torpedo tube (bow), total 3 torpedoes
COMPLEMENT: 12
NOTES: Richson designed this class as an enlarged version of the earlier *Hajen* single-hull type. From the outset these boats featured substantial casings and large bridge superstructures. They served in the Swedish archipelago until they were stricken between June 1929 and November 1930.

## *DELFINEN* (1914)

BUILDER: Bergsunds
DISPLACEMENT: 260 tons (surfaced), 370 tons (submerged)
DIMENSIONS: 139'5" x 14'1" x ?
MACHINERY: 2 Hesselman diesel engines, 2 electric motors, 2 shafts. 1000 bhp/300 shp = 13.5/9.5 knots
ARMAMENT: 2 x 450mm torpedo tubes (bow), total 4 torpedoes

COMPLEMENT: 21
NOTES: Richson developed this much larger single-hull boat from his earlier designs to create a submarine suitable for use beyond coastal waters. It again featured a large casing and bridge structure. The *Delfinen* was stricken on 1 October 1930.

## *LAXEN* CLASS (1914)

*Laxen* (1914), *Gädden* (1915)
BUILDER: Karlskrona
DISPLACEMENT: 140 tons (surfaced), 170 tons (submerged)
DIMENSIONS: 87'11" x 11'10" x ?
MACHINERY: 2 diesel engines, 2 electric motors, 2 shafts. 700 bhp/200 shp = 8.75/6.5 knots
ARMAMENT: 1 x 450mm torpedo tube (bow), 3 torpedoes

COMPLEMENT: 10
NOTES: These boats were a further development of Richson's coastal design for the *Undervattensbåten No. 2* class, with improved machinery and superstructure. The *Gädden* was stricken in 1931 and the *Laxen* in 1935.

## *ABBOREN* CLASS (1916)

*Abboren* (25 May 1916), *Braxen* (5 May 1916)
BUILDER: Karlskrona
DISPLACEMENT: 174 tons (surfaced), 310 tons (submerged)
DIMENSIONS: 101'8" x 11'10" x 10'2"
MACHINERY: 2 diesel engines, 2 electric motors, 2 shafts. 920 bhp/280 shp = 9.5/7.5 knots

ARMAMENT: 2 x 450mm torpedo tubes (bow), 4 torpedoes
COMPLEMENT: 14
NOTES: This class was the final development of Richson's coastal submarine design. It was enlarged to accommodate two bow torpedo tubes and more powerful machinery. Both boats were stricken on 18 June 1937.

## UNITED KINGDOM
## [GREECE]—NORDENFELT I (1885)

BUILDER: Ekensberg
DISPLACEMENT: 60 tons (surfaced); submerged characteristics unknown
DIMENSIONS: 64'0" x 9'0" x 7'0"
MACHINERY: 1 Lamm compound steam engine, 1 cylindrical return tube boiler, 1 shaft. 100 ihp = 9/4 knots
RANGE: 100 nm at 5 knots surfaced, 14 nm at 4 knots submerged
ARMAMENT: 1 x 14" torpedo tube (bow), 1 x 25mm gun
COMPLEMENT: 3
NOTES: The Reverend George Garrett developed the basic design for this submarine from his earlier *Resurgam* and completed the detail design jointly with Torsten Nordenfelt, the Swedish industrialist. The boat used ballast tanks, horizontal planes fore and aft, and vertical screws for diving and depth control. The steam plant, built by Bolinders Mekaniska Verkstad, propelled the submarine both on the surface and when submerged. The boiler furnace was shut down before diving, and steam was stored in special pressurized tanks at the bow and stern to power the engine while the boat was under water.

The submarine ran extensive trials in September 1885 with the Swedish Navy. Consistent depth control proved a problem, as did very high internal temperatures while the boat was submerged. Nevertheless, the trials were viewed as quite successful, and Nordenfelt sold the boat to the Greek government in 1886. The Greek Fleet rarely used its submarine, and was broken up in 1901.

## [TURKEY]—NORDENFELT II CLASS, *ABDUL HAMID* (1886)
*(Courtesy of Art-Tech)*

*Abdul Hamid* (6 September 1886), *Abdul Medjid* (4 August 1887),
BUILDER: Barrow
DISPLACEMENT: 100 tons (surfaced), 160 tons (submerged)
DIMENSIONS: 100'0" x 12'0" x 10'0"
MACHINERY: 1 Lamm compound steam engine, 1 cylindrical return tube boiler, 1 shaft. 250 ihp = 8/4 knots
RANGE: 100 nm at 5 knots surfaced, 14 nm at 4 knots submerged
ARMAMENT: 2 x 14" torpedo tube (bow), 2 x 25mm gun
COMPLEMENT: 7

NOTES: These boats were enlarged versions of the earlier Garrett and Nordenfelt design with an additional vertical screw on either beam to improve depth control and longitudinal stability. They were ordered by the Turkish government to counter the Nordenfelt boat deployed by Greece. Trials again were regarded as successful, although the boats still demonstrated longitudinal instability. Two boats were delivered to Turkey but saw virtually no service. They remained in storage until after World War I.

## [RUSSIA]—*NORDENFELT III* CLASS (1887)

*Nordenfelt* (26 March 1887)
BUILDER: Barrow
DISPLACEMENT: 160 tons (surfaced), 243 tons (submerged)
DIMENSIONS: 119'9" x 12'0" x 10'0"
MACHINERY: 1 Plenty and Scott compound steam engine, 1 cylindrical return tube boiler, 1 shaft. 1000 ihp = 14/5 knots
RANGE: 1000 nm at 8 knots surfaced, 14 nm at 4 knots submerged

ARMAMENT: 2 x 14" torpedo tube (bow), total 4 torpedoes, 2 x 25mm gun
COMPLEMENT: 9
NOTES: This was the final development of the Garrett and Nordenfelt design, sold to Russia. It ran aground off Jutland on 18 September 1888 while in transit to Russia and became a total loss.

## UNITED KINGDOM: A CLASS (1902), *A-13* (1905)
*(Courtesy of Art-Tech)*

A-1 (9 June 1902), A-3 (9 March 1903), A-2 (16 April 1903), A-4 (9 June 1903), A-5 (2 March 1904), A-6 (3 March 1904), A-7 (23 January 1905), A-8 (23 January 1905), A-9 (8 February 1905), A-10 (8 February 1905), A-11 (8 March 1905), A-12 (8 March 1905), A-13 (18 April 1905)

BUILDER: Barrow

DISPLACEMENT: 190 tons (surfaced), 205 tons (submerged)

DIMENSIONS: 105'0" x 12'9" x 10'8"

MACHINERY: 1 Wolseley gasoline (A-13 Hornsby-Ackroyd heavy oil) engine, 1 electric motor, 1 shaft. 450–600 bhp/125–150 shp = 11/7 knots

RANGE: 320 nm at 10 knots surfaced, 60 nm at 4 knots submerged

ARMAMENT: A-1–A-4: 1 x 18" torpedo tube (bow), total 3 torpedoes, A-5–A-13: 2 x 18" torpedo tubes (bow), total 4 torpedoes

COMPLEMENT: 11

NOTES: Vickers enlarged the design of the original Holland type, adding a full conning tower. These boats were largely experimental, with each successive unit incorporating improvements. They were used intensively for training throughout their careers. The A-1 was rammed and sunk by the liner Berwick Castle off the Nab on 18 March 1904, and the A-3 was rammed and sunk by the depot ship *Hazard* off the Isle of Wight on 2 February 1912. Both were raised and expended as targets. In 1905 the A-5 and the A-8 sank after internal explosions, and the A-4 sank during sound experiments as a result of flooding; all were raised and returned to service. An accident sank the A-7 in Whitesands Bay on 16 January 1914. All the surviving boats were sold for scrap in 1920.

## UNITED KINGDOM: B CLASS (1904), *B-4* (1905)
*(Courtesy of Art-Tech)*

*B-1* (25 October 1904), *B-2* (30 October 1905), *B-3* (31 October 1905), *B-4* (14 November 1905), *B-5* (14 November 1905), *B-6* (30 November 1905), *B-7* (30 November 1905), *B-8* (23 January 1906), *B-9* (24 January 1906), *B-11* (21 February 1906), *B-10* (23 March 1906)

BUILDER: Barrow

DISPLACEMENT: 287 tons (surfaced), 316 tons (submerged)

DIMENSIONS: 142'3" x 13'7" x 11'7"

MACHINERY: 1 Vickers gasoline engine, 1 electric motor, 1 shaft. 600 bhp/290 shp = 12/6 knots

RANGE: 1000 nm at 8.75 knots surfaced, 60 nm at 4 knots submerged

ARMAMENT: 2 x 18" torpedo tubes (bow), total 4 torpedoes

COMPLEMENT: 15

NOTES: The design for this class was an enlargement of the previous group, with a more extensive casing and planes on the conning tower to improve depth control. They saw extensive service in home waters and the Mediterranean (the *B-11* penetrating the Dardanelles and sinking the Turkish coast defense ship *Messudieh* on 13 December 1914). The *B-6* through the *B-11* were converted to surface patrol vessels at Venice in 1917. The *B-2* was rammed and sunk by the liner *Amerika* off Dover on 4 October 1912, and the *B-10* was bombed and sunk by Austro-Hungarian aircraft at Venice on 5 August 1916. The other vessels in the class were sold for scrap in 1920.

## UNITED KINGDOM: C CLASS (1906), *C-22* (1908)
*(Courtesy of Art-Tech)*

*C-1* (10 June 1906), *C-2* (10 June 1906), *C-5* (20 August 1906), *C-6* (20 August 1906), *C-3* (3 October 1906), *C-4* (18 October 1906), *C-7* (15 February 1907), *C-8* (15 February 1907), *C-9* (3 April 1907), *C-10* (15 April 1907), *C-11* (27 May 1907), *C-12* (9 September 1907), *C-13* (9 November 1907), *C-14* (7 December 1907), *C-15* (21 January 1908), *C-16* (19 March 1908), *C-21* (26 September 1908), *C-22* (10 October 1908), *C-23* (26 November 1908), *C-24* (26 November 1908), *C-25* (10 March 1909), *C-26* (20 March 1909), *C-27* (22 April 1909), *C-28* (22 April 1909), *C-29* (19 June 1909), *C-30* (19 June 1909), *C-31* (2 September 1909), *C-32* (29 September 1909), *C-35* (2 November 1909), *C-36* (30 November 1909), *C-37* (1 January 1910), *C-38* (10 December 1910), [Japan]—*No. 8* (19 May 1908), *No. 9* (19 May 1908)

BUILDER: Barrow

*C-17* (13 August 1908), *C-18* (10 October 1908), *C-19* (20 March 1909), *C-20* (27 November 1909), *C-33* (10 May 1910), *C-34* (8 June 1910)

BUILDER: Chatham

[Japan]—*No. 10* (4 March 1911), *No. 11* (18 March 1911), *No. 12* (27 March 1911), *No. 16* (15 March 1916), *No. 17* (15 March 1916)

BUILDER: Kure

DISPLACEMENT: 287 tons (surfaced), 316 tons (submerged)

DIMENSIONS: 142′3″ x 13′7″ x 11′6″

MACHINERY: 1 Vickers gasoline (Japanese boats: Vickers diesel) engine, 1 electric motor, 1 shaft. 600 bhp/290 shp = 13/7.5 knots

RANGE: 1000 nm at 8.75 knots surfaced, 60 nm at 4 knots submerged

ARMAMENT: 2 x 18″ torpedo tubes (bow), total 4 torpedoes

COMPLEMENT: 16

NOTES: This class was a mass-production version of the previous group, though the conning tower diving planes were omitted. The Japanese boats introduced diesel engines for improved safety.

The British boats saw very extensive service in home waters and the Mediterranean, including working as antisubmarine ships in cooperation with surface escorts that led to the destruction of three U-boats. Four boats (the C-26, the C-27, the C-32, and the C-35) went to the Baltic in 1916. The C-32 was blown up by its crew in the Gulf of Riga after suffering heavy damage from German forces on 22 October, 1917, and the other boats were scuttled off Helsingfors on 4 April 1918.

The C-11 was rammed and sunk by the steamer *Eddystone* off Cromer on 14 July 1909. The C-12, the C-14, the C-16, and the C-17 all sank after collisions but were raised and returned to service. The C-29, the C-31, and the C-33 were lost in the North Sea in 1915, probably to mines. The U-boat U-52 torpedoed and sank the C-34 off the Shetland Isles on 17 July 1917. The C-3 was expended as an explosive charge during the raid on Zeebrugge on 23 April 1918. The surviving boats of the class were sold for scrap in 1920.

The Japanese boats were used primarily for training and were stricken on 1 December 1928.

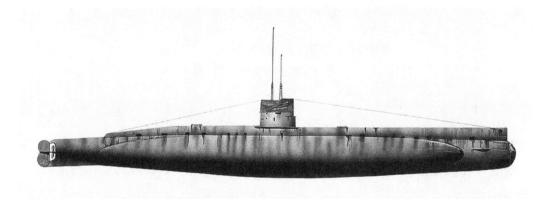

## UNITED KINGDOM: D CLASS (1908), *D-1* (1908)
*(Courtesy of Art-Tech)*

D-1 (16 May 1908), D-2 (25 May 1910), D-3 (17 October 1910), D-4 (27 May 1911), D-5 (28 August 1911), D-6 (23 October 1911)

BUILDER: Barrow

D-7 (14 January 1911), D-8 (23 September 1911)

BUILDER: Chatham

DISPLACEMENT: 495 tons (surfaced), 620 tons (submerged)

DIMENSIONS: 164'7" x 20'5" x 11'5"

MACHINERY: 2 diesel engines, 2 electric motors, 2 shafts. 1200 bhp/550 shp = 14/9 knots

RANGE: 2500 nm at 10 knots surfaced; submerged characteristics unknown

ARMAMENT: 3 x 18" torpedo tubes (2 bow, 1 stern), total 6 torpedoes

COMPLEMENT: 25

NOTES: The design for this class established the basic features of British submarine design until after World War II. It included the adoption of saddle ballast tanks, bow planes in addition to the stern units, a substantial casing and conning tower, relatively long range, diesel engines, and, in the case of the *D-4,* the installation of a deck gun. The *D-5* was mined off Yarmouth on 3 November 1914; the *D-2* was sunk by German antisubmarine craft off Borkum on 25 November 1914; the *D-3* was bombed in error and sunk by the French airship *AT-0* off Féchamp on 12 March 1918; and the *D-6* was torpedoed and sunk by the German *UB-73* off the Irish coast on 28 June 1918. The surviving members of the class were sold for scrap 1921.

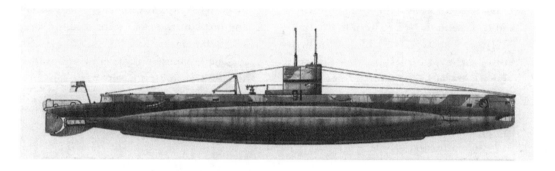

## UNITED KINGDOM: E CLASS (1912)
*(Courtesy of Art-Tech)*

**GROUP I**

*E-4* (5 February 1912), *E-5* (17 May 1912), *E-3* (29 October 1912), *E-6* (12 November 1912), [Australia]—*AE-2* (22 May 1913), *AE-1* (18 June 1913)

BUILDER: Barrow

*E-1* (9 November 1912), *E-2* (23 November 1912), *E-7* (2 October 1913), *E-8* (30 October 1913)

BUILDER: Chatham

**GROUP II**

*E-9* (29 November 1913), *E-10* (29 November 1913), *E-11* (23 April 1914), *E-15* (23 April 1914), *E-14* (7 June 1914), *E-16* (23 September 1914), *E-17* (16 January 1915), *E-18* (4 March 1915), *E-19* (13 May 1915), *E-20* (12 June 1915), *E-21* (24 June 1915), *E-22* (27 August 1915), *E-23* (28 September 1915),

BUILDER: Barrow

*E-12* (5 September 1914), *E-13* (22 September 1914)

BUILDER: Chatham

*E-29* (1 June 1915), *E-30* (29 June 1915)

BUILDER: Armstrong

*E-25* (23 August 1915), *E-26* (11 November 1915), *E-53* (1916), *E-54* (1916)

BUILDER: Beardmore

*E-31* (23 August 1915)

BUILDER: Scott

*E-37* (2 September 1915), *E-47* (29 May 1916), *E-38* (13 June 1916), *E-48* (2 August 1916)

BUILDER: Fairfield

*E-42* (22 October 1915)

BUILDER: Cammell Laird

*E-43* (11 November 1915), *E-44* (21 February 1916), *E-49* (18 September 1916)

BUILDER: Swan Hunter

*E-55* (5 February 1916), *E-56* (19 June 1916), *E-52* (25 January 1917)

BUILDER: Denny

*E-33* (18 April 1916)

BUILDER: Thornycroft

*E-35* (20 May 1916), *E-36* (16 September 1916), *E-50* (13 November 1916)

BUILDER: John Brown

*E-39* (18 May 1916), *E-40* (9 November 1916)

BUILDER: Palmer

*E-32* (16 August 1916)

BUILDER: White

*E-27* (9 June 1917)

BUILDER: Yarrow

**GROUP II MINELAYERS**

*E-41* (22 October 1915), *E-45* (25 January 1916), *E-46* (4 April 1916)

BUILDER: Cammell Laird

*E-24* (9 December 1915)

BUILDER: Barrow

*E-51* (30 November 1916)

BUILDER: Scott

*E-34* (27 January 1917)

BUILDER: Thornycroft

DISPLACEMENT: Group I: 655 tons (surfaced), 796 tons (submerged), Group II: 667 tons (surfaced), 807 tons (submerged)

DIMENSIONS: Group I: 178′1″ x 22′9″ x 12′7″, Group II: 182′6″ x 22′9″ x 12′7″

MACHINERY: 2 diesel engines, 2 electric motors, 2 shafts. 1600 bhp/840 shp = 15/9 knots

RANGE: 3000 nm at 10 knots surfaced; submerged characteristics unknown

ARMAMENT: Group I: 4 x 18″ torpedo tubes (1 bow, 2 beam, 1 stern), total 8 torpedoes, 1 x 12-pounder gun, Group II: 5 x 18″ torpedo tubes (2 bow, 2 beam, 1 stern), total 10 torpedoes, 1 x 12-pounder gun; minelayers: 3 x 18″ torpedo tubes (2 bow, 1 stern), total 3 torpedoes, 10 x mine tubes (20 mines)

COMPLEMENT: 30

NOTES: The E class design incorporated improvements from experience with the previous class and was continually updated during production. They saw extensive service in the North Sea and Mediterranean, forming the core of the British submarine force. They also operated successfully in the Sea of Marmara, the Adriatic, and the Baltic.

The *E-7*, the *E-14*, the *E-15*, and the *E-20* were lost in the Sea of Marmara. The *E-3*, the *E-5*, the *E-6*, the *E-10*, the *E-16*, the *E-22*, the *E-24*, the *E-26*, the *E-30*, the *E-34*, the *E-37*, the *E-47*, the *E-49*, and the *E-50* were lost in the North Sea to mines, or German antisubmarine forces or submarines. The *E-18* was lost in the Baltic on 24 May 1916 after attacking a German destroyer, and the *E-1*, the *E-8*, the *E-9*, and the *E-19* were blown up at Helsingfors on 3 April 1918 to avoid capture. Three boats, the *E-13*, the *E-17*, and the *E-36*, were lost through accidental collisions during World War I. The surviving boats of the class were sold for scrap in 1921–1922.

The Australian *AE-1* was lost (cause unknown) off New Britain on 14 September 1914, and the *AE-2* was scuttled in the Sea of Marmara after action with Turkish torpedo boats on 30 April 1915.

## UNITED KINGDOM: V CLASS (1914), *V-3* (1915)
*(Courtesy of Art-Tech)*

*V-1* (23 June 1914), *V-3* (1 April 1915), *V-4* (25 November 1915), *V-2* (17 February 1917)

BUILDER: Barrow

DISPLACEMENT: 391 tons (surfaced), 457 tons (submerged)

DIMENSIONS: 147′6″ x 16′3″ x 11′6″

MACHINERY: 2 diesel engines, 2 electric motors, 2 shafts. 900 bhp/450 shp = 14/8.5 knots

RANGE: 3000 nm at 9 knots surfaced; submerged characteristics unknown

ARMAMENT: 2 x 18″ torpedo tubes (bow), total 4 torpedoes, 1 x 12-pounder gun

COMPLEMENT: 20

NOTES: Vickers designed this class in response to an Admiralty request for a new coastal submarine. They had a partial double hull and rather small batteries that limited their underwater endurance. All served in the North Sea and were sold for scrap in 1920.

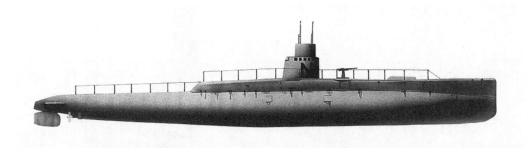

## UNITED KINGDOM: *NAUTILUS* (31 DECEMBER 1914)
*(Courtesy of Art-Tech)*

BUILDER: Barrow

DISPLACEMENT: 1441 tons (surfaced), 2026 tons (submerged)

DIMENSIONS: 258'5" x 26'0" x 17'9"

MACHINERY: 2 diesel engines, 2 electric motors, 2 shafts. 3700 bhp/1000 shp = 17/10 knots

RANGE: 5300 nm at 11 knots surfaced; submerged characteristics unknown

ARMAMENT: 8 x 18" torpedo tubes (2 bow, 4 beam, 2 stern), total 16 torpedoes, 1 x 3" AA gun

COMPLEMENT: 42

NOTES: This boat, designed by Vickers, was intended for long-range, high-speed operation. It served largely as an experimental platform for future development of large, fast submarines. The *Nautilus* was scrapped in 1922.

## UNITED KINGDOM: F CLASS (1915), *F-2* (1916)
*(Courtesy of Art-Tech)*

*F-1* (31 March 1915)
BUILDER: Chatham
*F-2* (7 June 1917)
BUILDER: White
*F-3* (19 February 1916)
BUILDER: Thornycroft
DISPLACEMENT: 363 tons (surfaced), 525 tons (submerged)
DIMENSIONS: 151'0" x 16'1" x 10'7"
MACHINERY: 2 diesel engines, 2 electric motors, 2 shafts. 900 bhp/400 shp = 14/8.5 knots

RANGE: 3000 nm at 9.5 knots surfaced; submerged characteristics unknown
ARMAMENT: 3 x 18" torpedo tubes (2 bow, 1 stern), total 6 torpedoes, 1 x 2-pounder gun
COMPLEMENT: 19
NOTES: This class was built to an Admiralty design for a coastal submarine and featured a partial double hull. These boats served in the North Sea and were sold for scrap in 1920.

## UNITED KINGDOM: G CLASS (1915), *G-13* (1916)
*(Courtesy of Art-Tech)*

*G-1* (14 August 1915), *G-2* (23 December 1915), *G-3* (22 January 1916), *G-4* (23 October 1915), *G-5* (23 November 1915)
BUILDER: Chatham
*G-6* (7 December 1915), *G-7* (4 March 1916)
BUILDER: Armstrong
*G-8* (1 May 1916), *G-9* (15 June 1916), *G-10* (11 January 1916), *G-11* (22 February 1916), *G-12* (24 March 1916), *G-13* (18 June 1916)
BUILDER: Barrow
*G-14* (17 May 1917)
BUILDER: Scott
DISPLACEMENT: 703 tons (surfaced), 837 tons (submerged)
DIMENSIONS: 187′1″ x 22′8″ x 13′4″
MACHINERY: 2 diesel engines, 2 electric motors, 2 shafts. 1600 bhp/840 shp = 14.5/9 knots

RANGE: 2400 nm at 12.5 knots surfaced; submerged characteristics unknown
ARMAMENT: 4 x 18″ torpedo tubes (2 bow, 2 beam), 1 x 21″ torpedo tube (stern), total 10 torpedoes, 1 x 3″ AA gun
COMPLEMENT: 30
NOTES: This Admiralty design for an overseas boat featured a partial double hull and introduced 21-inch torpedoes into submarine service. They served in the North Sea. The *G-9* was rammed and sunk accidentally by the destroyer *Paisley* on 16 September 1917; the *G-7* and the *G-8* were lost in the North Sea, probably to mines; the *G-11* was wrecked near Harwich on 22 November 1918. The class's surviving boats were sold for scrap in 1921–1922.

## UNITED KINGDOM: J CLASS (1915)
*(Courtesy of Art-Tech)*

J-1 (6 November 1915), J-2 (6 November 1915

BUILDER: Portsmouth DY

J-3 (4 December 1915), J-4 (2 February 1916)

BUILDER: Pembroke

J-5 (9 September 1915), J-6 (9 September 1915), [Australia]—J-7 (21 February 1917)

BUILDER: Devonport

DISPLACEMENT: 1204 tons (surfaced), 1820 tons (submerged)

DIMENSIONS: 275′6″ x 23′0″ x 14′0″

MACHINERY: 3 Vickers diesel engines, 3 electric motors, 3 shafts. 3600 bhp/1350 shp = 19.5/9.5 knots

RANGE: 5000 nm at 12.5 knots surfaced; submerged characteristics unknown

ARMAMENT: 6 x 18″ torpedo tubes (4 bow, 2 beam), total 12 torpedoes, 1 x 12-pounder gun, 1 x 3″ AA gun

COMPLEMENT: 44

NOTES: Vickers developed this class of fleet submarines with three shafts to allow use of standard, more reliable diesel engines to attain the specified speed. To improve the lines for speed, the design used a partial double hull. During World War I they served in the North Sea. The J-6 was sunk in error off Blyth by the Q-ship *Cymric* on 15 October 1918. The remaining British boats were transferred to Australia in 1919. All the Australia boats were sold for scrap between 1924 and 1929.

## UNITED KINGDOM: *SWORDFISH* (18 MARCH 1916)
*(Courtesy of Art-Tech)*

BUILDER: Scott

DISPLACEMENT: 932 tons (surfaced), 1105 tons (submerged)

DIMENSIONS: 231'3" x 22'11" x 14'11"

MACHINERY: 2 Parsons geared turbines, 1 Yarrow boiler, 2 electric motors, 2 shafts. 4000 shp/1400 shp = 18/10 knots

RANGE: 3000 nm at 8.5 knots surfaced; submerged characteristics unknown

ARMAMENT: 2 x 21" torpedo tubes (bow), 4 x 18" torpedo tubes (beam), total 10 torpedoes, 2 x 12-pounder guns

COMPLEMENT: 18

NOTES: Scott developed the *Swordfish* design from a Laurenti proposal for a steam-powered fleet submarine to meet Admiralty requirements. It featured a partial double hull over three-quarters of its length and a hull form very similar to that of contemporary large Italian boats. The *Swordfish* was used for experimental work until January 1917, then converted into a surface patrol boat. It was sold for scrap in 1922.

## UNITED KINGDOM: K CLASS (1913), *K-10* (1916)
*(Courtesy of Art-Tech)*

*K-1* (14 November 1916), K-2 (14 October 1916), *K-5* (16 December 1916)
BUILDER: Portsmouth DY
*K-3* (20 May 1916), *K-4* (15 June 1916), *K-8* (10 October 1916), *K-9* (8 November 1916), *K-10* (27 December 1916), *K-17* (10 April 1917), *K-26* (26 August 1919)
BUILDER: Barrow
*K-6* (31 May 1916), *K-7* (31 May 1916)
BUILDER: Devonport
*K-11* (16 August 1916), *K-12* (23 February 1917)
BUILDER: Armstrong
*K-13* (11 November 1916), *K-14* (8 February 1917)
BUILDER: Fairfield
*K-15* (31 October 1917)
BUILDER: Scott
*K-16* (5 November 1917)
BUILDER: Beardmore
DISPLACEMENT: 1980 (*K-26*: 2140) tons (surfaced), 2566 tons (submerged)
DIMENSIONS: 330'0" (*K-26*: 351'0") x 26'7" (*K-26*: 28'0") x 17'0" (*K-26*: 16'0")
MACHINERY: 2 geared turbines, 2 Yarrow boilers, 4 electric motors, 2 shafts. 10,500 shp/1440 shp = 24/9.5 knots
RANGE: 3000 nm at 13.5 knots surfaced; submerged characteristics unknown
ARMAMENT: 10 x 18" torpedo tubes (4 bow, 4 beam, 1 twin revolving mount in superstructure), total 18 torpedoes, 2 x 4" guns, 1 x 3" AA gun. *K-26*: 6 x 21" torpedo tubes (bow), 4 x 18" torpedo tubes (beam), total 20 torpedoes, 3 x 4" guns

COMPLEMENT: 59
NOTES: This class was the final wartime attempt to develop a fast fleet submarine. The Admiralty design featured a powerful steam plant, a complete upper hull above the main pressure hull, and a fully enclosed bridge. Wartime experience demonstrated the need for additional buoyancy forward, leading to the addition of a very prominent bulbous upper bow. Even though these submarines proved capable of meeting the speed and maneuverability requirements of the design, operating them with the battlefleet was extremely hazardous.

The *K-26* was the only unit completed from the Improved *K*-class, which was created to correct the original design's defects. It featured a much improved upper hull shape that conferred good seakeeping qualities on the surface, enlarged and heightened superstructure to better protect stacks and other openings, and redistributed ballast tanks arranged to enhance the rate of diving.

The *K-13* sank on trials, was refloated, and returned to service as the *K-22*. Three boats (the *K-1*, the *K-4*, and the *K-17*) were lost during World War I as a result of collisions, and the *K-5* sank in the Atlantic on 20 January 1921, probably after exceeding its safe dive depth. The surviving boats were sold for scrap between 1921 and 1926, except for the *K-26*, which survived until March 1931.

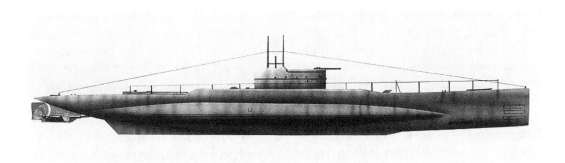

## UNITED KINGDOM: L CLASS (1917), *L-23* (1919)
*(Courtesy of Art-Tech)*

### GROUP I
*L-7* (24 April 1917), *L-8* (7 June 1917)
BUILDER: Cammell Laird
*L-1* (10 May 1917), *L-2* (6 June 1917), *L-3* (1 September 1917), *L-4* (17 November 1917)
BUILDER: Barrow
*L-6* (14 January 1918)
BUILDER: Beardmore
*L-5* (26 January 1918)
BUILDER: Swan Hunter
[Japan]—*No. 25* (10 October 1919), *No. 26* (9 March 1920), *No. 27* (6 June 1920), *No. 28* (13 October 1920), *No. 29* (10 February 1921), *No. 30* (11 May 1921)
BUILDER: Mitsubishi

### GROUP II
*L-15* (16 January 1918), *L-16* (9 April 1918)
BUILDER: Fairfield
*L-9* (29 January 1918), *L-10* (24 January 1918)
BUILDER: Denny
*L-18* (21 November 1918), *L-19* (4 February 1919), *L-20* (23 September 1918), *L-21* (11 October 1919), *L-22* (25 October 1919), *L-23* (1 June 1919), *L-24* (19 February 1919), *L-26* (29 May 1919), *L-27* (14 June 1919)
BUILDER: Barrow
*L-33* (29 May 1919)
BUILDER: Swan Hunter

### GROUP II MINELAYERS
*L-11* (26 February 1918), *L-12* (16 March 1918), *L-14* (10 June 1918), *L-17* (13 May 1918), *L-25* (13 February 1919)
BUILDER: Barrow

### GROUP III
*L-55* (21 September 1918), *L-56* (29 May 1919)
BUILDER: Fairfield
*L-52* (18 December 1918), *L-53* (12 August 1919), [Yugoslavia]—*Hrabri, Nebojsa* (1927)
BUILDER: Armstrong
*L-71* (17 May 1919)
BUILDER: Scott
*L-54* (20 August 1919)
BUILDER: Denny

### GROUP IV
[Japan]—*No. 46* (3 December 1921), *No. 47* (2 March 1922), *No. 57* (28 June 1922)
BUILDER: Mitsubishi

### GROUP V
[Japan]—*No. 59* (22 December 1922), *No. 72* (19 May 1923), *No. 73* (19 September 1923), *No. 84* (24 January 1924), *RO-64* (19 August 1924), *RO-68* (23 February 1925), *RO-65* (25 September 1925), *RO-67* (18 March 1926), *RO-66* (25 October 1926)
BUILDER: Mitsubishi

DISPLACEMENT: Groups I and II: 890 tons (surfaced), 1080 tons (submerged), Group III: 960 tons (surfaced), 1150 tons (submerged), Group IV: 897 tons (surfaced), 1195 tons (submerged), Group V: 996 tons (surfaced), 1322 tons (submerged)

DIMENSIONS: Group I: 231'1" x 23'6" x 13'3", Group II: 238'7" x 23'6" x 13'3", Group III: 235'0" x 23'6" 13.2", Group IV: 250'0" x 23'6" x 13'3", Group V: 250'0" x 24'3" x 12'4"

MACHINERY: 2 diesel engines, 2 electric motors, 2 shafts. 2400 bhp/1600 shp = 17/10.5 knots

RANGE: 3800 (Group IV: 7000, Group V: 5500) nm at 10 knots surfaced, 80 nm at 4 knots submerged

ARMAMENT: Group I: 6 x 18" torpedo tubes (4 bow, 2 beam), total 10 torpedoes, 1 x 4" gun, (final 4 Japanese boats omitted beam tubes), Group II: 4 x 21" torpedo tubes (bow), 2 x 18" torpedo tubes (beam), total 10 torpedoes, 1 x 4" gun, Group III: 6 x 21" torpedo tubes (bow), total 12 torpedoes, 2 x 4" guns, Group IV: 4 x 21" torpedo tubes (bow), total 8 torpedoes, 1 x 4" gun, Group V: 6 x 21" torpedo tubes (bow), total 10 torpedoes, 1 x 3" AA gun, 1 x 7.62mm machine gun; minelayers: 4 x 21" torpedo tubes (bow), total 4 torpedoes, 16 x mine tubes and mines

COMPLEMENT: Group I: 35, Group II: 38, Group III: 44, Group IV: 48, Group V: 60

NOTES: This design was developed as a replacement for the successful E-class. It reverted to the single-hull type with saddle ballast tanks that had proven itself with the earlier boats. Later series made the transition to 21-inch torpedo tubes. L-13 was not used in a superstitious reaction to the disasterous career of the K-13.

The L-10 was sunk by German warships north of Terschelling on 3 October 1918; the L-55 was sunk by Soviet warships off Kronstadt on 4 June 1919 (and was later recovered by the Soviets, commissioned in October 1931 as the Bezbozhnik, damaged and laid up in May 1941, and scrapped about 1953); the L-9 sank in a typhoon at Hong Kong on 18 January 1923; the L-24 was accidentally rammed and sunk by the battleship Resolution on 10 January 1924. The other boats, after serving actively into the 1930s, were sold for scrap between 1930 and 1936, apart from the L-23, the L-26, and the L-27, which were used for training during World War II and were not scrapped until 1946.

The Japanese boats were redesignated the RO-51 through the RO-63 in 1924. The RO-55 was stricken in 1939. The RO-62 collided with the RO-66 off Wake Island and sank it on 17 December 1941; the RO-60 wrecked at Kwajalein on 29 December; the U.S. destroyer Reid sank the RO-61 off Atka Island on 31 August 1942; U.S. aircraft sank the RO-65 in Kiska Harbor on 4 November. The other Group IV boats served as training vessels from 1941 and were joined by the remaining Group V boats from late 1942. The RO-64 was mined in Hiroshima Bay on 12 April 1945, and the other boats were scrapped in 1946.

The Hrabri was seized by the Italians in April 1941 but was broken up later that year. The Nebojsa escaped to Alexandria in April 1941 and operated with British forces. After World War II, the Nebosja returned to the Yugoslav Navy and was renamed the Tara. It was stricken in 1954.

## UNITED KINGDOM: M CLASS (1917), *M-2* (1918)
*(Courtesy of Art-Tech)*

*M-1* (9 June 1917), *M-2* (19 October 1918)
BUILDER: Barrow
*M-3* (19 October 1918), *M-4* (20 June 1919)
BUILDER: Armstrong
DISPLACEMENT: 1594 tons (surfaced), 1946 tons (submerged)
DIMENSIONS: 295'9" x 24'8" x 15'11"

MACHINERY: 2 Vickers diesel engines, 2 electric motors, 2 shafts. 2400 bhp/1600 shp = 15/9 knots
RANGE: 3840 nm at 10 knots surfaced; submerged characteristics unknown
ARMAMENT: 4 x 18" (*M-3*: 21") torpedo tubes (bow), total 8 torpedoes, 1 x 12" gun

COMPLEMENT: 65

NOTES: These boats were designed as submarine monitors for antiship operations with a secondary shore-bombardment role. Trials with the *M-1* were very successful, but the boats' mission was obsolete by that time and the *M-4* was canceled before completion. The *M-3* was converted to a minelayer in 1927, and the *M-2* was converted in 1928 to carry a seaplane in a hangar. The *M-1* served briefly during World War I; the class operated primarily on trials missions thereafter. The *M-1* was accidentally rammed and sunk by the Swedish collier *Vidar* in the English Channel on 12 November 1925; the *M-2* sank in an accident when the hangar door was incompletely sealed while operating off Portland on 26 January 1932; the *M-3* was sold for scrap in February 1932.

## R CLASS (1918)

*R-1* (24 April 1918), *R-2* (25 April 1918), *R-3* (8 June 1918), *R-4* (8 June 1918)

BUILDER: Chatham

*R-7* (14 May 1918), *R-8* (28 June 1918)

BUILDER: Barrow

*R-9* (12 August 1918), *R-10* (5 October 1918)

BUILDER: Armstrong

*R-11* (16 March 1918), *R-12* (9 April 1918)

BUILDER: Cammell Laird

DISPLACEMENT: 410 tons (surfaced), 503 tons (submerged)

DIMENSIONS: 153'9" x 15'3" x 11'6"

MACHINERY: 1 diesel engine, 1 electric motor, 1 shaft. 240 bhp/1200 shp = 9.5/15 knots

RANGE: 2000 nm at 8 knots surfaced; submerged characteristics unknown

ARMAMENT: 6 x 18" torpedo tubes (bow), total 12 torpedoes

COMPLEMENT: 22

NOTES: The Admiralty designed this class as fast boats that could overtake and sink enemy submarines. The hull cross-section duplicated that of the *H* class (see page 162): the hull form was similar, and the whole external form was streamlined for superior underwater performance. Machinery was half an *H*-class installation. The bow compartment contained five powerful, sensitive hydrophones with suitable direction-finding equipment to locate and target submarines underwater. These boats met all expectations, but the end of World War I seemed to terminate their mission; they were discarded in February 1923.

**NOTE:** *E-28, K-18–K-21, K-23–K-25, L-28–L-32, L-34–L-51, L-57–L-70, L-72–L-74, R-5,* and *R-6* all were cancelled at the end of World War I.

# UNITED STATES
## *HOLLAND* (17 MAY 1897)
*(Courtesy of Art-Tech)*

BUILDER: Crescent

DISPLACEMENT: 64 tons (surfaced), 74 tons (submerged)

DIMENSIONS: 53′10″ x 10′2″ x 8′6″

MACHINERY: 1 Otto gasoline engine, 1 Electro Dynamic electric motor, 1 shaft. 45 bhp/50 shp = 8/5 knots

ARMAMENT: 1 x 18″ torpedo tube (bow), total 3 torpedoes, 1 x 8″ dynamite gun

COMPLEMENT: 7

NOTES: The *Holland* was built as a private venture, the sixth of John P. Holland's submarines. The single hull contained a large ballast tank amidships, with small trim tanks fore and aft. As constructed it carried a dynamite gun fore and aft, and the rudders and diving planes were forward of the propeller.

Prior to its purchase for the U.S. Navy on 18 April 1900, the *Holland* was modified. The rudders and dive planes were moved abaft the propeller, and the after dynamite gun was removed.

The *Holland* served as a training vessel at the Naval Academy at Annapolis until 17 July 1905 (apart from a few months at the Naval Torpedo Station at Newport in 1901) and subsequently at Norfolk. It was stricken on 21 November 1910.

## UNITED STATES: A CLASS (1901), *PORPOISE* AND *SHARK* (1901)
*(Courtesy of Art-Tech)*

*Fulton* (12 June 1901), *Adder* (22 June 1901), *Moccasin* (28 August 1901), *Porpoise* (23 September 1901), *Shark* (19 October 1901), *Plunger* (1 February 1902)

BUILDER: Crescent

[United Kingdom]—*No. 1* (20 October 1901), *No. 2* (21 February 1902), *No. 3* (9 May 1902), *No. 4* (23 May 1902), *No. 5* (10 June 1902)

BUILDER: Barrow

*Grampus* (31 June 1902), *Pike* (14 January 1903)

BUILDER: Union Iron Works

[Russia]—*Shchuka* (15 October 1904), *Beluga* (1905), *Losos* (1905), *Peskar* (1905), *Sterlyad* (1905), *Sudak* (1907)

BUILDER: Nevskiy

[Japan]—*No. 1* (20 March 1905), *No. 2* (2 May 1905), *No. 5* (13 May 1905), *No. 3* (16 May 1905), *No. 4* (27 May 1905)

BUILDER: Fore River

[The Netherlands]—*O-1* (8 June 1905)

BUILDER: De Schelde

DISPLACEMENT: 107 tons (surfaced), 123 tons (submerged)

DIMENSIONS: 64′0″ x 11′10″ x 10′6″

MACHINERY: 1 gasoline engine, 1 electric motor, 1 shaft. 160 bhp/160 shp = 8/7 knots

RANGE: 184 nm at 8 knots surfaced, 21 nm at 4 knots submerged

ARMAMENT: 1 x 18″ (Russian boats: 15″) torpedo tube (bow), total 5 torpedoes

COMPLEMENT: 7

NOTES: Holland's seventh design was an enlarged version of his previous design. The prototype (the *Fulton*) later was sold to Russia and renamed the *Som*. There was greater internal space resulting from an increase in the single hull diameter and the elimination of the dynamite gun. The main ballast tank was concentrated amidships to enhance maneuverability, and a compensating tank was fitted to permit easy trim adjustment to suit different water salinity levels.

All of these boats were at least semiexperimental and acquired additional superstructure to enhance navigation on the surface, periscopes for submerged vision, and other enhancements. The Russian boats received diesel engines by 1910 (the *Sudak* was diesel-engined from the outset), and those serving in the Baltic added 47mm deck guns early in 1916. The Japanese boats received longitudinal bronze stiffening plates and bilge keels to increase their diving depth. The *O-1* received a 200-bhp MAN diesel engine in 1914.

All the U.S. boats, except the *Plunger,* operated with the Asiatic Fleet after service in home waters. The *Plunger* was stricken on 24 February 1913 and the others on 16 January 1922.

The British boats operated from Portsmouth on training missions. They were removed from the Effective List in August 1912.

The *Som* and the *Shschuka* were transported to Vladivostok by rail and were operational during the Russo-Japanese War. They remained in the Pacific until early 1915, when they transferred to the Black Sea and, later that same year, to the Baltic. The *Losos* and the *Sudak* went to the Black Sea in 1907 and were scuttled by the British on 26 April 1919 at Sevastopol. The *Som* collided with the Swedish steamer *Angermanland* off the Åland Islands on 23 May 1916 and sank. The remaining Baltic boats were scuttled at Reval on 25 February 1918.

The Japanese boats operated as training vessels. The *No. 4* sank at Kure on 14 November 1916 as a result of a gasoline explosion but was raised and returned to service. All boats were stricken in 1921.

The *O-1* conducted training missions until stricken in 1920.

## [RUSSIA]—*PROTECTOR* (1 NOVEMBER 1902)

BUILDER: Lake

DISPLACEMENT: 136 tons (surfaced), 174 tons (submerged)

DIMENSIONS: 65'0" x 11'0" x 12'3"

MACHINERY: 2 gasoline engines, 2 electric motors, 2 shafts. 250 bhp/100 shp = 12/7 knots

RANGE: 250 nm at 8 knots surfaced, 30 nm at 7 knots submerged

ARMAMENT: 3 x 15" torpedo tubes (2 bow, 1 stern), total 3 torpedoes

COMPLEMENT: 8

NOTES: Simon Lake built the *Protector* as a private venture. He entered it in the Imperial Russian Navy's international competition at Libau in 1904, leading to its purchase as *Osetr*. The *Osetr* served with the Baltic Fleet until stricken in 1913.

## [RUSSIA]—*OSETR* CLASS (1904)

*Kefal, Bychek, Paltus, Plotva, Sig* (1905)
BUILDER: Newport News
DISPLACEMENT: 153 tons (surfaced), 187 tons (submerged)
DIMENSIONS: 72′0″ x 12′0″ x 12′3″
MACHINERY: 2 gasoline engines, 2 electric motors, 2 shafts. 240 bhp/120 shp = 8.5/4.5 knots
RANGE: 385 nm at 8 knots surfaced, 35 nm at 4 knots submerged

ARMAMENT: 3 x 15″ torpedo tubes (2 bow, 1 stern)
COMPLEMENT: 24
NOTES: These boats were modestly improved production versions of the *Protector*. Newport News built the boats, which then were disassembled for shipping and reassembled at Libau. They all served with the Baltic Fleet until stricken in 1913.

## [JAPAN]—KAIGUN-HOLLAND TYPE (1905)

*No. 6* (28 September 1905), *No. 7* (28 September 1906)
BUILDER: Kawasaki
DISPLACEMENT: 57 (*No. 7*: 78) tons (surfaced), 63 (*No. 7*: 95) tons (submerged)
DIMENSIONS: 73′10″ (*No. 7*: 74′6″) x 7′0″ (*No. 7*: 8′0″) x 6′8″ (*No. 7*: 7′6″)
MACHINERY: 1 gasoline engine, 1 electric motor, 1 shaft. 250 bhp/22 shp = 8.5/4 knots
RANGE: 184 nm at 8 knots surfaced, 12 nm at 4 knots submerged
ARMAMENT: 1 x 18″ torpedo tube (bow), total 1 torpedo

COMPLEMENT: 14
NOTES: Imperial Japanese Navy designers successfully worked with Holland designers to develop a lighter, stronger hull for these boats to increase their operational depth, and placed more emphasis on surface performance.

These boats were used mainly for training and trials. The *No. 6* accidentally flooded and sank in Hiroshima Bay on 15 April 1910 but was raised and returned to service. Both boats were stricken in 1920.

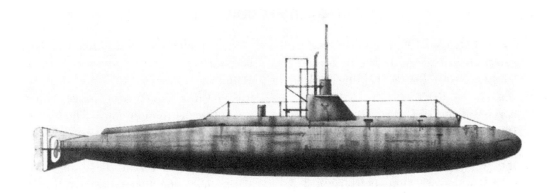

## UNITED STATES: B CLASS (1906)

*(Courtesy of Art-Tech)*

*Cuttlefish* (1 September 1906), *Viper* (30 March 1907), *Tarantula* (30 March 1907)

BUILDER: Fore River

DISPLACEMENT: 145 tons (surfaced), 173 tons (submerged)

DIMENSIONS: 82′4″ x 12′6″ x 10′6″

MACHINERY: 1 Craig gasoline engine, 1 Electro Dynamic electric motor, 1 shaft. 250 bhp/150 shp = 9/8 knots

RANGE: 540 nm at 9 knots surfaced, 12 nm at 4 knots submerged

ARMAMENT: 2 x 18″ torpedo tubes (bow), total 4 torpedoes

COMPLEMENT: 10

NOTES: An enlargement of the previous Holland single-hull design fitted with two side-by-side bow torpedo tubes and a more substantial conning tower and bridge structure. They latter were fitted with a second periscope.

After brief service in home waters all of these boats were transferred to the Asiatic Fleet, where they operated until stricken between 1919 and 1921.

## C CLASS (1906)

*Octopus* (4 October 1906), *Stingray* (8 April 1909), *Tarpon* (8 April 1909), *Snapper* (16 June 1909), *Bonita* (17 June 1909)

BUILDER: Fore River

[Austria-Hungary]—*U-5* (10 February 1909), *U-6* (12 June 1909), *U-12* (14 March 1911)

BUILDER: Whitehead

DISPLACEMENT: 238 tons (surfaced), 275 tons (submerged)

DIMENSIONS: 105′4″ x 13′9″ x 9′10″

MACHINERY: 2 gasoline engines, 1 electric motor, 2 shafts. 500 bhp/300 shp = 10.5/9 knots

RANGE: 800 nm at 10.5 knots surfaced, 80 nm at 5 knots submerged

ARMAMENT: 2 x 18″ torpedo tubes (bow), total 4 torpedoes

COMPLEMENT: 15

NOTES: An enlarged version of the earlier single-hull type, this class, designed by Lawrence Y. Spear, introduced two-shaft machinery that greatly extended its range. The U.S. boats later were fitted with a second periscope. Components for the first two Austrian boats were manufactured by the Electric Boat Company and assembled at Fiume, while the third boat was a speculative private venture by Whitehead that failed to find a buyer and was purchased by Austria-Hungary upon the outbreak of World War I. The *U-5* received a large conning tower and a 75mm deck gun when repaired after sinking in 1917.

The U.S. boats operated with the Atlantic Submarine Flotilla until mid-1913, when they transferred to Guantanamo in Cuba. In early 1914 they moved to the Panama Canal Zone, where they served until decommissioned and stricken at the end of 1919.

The earlier Austrian boats served to train crews prior to the war. The *U-6* became trapped in the Otranto barrage nets and was scuttled on 13 May 1916. The *U-12* was mined and sunk on 12 August 1916 while attempting to penetrate the harbor at Venice. The *U-5* struck a mine and sank on 16 May 1917, was raised, returned to service, and was ceded to Italy as war reparations; it was scrapped in 1920.

## [RUSSIA]—*KAIMAN* CLASS (1907)

*Kaiman* (November 1907), *Krokodil* (1908), *Alligator* (1908), *Drakon* (27 June 1908)
BUILDER: Crichton
DISPLACEMENT: 409 tons (surfaced), 482 tons (submerged)
DIMENSIONS: 132′0″ x 14′0″ x 16′0″
MACHINERY: 2 gasoline engines, 2 electric motors, 2 shafts. 1200 bhp/400 shp = 10.5/7 knots
RANGE: 1050 nm at 8 knots surfaced, 40 nm at 5 knots submerged
ARMAMENT: 4 x 450mm torpedo tubes (2 bow, 2 stern), 2 x 450mm torpedoes (Drzewiecki drop-collars). 1 x 47mm guns
COMPLEMENT: 34
NOTES: Lake designed these boats as powerful long-range submarines for Russia (they were termed "cruisers" at the time). Defects required a prolonged period for correction, and they were not accepted for service until 1910. All served with the Baltic Fleet until they were laid up on 15 November 1916. They were scuttled at Reval on 25 February 1918.

## [AUSTRIA-HUNGARY]—*U-1* CLASS (1909)

*U-1* (10 February 1909), *U-2* (3 April 1909)
BUILDER: Pola
DISPLACEMENT: 230 tons (surfaced), 249 tons (submerged)
DIMENSIONS: 100′0″ x 15′9″ x 12′8″
MACHINERY: 2 Lake gasoline engines, 2 electric motors, 2 shafts. 720 bhp/200 shp = 10.25/6 knots
RANGE: 950 nm at 6 knots surfaced, 40 nm at 2 knots submerged
ARMAMENT: 3 x 450mm torpedo tubes (2 bow, 1 stern), total 5 torpedoes, 1 x 37mm gun
COMPLEMENT: 17
NOTES: When the Austro-Hungarian Navy decided to add submarines to its fleet, it elected to acquire examples from each of the leading manufacturers of the time. This class was built under license from Lake and featured his trademark retractable wheels for running on the seabed, a diver's egress chamber, and variable pitch propellers. Overall, the Lake boats had the best diving and handling qualities, but their engines were unreliable and were replaced by diesel engines in 1913. Both boats served primarily as trials and training vessels until they were stricken on 11 January 1918.

## *D* CLASS (1909)

*Narwhal* (8 April 1909), *Grayling* (16 June 1909), *Salmon* (12 March 1910)
BUILDER: Fore River
DISPLACEMENT: 288 tons (surfaced), 337 tons (submerged)
DIMENSIONS: 135'10" x 13'9" x 11'10"
MACHINERY: 2 Craig gasoline engines, 2 Electro Dynamic electric motors, 2 shafts. 600 bhp/260 shp = 12/9.5 knots
RANGE: 1240 nm at 10 knots surfaced, 80 nm at 5 knots submerged
ARMAMENT: 2 x 18" torpedo tubes (bow), total 4 torpedoes
COMPLEMENT: 15
NOTES: This design was a greatly enlarged version of the previous two-shaft single-hull Electric Boat type. It featured a very substantial deck casing and bridge structure to enhance seaworthiness and included two periscopes from the outset. This was the first submarine design to include internal watertight bulkheads dividing the hull into compartments.

These boats served with the Atlantic Fleet, primarily undertaking training missions, until they were stricken in 1922.

## [THE NETHERLANDS]—*O-2* CLASS (1911)

*O-2* (30 January 1911), *O-3* (30 June 1912), *O-4* (5 August 1913), *O-5* (2 October 1913)
BUILDER: De Schelde
DISPLACEMENT: 130 tons (surfaced), 150 tons (submerged)
DIMENSIONS: 102'1" x 10'2" x 9'6"
MACHINERY: 1 MAN diesel engine, 1 electric motor, 1 shaft. 350 bhp/200 shp = 11/8.5 knots
RANGE: 500 nm at 10 knots surfaced, 26 nm at 8.5 knots submerged
ARMAMENT: 2 x 450mm torpedo tubes (bow), total 4 torpedoes
COMPLEMENT: 10
NOTES: Whitehead and Company at Fiume acquired a license from the Electric Boat Company to construct Holland type submarines in 1906. It hired Marley F. Hay—who had overseen construction of two Holland Type VII submarines between 1900 and 1904 at Union Iron Works in San Francisco and another at the Koninklijke Maatschappij De Schelde between 1904 and 1906—to supervise construction of two such boats for the Austro-Hungarian Navy. Hay subsequently developed a modified version of the single-hull Holland design, adding a full-length deck casing and a substantial bridge to improve seaworthiness. Whitehead licensed Hay's design to The Netherlands for construction of its second class of submarines.

The O-2 sank after colliding with a fishing vessel on 26 February 1919 but was refloated and returned to service. All four boats were stricken between 1931 and 1935.

## *SEAL* (8 FEBRUARY 1911)

BUILDER: Newport News

DISPLACEMENT: 400 tons (surfaced), 516 tons (submerged)

DIMENSIONS: 161'0" x 13'1" x 12'6"

MACHINERY: 4 White and Middleton gasoline engines, 2 Diehl electric motors, 2 shafts. 1200 bhp/520 shp = 14/10 knots

RANGE: 2500 nm at 8 knots surfaced, 70 nm at 5 knots submerged

ARMAMENT: 6 x 18" torpedo tubes (2 bow, 2 twin trainable deck mounts), total 6 torpedoes

COMPLEMENT: 24

NOTES: The first Lake boat accepted by the U.S. Navy, the *Seal* was a single-hull design with internal ballast tanks, retractable wheels for running on the bottom, an airlock allowing a diver egress and ingress, and three sets of hydroplanes along the length of the hull. There was a substantial watertight superstructure, and four of the torpedo tubes were in twin trainable deck mountings fore and aft of the bridge/conning tower structure.

One pair of engines and the deck torpedo tube mounts were removed in a December 1916 refit.

The *Seal* operated with the Atlantic Fleet primarily on training missions until decommissioned on 6 March 1920.

## E CLASS (1911)

*Skipjack* (27 May 1911), *Sturgeon* (15 June 1911)

BUILDER: Fore River

DISPLACEMENT: 287 tons (surfaced), 342 tons (submerged)

DIMENSIONS: 135'2" x 14'5" x 11'10"

MACHINERY: 2 NLSECO diesel engines, 2 Electro Dynamic electric motors, 2 shafts. 700 bhp/600 shp = 13.5/11.5 knots

RANGE: 2100 nm at 11 knots surfaced, 100 nm at 5 knots submerged

ARMAMENT: 2 x 18" torpedo tubes (bow), total 4 torpedoes

COMPLEMENT: 20

NOTES: These boats were essentially diesel-engined diminutives of the earlier single-hull Electric Boat–type *D* class submarines. In addition to introducing diesel engines into U.S. submarines, they also were the first both to use bow hydroplanes in addition to the planes at the stern and to carry radio on delivery. The diesel engines proved unreliable and were replaced in 1915.

Both boats operated with the Atlantic Fleet on training missions until the end of 1917. They then undertook war patrols until the end of World War I, when they reverted to training status until decommissioned and stricken in late 1921.

# F CLASS (1911)

*Carp* (6 September 1911), *Barracuda* (19 March 1912)

BUILDER: Union Iron Works

*Pickerel* (6 January 1912), *Skate* (6 January 1912)

BUILDER: Seattle

DISPLACEMENT: 330 tons (surfaced), 400 tons (submerged)

DIMENSIONS: 142'9" x 15'5" x 12'2"

MACHINERY: 2 NLSECO diesel engines, 2 Electro Dynamic electric motors, 2 shafts. 800 bhp/620 shp = 13.5/11.5 knots

RANGE: 2300 nm at 11 knots surfaced, 100 nm at 5 knots submerged

ARMAMENT: 2 x 18" torpedo tubes (bow), total 4 torpedoes

COMPLEMENT: 22

NOTES: These were slightly larger versions of the *E* class boats with bigger conning towers within the bridge structure. These boats too suffered from diesel engine problems and were re-engined in 1915.

All four boats served with the Pacific Fleet. The *F-1* (formerly the *Carp*) ran ashore near Watsonville, California, on 11 October 1912 and was refloated a week later. On 17 December 1917 it collided with its sister *F-3* (formerly the *Pickerel*) and sank with the loss of 19 of its crew. The *F-4* (formerly the *Skate*) sank with the loss of all of its crew off Honolulu on 25 March 1915 as a result of mechanical failure. The two other boats were stricken in 1922.

# [DENMARK]—*HAVMANDEN* CLASS (1911)

*Havmanden* (23 December 1911), *Thetis* (19 June 1912), *2den April* (31 March 1913)

BUILDER: Whitehead

*Havfruen* (31 August 1912), *Najaden* (9 June 1913), *Nymfen* (10 February 1914)

BUILDER: Copenhagen

DISPLACEMENT: 164 tons (surfaced), 204 tons (submerged)

DIMENSIONS: 127'8" x 11'10" x 7'7"

MACHINERY: 1 MAN (Whitehead boats: Fiat) diesel engine, 2 electric motors, 1 shaft. 450 bhp/275 shp (Whitehead boats: 430 bhp/270 shp) = 13/10 knots

ARMAMENT: 2 x 457mm torpedo tubes (bow)

COMPLEMENT: 10

NOTES: The Royal Danish Navy adopted an enlarged version of the original Hay-Whitehead single-hull design for its first submarines, contracting with Whitehead for three boats and purchasing a license to construct further examples itself. Two 8mm machines guns were fitted in 1917.

These boats spent most of their careers in the naval reserve and were scrapped between 1928 and 1929.

## UNITED STATES: G CLASS (1912), *TURBOT* (1913)
*(Courtesy of Art-Tech)*

*Tuna* (10 January 1912), *Turbot* (27 December 1913)

BUILDER: Lake

DISPLACEMENT: 400 tons (surfaced), 516 tons (submerged)

DIMENSIONS: 161'0" x 13'1" x 12'6"

MACHINERY: 4 White and Middleton gasoline (*Turbot*: Sulzer diesel) engines, 2 Diehl electric motors, 2 shafts. 1200 bhp/600 shp = 14/10.5 knots

RANGE: 2500 nm at 8 knots surfaced, 70 nm at 5 knots submerged

ARMAMENT: 4 (*Turbot*: 6) x 18" torpedo tubes (2/4 bow, 2 stern), total 4/6 torpedoes

COMPLEMENT: 24

NOTES: The second Lake design for the navy was very similar to the *Seal* but dispensed with the wheels and diver's lock. Two fixed torpedo tubes at the stern replaced the two twin deck tube mounts, reducing the extent of the superstructure considerably. The *Turbot* required the addition of midship blisters to compensate for excessive top weight.

These boats operated as training and experimental vessels throughout their careers with the Atlantic Fleet.

## UNITED STATES: H CLASS (1913), *H-2* (1916)
*(Courtesy of Art-Tech)*

*Seawolf* (6 May 1913), *Nautilus* (4 June 1913)

BUILDER: Union Iron Works

*Garfish* (3 June 1913), [Canada]—*CC-1, CC-2* (1913)

BUILDER: Seattle

[United Kingdom]—*H-1–H-10* (1915), [Italy]—*H-1* (16 October 1916), *H-2* (19 October 1916), *H-3* (26 April 1917), *H-4* (17 April 1917), *H-5* (25 April 1917), *H-6* (23 April 1917), *H-7* (24 April 1917), *H-8* (24 April 1917), [Russia]—*AG-21–AG-26* (1917–1921)

BUILDER: Canadian Vickers

[United Kingdom]—*H-11, H-12, H-14, H-15* (1916), [Chile]—*H 1–H 6* (1916)

BUILDER: Fore River

[Russia]—*AG-11–AG-15* (1916), [United States]—*H-4* (9 October 1918), *H-5* (24 September 1918), *H-6* (26 August 1918), *H-7* (17 October 1918), *H-8* (14 November 1918), *H-9* (23 November 1918)

BUILDER: British Pacific

DISPLACEMENT: 358 (CC boats: 313) tons (surfaced), 467 (CC boats: 421) tons (submerged)

DIMENSIONS: 150′3″ (CC-1: 144′6″) x 15′3″ x 12′6″ (CC boats: 11′0″)

MACHINERY: 2 NLSECO (first 5 boats: MAN) diesel engines, 2 electric motors, 2 shafts. 960 (first 5 boats: 600) bhp/600 (CC boats: 260) shp = 14 (first five boats: 13)/11 (CC boats: 10) knots

RANGE: 2300 nm at 11 knots surfaced, 100 nm at 5 knots submerged

ARMAMENT: 4 x 18″ (Italian boats: 450mm) torpedo tubes (bow), total 8 torpedoes. (*CC-1*: 5 x 18″ torpedo tubes [4 bow, 1 stern], total 5 torpedoes, *CC-2*: 3 x 18″ torpedo tubes [2 bow, 1 stern], total 3 torpedoes)

COMPLEMENT: 25

NOTES: This Electric Boat–type, single-hull design was prepared originally for the Chilean Navy, which ordered two boats as the *Iquique* and the *Antofagasta* in 1911. Chile rejected them, however, and they were purchased by Canada upon the outbreak of World War I. The U.S. Navy shortly afterward ordered three boats that combined the four bow tubes of the *Iquique* and the longer hull of the *Antofagasta*. These three U.S. boats were re-engined with NLSECO 480-bhp engines in 1918.

In 1914 the Royal Navy ordered twenty similar submarines from Electric Boat. To circumvent U.S. neutrality the first ten, ordered in October, were assembled by Canadian Vickers, but the second group, ordered in December, was impounded until the United States entered the war. Four of this group then joined the Royal Navy, while Britain gave five to Chile as compensation for warships under construction in the United Kingdom that had been seized when war began; Chile also purchased one additional British boat. Italy also placed an order in the summer of 1915 for eight boats supplied via Canadian Vickers.

The Imperial Russian Navy also ordered boats of this type. Five were ordered from the British Pacific Construction and Engineering Company at Vancouver in September 1915, three early in 1916, three more that summer, and a final group of eight in March 1917. The first three orders were delivered for final assembly in Russia (the British Pacific boats at Petrograd and the Canadian Vickers boats at Nikolayev), but the order for the final eight boats was canceled after the Russian Revolution and they were completed for the U.S. Navy at Puget Sound Navy Yard.

The three U.S. named boats became *H-1*, *H-2*, and *H-3* before completion. They served on the West Coast during World War I. *H-1* was wrecked off Baja California in March 1920, and all the other U.S. boats were stricken in 1930.

The Canadian boats served on the West Coast and were joined by the British *H-14* and *H-15*, which became the *CH-14* and the *CH-15*. All four boats were scrapped in 1925. The other British boats were very active in the North Sea and Mediterranean during World War I. The *H-6* grounded on the Dutch coast on 18 January 1916 and was interned. In May it was purchased and became the *O-8*. The *O-8* sank in port at Den Helder in October 1921 and was raised and repaired by September 1922. It was seized by German forces in May 1940 and became the *UD-1*, serving as a trials boat until it was scuttled at Kiel on 3 May 1945. The *H-3* was mined in the Gulf of Cattaro on 15 July 1916; the *H-10* was lost in the North Sea on 19 January 1918, probably to a mine; the *H-5* was rammed and sunk by the steamer *Rutherglen* on 15 July 1918 in the Irish Sea when it was mistaken for a U-boat. The remaining British boats were sold for scrap in 1921.

The Italian boats saw extensive service in the Mediterranean and Adriatic. The *H-5* was mistakenly torpedoed and sunk by the British *H-1* in the Adriatic on 16 April 1918; the *H-8* was bombed and sunk at La Spezia on 5 June 1943; the *H-6* was sunk at Bonifacio on 14 September 1943. The *H-7* was stricken in 1930, the *H-3* in 1937, and the remaining boats in 1947.

The Chilean boats were named the *Guacolda*, the *Tegualda*, the *Rucumilla*, the *Quidora*, the *Fresia*, and the *Guale* in 1936. The *Rucumilla* sank in an accident on 2 June 1937 with the loss of the entire crew but was raised and returned to service. All six boats were stricken between 1945 and 1953.

The Russian Baltic Fleet boats served actively until scuttled at Hango on 3 April 1918, apart from the *AG-14*, which was mined and sunk off Libau on 6 July 1917. The Black Sea Fleet boats did not commission prior to the Russian Revolution. The *AG-21* was seized by German forces at Sevastopol in April 1918, transferred to Allied control in November, and scuttled there on 26 April 1919. It was salved in 1928, rebuilt, and commissioned into the Soviet Fleet as the *No. 16* on 30 December 1930. The *AG-22* was commissioned in Admiral Wrangel's White Russian Fleet in 1919, escaped the Black Sea to Bizerta in 1920, and was abandoned and sold for scrap in November 1923. The other Black Sea submarines were completed and commissioned in the Soviet Navy as the *Trotsky* (later the *Nezamozhniy* and then the *Shakter*), the *Kommunist*, the *Marksist*, and the *Politrabotnik*. On 1 July 1923 they were renamed the *No. 12* through the *No. 15*. The five Soviet boats became the *A-1* to the *A-5* on 15 September 1934. The *A-1* was scuttled at Sevastopol in June 1942; the *A-3* was sunk by the German submarine chaser *UJ-117* off the Tendra Peninsular on 4 November 1943; and the other boats were stricken in late 1943 and scrapped after World War II.

## [THE NETHERLANDS]—*K-1* (20 MAY 1913)

BUILDER: De Schelde

DISPLACEMENT: 330 tons (surfaced), 386 tons (submerged)

DIMENSIONS: 159′5″ x 15′5″ x 10′2″

MACHINERY: 2 MAN diesel engines, 2 electric motors, 2 shafts. 1800 bhp/500 shp = 16/8.5 knots

RANGE: 3500 nm at 11 knots surfaced, 30 nm at 8.5 knots submerged

ARMAMENT: 3 x 450mm torpedo tubes (2 bow, 1 stern), total 6 torpedoes

COMPLEMENT: 17

NOTES: Hay enlarged his original Whitehead design and modified it to incorporate a two-shaft machinery arrangement that allowed fitting a stern torpedo tube. The single-hull design incorporated three ballast tanks and also carried both bow and stern rudders for increased maneuverability. Whitehead and Company licensed this new design to The Netherlands for use in the construction of its first submarine for service in the East Indies.

The *K-1* operated in home waters for two years. It transferred to the Dutch East Indies, arriving at Sabang on 6 November 1916. It served in the East Indies until stricken in 1928.

## UNITED STATES: K CLASS (1913), *K-5* (1914)
*(Courtesy of Art-Tech)*

*Haddock* (3 September 1913), *Cachalot* (4 October 1913), *K-5* (17 March 1914), *K-6* (26 March 1914)

BUILDER: Fore River

*Orca* (14 March 1914), *K-7* (20 June 1914), *K-8* (11 June 1914)

BUILDER: Union Iron Works

*Walrus* (19 March 1914)

BUILDER: Seattle

DISPLACEMENT: 392 tons (surfaced), 521 tons (submerged)

DIMENSIONS: 153'7" x 16'9" x 13'1"

MACHINERY: 2 diesel engines, 2 electric motors, 2 shafts. 950 bhp/600 shp = 14/10.5 knots

RANGE: 4500 nm at 10 knots surfaced, 120 nm at 5 knots submerged

ARMAMENT: 4 x 18" torpedo tubes (bow), total 8 torpedoes

COMPLEMENT: 28

NOTES: Modestly enlarged versions of earlier Electric Boat single-hull boats, these submarines encountered major problems with their engines, considerably delaying their entry into service. Nevertheless, the West Coast boats cruised as far as Hawai'i, while the Atlantic Fleet boats operated in the Azores during World War I. All boats were decommissioned in 1923, laid up, and scrapped in 1931.

## [DENMARK]—*ÆGIR* CLASS (1914)

*Ægir* (8 December 1914), *Ran* (30 May 1915), *Triton* (29 June 1915), *Neptun* (22 December 1915), *Galathea* (15 April 1916)
BUILDER: Copenhagen
DISPLACEMENT: 185 tons (surfaced), 235 tons (submerged)
DIMENSIONS: 133′2″ x 12′2″ x 7′11″
MACHINERY: 1 diesel engine, 1 electric motor, 1 shaft. 450 bhp/340 shp = 13.5/9.75 knots
ARMAMENT: 3 x 457mm torpedo tubes (bow), 1 x 57mm gun
COMPLEMENT: 11
NOTES: Marley F. Hay moved to the Dumbarton shipyard of William Denny and Brothers in 1913 and developed a slightly modified version of his earlier Whitehead single-hull design, enlarged to accommodate an additional torpedo tube in the bow. This was adopted for the second class of Danish submarines. Construction of a sixth vessel was canceled with the end of World War I.

These boats served actively with the Submarine Flotilla. The *Ægir* and the *Neptun* were stricken on 26 April 1933, and the other boats went into the reserve. They became floating oil depots at Holmen in 1943 and were scrapped in 1946.

## L CLASS (1915)

*L-1* (20 January 1915), *L-2* (11 February 1915), *L-3* (15 March 1915), *L-4* (3 April 1915), *L-9* (27 October 1915), *L-10* (16 March 1916), *L-11* (16 May 1916)
BUILDER: Fore River
*L-5* (1 May 1916)
BUILDER: Lake
*L-6* (11 August 1916), *L-7* (28 September 1916)
BUILDER: Craig
*L-8* (23 April 1917)
BUILDER: Portsmouth
[Norway]—*B1* (1 August 1922), *B2* (15 August 1923), *B3* (25 January 1924), *B4* (19 December 1923), *B5* (17 June 1929), *B6* (4 September 1929)
BUILDER: Horten
DISPLACEMENT: 450 tons (surfaced), 548 tons (submerged)
DIMENSIONS: 167′4″ x 17′5″ x 13′5″
MACHINERY: 2 diesel engines, 2 electric motors, 2 shafts. 1200 bhp/800 shp = 14/10.5 knots
RANGE: 3300 nm at 11 knots surfaced, 150 nm at 5 knots submerged
ARMAMENT: 4 x 18″ torpedo tubes (bow), total 8 torpedoes, 1 x 3″ gun (AA gun in Norwegian boats)
COMPLEMENT: 28
NOTES: These further enlargements of Electric Boat single hull–type submarines also encountered major machinery problems, delaying their entry into service. They were the first U.S. Navy submarines designed to carry a deck gun, which was on a semiretractable mount to minimize drag under water. The Norwegian boats used essentially the same design. Their building times were very extended (*B1* was laid down in 1915 and *B6* in 1925) because of the Horten Navy Yard's lack of submarine construction experience.

*L-6*–*L-8* were built to a Lake design, incorporating a double hull, diving planes amidships, a wide stern, and egress chamber for divers. Their building times were protracted because Lake's original company went into bankruptcy in the summer of 1916.

The Fore River boats operated from Bantry Bay in Ireland during World War I. All the U.S. Navy boats were decommissioned in the early 1920s and sold for scrap. The Norwegian boats served in the North Sea until the outbreak of World War II. The *B1* and the *B2* escaped the German invasion in 1940 and reached Britain, where they served as antisubmarine training vessels until April 1944. The *B3* was scuttled on 9 June 1940. The remaining Norwegian submarines were captured by Germany, and two, the *B5* and the *B6*, entered German service as the *UC-1* and the *UC-2*. The *UC-1* was stricken in 1942 and the *UC-2* in 1944.

## [RUSSIA]—*NARVAL* CLASS (1915)

*Narval* (10 May 1915), *Kashalot* (1915), *Kit* (1915)

BUILDER: Nevski Nikolayev

DISPLACEMENT: 621 tons (surfaced), 760 tons (submerged)

DIMENSIONS: 230'4" x 21'8" x 11'6"

MACHINERY: 4 diesel engines, 2 electric motors, 2 shafts. 640 bhp/980 shp = 13/9.75 knots

RANGE: 1900 nm at 7 knots surfaced, 120 nm at 4 knots submerged

ARMAMENT: 4 x 18" torpedo tubes (2 bow, 2 stern), 8 (*Narval:* 4) x 18" torpedoes (Drzewiecki drop collars), total 12/8 torpedoes, 1 x 75mm gun, 1 x 63mm gun (not *Narval*)

COMPLEMENT: 47

NOTES: The first double-hull Electric Boat design was originally specified to have more powerful engines, for a surface speed of 16 knots. The new arrangement of ballast and trim tanks, made possible by the double hull, dramatically improved diving time to 60 seconds to reach periscope depth, one-third the time required for earlier single-hull Holland boats, but the boats were cramped internally. These boats all served with the Black Sea Fleet. Germany captured these submarines in May 1918 and surrendered them to Britain in November 1918. They were scuttled off Sevastopol on 26 April 1919.

## UNITED STATES: M CLASS (1915)
*(Courtesy of Art-Tech)*

*M-1* (14 September 1915), [Spain]—*Isaac
    Peral* (27 June 1916)
BUILDER: Fore River
DISPLACEMENT: 488 tons (surfaced), 676
    tons (submerged)
DIMENSIONS: 196′3″ x 19′0″ x 11′2″
MACHINERY: 2 diesel engines, 2 electric
    motors, 2 shafts. 840 bhp/680 shp =
    14/10.5 knots
RANGE: 2750 nm at 11 knots surfaced, 150
    nm at 5 knots submerged
ARMAMENT: 4 x 18″ (*Isaac Peral:* 450mm)
    torpedo tubes (bow), total 8 torpedoes, 1
    x 3″ gun
COMPLEMENT: 28
NOTES: *M-1* was the first double-hull Elec-
    tric Boat design for the U.S. Navy, a
change adopted to give greater reserve
buoyancy and a faster diving time than
the firm's single-hull models. The change
also required the submarine to be larger
than its precursors, yet it was considered
cramped for internal space. The design
essentially was repeated for the Spanish
submarine, though that boat initially featured a deck along the center of the boat
above the casing that was deleted soon
after it entered service.

*M-1* served in the Atlantic until it was
stricken in 1922. The *Isaac Peral* was
stricken in 1930.

## [THE NETHERLANDS]—*O-6* (10 JUNE 1916)

BUILDER: De Schelde

DISPLACEMENT: 189 tons (surfaced), 229 tons (submerged)

DIMENSIONS: 117'0" x 12'6" x 10'0"

MACHINERY: 1 MAN diesel engine, 1 electric motor, 1 shaft. 375 bhp/185 shp = 12/8.5 knots

RANGE: 750 nm at 10 knots surfaced, 26 nm at 8.5 knots submerged

ARMAMENT: 3 x 450mm torpedo tubes (2 bow, 1 stern), total 5 torpedoes, 1 x 12.7mm machine gun

COMPLEMENT: 15

NOTES: This boat was built to a single-hull design by the Electric Boat Company with two ballast tanks and a lead drop-keel. The O-6 operated in the North Sea and English Channel until stricken in November 1936.

## [THE NETHERLANDS]—*O-7* (22 JUNE 1916)

BUILDER: Fijenoord

DISPLACEMENT: 176 tons (surfaced), 206 tons (submerged)

DIMENSIONS: 112'4" x 12'0" x 9'6"

MACHINERY: 1 MAN diesel engine, 1 electric motor, 1 shaft. 350 bhp/185 shp = 12/8.5 knots

RANGE: 750 nm at 10 knots surfaced, 26 nm at 8.5 knots submerged

ARMAMENT: 3 x 450mm torpedo tubes (2 bow, 1 stern), total 5 torpedoes

COMPLEMENT: 15

NOTES: This boat used another variant of Hay's single-hull design under license from Denny. It was unusual in incorporating an auxiliary steering propeller (a type of side thruster) just forward of the standard propeller and rudder at the stern.

The O-7 operated in the North Sea and English Channel until 1935, when it became the navy's training submarine. It was stricken on 21 December 1939.

## [AUSTRIA-HUNGARY]—*U-20* CLASS (1916)

*U-21* (15 August 1916), *U-20* (18 September 1916)

BUILDER: Pola

*U-23* (5 January 1917), *U-22* (27 January 1917)

BUILDER: UBAG

DISPLACEMENT: 173 tons (surfaced), 210 tons (submerged)

DIMENSIONS: 127'2" x 13'0" x 9'0"

MACHINERY: 1 diesel engine, 1 electric motor, 1 shaft. 450 bhp/160 shp = 12/9 knots

ARMAMENT: 2 x 450mm torpedo tubes (bow), total 2 torpedoes, 1 x 66mm gun, 1 x 8mm machine gun

COMPLEMENT: 18

NOTES: On the outbreak of war the Austro-Hungarian government confiscated the plans for the prewar Danish *Havmanden* class boats from Whitehead and Company at Fiume and used essentially the same design to construct these submarines. Political tension between the Hungarian and Austrian components of the empire prolonged construction, so they did not enter service until late 1917.

The *U-23* was destroyed by an explosive paravane towed by an escort while attacking a convoy in the Straits of Otranto on 21 February 1918. The Italian submarine *F-12* torpedoed and sank the *U-20* near the estuary of the Tagliamento River on 6 July 1918. The Treaty of Paris ceded the *U-21* to Italy and the *U-22* to France. Both were handed over in 1920 and scrapped.

## UNITED STATES: N CLASS (1916), *N-2* (1917)
*(Courtesy of Art-Tech)*

*N-1* (30 December 1916), *N-2* (16 January 1917), *N-3* (21 February 1917)
BUILDER: Seattle

*N-4* (27 November 1916), *N-5* (22 March 1917), *N-6* (21 April 1917), *N-7* (19 May 1917)
BUILDER: Lake
DISPLACEMENT: 348 tons (surfaced), 414 tons (submerged)
DIMENSIONS: 147′4″ x 15′9″ x 12′6″
MACHINERY: 2 diesel engines, 2 electric motors, 2 shafts. 600 bhp/300 shp = 13/11 knots
RANGE: 3500 nm at 11 knots surfaced, 30 nm at 5 knots submerged

ARMAMENT: 4 x 18″ torpedo tubes (bow), total 8 torpedoes
COMPLEMENT: 25
NOTES: The design for the Electric Boat single-hull class was based on the *H*-class design, enhanced by adding a steel bridge structure and reducing power output to improve reliability. The Lake-built boats were double-hull submarines with diving planes amidships and wide sterns. They were stricken in 1922, and the others in 1931.

## [UNITED KINGDOM]—IMPROVED H CLASS (1917), *H-31* (1918)
*(Courtesy of Art-Tech)*

*H-21* (20 October 1917), *H-22* (14 November 1917), *H-23* (29 January 1918), *H-24* (14 November 1917), *H-25* (27 April 1918), *H-26* (15 November 1917), *H-27* (25 September 1918), *H-28* (12 March 1918), *H-29* (8 June 1918), *H-30* (9 May 1918), *H-31* (16 November 1918), *H-32* (19 November 1918)

BUILDER: Barrow

*H-33* (24 August 1918), *H-34* (5 November 1918)

BUILDER: Cammell Laird

*H-42* (21 October 1918), *H-43* (3 February 1919), *H-44* (17 February 1919)

BUILDER: Armstrong

*H-47* (19 November 1918), *H-48* (31 March 1919), *H-49* (15 June 1919), *H-50* (25 October 1919)

BUILDER: Beardmore

*H-51* (15 November 1918), *H-52* (31 March 1919)

BUILDER: Pembroke

DISPLACEMENT: 423 tons (surfaced), 510 tons (submerged)

DIMENSIONS: 171′9″ x 15′9″ x 13′3″

MACHINERY: 2 diesel engines, 2 electric motors, 2 shafts. 480 bhp/620 shp = 11/10.5 knots

RANGE: 1600 nm at 10 knots surfaced; submerged characteristics unknown

ARMAMENT: 4 x 21″ torpedo tubes (bow), total 8 torpedoes

COMPLEMENT: 22

NOTES: Vickers developed these boats from the original *H*-class design by lengthening it to accommodate 21-inch torpedo tubes. The machinery and much of the equipment was identical to that of the earlier boats and was obtained from the same U.S. suppliers for the Vickers craft and from British firms for the others. Twelve additional submarines were canceled in October 1917 and their machinery and equipment transferred for use in *R*-class boats.

This class served extensively in the North Sea and Mediterranean during the last part of World War I and between the wars. The *H-42* and the *H-47* were sunk in collisions in 1922 and 1929. Eight boats (the *H-31–H-34, H-43–H-44, H-49–H-50*) served in World War II, and the others were scrapped between 1934 and 1936. German antisubmarine vessels sank the *H-31* and the *H-49* off the Dutch coast on 18 October 1940, and the surviving boats were scrapped between October 1944 and July 1945.

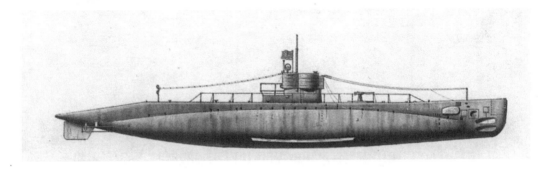

## UNITED STATES: O CLASS (1917)
*(Courtesy of Art-Tech)*

*O-1* (9 June 1918)
BUILDER: Portsmouth
*O-2* (24 May 1918)
BUILDER: Puget Sound
*O-3* (29 September 1917), *O-4* (20 October 1917), *O-5* (11 November 1917), *O-6* (25 November 1917), *O-7* (16 December 1917), *O-8* (31 December 1917), *O-9* (27 January 1918), *O-10* (21 February 1918)
BUILDER: Quincy
*O-11* (29 October 1917), *O-12* (29 September 1917), *O-13* (27 December 1917)
BUILDER: Lake
*O-14* (6 May 1918), *O-15* (12 February 1918), *O-16* (9 February 1918)
BUILDER: California
DISPLACEMENT: 521 tons (surfaced), 629 tons (submerged)
DIMENSIONS: 172'3" x 18'1" x 14'5"
MACHINERY: 2 diesel engines, 2 electric motors, 2 shafts. 880 bhp/740 shp = 14/10.5 knots

RANGE: 5500 nm at 11.5 knots surfaced, 150 nm at 5 knots submerged
ARMAMENT: 4 x 18" torpedo tubes (bow), total 8 torpedoes, 1 x 3" gun
COMPLEMENT: 29
NOTES: The design for this single-hull class was essentially a slightly enlarged *L*-class boat with the lower-rated power plant incorporated for greater reliability. The boats built by California Shipbuilding and Lake, built to a typical Lake double-hull design with diving planes amidships and wide sterns, were discarded in 1930. Those built by Electric Boat (except for the *O-5*, rammed and sunk by the steamer *Abangarez* in the Canal Zone on 28 October 1923; the *O-1*, stricken on 18 March 1938; the *O-9*, lost because of a mechanical failure on 20 June 1941) served during World War II as training vessels and were stricken in 1946.

## UNITED STATES: R CLASS (1917)

*(Courtesy of Art-Tech)*

*R-15* (10 December 1917) *R-16* (15 December 1917), *R-17* (24 December 1917), *R-18* (8 January 1918), *R-19* (28 January 1918), *R-20* (21 August 1918)

BUILDER: Union Iron Works

*R-21* (10 June 1918), *R-22* (24 September 1918), R-23 (5 November 1918), *R-24* (21 August 1918), *R-25* (15 May 1919), *R-26* (18 June 1919), *R-27* (23 September 1919)

BUILDER: Lake

*R-1* (24 August 1918), *R-2* (23 September 1918), *R-3* (18 January 1919), *R-4* (26 October 1918), *R-5* (24 November 1918), *R-6* (1 March 1919), *R-7* (5 April 1919), *R-8* (17 April 1919), *R-9* (14 May 1919), *R-10* (28 June 1919), *R-11* (12 June 1919), *R-12* (15 August 1919), *R-13* (27 August 1919), *R-14* (10 October 1919)

BUILDER: Quincy

[Peru]—*R1* (12 June 1926), *R2* (29 March 1926), *R3* (21 April 1928), *R4* (10 May 1928)

BUILDER: Electric Boat

DISPLACEMENT: 569 (*R-21–R-27*: 510) tons (surfaced), 680 (*R-21–R-27*: 583) tons (submerged)

DIMENSIONS: 186′5″ x 18′1″ x 14′5″

MACHINERY: 2 diesel engines, 2 electric motors, 2 shafts. 1200 bhp/934 shp = 13.5/10.5 knots (*R-21–R-27*: 1000 bhp/800 shp = 14/11 knots)

RANGE: 4700 nm at 6 knots surfaced, 100 nm at 5 knots submerged

ARMAMENT: 4 x 21″ (*R-21–R-27*: 18″) torpedo tubes (bow), total 8 torpedoes, 1 x 3″ gun

COMPLEMENT: 29

NOTES: These single-hull Electric Boat submarines were very similar to the preceding O class, with the addition of 21-inch torpedo tubes and a fixed rather than retractable gun mount. The double-hull Lake boats had their diving planes more conventionally positioned fore and aft, but they retained the characteristic wide stern and 18-inch torpedo tubes. The boats for Peru were built after World War I using material assembled for canceled S-class submarines. They were refitted in 1935–1936 and 1955–1956, renamed the *Islay*, the *Casma*, the *Pacocha*, and the *Arica* in 1957, and discarded in 1960.

The Lake boats were discarded in 1930. The *R-6* was stricken in 1936, but the other single-hull boats survived to serve in World War II. The *R-3*, the *R-17*, and the *R-19* were transferred to the Royal Navy under Lend-Lease and renamed the *P-511*, the *P-512*, and the *P-514* (accidentally rammed and sunk by the minesweeper *Georgian* on 21 June 1942). The *R-12* was lost as a training vessel near Key West on 12 June 1943. The remaining vessels were broken up in 1946.

## AA CLASS (1918)

*Schley* (25 June 1918), *AA-2* (6 September 1919), *AA-3* (24 May 1919)

BUILDER: Quincy

DISPLACEMENT: 1107 tons (surfaced), 1482 tons (submerged)

DIMENSIONS: 269'0" x 23'0" x 14'1"

MACHINERY: 4 diesel engines, 2 electric motors, 2 shafts. 4000 bhp/1350 shp = 20/10.5 knots

RANGE: 3000 nm at 14 knots surfaced, 100 nm at 5 knots submerged

ARMAMENT: 4 x 18" torpedo tubes (bow), total 12 torpedoes, 2 x 3" gun

COMPLEMENT: 38

NOTES: The U.S. Navy's interest in fast submarines capable of accompanying the battle fleet first emerged in 1911 and led to the development of this class, intended to meet requirements for high surface speed, good sea keeping, and long range. Although the class came close to meeting these requirements, the boats were plagued with unreliable machinery and the form of the bow made them extremely wet at sea. The first boat, initially named the *Schley*, carried four additional torpedo tubes on deck, but these quickly were removed and were not fitted to the later boats. They were re-armed with a single 4-inch gun in place of the 3-inch weapons soon after completion. The boats were renumbered the *T-1* through the *T-3* in 1920. The *T-3* was re-engined in 1925–1927, but its mechanical reliability did not improve. These submarines were stricken in 1930 after very little active service and scrapped.

## [DENMARK]—*ROTA* CLASS (1918)

*Rota* (16 August 1918), *Bellona* (14 March 1919), *Flora* (23 April 1920)

BUILDER: Copenhagen

DISPLACEMENT: 301 tons (surfaced), 369 tons (submerged)

DIMENSIONS: 155'10" x 14'5" x 8'10"

MACHINERY: 2 Burmeister and Wain diesel engines, 2 Titan Electro electric motors, 1 shaft. 900 bhp/640 shp = 14.5/10.5 knots

ARMAMENT: 4 (*Rota* 5) x 457mm torpedo tubes (3 bow, 1 stern, *Rota*: 1 trainable in conning tower), 1 x 57mm gun

COMPLEMENT: 17

NOTES: This class used essentially the same single-hull saddle-tank Hay design as the Dutch overseas submarine *K-I*, under license from Denny, modified to carry three bow torpedo tubes and a traversing deck mount.

The *Rota* carried a traversing torpedo tube in its conning tower, but this proved unsatisfactory in service and was omitted from the rest of the class. In its place the *Bellona* carried an enlarged radio room, and the *Flora* was equipped for minelaying.

All three boats served actively with the Submarine Flotilla until 1936, when they transferred to the reserve. They were scuttled at Holmen on 29 August 1943 and scrapped in 1952.

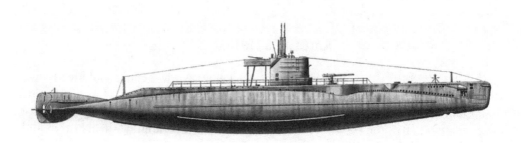

## UNITED STATES: S CLASS (1918)
*(Courtesy of Art-Tech)*

**ELECTRIC BOAT TYPE I**
*S-1* (26 October 1918), *S-18* (29 April 1920), *S-19* (21 June 1920), *S-20* (9 June 1920), *S-21* (18 August 1920), S-22 (15 June 1920), S-23 (27 October 1920), *S-24* (27 June 1922), *S-25* (29 May 1922), S-26 (22 August 1922), S-27 (18 October 1922), S-28 (20 September 1922), S-29 (9 November 1922)
BUILDER: Quincy
*S-30* (21 November 1918), *S-31* (28 December 1918), S-32 (11 January 1919), S-33 (5 December 1918), S-34 (13 February 1919), S-35 (27 February 1919), S-36 (3 June 1919), S-37 (20 June 1919), S-38 (17 June 1919), S-39 (2 June 1919), *S-40* (5 January 1921), *S-41* (21 February 1921)
BUILDER: Union Iron Works
**ELECTRIC BOAT TYPE II**
*S-42* (30 April 1923), *S-43* (31 March 1923), S-44 (27 October 1923), S-45 (26 June 1923), S-46 (11 September 1923), S-47 (5 January 1924)
BUILDER: Quincy
**LAKE TYPE I**
S-2 (15 February 1919)
BUILDER: Lake
**LAKE TYPE II**
*S-48* (26 February 1921), *S-49* (23 April 1921), *S-50* (18 June 1921), *S-51* (20 August 1921)
BUILDER: Lake
**BUREAU OF CONSTRUCTION AND REPAIR TYPE**
*S-3* (21 December 1918), *S-4* (27 August 1919), S-5 (10 November 1919), S-6 (23 December 1919), S-7 (5 February 1920), S-8 (21 April 1920), S-9 (17 June 1920), *S-10* (9 December 1920), *S-11* (7 February 1921), S-12 (4 August 1921), *S-13* (20 October 1921)
BUILDER: Portsmouth

S-*14* (22 October 1919), S-*15* (8 March 1920), S-*16* (23 December 1919), S-*17* (22 May 1920)

BUILDER: Lake

DISPLACEMENT: EBI: 854 tons (surfaced), 1062 tons (submerged), EBII: 906 tons (surfaced), 1126 tons (submerged), Lake I: 800 tons (surfaced), 977 tons (submerged), Lake II: 903 tons (surfaced), 1230 tons (submerged), C&R: 876 tons (surfaced), 1092 tons (submerged)

DIMENSIONS: EBI: 219'5" x 20'8" x 15'9", EBII: 225'5" x 20'8" x 16'1", Lake I: 207'0" x 19'8" x 16'1", Lake II: 240'2" x 21'8" x 13'5", C&R: 231'0" x 22'0" x 13'1"

MACHINERY: 2 diesel engines, 2 electric motors, 2 shafts. EBI: 1200 bhp/1500 shp = 14/11 knots, EBII: 1200 bhp/1200 shp = 14.5/11 knots, Lake I: 1800 bhp/1200 shp = 15/11 knots, Lake II: 1800 bhp/1500 shp = 14.4/11 knots, C&R: 2000 bhp/1500 shp = 15/11 knots

RANGE: 2500–5900 nm at 6.5 knots surfaced, 100 nm at 5 knots submerged

ARMAMENT: 4 (Lake II: 5) x 21" torpedo tubes (bow), total 12 (Lake II: 14) torpedoes, 1 x 4" gun

COMPLEMENT: 38

NOTES: The first three boats of this class were built to competing designs from Electric Boat (a single-hull type), Lake, and the Bureau of Construction and Repair (both double-hull types). The Lake design was found unsatisfactory, and the firm built two series of boats to the bureau's design, the original and an enlarged version. Two series of boats also used the Electric Boat design, the second series being enlarged.

The S-5 was lost in an accident on 1 September 1920. The steamer *City of Rome* sank the S-51 in a collision on 25 September 1925 off Block Island. The S-4 sank after colliding with the destroyer *Paulding* (then serving with the Coast Guard) on 17 December 1927, with the loss of the entire crew. It was salved, repaired, and returned to service in October 1928 and stricken in 1936, along with the S-10 and the S-19. The S-49 and the S-50 were stricken in 1931; the S-6 through the S-9 were stricken in 1937; and the remainder of the class served during World War II.

The S-1, the S-21, the S-22, the S-24, the S-25, and the S-29 were transferred to Britain under Lend-Lease, becoming the P-552, the P-553, the P-555, the *Jastrzab* (in Polish service), and the P-556. The S-36 was wrecked in the Makassar Strait on 20 January 1942; the S-26 was sunk in collision with the PC-460 in the Gulf of Panama on 24 January 1942; the S-27 was wrecked on Amchitka Island in Alaska on 19 June 1942; the S-39 was wrecked near Rossel Island on 14 August 1942; the S-44 was sunk by the Japanese escort *Ishigaki* on 7 October 1943; the S-28 was lost at sea (cause unknown) on 4 July 1944. The S-16, the S-17, the S-37, and the S-38 were sunk as targets in 1945. The surviving boats of the class were stricken in 1946.

## [THE NETHERLANDS]—*K-II* (24 FEBRUARY 1919)

BUILDER: Fijenoord

DISPLACEMENT: 569 tons (surfaced), 649 tons (submerged)

DIMENSIONS: 177′2″ x 16′9″ x 12′6″

MACHINERY: 2 MAN diesel engines, 2 electric motors, 2 shafts. 1800 bhp/500 shp = 16/8.5 knots

RANGE: 3500 nm at 16 knots surfaced, 26 nm at 8.5 knots submerged

ARMAMENT: 4 x 450mm torpedo tubes (2 bow, 2 stern), total 12 torpedoes, 1 x 75mm AA gun, 1 x 12.7mm machine gun

COMPLEMENT: 29

NOTES: Hay prepared an enlarged version of his single-hull saddle-tank design for the *K-I* for this boat, whose construction again was licensed by Denny. In 1923–1924 the Royal Netherlands Navy conducted trials of a diesel air intake tube system that extended above the periscope, but they removed the equipment because of problems with the valve arrangement intended to prevent ingress of water if a wave washed over the top of the tube.

The *K-II*'s commissioning was delayed by problems with completing and installing its German diesel engines in wartime. From 1923 it operated extensively in the East Indies and Far East until stricken in August 1937.

## [THE NETHERLANDS]—*K-III* CLASS (1919)

*K-III* (12 August 1919), *K-IV* (2 June 1920), *K-VIII* (28 March 1922), *K-IX* (23 December 1922), *K-X* (2 May 1923)

BUILDER: De Schelde

DISPLACEMENT: 574 tons (surfaced), 710 tons (submerged)

DIMENSIONS: 210′0″ x 18′4″ x 11′10″

MACHINERY: 2 Sulzer (*K-III* and *K-VIII*: MAN) diesel engines, 2 electric motors, 2 shafts. 1200 (*K-III* and *K-VIII*: 1800, *K-IX* and *K-X*: 1550) bhp/630 shp = 15 (*K-III* and *K-VIII*: 16.5)/9 knots

RANGE: 3500 nm at 11 knots surfaced, 26 nm at 9 knots submerged

ARMAMENT: 4 x 450mm torpedo tubes (2 bow, 1 twin training external mount [*K-III* and *K-IV*], 2 stern [*K-VII*–*K-X*]), total 12 torpedoes), 1 x 75mm AA (*K-VIII*–*K-X*: 88mm DP) gun, 1 x 12.7mm machine gun

COMPLEMENT: 29

NOTES: These boats used an Electric Boat Company double-hull design with five ballast tanks. The later group had a modified arrangement of the torpedo tubes to reduce vulnerability to depth-charge damage, an enlarged conning tower and bridge, longer periscopes, and a heavier deck gun.

## [THE NETHERLANDS]—*K-V* CLASS (1919)

*K-V* (2 November 1919), *K-VI* (23 December 1920), *K-VII* (8 March 1921)
BUILDER: Fijenoord
DISPLACEMENT: 560 tons (surfaced), 640 tons (submerged)
DIMENSIONS: 177'0" x 16'9" x 12'6"
MACHINERY: 2 Sulzer diesel engines, 2 electric motors, 2 shafts. 1200 bhp/500 shp = 15/8 knots
RANGE: 3500 nm at 11 knots surfaced, 26 nm at 9 knots submerged
ARMAMENT: 6 x 450mm torpedo tubes (2 bow, 2 stern, 1 twin training external mount), total 12 torpedoes, 1 x 75mm AA gun, 1 x 12.7mm machine gun
COMPLEMENT: 31

NOTES: This was a more heavily armed variant of Hay's single-hull saddle-tank design for the *K-II*. Originally a pair of 900-bhp MAN diesel engines were specified but were not available in wartime, so less powerful 600-bhp Sulzer engines were installed.

All three boats operated extensively in the East Indies and Far East until decommissioned in August 1937. The *K-V* and the *K-VI* were scrapped, but the *K-VII* was retained in reserve at Soerabaja, where it was bombed and sunk by Japanese aircraft on 18 February 1942.

## [SPAIN]—B CLASS (1921)

*B-1* (2 June 1921), *B-2* (10 October 1921), *B-3* (17 March 1922), *B-4* (31 October 1922), *B-6* (5 June 1923), *B-5* (4 April 1925)
BUILDER: Cartagena
DISPLACEMENT: 491 tons (surfaced), 715 tons (submerged)
DIMENSIONS: 210'4" x 17'4" x 11'3"
MACHINERY: 2 diesel engines, 2 electric motors, 2 shafts. 1400 bhp/850 shp = 16/10 knots
RANGE: 8000 nm at 10.5 knots surfaced, 125 nm at 4.5 knots submerged
ARMAMENT: 4 x 450mm torpedo tubes (bow), total 8 torpedoes, 1 x 75mm gun
COMPLEMENT: 28

NOTES: Electric Boat licensed the construction of these boats as a slightly enlarged version of the *Isaac Peral*. Construction began in July 1916 and was delayed by the yard's inexperience in submarine work. The *B-6* was sunk by the Spanish Nationalist destroyer *Velasco* near Santander on 19 September 1936, and the *B-5* was sunk by Nationalist aircraft off Malaga on 12 October 1936. The Republicans scuttled the surviving boats in April 1939.

# A War-Winning Weapon?

## DENMARK
### *DAPHNE* CLASS (1925)

*Daphne* (December 1925), *Dryaden* (3 June 1926)

BUILDER: Copenhagen

DISPLACEMENT: 308 tons (surfaced), 381 tons (submerged)

DIMENSIONS: 160'9" x 17'1" x 8'2"

MACHINERY: 2 Burmeister and Wain diesel engines, 2 Titan electric motors, 2 shafts. 1200 bhp/400 shp = 13.5/6.75 knots

ARMAMENT: 6 x 450mm torpedo tubes (4 bow, 2 stern), 1 x 75mm gun, 1 x 20mm AA gun

COMPLEMENT: 25

NOTES: This class was designed by the Orlogsværftet and was very heavily armed for its size. These submarines were scuttled at Holmen on 29 August 1943, salved subsequently, and scrapped in 1946.

### *HAVMANDEN* CLASS (1937)

*Havmanden* (19 June 1937), *Havfruen* (6 November 1937), *Havkalen* (3 March 1938), *Havhesten* (11 July 1940)

BUILDER: Copenhagen

DISPLACEMENT: 320 tons (surfaced), 402 tons (submerged)

DIMENSIONS: 157'6" x 15'5" x 9'2"

MACHINERY: 2 Burmeister and Wain diesel engines, 2 Brown-Boveri electric motors, 2 shafts. 1200 bhp/450 shp = 15/8 knots

ARMAMENT: 5 x 450mm torpedo tubes (3 bow, 2 stern), 2 x 40mm AA guns, 2 x 8mm machine guns

COMPLEMENT: 20

NOTES: This class was designed by the Orlogsværftet as an improved version of the previous boats. A fifth boat of this class was canceled. They were scuttled at Holmen on 29 August 1943.

# FRANCE
## *PIERRE CHAILLEY* (19 DECEMBER 1921)

BUILDER: Normand

DISPLACEMENT: 884 tons (surfaced), 1191 tons (submerged)

DIMENSIONS: 229'8" x 24'7" x 13'1"

MACHINERY: 2 Sulzer diesel engines, 2 electric motors, 2 shafts. 1800 bhp/1400 shp = 13.75/8.5 knots

RANGE: 2800 nm at 11 knots surfaced, 80 nm at 5 knots submerged

ARMAMENT: 4 x 450mm torpedo tubes (2 bow, 1 twin trainable external mount), total 6 torpedoes, 40 mines

COMPLEMENT: 44

NOTES: This large double-hull minelaying submarine was designed by Augustin Normand and Fernand Fenaux. The mines were carried in vertical external tubes, ten on each side, that became the French Navy's standard method, as it was extremely safe. The *Pierre Chailley* operated mainly in the Mediterranean and was stricken on 13 May 1936.

## *REQUIN* CLASS (1924)

*Requin* (19 July 1924), *Souffleur* (1 October 1924), *Narval* (9 May 1925), *Morse* (11 November 1925), *Caïman* (3 March 1927)

BUILDER: Cherbourg

*Marsouin* (27 December 1924), *Phoque* (16 March 1926)

BUILDER: Brest

*Dauphin* (2 April 1925), *Espadon* (28 May 1926)

BUILDER: Toulon

DISPLACEMENT: 1150 tons (surfaced), 1441 tons (submerged)

DIMENSIONS: 256'8" x 22'5" x 16'8"

MACHINERY: 2 Sulzer or Schneider diesel engines, 2 electric motors, 2 shafts. 2900 bhp/1800 shp = 15/9 knots

RANGE: 7700 nm at 9 knots surfaced, 70 nm at 5 knots submerged

ARMAMENT: 10 x 550mm torpedo tubes (4 bow, 2 stern, 2 twin trainable external mount), total 16 torpedoes, 1 x 100mm gun, 2 x 8mm machine guns

COMPLEMENT: 51

NOTES: Jean-Jacques Roquebert was responsible for the design of these double-hull submarines, intended for long-range operations, cooperation with the battlefleet, and colonial service. In service they suffered from inadequate surface speed and handling.

The *Morse* and the *Narval* were mined off the Tunisian coast on 16 June and 12 December 1940, and the submarine *Parthian* torpedoed the *Souffleur* off Beirut on 24 June 1941. The *Caïman* was scuttled at Toulon on 27 November 1942, salved, and bombed by USAAF aircraft on 11 March 1944. The *Phoque*, the *Requin*, the *Espadon*, and the *Dauphin* were seized at Bizerta on 8 December 1942 and commissioned by Italy as the *FR-111*, the *FR-113*, the *FR-114*, and the *FR-115*. They were transferred to Genoa but saw no service, were seized by Germany on 9 September 1943, and were scuttled on 15 September. The *Marsouin* escaped from Toulon on 27 November 1942 and served with the Free French forces. It was stricken on 18 February 1946.

## *SIRÈNE* CLASS (1925)

*Sirène* (6 August 1928), *Naïade* (20 October 1925), *Galatée* (18 December 1925), *Nymphe* (1 April 1926)

BUILDER: Loire

DISPLACEMENT: 609 tons (surfaced), 757 tons (submerged)

DIMENSIONS: 209'11" x 17'1" x 14'1"

MACHINERY: 2 Sulzer diesel engines, 2 electric motors, 2 shafts. 1300 bhp/1000 shp = 14/7.5 knots

RANGE: 3500 nm at 9 knots surfaced, 75 nm at 5 knots submerged

ARMAMENT: 7 x 550mm torpedo tubes (4 bow, 1 stern, 1 twin trainable external mount), total 13 torpedoes, 1 x 75mm gun, 2 x 8mm machine guns

COMPLEMENT: 41

NOTES: Jean Simonot designed these double-hull boats to a specification for a "600-tonne" second-class seagoing submarine. They were very maneuverable but dived slowly and had poor internal arrangements that made them cramped and uncomfortable for their crews. They served primarily in the Mediterranean.

The *Nymphe* was stricken on 25 June 1941. The *Naïade*, the *Sirène*, and the *Galatée* were scuttled at Toulon on 27 November 1942. They were refloated and later bombed by USAAF aircraft, the first pair on 24 November 1943 and the last on 5 July 1944.

## *ARIANE* CLASS (1925)

*Ariane* (6 August 1925), *Ondine* (8 May 1925), *Eurydice* (31 May 1927), *Danaé* (11 September 1927)

BUILDER: Normand

DISPLACEMENT: 626 tons (surfaced), 787 tons (submerged)

DIMENSIONS: 216'6" x 20'4" x 13'6"

MACHINERY: 2 Normand-Vickers diesel engines, 2 electric motors, 2 shafts. 1250 bhp/1000 shp = 14/7.5 knots

RANGE: 3500 nm at 9 knots surfaced, 75 nm at 5 knots submerged

ARMAMENT: 7 x 550mm torpedo tubes (4 bow, 1 stern, 1 twin trainable external mount), total 13 torpedoes, 1 x 100mm gun, 2 x 8mm machine guns

COMPLEMENT: 41

NOTES: These Normand-Fenaux boats were designed to the "600-tonne" specification. They too were very maneuverable but dived slowly and had poor internal arrangements that made them cramped and uncomfortable for their crews. They served primarily in the Mediterranean.

The Greek steamer *Aikaterini Gouloudris* accidentally rammed and sank the *Ondine* near Vigo on 2 October 1928. The *Ariane* and the *Danaé* were scuttled at Oran on 9 November 1942. The *Eurydice* was scuttled at Toulon on 27 November, refloated, and bombed by USAAF aircraft on 5 July 1944.

## *CIRCÉ* CLASS (1925)

*Circé* (29 October 1925), *Calypso* (15 January 1926), *Thétis* (20 June 1927), *Doris* (25 November 1927)
BUILDER: Schneider
DISPLACEMENT: 615 tons (surfaced), 776 tons (submerged)
DIMENSIONS: 204'11" x 20'4" x 13'1"
MACHINERY: 2 Schneider diesel engines, 2 electric motors 2 shafts. 1250 bhp/1000 shp = 14/7.5 knots
RANGE: 3500 nm at 9 knots surfaced, 75 nm at 5 knots submerged
ARMAMENT: 7 x 550mm torpedo tubes (4 bow, 1 stern, 1 twin trainable external mount), total 13 torpedoes, 1 x 75mm gun, 2 x 8mm machine guns
COMPLEMENT: 41

NOTES: These Simonot boats were designed to the "600-tonne" specification. They too were very maneuverable but dived slowly and had poor internal arrangements that made them cramped and uncomfortable for their crews. They served primarily in the Mediterranean.

The *U-9* torpedoed the *Doris* off the Dutch coast on 8 May 1940. The *Thétis* was scuttled at Toulon on 27 November 1942. The Italians seized the *Calypso* and the *Circé* at Bizerta on 8 December 1942. USAAF aircraft bombed the *Calypso* on 20 January 1943. The *Circé* became the *FR-117* and was scuttled at Bizerta on 6 May 1943.

## [GREECE]—*KATSONIS* CLASS (1926)

*Katsonis* (20 March 1926)
BUILDER: Gironde
*Papamicolis* (19 November 1926)
BUILDER: Loire
DISPLACEMENT: 595 tons (surfaced), 778 tons (submerged)
DIMENSIONS: 204'9" x 17'6" x 11'0"
MACHINERY: 2 Schneider-Carels diesel engines, 2 electric motors 2 shafts. 1300 bhp/1000 shp = 14/9.5 knots
RANGE: 3500 nm at 10 knots surfaced, 100 nm at 5 knots submerged

ARMAMENT: 6 x 550mm torpedo tubes (4 bow, 2 stern), 1 x 100mm gun, 1 x 3-pdr AA gun
COMPLEMENT: 39
NOTES: These boats were very similar to the *Circé* class with a larger conning tower. They operated within the British Mediterranean Fleet after the fall of Greece. The German antisubmarine vessel *Uj–2101* sank the *Katsonis* in the Aegean on 14 September 1943, and the *Papamicolis* was discarded in 1945.

## [LATVIA]—*RONIS* CLASS (1926)

*Ronis* (1 July 1926)
BUILDER: Loire
*Spidola* (6 October 1926)
BUILDER: Normand
DISPLACEMENT: 390 tons (surfaced), 514 tons (submerged)
DIMENSIONS: 180′5″ x 15′9″ x 11′10″
MACHINERY: 2 Sulzer diesel engines, 2 electric motors, 2 shafts. 1300 bhp/700 shp = 14/9 knots

ARMAMENT: 6 x 450mm torpedo tubes (4 bow, 2 stern) 1 x 75mm AA gun, 2 x 8mm machine guns
COMPLEMENT: 27
NOTES: Simonot designed these small double-hull submarines. The Soviet Union took them over in August 1940. They were blown up at Liepaya on 14 June 1941.

## [GREECE]—*PROTEUS* CLASS (1927)

*Proteus* (24 October 1927), *Nereus* (December 1927), *Triton* (4 April 1928)
BUILDER: Loire
*Glavkos* (1928)
BUILDER: CNF
DISPLACEMENT: 750 tons (surfaced), 960 tons (submerged)
DIMENSIONS: 225′0″ x 18′10″ x 13′8″
MACHINERY: 2 Sulzer diesel engines, 2 electric motors 2 shafts. 1420 bhp/1200 shp = 14/9.5 knots
RANGE: 3500 nm at 10 knots surfaced, 100 nm at 5 knots submerged
ARMAMENT: 8 x 550mm torpedo tubes (6 bow, 2 stern), 1 x 100mm gun, 1 x 3-pdr AA gun

COMPLEMENT: 41
NOTES: These submarines were enlargements of the *Katsonis* class with all torpedo tubes mounted internally. The Italian torpedo boat *Antares* rammed and sank the *Proteus* off Valona on 19 December 1940. The other boats operated with the British Mediterranean Fleet after the fall of Greece. The *Glavkos* was bombed at Malta on 4 April 1942; the German antisubmarine vessel *Uj–3102* sank the *Triton* near Andos on 16 November; the *Nereus* was discarded in 1945.

## FRANCE: *REDOUTABLE* CLASS (1928), *SFAX* (1934)
*(Courtesy of Art-Tech)*

*Redoutable* (24 February 1928), *Vengeur* (1 September 1928), *Prométhée* (12 April 1930), *L'Espoire* (18 July 1931), *Agosta* (20 April 1934), *Bévéziers* (14 October 1935), *Ouessant* (30 November 1936), *Sidi Ferruch* (9 July 1937)
BUILDER: Cherbourg
*Henri Poincaré* (10 April 1929), *Poncelet* (10 April 1929)
BUILDER: Lorient
*Argo* (11 April 1929), *Phénix* (12 April 1930)
BUILDER: Dubigeon
*Actéon* (10 April 1929), *Achéron* (6 August 1929), *Pégase* (28 July 1930), *Le Conquérant* (26 June 1934), *Sfax* (6 December 1934), *Casabianca* (2 February 1935)

BUILDER: Loire
*Fresnel* (8 June 1929), *Le Glorieux* (29 November 1931)
BUILDER: St. Nazaire
*Monge* (25 June 1929), *Protée* (31 July 1930), *Le Tonnant* (15 December 1934)
BUILDER: La Seyne
*Pascal* (19 July 1928), *Pasteur* (19 July 1928), *Achille* (28 May 1930), *Ajax* (28 May 1930), *Le Centaure* (14 October 1932), *Le Héros* (14 October 1932)
BUILDER: Brest
*Archimède* (6 September 1930), *Persée* (23 May 1931)
BUILDER: CNF
DISPLACEMENT: 1570 tons (surfaced), 2084 tons (submerged)

DIMENSIONS: 302'10" x 26'11" x 15'5"

MACHINERY: 4 Sulzer or Schneider diesel engines, 2 electric motors, 2 shafts. 6000-8000 bhp/2000 shp = 17-20/10 knots

RANGE: 10,000 nm at 10 knots surfaced, 100 nm at 5 knots submerged

ARMAMENT: 9 x 550mm plus 2 x 400mm torpedo tubes (4 bow, 1 triple trainable external mount, 1 quadruple trainable external 550mm/400mm mount), total 11 x 550mm plus 2 x 400mm torpedoes, 1 x 100mm gun, 2 x 13.2mm machine guns

COMPLEMENT: 61

NOTES: Roquebert designed these large double-hull, oceangoing, first-class submarines. They were fast, maneuvered easily, and took about 45 seconds to dive, but suffered from poor habitability and stowage for provisions and munitions. Nevertheless, they were regarded as successful vessels. Later boats received more powerful diesels and were faster on the surface. This class served primarily in the Atlantic and Mediterranean.

The *Prométhée* sank in an accident at Cherbourg on 8 July 1932, and the *Phénix* sank in an accident at Cam Ranh Bay on 15 June 1939. The *Achille*, the *Agosta*, the *Ouessant*, and the *Pasteur* were scuttled at Brest on 18 June 1940; aircraft from the carrier *Ark Royal* sank the *Persée* at Dakar on 23 September; the destroyer *Foxhound* sank the *Ajax* off Dakar on 24 September; a British bomber sank the *Poncelet* near Port-Gentil on 8 November; the *U-37* torpedoed the *Sfax* off Cape Juby on 19 December. British carrier aircraft sank the *Béveziers* and *Le Heros* off Diego Suarez on 5 and 7 May 1942; the destroyers *Active* and *Panther* sank the *Monge* off Diego Suarez on 8 May; the destroyer *Westcott* sank the *Actéon* off Oran on 8 November 1942; U.S. Navy aircraft sank the *Sidi Ferruch* near Casablanca on 11 November; U.S. Navy PBYs sank *Le Conquérant* between Casablanca and Dakar on 13 November; *Le Tonnant* was scuttled off Cadiz on 15 November; the *Achéron*, the *Espoire*, the *Fresnel*, the *Pascal*, the *Rédoutable*, and the *Vengeur* were scuttled at Toulon on 27 November (the *Achéron* and the *Pascal* were refloated and later bombed by USAAF aircraft on 24 November 1943 and 11 March 1944). The *Henri Poincaré* was captured at Toulon, became the Italian *FR-118*, and was scuttled at La Spezia on 9 September 1943. The *Protée* was interned at Alexandria from June 1940 until January 1943, when it joined the Free French forces. It was mined near Marseilles on 29 December 1943. The surviving boats were stricken in 1952.

## [YUGOSLAVIA]—*OSVETNIK* CLASS (1928)

*Smeli* (1 December 1938), *Osvetnik* (14 January 1929)
BUILDER: Loire
DISPLACEMENT: 630 tons (surfaced), 809 tons (submerged)
DIMENSIONS: 218'2" x 17'9" x 12'6"
MACHINERY: 2 MAN diesel engines, 2 Nancy electric motors 2shafts. 1480 bhp/1000 shp = 14.5/9.25 knots
RANGE: 3500 nm at 9 knots surfaced, 75 nm at 5 knots submerged
ARMAMENT: 6 x 550mm torpedo tubes (4 bow, 2 stern), 1 x 100mm gun, 1 x 40mm AA gun
COMPLEMENT: 43
NOTES: These submarines were similar to the French *Circé* class. The Italians took them over in April 1941 and renamed them the *Antonio Baiamonti* and the *Francesco Rismondo*. The former was scuttled at La Spezia on 9 September 1943, and the latter at Bonifacio on 18 September.

## *SAPHIR* CLASS (1928)

*Saphir* (20 December 1928), *Turquoise* (16 May 1929), *Nautilus* (21 March 1930), *Rubis* (30 September 1931), *Diamant* (18 May 1933), *Perle* (30 July 1935)
BUILDER: Toulon
DISPLACEMENT: 761 tons (surfaced), 925 tons (submerged)
DIMENSIONS: 216'2" x 23'7" x 14'1"
MACHINERY: 2 Normand-Vickers diesel engines, 2 electric motors, 2 shafts. 1300 bhp/1000 shp = 12/9 knots
RANGE: 7000 nm at 7.5 knots surfaced, 80 nm at 4 knots submerged
ARMAMENT: 3 x 550mm plus 2 x 400mm torpedo tubes (2 bow, 1 triple trainable external 550mm/400mm mount), total 5 x 550mm plus 2 x 400mm torpedoes, 32 mines, 1 x 75mm gun, 2 x 13.2mm machine guns
COMPLEMENT: 42
NOTES: These double-hull minelaying submarines were designed by Normand-Fenaux and were very successful boats. They served mainly in the Mediterranean before World War II.

The *Diamant* was scuttled at Toulon on 27 November 1942. The Italians captured the *Saphir*, the *Turquoise*, and the *Nautilus* at Bizerta on 8 December 1942. The *Nautilus* was bombed on 31 January 1943, but the other two became the Italian *FR-112* and *FR-116* and were scuttled at Naples on 15 September and Bizerta on 6 May 1943. Allied aircraft mistakenly sank the *Perle* in the North Atlantic on 8 July 1944. The *Rubis*, the most successful minelaying submarine of the war, served with Free French forces from June 1940 and survived the war. It was stricken on 10 April 1949.

## [POLAND]—*WILK* CLASS (1929)

*Wilk* (12 April 1929)
BUILDER: Normand
*Rys* (22 April 1929)
BUILDER: Loire
*Zbik* (14 June 1931)
BUILDER: CNF
DISPLACEMENT: 980 tons (surfaced), 1250 tons (submerged)
DIMENSIONS: 257'6" x 19'4" x 13'9"
MACHINERY: 2 Normand-Vickers diesel engines, 2 electric motors, 2 shafts. 1800 bhp/1200 shp = 14/9 knots
RANGE: 7000 nm at 7.5 knots surfaced, 80 nm at 4 knots submerged
ARMAMENT: 6 x 550mm torpedo tubes (4 bow, 1 twin trainable external mount), total 10 torpedoes, 40 mines, 1 x 100mm gun, 1 x 40mm AA gun

COMPLEMENT: 54
NOTES: These submarines were larger versions of the French *Saphir* class. The *Rys* and the *Zbik* were interned in Sweden in September 1939, returned to Poland at the war's end, and were scrapped in 1951 and 1954. The *Wilk* escaped to Britain in September 1939, became a training vessel a year later, and returned to Poland after World War II. It was scrapped in 1951.

**FRANCE: *SURCOUF* (18 OCTOBER 1929)**
*(Courtesy of Art-Tech)*

BUILDER: Cherbourg
DISPLACEMENT: 3250 tons (surfaced), 4304 tons (submerged)
DIMENSIONS: 360'10" x 29'6" x 23'10"
MACHINERY: 4 Sulzer diesel engines, 2 electric motors, 2 shafts. 7600 bhp/3400 shp = 18.5/10 knots
RANGE: 10,000 nm at 10 knots surfaced, 70 nm at 5 knots submerged
ARMAMENT: 8 x 550mm plus 4 x 400mm torpedo tubes (4 bow, 1 quadruple trainable external 550mm mount, 1 quadruple trainable external 400mm mount), total 14 x 550mm plus 8 x 400mm torpedoes, 1 x twin 8" gun turret, 2 x 37mm AA guns, 2 x twin 13.2mm machine guns, 1 aircraft
COMPLEMENT: 118
NOTES: Roquebert designed the *Surcouf* as a very long range commerce-raiding submarine. It had a double hull, heavy gun armament and fire control, a hangar for a scouting aircraft, and a special compartment to accommodate prisoners. The design was very successful. The *Surcouf* served with the Free French forces from June 1940. The U.S. steamer *Thomson Lykes* accidentally rammed and sank the *Surcouf* in the Gulf of Mexico on 18 February 1942.

## *ARGONAUTE* CLASS (1929)

*Argonaute* (23 May 1929), *Aréthuse* (8 August 1929), *Atalante* (5 August 1930), *La Vestale* (25 May 1932), *La Sultane* (5 August 1932)

BUILDER: Schneider

DISPLACEMENT: 630 tons (surfaced), 798 tons (submerged)

DIMENSIONS: 208'0" x 21'0" x 13'10"

MACHINERY: 2 Schneider-Carel diesel engines, 2 electric motors, 2 shafts. 1300 bhp/1000 shp = 14/9 knots

RANGE: 4000 nm at 10 knots surfaced, 85 nm at 5 knots submerged

ARMAMENT: 6 x 550mm plus 2 x 400mm torpedo tubes (3 bow, 1 stern, 1 twin trainable external 550mm mount, 1 twin trainable external 400mm mount), 1 x 75mm gun, 1 x 13.2mm machine gun

COMPLEMENT: 41

NOTES: Schneider-Laubeuf designed these double-hull boats to a specification for a "630-tonne" second-class seagoing submarine, an enlarged and improved version of the "600-tonne" type that corrected the problems of the earlier design. They were very maneuverable, dived quickly, and had much improved internal arrangements that endowed them with acceptable habitability. They served primarily in the Mediterranean.

The destroyer *Achates* sank the *Argonaute* off Oran on 8 November 1942. The other boats were stricken in 1946.

## *DIANE* CLASS (1930)

*Diane* (13 May 1930), *Méduse* (26 August 1930), *Amphitrite* (20 December 1930), *Orphée* (10 November 1931), *La Psyché* (4 August 1932)

BUILDER: Normand

*Antiope* (19 August 1930), *Amazone* (28 December 1931), *La Sybille* (28 January 1932), *Oréade* (23 May 1932)

BUILDER: Seine-Maritime

DISPLACEMENT: 571 tons (surfaced), 809 tons (submerged)

DIMENSIONS: 211'4" x 20'4" x 14'1"

MACHINERY: 2 Normand-Vickers diesel engines, 2 electric motors, 2 shafts. 1400 bhp/1000 shp = 14/9 knots

RANGE: 4000 nm at 10 knots surfaced, 85 nm at 5 knots submerged

ARMAMENT: 6 x 550mm plus 2 x 400mm torpedo tubes (3 bow, 1 stern, 1 twin trainable external 550mm mount, 1 twin trainable external 400mm mount), 1 x 75mm gun, 1 x 13.2mm machine gun

COMPLEMENT: 41

NOTES: Normand-Fenaux designed these double-hull boats to a specification for a "630-tonne" second-class seagoing submarine, an enlarged and improved version of the "600-tonne" type that corrected the problems of the earlier design. They were very maneuverable, dived quickly, and had much improved internal arrangements that endowed them with acceptable habitability. They served primarily in the Mediterranean.

U.S. Navy carrier aircraft sank the *Amphitrite*, the *Oréade*, and *La Psyche* near Casablanca on 8 November 1942; British carrier aircraft sank the *Diane* at Oran the next day; the destroyer *Rowan* drove the *Méduse* ashore near Casablanca on 10 November; *La Sybille*, after sinking a transport off Casablanca, was torpedoed by the *U-173* on 11 November. The surviving boats were stricken in 1946.

## *ORION* CLASS (1931)

*Orion* (21 April 1931)
BUILDER: Loire
*Ondine* (4 May 1931)
BUILDER: Dubigeon
DISPLACEMENT: 558 tons (surfaced), 787 tons (submerged)
DIMENSIONS: 219'0" x 20'4" x 14'5"
MACHINERY: 2 Sulzer diesel engines, 2 electric motors, 2 shafts. 1400 bhp/1000 shp = 14/9 knots
RANGE: 4000 nm at 10 knots surfaced, 85 nm at 5 knots submerged
ARMAMENT: 6 x 550mm plus 2 x 400mm torpedo tubes (3 bow, 1 stern, 1 twin trainable external 550mm mount, 1 twin trainable external 400mm mount), 1 x 75mm gun, 1 x 13.2mm machine gun

COMPLEMENT: 41
NOTES: Simonot designed these double-hull boats to a specification for a "630-tonne" second-class seagoing submarine, an enlarged and improved version of the "600-tonne" type that corrected the problems of the earlier design. They were very maneuverable, dived quickly, and had much improved internal arrangements that endowed them with acceptable habitability. They served primarily in the Mediterranean before World War II. In June 1940 they escaped to Britain but did not become operational because of lack of equipment and were scrapped in April 1943.

## *MINERVE* CLASS (1934)

*Iris* (23 September 1934)
BUILDER: Dubigeon
*Minerve* (23 October 1934)
BUILDER: Cherbourg
*Vénus* (6 April 1935), *Cérès* (9 December 1938)
BUILDER: Seine-Maritime
*Junon* (15 September 1935), *Pallas* (25 August 1938)
BUILDER: Normand
DISPLACEMENT: 662 tons (surfaced), 856 tons (submerged)
DIMENSIONS: 223'5" x 18'5" x 13'3"
MACHINERY: 2 Normand-Vickers diesel engines, 2 electric motors, 2 shafts. 1800 bhp/1230 shp = 14.5/9 knots
RANGE: 4000 nm at 10 knots surfaced, 85 nm at 5 knots submerged
ARMAMENT: 6 x 550mm plus 3 x 400mm torpedo tubes (4 bow, 2 stern, 1 triple trainable external 400mm mount), 1 x 75mm gun, 2 x 13.2mm machine guns

COMPLEMENT: 42
NOTES: Roquebert designed these double-hull boats to a specification for a "630-tonne" second-class seagoing submarine, an enlarged and improved version of the "600-tonne" type that corrected the problems of the earlier design. They were very maneuverable, dived quickly, and had much improved internal arrangements that endowed them with acceptable habitability. They served primarily in the Mediterranean.

The *Cérès*, the *Pallas*, and the *Vénus* were scuttled at Toulon on 27 November 1942. The *Junon* and the *Minerve* escaped to Britain in June 1940 and served with the Free French forces, and the *Iris* was interned in Spain. The *Minerve* wrecked on 19 September 1945 and the two other boats were stricken in the early 1950s.

## *AURORE* CLASS (1939)

*Aurore* (26 July 1939)
BUILDER: Toulon
*La Créole* (8 June 1940), *L'Artémis* (28 July 1942)
BUILDER: Normand
*La Favorite* (5 November 1942), *L'Africaine* (7 December 1946)
BUILDER: Seine-Maritime
*L'Astrée* (3 May 1946), *L'Andromède* (17 November 1949)
BUILDER: Dubigeon
DISPLACEMENT: 893 tons (surfaced), 1170 tons (submerged)
DIMENSIONS: 241'2" x 21'4" x 13'9"
MACHINERY: 2 Sulzer or Schneider diesel engines, 2 electric motors, 2 shafts. 3000 bhp/1400 shp = 14.5/9 knots
RANGE: 5600 nm at 10 knots surfaced, 85 nm at 5 knots submerged
ARMAMENT: 9 x 550mm torpedo tubes (4 bow, 2 stern, 1 triple trainable external mount), 1 x 100mm gun, 2 x 13.2mm machine guns
COMPLEMENT: 44

NOTES: Pierre Paoli designed these double-hull submarines as an improved version of the earlier "630-tonne" type to correct the remaining problems of the series. Eight additional boats were canceled or broken up incomplete.

The *Aurore* was scuttled at Toulon on 27 November 1942. The Germans completed *La Favorite* as the *UF-1*. It was bombed at Gotenhafen on 7 July 1944.

The five remaining submarines were completed after World War II to a revised design with a streamlined sail, snorkels, and revised armament. Displacement increased to 870 tons (surfaced) and 1250 tons (submerged); there were two twin trainable mounts in place of the triple mount; and an 88mm gun and two 20mm antiaircraft guns replaced the original artillery. They were scrapped between 1961 and 1967.

## GERMANY
## [SWEDEN]—*VALEN* (5 MAY 1925)

BUILDER: Karlskrona
DISPLACEMENT: 548 tons (surfaced), 730 tons (submerged)
DIMENSIONS: 187'4" x 23'4" x 10'2"
MACHINERY: 2 diesel engines, 2 electric motors, 2 shafts. 1340 bhp/700 shp = 14.75/7.5 knots
ARMAMENT: 4 x 450mm torpedo tubes (bow), total 8 torpedoes, 20 mines, 1 x 75mm AA gun, 1 x 25mm AA gun

COMPLEMENT: 31
NOTES: The *Valen* essentially was a minelaying version of the A.G. Weser–designed *Bävern* class. It carried its mines in five vertical tubes on each side within the main ballast tanks using the Normand-Fenaux system. It was stricken on 6 October 1944.

## [SWEDEN]—*DRAKEN* CLASS (1926)

*Draken* (21 October 1926), *Gripen* (21 August 1928), *Ulven* (6 March 1930)
BUILDER: Karlskrona
DISPLACEMENT: 667 tons (surfaced), 850 tons (submerged)
DIMENSIONS: 216'10" x 21'0" x 10'10"
MACHINERY: 2 Götaverken diesel engines, 2 electric motors, 2 shafts. 1920 bhp/1000 shp = 13.75/8.25 knots
ARMAMENT: 4 x 533mm torpedo tubes (bow), total 8 torpedoes, 1 x 105mm gun, 1 x 25mm AA gun

COMPLEMENT: 35
NOTES: These submarines were enlarged versions of the *Bävern* type. They introduced 533mm torpedoes and a heavy deck gun into the Swedish submarine fleet. The *Ulven* was mined on 16 April 1943. The *Gripen* and the *Draken* were stricken in 1947–1948.

## [TURKEY]—*BIRINCI INÖNÜ* CLASS

*Birinci Inönü* (1 February 1927), *Ikinci Inönü* (12 March 1927)
BUILDER: Fijenoord
DISPLACEMENT: 505 tons (surfaced), 620 tons (submerged)
DIMENSIONS: 192'6" x 19'0" x 11'6"
MACHINERY: 2 MAN diesel engines, 2 electric motors, 2 shafts. 1100 bhp/700 shp = 13.5/8.5 knots
RANGE: 7200 nm at 6 knots surfaced, 55 nm at 4 knots submerged

ARMAMENT: 6 x 450mm torpedo tubes (4 bow, 2 stern), 1 x 75mm gun, 1 x 20 mm AA
COMPLEMENT: 29
NOTES: The Ingenieurskantoor voor Scheepsbouw (IvS) in The Netherlands developed this design as an update of the wartime UB-III type. They were discarded in 1950.

## [FINLAND]—*VETEHINEN* CLASS (1930)

*Vetehinen* (1 June 1930), *Vesihiisi* (1 August 1930), *Iku-Tursu* (5 May 1931)
BUILDER: Crichton-Vulcan
DISPLACEMENT: 493 tons (surfaced), 716 tons (submerged)
DIMENSIONS: 208'4" x 20'4" x 11'10"
MACHINERY: 2 Polar-Atlas diesel engines, 2 Brown-Boveri electric motors, 2 shafts. 1160 bhp/600 shp = 12.5/8.5 knots
RANGE: 1500 nm at 10 knots surfaced, 75 nm at 5 knots submerged

ARMAMENT: 6 x 533mm torpedo tubes (4 bow, 2 stern), total 6 torpedoes, 20 mines, 1 x 76mm gun, 1 x 20mm AA gun, 1 x 12.7mm machine gun
COMPLEMENT: 30
NOTES: The IvS developed the design for this class as an updated version of the wartime UC-III type coastal minelayers. They operated in the Baltic during World War II and were stricken in 1947.

## [FINLAND]—*SAUKKO* (2 JULY 1930)

BUILDER: HSK

DISPLACEMENT: 114 tons (surfaced), 142 tons (submerged)

DIMENSIONS: 106'4" x 13'6" x 9'6"

MACHINERY: 1 Krupp-Germania diesel engine, 1 electric motor, 1 shaft. 170 bhp/120 shp = 7/5.75 knots

RANGE: 375 nm at 8 knots surfaced, 45 nm at 4 knots submerged

ARMAMENT: 2 x 450mm torpedo tubes (bow), 9 mines, 1 x 12.7mm machine gun

COMPLEMENT: 15

NOTES: This boat was designed by the IvS for service on Lake Ladoga. Because it exceeded the tonnage limits stipulated by the Treaty of Dorpat, it never served on the lake and operated in the Baltic. It was stricken in 1947.

## TYPE IA (1930)

U-25 (14 February 1936), U-26 (14 March 1936)

[Turkey]—*Gur* (22 October 1930)

BUILDER: Echovarrieta y Larringa)

DISPLACEMENT: 862 tons (surfaced), 983 tons (submerged)

DIMENSIONS: 237'6" x 20'4" x 13'6"

MACHINERY: 2 MAN diesel engines, 2 Brown-Boveri electric motors, 2 shafts. 2800 bhp/780 shp = 20/9 knots

RANGE: 7900 nm at 10 knots surfaced, 78 nm at 4 knots submerged

ARMAMENT: 6 x 533mm torpedo tubes (4 bow, 2 stern), total 14 torpedoes, 1 x 105mm (*Gur*: 100mm) gun, 1 x 20mm AA gun

COMPLEMENT: 42

NOTES: The IvS prepared this design for Spain as its *E-1*. Much of its structure was prefabricated in The Netherlands and shipped to Spain for assembly. The new Spanish Republic, established in 1932, declined to accept the boat, and it was sold to Turkey in 1934, just before completion. The same design was used for new oceangoing submarines for the Kriegsmarine when Germany resumed U-boat construction.

The corvette *Gladiolus* and an Australian flying boat crippled the *U-26* near Ireland, and it was scuttled on 1 July 1940. The *U-25* was mined near Terschelling on 1 August 1940. The *Gur* was stricken in 1950.

## GERMANY: TYPE IIA (1921), *U-1* (1935)
*(Courtesy of Art-Tech)*

*U-1* (15 June 1935), *U-2* (1 July 1935), *U-3* (19 July 1935), *U-4* (31 July 1935), *U-5* (14 August 1935), *U-6* (21 August 1935),
BUILDER: Kiel
[Finland]—*Vesikko* (1 August 1931)
BUILDER: Crichton-Vulcan
DISPLACEMENT: 254 tons (surfaced), 303 tons (submerged)
DIMENSIONS: 134'2" x 13'5" x 12'6"
MACHINERY: 2 MWM diesel engines, 2 Siemens electric motors, 2 shafts. 700 bhp/300 shp = 13/7 knots
RANGE: 1600 nm at 8 knots surfaced, 35 nm at 4 knots submerged
ARMAMENT: 3 x 533mm torpedo tubes (bow), total 5 torpedoes, 1 x 20mm AA gun
COMPLEMENT: 25 (*Vesikko*: 16)
NOTES: The prototype for this class was de-signed by the IvS for Finland and was based on the UBII type from World War I. The same design was used for new coastal submarines when Germany recommenced U-boat construction.

The German boats operated primarily in training and trials roles, although they undertook operational patrols during the first eight months of World War II. The *U-1* was mined off Terschelling on 8 April 1940; a training accident sank the *U-5* outside Pillau on 19 March 1943; the fishing vessel *Helmi Söhle* accidentally rammed and sank the *U-2* near Pillau on 8 April 1944. The other three boats decommissioned on 1 August 1944.

The *Vesikko* was stricken in 1947 and preserved as a memorial.

## [SWEDEN]—*DELFINEN* CLASS (1934)

*Delfinen* (20 December 1934), *Nordkaparen* (9 February 1935), *Springaren* (27 April 1935)

BUILDER: Kockums

DISPLACEMENT: 540 tons (surfaced), 720 tons (submerged)

DIMENSIONS: 207'0" x 21'0" x 11'2"

MACHINERY: 2 MAN diesel engines, 2 Brown-Boveri electric motors, 2 shafts. 1200 bhp/800 shp = 15/9 knots

ARMAMENT: 4 x 533mm torpedo tubes (3 bow, 1 stern), total 8 torpedoes, 20 mines, 1 x 57mm gun, 1 x 25mm AA gun

COMPLEMENT: 35

NOTES: These minelayers were designed by the IvS with the detail design work undertaken in Sweden by B. Swenzén. Five vertical tubes on each side in the main ballast tanks carried the mines using the Normand-Fenaux system. These submarines were stricken on 24 February 1953.

## TYPE IIB (1935)

*U-7* (28 June 1935), *U-8* (18 July 1935), *U-9* (30 July 1935), *U-10* (13 August 1935), *U-11* (27 August 1935), *U-12* (11 September 1935), *U-13* (9 November 1935), *U-17* (15 November 1935), *U-18* (6 December 1935), *U-19* (21 December 1935), *U-14* (28 December 1935), *U-20* (14 January 1936), *U-15* (15 February 1936), *U-16* (28 April 1936), *U-21* (13 July 1936), *U-22* (28 July 1936), *U-23* (28 August 1936), *U-24* (24 September 1936)

BUILDER: Germania

*U-120* (16 March 1940), *U-121* (20 April 1940)

BUILDER: Flenderwerke

DISPLACEMENT: 279 tons (surfaced), 328 tons (submerged)

DIMENSIONS: 140'0" x 13'5" x 12'6"

MACHINERY: 2 MWM diesel engines, 2 Siemens electric motors, 2 shafts. 700 bhp/300 shp = 13/7 knots

RANGE: 3100 nm at 8 knots surfaced, 43 nm at 4 knots submerged

ARMAMENT: 3 x 533mm torpedo tubes (bow), total 6 torpedoes, 1 x 20mm AA gun

COMPLEMENT: 25

NOTES: These submarines were modestly lengthened versions of the previous Type IIA boats. They served mainly as training vessels except in the early months of World War II, when they undertook operational patrols. The *U-12* was mined in the English Channel on 5 October 1939, and the trawler *Cayton Wyke* and patrol vessel *Puffin* sank the *U-16* there on 25 October. The torpedo boat *Iltis* accidentally rammed and sank the *U-15* off Heligoland Bight on 30 January 1940; the *U-22* was mined in the North Sea on 23 March; the sloop *Weston* sank the *U-13* near Newcastle-upon-Tyne on 31 May. A training accident sank the *U-7* in the Baltic on 18 February 1944; the *U-19* and the *U-20* were scuttled off the Turkish coast in the Black Sea on 10 September; Soviet aircraft sank the *U-9* there on 20 September. The surviving boats were scuttled in port in May 1945.

## [SOVIET UNION]—SERIES IX (1935), SERIES IXBIS (1936), AND SERIES XVI (1945)

*N-1 Voroshilovets* (8 August 1935), *N-2 Molotovets* (21 December 1935), *N-3 Kalininets* (30 April 1936), *S-4* (17 September 1936), *S-5* (16 October 1936), *S-6* (31 March 1938)

BUILDER: Baltic

*S-7–S-8* (5 April 1937), *S-9–S-11* (20 April 1938), *S-12* (20 April 1939), *S-15–S-18* (24 April 1940), *S-13–S-14* (25 April 1940), *S-19–S-20* (14 March 1941), *S-46–S-48* (1947)

BUILDER: Gorkiy

*S-101–S-102* (20 April 1938), *S-103–S-104* (25 April 1939), *S-21* (26 June 1941), *S-22* (7 July 1941), *S-23, S-24* (1947)

BUILDER: Sudomekh

*S-31* (22 February 1939), *S-32* (27 April 1939), *S-33* (30 May 1939), *S-34* (30 September 1939), *S-35* (1940)

BUILDER: Nikolayev

*S-54* (5 November 1938), *S-50* (1939), *S-55* (27 November 1939), *S-56* (25 December 1939), *S-51–S-52* (30 August 1940), *S-53* (30 October 1941)

BUILDER: Dalzavod

*S-58* (1945), *S-59–S-60* (1946)

BUILDER: Severodvinsk

DISPLACEMENT: 840 (Series IXbis and Series XVI: 856) tons (surfaced), 1070 (Series IXbis and Series XVI: 1090) tons (submerged)

DIMENSIONS: 255′1″ x 21′0″ x 13′3″ (Series IXbis and Series XVI: 13′4″)

MACHINERY: 2 diesel engines, 2 electric motors, 2 shafts. 4000 bhp/1100 shp = 19.5 (Series IXbis and Series XVI: 18.75)/9 (Series IXbis and Series XVI: 8.75) knots

RANGE: 9800 nm at 10.5 knots surfaced, 148 nm at 3 knots submerged

ARMAMENT: 6 x 533mm torpedo tubes (4 bow, 2 stern), total 12 torpedoes, 1 x 100mm gun, 1 x 45mm AA gun, 1 x 7.62mm machine gun (Series IXbis and Series XVI)

COMPLEMENT: 45

NOTES: For this class, the IvS modified its *E-1* design for Spain to suit Soviet requirements, especially for higher surface speed that necessitated more powerful diesel engines and larger machinery spaces. Deschimag engineers provided technical assistance during the construction of the first three boats. The Series IXbis featured more powerful batteries and deleted the shield for the 100mm gun. The Series XVI introduced all-welded construction in place of riveting, and also used high-tensile steel, thus increasing their diving depth. Two additional boats were destroyed on the slip to prevent their capture by German forces, and construction of seven other units was abandoned.

The *N-2* was mined off Märket Island on 3 January 1940. German S-boats sank the *N-3* off Steinort on 24 June 1941 and the *S-10* in Danzig Bight the following day; the *N-1* was blown up at Liepaya on 27 June; the *S-11* was mined near Soelavain Bay on 2 August; the *S-5* was mined off Cape Juminda on 28 August; German aircraft sank the *S-6* off Kassarwik on 30 August; the *S-8* was mined near Suursaari Island on 21 October; the *S-34* was mined in Burgas Bay on 14

November. German aircraft sank the *S-32* south of Feodosiya on 26 June 1942, and the Finnish submarine *Vesehiisi* torpedoed the *S-7* off Soderarm on 21 October. German and Finnish antisubmarine vessels sank the *S-12* off Keri on 10 August 1943 and the *S-9* off Porkkala on 8 September. The German torpedo boat *T-33* rammed and sank the *S-4* in Danzig Bight on 6 January 1945. The surviving boats were decommissioned between 1956 and 1962.

## TYPE VIIA (1936)

*U-33* (11 June 1936), *U-34* (17 July 1936), *U-35* (29 September 1936), *U-36* (4 November 1936)

BUILDER: Germania

*U-27* (24 June 1936), *U-28* (14 July 1936), *U-30* (4 August 1936), *U-29* (29 August 1936), *U-31* (25 September 1936), *U-32* (25 February 1937)

BUILDER: Bremen

DISPLACEMENT: 626 tons (surfaced), 745 tons (submerged)

DIMENSIONS: 211'7" x 19'0" x 14'5"

MACHINERY: 2 MAN diesel engines, 2 Brown-Boveri electric motors, 2 shafts. 2300 bhp/560 shp = 16/8 knots

RANGE: 6200 nm at 10 knots surfaced, 94 nm at 4 knots submerged

ARMAMENT: 5 x 533mm torpedo tubes (4 bow, 1 stern), total 11 torpedoes, 1 x 88mm gun, 1 x 20mm AA gun

COMPLEMENT: 44

NOTES: These boats used an improved version of the IvS design for the Finnish *Vetehinen*, and were the precursors of the Kriegsmarine's most important type of Atlantic submarine during World War II. They conducted operational patrols until the end of 1940, when surviving boats became training vessels.

The destroyers *Forester* and *Fortune* sank the *U-27* off the Scottish coast on 20 September 1939; the destroyers *Icarus*, *Kashmir*, and *Kingston* sank the *U-35* off the Norwegian coast on 29 November; the submarine *Salmon* torpedoed the *U-36* near Kristiansand on 4 December. The minesweeper *Gleaner* sank the *U-33* in the Firth of Clyde on 12 February 1940; a British aircraft sank the *U-31* in the Jade on 11 March; the destroyers *Harvester* and *Highlander* sank the *U-32* off the Irish coast on 30 October. The submarine tender *Lech* accidentally rammed and sank the *U-34* at Memel on 5 August 1943, and an accident sank the *U-28* at Neustadt on 17 March 1944. The two surviving boats were scuttled on 4 May 1945 at Flensburg.

## [SWEDEN]—*SJÖLEJONET* CLASS (1936)

*Sjölejonet* (25 July 1936), *Sjöbjörnen* (15 January 1937), *Sjöhunden* (26 November 1938), *Svärdfisken* (18 May 1940), *Tumlaren* (8 September 1940), *Sjöhästen* (19 October 1940), *Dykaren* (17 December 1940), *Sjöormen* (5 May 1941), *Sjöborren* (14 June 1941)
BUILDER: Kockums
DISPLACEMENT: 580 tons (surfaced), 760 tons (submerged)
DIMENSIONS: 210'8" x 21'0" x 11'2"
MACHINERY: 2 MAN diesel engines, 2 electric motors, 2 shafts. 2100 bhp/1000 shp = 16.25/10 knots

ARMAMENT: 6 x 533mm torpedo tubes (3 bow, 1 stern, 1 x twin external training mount), total 10 torpedoes, 2 x 40mm AA gun
COMPLEMENT: 38
NOTES: These submarines were very similar to the *Delfinen* class with minelaying capability deleted. They were reconstructed in the 1950s with streamlined sails, snorkels, and the external tubes and guns removed. They were stricken between 1959 and 1964.

## TYPE VIIB (1938)

*U-45* (27 April 1938), *U-51* (11 June 1938), *U-46* (10 September 1938), *U-47* (29 October 1938), *U-52* (21 December 1938), *U-48* (5 March 1939), *U-53* (6 May 1939), *U-49* (24 June 1939), *U-54* (15 August 1939), *U-55* (11 October 1939), *U-50* (1 November 1939), *U-100* (13 January 1940), *U-101* (10 February 1940), *U-99* (12 March 1940), *U-102* (21 March 1940)
BUILDER: Germania
*U-73* (27 July 1940), *U-74* (31 August 1940), *U-76* (9 October 1940), *U-75* (18 October 1940)
BUILDER: Vegesack
*U-83* (9 December 1940), *U-84* (26 February 1941), *U-85* (10 April 1941), *U-86* (16 May 1941), *U-87* (21 June 1941)
BUILDER: Flenderwerke
DISPLACEMENT: 753 tons (surfaced), 857 tons (submerged)
DIMENSIONS: 218'2" x 20'4" x 15'5"
MACHINERY: 2 MAN diesel engines, 2 Brown-Boveri or AEG electric motors, 2 shafts. 3200 bhp/560 shp = 17.25/8.75 knots

RANGE: 8700 nm at 10 knots surfaced, 90 nm at 4 knots submerged
ARMAMENT: 5 x 533mm torpedo tubes (4 bow, 1 stern), total 14 torpedoes, 1 x 88mm gun, 1 x 20mm AA gun
COMPLEMENT: 44
NOTES: These were slightly enlarged versions of the Type VIIA with greater range and space for more reload torpedoes. They undertook operational patrols until late 1943, when the surviving boats became training vessels. The *U-48* was the most successful U-boat of World War II, sinking 306,875 tons of shipping.

The destroyers *Inglefield*, *Intrepid*, and *Ivanhoe* sank the *U-45* off the Irish coast on 14 October 1939. British and French antisubmarine vessels sank the *U-55* near the Scilly Isles on 30 January 1940; the *U-54* was mined in the North Sea on 14 February; the destroyer *Gurkha* sank the *U-53* in the Orkney Islands on 23 February; the *U-50* was mined off Terschelling on 7 April; the destroyers *Brazen* and *Fearless* sank the *U-49* near Narvik on 15 April; the destroyer *Vansittart* sank the *U-102* in the Bay of Biscay on 1 July. The *U-47* was lost near Rockall on 7 March 1941; the destroyers *Vanoc* and *Walker* sank the *U-99* and the *U-100* south of Iceland on 17 March; the sloop *Scarborough* and destroyer *Wolverine* sank the *U-76* in the same area on 5 April. The destroyer *Roper* sank the *U-85* off Cape Hatteras on 14 April 1942; the destroyers *Wishart* and *Wrestler* sank the *U-74* east of Cartagena on 2 May, and the destroyer *Kipling* sank the *U-75* near Mersa Matruh on 28 December. A British aircraft sank the *U-83* near Cartagena on 4 March 1943, and the Canadian destroyer *St. Croix* and corvette *Shediac* sank the *U-87* the same day off Leixoes. A U.S. aircraft sank the *U-84* in the western Atlantic on 7 August; the *U-86* failed to return from an Atlantic patrol in November; the destroyers *Trippe* and *Woolsey* sank the *U-73* near Oran on 16 December. The four surviving boats were scuttled in May 1945.

## TYPE IX (1938)

*U-37* (14 May 1938), *U-38* (9 August 1938), *U-39* (22 September 1938), *U-40* (9 November 1938), *U-41* (20 January 1939), *U-42* (16 February 1939), *U-43* (23 May 1939), *U-44* (5 August 1939)

BUILDER: Bremen

DISPLACEMENT: 1032 tons (surfaced), 1153 tons (submerged)

DIMENSIONS: 251'0" x 21'4" x 15'5"

MACHINERY: 2 MAN diesel engines, 2 Siemens electric motors, 2 shafts. 4400 bhp/740 shp = 18.25/7.75 knots

RANGE: 10,500 nm at 10 knots surfaced, 78 nm at 4 knots submerged

ARMAMENT: 6 x 533mm torpedo tubes (4 bow, 2 stern), total 22 torpedoes, 1 x 105mm gun, 1 x 37mm AA gun, 1 x 20mm AA gun

COMPLEMENT: 48

NOTES: The design for these long-range oceanic boats was developed from the Type IA to incorporate greater range and a heavier gun armament. The first two became training boats in December 1941.

The destroyers *Faulknor*, *Firedrake*, and *Foxhound* sank the *U-39* northwest of Ireland on 14 September 1939; the *U-40* was mined in the English Channel on 13 October; the destroyers *Ilex* and *Imogen* sank the *U-42* southwest of Ireland on the same day. The destroyer *Antelope* sank the *U-41* south of Ireland on 5 February 1940, and the *U-44* was mined off Terschelling on 13 March. Aircraft from the escort carrier *Santee* sank the *U-43* near the Azores on 30 July 1943. The two surviving boats were scuttled in May 1945.

## [TURKEY]—*SALDIRAY* CLASS (1938)

*Saldiray* (23 July 1938)
BUILDER: Germania
*Atilay* (19 May 1939), *Yildiray* (23 August 1939)
BUILDER: Istanbul
DISPLACEMENT: 934 tons (surfaced), 1210 tons (submerged)
DIMENSIONS: 262′6″ x 21′0″ x 14′0″
MACHINERY: 2 Burmeister and Wain diesel engines, 2 Brown-Boveri electric motors, 2 shafts. 3500 bhp/1000 shp = 20/9 knots
RANGE: 13,100 nm at 10 knots surfaced, 75 nm at 4 knots submerged
ARMAMENT: 6 x 533mm torpedo tubes (4 bow, 2 stern), total 14 torpedoes, 1 x 100mm gun, 1 x 20mm AA gun
COMPLEMENT: 44
NOTES: These boats were designed by the IvS as enlarged versions of its earlier E-1 for Spain. They were faster thanks to more powerful machinery and had substantially greater range. Germania provided engineers and technicians to support the construction of the two boats in Turkey, and their departure when war came delayed the *Yildiray*'s completion. The *Atilay* was mined outside the Dardanelles on 14 July 1942, and the two other boats were discarded in 1957.

## TYPE IIC (1938)

*U-56–U-57* (3 September 1938), *U-59* (12 October 1938), *U-58* (14 October 1938), *U-60* (1 June 1939), *U-61* (15 June 1939), *U-62* (16 November 1939), *U-63* (6 December 1939)
BUILDER: Bremen
DISPLACEMENT: 291 tons (surfaced), 341 tons (submerged)
DIMENSIONS: 144′0″ x 13′5″ x 12′6″
MACHINERY: 2 MWM diesel engines, 2 Siemens electric motors, 2 shafts. 700 bhp/300 shp = 12/7 knots
RANGE: 3800 nm at 8 knots surfaced, 42 nm at 4 knots submerged
ARMAMENT: 3 x 533mm torpedo tubes (bow), total 5 torpedoes, 1 x 20mm AA gun
COMPLEMENT: 25
NOTES: This type was a developed version of the previous Type IIB. They became training vessels from the end of 1940.

The destroyers *Escort*, *Imogen*, and *Inglefield* and the submarine *Narwhal* sank the *U-63* off the Shetland Islands on 25 February 1940, and the rest of the class were scuttled in May 1945.

## [TURKEY]—*BATIRAY* (28 SEPTEMBER 1938)

BUILDER: Germania

DISPLACEMENT: 1128 tons (surfaced), 1284 tons (submerged)

DIMENSIONS: 284′5″ x 22′3″ x 13′5″

MACHINERY: 2 Burmeister and Wain diesel engines, 2 Brown-Boveri electric motors, 2 shafts. 4200 bhp/960 shp = 18/8.5 knots

RANGE: 13,100 nm at 10 knots surfaced, 75 nm at 4 knots submerged

ARMAMENT: 6 x 533mm torpedo tubes (4 bow, 2 stern), total 14 torpedoes, 1 x 105mm gun, 2 x 20mm AA guns, 40 mines.

COMPLEMENT: 45

NOTES: The IvS designed the *Batiray* as a minelaying version of its *Atilay* type for Turkey with five vertical mine tubes on each side in the main ballast tanks. It still was running trials when war broke out and it was taken over by Germany. The mine tubes were converted to fuel tanks and the boat commissioned as the *UA* on 12 September 1939. After operating in the Atlantic it became a training boat in August 1942 and was scuttled at Kiel on 2 May 1945.

## TYPE IXB (1939)

*U-64* (20 September 1939), *U-65* (6 November 1939), *U-122* (30 December 1939), *U-123* (2 March 1940), *U-124* (9 March 1940), *U-103* (12 April 1940), *U-104* (25 May 1940), *U-105* (15 June 1940), *U-106* (17 June 1940), *U-107* (2 July 1940), *U-108* (15 July 1940), *U-110* (25 August 1940), *U-111* (6 September 1940), *U-109* (14 September 1940)

BUILDER: Bremen

DISPLACEMENT: 1051 tons (surfaced), 1178 tons (submerged)

DIMENSIONS: 251′0″ x 22′4″ x 15′5″

MACHINERY: 2 MAN diesel engines, 2 Siemens electric motors, 2 shafts. 4400 bhp/740 shp = 18.25/7.25 knots

RANGE: 12,000 nm at 10 knots surfaced, 64 nm at 4 knots submerged

ARMAMENT: 6 x 533mm torpedo tubes (4 bow, 2 stern), total 22 torpedoes, 1 x 105mm gun, 1 x 37mm AA gun, 1 x 20mm AA gun

COMPLEMENT: 48

NOTES: This class had slightly greater range than the previous Type IX.

An aircraft from the battleship *Warspite* sank the *U-64* off Narvik on 13 April 1940; the *U-122* failed to return from a patrol in June, as did the *U-104* in November. The destroyer *Douglas* sank the *U-64* southeast of Iceland on 28 April 1941; the destroyers *Broadway* and *Bulldog* and the corvette *Aubretia* captured the *U-110* south of Iceland on 9 May and sank it the next day, and the trawler *Lady Shirley* sank the *U-111* southwest of Tenerife on 4 October. The sloop *Black Swan* and the corvette *Stonecrop* sank the *U-124* off Oporto on 2 April 1943; a British aircraft sank the *U-109* south of Ireland on 4 May; a French aircraft sank the *U-105* off Dakar on 2 June, and Australian and British aircraft sank the *U-106* in the Bay of Biscay on 2 August. The *U-108* was bombed at Stettin on 11 April 1944, and British aircraft sank the *U-107* in the Bay of Biscay on 18 August. The *U-103* was bombed at Kiel on 15 April 1945.

The *U-123* was scuttled at Lorient on 19 August 1944. It was raised, became the French *Blaison*, and was decommissioned on 18 August 1959.

## TYPE IID (1940)

*U-137* (18 May 1940), *U-138* (18 May 1940), *U-139* (28 June 1940), *U-140* (28 June 1940), *U-141* (27 July 1940), *U-142* (27 July 1940), *U-143* (10 August 1940), *U-144* (24 August 1940), *U-145* (21 September 1940), *U-146* (21 September 1940), *U-149* (19 October 1940), *U-150* (19 October 1940), *U-147* (16 November 1940), *U-148* (16 November 1940), *U-151* (14 December 1940), *U-152* (14 December 1940)

BUILDER: Kiel
DISPLACEMENT: 314 tons (surfaced), 364 tons (submerged)
DIMENSIONS: 144'4" x 16'0" x 12'9"
MACHINERY: 2 MWM diesel engines, 2 Siemens electric motors, 2 shafts. 700 bhp/300 shp = 13/7 knots
RANGE: 5650 nm at 8 knots surfaced, 56 nm at 4 knots submerged

ARMAMENT: 3 x 533mm torpedo tubes (bow), total 5 torpedoes, 1 x 20mm AA gun
COMPLEMENT: 25
NOTES: These final conventional coastal boats operated mainly as training submarines.

The corvette *Periwinkle* and the destroyer *Wanderer* sank the *U-147* northwest of Ireland on 2 June 1941; the destroyers *Faulknor*, *Fearless*, *Foresight*, *Forester*, and *Foxhound* sank the *U-138* off Cadiz on 18 June, and the Russian submarine *Schc–307* torpedoed the *U-144* in the Gulf of Finland on 10 August. The surviving boats were scuttled or surrendered at the end of World War II.

**GERMANY: TYPE VIIC (1940), *U-251* (1941)**
*(Courtesy of Art-Tech)*

*U-93* (8 June 1940), *U-94* (12 June 1940), *U-95* (18 July 1940), *U-96* (1 August 1940), *U-97* (15 August 1940), *U-98* (31 August 1940), *U-69* (19 September 1940), *U-70* (12 October 1940), *U-71* (31 October 1940), *U-72* (22 November 1940), *U-201* (7 December 1940), *U-203* (4 January 1941), *U-204* (23 January 1941), *U-202* (10 February 1941), *U-205* (20 March 1941), *U-206* (4 April 1941), *U-207* (24 April 1941), *U-208* (21 May 1941), *U-209* (28 August 1941), *U-210* (23 December 1941), *U-211* (15 January 1942), *U-212* (11 March 1942), *U-221* (14 March 1942), *U-222* (28 March 1942), *U-223* (16 April 1942), *U-224* (7 May 1942), *U-225* (28 May 1942), *U-226* (18 June 1942), *U-227* (9 July 1942), *U-228* (30 July 1942), *U-229* (20 August 1942), *U-230* (10 September 1942), *U-231* (1 October 1942), *U-232* (15 October 1942), *U-235* (4 November 1942), *U-236* (24 November 1942), *U-237* (17 December 1942), *U-238* (7 January 1943), *U-239* (28 January 1943), *U-240* (18 February 1943), *U-241* (25 June 1943), *U-242* (20 July 1943), *U-243–U-244* (2 September 1943), *U-247* (23 September 1943), *U-248* (7 October 1943), *U-249* (23 October 1943), *U-250* (11 November 1943), *U-245* (25 November 1943), *U-246* (7 December 1943), *U-1052* (16 December 1943), *U-1053* (17 January 1944), *U-1051* (3 February 1944), *U-1054* (24 February 1944), *U-1055* (9 March 1944), *U-1056* (30 March 1944), *U-1058* (11 April 1944), *U-1057* (20 April 1944)

BUILDER: Germania

U-551–U-552 (14 September 1940), U-553 (7 November 1940), U-554 (7 November 1940), U-555–U-556 (7 December 1940), U-557 (22 December 1940), U-558 (23 December 1940), U-559 (8 January 1941), U-560 (10 January 1941), U-561 (23 January 1941), U-562 (24 January 1941), U-563 (5 February 1941), U-564 (7 February 1041), U-565–U-566 (20 February 1941), U-567–U-568 (6 March 1941), U-569–U-570 (20 March 1941), U-571 (4 April 1941), U-572 (5 April 1941), U-573 (17 April 1941), U-574 (18 April 1941), U-575–U-576 (30 April 1941), U-577–U-578 (15 May 1941), U-579–U-580 (28 May 1941), U-581–U-582 (12 June 1941), U-583 (26 June 1941), U-584 (28 June 1941), U-585 (9 July 1941), U-586 (10 July 1941), U-587–U-588 (23 July 1941), U-589–U-590 (6 August 1941), U-591–U-592 (20 August 1941), U-593–U-594 (3 September 1941), U-595–U-596 (17 September 1941), U-598 (2 October 1941), U-597 (11 October 1941), U-599 (15 October 1941), U-600 (16 October 1941), U-601 (29 October 1941), U-602 (30 October 1941), U-603–U-604 (16 November 1941), U-605–U-606 (27 November 1941), U-607–U-608 (11 December 1941), U-609 (23 December 1941), U-610 (24 December 1941), U-611 (8 January 1942), U-612 (9 January 1942), U-613–U-614 (29 January 1942), U-615–U-616 (8 February 1942), U-617 (19 February 1942), U-618–U-619 (9 March 1942), U-620 (9 March 1942), U-621–U-622 (29 March 1942), U-623–U-624 (31 March 1942), U-625–U-626 (15 April 1942), U-627–U-628 (29 April 1942), U-629–U-630 (12 May 1942), U-631–U-632 (27 May 1942), U-633–U-634 (10 June 1942), U-635 (24 June 1942), U-636 (25 June 1942), U-637 (7 July 1942), U-638 (8 July 1942), U-639 (22 July 1943), U-640 (23 July 1942), U-641–U-642 (6 August 1942), U-643–U-644 (20 August 1942), U-645–U-646 (3 September 1942), U-647–U-648 (16 September 1942), U-649 (30 September 1942), U-650 (11 October 1942), U-951–U-952 (14 October 1942), U-953–U-954 (28 October 1942), U-955 (13 November 1942), U-956 (14 November 1942), U-957–U-958 (21 November 1942), U-959–U-960 (3 December 1942), U-961–U-962 (17 December 1942), U-963–U-964 (30 December 1942), U-965–U-966 (14 January 1943), U-967–U-968 (28 January 1943), U-969–U-970 (11 February 1943), U-971–U-972 (22 February 1943), U-973 (10 March 1943), U-974 (11 March 1943), U-975 (24 March 1943), U-976 (25 March 1943), U-977 (31 March 1943), U-978 (1 April 1943), U-984 (12 April 1943), U-979–U-980 (15 April 1943), U-981–U-982 (29 April 1943), U-983 (13 May 1943), U-985–U-986 (20 May 1943), U-987 (2 June 1943), U-988 (3 June 1943), U-989–U-990 (16 June 1943), U-991–U-992 (24 June 1943), U-993 (5 July 1943), U-994 (6 July 1943)

BUILDER: Blohm und Voss

U-751 (16 November 1940), U-752 (29 March 1941), U-753 (26 April 1941), U-754 (5 July 1941), U-755 (23 August 1941), U-756 (18 October 1941), U-757 (14 December 1941), U-758 (1 March 1942), U-759 (30 May 1942), U-760 (21 June 1942), U-761 (26 September 1942), U-762 (21 November 1942), U-763 (16 January 1943), U-764 (13 March 1943), U-765 (22 April 1943), U-766 (29 May 1943), U-767 (10 July 1943), U-768 (22 August 1943), U-771 (26 September 1943), U-772 (31 October 1943), U-773 (8 December 1942),

U-774 (23 December 1943), U-775 (11 February 1944), U-776 (4 March 1944), U-777 (25 March 1944), U-778 (6 May 1944), U-779 (17 June 1944)

BUILDER: Wilhelmshaven

U-77 (23 November 1940), U-78 (7 December 1940), U-79 (25 January 1941), U-80 (11 February 1941), U-81 (22 February 1941), U-82 (15 March 1941), U-132 (10 April 1941), U-133 (28 April 1941), U-134 (17 May 1941), U-135 (12 June 1941), U-136 (5 July 1941), U-251 (26 July 1941), U-252 (14 August 1941), U-253 (30 August 1941), U-254 (20 September 1941), U-255 (8 October 1941), U-256 (28 October 1941), U-257 (19 November 1941), U-258 (13 December 1941), U-259 (30 December 1941), U-260 (9 February 1942), U-261 (16 February 1942), U-262 (10 March 1942), U-263 (18 March 1942), U-264 (2 April 1942), U-265 (23 April 1942), U-266 (11 May 1942), U-267 (23 May 1942), U-268 (9 June 1942), U-269 (24 June 1942), U-270 (11 July 1942), U-271 (29 July 1942), U-272 (15 August 1942), U-273 (2 September 1942), U-274 (19 September 1942), U-275 (8 October 1942), U-276 (24 October 1942), U-277 (7 November 1942), U-278 (2 December 1942), U-279 (16 December 1942), U-280 (4 January 1943), U-281 (16 January 1943), U-282 (8 February 1943), U-283 (17 February 1943), U-284 (6 March 1943), U-285 (3 April 1943), U-288 (15 April 1943), U-286 (21 April 1943), U-289 (29 May 1943), U-290 (16 June 1943), U-291 (30 June 1943), U-287 (13 August 1943)

BUILDER: Vegesack

U-401 (16 December 1940), U-402 (28 December 1940), U-403 (26 February 1941), U-404 (6 April 1941), U-405 (4 June 1941), U-406 (16 June 1941), U-408 (16 July 1941), U-407 (16 August 1941), U-409 (23 September 1941), U-410 (14 October 1941), U-411 (15 November 1941), U-412 (15 December 1941), U-413 (15 January 1942), U-414 (25 March 1942), U-415–U-416 (9 May 1942), U-417 (6 June 1942), U-418 (11 July 1942), U-420 (12 August 1942), U-419 (22 August 1942), U-421 (24 September 1942), U-422 (10 October 1942), U-423 (7 November 1942), U-424 (28 November 1942), U-425 (19 December 1942), U-426–U-427 (6 February 1943), U-428 (11 March 1943), U-429 (30 March 1943), U-430 (22 April 1943), U-1161 (8 May 1943), U-1162 (29 May 1943),

BUILDER: Danziger

U-331 (20 December 1940), U-332 (20 March 1941), U-333 (14 June 1941), U-334 (15 August 1941), U-335 (15 October 1941), U-336 (1 December 1941), U-337 (25 March 1942), U-338 (20 April 1942), U-339 (30 June 1942), U-340 (20 August 1942), U-341 (10 October 1942), U-342 (10 November 1942), U-343 (21 December 1942), U-344 (29 January 1943), U-345 (11 March 1943), U-346 (13 April 1943), U-347 (24 May 1943), U-348 (25 June 1943), U-349 (22 July 1943), U-1101 (13 September 1943), U-1103 (12 October 1943), U-1104 (7 December 1943), U-1102 (15 January 1944), U-1105 (20 April 1944), U-1106 (26 May 1944), U-1109 (19 June 1944), U-1107 (30 June 1944), U-1110 (21 July 1944), U-1108 (6 September 1944)

BUILDER: Nordseewerke

U-651 (21 December 1940), U-652 (7 February 1941), U-653 (31 March 1941), U-654 (3 May 1941), U-655 (5 June 1941), U-656 (6 July 1941), U-657 (12 August 1941), U-658 (11 September 1941),

U-659 (14 October 1941), U-660 (17 November 1941), U-661 (11 December 1941), U-662 (22 January 1942), U-663 (26 March 1942), U-664 (28 April 1942), U-665 (9 June 1942), U-666 (18 July 1942), U-667 (29 August 1942), U-668–U-669 (5 October 1942), U-670–U-671 (15 December 1942), U-672–U-673 (27 February 1943), U-674–U-675 (8 May 1943), U-676–U-677 (6 July 1943), U-678–U-679 (18 September 1943), U-680–U-681 (20 November 1943), U-682–U-683 (7 March 1944)

BUILDER: Hamburg

U-371 (27 January 1941), U-372 (8 March 1941), U-373 (5 April 1941), U-374 (10 May 1941), U-375 (7 June 1941), U-376 (10 July 1941), U-377 (12 August 1941), U-378 (13 September 1941), U-379 (16 October 1941), U-380 (15 November 1941), U-381 (14 January 1942), U-382 (21 March 1942), U-383 (22 April 1942), U-384 (28 May 1942), U-385 (8 July 1942), U-386 (19 August 1942), U-387 (1 October 1942), U-388 (12 November 1942), U-389 (11 December 1942), U-390 (23 January 1943), U-391 (5 March 1943), U-392 (10 April 1943), U-393 (15 May 1943), U-394 (19 June 1943), U-396 (27 August 1943), U-397 (6 October 1943), U-398 (6 November 1943), U-399 (4 December 1943), U-400 (8 January 1944), U-1131 (3 April 1944), U-1132 (29 April 1944)

BUILDER: Howaldtswerke

U-431 (2 February 1941), U-432 (3 February 1941), U-433 (15 March 1941), U-434 (1 April 1941), U-435 (31 May 1941), U-437 (15 June 1941), U-436 (21 June 1941), U-438 (July 1941), U-439–U-440 (10 August 1941), U-441 (13 December 1941), U-444 (1 January 1942), U-442 (12 January 1942), U-443 (31 January 1942), U-445 (1 February 1942), U-446 (11 April 1942), U-447 (30 April 1942), U-448 (10 May 1942), U-449 (13 June 1942), U-450 (4 July 1942), U-731 (25 July 1942), U-732 (25 August 1942), U-733 (5 September 1942), U-734 (19 September 1942), U-735 (10 October 1942), U-736 (31 October 1942), U-737 (21 November 1942), U-738 (12 December 1942), U-739–U-740 (23 December 1942), U-741–U-742 (4 February 1943), U-743–U-744 (11 March 1943), U-745–U-746 (16 April 1943), U-747–U-748 (13 May 1943), U-749 (1 June 1943), U-750 (10 June 1943), U-1191 (6 July 1943), U-1192 (16 July 1943), U-1193–U-1194 (5 August 1943), U-1195–U-1196 (2 September 1943), U-1197–U-1198 (30 September 1943), U-1199 (12 October 1943), U-1200 –U-1201 (4 November 1943), U-1202 (11 November 1943), U-1203–U-1204 (9 December 1943), U-1205–U-1206 (30 December 1943), U-1207 (6 January 1944), U-1208 (13 January 1044), U-1209–U-1210 (9 February 1944), U-825 (27 February 1944), U-826–U-827 (9 March 1944), U-828 (16 March 1944)

BUILDER: Schichau

U-451 (5 March 1941), U-452 (29 March 1941), U-453–U-454 (30 April 1941), U-455–U-456 (21 June 1941), U-457–U-458 (4 October 1941), U-465–U-466 (30 March 1942), U-467–U-468 (16 May 1942), U-469–U-470 (8 August 1942), U-471–U-472 (6 March 1943), U-473–U-474 (17 April 1943), U-475 (28 May 1943), U-476 (5 June 1943), U-477 (3 July 1943), U-478 (17 July 1943), U-479–U-480 (14 August 1943), U-481 (25 September 1943), U-482 (28 September 1943), U-483 (30 October 1943), U-484 (20 November 1943), U-485 (15 January 1944), U-486 (12 February 1944)

BUILDER: Kiel

U-351 (27 March 1941), U-352 (7 May 1941), U-355 (5 July 1941), U-356 (16 September 1941), U-353 (11 November 1941), U-354 (6 January 1942), U-357 (31 March 1942), U-358 (21 April 1942), U-359 (11 June 1942), U-360 (28 July 1942), U-361 (9 September 1942), U-362 (21 October 1942), U-363 (17 December 1942), U-364 (21 January 1943), U-365 (9 March 1943), U-366 (16 April 1943), U-367 (11 June 1943), U-350 (17 August 1943), U-369 (17 August 1943), U-370 (24 September 1943), U-368 (16 November 1943)

BUILDER: Flensburger

U-701 (16 April 1941), U-702 (24 May 1941), U-703 (16 July 1941), U-704 (29 August 1941), U-705 (23 October 1941), U-706 (24 November 1941), U-707 (18 December 1941), U-708 (24 March 1942), U-709 (14 April 1942), U-710 (11 May 1942), U-711 (25 June 1942), U-712 (10 August 1942), U-713 (23 September 1942), U-714 (12 November 1942), U-715 (14 December 1942), U-716 (15 January 1943), U-717 (19 February 1943), U-718 (26 March 1943), U-719 (28 April 1943), U-720 (5 June 1943), U-721 (22 July 1943), U-722 (18 September 1943), U-905 (20 November 1943), U-907 (1 March 1944), U-906 (28 June 1944)

BUILDER: Stülcken

U-88 (16 August 1941), U-89 (20 September 1941), U-90 (25 October 1941), U-91 (30 November 1941), U-92 (10 January 1942), U-301 (25 March 1942), U-302 (25 April 1942), U-303 (16 May 1942), U-304 (13 June 1942), U-305 (25 July 1942), U-306 (29 August 1942), U-307 (30 September 1942), U-308 (31 October 1942), U-309 (14 December 1942), U-310 (31 December 1942), U-311 (1 February 1943), U-312 (27 February 1943), U-313 (27 March 1943), U-314 (17 April 1943), U-315 (29 May 1943), U-316 (19 June 1943), U-903 (17 July 1943), U-904 (7 August 1943), U-317 (1 September 1943)

BUILDER: Flenderwerke

U-921 (3 April 1943), U-922 (1 June 1943), U-923 (7 August 1943), U-924 (25 September 1943), U-925 (6 November 1943), U-926 (28 December 1943), U-928 (15 April 1944), U-927 (3 May 1944)

BUILDER: Neptun

U-821 (26 June 1943), U-901 (9 October 1943), U-822 (20 February 1944)

BUILDER: Vulcan

DISPLACEMENT: 769 tons (surfaced), 871 tons (submerged)

DIMENSIONS: 220'2" x 20'4" x 15'9"

MACHINERY: 2 MAN diesel engines, 2 AEG electric motors, 2 shafts. 3200 bhp/560 shp = 17/7.5 knots

RANGE: 8500 nm at 10 knots surfaced, 80 nm at 4 knots submerged

ARMAMENT: 5 x 533mm torpedo tubes (4 bow, 1 stern), total 14 torpedoes, 1 x 88mm gun, 1 x 20mm AA gun

COMPLEMENT: 44

NOTES: The Type VIIC was the backbone of the German submarine force during operations in the Atlantic and Mediterranean from 1940 onward. It was a further improvement on the basic Type VII design. Many received much heavier antiaircraft batteries, usually twin or quadruple 20mm mounts, after Dönitz made the decision to have U-boats fight their way past aircraft on the surface. They also received radar warning receivers and other electronic upgrades as the war continued.

This class suffered appalling casualties. Twenty-one boats were lost in 1941, two (the U-580 and the U-583) in accidents and one (the U-570) captured by the British and commissioned into the Royal Navy as the Graph. Sixty-one became casualties during 1942 and one, the U-573, was interned in Spain and became the Spanish G-7, remaining in service until 1970. During 1943 another 114 boats were lost, seven of them (the U-284, the U-649, the U-659, the U-670, the U-718, the U-768, and the U-983) in accidents. Casualties in 1944 were even higher, with 153 boats lost, only three (the U-673, the U-737, and the U-738) as a result of accidents. Finally, 57 boats were lost in 1945, two (the U-1053 and the U-1206) in accidents. More than half the 106 boats that survived until May 1945 were scuttled by their crews to prevent their seizure by Allied forces. Virtually all the others were destroyed by the Allies, although one, the U-977, fled to Argentina, where it was interned before being handed over to U.S. forces. In total, Allied antisubmarine forces sank no fewer than 370 of the 492 boats of this class that commissioned during World War II.

## GERMANY: TYPE IXC (1940)
*(Courtesy of Art-Tech)*

U-66 (10 October 1940), U-67 (30 October 1940), U-68 (22 November 1940), U-125 (10 December 1940), U-126 (31 December 1940), U-127 (4 February 1941), U-128 (20 February 1941), U-129 (28 February 1941), U-130 (14 March 1941), U-131 (1 April 1941), U-153 (5 April 1941), U-154 (21 April 1941), U-155 (12 May 1941), U-156 (21 May 1941), U-157 (5 June 1941), U-158 (21 June 1941), U-159 (1 July 1941), U-160 (12 July 1941), U-171 (22 July 1941), U-172 (5 August 1941), U-173 (11 August 1941), U-174 (21 August 1941), U-175 (2 September 1941), U-176 (12 September 1941)

BUILDER: Bremen

U-501 (25 January 1941), U-502 (18 February 1941), U-503 (5 April 1941), U-504 (24 April 1941), U-505 (24 May 1941), U-506 (20 June 1941), U-507 (15 July 1941), U-508 (30 July 1941), U-509 (19 August 1941), U-510 (4 September 1941), U-511 (22 September 1941), U-512 (9 October 1941), U-513 (29 October 1941), U-514 (18 November 1941), U-515 (2 December 1941), U-516 (16 December 1941), U-517 (30 December 1941), U-518 (11 February 1942), U-519 (12 February 1942), U-520 (2 March 1942), U-521 (17 March 1942), U-522 (1 April 1942), U-523 (15 April 1942), U-524 (30 April 1942), U-525 (20 May 1942)

BUILDER: Deutschewerft

*U-161–U-162* (1 March 1941), *U-163–U-164* (1 May 1941), *U-165* (15 August 1941), *U-166* (1 November 1941)

BUILDER: Seebeckwerft

DISPLACEMENT: 1120 tons (surfaced), 1232 tons (submerged)

DIMENSIONS: 252'0" x 22'4" x 15'5"

MACHINERY: 2 MAN diesel engines, 2 electric motors, 2 shafts. 4400 bhp/740 shp = 18.25/7.25 knots

RANGE: 13,450 nm at 10 knots surfaced, 63 nm at 4 knots submerged

ARMAMENT: 6 x 533mm torpedo tubes (4 bow, 2 stern), total 22 torpedoes, 1 x 105mm gun, 1 x 37mm AA gun, 1 x 20mm AA gun

COMPLEMENT: 48

NOTES: These boats were slightly larger than the previous Type IXB group and had enhanced range and antiaircraft batteries.

The Canadian corvettes *Chambly* and *Moosejaw* sank the *U-501* in the Denmark Straits on 10 September 1941; the Australian destroyer *Nestor* sank the *U-127* near Gibraltar on 15 December; antisubmarine vessels and aircraft sank the *U-131* off Madeira on 17 December.

Aircraft sank the *U-503* and the *U-520* off Newfoundland on 15 March and 30 October 1942, the *U-158* near Bermuda on 30 June, the *U-502* and the *U-165* in the Bay of Biscay on 5 July and 27 September, the *U-512* off Cayenne on 2 October, and the *U-517* southwest of Ireland on 21 November. The cutter *Thetis* sank the *U-157* off Havana on 13 June, the *PC-566* sank the *U-166* in the Gulf of Mexico on 1 August; the *U-171* was mined near Lorient on 8 October; the destroyers *Quick*, *Swanson*, and *Woolsey* sank the *U-173* near Casablanca on 16 November.

Almost half the class were lost during 1943. The *U-519* failed to return from an Atlantic patrol in January. Aircraft sank the *U-164* off Pernambuco on 6 January, the *U-507* northwest of Natal on 13 January, the *U-156* east of Barbados on 8 March, the *U-524* near Madeira on 22 March, the *U-174* off Newfoundland on 27 April, the *U-514* in the Bay of Biscay on 8 July, the *U-506* west of Vigo on 12 July, the *U-513* off the Brazilian coast on 19 July, the *U-159* east of Jamaica on 28 July, the *U-161* near Bahia on 27 September, and the *U-508* in the Bay of Biscay on 12 November. Escort carrier aircraft sank the *U-160* south of the Azores, the *U-509* near Madeira, and the *U-67* in the Sargasso Sea between 14 July and 16. The sloop *Totland* sank the *U-522* off Madeira on 22 February; the destroyer *Champlin* sank the *U-130* near the Azores on 12 March; the Canadian corvette *Prescott* sank the *U-163* northwest of Cape Finisterre the next day; the cutter *Spencer* sank the *U-175* off Ireland on 17 April; the destroyer *Oribi* and the corvette *Snowflake* sank the *U-125* east of Newfoundland on 6 May; the Cuban patrol boat *CS-13* sank the *U-176* near Havana on 15 May; the destroyers *Jouett* and *Moffett* and aircraft sank the *U-128* near Pernambuco on 17 May; the *PC-565* sank the *U-521* off the Maryland coast on 2 June; the sloops *Kite*, *Wild Goose*, *Woodpecker*, and *Wren* sank the *U-504* northwest of Cape Ortegal on 30 July; the corvette *Wallflower* and the destroyer *Wanderer* sank the *U-523* west of Vigo on 25 August; the destroyers *Pathfinder*, *Quentin*, and *Vimy* sank the *U-162* near Trinidad on 3 September; the *Bogue* group sank the *U-172* off the Canary Islands on 13 December.

U.S. hunter-killer groups sank the *U-515* and the *U-68* near Madeira on 9 and 10 April 1944 and the *U-66* near the Cape Verde Islands on 6 May, and they captured the *U-505* west of Africa on 4 June. Aircraft sank the *U-126* in the Bay of Biscay on 3 July, and the destroyer escorts *Frost* and *Inch* sank the *U-154* west of Madeira the same day. The *U-129* was scuttled at Lorient on 18 August.

The destroyer escorts *Carter* and *Neal A. Scott* sank the *U-518* west of the Azores on 22 April 1945. The *U-511* was transferred to Japan on 16 September 1943 as the *RO-500*, was surrendered, and scuttled postwar. The *U-155* and the *U-516* surrendered and were scuttled postwar. The *U-510* surrendered on 12 May 1945, became the French *Bouan*, and was stricken on 1 May 1959.

## TYPE XB (1941)

*U-116* (3 May 1941), *U-117* (26 July 1941), *U-118* (23 September 1941), *U-119* (6 January 1942), *U-219* (6 October 1942), *U-220* (16 January 1943), *U-233* (8 May 1943), *U-234* (23 December 1943)

BUILDER: Germania
DISPLACEMENT: 1763 tons (surfaced), 2177 tons (submerged)
DIMENSIONS: 294'7" x 30'2" x 15'5"
MACHINERY: 2 Germania diesel engines, 2 AEG electric motors, 2 shafts. 4200 bhp/800 shp = 16.5/7 knots
RANGE: 18,450 nm at 10 knots surfaced, 93 nm at 4 knots submerged
ARMAMENT: 2 x 533mm torpedo tubes (stern), total 2 torpedoes, 66 mines, 1 x 105mm gun, 1 x 37mm AA gun, 1 x 20mm AA gun
COMPLEMENT: 52
NOTES: These very large minelayers (Germany's largest wartime boats) carried their mines in vertical tubes, twelve on each side (each containing two mines) built into the main ballast tanks and six (each containing three mines) in a large forward hull compartment. They were used extensively as supply submarines to support Atlantic operations and for blockade running.

The *U-116* failed to return from an Atlantic patrol in October 1942. Escort carrier aircraft sank the *U-118*, the *U-117*, and the *U-220* in the Atlantic on 12 June, 7 August, and 28 October 1943 respectively. The sloop *Starling* sank the *U-119* in the Bay of Biscay on 24 June 1943, and the destroyer escorts *Baker* and *Thomas* sank the *U-233* southeast of Halifax on 5 July 1944. The *U-219* became the Japanese *I-505* in May 1945 and was surrendered in August at Djakarta. The *U-234* surrendered in May 1945 and was scuttled.

## [ROMANIA]—*MARSUINUL* (4 MAY 1941)

BUILDER: Galati
DISPLACEMENT: 620 tons (surfaced); submerged displacement unknown
DIMENSIONS: 190'3" x 18'4" x 11'10"
MACHINERY: 2 MAN diesel engines, 2 electric motors, 2 shafts. 3680 bhp/1000 shp = 16/9 knots
ARMAMENT: 6 x 533mm torpedo tubes (4 bow, 2 stern), 1 x 102mm gun, 1 x 37mm AA gun
COMPLEMENT: 45

NOTES: The IvS prepared this design as an improvement of its earlier *Vetehinen* for Finland. Deschimag engineers oversaw its construction in Romania. Soviet forces seized it on 30 August 1944 and it became their *TS-2*. It was sunk by an onboard torpedo explosion at Poti on 20 February 1945, raised, repaired, and renamed the *N-40* in August 1947 and the *S-40* in June 1949. It was deleted on 28 November 1950 and scrapped.

## [ROMANIA]—*REQUINUL* (22 MAY 1941)

BUILDER: Galati
DISPLACEMENT: 585 tons (surfaced), 870 tons (submerged)
DIMENSIONS: 216'8" x 19'4" x 11'10"
MACHINERY: 2 MAN diesel engines, 2 electric motors, 2 shafts. 1840 bhp/1000 shp = 17/9 knots
ARMAMENT: 4 x 533mm torpedo tubes (bow), 40 mines, 1 x 88mm gun, 1 x 20mm AA gun
COMPLEMENT: 40

NOTES: A minelaying version of the *Marsuinul*, also by the IvS, with the mines carried in five vertical tubes on each side in the main ballast tanks. It too was seized by Soviet forces on 30 August 1944 and became their *TS-1*. It was renamed the *N-39* in August 1947 and the *S-39* in June 1949. It was returned to Romania in July 1951, reverted to its original name, and was stricken in the late 1950s.

## TYPE XIV (1941)

U-459–U-460 (13 September 1941), *U-461* (8 November 1941), *U-462* (29 November 1941), *U-463* (20 December 1941), *U-464* (20 December 1941), *U-487* (17 October 1942), *U-488* (17 October 1942), *U-489* (24 December 1942), *U-490* (24 December 1942)

BUILDER: Kiel

DISPLACEMENT: 1688 tons (surfaced), 1932 tons (submerged)

DIMENSIONS: 220′2″ x 30′10″ x 21′4″

MACHINERY: 2 Germania diesel engines, 2 Siemens electric motors, 2 shafts. 1400 bhp/375 shp = 14.5/6.25 knots

RANGE: 12,350 nm at 10 knots surfaced, 55 nm at 4 knots submerged

ARMAMENT: 2 x 37mm AA guns, 1 x 20mm AA gun

COMPLEMENT: 53

NOTES: These boats were designed as specialized supply submarines to support Atlantic operations and were known popularly as *milchkuh* (milk cow).

Allied antisubmarine forces made a successful concerted effort to destroy these boats. Aircraft sank the *U-464* and the *U-489* southeast of Iceland on 20 August 1942 and 5 August 1943, and the *U-463*, the *U-459*, and the *U-461* in the Bay of Biscay on 16 May, 24 July, and 30 July 1943. Escort carrier aircraft sank the *U-460*, the *U-487*, and the *U-490* in the Atlantic on 16 April and 13 July 1943 and 12 June 1944. The sloops *Kite*, *Wild Goose*, *Woodcock*, and *Woodpecker* sank the *U-462* in the Bay of Biscay on 30 July 1943, and the destroyer escorts *Barber*, *Frost*, *Huse*, and *Snowden* sank the *U-488* west of the Cape Verde Islands on 26 April 1944.

## TYPE VIID (1941)

U-213 (24 July 1941), *U-214* (18 September 1941), *U-215* (9 October 1941), *U-216* (23 October 1941), *U-217* (15 November 1941), *U-218* (5 December 1941)

BUILDER: Germania

DISPLACEMENT: 965 tons (surfaced), 1080 tons (submerged)

DIMENSIONS: 252′3″ x 21′0″ x 16′5″

MACHINERY: 2 Germania diesel engines, 2 AEG electric motors, 2 shafts. 3200 bhp/560 shp = 17/7.5 knots

RANGE: 11,200 nm at 10 knots surfaced, 69 nm at 4 knots submerged

ARMAMENT: 5 x 533mm torpedo tubes (4 bow, 1 stern), total 14 torpedoes, 15 mines, 1 x 88mm gun, 1 x 20mm AA gun

COMPLEMENT: 44

NOTES: These minelayers were based on the Type VIIC design with an additional compartment inserted abaft the conning tower to accommodate five vertical mine tubes.

The trawler *Le Tiger* sank the *U-215* east of Boston on 3 July 1942; the sloops *Erne*, *Rochester*, and *Sandwich* sank the *U-213* east of the Azores on 31 July, and aircraft sank the *U-216* southwest of Ireland on 20 October. Aircraft from the escort carrier *Bogue* sank the *U-217* in the central Atlantic on 5 June 1943, and the frigate *Cooke* sank the *U-214* in the English Channel on 26 July 1944. The *U-218* surrendered in May 1945 and was scuttled.

## TYPE IXD-2 (1941)

*U-177* (1 October 1941), *U-178* (28 October 1941), *U-179* (18 November 1941), *U-181* (30 December 1941), *U-182* (3 March 1942), *U-196* (24 April 1942), *U-197* (21 May 1942), *U-198* (15 June 1942), *U-199* (12 July 1943), *U-200* (20 August 1942), *U-847* (5 September 1942), *U-848* (6 October 1942), *U-849* (31 October 1942), *U-850* (7 December 1942), *U-851* (15 January 1943), *U-852* (28 January 1943), *U-859* (2 March 1943), *U-860* (23 March 1943), *U-861* (29 April 1943), *U-862* (5 June 1943), *U-863* (29 June 1943), *U-864* (12 August 1943), *U-871* (7 September 1943), *U-872* (20 October 1943), *U-873* (16 November 1943), *U-874* (21 December 1943), *U-875* (16 February 1944), *U-876* (29 February 1944), *U-883* (28 April 1944)

BUILDER: Bremen

DISPLACEMENT: 1616 tons (surfaced), 1804 tons (submerged)

DIMENSIONS: 287′5″ x 24′7″ x 17′9″

MACHINERY: 2 MAN diesel engines, 2 MWM diesel generators, 2 Siemens electric motors, 2 shafts. 4400 plus 1000 bhp/740 shp = 19.25/7 knots

RANGE: 13,450 nm at 10 knots surfaced, 63 nm at 4 knots submerged

ARMAMENT: 6 x 533mm torpedo tubes (4 bow, 2 stern), total 24 torpedoes, 1 x 105mm gun, 1 x 37mm AA gun, 1 x 20mm AA gun

COMPLEMENT: 57

NOTES: These boats used a conventional power plant to achieve a slightly higher surfaced speed than the earlier Type IXC. The *U-883* was the only example commissioned of the Type IXD/42, which had a greatly increased range of 31,000 nautical miles. Twenty-three additional Type IXD/42 boats were canceled.

Aircraft sank the *U-200* southwest of Iceland on 24 June 1943, the *U-199* east of Rio de Janeiro on 31 July, the *U-197* near Madagascar on 20 August, the *U-849* west of the Congo river on 25 November, the *U-848* and the *U-177* off Acension Island on 5 November 1943 and 6 February 1944, the *U-871* northwest of the Azores on 26 September and the *U-863* near Recife three days later, and drove the *U-852* ashore on the Somali coast on 3 May. Escort carrier aircraft sank the *U-847* in the Sargasso Sea on 27 August 1943, the *U-850* west of Madeira on 20 December, and the *U-860* off St. Helena on 15 June 1944. The destroyer *Active* sank the *U-179* near Capetown on 8 October 1942; the destroyer *Mackenzie* sank the *U-182* near Madeira on 16 May 1943; the frigate *Findhorn* and the Indian sloop *Godavari* sank the *U-198* near the Seychelles on 12 August 1944; the submarine *Trenchant* torpedoed the *U-859* in the Malacca Straits on 23 September; the submarine *Venturer* torpedoed the *U-864* while both were submerged off Bergen on 9 February 1945. The *U-851* and the *U-196* failed to return from patrols to the Indian Ocean in April and November 1944.

The *U-872* was stricken after USAAF bombers badly damaged it at Bremen on 29 July 1944, and the *U-178* was scuttled at Bordeaux on 25 August. The *U-181* and the *U-862* became the Japanese *I-501* and *I-502* in May 1945 and were surrendered at Singapore in August. The surviving boats were surrendered at war's end.

## TYPE IXD-1 (1941)

*U-180* (10 December 1941), *U-195* (8 April 1942)

BUILDER: Bremen

DISPLACEMENT: 1610 tons (surfaced), 1799 tons (submerged)

DIMENSIONS: 287'5" x 24'7" x 17'9"

MACHINERY: 6 Daimler-Benz diesel engines, 2 Siemens electric motors, 2 shafts. 9000 bhp/740 shp = 20.75/7 knots

RANGE: 9500 nm at 14 knots surfaced, 115 nm at 4 knots submerged

ARMAMENT: 6 x 533mm torpedo tubes (4 bow, 2 stern), total 24 torpedoes, 1 x 105mm gun, 1 x 37mm AA gun, 1 x 20mm AA gun

COMPLEMENT: 57

NOTES: These boats were designed as faster versions of the Type IXC and used six S-boat engines. They were converted to transport submarines to carry 250 tons of freight in 1943 with two replacement Germania diesel engines generating 1400 bhp (top speed: 15.75 knots) and all torpedo tubes removed. The *U-180* was lost in the Bay of Biscay in August 1944. The *U-195* became the Japanese *I-506* in May 1945 and was surrendered in August at Djarkarta.

## TYPE IXC/40 (1942)

*U-183* (9 January 1942), *U-184* (21 February 1942), *U-185* (2 March 1942), *U-186* (11 March 1942), *U-187* (16 March 1942), *U-188* (31 March 1942), *U-189* (1 May 1942), *U-190* (8 June 1942), *U-191* (3 July 1942), *U-192* (31 July 1942), *U-193* (24 August 1942), *U-194* (22 September 1942), *U-841* (21 October 1942), *U-842* (14 November 1942), *U-843* (15 December 1942), *U-844* (30 December 1942), *U-845* (22 January 1943), *U-846* (17 February 1943), *U-853* (11 March 1943), *U-854* (5 April 1943), *U-855* (17 April 1943), *U-856* (11 May 1943), *U-857* (23 May 1943), *U-858* (17 June 1943), *U-865* (11 July 1943), *U-866* (29 July 1943), *U-867* (24 August 1943), *U-868* (18 September 1943), *U-869* (5 October 1943), *U-870* (29 October 1943), *U-877* (10 December 1943), *U-878* (6 January 1944), *U-879* (11 January 1944), *U-880* (10 February 1944), *U-881* (4 March 1944), *U-889* (5 April 1944)

BUILDER: Bremen

*U-167–U-168* (5 March 1942), *U-169–U-170* (6 June 1942), *U-801–U-802* (31 October 1942), *U-803–U-804* (1 April 1943), *U-805* (1943), *U-806* (1943)

BUILDER: Seebeckwerft

*U-526–U-527* (3 June 1942), *U-528* (1 July 1942), *U-529* (15 July 1942), *U-530* (28 July 1942), *U-531* (12 August 1942), *U-532* (26 August 1942), *U-533* (11 September 1942), *U-534* (23 September 1942), *U-535* (8 October 1942), *U-536* (21 October 1942), *U-537* (7 November 1942), *U-538* (20 November 1942), *U-539* (4 December 1942), *U-540* (18 December 1942), *U-541* (5 January 1943), *U-542* (19 January 1943), *U-543* (3 February 1943), *U-544* (17 February 1943), *U-545* (3 March 1943), *U-546* (17 March 1943), *U-547* (3 April 1943), *U-548* (14 April 1943), *U-549* (28 April 1943), *U-1221* (2 May 1943), *U-550* (12 May 1943), *U-1222* (9 June 1943), *U-1223* (16 June 1943), *U-1224* (7 July 1943), *U-1225* (21 July 1943),

*U-1226* (21 August 1943), *U-1227* (18 September 1943), *U-1228* (2 October 1943), *U-1229* (22 October 1943), *U-1230* (8 November 1943), *U-1231* (18 November 1943), *U-1232* (20 December 1943), *U-1233* (23 December 1943), *U-1234* (7 January 1944), *U-1235* (25 January 1944)

BUILDER: Deutschewerft

DISPLACEMENT: 1144 tons (surfaced), 1257 tons (submerged)

DIMENSIONS: 252′0″ x 22′8″ x 15′5″

MACHINERY: 2 MAN diesel engines, 2 Siemens electric motors, 2 shafts. 4400 bhp/740 shp = 18.25/7.25 knots

RANGE: 13,850 nm at 10 knots surfaced, 63 nm at 4 knots submerged

ARMAMENT: 6 x 533mm torpedo tubes (4 bow, 2 stern), total 22 torpedoes, 1 x 105mm gun, 1 x 37mm AA gun, 1 x 20mm AA gun

COMPLEMENT: 48

NOTES: These boats were similar to the earlier Type IXC, with heavier antiaircraft batteries and slightly greater range. An additional 59 units were either destroyed on the slip or canceled.

The *U-183* failed to return from an Atlantic patrol in November 1942, as did the *U-529* in February 1943, the *U-193* in April 1944, the *U-866* and the *U-865* in September 1944, the *U-1226* in October 1944, and the *U-857* in April 1945,

The *U-526* was mined off Lorient on 14 April 1943, as were the *U-854* and the *U-803* in the Baltic on 4 February and 27 April 1944.

Aircraft sank the *U-169*, the *U-194*, and the *U-844* south of Iceland on 27 March, 14 June, and 16 October 1943, the *U-167* near the Canary Islands on 6 April, the *U-189* and the *U-540* off Greenland on 23 April and 17 October, the *U-585* in the Bay of Biscay on 5 July, the *U-533* in the Gulf of Oman on 16

October, and the *U-542* off Madeira on 28 November. Escort carrier aircraft sank the *U-527*, the *U-628*, and the *U-185* west of the Azores on 23 July, 11 August, and 24 August. The destroyers *Beverley* and *Vimy* sank the *U-187* in the North Atlantic on 4 February; the destroyer *Hesperus* sank the *U-191* off Greenland and the *U-186* west of the Azores on 23 April and 12 May; the corvette *Loosestrife* sank the *U-192* off Greenland on 6 May; the destroyer *Vidette* sank the *U-531* off Newfoundland the same day; the sloop *Fleetwood* and aircraft sank the *U-528* southwest of Ireland on 11 May; the frigate *Byard* sank the *U-841* off Greenland on 17 October; the sloops *Starling* and *Wild Goose* sank the *U-842* in the western North Atlantic on 6 November; the frigate *Nene* and the Canadian corvettes *Calgary* and *Snowberry* sank the *U-536* off the Azores on 20 November; the sloop *Crane* and the frigate *Foley* sank the *U-538* southwest of Ireland the next day.

Aircraft sank the *U-545* off the Hebrides on 10 February 1944, the *U-846* and the *U-1222* in the Bay of Biscay on 4 May and 11 July, and the *U-1225* and the *U-867* off Bergen on 24 June and 19 September. Escort carrier aircraft sank the *U-544*, the *U-543*, and the *U-1229* in the central Atlantic on 16 January, 2 July, and 20 August, and the *Block Island* group sank the *U-801* there on 17 March. British and Canadian antisubmarine vessels sank the *U-845* in the North Atlantic on 10 March; the destroyer *Champlin* and the destroyer escort *Huse* sank the *U-856*; the destroyer escorts *Gandy*, *Joyce*, and *Peterson* sank the *U-550* off New York on 7 and 16 April; the destroyer escorts *Ahrens* and *Eugene E. Elmore* sank the *U-559* off Madeira on 29 May; the Dutch submarine

Zwaardvisch and the U.S. submarine Flounder sank the U-168 and the U-537 in the Java Sea on 6 October and 9 November; the Canadian corvette St. Thomas sank the U-877 northwest of the Azores on 27 December.

Aircraft sank the U-843 and the U-534 in the Kattegat on 9 April and 5 May 1945. USAAF aircraft bombed the U-870 and the U-1221 in Bremen and Kiel on 30 March and 3 April. Hunter-killer groups in the North Atlantic sank the U-866 on 18 March, the U-1235 on 15 April, the U-880 on 16 April, the U-546 and the U-548 on 24 April, and the U-879 on 30 April. The destroyer escorts Howard D. Crow and Koiner sank the U-869 off New Jersey on 11 February; the corvette Tintagel Castle and the destroyer Vanquisher sank the U-878 in the Bay of Biscay on 10 April; the submarine Besugo torpedoed the U-183 in the Java Sea on 23 April; the destroyer escort Farquhar sank the U-881 off Newfoundland on 6 May; and the destroyer escort Atherton and the frigate Moberly sank the U-853 off New London the same day.

The U-1224 became the Japanese RO-501 in February 1944 and was sunk by the destroyer escort Francis M. Robinson off the Cape Verde Islands on 13 May 1944.

The surviving boats were surrendered or scuttled in May 1945, apart from the U-1231, which became the Soviet B-26 in 1947 and was stricken in 1960.

## [SWEDEN]—*NEPTUN* CLASS (1942)

Najad (26 June 1942), Näcken (26 June 1942), Neptun (17 November 1942)

BUILDER: Kockums

DISPLACEMENT: 530 tons (surfaced), 730 tons (submerged)

DIMENSIONS: 205'5" x 21'0" x 11'2"

MACHINERY: 2 MAN diesel engines, 2 electric motors, 2 shafts. 1800 bhp/1000 shp = 15/10 knots

ARMAMENT: 5 x 533mm torpedo tubes (3 bow, 2 stern), total 10 torpedoes, 20 mines, 1 x 40mm AA gun, 1 x 20mm AA gun

COMPLEMENT: 35

NOTES: This class virtually repeated the earlier Delfinen type but incorporated an additional stern torpedo tube. They were reconstructed in the early 1950s with streamlined sails, snorkels, and no deck guns. These boats were stricken on 1 April 1966.

## GERMANY: TYPE VIIC 41 (1943)

*U-1163* (12 June 1943), *U-1164* (3 July 1943), *U-1165* (20 July 1943), *U-1166–U-1167* (28 August 1943), *U-1168–U-1169* (2 October 1943), *U-1170* (14 October 1943), *U-1171* (23 November 1943), *U-1172* (3 December 1943)

BUILDER: Danziger

*U-292* (17 July 1943), *U-293* (30 July 1943), *U-294* (27 August 1943), *U-295* (13 September 1943), *U-296* (25 September 1943), *U-297* (9 October 1943), *U-298* (25 October 1943), *U-299* (6 November 1943), *U-300* (23 November 1943), *U-1271* (8 December 1943), *U-1272* (23 December 1943), *U-1273* (10 January 9144), *U-1274* (25 January 1944), *U-1275* (8 February 1944), *U-1276* (25 February 1944), *U-1277* (18 March 1944), *U-1278* (15 April 1944), *U-1279* (May 1944)

BUILDER: Vegesack

*U-995–U-996* (22 July 1943), *U-997–U-998* (18 August 1943), *U-999–U-1000* (17 September 1943), *U-1001–U-1002* (6 October 1943), *U-1003–U-1004* (27 October 1943), *U-1005–U-1006* (17 November 1943), *U-1007–U-1008* (8 December 1943), *U-1009–U-1010* (5 January 1944), *U-1013* (19 January 1944), *U-1014* (30 January 1944), *U-1015* (7 February 1944), *U-1016* (8 February 1944), *U-1017–U-1018* (1 March 1944), *U-1019* (22 March 1944), *U-1020* (22 March 1944), *U-1021–U-1022* (12 April 1944), *U-1023–U-1024* (3 May 1944), *U-1025* (24 May 1944)

BUILDER: Blohm und Voss

*U-929* (23 July 1944), *U-930* (5 October 1944)

BUILDER: Neptun

*U-318* (25 September 1943), *U-319* (16 October 1943), *U-320* (6 November 1943), *U-321* (17 November 1943), *U-322* (18 December 1943), *U-323* (8 January 1944), *U-324* (12 February 1944), *U-325* (25 March 1944), *U-326* (22 April 1944), *U-327* (27 May 1944), *U-328* (15 July 1944)

BUILDER: Flenderwerke

*U-1301* (22 December 1943), *U-1303* (10 February 1944), *U-1302* (4 April 1944), *U-1305* (10 July 1944), *U-1304* (4 August 1944), *U-1307* (29 September 1944), *U-1306* (25 October 1944), *U-1308* (22 November 1944)

BUILDER: Flensburger

*U-1063* (8 June 1944), *U-1064* (22 June 1944), *U-1065* (3 August 1944)

BUILDER: Germania

DISPLACEMENT: 747 tons (surfaced), 847 tons (submerged)

DIMENSIONS: 220'6" x 20'4" x 15'9"

MACHINERY: 2 MAN diesel engines, 2 AEG electric motors, 2 shafts. 3200 bhp/560 shp = 17/7.5 knots

RANGE: 8500 nm at 10 knots surfaced, 80 nm at 4 knots submerged

ARMAMENT: 5 x 533mm torpedo tubes (4 bow, 1 stern), total 14 torpedoes, 1 x 88mm gun, 1 x 20mm AA gun

COMPLEMENT: 44

NOTES: This final production development of the basic Type VII design featured a stronger hull that permitted an increase in the diving depth to over 500 feet. Many boats also commissioned with heavier antiaircraft batteries, usually a single 37mm gun and four 20mm weapons.

This group also suffered heavy casualties. Nine boats were sunk during 1944, two (the *U-1013* and the *U-1015*) in accidents, and a further 23 in 1945. Sixteen boats were scuttled to prevent their seizure by Allied forces at the end of the war, and 31 boats were surrendered. One, the *U-995*, became a museum vessel postwar.

## TYPE VIIF (1943)

*U-1059* (12 March 1943), *U-1060* (18 April 1943), *U-1061* (22 April 1943), *U-1062* (8 May 1943)

BUILDER: Germania

DISPLACEMENT: 1094 tons (surfaced), 1181 tons (submerged)

DIMENSIONS: 254′7″ x 23′11″ x 16′0″

MACHINERY: 2 Germania diesel engines, 2 AEG electric motors, 2 shafts. 3200 bhp/560 shp = 17/7.5 knots

RANGE: 14,700 nm at 10 knots surfaced, 75 nm at 4 knots submerged

ARMAMENT: 5 x 533mm torpedo tubes (4 bow, 1 stern), total 39 torpedoes, 1 x 37mm AA gun, 2 x twin 20mm AA gun

COMPLEMENT: 46

NOTES: These boats were lengthened versions of the Type VIIC. They were designed to supply torpedoes to Atlantic boats and carried 24 torpedoes in the additional compartment, 10 in the torpedo rooms (five in the tubes and five reloads) and five more in pressure-tight compartments on top of the pressure hull.

Aircraft from the escort carrier *Block Island* sank the *U-1059* southwest of the Cape Verde Islands on 19 March 1944; the destroyer escort *Fessenden* sank the *U-1062* in the central Atlantic on 30 September; aircraft from the carrier *Implacable* drove the *U-1060* ashore at Bronnoysund on 27 October. The *U-1061* was surrendered in May 1945.

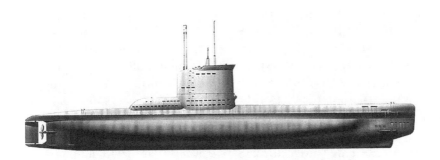

**GERMANY: TYPE XXIII (1944), *U-2326* (1944)**
*(Courtesy of Art-Tech)*

*U-2321* (17 April 1944), *U-2322* (30 April 1944), *U-2323* (31 May 1944), *U-2324* (16 June 1944), *U-2325* (13 July 1944), *U-2326* (17 July 1944), *U-2327* (29 July 1944), *U-2329* (11 August 1944), *U-2328* (17 August 1944), *U-2330* (19 August 1944), *U-2331* (22 August 1944), *U-2334* (26 August 1944), *U-2335* (31 August 1944), *U-2336* (10 September 1944), *U-2337* (15 September 1944), *U-2338* (18 September 1944), *U-2339* (22 September 1944), *U-2340* (28 September 1944), *U-2341* (3 October 1944), *U-2342* (13 October 1944), *U-2343* (18 October 1944), *U-2344* (24 October 1944), *U-2345* (28 October 1944), *U-2346* (31 October 1944), *U-2347* (6 November 1944), *U-2348* (11 November

1944), *U-2349* (20 November 1944), *U-2350* (22 November 1944), *U-2351* (25 November 1944), *U-2352* (5 December 1944), *U-2353* (6 December 1944), *U-2354* (10 December 1944), *U-2355* (13 December 1944), *U-2356–U-2357* (19 December 1944), *U-2358* (20 December 1944), *U-2359* (23 December 1944), *U-2360* (29 December 1944), *U-2361* (4 January 1945), *U-2362* (11 January 1945), *U-2363* (18 January 1945), *U-2364* (23 January 1945), *U-2365* (26 January 1945), *U-2366* (17 February 1945), *U-2367* (23 February 1945), *U-2368* (19 March 1945), *U-2369* (24 March 1945), *U-2370* (March 1945), *U-2371* (18 April 1945)

BUILDER: Deutschewerft

*U-2332* (18 October 1944), *U-2333* (16 November 1944), *U-4701* (14 December 1944), *U-4702* (20 December 1944), *U-4703* (3 January 1945), *U-4705* (11 January 1945), *U-4706* (19 January 1945), *U-4707* (25 January 1945), *U-4709* (8 February 1945), *U-4704* (13 February 1945), *U-4711* (21 February 1945), *U-4712* (1 March 1945), *U-4710* (14 April 1945), *U-4713* (19 April 1945), *U-4714* (26 April 1945)

BUILDER: Germania

DISPLACEMENT: 234 tons (surfaced), 258 tons (submerged)

DIMENSIONS: 113'10" x 9'10" x 12'2"

MACHINERY: 1 MWM diesel engine, 1 AEG electric motor, 1 BBC "creep" electric motor, 1 shaft. 575 bhp/575 plus 35 shp = 9.75/12.5/4 knots

RANGE: 2600 nm at 8 knots surfaced, 63 nm at 4 knots submerged

ARMAMENT: 2 x 533mm torpedo tubes (bow), total 2 torpedoes

COMPLEMENT: 14

NOTES: The Type XXIII boats were the coastal equivalents of the new Type XXI oceanic submarines. Like them, they brought together a hull designed for high underwater speed with more powerful batteries, powerful electric motors, and snorkels to maximize their operations while submerged. In addition to their main motors, these boats also used a low-power motor for silent, slow-speed operation. Their small size, however, was a major disadvantage, since they were very crowded internally and had no space for reload torpedoes, which limited their suitability for operations. A total of 491 units of this type were ordered, of which 61 were completed and commissioned, but only 6 undertook operations.

The *U-2323* and the *U-2341* were mined in the Baltic on 26 July and 26 December 1944. British aircraft sank the *U-2338* north of Frederika on 4 May 1945. The *U-2331*, the *U-2344*, and the *U-2367* were lost in accidents.

Almost all of the other boats were either scuttled or surrendered in May 1945. The *U-2353* became the Soviet *N-31* in 1948 and was scrapped in 1963, and the *U-4706* became the Norwegian *Knerter* in 1948 and was stricken in 1954. The Federal German Navy salved the *U-2365* and the *U-2367* in 1956, reconstructed them with 600-horsepower diesel-electric machinery and new superstructures, and commissioned them as the *Hai* and the *Hecht*. They were scrapped in 1968–1969.

## GERMANY: TYPE XXI (1944)
*(Courtesy of Art-Tech)*

*U-3501* (19 April 1944), *U-3502* (6 July 1944), *U-3503* (27 July 1944), *U-3504* (19 August 1944), *U-3505–U-3506* (25 August 1944), *U-3507* (16 September 1944), *U-3508* (22 September 1944), U-3509 (27 September 1944), U-3510 (4 October 1944), U-3511–U-3512 (11 October 1944), *U-3513–U-3514* (21 October 1944), *U-3515–U-3516* (4 November 1944), *U-3517* (6 November 1944), *U-3518* (11 November 1944), *U-3519–U-3520* (23 November 1944), *U-3521–U-3522* (3 December 1944), *U-3523–U-3524* (14 December 1944), *U-3525–U-3526* (23 December 1944), *U-3527–U-3528* (10 January 1945), *U-3529–U-3530* (26 January 1945)

BUILDER: Schichau

*U-2501* (12 May 1944), *U-2502* (15 June 1944), *U-2503* (29 June 1944), *U-2504* (18 July 1944), *U-2505* (27 July 1944), *U-2506* (5 August 1944), *U-2507* (14 August 1944), *U-2508* (19 August 1944), *U-2509* (27 August 1944), *U-2510* (29 August 1944), *U-2511* (2 September 1944), *U-2512* (7 September 1944), *U-2513* (14 September 1944), *U-2514* (17 September 1944), *U-2515* (22 September 1944), *U-2516* (27 September 1944), *U-2517–U-2518* (4 October 1944), *U-2520* (16 October 1944), *U-2519* (18 October 1944), *U-2521* (18 October 1944), *U-2522* (22 October 1944), *U-2523* (25 October 1944), *U-2524* (30 October 1944), *U-2525* (30 October 1944), *U-2528–U-2529* (18 November 1944), *U-2530* (23 November 1944), *U-2526–U-2527* (30 November 1944), *U-2531* (5 December 1944), *U-2532–U-2533* (7 December 1944), *U-2534* (11 December 1944), *U-2535–U-2536* (16 December 1944), *U-2537* (22 December 1944), *U-2538–U-2539* (6 January 1945), *U-2540–U-2541* (13 January 1945), *U-2542* (22 January 1945), *U-2543–U-2544* (Februrary 1945), *U-2545* (12 February 1945), *U-2546* (19 February 1945), *U-2548* (9 March 1945), *U-2551–U-2552* (31 March 1945)

BUILDER: Blohm und Voss

*U-3001* (30 May 1944), *U-3002* (9 July 1944), *U-3003* (18 July 1944), *U-3004* (26 July 1944), *U-3005* (18 August 1944), *U-3006* (25 August 1944), *U-3007* (4 September 1944), *U-3008* (15 September 1944), *U-3009* (30 September 1944), *U-3013* (19 October 1944), *U-3010–U-3012* (20 October 1944), *U-3014* (25 October 1944), *U-3015* (27 October 1944), *U-3016* (2 November 1944), *U-3017* (5 November 1944), *U-3019* (15 November 1944), *U-3020* (16 November 1944), *U-3021* (27 November 1944), *U-3018* (29 November 1944),

U-3022 (30 November 1944), U-3023 (2 December 1944), U-3024–U-3025 (6 December 1944), U-3026 (14 December 1944), U-3027 (18 December 1944), U-3028 (22 December 1944), U-3029 (28 December 1944), U-3030 (31 December 1944), U-3031 (6 January 1945), U-3032 (10 January 1945), U-3033 (20 January 1945), U-3034 (21 January 1945), U-3035 (24 January 1945), U-3036 (27 January 1945), U-3037 (31 January 1945), U-3038 (7 February 1945), U-3040 (10 February 1945), U-3039 (14 February 1945), U-3041 (23 February 1945), U-3044 (1 March 1945)

BUILDER: Bremen

DISPLACEMENT: 1595 tons (surfaced), 1790 tons (submerged)

DIMENSIONS: 251'8" x 21'8" x 20'8"

MACHINERY: 2 MAN diesel engines, 2 Siemens electric motors, 2 Siemens "creep" electric motors, 2 shafts. 4000 bhp/5500 plus 220 shp = 15.5/17.25/5 knots

RANGE: 15,500 nm at 10 knots surfaced, 30 nm at 15 knots/340 nm at 5 knots submerged

ARMAMENT: 6 x 533mm torpedo tubes (bow), total 23 torpedoes, 2 x twin 20mm AA guns

COMPLEMENT: 57

NOTES: The Type XXI boats were the most influential submarine type of World War II on postwar submarine development. The design brought together a hull optimized for high underwater speed with more powerful batteries, powerful electric motors, and snorkels to maximize their operations while submerged. In addition to their main motors, these boats also used low-power motors for silent, slow-speed operation. They had good torpedo batteries, antiaircraft mounts faired into the sail, and advanced radar and sensor suites that retracted into the sail for streamlining. Orders were placed for 739 boats, but only 118 were completed and commissioned; the U-2511 alone undertook an operational mission.

The U-3520 and the U-3519 were mined in the Baltic on 31 January and 2 March 1945. British aircraft sank or wrecked the U-2503, the U-2521, the U-2524, and the U-3032 in Flensburg Fjord on 3 May, and another sank the U-3523 in the Skagerrak on 6 May. Allied bombing raids sank 12 of the type in port during 1945 before they became operational for front-line duties.

Almost all the other boats were scuttled or surrendered in May 1945. The U-3008 went to the United States for trials and experiments and was sunk as a target in May 1954. The U-2529, the U-3035, the U-3041, and the U-3515 became the Soviet B-27 through the B-30 and were broken up in 1958. Components of at least 11 other boats were seized by the Soviets, but it is not certain that they were completed and put into service.

The U-2540 was salved by the Federal German Navy in 1957, reconstructed with new 1200-horsepower diesel-electric machinery and revised superstructure, and commissioned in 1960 as the Wilhelm Bauer. It was decommissioned on 15 March 1983 and transferred to the Deutsches Schiffahrtsmuseum in Bremerhaven as an exhibit.

## [SPAIN]—D CLASS (1944)

*D.1* (11 May 1944), *D.2* (21 December 1944), *D.3* (20 February 1952)

BUILDER: Cartagena

DISPLACEMENT: 1065 tons (surfaced), 1480 tons (submerged)

DIMENSIONS: 275'6" x 21'9" x 13'2"

MACHINERY: 2 Sulzer diesel engines, 2 electric motors, 2 shafts. 5000 bhp/1350 shp = 20.5/9.5 knots

RANGE: 9000 nm at 10 knots surfaced, 80 nm at 4 knots submerged

ARMAMENT: 6 x 533mm torpedo tubes (bow), 1 x 120mm gun, 4 x 37mm AA gun

COMPLEMENT: 60

NOTES: The IvS designed these boats as faster versions of its earlier *E-1* type with more powerful diesel engines and lengthened machinery spaces. They were ordered in 1933, but the Spanish Civil War halted work; their construction time consequently was very protracted. They were stricken between 1969 and 1971.

**NOTE:** *U-792–U-795* and *U-1405–U-1407* were experimental boats. *U-112 - U-115, U-329, U-330, U-395, U-491 - U-500, U-684–U-700, U-723–U-730, U-769, U-770, U-780–U-791, U-796–U-800, U-823, U-824, U-829–U-840, U-882, U-884–U-888, U-890–U-900, U-902, U-908–U-920, U-931–U-950, U-1011, U-1012, U-1026–U-1050, U-1066–U-1100, U-1111–U-1130, U-1133–U-1160, U-1173–U-1190, U-1211–U-1220, U-1236–U-1270, U-1280–U-1300, U-1309–1404, U-1408–U-2320, U-2372–U-2500, U-2547, U-2549, U-2550, U-2553–U-3000, U-3042, U-3043, U-3045–U-3500, U-3530–U-4700, U-4708, U-4713,* and *U-4714* were cancelled, or destroyed on the slip by enemy action before launching.

# ITALY
## *MAMELI* CLASS (1926)

*Goffredo Mameli* (9 December 1926), *Pier Capponi* (19 June 1927), *Giovanni da Procida* (1 April 1929), *Tito Speri* (25 May 1928)

BUILDER: Tosi

DISPLACEMENT: 810 tons (surfaced), 993 tons (submerged)

DIMENSIONS: 211'11" x 21'4" x 14'1"

MACHINERY: 2 Tosi diesel engines, 2 CGE electric motors, 2 shafts. 3000 bhp/1100 shp = 15/7.5 knots

RANGE: 3500 nm at 8 knots surfaced, 65 nm at 4 knots submerged

ARMAMENT: 6 x 533mm torpedo tubes (4 bow, 2 stern), total 10 torpedoes, 1 x 102mm gun, 2 x 13.2mm machine guns

COMPLEMENT: 49

NOTES: Cavallini designed these seagoing submarines after examining German designs and U-boats in detail. They featured a single hull with saddle main ballast tanks, a fine entrance for high surface speed, and a substantial conning tower. They were strongly built, handled and dived well, but initially suffered from some instability problems. The submarine *Rorqual* torpedoed the *Pier Capponi* off Stromboli on 31 March 1941. The three other boats received new 4000-bhp Tosi diesel engines in 1942, raising their surface speed to 17 knots. They were discarded on 1 February 1948.

## ITALY: *BALILLA* CLASS (1927), *ANTONIO SCIESA* (1928)
*(Courtesy of Art-Tech)*

*Balilla* (20 February 1927), *Domenico Millelire* (19 September 1927), *Enrico Toti* (14 April 1928), *Antonio Sciesa* (12 August 1928), [Brazil]—*Humaita* (11 June 1927)

BUILDER: Muggiano

DISPLACEMENT: 1427 tons (surfaced), 1874 tons (submerged)

DIMENSIONS: 283'9" (*Humaita*: 285'5") x 25'7" x 15'5"

MACHINERY: 2 Fiat (*Humaita*: Ansaldo) diesel engines, 2 Savigliano electric motors, 2 shafts. 4900 bhp/2200 shp = 16/7 knots

RANGE: 13,000 nm at 7 knots surfaced, 80 nm at 4 knots submerged

ARMAMENT: 6 x 533mm torpedo tubes (4 bow, 2 stern), total 16 torpedoes, 1 x 120mm gun, 2 x 13.2mm machine guns (not on *Humaita*)

COMPLEMENT: 77 (*Humaita*: 61)

NOTES: These double-hull cruiser submarines were designed for long-range operations in the Red Sea and Indian Ocean and for colonial service. Their design owed much to the German UE Type II minelayer U-120 that was in Italian hands after World War I. An unusual feature was the auxiliary 425-bhp Fiat diesel engine for cruising. They handled and dived well but suffered from some stability problems. During World War II they initially undertook offensive patrols but were too large for Mediterranean service and transferred to supply runs to North Africa. U.S. aircraft sank the *Antonio Sciesa* off Tobruk on 12 November 1942. The *Balilla* and the *Domenico Millelire* were laid up in April 1941, and the *Enrico Toti* was laid up two years later.

The Brazilian *Humaita* was discarded in 1951.

## *PISANI* CLASS (1927)

*Vettor Pisani* (24 November 1927), *Marcantonio Colonna* (26 December 1927), *Giovani Bausan* (24 March 1928), *Des Geneys* (14 November 1928), [Turkey]—*Dumlupinar* (4 March 1931)
BUILDER: CDT
DISPLACEMENT: 866 tons (surfaced), 1040 tons (submerged)
DIMENSIONS: 223'9" x 20'0" x 16'2"
MACHINERY: 2 Tosi (*Dumlupinar*: MAN) diesel engines, 2 CGE electric motors, 2 shafts. 3000 bhp/1100 (*Dumlupinar*: 1400) shp = 15/8.25 knots (*Dumlupinar*: 17.5/9 knots)
RANGE: 5000 nm at 8 knots surfaced, 108 nm at 4 knots submerged
ARMAMENT: 6 x 533mm torpedo tubes (4 bow, 2 stern), total 10 torpedoes, 1 x 102mm gun, 2 x 13.2mm machine guns (*Dumlupinar*: 1 machine gun)
COMPLEMENT: 48
NOTES: Bernardis was responsible for the design of these seagoing submarines to the same specification as the *Mameli* class. They were a single-hull type, with saddle main ballast tanks, and performed similarly, though their oil bunkerage was greater and endowed them with increased range. Their slow speed reduced their operational utility, and all but the *Vettor Pisani* (which remained in service and was scrapped in 1947) were laid up in April 1942.

Bernardis corrected the stability problems of the type in the design for the Turkish *Dumlupinar*. It remained in service until the early 1950s.

## *ETTORE FIERAMOSCA* (15 APRIL 1929)

BUILDER: Tosi
DISPLACEMENT: 1530 tons (surfaced), 2094 tons (submerged)
DIMENSIONS: 275'6" x 27'3" x 16'9"
MACHINERY: 2 Tosi diesel engines, 2 Marelli electric motors, 2 shafts. 5200 bhp/2300 shp = 15/8 knots
RANGE: 5000 nm at 9 knots surfaced, 80 nm at 4 knots submerged
ARMAMENT: 8 x 533mm torpedo tubes (4 bow, 4 stern), total 14 torpedoes, 1 x 120mm gun, 2 x twin 13.2mm machine guns
COMPLEMENT: 78
NOTES: Bernardis designed this cruiser submarine to meet the same requirements as the *Balilla* class. It was a single-hull type with saddle main ballast tanks. As delivered it featured a very long conning tower that carried the shielded 120mm gun on a platform forward and incorporated a seaplane hangar at its after end. The seaplane never materialized, and the boat's conning tower was rebuilt in 1931 without the hangar and with an unshielded gun. This submarine's speed was lower than designed, and it was slow to dive. It undertook offensive patrols at the start of World War II but suffered a battery explosion in October 1940, was laid up the following March, and scrapped in 1946.

## *BRAGADIN* CLASS (1929)

*Marcantonio Bragadin* (21 July 1929), *Filippo Corridoni* (30 March 1930)

BUILDER: Tosi

DISPLACEMENT: 965 tons (surfaced), 1068 tons (submerged)

DIMENSIONS: 235'7" x 20'2" x 16'4"

MACHINERY: 2 Tosi diesel engines, 2 Marelli electric motors, 2 shafts. 1500 bhp/1000 shp = 11.5/7 knots

RANGE: 9000 nm at 8 knots surfaced, 72 nm at 4 knots submerged

ARMAMENT: 4 x 533mm torpedo tubes (bow), total 6 torpedoes, 24 mines, 1 x 102mm gun, 2 x twin 13.2mm machine guns

COMPLEMENT: 55

NOTES: This was a Bernardis design for a single-hull submarine minelayer with saddle main ballast tanks. As delivered, their performance was not entirely satisfactory, and they received higher bows and had their sterns rebuilt with the mine tubes discharging at the extreme aft end of the hull. They operated primarily on supply runs to North Africa during World War II, were surrendered to the Allies in 1943, and were stricken on 1 February 1948.

**ITALY: *BANDIERA* CLASS, *LUCIANO MANARA* (1929)**
(*Courtesy of Art-Tech*)

*Fratelli Bandiera* (7 August 1929), *Luciano Manara* (5 October 1929)
BUILDER: CDT
*Santorre Santarosa* (22 October 1929), *Ciro Menotti* (29 December 1929)
BUILDER: Muggiano
DISPLACEMENT: 925 tons (surfaced), 1080 tons (submerged)
DIMENSIONS: 212'9" x 22'3" x 16'0"
MACHINERY: 2 Tosi (Muggiano boats: Fiat) diesel engines, 2 Savigliano electric motors, 2 shafts. 3000 bhp/1300 shp = 15/8 knots
RANGE: 4750 nm at 8.5 knots surfaced, 60 nm at 4 knots submerged
ARMAMENT: 8 x 533mm torpedo tubes (4 bow, 4 stern), total 12 torpedoes, 1 x 102mm gun, 2 x 13.2mm machine guns

COMPLEMENT: 53
NOTES: This Bernardis design was closely related to his contemporary minelayer type and was essentially an enlarged version of the *Pisani* class. They undertook offensive patrols during World War II until the end of 1941, when they switched to supply runs to North Africa. The *Santorre Santarosa* continued on these duties until it ran aground near Tripoli on 19 January 1943 and was scuttled the following day. The other boats became training units from September 1943 and were stricken on 1 February 1948.

## *SQUALO* CLASS (1930)

*Squalo* (15 January 1930), *Narvalo* (15 March 1930), *Delfino* (27 April 1930), *Tricheco* (11 September 1930)
BUILDER: Monfalcone
DISPLACEMENT: 920 tons (surfaced), 1125 tons (submerged)
DIMENSIONS: 212'9" x 22'0" x 15'10"
MACHINERY: 2 Fiat diesel engines, 2 CRDA electric motors, 2 shafts. 3000 bhp/1300 shp = 15/8 knots
RANGE: 4750 nm at 8.5 knots surfaced, 60 nm at 4 knots submerged
ARMAMENT: 8 x 533mm torpedo tubes (4 bow, 4 stern), total 12 torpedoes, 1 x 102mm gun, 2 x 13.2mm machine guns
COMPLEMENT: 55
NOTES: These boats were almost exact repeats of the earlier *Bandiera* class. The *Delfino* and the *Squalo* received a smaller conning tower in late 1942 to reduce their silhouette on the surface. The submarine *Upholder* torpedoed the *Tricheco* off Brindisi on 18 March 1942; the destroyers *Hursley* and *Pakenham* sank the *Narvalo* near Tripoli on 14 January 1943; and the *Delfino* was lost in a training accident at Taranto on 23 March 1943. The *Squalo* was stricken on 1 February 1948.

## [ROMANIA]—*DELFINUL* (22 JUNE 1930)

BUILDER: Fiume
DISPLACEMENT: 650 tons (surfaced), 900 tons (submerged)
DIMENSIONS: 223'1" x 19'4" x 11'10"
MACHINERY: 2 Sulzer diesel engines, 2 electric motors, 2 shafts. 800 bhp/800 shp = 14/9 knots
ARMAMENT: 8 x 533mm torpedo tubes (4 bow, 4 stern), total 12 torpedoes, 1 x 102mm gun, 2 x 13.2mm machine guns
COMPLEMENT: 55
NOTES: Romania required many corrections to the *Delfinul* before accepting its first submarine almost five years after its completion in 1931. It operated against Soviet shipping in the Black Sea during the early part of World War II but was under refit from July 1942. It was taken over by the Soviets as the *TS-3* in September 1944, returned to Romania in 1951, and stricken in 1957.

## *SETTEMBRINI* CLASS (1930)

*Luigi Settembrini* (28 September 1930), *Ruggiero Settimo* (29 March 1931)
BUILDER: Tosi
DISPLACEMENT: 938 tons (surfaced), 1135 tons (submerged)
DIMENSIONS: 226'6" x 21'8" x 14'7"
MACHINERY: 2 Tosi diesel engines, 2 Ansaldo electric motors, 2 shafts. 3000 bhp/1400 shp = 17.5/7.75 knots
RANGE: 9000 nm at 8 knots surfaced, 80 nm at 4 knots submerged
ARMAMENT: 8 x 533mm torpedo tubes (4 bow, 4 stern), total 12 torpedoes, 1 x 102mm gun, 2 x 13.2mm machine guns
COMPLEMENT: 56
NOTES: This was an improved version of Cavallini's design for the *Mameli* class that corrected their instability issues. They operated extensively during World War II. The destroyer escort *Frament* sank the *Luigi Settembrini* in error in the western Atlantic on 15 November 1944; the *Ruggiero Settimo* was stricken on 23 March 1947.

## "600-TONNE" TYPE (GROUP I) (1931)

*Argonauta* (19 January 1931), *Fisalia* (2 May 1931), *Medusa* (10 December 1931)
BUILDER: Monfalcone
*Serpente* (28 February 1932), *Salpa* (8 May 1932)
BUILDER: Tosi
*Jantina* (16 May 1932), *Jalae* (15 June 1932)
BUILDER: Muggiano
DISPLACEMENT: 650 tons (surfaced), 800 tons (submerged)
DIMENSIONS: 201'9" x 18'8" x 15'5"
MACHINERY: 2 diesel engines, 2 electric motors, 2 shafts. 1200 bhp/800 shp = 14/8 knots
RANGE: 5000 nm at 8 knots surfaced, 74 nm at 4 knots submerged
ARMAMENT: 6 x 533mm torpedo tubes (4 bow, 2 stern), total 12 torpedoes, 1 x 102mm gun, 2 x 13.2mm machine guns
COMPLEMENT: 44
NOTES: Bernardis developed this "600-tonne" design as a diminutive of his earlier single-hull boats with saddle main ballast tanks. They proved to be a very effective type for Mediterranean service and operated continuously during World War II. The *Medusa* and the *Serpente* were fitted with smaller conning towers in late 1941 to reduce their silhouette on the surface.

A British flying boat sank the *Argonauta* in the eastern Mediterranean on 28 June 1940. The submarine *Triumph* torpedoed the *Salpa* off Sollum on 27 June 1941; the submarine *Torbay* torpedoed the *Jantina* in the Aegean on 5 July; the corvette *Hyacinth* sank the *Fisalia* near Haifa on 28 September. The submarine *Thorn* torpedoed the *Medusa* in the Adriatic on 20 January 1942; the *Serpente* was scuttled at Ancona on 12 September 1943 after Italy's surrender; the *Jalae* was stricken on 1 February 1948.

## [TURKEY]—*SAKARYA* (2 FEBRUARY 1931)

BUILDER: CDT
DISPLACEMENT: 710 tons (surfaced), 940 tons (submerged)
DIMENSIONS: 196'0" x 22'4" x 13'0"
MACHINERY: 2 MAN diesel engines, 2 electric motors, 2 shafts. 1600 bhp/1100 shp = 17/9.5 knots
RANGE: 5000 nm at 8 knots surfaced, 74 nm at 4 knots submerged
ARMAMENT: 6 x 533mm torpedo tubes (4 bow, 2 stern), total 12 torpedoes, 1 x 100mm gun, 1 x 20mm AA gun
COMPLEMENT: 41
NOTES: Bernardis designed this boat as a modest enlargement of his "600-tonne" type to accommodate more powerful machinery for higher speed. It was discarded in 1950.

## [ARGENTINA]—*SANTA FE* CLASS (1931)

*Santa Fe* (28 July 1931), *Salta* (17 January 1932), *Santiago del Estero* (28 March 1932)
BUILDER: Tosi
DISPLACEMENT: 775 tons (surfaced), 920 tons (submerged)
DIMENSIONS: 227'1" x 21'8" x 16'6"
MACHINERY: 2 Tosi diesel engines, 2 electric motors, 2 shafts. 3000 bhp/1400 shp = 17.5/9 knots

RANGE: 3500 nm at 8 knots surfaced, 65 nm at 4 knots submerged
ARMAMENT: 8 x 21" torpedo tubes (4 bow, 2 stern), total 10 torpedoes, 1 x 4" gun, 1 x 37mm AA gun
COMPLEMENT: 40
NOTES: These boats were a further enlargement of the Bernardis type for export. They were stricken between 1959 and 1961.

## ITALY: "600-TONNE" TYPE (GROUPS II – IV) (1933), *DESSIE* (1936)
*(Courtesy of Art-Tech)*

*Sirena* (26 January 1933), *Naiade* (27 March 1933), *Nereide* (25 May 1933), *Anfitrite* (5 August 1933), *Galatea* (5 October 1933), *Ondina* (2 December 1933), *Perla* (3 May 1936), *Gemma* (21 May 1936), *Berillo* (14 June 1936), *Diaspro* (5 July 1936), *Turchese* (19 July 1936),

*Corallo* (2 August 1936), *Adua* (13 September 1936), *Aradam* (18 October 1936), *Axum* (27 September 1936), *Alagi* (15 November 1936)
BUILDER: Monfalcone
*Diamante* (21 May 1933), *Smeralda* (23 July 1933), *Dagabur* (22 November

1936), *Dessie* (22 November 1936), *Uar-sciek* (19 September 1937), *Uebi Scebeli* (3 October 1937)

BUILDER: Tosi

*Rubino* (29 March 1933), *Topazio* (15 May 1933)

BUILDER: Fiume

*Ametista* (26 April 1933), *Zeffiro* (26 June 1933), *Ambra* (28 May 1936), *Onice* (15 June 1936), *Malachite* (15 July 1936), *Iride* (30 July 1936), *Macallé* (29 October 1936), *Gondar* (3 October 1937), *Neghelli* (7 November 1937), *Ascianghi* (5 December 1937), *Scire* (6 January 1938), *Tembien* (6 February 1938), *Durbo* (6 March 1938), *Lafolé* (10 April 1938), *Beilul* (22 May 1938), [Brazil]— *Tupi* (28 November 1936), *Timbira* (30 December 1936), *Tamoio* (14 February 1937)

BUILDER: Muggiano

DISPLACEMENT: 680 tons (surfaced), 837 tons (submerged)

DIMENSIONS: 197'6" x 21'2" x 15'5"

MACHINERY: 2 diesel engines, 2 electric motors, 2 shafts. 1200 bhp/800 shp = 14/7.75 knots

RANGE: 5000 nm at 8 knots surfaced, 74 nm at 4 knots submerged

ARMAMENT: 6 x 533mm torpedo tubes (4 bow, 2 stern), total 12 torpedoes, 1 x 100mm gun, 2 x single or twin 13.2mm machine guns

COMPLEMENT: 45

NOTES: The boats were repeats of Bernardis's "600-tonne" design with minor changes. The *Adua*, the *Alagi*, the *Ambra*, the *Ametista*, the *Corallo*, the *Diaspro*, the *Gondar*, the *Malachite*, the *Nereide*, the *Ondina*, the *Onice*, the *Perla*, the *Scire*, the *Sirena*, the *Tembien*, the *Topazio*, the *Turchese*, and the *Zeffiro* were fitted with smaller conning towers in late 1941 to reduce their silhouette on the surface. The *Ambra*, the *Gondar*, the

*Iride*, and the *Scire* were modified in 1940 to carry three to four "human torpedoes" (operated by divers who attached the warhead to its target) in canisters fore and aft of the conning tower.

The *Iride* and the *Onice* were transferred to the Spanish Nationalist Navy as the *Gonzalez Lopez* and the *Aquilar Tablada* in 1937. They operated with their original Italian crews and were returned to Italy in 1938.

The *Macallé* was wrecked in the Red Sea on 15 June 1940; the submarine *Parthian* torpedoed the *Diamante* off Tobruk on 20 June; British aircraft sank the *Rubino* in the Ionian Sea on 29 June; and the destroyers *Dainty* and *Ilex* sank the *Uebi Scebeli* southwest of Crete the same day; carrier aircraft torpedoed the *Iride* near Tobruk on 22 August; the Australian destroyers *Diamond* and *Stuart* sank the *Gondar* near Alexandria on 30 September; the destroyers *Havock* and *Hasty* sank the *Berillo* off the Egyptian coast on 2 October; the Italian submarine *Tricheco* torpedoed the *Gemma* in error on 6 October; the destroyers *Firedrake* and *Wrestler* sank the *Durbo* east of Gibraltar on 18 October; the destroyers *Gallant*, *Griffin*, and *Hotspur* sank the *Lafolé* near Melilla on 20 October; the destroyers *Hereward* and *Hyperion* sank the *Naiade* off the Cyrenaican coast on 14 December.

The destroyer *Greyhound* sank the *Neghelli* in the eastern Mediterranean on 19 January 1941 and the *Anfitrite* in the Aegean on 6 March; the cruiser *Hermione* rammed and sank the *Tembien* off Tunis on 2 August; the destroyers *Ghurka* and *Legion* sank the *Adua* off the Algerian coast on 30 September; the *Smeraldo* probably was mined in the Strait of Sicily the same month. British aircraft sank the *Zeffiro* off the Algerian coast on 9 June 1942; the South African escort vessels *Protea* and *Southern Maid* sank the *Ondina* off Beirut on 11 July; the destroyer *Wolverine* rammed and sank the *Dagabur* off Algiers on 12 August; the destroyers *Quentin* and *Quiberon* sank the *Dessie* off Bone on 28 November; the sloop *Enchantress* sank the *Corallo* in the western Mediterranean on 13 December; the destroyer *Petard* and the Greek destroyer *Vasilissa Olga* sank the *Uarsciek* south of Malta on 15 December.

The Dutch submarine *Dolfijn* torpedoed the *Malachite* off Sardinia on 9 February 1943; the destroyers *Echo* and *Ilex* sank the *Nereide* off Augusta on 13 July; the destroyers *Eclipse* and *Laforey* sank the *Ascianghi* off Sicily on 23 July; British aircraft sank the *Topazio* in error off Sardinia on 12 September. The *Ambra*, the *Ametista*, the *Axum*, and the *Sirena* were scuttled in 1943 after Italy's surrender. The *Aradam* and the *Beilul* were seized by the Germans in September 1943, and the latter was sunk at Monfalcone during an air raid in May 1944. The surviving boats were stricken in 1947–1948.

The Brazilian boats were originally the *Ascianghi*, the *Gondar*, and the *Neghelli* for the Italian fleet (the names were used for new boats ordered in their place). They served actively until discarded in 1960.

## *ARCHIMEDE* CLASS (1933)

*Archimede* (10 December 1933), *Galileo Galilei* (19 March 1934), *Evangelista Torricelli* (27 May 1934), *Galileo Ferraris* (11 August 1934)

BUILDER: Tosi

DISPLACEMENT: 970 tons (surfaced), 1239 tons (submerged)

DIMENSIONS: 231′4″ x 22′6″ x 13′6″

MACHINERY: 2 Tosi diesel engines, 2 Marelli electric motors, 2 shafts. 3000 bhp/1100 shp = 17/8 knots

RANGE: 10,500 nm at 8 knots surfaced, 105 nm at 3 knots submerged

ARMAMENT: 8 x 533mm torpedo tubes (4 bow, 4 stern), total 16 torpedoes, 2 x 100mm guns, 2 x 13.2mm machine guns

COMPLEMENT: 55

NOTES: This Cavallini design essentially was an enlarged version of his earlier *Settembrini* class of single hull boats with saddle main ballast tanks. Larger size endowed these submarines with greater range and reloads for all tubes. They served in the Red Sea and Indian and Atlantic oceans

The *Archimede* and the *Evangelista Torricelli* were transferred secretly to the Spanish Nationalist Navy in 1937. Renamed the *General Sanjurjo* and the *General Mola*, they were stricken in 1959.

The trawler *Moonstone* captured the *Galileo Galilei* in the Red Sea on 19 June 1940. It was commissioned in the Royal Navy as the *X-2* and operated as a training vessel until it was scrapped in 1946. The destroyer *Lamerson* sank the *Galileo Ferraris* in the Bay of Biscay on 25 October 1941.

## *GLAUCO* CLASS (1935)

*Glauco* (5 January 1935), *Otaria* (20 March 1935)

BUILDER: Monfalcone

DISPLACEMENT: 1054 tons (surfaced), 1305 tons (submerged)

DIMENSIONS: 239'6" x 23'3" x 16'10"

MACHINERY: 2 Fiat diesel engines, 2 CRDA electric motors, 2 shafts. 3000 bhp/1200 shp = 17/8 knots

RANGE: 10,500 nm at 8 knots surfaced, 105 nm at 3 knots submerged

ARMAMENT: 8 x 533mm torpedo tubes (4 bow, 4 stern), total 14 torpedoes, 2 x 100mm guns, 2 x 13.2mm machine guns

COMPLEMENT: 55

NOTES: Bernardis designed these submarines for Portugal, which ordered them as the *Delfin* and *Espadarte* in 1931 but canceled the order soon afterward. In 1932, Italy took them over for completion. They served in the North Atlantic until mid-1941, when the *Otaria* transferred to the Mediterranean, undertaking both offensive patrols and supply runs to North Africa. The destroyer *Wishart* sank the *Glauco* near Gibraltar on 27 June 1941. The *Otaria* was stricken on 1 February 1948.

## *PIETRO MICCA* (31 MARCH 1935)

BUILDER: Tosi

DISPLACEMENT: 1545 tons (surfaced), 1940 tons (submerged)

DIMENSIONS: 296'3" x 25'3" x 17'5"

MACHINERY: 2 Tosi diesel engines, 2 Marelli electric motors, 2 shafts. 3000 bhp/1150 shp = 15.5/8.5 knots

RANGE: 12,000 nm at 8 knots surfaced, 80 nm at 4 knots submerged

ARMAMENT: 6 x 533mm torpedo tubes (4 bow, 2 stern), total 10 torpedoes, 20 mines, 2 x 120mm guns, 2 x twin 13.2mm machine guns

COMPLEMENT: 72

NOTES: Cavallini designed this single-hull submarine with saddle main ballast tanks as a cruiser-minelayer. It was the largest Italian submarine before World War II and a very satisfactory design. It undertook minelaying operations and switched to supply runs to North Africa from early 1941. The submarine *Trooper* torpedoed the *Pietro Micca* in the Straits of Otranto on 29 July 1943.

## *CALVI* CLASS (1935)

*Pietro Calvi* (31 March 1935), *Giuseppe Finzi* (29 June 1935), *Enrico Tazzoli* (14 October 1935)

BUILDER: Muggiano

DISPLACEMENT: 1525 tons (surfaced), 2028 tons (submerged)

DIMENSIONS: 276'7" x 25'3" x 17'1"

MACHINERY: 2 Fiat diesel engines, 2 San Giorgio electric motors, 2 shafts. 4400 bhp/1800 shp = 17/8 knots

RANGE: 13,400 nm at 8 knots surfaced, 80 nm at 4 knots submerged

ARMAMENT: 8 x 533mm torpedo tubes (4 bow, 4 stern), total 16 torpedoes, 2 x 120mm guns, 2 x twin 13.2mm machine guns

COMPLEMENT: 77

NOTES: These double-hull submarines were an improved version of the *Balilla* class.

They had less powerful machinery and used the extra displacement as space to fit two additional stern torpedo tubes, a further 120mm deck gun, and stowage for additional fuel oil. Improved hull lines compensated for the lower power and gave them an almost identical performance. They operated extensively in the North Atlantic during World War II.

The sloop *Lulworth* sank the *Pietro Calvi* in the Atlantic on 15 July, and a British aircraft probably sank the *Enrico Tazzoli* in the Bay of Biscay on 16 May 1943. German forces seized the *Giuseppe Finzi* in September 1943 and commissioned it as the *UIT-21*. After a series of operations in the North Atlantic, it was scuttled at Bordeaux on 20 August 1944.

## *FOCA* CLASS (1937)

*Foca* (26 June 1937), *Zoea* (5 December 1937), *Atropo* (20 November 1938)

BUILDER: Tosi

DISPLACEMENT: 1305 tons (surfaced), 1625 tons (submerged)

DIMENSIONS: 271'10" x 23'6" x 17'1"

MACHINERY: 2 Fiat diesel engines, 2 Ansaldo electric motors, 2 shafts. 2880 bhp/1250 shp = 16/8 knots

RANGE: 8500 nm at 8 knots surfaced, 106 nm at 4 knots submerged

ARMAMENT: 6 x 533mm torpedo tubes (bow), total 8 torpedoes, 36 mines, 1 x 100mm gun, 2 x twin 13.2mm machine guns

COMPLEMENT: 60

NOTES: Cavallini designed this class as minelaying versions of his *Glauco* type. They operated extensively on minelaying missions in the Mediterranean during World War II.

The *Foca* failed to return from a minelaying operation off Haifa in October 1940. The two surviving boats were stricken on 23 March 1947.

## *MARCELLO* CLASS (1937)

*Marcello* (20 November 1937), *Dandolo* (20 November 1937), *Mocenigo* (20 November 1937), *Nani* (16 January 1938), *Veniero* (12 February 1938), *Provana* (16 March 1938), *Barbarigo* (13 June 1938), *Emo* (26 June 1938), *Morosini* (28 July 1938)

BUILDER: Monfalcone

*Commandante Cappellini* (14 May 1939), *Commandante Faa di Bruno* (18 June 1939)

BUILDER: Muggiano

DISPLACEMENT: 1054 tons (surfaced), 1305 tons (submerged)

DIMENSIONS: 239'6" x 23'7" x 16'8"

MACHINERY: 2 CRDA or Fiat diesel engines, 2 CRDA electric motors, 2 shafts. 3600 bhp/1100 shp = 17.5/8 knots

RANGE: 7500 nm at 9.5 knots surfaced, 120 nm at 3 knots submerged

ARMAMENT: 8 x 533mm torpedo tubes (4 bow, 4 stern), total 16 torpedoes, 2 x 100mm guns, 2 x twin 13.2mm machine guns

COMPLEMENT: 57

NOTES: The Bernardis design for these submarines added a partial double-hull section amidships containing the main ballast tanks, with supplemental saddle ballast tanks outside them. They were very maneuverable and dived quickly but suffered from some instability problems, largely a result of their large conning towers. They served extensively in the Mediterranean and North Atlantic during World War II. The *Barbarigo* and the *Commandante Cappellini* were reconfigured as transport submarines in 1943 to bring rubber from the Far East through the Allied blockade.

The French sloop *La Curieuse* rammed and sank the *Provana* off Oran on 17 June 1940, and the *Commandante Faa di Bruno* failed to return from an operation in the North Atlantic in October. The corvette *Anemone* sank the *Nani* in the North Atlantic on 7 January 1941, and convoy escorts sank the *Marcello* there on 22 February. Aircraft sank the *Veniero* in the western Mediterranean on 7 June 1942 and the *Morosini* in the Bay of Biscay on 11 August; the trawler *Lord Nuffield* sank the *Emo* off Algiers on 10 November. The *Mocenigo* was sunk during an air raid on Cagliari on 13 May 1943, and aircraft sank the *Barbarigo* in the Bay of Biscay at the end of June.

The *Commandante Cappellini* was seized by the Japanese at Sabang after Italy's surrender in September 1943, handed over to Germany, and became the *UIT-24*. After Germany's collapse it became the Japanese *I-503* and was surrendered at Kobe on 2 September 1945 to the United States, which scuttled the submarine offshore on 15 April 1946. The *Dandolo* survived the war and was stricken on 23 March 1947.

## *BRIN* CLASS (1938)

*Brin* (3 April 1938), *Galvani* (22 May 1938), *Guglielmotti* (5 March 1939), *Archimede* (5 March 1939), *Torricelli* (26 March 1939)
BUILDER: Tosi
DISPLACEMENT: 1000 tons (surfaced), 1245 tons (submerged)
DIMENSIONS: 237'8" x 21'11" x 14'11"
MACHINERY: 2 Tosi diesel engines, 2 Ansaldo electric motors, 2 shafts. 3400 bhp/1300 shp = 17.25/8 knots
RANGE: 10,500 nm at 8 knots surfaced, 105 nm at 3 knots submerged
ARMAMENT: 8 x 533mm torpedo tubes (4 bow, 4 stern), total 14 torpedoes, 1 x 120mm gun, 4 x 13.2mm machine guns
COMPLEMENT: 58
NOTES: This Cavallini design was an improved version of his *Archimede* class. The two final units were ordered to replace the boats transferred surreptitiously to Spanish Nationalist forces and used the same names to preserve the secret. They served widely in the Red Sea, Mediterranean, and Atlantic during World War II.

The destroyers *Kandahar*, *Khartoum*, and *Kingston* and the sloop *Shoreham* sank the *Torricelli* in the Red Sea on 23 June 1940, and the sloop *Falmouth* sank the *Galvani* in the Persian Gulf the following day. The submarine *Unbeaten* torpedoed the *Guglielmotti* off Calabria on 17 March 1942, and a U.S. flying boat sank the *Archimede* off the coast of Brazil on 16 April 1943. The *Brin* surrendered after Italy's collapse and operated as a training vessel in 1944–1945. It was stricken on 1 February 1948.

## *LIUZZI* CLASS (1939)

*Console Generale Liuzzi* (17 September 1939), *Alpino Bagnolini* (28 October 1939), *Reginaldo Giuliani* (3 December 1939), *Capitano Tarantini* (7 January 1940)
BUILDER: Tosi
DISPLACEMENT: 1148 tons (surfaced), 1460 tons (submerged)
DIMENSIONS: 249'8" x 22'11" x 14'11"
MACHINERY: 2 Tosi diesel engines, 2 Ansaldo electric motors, 2 shafts. 2500 bhp/1500 shp = 18/8 knots
RANGE: 10,500 nm at 8 knots surfaced, 105 nm at 3 knots submerged
ARMAMENT: 8 x 533mm torpedo tubes (4 bow, 4 stern), total 12 torpedoes, 1 x 100mm gun, 2 x twin 13.2mm machine guns
COMPLEMENT: 58
NOTES: This class was a further improvement on Cavallini's previous *Brin* type with more powerful machinery and a lighter deck gun. They operated in the Mediterranean and North Atlantic on offensive patrols. The *Alpino Bagnolini* and the *Reginaldo Giuliani* were converted into transport submarines in 1943 to bring rubber from the Far East.

The destroyers *Daring*, *Defender*, and *Ilex* sank the *Console Generale Liuzzi* near Crete on 27 June 1940, and the submarine *Thunderbolt* torpedoed the *Capitano Tarantini* in the Bay of Biscay on 15 December. The two transport submarines became the German *UIT-22* and *UIT-23*, respectively, in September 1943. The submarine *Tally Ho* torpedoed the *UIT-23* in the Malacca Straits on 14 February 1944, and a South African flying boat sank the *UIT-22* off the Cape of Good Hope on 11 March.

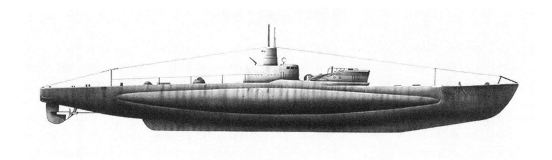

## ITALY: *MARCONI* CLASS, *LEONARDO DA VINCI* (1939)
*(Courtesy of Art-Tech)*

*Guglielmo Marconi* (30 July 1939), *Leonardo da Vinci* (16 September 1939)
BUILDER: Monfalcone
*Michele Bianchi* (3 December 1939), *Luigi Torelli* (6 January 1940), *Alessandro Malaspina* (18 February 1940), *Maggiore Baracca* (21 April 1940)
BUILDER: Muggiano
DISPLACEMENT: 1175 tons (surfaced), 1465 tons (submerged)
DIMENSIONS: 251'0" x 22'4" x 15'6"
MACHINERY: 2 CRDA diesel engines, 2 Marelli electric motors, 2 shafts. 3600 bhp/1500 shp = 17.75/8.25 knots
RANGE: 10,500 nm at 8 knots surfaced, 110 nm at 3 knots submerged
ARMAMENT: 8 x 533mm torpedo tubes (4 bow, 4 stern), total 12 torpedoes, 1 x 100mm gun, 2 x twin 13.2mm machine guns
COMPLEMENT: 57
NOTES: Bernardis developed this class as an improvement on his earlier *Marcello* design. It had more powerful machinery, a reduced gun armament, and a smaller conning tower. They operated primarily in the North Atlantic during World War II. The *Luigi Torelli* was converted to a transport submarine in 1943 to carry rubber from the Far East.

The submarine *Tigris* torpedoed the *Michele Bianchi* in the Bay of Biscay on 5 July 1941; the destroyer *Croome* rammed and sank the *Maggiore Baracca* west of Gibraltar on 8 September; and the *Alessandro Malaspina* and *Guglielmo Marconi* failed to return from North Atlantic patrols in September and October, respectively. The *Luigi Torelli* became the German *UIT-25* in September 1943 and was seized by Japan as the *I-504* in May 1945. It was surrendered at Kobe on 2 September 1945 and was scuttled offshore in April 1946.

## *CAGNI* CLASS (1940)

*Ammiraglio Saint-Bon* (6 June 1940), *Ammiraglio Cagni* (20 July 1949), *Ammiraglio Millo* (31 August 1940), *Ammiraglio Caracciolo* (16 October 1940)

BUILDER: Monfalcone

DISPLACEMENT: 1653 tons (surfaced), 2136 tons (submerged)

DIMENSIONS: 288′5″ x 25′5″ x 18′9″

MACHINERY: 2 CRDA diesel engines, 2 CRDA electric motors, 2 shafts. 4370 bhp/1800 shp = 17/8.5 knots

RANGE: 13,500 nm at 9 knots surfaced, 110 nm at 3 knots submerged

ARMAMENT: 14 x 450mm torpedo tubes (8 bow, 6 stern), total 36 torpedoes, 2 x 100mm guns, 2 x twin 13.2mm machine guns

COMPLEMENT: 85

NOTES: This class was designed for very-long-range antishipping operations. The boats carried a very large battery of smaller torpedoes to enhance their suitability for the mission. While under construction they were fitted with smaller conning towers to reduce their silhouette when on the surface. Initially they operated as transport submarines carrying supplies to North Africa, a role for which they were unsuited. The *Ammiraglio Cagni* then was deployed as designed and undertook some very long patrols in the South Atlantic that lasted as much as 135 days.

The destroyer *Farndale* sank the *Ammiraglio Caracciola* near Bardia on 11 December 1941; the submarine *Upholder* torpedoed the *Ammiraglio Saint-Bon* off Sicily on 5 January 1942; the submarine *Ultimatum* torpedoed the *Ammiraglio Millo* in the Ionian Sea on 14 March. The *Ammiraglio Cagni* surrendered to the Allies in September 1943 and was employed as a training vessel until 1944. It was stricken on 1 February 1948.

## ITALY: "600-TONNE" TYPE (GROUP V) (1941), *NICHELIO* (1942)
*(Courtesy of Art-Tech)*

*Platino* (1 June 1941), *Acciaio* (20 July 1941), *Cobalto* (20 July 1941), *Nichelio* (12 April 1942)

BUILDER: Muggiano

*Asteria* (25 June 1941), *Giada* (10 July 1941), *Granito* (7 August 1941), *Porfido* (23 August 1941), *Avorio* (6 September 1941), *Alabastro* (18 December 1941)

BUILDER: Monfalcone

*Bronzo* (28 September 1941), *Volframio* (9 November 1941), *Argento* (22 February 1942)

BUILDER: Tosi

DISPLACEMENT: 697 tons (surfaced), 850 tons (submerged)

DIMENSIONS: 197′6″ x 21′2″ x 15′8″

MACHINERY: 2 Fiat (Tosi boats: Tosi) diesel engines, 2 CRDA (Tosi boats: Ansaldo) electric motors, 2 shafts. 1400 (Tosi boats: 1600) bhp/800 shp = 14 (Tosi boats 14.75)/7.75 knots

RANGE: 5000 nm at 8 knots surfaced, 74 nm at 4 knots submerged

ARMAMENT: 6 (Tosi boats: 4) x 533mm torpedo tubes (4 bow, 2 stern), total 12 torpedoes, 1 x 100mm gun, 2 x single or twin 13.2mm machine guns or 1–2 x 20mm AA guns

COMPLEMENT: 45

NOTES: This was the final series of Bernardis's "600-tonne" type. They had more powerful machinery and smaller conning towers to reduce their silhouette on the surface. They operated mainly in the Mediterranean during World War II.

The destroyer *Ithuriel* rammed and sank the *Cobalto* off Bizerta on 12 August 1942; a British aircraft sank the *Alabastro* off the Algerian coast on 14 September; the submarine *Saracen* torpedoed the *Granito* near Sicily on 9 November; the submarine *Tigris* torpedoed the *Porfido* off Bone on 6 December. The Canadian corvette *Regina* sank the *Avorio* off Bougie on 8 February 1943; the destroyers *Easton* and *Wheatland* sank the *Asteria* in the same area on 17 February; the submarine *Unruly* torpedoed the *Acciaio* in the Straits of Messina on 13 July; the destroyer *Buck* sank the *Argento* south of Sicily on 3 August. The *Volframio* was scuttled at La Spezia on 8 September 1943, raised by the Germans, and sunk in an air raid on the port in September 1944.

Four British minesweepers captured the *Bronzo* on 12 July 1943. It was commissioned as the *P-714* in the Royal Navy, then transferred as a training vessel to France as the *Narval*, and scrapped in 1948. The *Platino* was stricken on 1 February 1948, and the *Nichelio* was ceded to the Soviet Union in February 1949 as the *S-41* and stricken in the mid-1950s. The *Giada* was retained by the Italian Navy. It was rebuilt as a training vessel in 1951–1953 and finally discarded on 1 January 1966.

## *FLUTTO* CLASS (1942)

*Tritone* (3 January 1942), *Gorgo* (31 January 1942), *Flutto* (19 November 1942), *Marea* (10 December 1942), *Vortice* (23 February 1943), *Nautilo* (20 March 1943), *Bario* (23 January 1944), *Litio* (19 February 1944), *Sodio* (16 March 1944)
BUILDER: Monfalcone
*Sparide* (21 February 1943), *Murena* (11 April 1943), *Grongo* (6 May 1943)
BUILDER: Muggiano
DISPLACEMENT: 930 tons (surfaced), 1093 tons (submerged)
DIMENSIONS: 207′4″ x 22′11″ x 16′0″
MACHINERY: 2 Fiat diesel engines, 2 CRDA electric motors, 2 shafts. 2400 bhp/800 shp = 16/8 knots
RANGE: 5400 nm at 8 knots surfaced, 80 nm at 4 knots submerged
ARMAMENT: 6 x 533mm torpedo tubes (4 bow, 2 stern), total 12 torpedoes, 1 x 100mm gun, 2 x 20mm AA guns
COMPLEMENT: 50
NOTES: Bernardis improved his "600-tonne" design for this class by enlarging it to accommodate more powerful machinery, additional torpedo reloads, and modifications to enhance diving and underwater handling. Three additional boats were incomplete in September 1943 when the Allies concluded an armistice with Italy.

The destroyer *Antelope* and the Canadian corvette *Port Arthur* sank the *Tritone* near Bougie on 19 January 1943; the destroyer *Nields* sank the *Gorgo* off the Algerian coast on 21 May; British motor torpedo boats sank the *Flutto* in the Straits of Messina on 11 July. The *Nautilo* was scuttled at Venice, and the *Grongo*, the *Murena*, and the *Sparide* at La Spezia in September 1943. German forces refloated them and designated them the *UIT-19*, the *UIT-20*, the *UIT-16*, and the *UIT-15*, respectively. All were sunk again in port by Allied air raids in January and September 1944.

The *UIT-19* was salved and commissioned as the Yugoslavian *Sava*. Between 1958 and 1960 it underwent a major reconstruction, surrendering its deck gun and gaining a streamlined sail and then became a training vessel until it was stricken in 1971.

The *Marea* was ceded to the Soviet Union on 7 February 1949 as the *S-43* and stricken in the mid-1950s. The *Vortice* was retained by the Italian Navy. It was rebuilt as a training vessel in 1950–1952 and finally discarded on 1 August 1967.

## *ROMOLO* CLASS (1943)

*Romolo* (21 March 1943), *Remo* (28 March 1943), *R-3* (7 September 1946), *R-4* (30 September 1946)
BUILDER: Tosi
*R-7* (21 October 1943), *R-8* (28 December 1943), *R-9* (27 February 1944)
BUILDER: Monfalcone
*R-10* (12 July 1944), *R-11* (6 August 1944), *R-12* (29 September 1944)
BUILDER: Muggiano
DISPLACEMENT: 2155 tons (surfaced), 2560 tons (submerged)
DIMENSIONS: 283'10" x 25'9" x 17'6"
MACHINERY: 2 Tosi diesel engines, 2 Marelli electric motors, 2 shafts. 2600 bhp/900 shp = 14/6.5 knots
RANGE: 12,000 nm at 9 knots surfaced, 90 nm at 4 knots submerged
ARMAMENT: 2 x 450mm torpedo tubes (bow), 3 x 20mm AA guns
COMPLEMENT: 63

NOTES: Cavallini designed these large single hull submarines with saddle ballast tanks as transports to carry high-priority cargoes, especially rubber, from the Far East. They could carry 600 tons of cargo. Two additional hulls (the *R-5* and *R-6*) were never launched at the Tosi yard, and only two boats were ever delivered complete for service.

The submarine *United* torpedoed the *Remo* on 15 July 1943 in the Gulf of Taranto, and Allied aircraft sank the *Romolo* off Augusta on 18 July. The Germans seized the *R-7* through the *R-12* in September 1943 as the *UIT-4* through the *UIT-6* and the *UIT-1* through the *UIT-3*, respectively. Allied air raids on Monfalcone sank the *UIT-4* through the *UIT-6*, and the other three boats were scuttled in April 1945. The *R-3* and the *R-4* were broken up incomplete in 1947.

## JAPAN
### TYPE KD1, *NO. 44* (1921)
*(Courtesy of Art-Tech)*

*No. 44* (29 November 1921)
BUILDER: Kure
DISPLACEMENT: 1500 tons (surfaced), 2430 tons (submerged)
DIMENSIONS: 300′0″ x 28′10″ x 15′1″
MACHINERY: 4 diesel engines, 4 electric motors, 4 shafts. 5200 bhp/2000 shp = 20/10 knots
RANGE: 20,000 nm at 10 knots surfaced, 100 nm at 4 knots submerged
ARMAMENT: 8 x 21″ torpedo tubes (bow), total 24 torpedoes, 1 x 4.7″ gun, 1 x 3″ AA gun

COMPLEMENT: 60
NOTES: This submarine's design was based on the British J class enlarged to accommodate an extra engine and shaft for high surface speed and very long range. It was partially reconstructed in 1932 with two engines and shafts only.

In 1924 it became the *I-51*. It was largely an experimental boat and was used for training from 1930 to 1939. The *I-51* was stricken in 1941.

## TYPE KD2 (1922)

*No. 51* (12 June 1922)

BUILDER: Kure

DISPLACEMENT: 1500 tons (surfaced), 2500 tons (submerged)

DIMENSIONS: 330'10" x 25'1" x 16'10"

MACHINERY: 2 diesel engines, 2 electric motors, 2 shafts. 6800 bhp/2000 shp = 22/10 knots

RANGE: 10,000 nm at 10 knots surfaced, 100 nm at 4 knots submerged

ARMAMENT: 8 x 21" torpedo tubes (6 bow, 2 stern), total 16 torpedoes, 1 x 4.7" gun, 1 x 3" AA gun

COMPLEMENT: 60

NOTES: This boat's design was based on the German *U-139* class submarine cruiser type. Five additional boats were canceled after the signature of the Washington Treaty. It became the *I-52* in 1924 and the *I-152* in 1942. It became a training vessel in 1940, was disarmed in July 1942, and scrapped in 1948.

## JAPAN: TYPE J1 (1924), *I-3* (EX–NO. 76) (1925)
*(Courtesy of Art-Tech)*

*No.* 74 (15 October 1924), *No.* 75 (23 February 1925), *No.* 76 (8 June 1925), *I-4* (22 May 1928)

BUILDER: Kawasaki

DISPLACEMENT: 2135 tons (surfaced), 2791 tons (submerged)

DIMENSIONS: 319'11" x 30'3" x 16'5"

MACHINERY: 2 MAN diesel engines, 2 electric motors, 2 shafts. 6000 bhp/2600 shp = 18/8 knots

RANGE: 24,400 nm at 10 knots surfaced, 60 nm at 3 knots submerged

ARMAMENT: 6 x 21" torpedo tubes (bow), total 20 torpedoes, 2 x 5.5" guns

COMPLEMENT: 92

NOTES: These large cruiser submarines were designed with substantial assistance from German engineers as developed versions of the Type KD2 with very long range and heavier deck guns. They were redesignated the *I-1* through the *I-4* before launching.

The *PT-59* sank the *I-3* off Guadalcanal on 10 December 1942, and the submarine *Seadragon* torpedoed the *I-4* off Cape Esperance on 20 December. The two surviving boats were converted to transport submarines with the after gun removed, a reduced torpedo load, and space to transport a small landing craft on deck. The New Zealand trawlers *Kiwi* and *Moa* sank the *I-1* off Guadalcanal on 29 January 1943, and the destroyer *Saufley* sank the *I-2* off New Ireland on 7 April 1944.

## TYPE KD3A (1925–1926), TYPE KD3B (1927–1929)

*No. 64* (5 August 1925), *No. 78* (2 September 1925), *I-56* (23 March 1928), *I-57* (1 October 1928)

BUILDER: Kure

*I-58* (3 October 1925), *I-59* (25 March 1929)

BUILDER: Yokosuka

*No. 77* (15 March 1926), *I-63* (28 September 1927), *I-60* (24 April 1929)

BUILDER: Sasebo

DISPLACEMENT: 1800 tons (surfaced), 2300 tons (submerged)

DIMENSIONS: 330'0" (Type KD3b: 331'4") x 26'2" x 15'10"

MACHINERY: 2 diesel engines, 2 electric motors, 2 shafts. 6800 bhp/1800 shp = 20/8 knots

RANGE: 10,000 nm at 10 knots surfaced, 90 nm at 3 knots submerged

ARMAMENT: 8 x 21" torpedo tubes (bow), total 16 torpedoes, 1 x 4.7" gun

COMPLEMENT: 64

NOTES: These boats were slightly modified versions of the Type KD2. The later boats had raking bows to improve sea-keeping. The first three boats were redesignated the *I-53* through the *I-55* in 1924 before launching.

The *I-60* collided with the *I-63* and sank it in Bingo Strait on 2 February 1939. The destroyer *Jupiter* sank the *I-60* in Sunda Strait on 17 January 1942. The surviving boats were redesignated the *I-153* through the *I-159* in 1942. They were surrendered in 1945 and either scrapped or scuttled.

## TYPE KRS (1926)

*No. 48* (30 March 1926), *No. 49* (8 November 1926), *No. 50* (19 March 1927), *I-24* (12 December 1927)

BUILDER: Kawasaki

DISPLACEMENT: 1383 tons (surfaced), 1768 tons (submerged)

DIMENSIONS: 279'6" x 24'8" x 14'6"

MACHINERY: 2 diesel engines, 2 electric motors, 2 shafts. 2400 bhp/1100 shp = 14.5/7 knots

RANGE: 10,500 nm at 8 knots surfaced, 40 nm at 4.5 knots submerged

ARMAMENT: 4 x 21" torpedo tubes (bow), total 12 torpedoes, 42 mines, 1 x 5" gun

COMPLEMENT: 70

NOTES: The German Type UE II minelayer *U-125* served as the basis for the design of this class. The mines were stowed in a large compartment at the stern and discharged through two horizontal tubes aft. In 1924 the early boats were redesignated the *I-21* through the *I-23* before launching. They were redesignated the *I-121* through the *I-124* in 1939 and modified the following year by adding large aviation gasoline storage tanks so they could refuel flying boats.

The destroyer *Edsall* and the Australian minesweepers *Deloraine* and *Katoomba* sank the *I-124* off Darwin on 20 January 1942; the high-speed minelayer *Gamble* sank the *I-123* off Savo Island on 29 August; and the submarine *Skate* torpedoed the *I-122* in Toyama Bay on 10 June 1945. The *I-121* was surrendered in 1945 and scrapped.

## JAPAN: TYPE KD4 (1927), *I-61* (1927)
*(Courtesy of Art-Tech)*

*I-61* (12 November 1927), *I-62* (29 November 1928)

BUILDER: Mitsubishi

*I-64* (5 October 1929)

BUILDER: Kure

DISPLACEMENT: 1720 tons (surfaced), 2300 tons (submerged)

DIMENSIONS: 320'6" x 25'7" x 15'10"

MACHINERY: 2 diesel engines, 2 electric motors, 2 shafts. 6000 bhp/1800 shp = 20/8.5 knots

RANGE: 10,800 nm at 10 knots surfaced, 60 nm at 3 knots submerged

ARMAMENT: 6 x 21" torpedo tubes (bow), total 14 torpedoes, 1 x 4.7" gun

COMPLEMENT: 58

NOTES: This class was a smaller version of the previous Type KD3 with two fewer torpedo tubes. A merchant ship accidentally rammed and sank the *I-61* in the Iki Strait on 2 October 1941. The other two boats were redesignated the *I-162* and the *I-164* in 1942. The submarine *Triton* torpedoed the *I-164* off Kagoshima on 17 May 1942, and the *I-162* was surrendered in 1945 and scuttled.

## TYPE KD5 (1931)

*I-67* (7 April 1931)
BUILDER: Mitsubishi
*I-65* (2 June 1931)
BUILDER: Kure
*I-66* (2 June 1931)
BUILDER: Sasebo
DISPLACEMENT: 1705 tons (surfaced), 2330 tons (submerged)
DIMENSIONS: 320'6" x 26'11" x 15'5"
MACHINERY: 2 diesel engines, 2 electric motors, 2 shafts. 6000 bhp/1800 shp = 20.5/8.25 knots
RANGE: 10,800 nm at 10 knots surfaced, 60 nm at 3 knots submerged

ARMAMENT: 6 x 21" torpedo tubes (bow), total 14 torpedoes, 1 x 3.9" gun, 1 x 13.2mm machine gun
COMPLEMENT: 82
NOTES: This class was very similar to its precursor but had a heavier structure to increase the diving depth. The *I-67* was lost in an accident off Marcus Island on 29 August 1940. The other boats became the *I-165* and the *I-166* in 1942. The submarine *Telemachus* torpedoed the *I-166* near Singapore on 17 July 1944, and U.S. carrier aircraft sank the *I-165* east of Saipan on 27 June 1945.

## TYPE J1M (1931)

*I-5* (19 June 1931)
BUILDER: Kawasaki
DISPLACEMENT: 2243 tons (surfaced), 2921 tons (submerged)
DIMENSIONS: 319'11" x 29'9" x 16'2"
MACHINERY: 2 diesel engines, 2 electric motors, 2 shafts. 6000 bhp/2600 shp = 18/8 knots
RANGE: 24,400 nm at 10 knots surfaced, 60 nm at 3 knots submerged

ARMAMENT: 6 x 21" torpedo tubes (bow), total 20 torpedoes, 1 x 5.5" gun, 1 aircraft
COMPLEMENT: 93
NOTES: The *I-5* was a version of the Type J1 enlarged to accommodate two tubular hangars for a dismantled seaplane and a launching catapult. The destroyer escort *Wyman* sank it east of Guam on 19 July 1944.

## TYPES KD6A (1933) AND KD6B (1936)

*I-68* (26 June 1933)
BUILDER: Kure
*I-69* (15 February 1934), *I-72* (20 June 1935), *I-75* (16 September 1936)
BUILDER: Mitsubishi
*I-70* (14 June 1934), *I-74* (28 March 1937)
BUILDER: Sasebo
*I-71* (25 August 1934), *I-73* (20 June 1935)
BUILDER: Kawasaki
DISPLACEMENT: 1785 (Type KD6b: 1810) tons (surfaced), 2440 (Type KD6b: 2564) tons (submerged)
DIMENSIONS: 344'6" x 26'11" x 15'1"
MACHINERY: 2 diesel engines, 2 electric motors, 2 shafts. 9000 bhp/1800 shp = 23/8.25 knots
RANGE: 14,000 nm at 10 knots (Type KD6b: 10,000 nm at 16 knots) surfaced, 65 nm at 3 knots submerged
ARMAMENT: 6 x 21" torpedo tubes (bow), total 14 torpedoes, 1 x 3.9" (*I-71* – *I-73*: 4.7") gun, 1 (Type KD6b: 4) x 13.2mm machine gun(s)

COMPLEMENT: 84
NOTES: This group of submarines was a further development of the KD type, with higher surface speed, deeper diving depth, and longer range.

Aircraft from the carrier *Enterprise* sank the *I-70* off Oahu on 10 December 1941, and the submarine *Gudgeon* torpedoed the *I-73* east of Midway on 27 January 1942. The remainder of the class became the *I-168* through the *I-175* in 1942. The fast minesweeper *Southard* sank the *I-172* near Guadalcanal on 11 November 1942 and the submarine *Scamp* torpedoed the *I-168* off New Ireland on 27 July 1943. The destroyers *Guest* and *Hudson* sank the *I-171* near Buka Island on 1 February 1944; the destroyer *Charette* and destroyer escort *Fair* sank the *I-175* off Jaluit on 5 February; aircraft sank the *I-174* on 3 April and the *I-169* the following day at Truk.

## TYPE J2 (1934)

*I-6* (31 March 1934)
BUILDER: Kawasaki
DISPLACEMENT: 2243 tons (surfaced), 3061 tons (submerged)
DIMENSIONS: 323'2" x 29'9" x 17'5"
MACHINERY: 2 diesel engines, 2 electric motors, 2 shafts. 8000 bhp/2600 shp = 20/7.5 knots
RANGE: 20,000 nm at 10 knots surfaced, 60 nm at 3 knots submerged

ARMAMENT: 6 x 21" torpedo tubes (bow), total 17 torpedoes, 1 x 5" DP gun, 1 x 13.2mm machine gun, 1 aircraft
COMPLEMENT: 97
NOTES: The *I-6* was similar to the *I-5* but fitted with a dual-purpose deck gun. The destroyer escort *William C. Miller* sank it off Saipan on 14 July 1944.

## TYPE *K5* (1934)

*RO*–33 (10 October 1934)
BUILDER: Kure
*RO*–34
BUILDER: Mitsubishi
DISPLACEMENT: 700 tons (surfaced), 940 tons (submerged)
DIMENSIONS: 248'4" x 22'0" x 12'11"
MACHINERY: 2 diesel engines, 2 electric motors, 2 shafts. 2900 bhp/1200 shp = 19/8.25 knots
RANGE: 8000 nm at 12 knots surfaced, 90 nm at 3.5 knots submerged
ARMAMENT: 4 x 21" torpedo tubes (bow), total 10 torpedoes, 1 x 3" AA gun, 1 x 13.2mm machine gun
COMPLEMENT: 42
NOTES: This class was developed as a prototype medium submarine design for mass production in wartime, emphasizing surface speed and ease of construction. The Australian destroyer *Arunta* sank the *RO*-33 near Port Moresby on 29 August 1942, and the destroyers *O'Bannon* and *Strong* sank the *RO*-34 off Russell Island on 5 April 1943.

## JAPAN: TYPE J3, *I-7* (1935)
*(Courtesy of Art-Tech)*

*I*-7 (3 July 1935)
BUILDER: Kure
*I*-8 (20 July 1936)
BUILDER: Kawasaki
DISPLACEMENT: 2525 tons (surfaced), 3538 tons (submerged)
DIMENSIONS: 358'7" x 29'10" x 17'3"
MACHINERY: 2 diesel engines, 2 electric motors, 2 shafts. 11,200 bhp/2800 shp = 23/8 knots
RANGE: 14,000 nm at 16 knots surfaced, 60 nm at 3 knots submerged
ARMAMENT: 6 x 21" torpedo tubes (bow), total 20 torpedoes, 1 x 5.5" gun, 2 x 13.2mm machine guns, 1 aircraft
COMPLEMENT: 100
NOTES: This class was an enlargement of the Type J2. They were fitted as squadron flagships. In 1943 one 13.2mm mount was replaced with a twin 25mm antiaircraft mount. The *I*-8 received a twin 5.5" mount in place of its single weapon in mid-1943 and was converted to a *kaiten* carrier in late 1944 by removing the 5.5" weapons, the hangar, and the catapult and replacing them with cradles for four human torpedoes.

The destroyer *Monaghan* sank the *I*-7 near Kiska on 5 July 1943, and the destroyers *Morrison* and *Stockton* sank the *I*-8 near Okinawa on 31 March 1945.

## JAPAN: TYPES C1 (1938) AND C2 (1943), *I-16* (1938)
*(Courtesy of Art-Tech)*

*I-16* (28 July 1938), *I-20* (25 January 1939)
BUILDER: Mitsubishi
*I-18* (12 November 1938), *I-24* (12 November 1939), *I-46–I-48* (1943)
BUILDER: Sasebo
*I-22* (23 December 1938)
BUILDER: Kawasaki
DISPLACEMENT: 2554 tons (surfaced), 3561 tons (submerged)
DIMENSIONS: 358'7" x 29'10" x 17'7"
MACHINERY: 2 diesel engines, 2 electric motors, 2 shafts. 12,400 bhp/2000 shp = 23.5/8 knots
RANGE: 14,000 nm at 16 knots surfaced, 60 nm at 3 knots submerged
ARMAMENT: 8 x 21" torpedo tubes (bow), total 20 torpedoes, 1 x 5.5" gun, 2 x 25mm AA guns
COMPLEMENT: 101
NOTES: The Imperial Japanese Navy developed a design for a large long-range submarine in the late 1930s from the Type J3. Different detail arrangements suited the design for service as torpedo attack, scouting, or headquarters submarines. The C type was the torpedo attack design, the Type C1 being equipped to carry a midget submarine as well. Seven additional Type C2 boats were canceled in 1942–1943.

The *I-16* was converted in late 1942 as a transport submarine capable of carrying a small landing craft abaft the conning tower. The *I-47* and the *I-48* were converted to *kaiten* carriers in late 1944, losing their deck gun and receiving cradles for four to six human torpedoes.

The *I-22* failed to return from a patrol in the Solomons in October 1942. The destroyer *Fletcher* sank the *I-18* off San Cristobal on 11 February 1943; the submarine chaser *PC-487* sank the *I-24* near

Attu on 11 June; the *I-20* failed to return from a patrol in the New Hebrides in October. The destroyer escort *England* sank the *I-16* northeast of Choiseul on 19 May 1944, and the destroyers *Gridley* and *Helm* sank the *I-46* off Leyte on 28 October. The destroyer escorts *Conklin*, *Corbesier*, and *Raby* sank the *I-48* near Yap on 23 January 1945, and the *I-47* was surrendered in August and scuttled.

## *NO. 71* (1938)

BUILDER: Kure

DISPLACEMENT: 213 tons (surfaced), 240 tons (submerged)

DIMENSIONS: 140′5″ x 10′10″ x 10′2″

MACHINERY: 1 diesel engine, 2 electric motors, 1 shaft. 300 bhp/1800 shp = 13/21.25 knots

RANGE: 2200 nm at 12 knots surfaced, 38 nm at 7 knots submerged

ARMAMENT: 3 x 18″ torpedo tubes (bow), total 3 torpedoes

COMPLEMENT: 11

NOTES: The *No. 71* was designed as an experimental boat with high submerged speed. It had a streamlined hull form and was powered underwater by a powerful electric motor drawing on a new type of high-capacity battery. After extensive trials it was scrapped in 1940, but the data was used in designing later Japanese high-speed boats.

## JAPAN: TYPES B1 (1939), B2 (1942), AND B3 (1943), *I-30* (1940)
*(Courtesy of Art-Tech)*

*I-15* (7 March 1939), *I-26* (10 April 1940), *I-30* (17 September 1940), *I-37* (22 October 1941), *I-40* (1942), *I-41, I-42* (1943)

**BUILDER:** Kure

*I-17* (19 July 1939), *I-23* (24 November 1939), *I-29* (29 September 1940), *I-31* (13 March 1941), *I-36* (1 November 1941), *I-44* (1943), *I-54, I-55, I-56* (1943), *I-58* (1944)

**BUILDER:** Yokosuka

*I-19* (16 September 1939), *I-25* (8 June 1940), *I-28* (18 December 1940), *I-33* (1 May 1941), *I-35* (24 September 1941)

**BUILDER:** Mitsubishi

*I-21* (24 February 1940)

**BUILDER:** Kawasaki

*I-27* (6 June 1940), *I-32* (17 December 1940), *I-34* (24 September 1941), *I-38* (15 April 1942), *I-39* (15 April 1942), *I-43, I-45* (1943)

**BUILDER:** Sasebo

**DISPLACEMENT:** 2589 (Type B2: 2624, Type B3: 2607) tons (surfaced), 3654 (Type B2: 3700, Type B3: 3688) tons (submerged)

**DIMENSIONS:** 356′7″ x 30′6″ x 16′10″

**MACHINERY:** 2 diesel engines, 2 electric motors, 2 shafts. 12,400 (Type B3: 4700) bhp/2000 (Type B3: 1200) shp = 23.5/8 knots (Type B3: 17.75/6.5 knots)

**RANGE:** 14,000 (Type B3: 21,000) nm at 16 knots surfaced, 96 (Type B3: 105) nm at 3 knots submerged

**ARMAMENT:** 6 x 21″ torpedo tubes (bow), total 17 torpedoes, 1 x 5.5″ gun, 2 x 25mm AA guns, 1 aircraft

**COMPLEMENT:** 101

NOTES: The Type B submarines were long-range scouting boats equipped with a seaplane hangar and catapult. The Type B3 boats had less powerful diesel engines and were slower but had a greatly enhanced range. The I-36, the I-37, the I-44, the I-56, and the I-58 were converted to *kaiten* carriers in late 1944, losing their deck guns, hangars, and catapults and receiving cradles for four to six human torpedoes. An additional 8 Type B2, 18 Type B3, and 18 Type B4 (enlarged Type B3) boats were canceled in 1943.

The I-23 failed to return from a patrol to Hawai'i in February 1942; the U.S. submarine *Tautog* torpedoed the I-28 near Truk on 17 May; the I-30 was mined near Singapore on 13 October; the destroyer *McCalla* sank the I-15 off San Cristobal on 2 November.

The destroyers *Edwards* and *Farragut* sank the I-31 off Kiska on 12 May 1943; the New Zealand trawler *Tui* sank the I-17 near Noumea on 19 August; the destroyer *Patterson* sank the I-25 in the New Hebrides on 3 September; U.S. aircraft sank the I-19 near Makin on 18 October; the submarine *Taurus* torpedoed the I-34 off Penang on 13 November; the destroyers *Frazier* and *Meade* sank the I-35 off Tarawa on 23 November; the destroyer *Radford* sank the I-40 near Makin on 25 November; the destroyer *Boyd* sank the I-39 in the same area the next day;

aircraft from the escort carrier *Chenango* sank the I-21 in the Gilbert Islands on 29 November.

The British destroyers *Paladin* and *Petard* sank the I-27 near Addu Atoll on 12 February 1944; the submarine *Aspro* torpedoed the I-43 east of Guam on 15 February; the U.S. submarine *Tunny* torpedoed the I-42 near Anguar on 23 March; the destroyer escort *Manlove* and the submarine chaser *PC-1135* sank the I-32 off Wotje the following day; the I-33 was lost in an accident near Iyo Nada on 13 June; the submarine *Sawfish* torpedoed the I-29 in Balintang Channel on 26 July; the I-26 failed to return from a patrol off Leyte in October; the destroyer escort *Richard M. Rowell* sank the I-54 in Surigao Strait on 26 October; the destroyer escort *Whitehurst* sank the I-45 there on 29 October; the destroyer *Nicholas* sank the I-38 south of Yap on 12 November; the destroyer escort *Lawrence C. Taylor* sank the I-41 east of Samar on 18 November; the destroyer escorts *Conklin* and *McCoy Reynolds* sank the I-37 off Leyte on 19 November.

The destroyers *Collett*, *Heerman*, *McCord*, *Mertz*, and *Uhlmann* sank the I-56 off Okinawa on 18 April 1945, and aircraft from the escort carrier *Tulagi* sank the I-44 there on 29 April. The I-36 and the I-58 were surrendered in August and scuttled.

## TYPE A1 (1939)

*I-9* (20 May 1939)

BUILDER: Kure

*I-10* (20 September 1939), *I-11* (28 February 1941)

BUILDER: Kawasaki

DISPLACEMENT: 2919 tons (surfaced), 4149 tons (submerged)

DIMENSIONS: 373′0″ x 31′4″ x 17′7″

MACHINERY: 2 diesel engines, 2 electric motors, 2 shafts. 12,400 bhp/2400 shp = 23.5/8 knots

RANGE: 16,000 nm at 16 knots surfaced, 60 nm at 3 knots submerged

ARMAMENT: 6 x 21″ torpedo tubes (bow), total 16 torpedoes, 1 x 5.5″ gun, 2 x 25mm AA guns, 1 aircraft

COMPLEMENT: 114

NOTES: These boats were fitted as flagships for submarine squadrons with extra staff accommodations and more powerful communications equipment. Two additional boats were canceled in 1942.

The destroyer *Frazier* sank the *I-9* off Kiska on 11 June 1943; the *I-11* failed to return from a patrol to the Ellis Islands in January 1944; the destroyer *David W. Taylor* and the destroyer escort *Riddle* sank the *I-10* east of Saipan on 4 July.

## TYPE KS (1941)

*RO-100* (6 December 1941), *RO-103* (6 December 1941), *RO-106–RO-107* (30 May 1942)

BUILDER: Kure

*RO-101–RO-102* (17 May 1942), *RO-104–RO-105* (11 July 1942), *RO-108* (26 October 1942), *RO-109* (1942), *RO-110–RO-117* (1943)

BUILDER: Kawasaki

DISPLACEMENT: 601 tons (surfaced), 782 tons (submerged)

DIMENSIONS: 199′10″ x 19′8″ x 11′6″

MACHINERY: 2 diesel engines, 2 electric motors, 2 shafts. 1100 bhp/760 shp = 14.25/8 knots

RANGE: 3500 nm at 12 knots surfaced, 60 nm at 3 knots submerged

ARMAMENT: 4 x 21″ torpedo tubes (bow), total 10 torpedoes, 1 x 3″ AA gun

COMPLEMENT: 38

NOTES: These small submarines were designed for short-range defensive missions. Nine additional boats were projected but not built.

The *PT-150* and *PT-152* sank the *RO-102* near Lae on 14 May 1943; the destroyer *Taylor* sank the *RO-107* near Kolombangara Island on 12 July; the *RO-103* was mined in the Solomons on 28 July; the destroyer *Saufley* sank the *RO-101* off San Cristobal on 15 September; the *RO-100* was mined near Buin on 25 November.

The Australian minesweepers *Ipswich* and *Launceston* and the Indian sloop *Jumna* sank the *RO-110* near Vizgapatam on 11 February 1944; the destroyer escort *England* sank the *RO-104*, the *RO-105*, the *RO-106*, the *RO-108*, and the *RO-116* off Kavieng between 22 and 31 May; the destroyer *Taylor* sank the *RO-111* north of Kavieng on 11 June; the destroyers *Melvin* and *Wadleigh* sank the *RO-114* west of Tinian on 17 June; a

U.S. Navy Liberator sank the *RO-117* off Saipan the same day.

The destroyers *Bell*, *Jenkins*, and *O'Bannon* and the destroyer escort *Ulvert M. Moore* sank the *RO-115* near Manila on 31 January 1945; north of Luzon the submarine *Batfish* torpedoed the *RO-112* on 11 February and the *RO-113* the next day; the destroyer escort *Horace A. Bass* sank the *RO-109* near Okinawa on 25 April.

## JAPAN: TYPE KD7, *I-176* (*EX–I-176*) (1941)

*(Courtesy of Art-Tech)*

*I-76* (7 June 1941), *I-81* (2 May 1942)
BUILDER: Kure
*I-77* (20 December 1941), *I-79* (16 July 1942), *I-83* (21 January 1943)
BUILDER: Kawasaki
*I-80* (7 February 1942), *I-82* (30 May 1942), *I-85* (16 September 1943), *I-84* (12 December 1943)
BUILDER: Yokosuka

*I-78* (24 February 1942)
BUILDER: Mitsubishi
DISPLACEMENT: 1833 tons (surfaced), 2602 tons (submerged)
DIMENSIONS: 346'2" x 27'1" x 15'1"
MACHINERY: 2 diesel engines, 2 electric motors, 2 shafts. 89,000 bhp/1800 shp = 23/8 knots

RANGE: 8000 nm at 16 knots surfaced, 50 nm at 5 knots submerged

ARMAMENT: 6 x 21″ torpedo tubes (bow), total 12 torpedoes, 1 x 4.7″ gun, 2 x 25mm AA guns

COMPLEMENT: 86

NOTES: This class was developed from the earlier KD6 type. They became the *I-176* through the *I-185* in 1942. The *I-175*, the *I-177*, and the *I-181* became transport submarines in early 1943, landing their deck gun and gaining a cradle for a small landing craft.

The submarine chaser *SC-669* sank the *I-178* off Espiritu Santo on 29 May 1943; the *I-179* sank in an accident near Iyo Nada on 14 July; the destroyer *Wadsworth* sank the *I-182* near Espiritu Santo on 1 September. Destroyers sank the *I-181* in the St. Georges Channel on 16 January 1944; the destroyer escort *Gilmore* sank the *I-180* off Kodiak Island on 26 April; the submarine *Pogy* torpedoed the *I-183* in the Bungo Strait on 28 April; the destroyers *Franks*, *Haggard*, and *Johnston* sank the *I-176* in Buka Passage on 16 May; aircraft from the escort carrier *Suwannee* sank the *I-184* near Guam on 19 June; the destroyer *Newcomb* and the fast minesweeper *Chandler* sank the *I-185* near Saipan on 22 June; the destroyer escort *Samuel S. Miles* sank the *I-177* in the Palau Islands on 3 October.

## TYPE K6 (1942)

*RO-35* (4 June 1942), *RO-37* (30 June 1942), *RO-36* (14 October 1942), *RO-38* (24 December 1942), *RO-40* (6 March 1943), *RO-41* (5 May 1943), *RO-43* (5 June 1943), *RO-45*, *RO-46*, *RO-48* (1943), *RO-56* (1944)

BUILDER: Mitsubishi

*RO-42* (25 October 1942), *RO-39* (6 March 1943)

BUILDER: Sasebo

*RO-44*, *RO-47*, *RO-49*, *RO-50* (1943), *RO-55*, *RO-56* (19,440

BUILDER: Mitsui

DISPLACEMENT: 1115 tons (surfaced), 1447 tons (submerged)

DIMENSIONS: 264′1″ x 23′2″ x 13′4″

MACHINERY: 2 diesel engines, 2 electric motors, 2 shafts. 4200 bhp/1200 shp = 19.75/8 knots

RANGE: 5000 nm at 16 knots surfaced, 45 nm at 5 knots submerged

ARMAMENT: 4 x 21″ torpedo tubes (bow), total 10 torpedoes, 1 x 3″ AA gun, 2 x 25mm AA guns

COMPLEMENT: 54

NOTES: These boats were an improved version of the Type K5 with more powerful machinery, increased fuel, and stronger hull structure to increase diving depth. Sixteen additional boats were canceled in 1942–1943.

The destroyer *Patterson* sank the *RO-25* in the Solomon Sea on 25 August 1943, and the destroyer *Cotten* sank the *RO-38* near San Cristobal on 24 November. The destroyer *Buchanan* sank the *RO-37* near San Cristobal on 22 January 1944; the destroyer *Walker* sank the *RO-39* near Wotje on 2 February; the destroyer *Phelps* and the minesweeper *Sage* sank the *RO-40* off Kwajalein on 16 February; the destroyers *Macdonough* and *Stephen Potter* sank the *RO-45* off Truk on 30 April; the destroyer escort *Bangust* sank the *RO-42* off Kwajalein on 11 June; the destroyer *Melvin* sank the *RO-36* off Saipan on 13 June; the destroyer escort *Burden R. Hastings* sank the *RO-44* off Eniwetok on 16 June; the destroyer escort William C. Miller sank the

RO-48 off Saipan on 14 July; the destroyer escort *McCoy Reynolds* sank the RO-47 off Yap on 25 September. The destroyer escort *Thomason* sank the RO-55 off Luzon on 7 February 1945; aircraft from the escort carrier *Anzio* sank the RO-43 off Iwo Jima on 26 February; the destroyer *Haggard* sank the RO-41 off

Okinawa on 23 March; off Okinawa the destroyer *Hudson* sank the RO-49 on 5 April; the destroyers *Mertz* and *Monssen* sank the RO-56 on 9 April; the submarine *Sea Owl* torpedoed the RO-46 off Wake Island on 18 April. The RO-50 was surrendered in August and scuttled.

## TYPE A2 (1943)

*I-12* (1943)
BUILDER: Kawasaki
DISPLACEMENT: 2919 tons (surfaced), 4149 tons (submerged)
DIMENSIONS: 373'0" x 31'4" x 17'8"
MACHINERY: 2 diesel engines, 2 electric motors, 2 shafts. 4700 bhp/1200 shp = 17.75/6.25 knots
RANGE: 22,000 nm at 16 knots surfaced, 75 nm at 3 knots submerged

ARMAMENT: 6 x 21" torpedo tubes (bow), total 16 torpedoes, 1 x 5.5" gun, 2 x 25mm AA guns, 1 aircraft
COMPLEMENT: 114
NOTES: This boat received less powerful engines than the Type A1 class, sacrificing speed on the surface but greatly increasing its range. It failed to return from a patrol to the central Pacific in January 1945.

## TYPE C3 (1943)

*I-52, I-53, I-55* (1943)
BUILDER: Kure
DISPLACEMENT: 2564 tons (surfaced), 3644 tons (submerged)
DIMENSIONS: 356'7" x 30'6" x 16'10"
MACHINERY: 2 diesel engines, 2 electric motors, 2 shafts. 4700 bhp/1200 shp = 17.75/6.5 knots
RANGE: 21,0000 nm at 16 knots surfaced, 105 nm at 3 knots submerged
ARMAMENT: 6 x 21" torpedo tubes (bow), total 20 torpedoes, 2 x 5.5" guns, 2 x 25mm AA guns
COMPLEMENT: 101
NOTES: These boats received less powerful engines than the Type C2 class, sacrificing

speed on the surface but greatly increasing their range. They also were fitted with snorkels. An additional 22 boats were canceled. The I-53 became a *kaiten* carrier in early 1945, landing its deck gun and carrying cradles for up to six human torpedoes.

Aircraft from the escort carrier *Bogue* sank the I-52 off the Azores on 24 June 1944, and the destroyer escorts *Reynolds* and *Wyman* sank the I-55 near Tinian on 28 July. The I-53 was surrendered in August 1945 and scuttled.

## TYPES D1 (1943) AND D2 (1944)

*I-361, I-363* (1943)
BUILDER: Kure
*I-362, I-364* (1943), *I-366, I-367, I-370, I-371* (1944)
BUILDER: Mitsubishi
*I-365, I-368, I-369, I-372, I-373, I-374* (1944)
BUILDER: Yokosuka
DISPLACEMENT: 1779 (Type D2: 1926) tons (surfaced), 2215 (Type D2: 2240) tons (submerged)
DIMENSIONS: 241'2" (Type D2: 242'9") x 29'2" x 15'7" (Type D2: 16'7")
MACHINERY: 2 diesel engines, 2 electric motors, 2 shafts. 1850 (Type D2: 1750) bhp/1200 shp = 13/6.5 knots
RANGE: 15,000 nm at 10 knots surfaced, 120 (Type D2: 100) nm at 3 knots submerged
ARMAMENT: 1 x 5.5" gun, 2 x 25mm AA guns
COMPLEMENT: 60
NOTES: These types were developed as transport submarines to carry troops, equipment, and supplies to forward garrisons. They carried small landing craft and inflatable boats to transport supplies to the shore. An additional 92 units of Type D1 and 144 of Type D2 were planned but canceled before construction began, and construction ceased on the *I-374* in March 1945.

The submarine *Sea Devil* torpedoed the *I-364* east of Yokosuka on 16 September 1944, and the submarine *Scabbardfish* torpedoed the *I-365* closer in on 28 November. The destroyer escort *Fleming* sank the *I-362* north of Truk on 18 January 1945; the submarine *Lagarto* torpedoed the *I-371* in Bungo Strait on 24 February; off Iwo Jima the destroyer escort *Finnegan* sank the *I-370* on 26 February; aircraft from the escort carrier *Anzio* sank the *I-368* on 27 February and also the *I-361* off Okinawa on 30 May. Carrier aircraft sank the *I-372* at Yokosuka on 18 July, and the submarine *Snakefish* torpedoed the *I-373* off Shanghai on 14 August. The three surviving boats were surrendered in August 1945.

## JAPAN: TYPE AM, *I-14* (1944)
*(Courtesy of Art-Tech)*

*I-15* (12 April 1944), *I-1* (10 June 1944), *I-13*, *I-14* (1944)

BUILDER: Kawasaki

DISPLACEMENT: 3603 tons (surfaced), 4762 tons (submerged)

DIMENSIONS: 373'0" x 38'5" x 19'4"

MACHINERY: 2 diesel engines, 2 electric motors, 2 shafts. 4400 bhp/600 shp = 16.75/5.5 knots

RANGE: 21,000 nm at 16 knots surfaced, 60 nm at 3 knots submerged

ARMAMENT: 6 x 21" torpedo tubes (bow), total 12 torpedoes, 1 x 5.5" gun, 2 x triple 25mm AA guns, 1 x single 25mm AA gun, 2 aircraft

COMPLEMENT: 114

NOTES: This class was a substantial expansion of the earlier Type A headquarters submarine design with two aircraft and a heavier antiaircraft battery. Only the *I-13* and *I-14* were completed; construction of the other boats was halted in March 1945. Three additional submarines were canceled in 1943.

Aircraft from the escort carrier *Anzio* sank the *I-13* near Truk on 16 July 1945, and the *I-14* was surrendered in August and scrapped.

## TYPE SH (1944)

*I-351* (1944), *I-352* (23 April 1944)
BUILDER: Kure
DISPLACEMENT: 3512 tons (surfaced),
4290 tons (submerged)
DIMENSIONS: 364'2" x 33'4" x 20'2"
MACHINERY: 2 diesel engines, 2 electric
motors, 2 shafts. 3700 bhp/1200 shp =
15.75/6.25 knots
RANGE: 13,000 nm at 14 knots surfaced,
100 nm at 3 knots submerged
ARMAMENT: 4 x 21" torpedo tubes (bow),
total 4 torpedoes, 2 x 3" trench mortars, 2
x triple 25mm AA guns, 1 x 25mm AA
gun

COMPLEMENT: 90
NOTES: This class was designed to support
flying boats and carried large supplies of
aviation gasoline, bombs, and aircraft torpedoes. Four additional boats were canceled in 1942–1943.

USAAF B-29 bombers sank the incomplete *I-352* at Kure on 22 June 1945,
and the submarine *Bluefin* torpedoed the
*I-351* in the South China Sea on 14 July
1945.

## JAPAN: TYPE STO (1944)

*(Courtesy of Art-Tech)*

*I-400* (1944), *I-404* (7 July 1944)
BUILDER: Kure
*I-401, I-402* (1944)
BUILDER: Sasebo
DISPLACEMENT: 5223 tons (surfaced),
6560 tons (submerged)
DIMENSIONS: 400'3" x 39'4" x 23'0"
MACHINERY: 2 diesel engines, 2 electric
motors, 2 shafts. 7700 bhp/2400 shp =
18.75/6.5 knots
RANGE: 30,000 nm at 16 knots surfaced, 60
nm at 3 knots submerged
ARMAMENT: 8 x 21" torpedo tubes (bow),
total 20 torpedoes, 1 x 5.5" gun, 3 x triple
25mm AA guns, 1 x single 25mm AA gun,
3 aircraft
COMPLEMENT: 144

NOTES: This class was designed to launch
aircraft for operations against cities of
the U.S. mainland. These boats were the
largest submarines built until after World
War II. They had double pressure hulls
over three-quarters of their length,
placed one above the other forward and
side by side over their midships section.
They were commissioned with search
radar and snorkel equipment. One additional unit was canceled in 1942 and 14
further boats in 1945. U.S. carrier aircraft sank the incomplete *I-404* at Kure
on 28 July 1945. The three other boats
were surrendered in August and used for
trials by the U.S. Navy before they were
scuttled in 1946.

## TYPE ST (1944)

*I-201, I-202, I-203* (1944), *I-204* (16 December 1944), *I-205* (15 February 1945), *I-206* (26 March 1945)

BUILDER: Kure

DISPLACEMENT: 1291 tons (surfaced), 1450 tons (submerged)

DIMENSIONS: 259'2" x 19'0" x 17'11"

MACHINERY: 2 diesel engines, 2 electric motors, 2 shafts. 2750 bhp/5000 shp = 15.75/19 knots

RANGE: 5800 nm at 14 knots surfaced, 135 nm at 3 knots submerged

ARMAMENT: 4 x 21" torpedo tubes (bow), total 10 torpedoes, 2 x 25mm AA guns

COMPLEMENT: 31

NOTES: The design for this class was developed using data from the experimental *No. 71* to create a torpedo attack type with high underwater speed. It featured a streamlined hull, retractable deck fittings and weapons (including a snorkel), spring-loaded cover plates for limber holes, powerful electric motors, and a new high-capacity battery that enabled it to maintain full speed for up to 55 minutes followed by a cruise at 3 knots for up to 12 hours. The design was optimized for mass production with extensive use of prefabrication and an all-welded hull.

The incomplete *I-204* and *I-205* were wrecked by USAAF B-29 bombers, and the incomplete *I-206* was wrecked in a storm. The *I-201* through the *I-203* were surrendered in August 1945 and scuttled after testing by the U.S. Navy. An additional 17 boats were either not completed or canceled.

## TYPE SS (1944)

*Ha–101, Ha–104, Ha–106* (1944), *Ha–107, Ha–108, Ha–110* (1945)

BUILDER: Tanagawa

*Ha–102, Ha–103* (1944), *Ha–105, Ha–109, Ha–111, Ha–112* (1945)

BUILDER: Mitsubishi

DISPLACEMENT: 429 tons (surfaced), 493 tons (submerged)

DIMENSIONS: 146'0" x 20'0" x 13'3"

MACHINERY: 1 diesel engine, 1 electric motor, 1 shaft. 400 bhp/150 shp = 10/5 knots

RANGE: 3000 nm at 10 knots surfaced, 146 nm at 3 knots submerged

ARMAMENT: 1 x 25mm AA gun

COMPLEMENT: 21

NOTES: Heavy losses of the Type D1 transport submarines led to the development of this smaller type. It was optimized for mass production, making extensive use of prefabrication, and featured all-welded construction. Twenty-eight additional units were canceled in favor of high-speed attack boats, and the *Ha–110* and the *Ha–112* were not completed. All boats were surrendered in August 1945 and scrapped or scuttled.

## TYPE STS (1945)

*Ha–201, Ha–202, Ha–203, Ha–204, Ha–205, Ha–207, Ha–208, Ha–209, Ha–210, Ha–216* (1945), *Ha–215* (15 June 1945), *Ha–217* (26 June 1945), *Ha–218* (2 July 1945), *Ha–219* (12 July 1945), *Ha–228* (18 July 1945), *Ha–229* (27 July 1945), *Ha–230* (1946)

BUILDER: Sasebo

*Ha–212* (25 June 1945), *Ha–221* (4 August 1945)

BUILDER: Kawasaki

*Ha–206* (10 July 1945), *Ha–211* (24 April 1946)

BUILDER: Tanagawa

*Ha–213* (29 July 1945), *Ha–214* (15 August 1945)

BUILDER: Mitsubishi

DISPLACEMENT: 377 tons (surfaced), 440 tons (submerged)

DIMENSIONS: 173′11″ x 13′1″ x 11′3″

MACHINERY: 1 diesel engine, 2 electric motors, 1 shaft. 400 bhp/1250 shp = 10.5/13 knots

RANGE: 3000 nm at 10 knots surfaced, 100 nm at 2 knots submerged

ARMAMENT: 2 x 21″ torpedo tubes (bow), total 4 torpedoes, 1 x 7.7mm machine gun

COMPLEMENT: 22

NOTES: The design for these high-speed coastal submarines employed the data collected from the trials of the *No. 71.* Mass production using prefabrication and all-welded construction was a feature of this type. They had streamlined hulls, high-power electric motors, and high-capacity batteries. Their test depth was 500 feet, and many units received snorkels. A total of 90 boats were ordered, but only 10 were completed; none undertook any operational patrols.

## THE NETHERLANDS
## *K.XI* CLASS (1924)

*K.XI* (24 April 1924), *K.XII* (15 July 1924), *K.XIII* (23 December 1924)

BUILDER: Fijenoord

DISPLACEMENT: 670 tons (surfaced), 815 tons (submerged)

DIMENSIONS: 218′10″ x 20′2″ x 12′2″

MACHINERY: 2 MAN diesel engines, 2 electric motors, 2 shafts. 2400 bhp/725 shp = 15/8 knots

RANGE: 3500 nm at 11 knots surfaced, 13 nm at 8 knots submerged

ARMAMENT: 2 x 530mm plus 4 x 450mm torpedo tubes (4 bow. 2 x 450mm stern), total 12 torpedoes, 1 x 88mm AA gun, 1 x 12.7mm machine gun

COMPLEMENT: 31

NOTES: This was the first indigenous Dutch submarine design, by J. J. van der Struyff. It was a double-hull type, with three main ballast tanks amidships, for colonial service in the Dutch East Indies.

Japanese aircraft sank the *K.XII* at Soerabaya on 18 February 1942. The other boats escaped to Australia. They were operational until 1944, when they transferred to the training role, and were stricken in 1946.

## *O.9* CLASS (1925)

O.9 (7 April 1925)
BUILDER: De Schelde
O.10 (30 July 1925)
BUILDER: Nederlandsche
O.11 (19 March 1925)
BUILDER: Fijenoord
DISPLACEMENT: 568 tons (surfaced), 715 tons (submerged)
DIMENSIONS: 198′6″ x 18′4″ x 11′10″
MACHINERY: 2 MAN diesel engines, 2 electric motors, 2 shafts. 1800 bhp/620 shp = 15/8 knots
RANGE: 3500 nm at 10 knots surfaced, 26 nm at 8 knots submerged

ARMAMENT: 2 x 530mm plus 3 x 450mm torpedo tubes (4 bow. 1 x 450mm stern), total 10 torpedoes, 2 x 40mm AA guns
COMPLEMENT: 31
NOTES: J. J. van der Struyff designed these boats as home service equivalents of his first colonial submarines. The O.9 and the O.10 escaped to the United Kingdom in 1940 and served operationally until they decommissioned in 1944. The O.11 was seized by the Germans and scuttled in September 1944. It was raised and scrapped postwar, along with its sisters.

## *K.XIV* CLASS (1932)

K.XIV (11 July 1932), K.XV (December 1932), K.XVI (April 1933)
BUILDER: Rotterdamse
K.XVII (July 1932), K.XVIII (July 1932)
BUILDER: Fijenoord
DISPLACEMENT: 771 tons (surfaced), 1008 tons (submerged)
DIMENSIONS: 242′9″ x 25′0″ x 12′10″
MACHINERY: 2 MAN diesel engines, 2 electric motors, 2 shafts. 3200 bhp/1000 shp = 17/9 knots
RANGE: 3500 nm at 11 knots surfaced, 26 nm at 8.5 knots submerged
ARMAMENT: 8 x 533mm torpedo tubes (4 bow, 2 stern, 1 x twin external trainable mount), total 14 torpedoes, 1 x 88mm AA gun, 2 x 40mm AA guns
COMPLEMENT: 38
NOTES: Van der Struyff's improved and enlarged version of his previous colonial boat design carried a uniform armament of 533mm torpedo tubes and added an external trainable twin mount forward of the conning tower. When the K.XIV and the K.XV were refitted at Philadelphia in late 1942 and early 1943, the external mounts were deleted.

The K.XVII was mined in the Gulf of Siam on 21 December 1941; the Japanese submarine I-66 torpedoed the K.XVI off the coast of Borneo on 25 December; the K.XVIII was scuttled at Soerabaja on 24 January 1942. Japanese forces raised the boat, partially repaired it, and stationed it as a radar picket in Madoera Strait, where it was torpedoed by the submarine *Taciturn* on 16 June 1945. The other two boats escaped to Ceylon and remained operational until April 1946. They were stricken on 1 June 1946.

## *O.16* (27 JANUARY 1936)

BUILDER: De Schelde

DISPLACEMENT: 896 tons (surfaced), 1170 tons (submerged)

DIMENSIONS: 254'3" x 21'9" x 13'3"

MACHINERY: 2 MAN diesel engines, 2 electric motors, 2 shafts. 3200 bhp/1000 shp = 18/9 knots

RANGE: 3500 nm at 11 knots surfaced, 26 nm at 8.5 knots submerged

ARMAMENT: 8 x 533mm torpedo tubes (4 bow, 2 stern, 1 x twin external trainable mount), total 14 torpedoes, 1 x 88mm AA gun, 2 x 40mm AA guns

COMPLEMENT: 38

NOTES: Gerhard de Rooy designed this double-hull submarine for home service. It was constructed from high-tensile steel and 49 percent welded, which increased its diving depth. It also was fitted with a snorkel, to allow the diesel engines to run underwater in good weather conditions. In June 1939 the *O-16* transferred to the East Indies. It was mined in the Gulf of Siam on 15 December 1941

## [POLAND]—*ORZEL* CLASS (1938)

*Orzel* (15 January 1938)

BUILDER: De Schelde

*Sept* (17 October 1938)

BUILDER: Rotterdamse

DISPLACEMENT: 1100 tons (surfaced), 1650 tons (submerged)

DIMENSIONS: 275'7" x 22'0" x 13'4"

MACHINERY: 2 Sulzer diesel engines, 2 electric motors, 2 shafts. 4740 bhp/1100 shp = 20/9 knots

RANGE: 7000 nm at 10 knots surfaced, 100 nm at 3 knots submerged

ARMAMENT: 12 x 550mm torpedo tubes (4 bow, 4 stern, 1 x quadruple external trainable mount), total 20 torpedoes, 1 x 105mm gun, 1 x twin 40mm AA gun

COMPLEMENT: 60

NOTES: These submarines were designed by the Nederlandsche Verenigde Scheepsbouw Bureaux in 's-Gravenhage, in cooperation with a team from the Polish Navy. They incorporated many features of the earlier Dutch *O.16*, including the external trainable mount. The hulls were entirely welded, and all controls were hydraulically operated.

The *Orzel* escaped the German invasion of Poland to the United Kingdom and was mined in the North Sea on 8 June 1940. The *Sept* escaped and was interned in Sweden until the war's end, when it returned to Polish service until it decommissioned on 15 September 1969.

## *O.19* CLASS (1938)

*O.19* (22 September 1938), *O.20* (31 January 1939)

BUILDER: Wilton-Fijenoord

DISPLACEMENT: 998 tons (surfaced), 1536 tons (submerged)

DIMENSIONS: 265'9" x 24'7" x 13'1"

MACHINERY: 2 Sulzer diesel engines, 2 electric motors, 2 shafts. 5200 bhp/1000 shp = 19.25/9 knots

RANGE: 3500 nm at 11 knots surfaced, 26 nm at 8.5 knots submerged

ARMAMENT: 8 x 533mm torpedo tubes (4 bow, 2 stern, 1 x twin external trainable mount), total 14 torpedoes, 40 mines, 1 x 88mm AA gun, 2 x 40mm AA guns, 1 x 12.7mm machine gun

COMPLEMENT: 55

NOTES: These submarines were very similar to the *Orzel* class, with a reduced torpedo battery and 10 vertical mine tubes fitted on each beam. They were equipped with a more sophisticated snorkel system than their precursor.

Both boats served in the East Indies. The destroyer *Uranami* forced the *O.20* to the surface off the coast of Malaya on 19 December 1941, and it was scuttled. The *O.19* wrecked on Ladd Reef in the South China Sea on 8 July 1945 and was scuttled.

## *O.21* CLASS (1939)

*O.21* (21 October 1939), *O.22* (20 January 1940)

BUILDER: De Schelde

*O.23* (5 December 1939), *O.24* (18 March 1940), *O.26* (23 November 1940), *O.27* (26 September 1941)

BUILDER: Rotterdamse

*O.25* (1 May 1940)

BUILDER: Wilton-Fijenoord

DISPLACEMENT: 934 tons (surfaced), 1350 tons (submerged)

DIMENSIONS: 255'11" x 21'4" x 12'6"

MACHINERY: 2 Sulzer diesel engines, 2 electric motors, 2 shafts. 5200 bhp/1000 shp = 19.5/9 knots

RANGE: 7100 nm at 10 knots surfaced, 26 nm at 8.5 knots submerged

ARMAMENT: 8 x 533mm torpedo tubes (4 bow, 2 stern, 1 x twin external trainable mount), total 14 torpedoes, 1 x 88mm AA gun, 2 x 40mm AA guns, 1 x 12.7mm machine gun

COMPLEMENT: 55

NOTES: This design was essentially the same as the *O.19* class, with minelaying capability deleted. Their ballast tank valve arrangements were improved to enable them to dive more quickly.

The *O.21* through the *O.24* escaped to Britain when German forces invaded The Netherlands in May 1940, and they saw extensive service in the Atlantic, Mediterranean, and East Indies. The *O.22* most probably was mined in early November 1940. The *O.23* decommissioned on 1 December, 1948, the *O.24* on 22 February 1954, and the *O.21* on 2 November 1957.

The *O.25* through the *O.27* were seized and became the German *UD-3* through *UD-5*. They became training boats in 1943. The *UD-3* and the *UD-4* were scuttled on 3 May 1945, while the *UD-5* was surrendered. It recommissioned as the Dutch *O.27*, served as a training and trials boat, and was stricken on 14 November 1959.

## SOVIET UNION
## SERIES I (1928)

*Dekabrist* (3 November 1928), *Naradovoylets* (19 May 1929), *Krasnogvardeyets* (12 July 1929)

BUILDER: Baltic

*Revolyutsioner* (16 April 1929), *Spartakovets* (28 September 1929), *Yakobinets* (12 May 1930)

BUILDER: Nikolayev

DISPLACEMENT: 933 tons (surfaced), 1354 tons (submerged)

DIMENSIONS: 249′4″ x 21′4″ x 12′6″

MACHINERY: 2 Kolomna diesel engines, 2 electric motors, 2 shafts. 2600 bhp/1600 shp = 14/9 knots

RANGE: 7500 nm at 9 knots surfaced, 132 nm at 2 knots submerged

ARMAMENT: 8 x 533mm torpedo tubes (6 bow, 2 stern), total 14 torpedoes, 1 x 100mm gun, 1 x 45mm AA gun, 1 x 7.62mm machine gun

COMPLEMENT: 53

NOTES: Boris Mikhailovich Malinin designed this double-hull class, the first submarines built by the Soviet Union.

They were good sea boats but suffered from stability problems, dived very slowly, and also displayed poor quality control in their construction. Numerous refits were necessary to correct these deficiencies, after which their time to dive was reduced from 3 minutes to 30 seconds.

The first three boats went to the Baltic Fleet and the second group to the Black Sea. The Baltic Fleet units transferred to the Northern Fleet in 1933. The *Dekabrist* sank during exercises in Molotovskiy Bay in November 1940; the *Yakobinets* was bombed while dry-docked at Sevastopol on 12 November 1941; the *Krasnogvardets* failed to return from a patrol off the Norwegian coast in June 1942; the antisubmarine vessels *UJ-102* and *UJ-103* sank the *Revolutsioner* off Yevpatoria on 4 December 1943. The two surviving boats were stricken in the late 1950s, the *Naradovoylets* becoming a museum ship at Kronshtadt in the 1980s.

## SERIES III (1930)

*Shch–1 Shchuka* (1 December 1930), *Shch–2 Okun'* (6 November 1931), *Shch–4 Komsomolets* (2 May 1931), *Shch–3 Yorsh* (6 November 1931)

BUILDER: Baltic

DISPLACEMENT: 578 tons (surfaced), 704 tons (submerged)

DIMENSIONS: 187′0″ x 20′4″ x 12′5″

MACHINERY: 2 diesel engines, 2 electric motors, 2 shafts. 1370 bhp/800 shp = 12.5/8.5 knots

RANGE: 3250 nm at 8 knots surfaced, 110 nm at 2 knots submerged

ARMAMENT: 6 x 533mm torpedo tubes (4 bow, 2 stern), total 10 torpedoes, 1 x 45mm AA gun, 2 x 7.62mm machine guns

COMPLEMENT: 35

NOTES: This class, with a partial double hull and saddle ballast tanks, served as prototypes for several large series of successful coastal submarines of similar design. They were redesignated the *Shch–31* through the *Shch–34* and then the *Shch–301* through the *Shch–304* in 1934. All four boats operated in the Baltic. The *Shch–301* was mined off Cape Juminda on 27 August 1941; the *Shch–302* near Somen Island on 13 Oc-

tober 1942; the *Shch–304* in the Gulf of Finland in December 1942. The *Shch–303* became the *S-303* in October 1949 and was scrapped in 1959 (the conning tower was preserved as a memorial at Kronshtadt).

## SERIES II (1931) AND SERIES XI (1935)

*Leninets* (28 February 1931), *Marksist* (21 May 1931), *Bolshevik* (8 July 1931)
BUILDER: Baltic
*Garibaldiets* (31 August 1931), *Chartist* (5 June 1932), *Karbonari* (3 November 1932)
BUILDER: Nikolayev
*Voroshilovets* (15 May 1935), *Kirovets* (25 August 1935), *Dzerzhinets* (10 September 1935), *L-12* (7 November 1936), *L-11* (4 December 1936), *L-10* (18 December 1936)
BUILDER: Dalzavod
DISPLACEMENT: 1051 (Series XI: 1100) tons (surfaced), 1327 (Series XI: 1400) tons (submerged)
DIMENSIONS: 265′9″ x 21′8″ x 13′9″ (Series XI: 14′5″)
MACHINERY: 2 diesel engines, 2 electric motors, 2 shafts. 2200 bhp/1050 (Series XI: 1450) shp = 14/9 knots
RANGE: 6000 nm at 9 knots surfaced, 135 nm at 2 knots submerged
ARMAMENT: 6 x 533mm torpedo tubes (bow), total 12 torpedoes, 20 mines, 1 x 100mm gun, 1 x 45mm AA gun
COMPLEMENT: 54

NOTES: These double-hull minelayers with saddle main ballast tanks were designed by Malinin on the basis of his earlier Series I class, with many features incorporated from the former British *L-55*. Mines were carried in two horizontal tubes and ejected at the stern, either on the surface or while submerged. The first three boats went to the Baltic, the next three to the Black Sea, and the final six to the Pacific fleets. The named boats were redesignated the *L-1* through the *L-10* in 1934.

The *L-2* was mined off Keri Island on 14 November 1941; German artillery sank the *L-1* in the Neva River in the same month; the *L-9* failed to return from a Pacific patrol in 1941–1942; the antisubmarine vessel *UJ-104* sank the *L-6* near Constanza on 18 April 1944. In 1949 the *L-3* through the *L-6* were redesignated the *B-3* through the *B-6*; the *L-7* and the *L-8* were redesignated the *B-24* and the *B-25*; the *L-12* was redesignated the *B-12*. All were stricken between 1956 and 1963.

## SERIES V (1932)

*Shch–101 Losos* (25 December 1932), *Shch–102 Leshch* (19 April 1933), *Shch–103 Karp* (1933), *Shch–104* (May 1933), *Shch–106* (May 1933), *Shch–107* (July 1933), *Shch–108* (July 1933), *Shch–111 Karas* (July 1933), *Shch–105* (August 1933), *Shch–109* (August 1933), *Shch–110* (October 1933), *Shch–113 Sterlyad* (12 December 1933), *Shch–112* (April 1934), *Shch–114* (1934), *Shch–121 Zubatka* (3 April 1934), *Shch–115* (4 April 1934), *Shch–116 Osetr* (1934), *Shch–117 Makrel* (15 April 1934), *Shch–118 Kefal'* (1934), *Shch–119 Beluga* (7 May 1934), *Shch–120* (June 1934), *Shch–123 Ugor* (26 August 1934), *Shch–125* (26 August 1934), *Shch–122 Saida* (29 August 1934), *Shch–124* (29 December 1934)
BUILDER: Dalzavod

*Shch–305 Lin* (31 December 1933), *Shch–306 Piksha* (1 August 1934), *Shch–307 Treska* (1 August 1934)
BUILDER: Admiralty

*Shch–201 Sazan* (3 April 1934), *Shch–202 Seld* (25 May 1934), *Shch–203 Kambala* (29 May 1934), *Shch–205 Nerpa* (6 November 1934), *Shsch–206* (6 November 1934), *Shch–204 Minoga* (31 December 1934)
BUILDER: Nikolayev

*Shch–308 Siyomga* (December 1933), *Shch–309 Delfin* (10 April 1935), *Shch–310 Bielukha* (10 April 1935), *Shch–311 Kumzha* (10 April 1935)
BUILDER: Baltic

*Shch–207* (25 March 1935)
BUILDER: 61 Kommuna

DISPLACEMENT: 589 tons (surfaced), 708 tons (submerged)
DIMENSIONS: 191'11" x 20'4" x 14'1"
MACHINERY: 2 diesel engines, 2 electric motors, 2 shafts. 1600 bhp/800 shp = 14/8 knots
RANGE: 5750 nm at 8.5 knots surfaced, 125 nm at 2 knots submerged
ARMAMENT: 6 x 533mm torpedo tubes (4 bow, 2 stern), total 10 torpedoes, 2 x 45mm AA guns, 1 x 7.62mm machine gun
COMPLEMENT: 40
NOTES: This series was the production version of the earlier *Shchuka* type. The *Shch–101* through the *Shch–124* went to the Pacific, the *Shch–201* through the *Shch–207* went to the Black Sea, and the *Shch–305* through the *Shch–311* went to the Baltic fleets.

The *Shch–204* was mined off the Bulgarian coast on 3 July 1941, and the *Shch–206* was mined off Sulina in September 1941. The *Shch–307* was mined near Suursaari on 17 August 1942; the minesweeper *M-37* sank the *Shch–308* in the Gulf of Finland on 31 August; the Finnish submarine chasers *VMV-13* and *VMV-15* sank the *Shch–311* off Porkkala on 15 October; the Finnish submarine *Vetehinen* sank the *Shch–305* in the Åland Sea on 5 November; the *Shch–307* was mined there later the same month. The *Shch–304* was mined off Cape Tarkhanskutskiy in September 1943.

The surviving boats' designations were changed from *Shch-* to *S-* in 1949, and they were stricken in the mid-1950s.

## SERIES VI (1933) AND VIbis (1934)

*M-1* (8 April 1933), *M-2* (8 April 1933), *M-6* (24 April 1933), *M-3* (8 June 1933), *M-7* (5 August 1933), *M-8* (11 August 1933), *M-10* (24 August 1933), *M-51* (8 September 1933), *M-9* (27 September 1933), *M-13* (3 October 1933), *M-5* (29 October 1933), *M-4* (18 November 1933), *M-11* (29 November 1933), *M-12* (2 December 1933), *M-18* (24 December 1933), *M-14* (26 December 1933), *M-15* (26 December 1933), *M-17* (27 December 1933), *M-16* (28 December 1933), *M-52* (18 January 1934), *M-20* (17 March 1934), *M-26* (14 April 1934), *M-25* (16 April 1934), *M-21* (11 May 1934), *M-19* (14 May 1934), *M-22* (15 May 1934), *M-23* (16 May 1934), *M-24* (1 June 1934), *M-28* (21 June 1934), *M-27* (23 July 1934)

BUILDER: Sverdlovsk

*M-53* (10 February 1934), *M-54* (15 September 1935), *M-55* (20 November 1935), *M-56* (20 November 1935)

BUILDER: Nikolayev

*M-72* (23 December 1934), *M-71* (31 December 1 34), *M-74* (31 December 1934), *M-73* (5 January 1935), *M-75* (5 February 1935), *M-76* (8 February 1935), *M-78* (21 March 1935), *M-77* (2 September 1935), *M-79–M-80* (15 September 1935)

BUILDER: Zhdanov

*M-83* (1 June 1935), *M-82* (10 June 1935), *M-84–M-86* (15 July 1935), *M-81* (15 September 1935)

BUILDER: Sudomekh

DISPLACEMENT: 160 tons (surfaced), 200 tons (submerged)

DIMENSIONS: 124'0" x 10'3" x 8'6"

MACHINERY: 1 diesel engine, 1 electric motor, 1 shaft. 685 bhp/235 shp = 13/6 knots

RANGE: 900 nm at 8 knots surfaced, 60 nm at 2 knots submerged

ARMAMENT: 2 x 533mm torpedo tubes (bow), total 2 torpedoes, 1 x 45mm AA gun

COMPLEMENT: 16

NOTES: The design of these small single-hull boats allowed them to be transported between the various fleet operating areas on special rail cars. They were not very effective, however, especially as they could not carry reload torpedoes and had a very limited range. The *M-1* through the *M-28*, the *M-53*, the *M-56*, the *M-82*, and the *M-84* through the *M-86* served in the Pacific Fleet; the *M-51*, the *M-52*, and the *M-55* operated in the Caspian Sea; and the other boats served in the Baltic Fleet. The *M-72*, the *M-73*, the *M-75*, and the *M-76* were decommissioned in early 1941.

The *U-144* torpedoed the *M-78* off Ventspils on 24 June 1941; the *M-71*, the *M-80*, and the *M-83* were blown up at Liepaya the same day to prevent their capture; the *M-81* was mined near Laine Bank on 1 July; German aircraft sank the *M-74* at Kronshtadt on 23 September. The surviving boats were scrapped immediately after World War II.

## SERIES IV (1934)

*Pravda* (3 January 1934), *Zvezda* (15 February 1934), *Iskra* (4 December 1934)
BUILDER: Baltic
DISPLACEMENT: 1200 tons (surfaced), 1870 tons (submerged)
DIMENSIONS: 295'3" x 26'3" x 10'2"
MACHINERY: 2 MAN diesel engines, 2 electric motors, 2 shafts. 5400 bhp/1000 shp = 18.5/7.75 knots
RANGE: 5700 nm at 10 knots surfaced, 105 nm at 4 knots submerged
ARMAMENT: 6 x 533mm torpedo tubes (4 bow, 2 stern), total 10 torpedoes, 2 x 100mm guns, 1 x 45mm AA gun

COMPLEMENT: 54
NOTES: These double-hull submarines, designed by A. N. Asafov, were intended to operate with the fleet. They were poor sea boats, dived slowly, and required multiple refits to suit them for service. A fourth example was canceled.

The *Pravda* probably was mined in the Baltic in September 1941. The two surviving boats were redesignated the *B-31* and the *B-1*, respectively, in 1949 and were stricken in the mid-1950s.

## SERIES X (1935)

*Shch-322* (10 April 1935), *Shch-323–Shch-324* (10 April 1935), *Shch-321* (21 April 1935), *Shch-327* (27 April 1935), *Shch-313–Shch-314* (28 June 1935), *Shch-312* (1936), *Shch-329* (1939)
BUILDER: Baltic
*Shch-326* (12 April 1935), *Shch-328* (27 April 1935), *Shch-325* (12 May 1935), *Shch-318* (11 August 1935), *Shch-317* (24 September 1935), *Shch-320* (12 February 1936), *Shch-319* (15 February 1936), *Shch-406* (17 December 1939), *Shch-405* (1940), *Shch-407* (1941), *Shch-408* (1941), *Shch-409* (1941), *Shch-410* (1941), *Shch-411* (July 1941), *Shch-412* (July 1941), *Shch-413* (1946), *Shch-414* (1946), *Shch-415* (1946), *Shch-417* (1947), *Shch-419* (1947)
BUILDER: Admiralty
*Shch-126* (20 April 1935), *Shch-130* (8 June 1935), *Shch-128* (9 June 1935), *Shch-127* (13 June 1935), *Shch-131* (4 July 1935), *Shch-132* (4 July 1935),

*Shch-137* (22 July 1935), *Shch-138* (22 July 1935), *Shch-133* (8 August 1935), *Shch-129* (10 October 1935)
BUILDER: Dalzavod
*Shch-208* (7 October 1935), *Shch-209* (2 March 1936), *Shch-215* (11 January 1937), *Shch-213* (13 April 1937), *Shch-214* (23 April 1937), *Shch-216* (1940)
BUILDER: 61 Kommuna
*Shch-315* (27 December 1935), *Shch-316* (27 December 1935)
BUILDER: Zhdanov
*Shch-210* (13 March 1936), *Shch-211* (3 September 1936), *Shch-210* (28 December 1936)
BUILDER: Nikolayev
*Shch-428* (1940), *Shch-426* (1941), *Shch-420* (1946), *Shch-425* (1946), *Shch-429* (1946), *Shch-427* (1947), *Shch-430* (1947), *Shch-431* (1947)
BUILDER: Sudomekh
DISPLACEMENT: 607 tons (surfaced), 749 tons (submerged)

DIMENSIONS: 192'9" x 20'4" x 14'1"

MACHINERY: 2 diesel engines, 2 electric motors, 2 shafts. 1600 bhp/800 shp = 13.5/8 knots

RANGE: 3650 nm at 8 knots surfaced, 125 nm at 2 knots submerged

ARMAMENT: 6 x 533mm torpedo tubes (4 bow, 2 stern), total 10 torpedoes, 2 x 45mm AA guns

COMPLEMENT: 40

NOTES: These were improved versions of the Series VI type. The *Shch-126* through the *Shch-140* went to the Pacific Fleet, the *Shch-312* through the *Shch-316* and the *Shch-325* through the *Shch-329* to the Northern Fleet, the *Shch-208* through the *Shch-216* to the Black Sea Fleet, and the remainder to the Baltic Fleet. Two additional boats were abandoned on the slips at Leningrad during World War II and scrapped incomplete.

A Soviet fishing vessel accidentally rammed and sank the *Shch-328* in Kola Inlet in October 1939. The *Shch 211* probably was mined off the Bulgarian coast on 16 November 1941, and the *Shch-324* probably was mined in the Gulf of Finland the same month. German aircraft sank the *Shch-210* south of the Crimea on 13 March, 1942; the *Shch-325* was scuttled after hitting a mine near Porsanger Fjord on 8 April; an internal explosion wrecked the *Shch-212* at Sevastopol in May; the Italian motor torpedo boat *MAS-571* sank the *Shch-214* off Cape Aitodor on 19 June; the *Shch-213* was blown up after stranding at Sochi on 12 July; the Finnish minelayer *Ruotsinsalmi* sank the *Shch-317* in the Baltic on 14 July; the *Shch-208*, the *Shch-313*, and the *Shch-405* were mined in August and the *Shch-319* in September; the Finnish submarine *Iku-Turso* torpedoed the *Shch-320* in the Åland Sea on 27 October; the *Shch-322* was mined in November. The *Shch-323* was probably mined off Peterhof on 1 May 1943; the Finnish minelayer *Ruotsinsalmi* sank the *Shch-408* near Vaindlo Island on 25 May; the Finnish minelayer *Rulahti* sank the *Shch-406* off Steinskar Island the next day; the *Shch-326* failed to return from a patrol off the Norwegian coast in July; the *Shch-315* failed to return from a similar mission in October. A German submarine chaser sank the *Shch-216* west of Cape Tarkhankutskiy on 17 February 1944, and Soviet aircraft sank the *Shch-314* in the Barents Sea in error on 21 September.

The surviving boats' designations were changed from *Shch-* to *S-* in 1949, and they were stricken in the mid-1950s.

## SERIES XIII (1936)

*L-13* (2 August 1936), *L-14* (10 December 1936), *L-15* (26 December 1936), *L-16* (9 July 1937), *L-17* (5 November 1937), *L-18* (12 May 1938), *L-19* (26 May 1938)

BUILDER: Dalzavod

*L-22* (23 September 1939), *L-20* (14 April 1940), *L-21* (17 July 1940)

BUILDER: Baltic

*L-23* (29 April 1940), *L-24* (17 December 1940), *L25* (1941)

BUILDER: Nikolayev

DISPLACEMENT: 1123 tons (surfaced), 1416 tons (submerged)

DIMENSIONS: 273'3" x 23'0" x 13'5"

MACHINERY: 2 diesel engines, 2 electric motors, 2 shafts. 4200 bhp/2400 shp = 18/10 knots

RANGE: 14,000 nm at 9 knots surfaced, 130 nm at 2 knots submerged

ARMAMENT: 8 x 533mm torpedo tubes (6 bow, 2 stern), total 14 torpedoes, 20 mines, 1 x 100mm gun, 1 x 45mm AA gun, 2 x 7.62mm machine guns

COMPLEMENT: 55

NOTES: This series was an improved version of the Series XI, with a pair of torpedo tubes added in the stern and greater test-depth. All boats served in the Pacific Fleet.

The submarine *I-25* sank the *L-16* off the Oregon coast in error on 11 October 1942, and the *L-19* probably was mined in the La Perouse Straits on 23 August 1945. The surviving boats were stricken in the late 1950s.

## SERIES XII (1937)

*M-88* (12 June 1937) *M-87* (10 July 1937), *M-89* (9 October 1937), *M-91* (12 October 1937), *M-92* (12 October 1937), *M-93* (12 October 1937), *M-90* (28 November 1937), *M-100* (5 September 1939), *M-98* (15 April 1940), *M-99* (15 April 1940), *M-101* (1940), *M-102* (12 October 1940), *M-103* (12 October 1940)

BUILDER: Sudomekh

*M-57* (25 January 1939), *M-58* (28 April 1939), *M-59* (13 June 1939), *M-60* (28 August 1939), *M-62* (5 October 1939), *M-63* (5 October 1939), *M-31* (25 February 1940), *M-32* (26 February 1940), *M-33* (23 June 1940), *M-34* (23 June 1940), *M-35* (20 August 1940), *M-36* (20 August 1940)

BUILDER: Nikolayev

*M-111* (31 December 1940), *M-112* (31 December 1940), *M-113* (31 December 1940), *M-114* (31 December 1940), *M-115* (31 December 1940), *M-116* (31 December 1940), *M-117* (12 February 1941), *M-118* (12 February 1941), *M-120* (12 February 1941), *M-122* (12 February 1941), *M-104 Yaroslavskiy Komsomolets* (10 April 1941), *M-105 Chelyabinskiy Komsomolets* (10 April 1941), *M-106 Leninskiy Komsomolets* (10 April 1941), *M-107 Novosibirskiy Komsomolets* (16 April 1941), *M-108 Penzenskiy Komsomolets* (16 April 1941), *M-401* (31 May 1941), *M-119* (26 June 1941), *M-121* (19 August 1941)

BUILDER: Gorkiy

DISPLACEMENT: 206 tons (surfaced), 218 tons (submerged)

DIMENSIONS: 146'0" x 10'10" x 9'10"

MACHINERY: 1 diesel engine, 1 electric motor, 1 shaft. 800 bhp/400 shp = 13.5/7.75 knots

RANGE: 3440 nm at 8 knots surfaced, 107 nm at 2 knots submerged

ARMAMENT: 2 x 533mm torpedo tubes (bow), total 2 torpedoes, 1 x 45mm AA gun, 1–2 x 7.62mm machine gun(s)

COMPLEMENT: 20

NOTES: These boats were built to an improved coastal submarine design with substantially more range but still no torpedo reloads. The *M-31* through the *M-63*, the *M-111* through the *M-113*, the *M-117*, the *M-118*, and the *M-120* went to the Black Sea Fleet; the *M-87* through the *M-93*, the *M-104* through the *M-108*, and the *M-119*, the *M-121*, and the *M-122* went to the Northern Fleet; the *M-114* through the *M-116* went to the Pacific Fleet; the *M-401* went to the Caspian Sea; the other boats went to the Baltic Fleet. Two additional boats were lost incomplete in 1941.

The *U-149* torpedoed the *M-101* off Dago Island on 26 June 1941; the *M-99* was mined in the Gulf of Finland on 29 June; the *U-104* torpedoed the *M-94* off Dago Island on 21 July; the *M-103* was mined in the Gulf of Finland on 28 August; the *M-34* failed to return from a Black Sea patrol in December. The *U-584* torpedoed the *M-92* off the North Cape on 10 January 1942; the *M-95* was mined near Suursaari Island on 15 June;

the *M-93* failed to return from a patrol off the Norwegian coast the same month; the *M-97* was mined near Lavansaari Island on 14 August; German submarine chasers sank the *M-89* at Batsfjord on 24 August and the *M-33* was mined off Odessa the same day; the *M-121* failed to return from a patrol off the Norwegian coast in November; the Romanian destroyer *Regele Ferdinand I* sank the *M-59* in the Black Sea on 17 December, and the *M-58* was mined there the next day. The *M-106* was lost off the North Cape on 5 July 1943; the *M-36* was lost off Sevastopol on 11 September; German aircraft sank the *M-31* south of Takil on 2 October; the *M-88* failed to return from a patrol off the Norwegian coast the same month, as did the *M-91* and the *M-122* the following month. The *M-108* also failed to return from a Norwegian coast patrol in April 1944, and the *M-96* was mined off Narva on 10 September.

Three boats were transferred to Bulgaria in the early 1950s and commissioned as its *M-1* through *M-3*. Two were returned to the Soviet Union in 1958 in exchange for two Project 613 boats, and the third example was stricken in 1967.

The surviving boats were stricken after World War II.

## SERIES XIV (1938)

*K-1* (29 April 1938), *K-2* (29 April 1938), *K-3* (31 July 1938), *K-56* (29 December 1940), *K-55* (7 February 1941), *K-54* (March 1941), *K-57* (1946)
BUILDER: Admiralty
*K-22* (4 November 1938), *K-23* (28 April 1939), *K-52* (5 July 1939), *K-51* (30 July 1939), *K-21* (14 August 1939), *K-53* (2 September 1939), *K-24* (1940)
BUILDER: Baltic
*K-58, K-60, K-77, K-78* (1946)
BUILDER: Zhdanov
DISPLACEMENT: 1490 tons (surfaced), 2140 tons (submerged)
DIMENSIONS: 320'4" x 24'3" x 14'10"
MACHINERY: 4 diesel engines, 2 electric motors, 2 shafts. 8400 bhp/2400 shp = 21/10 knots
RANGE: 14,000 nm at 9 knots surfaced, 160 nm at 3 knots submerged
ARMAMENT: 10 x 533mm torpedo tubes (6 bow, 2 stern, 2 trainable external mounts), total 24 torpedoes, 20 mines, 2 x 100mm guns, 2 x 45mm AA guns
COMPLEMENT: 60

NOTES: Mikhail Alekseevich Rudnitskiy designed these large double-hull cruiser submarines. In addition to mines laid through two vertical tubes amidships, these boats originally were to carry a seaplane in a hangar abaft the conning tower, but the aviation proposal was abandoned. These submarines performed well and were the best Soviet-designed boats in service during World War II. All the class operated with the Northern Fleet. One additional boat building at Leningrad was not completed because of the German siege.

The *K-22* was mined off Cape Harbaken on 6 February 1942; the *K-23* was lost off Okse Fjord on 12 May; the *K-2* failed to return from a patrol off the Norwegian coast in September. The *K-3* was lost off Batsfjord on 21 March 1943, and the *K-1* probably was mined in the Kara Sea in October. The surviving boats were stricken in the late 1950s, and the *K-21* became a memorial at Severomorsk.

## SERIES XV (1940)

*M-200 Mest* (4 February 1941), *M-201* (4 February 1941), *M-202 Rybnik Donbasa* (4 April 1941), *M-203 Irkutskiy Rybak* (7 July 1941), *M-204* (1946), *M-205–M-216, M-219, M-231, M-234–253, M-257, M-258, M-260, M-262, M-266, M-270–M-291* (1947–1949)
BUILDER: Sudomekh
DISPLACEMENT: 281 tons (surfaced), 351 tons (submerged)
DIMENSIONS: 162'5" x 14'5" x 9'0"
MACHINERY: 2 diesel engines, 2 electric motors, 2 shafts. 1600 bhp/875 shp = 15.75/7.75 knots
RANGE: 4500 nm at 8 knots surfaced, 90 nm at 2 knots submerged

ARMAMENT: 4 x 533mm torpedo tubes (bow), total 4 torpedoes, 1 x 45mm AA gun, 2 x 7.62mm machine guns
COMPLEMENT: 24
NOTES: F. F. Polushkin designed this series of coastal submarines. They had a single all-welded pressure hull with saddle ballast tanks. The design was a great improvement on earlier coastal boats with its much greater range and heavier torpedo battery. None of the class were completed during World War II.

Those remaining in Soviet Navy service were stricken in the 1960s.

## SWEDEN
## *U-1* CLASS (1941)

*U-1* (14 June 1941), *U-4* (5 June 1943), *U-5* (8 July 1943), *U-6* (18 August 1943), *U-7* (25 November 1943)

BUILDER: Kockums

*U-2* (16 May 1942), *U-3* (11 June 1942), *U-8* (25 April 1944), *U-9* (23 May 1944)

BUILDER: Karlskrona

DISPLACEMENT: 367 tons (surfaced), 450 tons (submerged)

DIMENSIONS: 162'9" x 15'5" x 12'6"

MACHINERY: 1 MAN diesel-electric generator, 2 electric motors, 2 shafts. 1350 shp = 13/7.5 knots

ARMAMENT: 4 x 533mm torpedo tubes (3 bow, 1 external training mount), 1 x 20mm AA gun

COMPLEMENT: 23

NOTES: Swenzén designed these small coastal submarines, which introduced diesel-electric drive and were Sweden's first all-welded boats. In 1952–1953 these boats were refitted. One periscope was removed and replaced with a snorkel, and the external mount and antiaircraft gun were landed. The *U-4* through the *U-6* again were reconstructed between 1951 and 1954 as streamlined hunter-killer submarines and named the *Forellen*, the *Aborren*, the *Siken*, the *Gädden*, the *Laxen*, and the *Makrillen*. Displacement rose to 388 tons, and submerged speed increased to 9 knots. The three early boats were stricken in the early 1960s, and the later hunter-killers between 1970 and 1976. The *U-3* is preserved in a museum at Malmö.

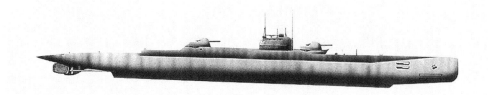

# UNITED KINGDOM
## *X-1* (16 JUNE 1923)
*(Courtesy of Art-Tech)*

BUILDER: Chatham

DISPLACEMENT: 2425 tons (surfaced), 3600 tons (submerged)

DIMENSIONS: 363′6″ x 29′10″ x 15′9″

MACHINERY: 2 Admiralty diesel engines plus 2 former *U-126* diesel engines, 2 electric motors, 2 shafts. 7000 bhp/2400 shp = 19.5/8 knots

ARMAMENT: 6 x 21″ torpedo tubes (bow), total 12 torpedoes, 2 x twin 5.25″ guns

COMPLEMENT: 110

NOTES: The *X-1* was a cruiser submarine, almost a complete double-hull type, equipped with gun armament and fire control equipment suitable for a surface action. The former German diesel engines drove the battery-charging generators, which also could power the electric motors to boost speed on the surface. The machinery arrangements gave almost continuous trouble, and the boat was laid up in December 1933 and scrapped in 1937.

## UNITED KINGDOM: *OBERON* (24 SEPTEMBER 1926)
*(Courtesy of Art-Tech)*

BUILDER: Chatham

DISPLACEMENT: 1311 tons (surfaced), 1831 tons (submerged)

DIMENSIONS: 269′8″ x 28′0″ x 15′6″

MACHINERY: 2 Admiralty diesel engines, 2 electric motors 2 shafts. 2950 bhp/1350 shp = 13.75/7.5 knots

ARMAMENT: 8 x 21″ torpedo tubes (6 bow, 2 stern), total 16 torpedoes, 1 x 4″ gun

COMPLEMENT: 54

NOTES: The *Oberon* was the prototype for an improved overseas patrol submarine, a substantial enlargement of the L-class, with saddle main ballast tanks and oil fuel tanks outside the pressure hull. It operated with the Atlantic Fleet until 1937, went into the reserve fleet, and was recommissioned for training duties during World War II. The *Oberon* was laid up in July 1944 and scrapped in 1945.

## UNITED KINGDOM: *OXLEY* CLASS, *OTWAY* (1926)
*(Courtesy of Art-Tech)*

[Australia]—*Oxley* (29 June 1926), *Otway* (7 September 1926)

BUILDER: Barrow

DISPLACEMENT: 1354 tons (surfaced), 1872 tons (submerged)

DIMENSIONS: 275'0" x 27'8" x 15'9"

MACHINERY: 2 Admiralty diesel engines, 2 electric motors, 2 shafts. 3100 bhp/1350 shp = 15/8.5 knots

ARMAMENT: 8 x 21" torpedo tubes (6 bow, 2 stern), total 16 torpedoes, 1 x 4" gun

COMPLEMENT: 55

NOTES: These were modestly enlarged versions of the *Oberon* for the Royal Australian Navy. They were transferred to the Royal Navy in 1931 and served with the Atlantic Fleet. The submarine *Triton* mistakenly torpedoed the *Oxley* off the Norwegian coast on 10 September 1939, and the *Otway* was scrapped in 1945.

## *ODIN* CLASS (1928)

*Odin* (5 May 1928)
BUILDER: Chatham
*Osiris* (19 May 1928), *Oswald* (19 June 1928), *Otus* (31 August 1928)
BUILDER: Barrow
*Olympus* (11 December 1928), *Orpheus* (26 February 1929)
BUILDER: Beardmore
DISPLACEMENT: 1475 tons (surfaced), 2038 tons (submerged)
DIMENSIONS: 283'6" x 29'11" x 16'1"
MACHINERY: 2 Admiralty diesel engines, 2 electric motors, 2 shafts. 4520 bhp/1390 shp = 17.5/8 knots
ARMAMENT: 8 x 21" torpedo tubes (6 bow, 2 stern), total 14 torpedoes, 1 x 4" gun

COMPLEMENT: 53
NOTES: These were production versions of the *Oberon* with greater speed. During World War II they served primarily in the Mediterranean. The destroyers *Baleno* and *Strale* sank the *Odin* in the Gulf of Taranto on 13 June 1940; the destroyer *Turbine* sank the *Orpheus* off Tobruk on 19 June; the destroyer *Ugolino Vivaldi* rammed and sank the *Oswald* off Cape Spartivento on 1 August. The *Olympus* was mined off Malta on 8 May 1942, and the two surviving boats were discarded in 1946.

## [CHILE]—*CAPITAN O'BRIEN* CLASS (1928)

*Capitan O'Brien* (2 October 1928), *Almirante Simpson* (15 January 1929), *Capitan Thompson* (15 January 1929)
BUILDER: Barrow
DISPLACEMENT: 1540 tons (surfaced), 2020 tons (submerged)
DIMENSIONS: 260'0" x 28'0" x 13'6"
MACHINERY: 2 diesel engines, 2 electric motors, 2 shafts. 2750 bhp/1300 shp = 15/9 knots

ARMAMENT: 8 x 21" torpedo tubes (6 bow, 2 stern), total 16 torpedoes, 1 x 4.7" gun
COMPLEMENT: 54
NOTES: These were export versions of the *Olympus*, with greater speed and fitted with enlarged conning towers. They were discarded in 1957–1958.

## UNITED KINGDOM: IMPROVED OVERSEAS TYPE, *PARTHIAN* (1929)
*(Courtesy of Art-Tech)*

*Perseus* (22 May 1929), *Poseidon* (21 June 1929), *Proteus* (23 July 1929), *Pandora* (22 August 1929), *Regent* (11 June 1930), *Regulus* (11 June 1930), *Rover* (11 June 1930)

BUILDER: Barrow

*Parthian* (22 June 1929), *Rainbow* (14 May 1930)

BUILDER: Chatham

*Phoenix* (3 October 1929)

BUILDER: Cammell Laird

DISPLACEMENT: 1475 tons (surfaced), 2040 tons (submerged)

DIMENSIONS: 289′2″ (R boats: 287′2″) x 29′11″ x 15′11″

MACHINERY: 2 Admiralty diesel engines, 2 electric motors, 2 shafts. 4640 bhp/1635 shp = 17.5/8.5 knots

ARMAMENT: 8 x 21″ torpedo tubes (6 bow, 2 stern), total 14 torpedoes, 1 x 4″ gun

COMPLEMENT: 53

NOTES: Improved versions of the *Odin* class. They were designed for deployment to the Far East, where they served until World War II. The steamer *Yuta* accidentally rammed and sank the *Poseidon* off Wei Hai Wei on 9 June 1931. The other boats transferred to the Mediterranean during World War II. The torpedo boat *Albatros* sank the *Phoenix* off Augusta, Sicily, on 16 July 1940; the motor vessel *Antonietta Costa* rammed and sank the *Rainbow* off the Libyan coast in 10 October; the *Regulus* was mined in the Straits of Otranto on 26 November. The *Perseus* was mined off Cephalonia on December 6, 1941; the *Pandora* was bombed at Malta on 1 April 1942; the *Regent* and the *Parthian* were mined in the Adriatic on 18 April and 10 August 1943. The two surviving boats were broken up in 1946.

## *THAMES* CLASS (1932)

*Thames* (26 January 1932), *Severn* (16 January 1934), *Clyde* (15 March 1934)

BUILDER: Barrow

DISPLACEMENT: 1850 tons (surfaced), 2723 tons (submerged)

DIMENSIONS: 345'0" x 28'3" x 15'11"

MACHINERY: 2 Admiralty supercharged diesel engines, 2 electric motors, 2 shafts. 10,000 bhp/2500 shp = 22/10 knots

ARMAMENT: 6 x 21" torpedo tubes (bow), total 12 torpedoes, 1 x 4" gun

COMPLEMENT: 61

NOTES: These high-speed fleet submarines were of almost double-hull form and introduced welded external fuel tanks to eliminate the leakage problem present in earlier boats with riveted tanks. The Admiralty planned to order as many as twenty of this class but changed its policy. These boats operated with the Atlantic and Home fleets. The *Thames* was mined in the North Sea on 3 August 1940, and the other boats were scrapped in 1946.

**UNITED KINGDOM: EARLY S CLASS (1931), *SALMON* (1934)**
*(Courtesy of Art-Tech)*

*Swordfish* (10 November 1931), *Sturgeon* (8 January 1932), *Seahorse* (15 November 1932), *Starfish* (14 March 1933), *Shark* (31 May 1934), *Snapper* (25 October 1934), *Sunfish* (30 September 1936), *Sterlet* (22 September 1937)
BUILDER: Chatham
*Sealion* (16 March 1934), *Salmon* (30 April 1934), *Spearfish* (21 April 1936)
BUILDER: Cammell Laird
*Seawolf* (28 November 1935)
BUILDER: Scott
DISPLACEMENT: 670 (first four boats: 640) tons (surfaced), 960 (first four boats: 927) tons (submerged)
DIMENSIONS: 208′8″ (first four boats: 202′2″) x 24′0″ x 11′11″

MACHINERY: 2 Admiralty diesel engines, 2 electric motors, 2 shafts. 1550 bhp/1440 shp = 14/10 knots
ARMAMENT: 6 x 21″ torpedo tubes (bow), total 12 torpedoes, 1 x 3″ gun
COMPLEMENT: 38–39
NOTES: These boats were designed for short-range operations. They had a single hull with saddle main ballast tanks and internal fuel tanks. They served primarily in the Home Fleet. The *Sturgeon* was transferred to The Netherlands in October 1943 as the *Zeehond,* and the *Sunfish* to the Soviet Union in June 1944 as the *V-1.* German minesweepers sank the *Seahorse* off the Elbe and the *Starfish* off Heligoland on 7 January and 9 January

1940; the minesweeper *M-75* sank the *Sterlet* in the Skagerrak on 14 April; aircraft so seriously damaged the *Shark* off Stavanger that it was scuttled on 6 July; the *Salmon* was mined in the North Sea on 9 July; the *U-34* torpedoed the *Spearfish* in the North Sea on 1 August; the *Swordfish* was mined in the English Channel on 7 November. German minesweepers sank the *Snapper* off Ushant on 11 February 1941, and the *V-1* was sunk in error by British aircraft off Norway on 27 July 1944. The *Sealion* was scuttled on 3 March 1945, and the two surviving boats were broken up 1945–1946.

## UNITED KINGDOM: *PORPOISE* (1932)
*(Courtesy of Art-Tech)*

BUILDER: Barrow
DISPLACEMENT: 1500 tons (surfaced), 2053 tons (submerged)
DIMENSIONS: 289'0" x 29'10" x 15'11"
MACHINERY: 2 Admiralty diesel engines, 2 electric motors, 2 shafts. 3300 bhp/1630 shp = 15.5/8.75 knots
ARMAMENT: 6 x 21" torpedo tubes (bow), total 12 torpedoes, 50 mines, 1 x 4" gun

COMPLEMENT: 59
NOTES: This submarine essentially was a minelayer version of the overseas patrol design with the mines carried in the superstructure on a chain conveyor. It served in the Mediterranean and Far East and was sunk by Japanese aircraft in the Malacca Strait on 16 January 1945.

## [PORTUGAL]—*DELFIM* CLASS (1934)

*Delfim* (1 May 1934), *Espardarte* (30 May 1934), *Golginho* (30 May 1934)
BUILDER: Barrow
DISPLACEMENT: 800 tons (surfaced), 1092 tons (submerged)
DIMENSIONS: 227′2″ x 21′4″ x 12′8″
MACHINERY: 2 Vickers diesel engines, 2 electric motors, 2 shafts. 2300 bhp/1000 shp = 16.5/9.25 knots
RANGE: 5000 nm at 10 knots surfaced, 110 nm at 4 knots submerged

ARMAMENT: 6 x 533mm torpedo tubes (4 bow, 2 stern), 1 x 4″ gun, 2 x 7.62mm machine guns
COMPLEMENT: 36
NOTES: Vickers designed these submarines as diminutives of contemporary British overseas boats. They were discarded in the 1950s.

## *GRAMPUS* CLASS (1935)

*Narwhal* (29 August 1935), *Rorqual* (21 July 1936)
BUILDER: Barrow
*Grampus* (25 February 1936), *Seal* (27 September 1938)
BUILDER: Chatham
*Cachalot* (2 December 1937)
BUILDER: Scott
DISPLACEMENT: 1520 tons (surfaced), 2157 tons (submerged)
DIMENSIONS: 293′0″ x 25′6″ x 16′10″
MACHINERY: 2 Admiralty diesel engines, 2 electric motors, 2 shafts. 3300 bhp/1630 shp = 15.75/8.75 knots
ARMAMENT: 6 x 21″ torpedo tubes (bow), total 12 torpedoes, 50 mines, 1 x 4″ gun
COMPLEMENT: 59

NOTES: These minelayers used a hull form similar to the *Thames* class with internal fuel tanks and an almost complete double hull. They served with the Mediterranean and Home fleets. The *Seal* was damaged by a mine in the Kattegat on 4 May 1940 and surrendered to German forces the following day. It served briefly for training as the *UB* and was scuttled in May 1945. The torpedo boat *Polluce* sank the *Grampus* off Syracuse on 16 June 1940; German aircraft sank the *Narwhal* off Norway on 23 July; and the torpedo boat *Generale Achille Papa* rammed and sank the *Cachalot* off Benghazi on 30 July 1941. The *Rorqual* was broken up in 1946.

## [ESTONIA]—*KALEV* CLASS (1936)

*Lembit* (7 July 1936), *Kalev* (1937)
BUILDER: Barrow
DISPLACEMENT: 620 tons (surfaced), 850 tons (submerged)
DIMENSIONS: 190′3″ x 23′11″ x 10′10″
MACHINERY: 2 Vickers diesel engines, 2 electric motors, 2 shafts. 1200 bhp/790 shp = 13.5/8.5 knots
ARMAMENT: 4 x 533mm torpedo tubes (bow), 20 mines, 1 x 45mm AA gun, 1 x 20mm AA gun

COMPLEMENT: 38
NOTES: Vickers designed these submarine minelayers with single hulls, saddle main ballast tanks, and mine chutes in the tanks. They were taken over by the Soviet Union in August 1940. The *Kalev* was mined off Hangö in November 1940. The *Lembit* was renamed the *U-1* in 1945 and the *S-85* in 1949. It was used for experimental trials until 1956 and became a memorial ship at Tallinn in 1979.

**UNITED KINGDOM: T CLASS (1937), *THERMOPYLAE* (1945)**
**(as reconstructed postwar)**
*(Courtesy of Art-Tech)*

*Triton* (5 October 1937), *Triumph* (16 February 1938), *Thistle* (25 October 1938), *Triad* (5 May 1939), *Truant* (5 May 1939), *Tetrarch* (14 November 1939), *Trusty* (14 March 1941), *Turbulent* (12 May 1941), *Tutankhamen* (5 March 1942), *Trespasser* (29 May 1942), *Taurus* (27 June 1942), *Tactician* (29 July 1942), *Truculent* (12 September 1942), *Templar* (26 October 1942), *Tally Ho* (23 December 1942), *Tantalus* (24 February 1943), *Tantivy* (6 April 1943), *Telemachus* (19 June 1943), *Talent* (17 July 1943), *Terrapin* (31 August 1943), *Thorough* (30 October 1943), *Tiptoe* (25 February 1944), *Trump* (25 March 1944), *Taciturn* (7 June 1944), *Tapir* (21 August 1944), *Tarn* (29 November 1944), *Tasman* (13 February 1945), *Teredo* (27 April 1945)
BUILDER: Barrow

*Thetis* (29 June 1938), *Trident* (7 December 1938), *Taku* (20 May 1939), *Talisman* (29 January 1940), *Thrasher* (28 November 1940), *Thorn* (18 March 1941), *Tempest* (10 June 1940)
BUILDER: Cammell Laird

*Tribune* (8 December 1938), *Tarpon* (17 October 1939), *Tuna* (10 May 1940), *Traveller* (27 August 1941), *Trooper* (5 March 1942), *Tabard* (21 November 1945)
BUILDER: Scott

*Tigris* (31 October 1939), *Torbay* (9 April 1940), *Tradewind* (11 December 1942), *Trenchant* (24 March 1943), *Turpin* (5 August 1944), *Thermopylae* (27 June 1945)
BUILDER: Chatham

*Tudor* (23 September 1942), *Thule* (22 October 1942), *Totem* (28 September 1943), *Truncheon* (22 February 1944)

BUILDER: Devonport

*Tireless* (19 March 1943), *Token* (19 March 1943), *Thor* (18 April 1944), *Tiara* (18 April 1944)

BUILDER: Portsmouth DY

DISPLACEMENT: 1090 tons (surfaced), 1575 tons (submerged)

DIMENSIONS: 275′0″ x 26′7″ x 14′8″

MACHINERY: 2 diesel engines, 2 electric motors, 2 shafts. 2500 bhp/1450 shp = 15.25/9 knots

ARMAMENT: 11 (first twelve boats: 10) x 21″ torpedo tubes (6 bow, 4–5 external), total 16–17 torpedoes, 1 x 4″ gun

COMPLEMENT: 59–61

NOTES: This class of patrol submarines constantly evolved as construction continued through World War II. It was a single-hull design with saddle main ballast tanks and a very heavy torpedo battery. All but the first few boats had welded framing, and the final dozen were of all-welded construction. The *Thetis* sank on trials in Liverpool Bay on 1 June 1939 and was salved and recommissioned as the *Thunderbolt*.

The *U-4* torpedoed the *Thistle* off the Norwegian coast on 10 April 1940; the Q-ship *Schiff 40* sank the *Tarpon* in the North Sea on the same day; the submarine *Enrico Toti* sank the *Triad* off Calabria on 15 October; Italian torpedo boats probably sank the *Triton* in the Adriatic on 6 December. The *Tetrarch* and the *Triumph* probably were mined off the Sicilian coast and in the Cyclades on 27 October and 31 December 1941. The

torpedo boat *Circe* sank the *Tempest* in the Gulf of Taranto on 12 February 1942; the torpedo boat *Pegaso* sank the *Thorn* near Crete on 7 August; the *Talisman* was mined near Sicily on 17 September; the *Traveller* probably was mined in the Gulf of Taranto on 4 December. The *Tutankhamen* was mined off Sardinia on 2 January 1943; the antisubmarine vessel *Uj–2210* sank the *Tigris* off Capri on 27 February; the corvette *Cicogna* sank the *Thunderbolt* off Sicily on 14 March; the *Turbulent* was mined off Sardinia on the same date, and the *Trooper* was mined in the Aegean on 10 October. Japanese antisubmarine vessels badly damaged the *Terrapin* off Batavia on 19 May 1945, and it was scrapped without being repaired.

The merchant ship *Dvina* accidentally rammed and sank the *Truculent* in the Thames estuary on 12 January 1950, and the *Templar* and the *Tantivy* were sunk as targets in the 1950s. The surviving prewar boats were scrapped between 1945 and 1947, while 13 of the later boats were partially reconstructed for improved underwater performance. They were scrapped between 1960 and 1970.

The *Taurus*, the *Talent*, the *Tapir*, and the *Tarn* were transferred to The Netherlands between 1943 and 1948 as the *Dolfijn*, the *Zwaardvisch*, the *Zeehond*, and the *Tijgerhaai*. The *Totem*, the *Truncheon*, and the *Turpin* were transferred to Israel between 1964 and 1968 as the *Dakar*, the *Dolphin*, and the *Leviathan*.

## SHORT HULL U CLASS (1937)

*Undine* (5 October 1937), *Unity* (16 February 1938), *Ursula* (16 February 1938), *Utmost* (20 April 1940), *Upright* (21 April 1940), *Unique* (6 June 1940), *Usk* (7 June 1940), *Upholder* (8 July 1940), *Unbeaten* (9 July 1940), *Urge* (19 August 1940), *Undaunted* (20 August 1940), *Urchin* (30 September 1940), *Union* (1 October 1940), *P-31* (27 November 1940), *P-32* (15 December 1940), *P-33* (28 January 1941), *P-34* (11 February 1941), *P-35* (15 March 1941), *P-36* (28 April 1941), *P-37* (12 May 1941), *P-38* (9 July 1941), *P-39* (23 August 1941), *P-41* (24 August 1941), *P-42* (4 November 1941), *P-43* (5 November 1941), *P-44* (18 December 1941), *P-46* (19 December 1941), *P-45* (16 February 1942), *P-54* (17 February 1942), *P-48* (15 April 1942), *P-51* (16 April 1942), *P-47* (27 July 1942), *P-49* (28 July 1942), *P-52* (11 October 1942), *P-53* (12 October 1942), *P-64* (23 November 1942), *P-65* (24 November 1942), *Varne* (22 January 1943), *Vox* (23 January 1943)

BUILDER: Barrow

*Umpire* (30 December 1940), *Una* (10 June 1941)

BUILDER: Chatham

*P-55* (28 July 1942), *P-56* (24 September 1942), *P-57* (10 November 1942), *P-58* (8 December 1942), *Untiring* (20 January 1943), *Varangian* (4 March 1943), *Uther* (6 April 1943), *Unswerving* (19 July 1943)

BUILDER: Armstrong

DISPLACEMENT: 540 tons (surfaced), 730 tons (submerged)

DIMENSIONS: 191′0″–196′10″ x 16′1″ x 15′2″

MACHINERY: 2 Paxman diesel engines, 2 electric motors, 2 shafts. 615 bhp/825 shp = 11.25/10 knots

ARMAMENT: 4 (first three boats: 6) x 21″ torpedo tubes (4 bow, 2 external), total 8–10 torpedoes, 1 x 3″ gun

COMPLEMENT: 27–33

NOTES: These single hull submarines with saddle main ballast tanks were designed for use as training vessels and for short-range patrol operations. They employed diesel-electric drive while surfaced. The bulk of their service was in the Mediterranean, where their small size proved an advantage and they were very successful.

German minesweepers sank the *Undine* off Heligoland on 7 January 1940, and the Norwegian steamer *Atle Jarl* accidentally rammed and sank the *Unity* off the Tyne on 29 April. The *Usk* was mined off Cape Bon on 26 April 1941; the torpedo boat *Pegaso* probably sank the *Undaunted* off the Libyan coast on 12 May; the trawler *Peter Hendricks* accidentally rammed and sank the *Umpire* off the Suffolk coast on 19 July; the torpedo boat *Circe* sank the Union off *Pantellaria* on 20 July; the *P-32* and the *P-33* were mined off Tripoli on 18 August and 20 August. The torpedo boat *Circe* sank the *P-38* off Tripoli on 23 February 1942; the *P-39* and the *P-36* were sunk by aircraft at Malta on 26 March and 1 April; the torpedo boat *Pegaso* sank the *Upholder* near Tripoli on 14 April and probably the *Urge* in the same area on 29 April; the *Unique* failed to return from a patrol in the Bay of Biscay in October; British aircraft accidentally sank the *Unbeaten* in the same area on 11 November; the torpedo boat *Groppo* sank the *Utmost* near Sicily on 25 November; the torpedo boat *Ardente* sank the *P-48* off Tunisia on 25 December. The *Vandal* sank in an accident in the Clyde on 24 February 1943, the *Untamed* in another near Campbeltown on 30 May, and the antisubmarine vessel *Uj–2208* sank the *Usurper* in the Gulf of Genoa on 3 October.

Several boats served with Allied navies during World War II (Poland–2, The Netherlands–1, Soviet Union–2, Norway–2). The *P-52* went to the Royal Danish Navy as the *Springeren* between 1946 and 1957, and the *Untiring* and the *Upstart* to the Greek Navy as the *Xifias* and the *Amfitritii* between 1945 and 1952. The remainder of the class were scrapped between 1946 and 1950.

## [TURKEY]—*ORUC REIS* CLASS (1940)

*Oruc Reis* (19 July 1940), *Murat Reis* (20 July 1940), *Burak Reis* (19 October 1940), *Ulac Ali Reis* (1 November 1940)
BUILDER: Barrow
DISPLACEMENT: 624 tons (surfaced), 856 tons (submerged)
DIMENSIONS: 201'7" x 22'4" x 11'10"
MACHINERY: 2 Vickers diesel engines, 2 electric motors, 2 shafts. 1200 bhp/780 shp = 13.75/8.5 knots
ARMAMENT: 5 x 21" torpedo tubes (4 bow, 1 external), total 9 torpedoes, 1 x 4" gun

COMPLEMENT: 35
NOTES: The design for these boats was a modestly enlarged version of the original S-class. They were taken over while under construction and commissioned as the *P-611*, the *P-612*, the *P-614*, and the *P-615*. The *U-123* torpedoed the *P-615* off the Liberian coast on 18 April 1943. The first two boats were returned to Turkey in 1942, and the *P-614* in 1945. They reverted to their original names and were discarded in 1957.

## UNITED KINGDOM: LATER S CLASS (1941)
*(Courtesy of Art-Tech)*

P-222 (20 September 1941), *Seraph* (25 October 1941), *Shakespeare* (8 December 1941)

BUILDER: Barrow

*Safari* (18 November 1941), *Sahib* (19 January 1942), *Saracen* (16 February 1942), *Sibyl* (29 April 1942), *Seadog* (11 June 1942), *Sea Nymph* (29 July 1942), *Sickle* (27 August 1942), *Simoom* (12 October 1942), *Stubborn* (11 November 1942), *Surf* (10 December 1942), *Syrtis* (4 February 1943), *Stonehenge* (23 March 1943), *Stoic* (9 April 1943), *Storm* (18 May 1943), *Stratagem* (21 June 1943), *Spirit* (20 July 1943), *Statesman* (14 September 1943), *Sturdy* (30 September 1943), *Stygian* (30 November 1943), *Subtle* (27 January 1944), *Supreme* (24 February 1944), *Sea Scout* (24 March 1944), *Selene* (24 April 1944), *Solent* (8 June 1944), *Sleuth* (6 July 1944), *Sidon* (4 September 1944), *Spearhead* (2 October 1944), *Spur* (17 November 1944), *Scorcher* (18 December 1944), *Sanguine* (15 February 1945), *Saga* (14 March 1945), *Springer* (14 May 1945)

BUILDER: Cammell Laird

*Satyr* (28 September 1942), *Sceptre* (9 January 1943), *Sea Rover* (18 February 1943), *Sirdar* (26 March 1943), *Spiteful* (5 June 1943), *Strongbow* (30 August 1943), *Spark* (28 December 1943), *Scythian* (14 April 1944), *Scotsman* (18 August 1944), *Sea Devil* (30 January 1944), *Seneschal* (23 April 1945), *Sentinel* (27 July 1945)

BUILDER: Scott

*Splendid* (19 January 1942), *Sportsman* (17 April 1942), *Shalimar* (22 April 1943)

BUILDER: Chatham

DISPLACEMENT: 715 tons (surfaced), 990 tons (submerged)

DIMENSIONS: 217'0" x 23'9" x 14'2"

MACHINERY: 2 diesel engines, 2 electric motors, 2 shafts. 1900 bhp/1300 shp = 14.75/9 knots

ARMAMENT: 7 (last 17 boats: 6) x 21″ torpedo tubes (6 bow, 1 external), total 12–13 torpedoes, 1 x 3″ or 4″ gun

COMPLEMENT: 48

NOTES: These submarines were improved versions of the earlier S class. They all featured welded framing, and the final 15 boats were of all-welded construction. Most added a 20mm antiaircraft gun during the war.

The torpedo boat *Fortunale* probably sank the *P-222* off Capri on 12 December 1942. The German destroyer *Hermes* sank the *Splendid* off Capri on 21 April 1943; the corvette *Euterpe* sank the *Sahib* off Sicily on 24 April; the corvette *Minerva* sank the *Saracen* off Bastia on 14 August; the *Simoom* was probably mined in the Aegean on 19 November. Mines claimed the *Stonehenge* in the Malacca Strait on 16 March 1944, the *Syrtis* off Bodo on 28 March, and the *Sickle* in the Aegean on 16 June, while a Japanese antisubmarine vessel sank the *Stratagem* off Malacca on 22 November.

The *Spearhead*, the *Saga*, and the *Spur* went to Portugal as the *Neptuno*, the *Nautilo*, and the *Narval* in 1948. The *Satyr*, the *Spiteful*, the *Sportsman*, and the *Statesman* went to France in 1951 as the *Saphir*, the *Sirène*, the *Sibylle*, and the *Sultane*. The *Springer* and the *Sanguine* went to Israel as the *Tanin* and the *Rahav* in 1958. The *Seraph*, the *Sceptre*, the *Selene*, the *Solent*, and the *Sleuth* were converted into high-speed underwater targets. The *Sidon* sank after an internal explosion on 16 June 1951 at Portsmouth. Most of the remaining boats were discarded by the early 1950s, and the final examples were scrapped by 1962.

## LONG HULL U CLASS (1943)

*Venturer* (4 May 1943), *Viking* (5 May 1943), *Veldt* (19 July 1943), *Vampire* (20 July 1943), *Vox* (28 September 1943), *Vigorous* (15 October 1943), *Virtue* (29 November 1943), *Visigoth* (30 November 1943), *Upshot* (24 February 1944), *Urtica* (23 March 1944), *Vineyard* (8 May 1944), *Variance* (22 May 1944), *Vengeful* (20 July 1944), *Vortex* (19 August 1944), *Vagabond* (19 September 1944)

BUILDER: Barrow

*Vivid* (15 September 1943), *Voracious* (11 November 1943), *Vulpine* (28 December 1943), *Varne* (24 February 1944), *Virulent* (23 May 1944), *Volatile* (20 June 1944), *Votary* (21 August 1944)

BUILDER: Armstrong

DISPLACEMENT: 545 tons (surfaced), 740 tons (submerged)

DIMENSIONS: 204′6″ x 16′1″ x 15′3″

MACHINERY: 2 Paxman diesel engines, 2 electric motors, 2 shafts. 615 bhp/825 shp = 11.25/10 knots

ARMAMENT: 4 x 21″ torpedo tubes (bow), total 8 torpedoes, 1 x 3″ gun

COMPLEMENT: 33

NOTES: This class repeated the earlier group but incorporated a longer bow with a finer entrance. Twenty additional boats were canceled. During and after World War II, France received three boats, Norway four, Greece four, and Denmark two. Most of the class were scrapped by 1950, and all were broken up by 1959.

## UNITED KINGDOM: A CLASS (1944), *ARTFUL* (1947)
*(Courtesy of Art-Tech)*

*Amphion* (31 August 1944), *Astute* (30 January 1945), *Auriga* (29 March 1945), *Alcide* (12 April 1945), *Alderney* (25 June 1945), *Alliance* (28 July 1945), *Aurochs* (28 July 1945), *Ambush* (24 September 1945), *Anchorite* (22 January 1946), *Andrew* (6 April 1946)
BUILDER: Barrow
*Affray* (12 April 1945), *Aeneas* (25 October 1945), *Alaric* (18 February 1946), *Acheron* (25 March 1947)
BUILDER: Cammell Laird
*Ace* (1945), *Achates* (1945)
BUILDER: Devonport
*Artemis* (26 August 1946), *Artful* (22 May 1947)
BUILDER: Scott
DISPLACEMENT: 1120 tons (surfaced), 1620 tons (submerged)

DIMENSIONS: 279′3″ x 22′3″ x 17′1″
MACHINERY: 2 supercharged diesel engines, 2 electric motors, 2 shafts. 4300 bhp/1250 shp = 18.5/8 knots
ARMAMENT: 10 x 21″ torpedo tubes (4 bow, 2 stern, 4 external), total 16 torpedoes, 1 x 4″ gun
COMPLEMENT: 61
NOTES: These boats were of all-welded construction and were designed for operation in the Far East. They had an almost complete double hull and introduced air conditioning and other habitability improvements. An additional 50 vessels of this class were ordered or projected. None of these boats saw any service during World War II.

The *Affray* sank in an accident in the English Channel on 16 April 1951. The rest of the class except the *Aurochs* were modernized between 1955 and 1960 with enlarged batteries, modified bows, streamlined sails, and upgraded electronics and sonar, increasing their submerged speed to 15 knots. They were scrapped between 1970 and 1974 except the *Alliance*, which is preserved as a memorial at Gosport.

## UNITED STATES
## *BARRACUDA* CLASS (1924)

*Barracuda* (17 July 1924), *Bass* (27 December 1924), *Bonita* (9 June 1925)

BUILDER: Portsmouth

DISPLACEMENT: 2119 tons (surfaced), 2506 tons (submerged)

DIMENSIONS: 334'6" x 27'7" x 15'2"

MACHINERY: 2 diesel engines, 2 diesel electric generators, 2 shafts. 6200 bhp = 18.75/9 knots

RANGE: 6000 nm at 11 knots surfaced, 50 nm at 5 knots submerged

ARMAMENT: 6 x 21" torpedo tubes (4 bow, 2 stern), 1 x 5" gun

COMPLEMENT: 85

NOTES: These very large submarines were designed to operate with the fleet. In an effort to endow them with high surface speed they used both direct drive diesel engines and diesel electric generators while operating on the surface (known as composite drive). They received new diesel engines in the mid-1930s. During World War II they served primarily as training submarines, and they were stricken on 10 March 1945.

## [SPAIN]—C CLASS (1927)

C1 (31 March 1927), C2 (4 May 1928), C3 (20 February 1929), C4 (6 July 1929), C5 (28 October 1929), C6 (26 December 1929)

BUILDER: Cartagena

DISPLACEMENT: 916 tons (surfaced), 1290 tons (submerged

DIMENSIONS: 247'0" x 20'10" x 13'6

MACHINERY: 2 diesel engines, 2 electric motors, 2 shafts. 2000 bhp/750 shp = 16/8.5 knots

RANGE: 4000 nm at 6.5 knots surfaced, 125 nm at 4.5 knots submerged

ARMAMENT: 6 x 533mm torpedo tubes (4 bow, 2 stern), total 12 torpedoes, 1 x 75mm AA gun.

COMPLEMENT: 46

NOTES: These boats were built to an Electric Boat design under license and were enlarged versions of the previous B class with 533mm torpedo tubes in place the earlier type's 450mm tubes. Four boats served with the Spanish Republican Navy during the Spanish Civil War. The German U-34 torpedoed the C3 off Malaga on 12 December 1936; the C5 was lost in the Bay of Biscay the same month; the C6 was scuttled at Gijon on 10 October 1937; Nationalist aircraft sank the C1 at Barcelona on 9 October 1938. The C2 and the C4 were refitting in France when the war began. They were interned until 1939 and returned to Spain. The C4 was lost in an accident in June 1946, and the C2 was discarded in 1952.

## *ARGONAUT* (10 NOVEMBER 1927)

BUILDER: Portsmouth

DISPLACEMENT: 2878 tons (surfaced), 4045 tons (submerged)

DIMENSIONS: 381'0" x 33'8" x 16'0"

MACHINERY: 2 MAN diesel engines, 2 diesel electric generators, 2 shafts. 3175 bhp/2200 shp = 13.5/7.5 knots

RANGE: 18,000 nm at 10 knots surfaced, 50 nm at 5 knots submerged

ARMAMENT: 4 x 21" torpedo tubes (bow), 60 mines, 2 x 6" guns, 2 x 0.3" machine guns

COMPLEMENT: 86

NOTES: The *Argonaut* was the U.S. Navy's only dedicated minelaying submarine and carried its mines in two horizontal tubes discharging at the stern. It had an exceptionally long range and was fitted with a bow modeled after the big German submarine cruisers to improve its surface performance. The *Argonaut* was converted to a transport submarine in September 1942. The destroyers *Isokaze* and *Maikaze*, assisted by aircraft, sank it in the Solomon Sea on 10 January 1943.

## UNITED STATES: *NARWHAL* CLASS (1927), *NAUTILUS* (1930)
*(Courtesy of Art-Tech)*

*Narwhal* (17 December 1927), *Nautilus* (15 March 1930)
BUILDER: Mare Island
DISPLACEMENT: 2987 tons (surfaced), 3960 tons (submerged)
DIMENSIONS: 371′0″ x 33′3″ x 16′11″
MACHINERY: 2 diesel engines, 2 diesel electric generators, 2 shafts. 5633 bhp/1600 shp = 17.5/8 knots
RANGE: 18,000 nm at 10 knots surfaced, 50 nm at 5 knots submerged

ARMAMENT: 6 x 21″ torpedo tubes (4 bow, 2 stern), 2 x 6″ guns, 2 x 0.3″ machine guns
COMPLEMENT: 89
NOTES: These submarines were the largest in the U.S. Navy until after World War II and were similar to the *Argonaut*, with two torpedo tubes replacing the mine tubes. In early 1943 they received four additional external torpedo tubes, two firing forward and two firing aft. They were stricken in May 1945.

## *DOLPHIN* (8 MARCH 1932)

BUILDER: Portsmouth
DISPLACEMENT: 1688 tons (surfaced), 2215 tons (submerged)
DIMENSIONS: 319′3″ x 27′11″ x 13′1″
MACHINERY: 2 diesel engines, 2 diesel electric generators, 2 shafts. 3500 bhp/1750 shp = 17/8 knots

RANGE: 6000 nm at 10 knots surfaced, 50 nm at 5 knots submerged
ARMAMENT: 6 x 21″ torpedo tubes (4 bow, 2 stern), total 18 torpedoes, 1 x 4″ gun, 4 x 0.3″ machine guns
COMPLEMENT: 63

NOTES: The *Dolphin* was designed as a relatively slow, long-range submarine for patrol operations in the Pacific. Its small size, relative to the earlier types, reduced its range and overall performance substantially. The *Dolphin* operated primarily in a training role during World War II and was stricken on 24 October 1945.

## UNITED STATES: *CACHALOT* CLASS, *CUTTLEFISH* (1933)
*(Courtesy of Art-Tech)*

*Cachalot* (19 October 1933)
BUILDER: Portsmouth
*Cuttlefish* (21 November 1933)
BUILDER: Electric Boat
DISPLACEMENT: 1120 tons (surfaced), 1650 tons (submerged)
DIMENSIONS: 271'1" x 24'9" x 14'0"
MACHINERY: 2 diesel engines, 2 electric motors, 2 shafts. 2770 bhp/1600 shp = 17/8 knots
RANGE: 11,000 nm at 10 knots surfaced, 50 nm at 5 knots submerged
ARMAMENT: 6 x 21" torpedo tubes (4 bow, 2 stern), total 16 torpedoes, 1 x 3" gun, 3 x 0.5" machine guns, 4 x 0.3" machine guns

COMPLEMENT: 51
NOTES: This class dispensed with composite drive and relied on diesel engine propulsion only on the surface, saving space and weight. It also featured extensive use of welded construction and carried a much lighter deck gun battery. These submarines were the first in the U.S. Navy to embark torpedo fire control computers. They undertook operational patrols until 1943, then transferred to training duties until they were stricken in November 1945.

## *SHARK* CLASS (1935)

*Shark* (21 May 1935), *Tarpon* (4 September 1935)
BUILDER: Electric Boat
DISPLACEMENT: 1315 tons (surfaced), 1968 tons (submerged)
DIMENSIONS: 298'0" x 25'1" x 15'1"
MACHINERY: 4 diesel-electric power units, 2 electric motors, 2 shafts. 4300 bhp/2085 shp = 19.5/8 knots

RANGE: 11,000 nm at 10 knots surfaced, 50 nm at 5 knots submerged
ARMAMENT: 6 x 21" torpedo tubes (4 bow, 2 stern), total 16 torpedoes, 1 x 3" gun, 2 x 0.5" machine guns, 4 x 0.3" machine guns
COMPLEMENT: 54

## *PORPOISE* CLASS (1935)

*Porpoise* (20 June 1935), *Pike* (12 September 1935)
BUILDER: Portsmouth
DISPLACEMENT: 1316 tons (surfaced), 1934 tons (submerged)
DIMENSIONS: 301'0" x 24'11" x 14'1"
MACHINERY: 4 diesel-electric power units, 2 electric motors, 2 shafts. 4300 bhp/2085 shp = 19/10 knots

RANGE: 11,000 nm at 10 knots surfaced, 50 nm at 5 knots submerged
ARMAMENT: 6 x 21" torpedo tubes (4 bow, 2 stern), total 16 torpedoes, 1 x 3" gun, 2 x 0.5" machine guns, 4 x 0.3" machine guns
COMPLEMENT: 54

## UNITED STATES: *PERCH* CLASS (1936), *POMPANO* (1937)
*(Courtesy of Art-Tech)*

*Perch* (9 May 1936), *Pickerel* (7 July 1936), *Permit* (5 October 1936)
BUILDER: Electric Boat
*Plunger* (8 July 1936), *Pollack* (15 September 1936)
BUILDER: Portsmouth
*Pompano* (11 March 1937)
BUILDER: Mare Island
DISPLACEMENT: 1330 tons (surfaced), 1997 tons (submerged)
DIMENSIONS: 300′6″ x 25′2″ x 15′2″
MACHINERY: 4 diesel-electric power units, 2 electric motors, 2 shafts. 4300 bhp/2366 shp = 19.25/8 knots
RANGE: 11,000 nm at 10 knots surfaced, 50 nm at 5 knots submerged
ARMAMENT: 6 x 21″ torpedo tubes (4 bow, 2 stern), total 16 torpedoes, 1 x 3″ gun, 2 x 0.5″ machine guns, 4 x 0.3″ machine guns
COMPLEMENT: 54
NOTES: These three classes (*Shark, Porpoise,* and *Perch*) introduced high-speed diesel engines, diesel-electric drive, and air conditioning into a hull slightly larger than that of the *Cachalot* class, to reduce machinery space crowding. They were very successful and set the pattern for subsequent production. Two additional external forward-firing torpedo tubes were added to the *Porpoise,* the *Pike,* the *Tarpon,* the *Pickerel,* and the *Permit* in early 1942, and all surviving boats received additional antiaircraft weapons and reduced superstructures from mid-1943.

The destroyer *Yamakaze* sank the *Shark* in the Celebes Islands on 11 February 1942; Japanese destroyers forced the *Perch* to the surface in the Java Sea on 3 March, and it was scuttled; the *Pickerel* failed to return from a patrol off Honshu in April 1943; the *Pompano* probably was mined off the Japanese coast on 29 August. The surviving boats were stricken in 1956.

## UNITED STATES: *SALMON* CLASS, *SNAPPER* (1937)
*(Courtesy of Art-Tech)*

*Salmon* (12 June 1937), *Seal* (25 August 1937), *Skipjack* (23 October 1937)
BUILDER: Electric Boat
*Snapper* (24 August 1937), *Stingray* (6 October 1937)
BUILDER: Portsmouth
*Sturgeon* (15 March 1938)
BUILDER: Mare Island
DISPLACEMENT: 1449 tons (surfaced), 2210 tons (submerged)
DIMENSIONS: 308'0" x 26'2" x 15'7"

MACHINERY: 4 diesel engines, 2 electric motors, 2 shafts. 5500 bhp/2660 shp = 21/9 knots
RANGE: 11,000 nm at 10 knots surfaced, 50 nm at 5 knots submerged
ARMAMENT: 8 x 21" torpedo tubes (4 bow, 4 stern), total 24 torpedoes, 1 x 3" gun, 2 x 0.5" machine guns, 2 x 0.3" machine guns
COMPLEMENT: 59

## UNITED STATES: *SARGO* CLASS (1938)

*(Courtesy of Art-Tech)*

*Sargo* (6 June 1938), *Saury* (20 August 1938), *Spearfish* (29 October 1938)

BUILDER: Electric Boat

*Sculpin* (27 July 1938), *Squalus* (14 September 1938)

BUILDER: Portsmouth

DISPLACEMENT: 1450 tons (surfaced), 2215 tons (submerged)

DIMENSIONS: 310'6" x 26'10" x 16'8"

MACHINERY: 4 diesel engines, 2 electric motors, 2 shafts. 5500 bhp/2740 shp = 20/8.75 knots

RANGE: 11,000 nm at 10 knots surfaced, 50 nm at 5 knots submerged

ARMAMENT: 8 x 21" torpedo tubes (4 bow, 4 stern), total 24 torpedoes, 1 x 3" gun, 2 x 0.5" machine guns, 2 x 0.3" machine guns

COMPLEMENT: 59

NOTES: These two classes (*Salmon* and *Sargo*) reverted to composite drive, using high-speed diesel engines, and added two torpedo tubes at the stern. An accident sank the *Squalus* at Portsmouth on 23 May 1939. It was raised, repaired, and recommissioned as the *Sailfish* in May 1940. Surviving boats received additional antiaircraft weapons and reduced superstructures from 1943.

The destroyer *Yamagumo* sank the *Sculpin* off Truk on 19 November 1943. The surviving boats were stricken 1946–1948.

## SEADRAGON CLASS (1939)

*Swordfish* (1 April 1939)
BUILDER: Mare Island
*Seadragon* (21 April 1939), *Sealion* (25 May 1939)
BUILDER: Electric Boat
*Searaven* (21 June 1939), *Seawolf* (15 August 1939)
BUILDER: Portsmouth
DISPLACEMENT: 1450 tons (surfaced), 2215 tons (submerged)
DIMENSIONS: 310'6" x 26'10" x 16'8"
MACHINERY: 4 diesel-electric power units, 2 electric motors, 2 shafts. 5200 bhp/2740 shp = 20/8.75 knots
RANGE: 11,000 nm at 10 knots surfaced, 50 nm at 5 knots submerged
ARMAMENT: 8 x 21" torpedo tubes (4 bow, 4 stern), total 24 torpedoes, 1 x 3" gun, 2 x 0.5" machine guns, 2 x 0.3" machine guns
COMPLEMENT: 59
NOTES: This class reintroduced diesel-electric drive, but otherwise duplicated the preceding group of submarines. Surviving boats received additional antiaircraft weapons and reduced superstructures from 1943.

The *Sealion* was scuttled at Cavite on 25 December 1941; the destroyer escort *Richard M. Rowell* sank the *Seawolf* in error off Morotai on 3 October 1944; the *Swordfish* failed to return from a patrol off Okinawa in January 1945. The surviving boats were stricken in 1948.

## TAMBOR CLASS (1939)

*Tambor* (20 December 1939), *Tautog* (27 January 1940), *Thresher* (27 March 1940), *Gar* (7 November 1940), *Grampus* (23 December 1940), *Grayback* (31 January 1941)
BUILDER: Electric Boat
*Triton* (25 March 1940), *Trout* (21 May 1940), *Grayling* (4 September 1940), *Grenadier* (29 November 1940)
BUILDER: Portsmouth
*Tuna* (2 October 1940), *Gudgeon* (25 January 1941)
BUILDER: Mare Island
DISPLACEMENT: 1475 tons (surfaced), 2370 tons (submerged)
DIMENSIONS: 307'2" x 27'3" x 15'0"
MACHINERY: 4 diesel-electric power units, 2 electric motors, 2 shafts. 5400 bhp/2740 shp = 20/8.75 knots
RANGE: 11,000 nm at 10 knots surfaced, 50 nm at 5 knots submerged
ARMAMENT: 10 x 21" torpedo tubes (6 bow, 4 stern), total 24 torpedoes, 1 x 3" gun, 2 x 0.5" machine guns
COMPLEMENT: 60
NOTES: This class was similar to the previous type and added two forward torpedo tubes. Surviving boats received additional antiaircraft weapons and reduced superstructures from 1943.

The destroyers *Minegumo* and *Murasame* sank the *Grampus* in Blackett Strait on 5 March 1943; the destroyer *Satsuki* sank the *Triton* north of the Admiralty Islands on 15 March; Japanese aircraft bombed the *Grenadier* in the Lem Voalan Strait on 21 April; the *Grayling* failed to return from a patrol in

Lingayen Gulf in September. Japanese carrier aircraft sank the *Grayback* in the East China Sea on 27 February 1944; the destroyers *Asashimo* and *Okinami* sank the *Trout* in the Philippine Sea two days later; the *Gudgeon* failed to return from a patrol in the Saipan area in April. The surviving boats were stricken after World War II.

## *MACKEREL* (28 SEPTEMBER 1940)

BUILDER: Electric Boat
DISPLACEMENT: 825 tons (surfaced), 1190 tons (submerged)
DIMENSIONS: 243'1" x 22'1" x 14'0"
MACHINERY: 2 diesel-electric power units, 2 electric motors, 2 shafts. 1680 bhp/ 1500 shp = 16.25/9 knots
RANGE: 6000 nm at 10 knots surfaced, 50 nm at 5 knots submerged
ARMAMENT: 6 x 21" torpedo tubes (4 bow, 2 stern), total 12 torpedoes, 1 x 3" gun, 2 x 0.5" machine guns, 2 x 0.3" machine guns
COMPLEMENT: 42

## *MARLIN* (29 JANUARY 1941)

BUILDER: Portsmouth
DISPLACEMENT: 800 tons (surfaced), 1165 tons (submerged)
DIMENSIONS: 238'11" x 21'8" x 13'0"
MACHINERY: 2 diesel-electric power units, 2 electric motors, 2 shafts. 1680 bhp/ 1500 shp = 16.25/9 knots
RANGE: 6000 nm at 10 knots surfaced, 50 nm at 5 knots submerged
ARMAMENT: 6 x 21" torpedo tubes (4 bow, 2 stern), total 12 torpedoes, 1 x 3" gun, 2 x 0.5" machine guns, 2 x 0.3" machine guns
COMPLEMENT: 42
NOTES: These two boats (*Mackerel* and *Marlin*) were built as prototypes for shorter range submarines intended to protect the Hawai'ian Islands and the Continental West Coast. They were not effective for Pacific operations and served primarily as training vessels until they were stricken in 1946–1947.

## UNITED STATES: *GATO* CLASS (1941)
## [ITALY]—*ENRICO TAZZOLI* (*EX-BARB*, 1942) AFTER GUPPY IB CONVERSION
*(Courtesy of Art-Tech)*

*Drum* (12 May 1941), *Flying Fish* (9 July 1941), *Finback* (25 August 1941), *Haddock* (20 October 1941), *Halibut* (3 December 1941), *Herring* (15 January 1942), *Kingfish* (2 March 1942), *Shad* (15 April 1942), *Runner* (30 May 1942), *Sawfish* (23 June 1942), *Scamp* (20 July 1942), *Scorpion* (20 July 1942), *Snook* (15 August 1942), *Steelhead* (11 September 1942)

BUILDER: Portsmouth

*Gato* (21 August 1941), *Greenling* (20 September 1941), *Grouper* (27 October 1941), *Growler* (22 November 1941), *Grunion* (22 December 1941), *Guardfish* (20 January 1942), *Albacore* (17 February 1942), *Amberjack* (6 March 1942), *Barb* (2 April 1942), *Blackfish* (18 April 1942), *Gunnel* (17 May 1942), *Gurnard* (1 June 1942), *Haddo* (21 June 1942), *Hake* (17 July 1942), *Harder* (19 August 1942), *Hoe* (17 September 1942), *Jack* (16 October 1942), *Lapon* (27 October 1942), *Mingo* (30 November 1942), *Muskallunge* (13 December 1942), *Paddle* (30 December 1942), *Pargo* (24 January 1943), *Bluefish* (21 February 1943), *Bonefish* (7 March 1943), *Cod* (21 March 1943), *Cero* (4 April 1943), *Dace* (25 April 1943), *Corvina* (9 May 1943), *Dorado* (23 May 1943), *Darter* (6 June 1943), *Flasher* (20 June 1943), *Angler* (4 July 1943), *Flier* (11 July 1943), *Bashaw* (25 July 1943), *Bluegill* (8 August 1943), *Flounder* (22 August 1943), *Gabilan* (19 September 1943), *Bream* (17 October 1943), *Cavalla* (14 November 1943), *Cobia* (28 November 1943), *Croaker* (19 December 1943)

BUILDER: Electric Boat

*Silversides* (26 August 1941), *Trigger* (22 October 1941), *Wahoo* (14 February 1942), *Whale* (14 March 1942), *Sunfish* (2 May 1942), *Tunny* (30 June 1942), *Tinosa* (7 October 1942), *Tullibee* (11 November 1942)

BUILDER: Mare Island

*Peto* (30 April 1942), *Pogy* (23 June 1942), *Pompon* (15 August 1942), *Puffer* (22 November 1942), *Rasher* (20 December 1942), *Raton* (24 January 1943), *Ray* (28 February 1943), *Redfin* (4 April 1943), *Robalo* (9 May 1943), *Rock* (20 June 1943)

BUILDER: Manitowoc

DISPLACEMENT: 1526 tons (surfaced), 2410 tons (submerged)

DIMENSIONS: 311′9″ x 27′3″ x 15′3″

MACHINERY: 4 diesel-electric power units, 2 electric motors, 2 shafts. 5400 bhp/2740 shp = 20.25/8.75 knots

RANGE: 11,000 nm at 10 knots surfaced, 96 nm at 2 knots submerged

ARMAMENT: 10 x 21″ torpedo tubes (6 bow, 4 stern), total 24 torpedoes, 1 x 3″ gun, 2 x 0.5″ machine guns

COMPLEMENT: 60

NOTES: This class was the initial standard war production version of the fleet submarine. The machinery space was divided with a watertight bulkhead and the hulls strengthened to increase diving depth to 300 feet from the prewar standard of 250 feet. During the course of World War II their armament was modified to embark 4-inch or 5-inch deck guns, and 40mm and 20mm antiaircraft weapons. The superstructure was cut down to reduce the silhouette on the surface, and search radar was added.

The steamer *Kano Maru* rammed and sank the *Grunion* off Kiska on 30 July 1942; Japanese submarine chasers sank the *Amberjack* off Rabaul on 16 February 1943; Japanese aircraft sank the *Wahoo* in La Perouse Strait on 11 October; the *Dorado* was lost in transit to the Pacific the same month; the submarine *I-176* torpedoed the *Corvina* near Truk on 16 November. The *Scorpion* was mined in the Yellow Sea in February 1944; the *Tullibee* was sunk by one of its own torpedoes in the Palaus on 26 March; the *Snook* failed to return from a patrol off Taiwan in April; shore batteries on Matsuwa Island sank the *Herring* on 1 June; the *Robalo* was mined off Palawan Island on 26 July; the *Flier* was mined in Balabac Strait on 13 August; the escort *No. 8* sank the *Harder* in Davol Bay on 24 August; Japanese aircraft bombed the *Darter* off Palawan Island on 24 October; the *Albacore* was mined off Hokkaido on 7 November; the destroyer *Shigure* and escorts *Chiburi* and *No. 19* sank the *Growler* off Mindoro the next day; a Japanese escort sank the *Scamp* in Tokyo Bay on 16 November. Japanese escorts sank the *Trigger* in the East China Sea on 28 March 1945, and the escorts *No. 63*, *No. 75*, and *No. 207* sank the *Bonefish* in Toyama Wan on 18 June.

The *Grouper*, the *Angler*, the *Bluegill*, the *Bream*, the *Cavalla*, and the *Croaker* were converted to hunter-killer submarines between 1951 and 1953 (two engines being removed, a streamlined sail and a snorkel fitted, much upgraded active and passive sonar systems added, and extensive silencing and sound isolation incorporated) and were stricken in 1968–1969. The *Pompon*, the *Rasher*, the *Raton*, the *Ray*, the *Redfin*, and the *Rock* were converted to radar picket submarines in 1951with large search radar arrays and were stricken in the 1960s. The *Tunny* was converted into a missile submarine in 1953 to launch Regulus missiles, became a transport submarine in 1966, and was stricken in 1969.

The *Muskallunge* and the *Paddle* were transferred to Brazil as the *Humaita* and the *Riachvelo* and discarded in 1968. The *Jack* and the *Lapon* were transferred to Greece as the *Amfitriti* and the *Poseidon* and were discarded in the mid-1970s. The *Trigger* and the *Harder* were transferred to Italy as the *Livio Piomarta* and the *Romeo Romei,* and they were stricken in the late 1980s. Italy also acquired the *Barb* and the *Dace* (GUPPY IB conversions) as the *Enrico Tazzoli* and the *Leonardo da Vinci,* and they were discarded in 1973. The *Mingo* was transferred to Japan as the *Kuroshio* and decommissioned in 1966. The remaining vessels were stricken by 1960.

## UNITED STATES: *BALAO* CLASS (1942), *PAMPANITO* (1943)
*(Courtesy of Art-Tech)*

*Balao* (27 October 1942), *Billfish* (12 November 1942), *Bowfin* (7 December 1942), *Cabrilla* (24 December 1942), *Cisco* (24 December 1942), *Capelin* (20 January 1943), *Crevalle* (22 February 1943), *Sand Lance* (25 June 1943), *Picuda* (12 July 1943), *Pampanito* (12 July 1943), *Parche* (24 July 1943), *Bang* (30 August 1943), *Pilotfish* (30 August 1943), *Pintado* (15 September 1943), *Pipefish* (12 October 1943), *Piranha* (27 October 1943), *Pomfret* (27 October 1943), *Sterlet* (27 October 1943), *Plaice* (15 November 1943), *Queenfish* (30 November 1943), *Razorback* (27 January 1944), *Redfish* (27 January 1944), *Ronquil* (27 January 1944), *Scabbardfish* (27 January 1944), *Segundo* (5 February 1944), *Sea Devil* (28 February 1944), *Atule* (6 March 1944), *Sea Dog* (28 March

1944), *Sea Fox* (28 March 1944), *Spike-fish* (26 April 1944), *Sea Owl* (7 May 1944), *Sea Poacher* (20 May 1944), *Sea Robin* (25 May 1944), *Sennet* (6 June 1944), *Piper* (26 June 1944), *Threadfin* (26 June 1944), *Sea Cat* (30 November 1944)

BUILDER: Portsmouth

*Seahorse* (9 January 1943), *Skate* (4 March 1943), *Tang* (17 August 1943), *Tilefish* (25 October 1943), *Spadefish* (8 January 1944), *Trepang* (8 January 1944), *Spot* (19 May 1944), *Springer* (3 August 1944), *Stickleback* (1 January 1945), *Tiru* (16 September 1947)

BUILDER: Mare Island

*Apogon* (10 March 1943), *Aspro* (7 April 1943), *Batfish* (5 May 1943), *Archerfish* (28 May 1943), *Burrfish* (18 June 1943), *Perch* (12 September 1943), *Shark* (17 October 1943), *Sealion* (31 October 1943), *Barbel* (14 November 1943), *Barbero* (12 December 1943), *Baya* (2 January 1944), *Becuna* (30 January 1944), *Besugo* (27 February 1944), *Blackfin* (12 March 1944), *Caiman* (30 March 1944), *Blenny* (9 April 1944), *Blower* (23 April 1944), *Blueback* (7 May 1944), *Boarfish* (21 May 1944), *Charr* (18 June 1944), *Chub* (18 June 1944), *Brill* (25 June 1944), *Bugara* (2 July 1944), *Bullhead* (16 July 1944), *Bumper* (6 August 1944), *Cabezon* (27 August 1944), *Dentuda* (10 September 1944), *Capitaine* (1 October 1944), *Carbonero* (15 October 1944), *Carp* (12 November 1944), *Catfish* (19 November 1944), *Bergall* (12 December 1944), *Entemedor* (17 December 1944), *Chivo* (14 January 1945), *Chipper* (4 February 1945), *Clamagore* (25 February 1945), *Cobbler* (1 April 1945), *Cochino* (20 April 1945), *Corporal* (10 June 1945), *Cubera* (17 June 1945), *Cusk* (28 July 1945), *Diodon* (10 September 1945), *Dogfish* (27 October 1945),

*Greenfish* (21 December 1945), *Halfbeak* (19 February 1946)

BUILDER: Electric Boat

*Dragonet* (18 April 1943), *Escolar* (18 April 1943), *Devilfish* (30 May 1943), *Hackleback* (30 May 1943), *Lancetfish* (15 August 1943), *Ling* (15 August 1943), *Lionfish* (7 November 1943), *Manta* (7 November 1943), *Moray* (14 May 1944), *Roncador* (14 May 1944), *Sabalo* (4 June 1944), *Sablefish* (4 June 1944)

BUILDER: Cramp

*Golet* (1 August 1943), *Guavina* (29 August 1943), *Guitarro* (26 September 1943), *Hammerhead* (24 October 1943), *Hardhead* (12 December 1943), *Hawksbill* (9 January 1944), *Icefish* (20 February 1944), *Jallao* (12 March 1944), *Kete* (9 April 1944), *Kraken* (30 April 1944), *Lagarto* (28 May 1944), *Lamprey* (18 June 1944), *Lizardfish* (16 July 1944), *Loggerhead* (13 August 1944), *Macabi* (19 September 1944), *Mapiro* (9 November 1944), *Menhaden* (20 December 1944), *Mero* (17 January 1945)

BUILDER: Manitowoc

DISPLACEMENT: 1525 tons (surfaced), 2415 tons (submerged)

DIMENSIONS: 311'9" x 27'3" x 15'3"

MACHINERY: 4 diesel-electric power units, 2 electric motors, 2 shafts. 5400 bhp/2740 shp = 20.25/8.75 knots

RANGE: 11,000 nm at 10 knots surfaced, 96 nm at 2 knots submerged

ARMAMENT: 10 x 21" torpedo tubes (6 bow, 4 stern), total 24 torpedoes, 1 x 4" gun, 1 x 40mm AA gun, 2 x 0.5" machine guns

COMPLEMENT: 80

NOTES: Careful attention to weight saving allowed stronger construction in this class, increasing diving depth to 400 feet.

The gunboat *Karatsu* and aircraft sank the *Cisco* in the Sulu Sea on 28 September 1943, and the *Capelin* failed to return from a patrol in the Celebes Sea in

December. Japanese antisubmarine vessels sank the *Golet* off Honshu on 14 June 1944; the *Escolar* probably was mined in the Yellow Sea on 17 October; the destroyer *Harukaze* sank the *Shark* in Luzon Strait on 24 October; the *Tang* was sunk by one of its own torpedoes near Turnabout Island on the same day. Japanese aircraft sank the *Barbel* near Palawan Island on 4 February 1945; the *Kete* failed to return from a patrol in Colnett Strait in March; the minelayer *Hatsutaka* sank the *Lagarto* in the Gulf of Siam on 3 May; Japanese aircraft sank the *Bullhead* off Bali on 6 August.

The *Barbero* was converted into a missile submarine in 1955 to launch Regulus missiles. The *Becuna*, the *Blackfin*, the *Caiman*, the *Blenny*, the *Chivo*, the *Atule*, the *Sea Poacher*, and the *Sea Robin* received GUPPY IA conversions (increased battery capacity, streamlined topsides and sails, and snorkels, increasing submerged speed to 15 knots). The *Catfish*, the *Entemedor*, the *Clamagore*, the *Cobbler*, the *Cochino*, the *Corporal*, the *Cubera*, the *Diodon*, the *Dogfish*, the *Greenfish*, the *Halfbeak*, the *Hardhead*, the *Jallao*, the *Menhaden*, the *Picuda*, the *Bang*, the *Pomfret*, the *Razorback*, the *Ronquil*, the *Sea Fox*, the *Threadfin*, the *Stickleback*, and the *Tiru* received GUPPY IIA conversions (as GUPPY IA with more advanced batteries increasing submerged speed to 16 knots). The *Clamagore*, the *Cobbler*, the *Cochino*, the *Greenfish*, and the *Tiru* later received Guppy III conversions with 10-foot hull sections inserted to provide space for new fire control systems. The *Sabalo*, the *Sablefish*, the *Tilefish*, the *Bergall*, the *Blower*, the *Brill*, the *Bumper*, the *Capitaine*, the *Carbonero*, the *Carp*, the *Cusk*, the *Guitarro*, the *Hammerhead*, the *Sterlet*, the *Scabbardfish*, the *Segundo*, the

*Sea Cat*, the *Sea Owl*, the *Sennet*, and the *Piper* received Fleet Snorkel conversions (as GUPPY IA without the hull streamlining). The *Perch* and the *Sealion* became transport submarines and the *Burrfish* a radar picket.

The *Apogon*, the *Pilotfish*, and the *Skate* were expended as targets at Bikini Atoll on 1 July 1946; a battery explosion sank the *Cochino* off Norway on 26 August 1949; and the destroyer escort *Silverstein* accidentally rammed and sank the *Stickleback* off Hawai'i on 29 May 1958.

The *Lamprey* and the *Macabi* were transferred to Argentina as the *Santa Fe* and the *Santiago del Estero* and were broken up in 1971–1972. They were replaced by the *Catfish* and the *Chivo*, which took their precursors' names. British aircraft sank the *Santa Fe* on South Georgia on 25 April 1982, and the *Santiago del Estero* was discarded in 1983. The *Dogfish*, the *Greenfish*, the *Sand Lance*, and the *Plaice* were transferred to Brazil as the *Guanabara*, the *Amazonas*, the *Rio Grande del Sul*, and the *Bahia* and discarded between 1975 and 1983. The *Burrfish* was transferred to Canada as the *Grilse* and stricken in 1969. The *Spot* and the *Springer* were transferred to Chile as the *Simpson* and the *Thomson* and deleted in the late 1970s. The *Scabbardfish* and the *Hardhead* were transferred to Greece as the *Triaina* and the *Papanikolos* and stricken in the early 1990s. The *Besugo*, the *Capitaine*, and the *Lizardfish* were transferred to Italy as the *Francesco Morosini*, the *Alfredo Cappellini*, and the *Evangelista Toricelli* and discarded in the mid-1970s. The *Hawkbill* and the *Icefish* were transferred to The Netherlands as the *Zeeleeuw* and the *Walrus* and stricken in 1970–1971. The *Atule* and the *Sea Poacher* were transferred to Peru as the *Pacocha* and *La Pedrera*. The *Pacocha* was sunk in a collision in 1988, and *La Pedrera* was deleted in 1995. The *Jallao*, the *Kraken*, the *Bang*, and the *Ronquil* were transferred to Spain as the *Narciso Monturiol*, the *Almirante Garcia de los Reyes*, the *Cosme Garcia*, and the *Isaac Peral* and stricken in the 1980s. Turkey acquired the *Brill*, the *Bumper*, the *Hammerhead*, the *Blower*, the *Chub*, the *Mero*, the *Blueback*, the *Mapiro*, the *Guitarro*, the *Boarfish*, and the *Bergall* as the *Birinci Inönü*, the *Canakkale*, the *Cerbe*, the *Dumlupinar*, the *Gur*, the *Hizar Reis*, the *Ikinci Inönü*, the *Piri Reis*, the *Preveze*, the *Sakarya*, and the *Turget Reis* between 1948 and 1960 and discarded them in the early 1970s. Turkey acquired the *Caiman*, the *Threadfin*, the *Sea Fox*, the *Razorback*, the *Pomfret,* the *Entemedor*, the *Cobbler*, and the *Corporal* in their place as the *Dumlupinar*, the *Birinci Inönü*, the *Burak Reis*, the *Murat Reis*, the *Oruc Reis*, the *Preveze*, the *Canakkale*, and the *Ikinci Inönü* and retained them into the 1990s. Venezuela acquired the *Tilefish* and the *Cubera* as the *Carite* and the *Tiburon*, discarding them in the late 1970s.

The other members of the class became training vessels in the 1960s and were discarded in the 1970s.

## UNITED STATES:
### *TENCH* CLASS, *ARGONAUT* (1944), AS A FLEET SNORKEL BOAT
*(Courtesy of Art-Tech)*

*Tench* (7 July 1944), *Thornback* (7 July 1944), *Tigrone* (20 July 1944), *Tigrante* (9 August 1944), *Trutta* (18 August 1944), *Toro* (23 August 1944), *Torsk* (6 September 1944), *Quillback* (1 October 1944), *Argonaut* (1 October 1944), *Runner* (17 October 1944), *Conger* (17 October 1944), *Cutlass* (5 November 1944), *Diablo* (1 December 1944), *Requin* (1 December 1944), *Medregal* (15 December 1944), *Irex* (26 January 1945), *Sea Leopard* (2 March 1945), *Odax* (10 April 1945), *Sirago* (11 May 1945), *Trumpetfish* (13 May 1945), *Pomodon* (12 June 1945), *Remora* (12 July 1945), *Sarda* (24 August 1945), *Spinax* (20 November 1945), *Volador* (17 January 1946)
BUILDER: Portsmouth

*Amberjack* (15 December 1944), *Grampus* (15 December 1944), *Grenadier* (15 December 1944), *Pickerel* (15 December 1944)
BUILDER: Boston
*Trumpetfish* (13 May 1945), *Tusk* (8 July 1945)
BUILDER: Cramp
*Corsair* (3 May 1946), *Unicorn* (1 August 1946), *Walrus* (20 September 1946)
BUILDER: Electric Boat
DISPLACEMENT: 1570 tons (surfaced), 2415 tons (submerged)
DIMENSIONS: 311'8" x 27'3" x 15'5"
MACHINERY: 4 diesel-electric power units, 2 electric motors, 2 shafts. 5400 bhp/2740 shp = 20.25/8.75 knots

RANGE: 11,000 nm at 10 knots surfaced, 96 nm at 2 knots submerged

ARMAMENT: 10 x 21″ torpedo tubes (6 bow, 4 stern), total 24 torpedoes, 1 x 5″ gun, 1 x 40mm AA gun, 1 x 20mm AA gun

COMPLEMENT: 80

NOTES: These boats featured still stronger construction, increasing the dive depth to 450 feet. The *Unicorn* and the *Walrus* were broken up incomplete and a further 17 boats were canceled.

The *Tench* and the *Pomodon* received GUPPY IA conversions; the *Thornback*, the *Tirante*, the *Trutta*, the *Quillback*, the *Trumpetfish*, the *Tusk*, the *Conger*, the *Sea Leopard*, the *Odax*, the *Sirago*, the *Pompodon*, the *Remora*, the *Volador*, the *Amberjack*, the *Grampus*, the *Pickerel*, and the *Grenadier* received GUPPY IIA conversions; the *Remora*, the *Volador*, and the *Pickerel* received GUPPY III conversions; and the *Torsk*, the *Argonaut*, the *Runner*, the *Diabolo*, the *Medregal*, and the *Irex* received Fleet Snorkel conversions; while the *Tigrone*, the *Requin*, and the *Spinax* became radar pickets.

Brazil acquired the *Trumpetfish*, the *Sea Leopard*, the *Odax*, the *Amberjack*, and the *Grampus* as the *Goias*, the *Bahia*, the *Rio de Janeiro*, the *Ceara*, and the *Rio Grande do Sul* and discarded them in the 1990s. The *Argonaut* was transferred to Canada as the *Rainbow* and stricken in 1974. Greece acquired the *Remora* as the *Katsonis*, discarding it in 1993. The *Volador* and the *Pickerel* were transferred to Italy as the *Primo Longobardo* and the *Gianfranco Gazzana Priaroggia,* and they were stricken in 1980–1981. Pakistan received the *Diabolo* as the *Ghazi*. It was sunk by the Indian destroyer *Rajput* near Vishakapatnam on 4 February 1971. The *Cutlass* and the *Tusk* went to Taiwan as the *Hai Shih* and the *Hai Pao,* and they were discarded in the late 1990s. Turkey acquired the *Trutta* and the *Thornback* as the *Cerbe* and the *Ulac Ali Reis* and discarded them in the late 1990s. Venezuela acquired the *Grenadier* as the *Picuda* and discarded it in 1990. The other members of the class were stricken in the late 1960s and early 1970s.

# The Advent of True Submarines

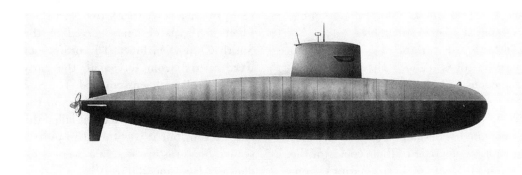

**CHINA**
**PROJECT 091 (NATO HAN CLASS) (1970)**
*(Courtesy of Art-Tech)*

*401* (26 December 1970), *402* (1977), *403* (1983), *404* (1987), *405* (April 1990)

BUILDER: Huludao

DISPLACEMENT: 4500 tons (surfaced), 5500 tons (submerged)

DIMENSIONS: 328'0" x 36'0" x 29'0"

MACHINERY: 1 pressurized water reactor, 1 electric motor, 1 shaft. 15,000 shp = 12/25 knots

Endurance: 60 days

ARMAMENT: 6 x 533mm torpedo tubes (bow), total 20 torpedoes or 36 mines

COMPLEMENT: 75

NOTES: China's first nuclear-powered submarines seem initially to have required an extended period of trials and upgrades to correct problems with their power plants that persisted into the early 1990s. The final three boats were completed to a modified design that lengthened the hull some 25 feet abaft the sail and probably upgraded torpedo weaponry and added antiship missile launch capability. Recent refits have enhanced these boats' sonar equipment and placed an anechoic tile covering over their hulls.

## PROJECT 035 (NATO MING CLASS) (1971)

*Unknown* (July 1971), 232 (November 1974), 233 (1978), 342, 352–354, 356–362 (1986–1995), 363 (May 1996), 305 (June 1997), 306 (September 1997), 307 (May 1998), 308 (October 1998), 309 (December 1999), 310 (June 2000) 4+ boats (2000–2002)

BUILDER: Wuhan

DISPLACEMENT: 1584 tons (surfaced), 2113 tons (submerged)

DIMENSIONS: 250'0" x 25'0" x 16'9"

MACHINERY: 2 diesel engines, 2 electric motors, 2 shafts. 5200 bhp/3500 shp = 15/18 knots

RANGE: 8000 nm at 8 knots snorkeling, 330 nm at 4 knots submerged

ARMAMENT: 8 (prototypes: 6) x 533mm torpedo tubes (6 bow, 2 stern), total 16 torpedoes or 32 mines

COMPLEMENT: 57

NOTES: The first three boats of this class functioned as development prototypes for a Chinese upgrade of their copies of the Soviet Project 633 submarines constructed earlier. The new design had greater submerged speed and range thanks to more powerful machinery, an expanded battery, and improved hull form. It also featured a more advanced sensor outfit. The prototypes were followed by an improved version that incorporated some hull contour modifications and two stern torpedo tubes. The final 10 boats were further upgraded with additional equipment installed in space created by a 6'6" longer hull.

Considerable uncertainty surrounds the operational deployment of these boats. Most of the first production craft seem to have served with the North Sea Fleet, while later boats served in the South China Sea Fleet. The prototypes were retired from service in the early 1980s and have been scrapped. The *361* suffered a major accident while on the surface in April–May 2003 that killed the entire crew, but it was towed to port; a second boat was involved in a major accident in May–June 2005.

## PROJECT 039 (NATO SONG CLASS) (1994)

*320* (25 May 1994), *321* (11 November 1999), *322* (28 June 2000), *314* (2003), *315* (3 June 2004), *316* (2004), *323* (2004), *318* (2005)

BUILDER: Wuhan

*324* (2004), *325* (2004)

BUILDER: Jiangnan

DISPLACEMENT: 1700 tons (surfaced), 2250 tons (submerged)

DIMENSIONS: 251'3" x 27'6" x 17'3"

MACHINERY: 4 MTU diesel engines, 2 generator sets, 2 electric motors, 1 shaft. 6092 shp = 15/22 knots

RANGE: 8000 nm at 8 knots snorkeling, 72 nm at 2 knots submerged

ARMAMENT: 6 x 533mm torpedo tubes (bow), torpedoes, antiship missiles, or mines

COMPLEMENT: 60

NOTES: The Project 039 design represents a major advance in Chinese submarine performance. It incorporates a teardrop hull shape coated with anechoic tiles. The raft-mounted German machinery drives a seven-bladed skewed propeller, making these boats as quiet as the U.S. Navy's *Los Angeles* class. These submarines are capable of firing wire-guided torpedoes or antiship missiles via their torpedo tubes. The first boat (*320*) is the only Project 039; all later boats are to Project 039G with improved sail contours and upgraded bow-mounted sonar equipment. All boats of this class serve with the East Sea Fleet, and there apparently are plans to build up to seven more of the type.

## PROJECT 093 (2001)

2 boats

BUILDER: Huludao

DISPLACEMENT: 6000 tons (surfaced), 8000 tons (submerged)

DIMENSIONS: 350'0" x 36'1" x 24'7"

MACHINERY: 2 pressurized water reactors, 1 electric motor, 1 shaft. 20,000 shp = 30 knots submerged

ARMAMENT: 6 x 533mm torpedo tubes (bow)

COMPLEMENT: 100

NOTES: Reports indicate that this second-generation nuclear-powered attack sub-marine was developed with appreciable Soviet assistance, especially for its power plant and quieting. It features a seven-bladed asymmetrical skewed propeller and anechoic tile coating to reduce underwater noise. At least one example was launched in 2001 and began trials in late 2002; a second boat has been completed of a total of six to eight vessels projected.

## PROJECT 039A (NATO YUAN CLASS) (2004)

*330* (31 May 2004), *unknown* (December 2004)

BUILDER: Wuhan

NOTES: Very little hard information on the Yuan class is available, and its very existence came as a surprise to Western intelligence when photographs appeared in 2004. It has a teardrop hull with a raised upper hump, anechoic tile coating to reduce underwater noise, an asymmetrical seven-blade skewed propeller, and a tail similar to that of the earlier Project 039 boats. It most likely is equipped with a passive/active noise reduction system and is capable of launching torpedoes and antiship missiles through its tubes.

## DENMARK
## *DELFINEN* CLASS (1956)

*Delfinen* (4 May 1956), *Spaekhuggeren* (20 February 1957), *Tumleren* (22 May 1958), *Springeren* (26 April 1963)

BUILDER: Copenhagen

DISPLACEMENT: 595 tons (surfaced), 643 tons (submerged)

DIMENSIONS: 178′10″ x 15′5″ x 13′0″

MACHINERY: 2 Burmeister and Wain diesel engines, 2 Brown-Boveri electric motors, 2 shafts. 1200 bhp/2100 shp = 13.5/16 knots

RANGE: 4000 nm at 8 knots snorkeling, 141 nm at 6 knots submerged

ARMAMENT: 4 x 533mm torpedo tubes (bow), total 8 torpedoes

COMPLEMENT: 33

NOTES: This class, designed by the Orlogsværftet, was the last indigenous type produced for the Danish fleet. It used systems derived from study of the German Type XXIII coastal boats and incorporated into a wholly local design. The *Tumleren* was stricken in 1981, the *Delfinen* in 1984, and the other boats in 1989.

# FRANCE
## *NARVAL* CLASS (1954)

*Narval* (11 December 1954), *Marsouin* (21 May 1955), *Dauphin* (12 September 1955), *Requin* (3 December 1955)
BUILDER: Cherbourg
*Espadon* (15 September 1958)
BUILDER: Normand
*Morse* (10 December 1958)
BUILDER: Seine-Maritime
DISPLACEMENT: 1635 tons (surfaced), 1910 tons (submerged)
DIMENSIONS: 257'0" x 26'0" x 17'0"
MACHINERY: 2 Schneider diesel engines, 2 electric motors, 2 shafts. 4400 bhp/5000 shp = 16/18 knots
RANGE: 15,000 nm at 8 knots snorkeling, 400 nm at 5 knots submerged
ARMAMENT: 8 x 550mm torpedo tubes (6 bow, 2 stern), total 14 torpedoes

COMPLEMENT: 63
NOTES: These double-hull boats, designed by Marie Clément Dupont de Dinechin, incorporated French experience from operating its two former German Type XXI submarines. The class was modernized between 1966 and 1970, receiving new machinery (three 2500-bhp Pielstick diesel engines and two 1500-shp electric motors) and a revised sail with upgraded sensors and fire control equipment, and landing the stern tubes. Displacement fell slightly, and these boats also could carry a mixed weapons load of 10 torpedoes and 18 mines or 14 torpedoes only. They were decommissioned between 1982 and 1986 and scrapped.

## *ARÉTHUSE* CLASS (1957)

*Aréthuse* (9 November 1957), *Argonaute* (26 June 1957), *Amazone* (3 April 1958), *Ariane* (12 September 1958)
BUILDER: Cherbourg
DISPLACEMENT: 543 tons (surfaced), 669 tons (submerged)
DIMENSIONS: 163'0" x 19'0" x 13'0"
MACHINERY: 2 SEMT-Pielstick diesel engines, 1 electric motor, 1 shaft. 1060 bhp/1300 shp = 12.5/16 knots
RANGE: 4500 nm at 5 knots snorkeling, 350 nm at 3.5 knots submerged

ARMAMENT: 4 x 550mm torpedo tubes (bow), total 8 torpedoes
COMPLEMENT: 39
NOTES: These boats were designed as small hunter-killer submarines, primarily for service in the Mediterranean. They were decommissioned between 1979 and 1982. The *Argonaute* became a museum ship, and the other boats were scrapped.

## FRANCE: *DAPHNÉ* CLASS (1959), [SPAIN]—*DELFIN* (1972)
*(Courtesy of Art-Tech)*

*Daphné* (20 June 1959), *Diane* (4 October 1960), *Minerve* (31 May 1961), [Portugal]—*Albacora* (15 October 1966), *Barracuda* (24 April 1967), *Cachalote* (16 February 1968), *Delfim* (25 September 1968), [South Africa]—*Maria van Riebeeck* (18 March 1969), *Emily Hobhouse* (24 October 1960), *Johanna van der Merwe* (21 July 1970)
BUILDER: Dubigeon
*Doris* (14 May 1960), *Eurydice* (19 June 1960), *Flore* (21 December 1960), *Galatée* (22 September 1961), *Junon* (11 May 1964), *Vénus* (24 September 1964)
BUILDER: Cherbourg
*Psyché* (28 June 1969), *Sirène* (28 June 1969), [Pakistan]—*Hangor* (June 1969)
BUILDER: Brest

[Pakistan]—*Shushuk* (July 1969), *Mangro* (February 1970)
BUILDER: La Ciotat
[Spain]—*Delfin* (25 March 1972), *Tonina* (3 October 1972), *Marsopa* (15 March 1974), *Narval* (14 December 1974)
BUILDER: Cartagena
DISPLACEMENT: 869 tons (surfaced), 1043 tons (submerged)
DIMENSIONS: 190'0" x 22'0" x 17'0"
MACHINERY: 2 SEMT-Pielstick diesel engines, 1 electric motor, 2 shafts. 1300 bhp/1600 shp = 13.5/16 knots
RANGE: 4500 nm at 5 knots snorkeling, 350 nm at 3.5 knots submerged
ARMAMENT: 12 x 550mm torpedo tubes (8 bow, 4 stern), total 12 torpedoes
COMPLEMENT: 45

NOTES: This class, designed by André Gempp, was an enlarged version of the previous hunter-killer type with substantially enhanced sensors and a diving depth of 1000 feet. They also proved very successful in the export market until the type suffered a series of accidents.

Diving accidents sank the *Minerve,* the *Eurydice,* and the *Flore* on 28 January 1968, 4 March 1970, and 19 February 1971, probably as a result of problems with their snorkels. The *Flore* was raised, returned to service, and decommissioned with the other French boats between 1987 and 1992 and scrapped.

The South African boats were renamed the *Spear,* the *Umkhonto,* and the *Assegaai* in 1994. The *Spear* was scrapped in 2002 and the other boats de-commissioned in 2003. The *Assegaai* is to become the centerpiece of a museum of submarine technology at Capetown.

Portugal sold the *Cachalote* to Pakistan in 1975 as the *Ghazi.* The *Albacora* was stricken on 14 July 2000. The other two boats still were in service in 2006.

The Pakistani boats received an upgrade refit in the late 1980s and were equipped to launch Sub-Harpoon missiles. They will remain in service until the delivery of the final Agosta 90B boats.

The Spanish boats received a modernization refit in the late 1980s, acquiring a new sonar outfit, fire control system, and noise suppression equipment. These boats were decommissioned in 2003, the *Delfin* becoming a museum ship.

## FRANCE: *AGOSTA* CLASS (1974), [PAKISTAN]—*HASHMAT* (1977)

*(Courtesy of Art-Tech)*

*Agosta* (19 October 1974), *Beveziers* (14 June 1975), *La Praya* (15 May 1976), *Ouessant* (23 October 1976)

BUILDER: Cherbourg

[Pakistan]—*Hashmat* (14 December 1977), *Hurmat* (1 December 1978)

BUILDER: Dubigeon

[Spain]—*Galerna* (5 December 1981), *Siroco* (13 November 1982), *Mistral* (14 November 1983), *Tramontana* (30 November 1984)

BUILDER: Cartagena

DISPLACEMENT: 1490 tons (surfaced), 1740 tons (submerged)

DIMENSIONS: 222′0″ x 22′0″ x 18′0″

MACHINERY: 2 SEMT-Pielstick diesel engines, 1 electric motor, 1 shaft. 3600 bhp/4600 shp = 12/17.5 knots

RANGE: 8500 nm at 9 knots snorkeling, 350 nm at 3.5 knots submerged

ARMAMENT: 4 x 550mm torpedo tubes (bow), total 20 torpedoes

COMPLEMENT: 54

NOTES: Jean Touffait oversaw the creation of this new design for an oceanic hunter-killer submarine with advanced sensors and fire control systems. They also were successful in the export market. Two boats ordered by South Africa were not delivered because of the UN embargo on arms sales to that nation and were purchased by Pakistan.

The French boats were withdrawn from service between 1997 and 2001 but remain in the fleet's special reserve. The *Ouessant* was reactivated in 2003 as a training vessel for Malaysian crews for the *Scorpène* type boats on order. The Pakistani boats were fitted to launch Sub-Harpoon missiles in 1984–1985 and remain in service. The Spanish boats underwent an upgrade refit that improved their fire control system and sonar outfits. They too remain operational.

**FRANCE: *AMÉTHYSTE* CLASS (1979), *PERLE* (1990)**
*(Courtesy of Art-Tech)*

*Rubis* (7 July 1979), *Saphir* (1 September 1981), *Casablanca* (22 December 1984), *Améthyste* (14 May 1985), *Émeraude* (12 April 1986), *Perle* (22 September 1990)

BUILDER: Cherbourg

DISPLACEMENT: 2410 tons (surfaced), 2680 tons (submerged)

DIMENSIONS: 237'0" x 25'0" x 23'0"

MACHINERY: 1 CAS pressurized water reactor, 2 turbo-alternator sets, 1 electric motor, 1 shaft. 9500 shp = 25 knots submerged

Endurance: 60 days

ARMAMENT: 4 x 533mm torpedo tubes (bow), total 14 torpedoes or missiles, or 32 mines

COMPLEMENT: 66

NOTES: Like the French ballistic missile submarines, these boats are unusual in using turbo-electric drive rather than steam turbines. The *Améthyste* and the *Perle* incorporated considerably improved noise reduction measures compared with the earlier boats, and all but the *Rubis* were brought up to the same standard between 1991 and 1995. These boats are much noisier than their U.S. and British counterparts and also have demonstrated less mechanical reliability. The first is not expected to leave service until 2012, and the last is scheduled to decommission in 2022.

## [PAKISTAN]—*AGOSTA* 90B CLASS, *KHALID* (1998)
*(Courtesy of Art-Tech)*

[Pakistan]—*Khalid* (8 August 1998), *Saad* (24 August 2002)

BUILDER: Cherbourg

[Pakistan]—*Hamza* (2005)

BUILDER: Karachi

DISPLACEMENT: 1570 tons (surfaced), 1760 tons (submerged)

DIMENSIONS: 222'0" (*Hamza:* 254'6") x 22'0" x 18'0"

MACHINERY: 2 SEMT-Pielstick diesel engines, 1 electric motor, 1 shaft. 3600 bhp/4600 shp = 12/17.5 knots. (*Hamza* also: MESMA air independent auxiliary power system, 270 shp = 4 knots)

RANGE: 7900 nm at 10 knots snorkeling, 178 nm at 3.5 knots submerged, 750 nm at 3 knots (AIP)

ARMAMENT: 4 x 550mm torpedo tubes (bow), total 20 torpedoes or Exocet missiles

COMPLEMENT: 36

NOTES: This class was developed from the earlier *Agosta* type. It incorporates very high tensile steel (equivalent to U.S. HY100 steel) hull construction for greater dive depth, extensive automation to reduce crew size, integrated fire control with an optronic periscope, an inertial navigation system, very advanced sensors, extensive noise suppression and integral quieting, and the capability of launching Exocet missiles while submerged. The *Hamza* also incorporates the modular MESMA air-independent propulsion system that burns diesel fuel and oxygen to generate high-pressure steam that drives a turbine. Using the MESMA system it can operate submerged for up to 18 days withoutsnorkeling. The earlier units are to be back-fitted with MESMA modules in the future.

## [SPAIN]—*SCORPÈNE* CLASS (2003)

(*Courtesy of Art-Tech*)

Type CM-2000
[Chile]—*O'Higgins* (November 2003),
   [Malaysia]—1 boat
BUILDER: Cherbourg
[Chile]—*Carerra* (November 2004),
   [Malaysia]—1+ boats
BUILDER: Cartagena
[India]—3 boats
BUILDER: Mazagon
Type AM-2000

[Spain]—4 boats
BUILDER: Cartagena and Cherbourg
[India]—3 boats
BUILDER: Mazagon
DISPLACEMENT: 1564 (AM-2000: 1670)
   tons (surfaced), 1710 (AM-2000: 1815)
   tons (submerged)
DIMENSIONS: 217'11" (AM-2000: 229'8")
   x 27'7" x 18'0"

MACHINERY: 4 MTU diesel engines, 1 Jeumont-Schneider electric motor, 1 shaft. 4694 shp = 17/20 knots (AM-2000 also: MESMA air independent auxiliary power system, 270 shp = 4 knots)

RANGE: 6500 nm at 8 knots snorkeling, 550 nm at 4 knots submerged, 750 nm at 4 knots (AIP)

ARMAMENT: 4 x 533mm torpedo tubes (bow), total 18 torpedoes or Exocet missiles

COMPLEMENT: 31

NOTES: This design was jointly developed by France and Spain, with construction shared between the two nations, the fore section being built at Navantia and the aft sections at DCN. It is optimized for ultra-quiet operation through the use of a streamlined hull form, suspended internal decks, extensive sound insulation of machinery, and noise suppression equipment. Operation is highly automated to minimize crew size and extend operational autonomy. The AM-200 version can operate submerged for up to 18 days without snorkeling. The final three Indian boats will incorporate AIP.

## *BARRACUDA* CLASS (2009)

6 boats

BUILDER: Cherbourg

DISPLACEMENT: 3500 tons (surfaced), 4600 tons (submerged)

DIMENSIONS: 318'0" x 29'11" x 24'0"

MACHINERY: 1 K15 pressurized water reactor, 2 turbo-reductors, 2 electric motors, 1 pumpjet propulsor. 41,500 shp = 25+ knots submerged

Endurance: 70 days

ARMAMENT: 4 x 533mm torpedo tubes (bow), total 18 torpedoes or Exocet missiles, 12 vertical launch missile tubes, 12 Scalp missiles

COMPLEMENT: 60

NOTES: Design work for these new boats began in 1998; the first order was placed in 2003; and the first hull was laid down in 2005, with an anticipated trials date in 2011. The machinery arrangement is unusual, using electric motors for propulsion at cruising speeds and direct turbine drive for maximum speed. Their dive depth will be 1600 feet, and they will incorporate extensive passive and active noise suppression measures.

## GERMANY
## TYPE 201 (1961)

*U-1* (21 October 1962), *U-2* (25 January 1962), *U-3* (7 May 1962)

BUILDER: HWK

DISPLACEMENT: 395 tons (surfaced), 433 tons (submerged)

DIMENSIONS: 142'9" x 15'0" x 13'0"

MACHINERY: 2 Mercedes-Benz diesel engines, 1 electric motor, 1 shaft. 1200 bhp/1500 shp = 10/17.5 knots

RANGE: 3800 nm at 8 knots snorkeling, 400 nm at 4 knots submerged

ARMAMENT: 8 x 533mm torpedo tubes (bow)

COMPLEMENT: 21

NOTES: The design for these boats, by the Ingenieurkontor Lübeck (IKL), drew heavily on the Type XXXIII coastal submarines that were in production at the end of World War II. Since it was anticipated that their principal area of operations would be the shallow waters of the Baltic, hull and equipment were required to have minimal magnetic signatures. The nonmagnetic steel chosen for their hull structures proved to have very little resistance to corrosion, and they were broken up in 1971.

## TYPE 202 (1965)

*Hans Techel* (15 March 1965), *Friedrich Schurer* (10 November 1965)

BUILDER: Atlas

DISPLACEMENT: 100 tons (surfaced), 137 tons (submerged)

DIMENSIONS: 75'9" x 11'3" x 9'0"

MACHINERY: 2 Mercedes-Benz diesel engines, 1 electric motor, 1 shaft. 330 bhp/243 shp = 6/13 knots

RANGE: 3800 nm at 8 knots snorkeling, 400 nm at 4 knots submerged

ARMAMENT: 2 x 533mm torpedo tubes (bow)

COMPLEMENT: 6

NOTES: The IKL produce this design for a small hunter-killer submarine at the same time as the Type 201. The diesel engine and the electric motor were mounted in parallel, driving the same gearbox. These boats suffered from the same corrosion problems as the larger submarines and proved too small to be effective weapons. They were decommissioned in 1966 and scrapped.

## TYPE 207 (1962), [NORWAY]—*ULA* (1964)
*(Courtesy of Art-Tech)*

*U-4* (25 August 1962), *U-5* (20 November 1962), *U-6* (30 January 1963), *U-7* (10 April 1963), *U-8* (19 June 1963), *U-2* (15 July 1966), *U-9* (20 October 1966), *U-1* (17 February 1967), *U-10* (5 June 1967), *U-11* (9 February 1968), *U-12* (10 September 1968)

BUILDER: HWK

[Norway]—*Kinn* (30 November 1963), *Kya* (20 February 1964), *Kobben* (26 April 1964), *Kunna* (16 July 1964), *Ula* (19 December 1964), *Kaura* (5 February 1965), *Utsira* (11 March 1965), *Utstein* (19 May 1965), *Utvaer* (30 June 1965), *Uthaug* (8 October 1965), *Sklinna* (21 January 1966), *Skolpen* (24 March 1966), *Stadt* (10 June 1966), *Stord* (2 September 1966), *Svenner* (27 January 1967)

BUILDER: Nordseewerke

[Denmark]—*Narhvalen* (10 September 1968), *Nordkaperen* (18 December 1969)

BUILDER: Copenhagen

DISPLACEMENT: 419 tons (surfaced), 455 tons (submerged)

DIMENSIONS: 143'9"–150'4" x 15'0" x 13'9"

MACHINERY: 2 Mercedes-Benz diesel engines, 1 electric motor, 1 shaft. 1200 bhp/1500 shp = 10/17.5 knots

RANGE: 3800 nm at 10 knots snorkeling, 200 nm at 5 knots submerged

ARMAMENT: 8 x 533mm torpedo tubes (bow)

COMPLEMENT: 21

NOTES: These boats were very slightly modified versions of the earlier Type 201 class with upgraded sensors. To protect against the corrosion problems of the earlier boats, the first five vessels' hulls received a coating of special zinc paint; the next four used a different, corrosion-resistant steel; and the *U-1* and *U-2* were new hulls built from magnetic steel incorporating all of the original machinery and basic equipment of the original *U-1* and *U-2*. The *U-4* through the *U-8* were broken up between 1975 and 1977 and the *U-1* and *U-2* in 1993. The *U-9* and *U-10* became museum ships in 1993; the *U-11* was modified as a target vessel that same year and became a museum ship in 2003; and the *U-12* became a sonar trials boat in 1993 and was stricken in 2005. The Danish boats had small changes to suit local requirements and were decommissioned in 2003–2004.

The Norwegian boats were classed as Type 207 and were built of magnetic high-tensile steel to endow them with deeper diving limits, and they had other minor variations from the German boats. The *Stadt* was scrapped in 1989; the *Kinn* was sunk as a target in 1990; the *Ula* was renamed the *Kinn* in 1988 and scrapped with the *Utsira* in 1998; the *Utstein* became a museum ship the same year; the *Sklinna* was scrapped in 2001. The *Uthaug*, the *Utvaer*, and the *Kya* were transferred to Denmark between 1989 and 1991 as the *Tumleren*, the *Saelen*, and the *Springeren*, and Denmark also received the *Kaura* for spare parts. They were decommissioned in 2004. The *Skolpen*, the *Stord*, the *Svenner*, and the *Kunna* were transferred between 2002 and 2004 to Poland as the *Sep*, the *Sokol*, the *Bielek*, and the *Kondor*, and Poland also received the *Kobben* for spare parts. The Polish boats remain in service.

## GERMANY: TYPE 206 CLASS, *U-29* (1971)

*(Courtesy of Art-Tech)*

*U-13* (28 September 1971), *U-15* (15 June 1972), *U-17* (10 October 1972), *U-19* (15 December 1972), *U-21* (9 March 1973), *U-25* (23 May 1973), *U-27* (21 August 1973), *U-29* (5 November 1973)

BUILDER: HWK

*U-14* (1 February 1972), *U-16* (29 August 1972), *U-18* (31 October 1972), *U-20* (16 January 1973), *U-22* (27 March 1973), *U-23* (22 May 1073), *U-24* (26 June 1973), *U-26* (20 November 1973), *U-28* (22 January 1974), *U-30* (26 March 1974)

BUILDER: Nordseewerke

[Israel]—*Gal* (2 December 1975), *Tanin* (25 October 1976), *Rahav* (8 May 1977)

BUILDER: Barrow

DISPLACEMENT: 456 tons (surfaced), 500 tons (submerged)

DIMENSIONS: 149′6″ x 15′0″ x 14′0″

MACHINERY: 2 Mercedes-Benz (Israeli boats: MTU) diesel engines, 1 electric motor, 1 shaft. 1200 bhp/1500 shp = 10/17.5 knots

RANGE: 4500 nm at 5 knots snorkeling, 200 nm at 5 knots submerged

ARMAMENT: 8 x 533mm torpedo tubes (bow), total 16 torpedoes, 24 mines

COMPLEMENT: 21

NOTES: The Type 206 was designed by the IKL as an improved Type 205 with a large sonar dome in the bow, enhanced maneuverability, quieter operations, and the capability to launch wire-guided torpedoes. The mines are carried in two external fiberglass containers.

The German boats were upgraded to Type 206A between 1988 and 1992 with updated sensors and improved crew accommodations. The *U-13*, the *U-14*, the *U-19* through the *U-21*, and the *U-27* were scrapped between 1996 and 1998, and the *U-28* was decommissioned in 2004. The other boats remain in service as of 2006.

The Israeli boats were built under license in Britain for political reasons. They were upgraded to operate Sub-Harpoon missiles in 1983 and received torpedo, fire control, and sensor improvements between 1987 and 1994. They were decommissioned in 1999 and offered for sale but remain unsold.

**GERMANY: TYPE 209 (1970) [INDIA]—*SHISHUMAR* (1984) TYPE 209/1500**
(*Courtesy of Art-Tech*)

Type 209/1100
[Greece]—*Glavkos* (15 September 1970), *Nereus* (7 June 1971), *Triton* (19 October 1971), *Proteus* (1 February 1972)
BUILDER: HWK

Type 209/1200
[Argentina]—*Salta* (9 November 1972), *San Luis* (5 April 1973), [Peru]—*Islay* (11 October 1973), *Arica* (5 April 1974), *Casma* (31 August 1979), *Antofagasta* (19 December

1979), *Pisagua* (19 October 1980), *Chipana* (19 May 1981), [Colombia]—*Pijao* (10 April 1974), *Tayrona* (16 July 1974), [Turkey]—*Atilay* (23 October 1974), *Saldiray* (14 February 1975), *Batiray* (26 October 1977), [South Korea]—*Jang Bogo* (18 June 1992), [Portugal]—2 boats

BUILDER: HWK

[Turkey]—*Yildiray* (20 July 1977), *Dogonay* (16 November 1983), *Dolunay* (21 July 1988)

BUILDER: Golcük

[South Korea]—*Lee Chun* (12 October 1992), *Choi Museon* (7 August 1993), *Park Wi* (21 May 1994), *Lee Jongmu* (17 May 1995), *Jeong Un* (5 May 1996), *Lee Shunsin* (21 May 1998), *Na Daeyong* (June 1999), *Lee Eokgi* (26 May 2000)

BUILDER: Daewoo

Type 209/1300

[Venezuela]—*Sabalo* (21 August 1975), *Caribe* (16 December 1975), [Ecuador]—*Shyri* (8 October 1976), *Huancavilva* (18 March 1977), [Indonesia]—*Cakra* (10 September 1980), *Nanggala* (10 September 1980)

BUILDER: HWK

Type 209/1400

[Chile]—*Thomson* (28 October 1982), *Simpson* (29 July 1983), [Brazil]—*Tupi* (28 April 1987), [South Africa]—2 boats

BUILDER: HWK

[Brazil]—*Tamoio* (18 November 1993), *Timbira* (5 January 1996), *Tapajó* (11 June 1998), *Tikuná* (December 2005)

BUILDER: Rio de Janeiro

[Turkey]—*Preveze* (27 November 1993), *Sakarya* (28 July 1994), *18 Mart* (25 August 1997), *Anafartalar* (2 September 1998), *Gür* (25 July 2001), *Çanakkale* (July 2002)

BUILDER: Golcük

[Turkey]—*Burakreis* (2004), *Inonü* (2005)

BUILDER: Istanbul

[South Africa]—1 boat

BUILDER: Blohm und Voss

Type 209/1500

[India]—*Shishumar* (15 December 1984), *Shankush* (11 May 1984)

BUILDER: HWK

[India]—*Shalki* (30 September 1989), *Shankul* (21 March 1992)

BUILDER: Mazagon

DISPLACEMENT: 1100: 1106 tons (surfaced), 1207 tons (submerged), 1200: 1140 tons (surfaced), 1248 tons (submerged), 1300: 1265 tons (surfaced), 1395 tons (submerged), 1400: 1285 tons (surfaced), 1395 tons (submerged), 1500: 1660 tons (surfaced), 1850 tons (submerged)

DIMENSIONS: 149'6" x 15'0" x 14'0"

MACHINERY: 4 MTU diesel engines, 1 Siemens electric motor, 1 shaft. 1200 bhp/1500 shp = 10/17.5 knots

RANGE: 8000 nm at 10 knots snorkeling, 400 nm at 4 knots submerged

ARMAMENT: 8 x 533mm torpedo tubes (bow), total 14 torpedoes

COMPLEMENT: 31

NOTES: The Type 209 has been the most successful export submarine design in the West, yet none have served with the German fleet. The design, by the IKL, was based on features of earlier German submarines and utilized well-proven components. Its clean layout gave a clear view from the torpedo room to the machinery compartments, enhancing operational control. Very high capacity batteries endowed the type with long range and high submerged speed. This sophisticated design also proved very flexible, able to grow, to accommodate upgraded sensors and equipment, and steadily to improve its quiet operation characteristics.

During the long production run of the type, Howaldtswerke-Deutsche Werke developed a series of upgrade packages. Many Type 209 boats were modified to the standards of the German Type 206A and also received Sub-Harpoon missile capabilities. When the Type 212 appeared, its improved performance and quieting through the use of a slow-speed permanent magnet electric motor driving an advanced near-silent propeller and the incorporation of air-independent propulsion through the insertion of a compartment for fuel cells became upgrade options. The later Greek and the South Korean boats are planned to receive air-independent propulsion modules during refits in the early 2000s, and the new Portuguese boats will incorporate AIP from the outset.

## TYPE TR1700 (1982)

[Argentina]—*Santa Cruz* (28 September 1982), *San Juan* (20 June 1983)

BUILDER: Nordseewerke

DISPLACEMENT: 2116 tons (surfaced), 2264 tons (submerged)

DIMENSIONS: 216′6″ x 24′0″ x 21′4″

MACHINERY: 4 MTU diesel engines, 1 Siemens electric motor, 1 shaft. 6720 bhp/6600 shp = 15/25 knots

RANGE: 12,000 nm at 8 knots snorkeling, 460 nm at 6 knots submerged

ARMAMENT: 6 x 533mm torpedo tubes (bow), total 22 torpedoes

COMPLEMENT: 26

NOTES: This class essentially was a substantially enlarged version of the Type 209, primarily to endow it with greater range for operations in the open waters of the south Atlantic and Pacific.

## TYPE 210 (1988)

[Norway]—*Ula* (28 July 1988), *Uredd* (22 September 1989), *Utvaer* (19 April 1990), *Uthaug* (18 October 1990), *Utstein* (25 April 1991), *Utsira* (21 November 1991)

BUILDER: Nordseewerke

DISPLACEMENT: 940 tons (surfaced), 1150 tons (submerged)

DIMENSIONS: 193′7″ x 17′9″ x 15′1″

MACHINERY: 2 MTU diesel engines, 1 Siemens electric motor, 1 shaft. 1700 bhp/1700 shp = 11/23 knots

RANGE: 5000 nm at 8 knots snorkeling, 200 nm at 5 knots submerged

ARMAMENT: 6 x 533mm torpedo tubes (bow), total 14 torpedoes

COMPLEMENT: 19

NOTES: This IKL design incorporated an X-tail for enhanced maneuverability. They had many problems with noisy machinery and weapons system malfunctions initially. All boats remain in service.

## TYPE 800 (1996)

[Israel]—*Dolphin* (15 April 1996), *Leviathan* (27 May 1997), *Tekuma* (9 July 1998)

BUILDER: HWK and Nordseewerke

DISPLACEMENT: 1565 tons (surfaced), 1720 tons (submerged)

DIMENSIONS: 188'0" x 25'0" x 20'4"

MACHINERY: 3 MTU diesel engines, 3 diesel generators sets, 2 Siemens electric motors, 1 shaft. 5000 shp = 11/20 knots

RANGE: 14,000 nm at 4 knots snorkeling, 420 nm at 8 knots submerged

ARMAMENT: 4 x 650mm torpedo tubes, 6 x 533mm torpedo tubes (bow), total 16 torpedoes, antiship, or antihelicopter missiles

COMPLEMENT: 30

NOTES: These boats represent a very considerable advance on the earlier Type 209. The hull is constructed of nonmagnetic high-tensile steel to increase diving depth. They have an improved hull form for better submerged performance, and bow-mounted planes and an X-tail endow them with enhanced maneuverability. The German government funded construction of the first two boats and paid half the cost of the third boat.

## GERMANY: TYPE 212A (2001), [ITALY]—*SALVATORE TODARO* (2003)
*(Courtesy of Art-Tech)*

*U-31* (20 March 2002), *U-33* (30 April 2001)
BUILDER: HWK
*U-32* (November 2003), *U-34* (May 2005)
BUILDER: Nordseewerke
[Italy]—*Salvatore Todaro* (6 November 2003), *Sirce* (April 2004) 2+ boats
BUILDER: Monfalcone
DISPLACEMENT: 1460 tons (surfaced), 1840 tons (submerged)
DIMENSIONS: 187′6″ x 23′0″ x 23′0″
MACHINERY: 1 MTU diesel generator set, 9 Siemens PEM fuel cells for air-independent cruising, 1 Siemens electric motor, 1 shaft. 2400 shp = 12/20 knots
RANGE: 8000 nm at 8 knots snorkeling, 420 nm at 8 knots submerged
ARMAMENT: 6 x 533mm torpedo tubes (bow), total 22 torpedoes or 24 mines

COMPLEMENT: 27
NOTES: The design for these boats was developed from the Type 800 and shares its nonmagnetic high-tensile steel construction. The planes were moved to the sail and, in conjunction with an X-tail, endow them with enhanced submerged maneuverability. They also are the first production submarines to feature air-independent propulsion using fuel cells, and they introduced new slow-speed permanent-magnet electric motors driving advanced near-silent propellers. Using fuel cells, these boats can operate submerged continuously for up to three weeks without snorkeling to recharge their batteries. Accommodations are considerably improved to suit them for long-term submerged operation.

## GERMANY: TYPE 214 CLASS (2004)

*(Courtesy of Art-Tech)*

[Greece]—*Papanikolis* (22 April 2004)
BUILDER: HWK
[Greece]—*Pipinos* (1 September 2006), *Matrozos* (2007), *Katsonis* (2007)
BUILDER: Hellenic
[South Korea]—*Son Won-Il* (2006), 2+ boats
BUILDER: Hyundai
DISPLACEMENT: 1700 tons (surfaced), 1860 tons (submerged)
DIMENSIONS: 213′3″ x 20′8″ x 20′8″
MACHINERY: 2 MTU diesel generator sets, 2 Siemens PEM fuel cell air-independent auxiliary propulsion units, 1 Siemens electric motor, 1 shaft. 2400 shp = 12/20 knots
RANGE: 12,000 nm at 8 knots snorkeling, 2400 nm at 4 knots submerged on fuel cells
ARMAMENT: 8 x 533mm torpedo tubes (bow), total 16 torpedoes or Sub-Harpoon missiles
COMPLEMENT: 27
NOTES: The Type 214 is an enlarged version of the Type 212 with a modified power plant and heavier armaments intended for export customers.

# ITALY
## *TOTI* CLASS (1967)

*Enrico Toti* (12 March 1967), *Attilio Bagnolini* (26 August 1967), *Enrico Dandolo* (16 December 1967), *Lazzaro Mocenigo* (20 April 1968)

BUILDER: Monfalcone

DISPLACEMENT: 535 tons (surfaced), 592 tons (submerged)

DIMENSIONS: 151′8″ x 15′5″ x 13′1″

MACHINERY: 2 diesel engines, 1 electric motor, 1 shaft. 1080 bhp/900 shp = 8.5/13.5 knots

RANGE: 3000 nm at 5 knots snorkeling, 180 nm at 4 knots submerged

ARMAMENT: 4 x 533mm torpedo tubes (bow), total 8 torpedoes

COMPLEMENT: 26

NOTES: The gestation of the design for these small hunter-killer submarines was very prolonged, lasting for eight years beginning in 1956. Initially they could carry four wire-guided antisubmarine torpedoes and four conventional antiship weapons, but those were replaced by six dual-purpose wire-guided torpedoes in 1972, when a passive ranging system was fitted. They were stricken between 1991 and 1993.

## ITALY: *SAURO* CLASS, *NAZARRO SAURO* (1976)

*(Courtesy of Art-Tech)*

*Nazarro Sauro* (9 October 1976), *Carlo Fecia di Cossato* (16 November 1977), *Leonardo da Vinci* (20 October 1979), *Guglielmo Marconi* (20 September 1980)

BUILDER: Monfalcone

DISPLACEMENT: 1455 tons (surfaced), 1640 tons (submerged)

DIMENSIONS: 209'7" x 22'5" x 18'9"

MACHINERY: 3 diesel engines, 1 electric motor, 1 shaft. 3210 bhp/3650 shp = 12/20 knots

RANGE: 2500 nm at 12 knots snorkeling, 250 nm at 4 knots submerged

ARMAMENT: 6 x 533mm torpedo tubes (bow), total 12 torpedoes

COMPLEMENT: 45

NOTES: The design for these boats drew considerably on contemporary German submarine experience to create an effective hunter-killer type. They had an effective active and passive sonar array and were armed with wire-guided torpedoes controlled through a modern fire control system integrated with the sonar and a passive ranging system. In the 1990s they received a substantial refit, upgrading fire control and sonar systems and incorporating substantial noise reduction. They also were fitted to launch Sub-Harpoon missiles, but Italy did not procure these weapons. They were stricken between 2002 and 2005.

## *PELOSI* CLASS (1986)

*Salvatore Pelosi* (29 November 1986), *Giuliano Prini* (12 December 1987)

BUILDER: Monfalcone

DISPLACEMENT: 1476 tons (surfaced), 1662 tons (submerged)

DIMENSIONS: 211′2″ x 22′5″ x 18′7″

MACHINERY: 3 diesel engines, 1 electric motor, 1 shaft. 3210 bhp/3650 shp = 11/19 knots

RANGE: 2500 nm at 12 knots snorkeling, 250 nm at 4 knots submerged

ARMAMENT: 6 x 533mm torpedo tubes (bow), total 12 torpedoes

COMPLEMENT: 50

NOTES: These boats were slightly lengthened versions of the previous class with a single watertight bulkhead incorporated into the pressure hull. They were equipped to launch Sub-Harpoon missiles from the outset, though Italy has yet to procure that weapon. These boats were modernized in the late 1990s with improved integrated sensors and fire control systems. They also received substantial noise reduction through hull casing improvements and an anechoic coating.

# ITALY: *LONGOBARDO* CLASS (1992), *GIANFRANCO GAZZANA PRIAROGGIA* (1993)

*(Courtesy of Art-Tech)*

*Primo Longobardo* (20 June 1992), *Gianfranco Gazzana Priaroggia* (26 June 1993)

BUILDER: Monfalcone

DISPLACEMENT: 1653 tons (surfaced), 1829 tons (submerged)

DIMENSIONS: 217'8" x 22'5" x 19'8"

MACHINERY: 3 diesel engines, 1 electric motor, 1 shaft. 3210 bhp/3650 shp = 11/19 knots

RANGE: 5100 nm at 5 knots snorkeling, 240 nm at 4.5 knots submerged

ARMAMENT: 6 x 533mm torpedo tubes (bow), total 12 torpedoes

COMPLEMENT: 50

NOTES: These boats represent a further improvement on the original *Sauro* design, with a longer hull of better hydrodynamic form to reduce noise, increased fuel supply, and an enlarged sail and casing. They were modernized in the late 1990s with an updated integrated combat system, and the hull received an anechoic coating.

# JAPAN
## *OYASHIO* (25 MAY 1959)

BUILDER: Kawasaki

DISPLACEMENT: 1139 tons (surfaced), 1420 tons (submerged)

DIMENSIONS: 258'6" x 22'11" x 15'0"

MACHINERY: 2 diesel engines, 2 electric motors, 2 shafts. 2700 bhp/5860 shp = 13/19 knots

ARMAMENT: 4 x 21" torpedo tubes (bow)

COMPLEMENT: 65

NOTES: Japan's first submarine design since World War II was very conservative and drew heavily on experience from earlier wartime Japanese boats. The *Oyashio* served as a training vessel from 1973 and was discarded in 1976.

## *HAYASHIO* CLASS (1961)

*Hayashio* (31 July 1961), *Natsushio* (18 September 1962)

BUILDER: Mitsubishi

*Wakashio* (28 June 1961), *Fuyushio* (14 December 1962)

BUILDER: Kawasaki

DISPLACEMENT: 650 tons (surfaced), 800 tons (submerged)

DIMENSIONS: 193'6" x 21'4" x 13'6"

MACHINERY: 2 diesel engines, 2 electric motors, 2 shafts. 1350 bhp/1700 shp = 12/15 knots

ARMAMENT: 3 x 21" torpedo tubes (bow)

COMPLEMENT: 43

NOTES: The design for these boats drew on U.S. experience with the small hunter-killer submarines of the *Barracuda* class. They were very maneuverable underwater and had good habitability, but their small size was not suited to Pacific conditions. They were discarded in 1978–1979.

## *OSHIO* CLASS (1964)

*Oshio* (30 April 1964), *Harushio* (25 February 1967), *Arashio* (24 October 1968)

BUILDER: Mitsubishi

*Asashio* (27 November 1965), *Michishio* (5 December 1967)

BUILDER: Kawasaki

DISPLACEMENT: 1650 tons (surfaced), 2150 tons (submerged)

DIMENSIONS: 288'8" x 26'11" x 16'0"

MACHINERY: 2 Kawasaki-MAN diesel engines, 2 electric motors, 2 shafts. 2300 bhp/6300 shp = 14/18 knots

ARMAMENT: 8 x 21" torpedo tubes (6 bow, 2 stern)

COMPLEMENT: 80

NOTES: These large boats drew on U.S. experience with the *Tang* class. They were equipped to operate as antisubmarine warfare targets. The stern tubes were set up to launch swim-out torpedoes. These boats were deleted between 1981 and 1986.

## JAPAN: *UZUSHIO* CLASS (1970), *NARUSHIO* (1972)
*(Courtesy of Art-Tech)*

*Uzushio* (11 March 1970), *Isoshio* (18 March 1972), *Kuroshio* (22 February 1974), *Yaeshio* (19 May 1977)

BUILDER: Kawasaki

*Makishio* (27 January 1971), *Narushio* (22 November 1972), *Takashio* (30 June 1975)

BUILDER: Mitsubishi

DISPLACEMENT: 1850 tons (surfaced), 2600 tons (submerged)

DIMENSIONS: 236′3″ x 32′6″ x 24′7″

MACHINERY: 2 Kawasaki-MAN diesel engines, 2 electric motors, 1 shaft. 3600 bhp/7200 shp = 12/20 knots

ARMAMENT: 6 x 21″ torpedo tubes (amidships)

COMPLEMENT: 80

NOTES: The *Uzushio* class introduced a teardrop double hull configuration. It used high-tensile steel construction to increase the diving depth and an automatic three-dimensional steering system for control at high submerged speeds. The main sonar array was in a bow dome and the torpedo tubes amidships. The first two boats were deleted in 1987 and 1988. The other class members became training vessels and were stricken between 1990 and 1996.

## *YUSHIO* CLASS (1979)

*Yushio* (29 March 1979), *Nadashio* (27 January 1983), *Akishio* (22 January 1985), *Yukishio* (23 January 1987)
BUILDER: Mitsubishi
*Mochishio* (12 March 1980), *Setoshio* (12 February 1981), *Okishio* (5 March 1982), *Hamashio* (1 January 1984), *Takeshio* (9 February 1986), *Sachishio* (17 February 1988)
BUILDER: Kawasaki
DISPLACEMENT: 2200 tons (surfaced), 2450 tons (submerged)
DIMENSIONS: 249'4" x 32'6" x 24'7"
MACHINERY: 2 Kawasaki-MAN diesel engines, 2 electric motors, 1 shaft. 3400 bhp/7200 shp = 13/20 knots
ARMAMENT: 6 x 21" torpedo tubes (amidships), total 20 torpedoes
COMPLEMENT: 80
NOTES: These boats were improved versions of the previous class with upgraded sensor systems and stronger hulls for deeper diving. The final six boats were equipped to launch Sub-Harpoon missiles through their torpedo tubes. All became training submarines between 1996 and 2006. Japan began discarding them in 1999, with the final boat scheduled to be stricken in 2010.

## *HARUSHIO* CLASS (1989)

*Harushio* (26 July 1989), *Hayashio* (17 January 1991), *Wakashio* (22 January 1993), *Asashio* (12 July 1995)
BUILDER: Mitsubishi
*Natsushio* (20 March 1990), *Arashio* (17 March 1992), *Fuyushio* (22 January 1993)
BUILDER: Kawasaki
DISPLACEMENT: 2450 tons (surfaced), 2750 tons (submerged)
DIMENSIONS: 252'7" x 32'10" x 25'4"
MACHINERY: 2 Kawasaki-MAN diesel engines, 2 electric motors, 1 shaft. 5520 bhp/7200 shp = 12/20 knots
ARMAMENT: 6 x 21" torpedo tubes (amidships), total 20 torpedoes or missiles
COMPLEMENT: 75
NOTES: These boats were still further improved versions of the previous type, with more advanced sensors, greater noise quieting, and hulls built of NS110 high-tensile steel, endowing them with a diving depth in excess of 1,650 feet. They were equipped to launch Sub-Harpoon missiles from the outset.

The *Asashio* was withdrawn from front-line operations in 2000 and was lengthened by 30 feet to accommodate an air-independent propulsion system module incorporating two 120-shp Stirling engines, more highly automated engineering control systems, and an anechoic covering for the hull. These modifications increased displacement by 400 tons.

## *OYASHIO* CLASS (1996)

*Oyashio* (15 October 1996), *Uzushio* (26 November 1998), *Isoshio* (27 November 2000), *Kuroshio* (23 October 2002), *Yaeshio* (4 November 2004), *SS-600* (October 2006)

BUILDER: Kawasaki

*Michishio* (18 September 1997), *Makishio* (22 September 1999), *Narushio* (4 October 2001), *Takashio* (September 2003), *Setoshio* (5 October 2005)

BUILDER: Mitsubishi

DISPLACEMENT: 2750 tons (surfaced), 3600 tons (submerged)

DIMENSIONS: 268′0″ x 33′9″ x 24′3″

MACHINERY: 2 Kawasaki diesel engines, 2 electric motors, 1 shaft. 3400 bhp/7750 shp = 12/20 knots

ARMAMENT: 6 x 21″ torpedo tubes (bow), 20 torpedoes or missiles

COMPLEMENT: 69

NOTES: This class adopted a new partial double hull form to optimize the sensor layout, which takes the form of two conformal arrays covering almost the full length of each side of the hull and a chin sonar dome. The hull also is optimized for quiet operation and covered with an anechoic layer except on the bottom. Fire control, machinery, and submerged operations are highly automated. The final boat of this class is scheduled to commission in March 2008.

## 2900-TON TYPE (2007)

*SS-601* (October 2007)

BUILDER: Mitsubishi

*SS-602* (October 2008)

BUILDER: Kawasaki

DISPLACEMENT: 2900 tons (surfaced), 4200 tons (submerged)

DIMENSIONS: 275′7″ x 35′10″ x 28′0″

MACHINERY: 2 Kawasaki diesel engines, 2 Stirling air-independent generator sets, 2 electric motors, 1 shaft. 3400 bhp/8000 shp = 13/20 knots

ARMAMENT: 6 x 21″ torpedo tubes (bow), 20 torpedoes or missiles

COMPLEMENT: 65

NOTES: Modified versions of the *Oyashio* class incorporating a Stirling engine air-independent propulsion system as tested in the *Asashio*.

## THE NETHERLANDS
### *DOLFIJN* CLASS (1959)

*Dolfijn* (20 May 1959), *Zeehond* (20 February 1960)

BUILDER: Rotterdamse

*Potvis* (12 January 1965), *Tonijn* (14 June 1965)

BUILDER: Fijenoord

DISPLACEMENT: 1494 tons (surfaced), 1826 tons (submerged)

DIMENSIONS: 262'0" x 26'0" x 14'0"

MACHINERY: 2 MAN diesel engines, 2 electric motors, 2 shafts. 2800 bhp/4200 shp = 14.5/17 knots

ARMAMENT: 8 x 533mm torpedo tubes (4 bow, 4 stern), total 16 torpedoes

COMPLEMENT: 67

NOTES: The unusual three-cylinder pressure hull design for these boats evolved from studies undertaken during World War II by the Nederlandsche Verenigde Scheepsbouw Bureaux for multicylinder submarines. The full-length upper cylinder housed crew, command and control, and weapons spaces, while the two shorter parallel, lower cylinders accommodated independent machinery modules (each comprising a diesel engine and an electric motor driving a single shaft, plus a 168-cell battery). A streamlined outer casing enclosed the entire structure. Construction of the second pair of boats was delayed to explore ultimately abortive nuclear power options.

All boats received upgraded sensor outfits in the 1970s, and the later pair received more powerful Pielstick diesel engines in the late 1980s. The *Dolfijn* decommissioned in 1982; the *Zeehond* became a test hulk in 1990 and was scrapped in 1997; and the final pair decommissioned in 1992, the *Tonijn* becoming a museum vessel in 1994.

## SOVIET UNION
## PROJECT 613 [NATO WHISKEY] (1951)

S-80 (1951), S-43–S-46 (1952), S-140–S-152 (1953), S-155 (1953), S-157–S-158 (1953), S-159–S-186 (1954), S-192 (1954), S-193 –S-200 (1955), S-261–S-289 (1955), S-290–S-297 (1956), S-300 (1956), S-325–S-329 (1956), S-338–S-349 (1956)

BUILDER: Gorkiy

S-61–S-65 (1952), S-66–S-76 (1953), S-77–S-80 (1954), S-86–S-91 (1954), S-95–S-97 (1954), S-100 (1954), S-217 (1954), S-98 (1955), S-218–S-234 (1955), S-235–S-246 (1956), S-250 (1956), S-374 (1956), S-376 (1956), S-375 (1957), S-277–S-384 (1957)

BUILDER: Nikolayev

S-153–S-154 (1953), S-156 (1953), S-187–S-191 (1955), S-355–S-357 (1955), S-358–S-361 (1956), S-362–S-364 (1957), S-365 (1958)

BUILDER: Baltic

S-331 (1954), S-332–S-335 (1955), S-336–S-337 (1956), S-390–S-391 (1956), S-392–S-393 (1957)

BUILDER: Komsomolsk

[China]—119–120, 122–123, 127, 129, 131, 201–207, 221, 241, 243–244, 265–267 (1956–1964)

BUILDER: Guangdong and Shanghai

DISPLACEMENT: 1055 tons (surfaced), 1350 tons (submerged)

DIMENSIONS: 249'2" x 20'8" x 15'1"

MACHINERY: 2 diesel engines, 2 electric motors, 2 shafts. 4000 bhp/2700 shp = 18.25/13 knots

RANGE: 22,000 nm at 9 knots surfaced, 443 nm at 2 knots submerged

ARMAMENT: 6 x 533mm torpedo tubes (4 bow, 2 stern), total 12 torpedoes, 2 x 57mm guns, 2 x 25mm guns

COMPLEMENT: 52

NOTES: Design work on this class began immediately after World War II as a medium submarine to replace the earlier S and Shch types. Detailed examination of German Type XXI boats strongly influenced the final design, which incorporated, in a less pronounced form, the figure-eight midsection and distinctive stern contours of these boats. There were many detail variations between different series of these submarines, mainly in the exact number and disposition of the guns.

Large numbers of these boats were modified for special missions or experiments. Many also went to fleets within the Soviet sphere of influence: 5 to China (in addition to the 21 assembled there from Soviet-supplied components), 8 to Egypt, 2 to Bulgaria, 14 to Indonesia, 4 to Albania, 5 to Poland, 4 to North Korea, and one each to Cuba and Syria. By the early 1980s about 60 boats of the 215 built in the Soviet Union remained in service, and 18 still existed 10 years later.

## SOVIET UNION: PROJECT 611 [NATO ZULU] (1953)
*(Courtesy of Art-Tech)*

*B-61–B-62* (1953), *B-63–B-67* (1954), *B-68* (1955)

BUILDER: Sudomekh

*B-69–B-70* (1955), *B-71–B-72* (1956), *B-74–B-77* (1956), *B-80–B-82* (1957), *B-88* (1957), *B-90* (1957), *B-91* (1958)

BUILDER: Severodvinsk

DISPLACEMENT: 1830 tons (surfaced), 2600 tons (submerged)

DIMENSIONS: 296'10" x 24'7" x 16'5"

MACHINERY: 3 diesel engines, 2 electric motors, 3 shafts. 6000 bhp/2700 shp = 17/15 knots

RANGE: 22,000 nm at 9 knots surfaced, 443 nm at 2 knots submerged, 9500 nm at 8 knots snorkeling

ARMAMENT: 10 x 533mm torpedo tubes (6 bow, 4 stern), total 22 torpedoes, 2 x 57mm guns, 1 x 25mm gun

COMPLEMENT: 72

NOTES: Design work on this class began immediately after World War II as a long-range submarine to replace the earlier K type. It featured greatly increased battery capacity and stronger hull construction to make possible deeper diving. The gun armament eventually was removed from all boats, and they were reconfigured with snorkels and larger sails.

Three to four boats were converted for oceanographic research, and others were adapted to experimental projects. All went out of service during the 1980s.

## PROJECT 615 [NATO QUEBEC] (1953)

*M-254* (1953), *M-255–M-259* (1955), *M-260–M-268* (1956), *M-351–M-354* (1956), *M-269* (1957), *M-295* (1957), *M-297–M-300* (1957), *M-355–M-356* (1957), *M-301* (1958), *M-321* (1958), *M-354* (1958)

BUILDER: Sudomekh

DISPLACEMENT: 460 tons (surfaced), 540 tons (submerged)

DIMENSIONS: 286'3" x 14'9" x 11'10"

MACHINERY: 1 diesel engine, 2 electric motors, 3 shafts. 3000 bhp/4400 shp = 18/16 knots

RANGE: 3150 nm at 8.25 knots surfaced, 410 nm at 3.5 knots submerged

ARMAMENT: 4 x 533mm torpedo tubes (bow), total 8 torpedoes, 2 x 25mm guns

COMPLEMENT: 33

NOTES: These boats were designed for service in the Baltic and Black seas as replacements for the wartime M type. The first few units received the Kreislauf closed-cycle oxygen-fueled diesel propulsion system, but that was not successful; it was replaced by a conventional diesel engine. The guns were removed in the late 1950s, and all the boats were stricken by the late 1960s.

## SOVIET UNION: PROJECT 627 [NATO NOVEMBER] (1957)
*(Courtesy of Art-Tech)*

K-3 *Leninskiy Komsomolets* (1 July 1958), K-14 (31 December 1959), K-5 (17 August 1960), K-8 (31 August 1960), K-115 (30 December 1960), K-11 (23 December 1961), K-21 (23 December 1961), K-133 (16 October 1962), K-181 (16 October 1962), K-42 *Rostovskiy Komsomolets* (4 November 1963), K-159 (4 November 1963), K-50 (20 December 1963), K-52 (23 December 1963)

BUILDER: Severodvinsk

DISPLACEMENT: 3087 tons (surfaced), 3986 tons (submerged)

DIMENSIONS: 352'3" x 26'1" x 21'0"

MACHINERY: 2 VM-A pressurized water reactors, 2 steam turbines, 2 shafts. 35,000 shp = 15.5/30 knots

Endurance: 60 days

ARMAMENT: 8 x 533mm torpedo tubes (bow), total 20 torpedoes

COMPLEMENT: 110

NOTES: The first boat (the K-3) was built to Project 627, and its successors to Project 627A. The double-hull design was characterized by its torpedolike form and streamlined sail. Initially it was to be armed with a single T-15 torpedo with a thermonuclear warhead but was redesigned for conventional torpedo tubes. The hull interior was lined to reduce noise emissions, and its exterior received an anechoic coating; nevertheless, these submarines still were noisier than contemporary U.S. boats. They carried two large sonars in the bow, one passive and the other capable of operating in either active or passive modes. Their test depth was 975 feet.

The Soviet power plant operated at higher temperatures and was more powerful than contemporary U.S. systems. This class nevertheless suffered from substantial machinery problems, often a consequence of inadequate quality control in production. At least three of the class suffered reactor accidents in the early 1960s.

A fire broke out on the K-8 while it was submerged off the Spanish coast on 8 April 1970. It surfaced but sank four days later with half of its crew. The other class members were stricken between 1989 and 1992. The K-3 is preserved as a memorial on the Kola Peninsula.

## SOVIET UNION: PROJECT 633 [NATO ROMEO] (1958)
*(Courtesy of Art-Tech)*

S-4 (1958), S-6 (1958), S-7 (1958) *S-11* (1959), *S-28* (1959), S-34 (1959), S-36–S-38 (1960), *S-41* (1960), S-49 (1960), S-53 (1961), S-57 (1961), *S-101* (1961), *S-123* (1961), *S-212* (1961), S-323 (1961), S-350–S-352 (1961), S-354 (1962)

BUILDER: Gorkiy

[China]—*126, 140, 142–143, 153, 172, 176, 208–218, 227–229, 237–239, 245, 249, 254, 260, 267–272, 275–283, 286, 287, 291–304, 343–350, 355 (1965–1984)*

BUILDER: Wuhan, Guangdong, Jiangnan, and Huludao

[North Korea]—12 to 15 boats (1976–1992)

BUILDER: Bong Dao Bo and Mayang Do

DISPLACEMENT: 1330 tons (surfaced), 1730 tons (submerged)

DIMENSIONS: 251'3" x 21'4" x 15'1"

MACHINERY: 2 diesel engines, 2 electric motors, 2 shafts. 2000 bhp/2700 shp = 15.5/13 knots

RANGE: 9000 nm at 9 knots snorkeling, 350 nm at 2 knots submerged

ARMAMENT: 8 x 533mm torpedo tubes (6 bow, 2 stern), total 14 torpedoes

COMPLEMENT: 52

NOTES: This class was developed to replace the earlier Project 613 boats and were the first Soviet type completed without any gun armament. They could dive appreciably deeper than their precursors and were equipped with considerably more advanced sonar systems.

Large numbers of these boats were transferred to other fleets: 6 to Egypt, 2 to Bulgaria, 2 to Algeria, and 2 to Syria. Of the 35 boats built in China, 7 were transferred to North Korea (in addition to the 12 to 15 built there) and 4 to Egypt.

## SOVIET UNION: PROJECT 641 [NATO FOXTROT] (1958)
(*Courtesy of Art-Tech*)

B-94 (1958), B-37, B-95, B-133, B-135 (1959), B-57, B-85, B-116, B-130, B-139, B-143 (1960), B-4 *Chalyabinskiy Komsomolets*, B-7, B-33, B-59, B-153, B-156, B-164 (1961), B-8, B-38, B-50, B-53, B-105, B-169 (1962), B-2, B-31, B-55 (1963), B-6, B-15, B-98, B-101, B-103 (1964), B-9, B-21, B-25, B-107, B-109, B-112 (1965), B-26 *Yaroslavskiy Komsomolets*, B-28–B-29, B-34, B-40–B-41 (1966), B-39, B-46, B-49 *Vladimirskiy Komsomolets*, B-397 (1967), B-400, B-413 (1968), B-205, B-416 (1969), B-213, B-435, B-440 (1970), B-409, B-427 (1971) [India]— *Kursura* (1968), *Karanj*, *Kandhera* (1969), *Kalvari* (1970), *Vela*, *Vagir* (1973), *Vagli* (1974), *Vagsheer* (1975), [Libya]—*Al Badr*, *Al Fatah*, *Al Ahad* (1978), *Al Matrega* (1981), *Al Khyber* (1982), *Al Hunyan* (1983), [Cuba]— 725 (1979), 727 (1980), 729 (1984)

BUILDER: Sudomekh

DISPLACEMENT: 1957 tons (surfaced), 2475 tons (submerged)

DIMENSIONS: 299'6" x 24'7" x 16'9"

MACHINERY: 3 diesel engines, 1 electric motor, 3 shafts. 6000 bhp/8100 shp = 16.75/16 knots

RANGE: 17,900 nm at 8 knots snorkeling, 400 nm at 2 knots submerged

ARMAMENT: 10 x 533mm torpedo tubes (6 bow, 4 stern), total 22 torpedoes

COMPLEMENT: 70

NOTES: This class of long-range submarines was developed to replace the earlier Project 611 type. Like the Project 633 type, they were equipped with a substantially more advanced sonar outfit and could dive deeper than their precursors.

In addition to the 17 boats built for export, 2 submarines were transferred to Poland in 1987 and 1988 as the *Wilk* and the *Dzik*. All the boats, both Soviet and foreign, were discarded in the 1990s.

## PROJECT 651 [NATO JULIETT] (1962)

*K-156* (31 July 1962), *K-70*, *K-85* (1963), *K-81* (7 August 1964), *K-68*, *K-77* (1964), *K-24* (11 March 1965), *K-58*, *K-63*, *K-73* (1965), *K-67*, *K-78*, *K-203* (1966), *K-120*, *K-304*, *K-318* (1967)

BUILDER: Gorkiy

DISPLACEMENT: 3140 tons (surfaced), 4240 tons (submerged)

DIMENSIONS: 281'9" x 31'10" x 22'8"

MACHINERY: 2 diesel engines, 2 electric motors, 2 shafts. 7000 bhp/5000 shp = 16/14 knots

RANGE: 9000 nm at 7 knots snorkeling, 810 nm at 2.75 knots submerged

ARMAMENT: 4 x P-6 antiship missiles, 6 x 533mm torpedo tubes (bow), 4 x 400mm torpedo tubes (stern), total 6 plus 12 torpedoes

COMPLEMENT: 78

NOTES: This class was designed for antiship missile attack against NATO surface warships, especially carrier groups. They proved very reliable and tough but were not optimized for either surface or submerged operation; also, they were too noisy for their primary mission. All were discarded between 1989 and 1994.

## SOVIET UNION: PROJECT 675 [NATO ECHO II] (1962)
*(Courtesy of Art-Tech)*

*K-1, K-22 Krasnovardeets, K-28, K-35, K-47, K-56, K-74, K-86, K-104, K-125, K-166* (1962–1968)

BUILDER: Severodvinsk

*K-7, K-10, K-23, K-31, K-34 Kefal, K-48, K-57, K-90, K-94, K-108, K-116, K-128, K-135, K-172, K-175, K-184, K-189* (1962–1968)

BUILDER: Komsomolsk

DISPLACEMENT: 4415 tons (surfaced), 5737 tons (submerged)

DIMENSIONS: 376'6" x 30'6" x 23'0"

MACHINERY: 2 VM-A pressurized water reactors, 2 geared steam turbines, 2 shafts. 35,000 shp = 14/22.75 knots

ENDURANCE: 70 days

ARMAMENT: 8 x P-6 antiship missiles, 4 x 533mm torpedo tubes (bow), 2 x 400mm torpedo tubes (stern), total 10 plus 6 torpedoes

COMPLEMENT: 109

NOTES: These boats were an enlargement of the Project 659 (NATO Echo I) design, with an additional pair of missile-launching tubes and an enlarged sail to accommodate the guidance radar for P-6 antiship missiles. Their primary mission was attacks against U.S. Navy carrier task forces, though they had a secondary land attack role.

Like other early Soviet nuclear submarines, boats of this class suffered from power plant accidents and breakdowns. The *K-116*, the *K-31* (by then redesignated the *K-431*), and the *K-192* all experienced serious reactor accidents (explosions or melt-downs), leading to their removal from service in 1978, 1986, and 1989, respectively. The whole class was decommissioned by the mid-1990s.

## PROJECT 645 ZHMT (NATO NOVEMBER) (1963)

K-27 (30 October 1963)

BUILDER: Severodvinsk

DISPLACEMENT: 3414 tons (surfaced), 5078 tons (submerged)

DIMENSIONS: 360'3" x 27'3" x 19'2"

MACHINERY: 2 VT liquid lead-bismuth reactors, 2 geared steam turbines, 2 shafts. 35,000 shp = 15/29 knots

ENDURANCE: 60 days

ARMAMENT: 8 x 533mm torpedo tubes (bow), total 20 torpedoes

COMPLEMENT: 105

NOTES: The K-27 used the Project 627A design lengthened to accommodate liquid lead-bismuth reactors, which offered the potential for higher power outputs as a result of more efficient heat transfer, although their operation was complicated by the need to keep the alloy liquid, either by running the reactors continuously or by providing an external heat supply while in port. The K-27 also was constructed of low-magnetic steel to reduce its vulnerability to mines, had an automated torpedo reloading system, and a self-sustaining turbo-generator. After initially successful trials, major repairs to fix hull cracks were necessary. When the K-27 returned to service, a series of major machinery problems culminated in a radioactive gas explosion on 24 May 1968 while the submarine was underwater. Required repairs were so extensive that the K-27 was stricken and scuttled in 1981.

## PROJECT 671 [NATO VICTOR I] (1965)

K-37 (October 1965), K-69, K-147 (1967), K-53, K-306 (1968), K-53 50 Let SSSR, K-370 (1969), K-367, K-438 (1970), K-314, K-398 (1971), K-454, K-462, K-469, K-481 (1972)

BUILDER: Admiralty

DISPLACEMENT: 3650 tons (surfaced), 4830 tons (submerged)

DIMENSIONS: 305'0" x 34'9" x 23'7"

MACHINERY: 2 VM-5P pressurized water reactors, 1 geared steam turbine, 1 shaft. 31,000 shp = 12/33 knots

ENDURANCE: 50 days

ARMAMENT: 6 x 533mm torpedo tubes (bow), total 18 torpedoes or 36 mines

COMPLEMENT: 76

NOTES: The use of a body-of-revolution hull form in this design permitted the installation of the two reactors side-by-side and the turbine and two turbo-reactors in a single compartment, reducing overall length and, therefore, wetted area. As a result the Project 6711 boats were 10 percent faster than their Project 627A precursors. The designers made a major effort to reduce noise generation through the use of a dampening coating internally, an external anechoic layer, and spring-loaded covers for limber holes. Higher tensile steel construction endowed the type with a test depth of 1300 feet. The large Rubin sonar system was installed in the bow hemisphere, with the torpedo tubes arranged above it. At least three boats (the K-314, the K-454, and the K-469) were upgraded to launch TEST-68 wire-guided torpedoes. All boats were taken out of service between 1989 and 1996.

## SOVIET UNION: PROJECT 670A [NATO CHARLIE I] (1967)
*(Courtesy of Art-Tech)*

*K-43* (1967), *K-25*, *K-87*, *K-121* (1968), *K-308*, *K-313* (1969), *K-303*, *K-320*, *K-325* (1970), *K-201*, *K-429* (1971)

BUILDER: Gorkiy

DISPLACEMENT: 3580 tons (surfaced), 4550 tons (submerged)

DIMENSIONS: 309'4" x 32'6" x 24'7"

MACHINERY: 1 VM-4 pressurized water reactors, 1 geared steam turbine, 1 shaft. 18,800 shp = 16/26 knots

ENDURANCE: 50 days

ARMAMENT: 8 x P-70 antiship missiles, 4 x 533mm torpedo tubes, 2 x 400mm torpedo tubes (all bow), total 12 plus 4 torpedoes

COMPLEMENT: 90

NOTES: Project 670 was developed specifically to attack U.S. Navy carrier groups. It used a streamlined double hull similar to that of the Project 671 but with a large domed bow to accommodate torpedo tubes and the large Kerch–670 sonar, used to track its targets. Four angled missile-launching tubes on each side flanked the torpedo compartment between the inner and outer hulls. The power plant was one-half of the installation used in Project 671. These submarines had a test depth of 1150 feet.

The *K-429* sank in the Bering Sea on 23 June 1983, was recovered, only to sink again while repairing on 13 September 1985. The *K-313* suffered a reactor meltdown in December 1985 but returned to service. The *K-43* was leased to India for three years from January 1988, serving as the *Chakri*. All surviving boats of the class were discarded by 1994.

## PROJECT 661 [NATO PAPA] (1968)

*K-162* (21 December 1968)
BUILDER: Severodvinsk
DISPLACEMENT: 5280 tons (surfaced), 6320 tons (submerged)
DIMENSIONS: 350'8" x 37'9" x 26'3"
MACHINERY: 2 VM-5 pressurized water reactors, 2 geared steam turbines, 2 shafts. 80,000 shp = 16/42 knots
ENDURANCE: 50 days
ARMAMENT: 10 x P-120 antiship missiles, 4 x 533mm torpedo tubes (bow), total 12 torpedoes
COMPLEMENT: 75

NOTES: Designed as a prototype for series construction, the Project 661 boat remained a unique example and served primarily as a test bed for advanced submarine features. Titanium was used for constructing the double hull; there was a very small sail, and a large bow sonar dome. This boat was among the fastest submarines built, attaining 44.75 knots during a series of experimental patrols in 1971, but it was too expensive, noisy, and unreliable for series production. It was withdrawn from service in 1988.

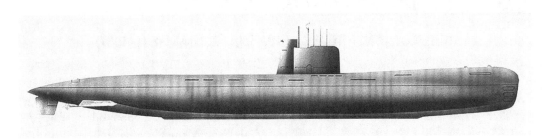

## SOVIET UNION: PROJECT 641BUKI [NATO TANGO] (1972)

*(Courtesy of Art-Tech)*

*B-380 Gorvovskiy Komsomolets* (1972), *B-30* (1972), *B-97*, *B-146* (1974), *B-215*, *B-225* (1975), *B-290* (1976), *B-303*, *B-307* (1977), *B-312*, *B-319*, *B-386* (1978), *B-443*, *B-474* (1979), *B-498*, *B-504*, *B-515* (1980), *B-519*, *B-546* (1981)
BUILDER: Gorkiy
DISPLACEMENT: 3100 tons (surfaced), 3900 tons (submerged)
DIMENSIONS: 295'10" x 28'3" x 18'8"
MACHINERY: 3 diesel engines, 3 electric motors, 3 shafts. 5570 bhp/8100 shp = 13/15 knots
RANGE: 14,400 nm at 7 knots snorkeling, 450 nm at 2.5 knots submerged
ARMAMENT: 10 x 533mm torpedo tubes (6 bow, 4 stern), total 24 torpedoes or antiship missiles

COMPLEMENT: 78
NOTES: These boats were developed as very-long-range submarines to supplement to Project 641 type. Their larger size resulted from the need to accommodate a large bow sonar, a sonar intercept and ranging system, and an underwater communication set, all linked to a fire control system for the RPK-2 Viyoga (NATO designation SS-N-15 Starfish) solid-fuel rocket missile launched through the torpedo tubes.

All but four boats went into reserve in 1998, and none remained operational by 2004.

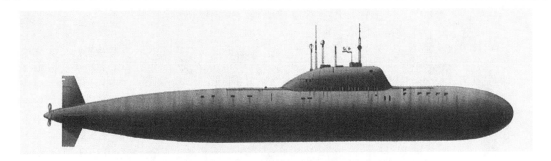

## SOVIET UNION: PROJECT 705 [NATO ALFA] (1972)
*(Courtesy of Art-Tech)*

*K-377* (1972), *K-373* (1978), *K-316* (1979), *K-463* (1982)
BUILDER: Sudomekh
*K-123* (1979), *K-432* (1982), *K-493* (1983)
BUILDER: Severodvinsk
DISPLACEMENT: 2324 tons (surfaced), 3210 tons (submerged)
DIMENSIONS: 261'2" x 31'1" x 23'3"
MACHINERY: 1 BM-40A (Severodvinsk boats—OK-550) liquid lead-bismuth reactor, 1 geared steam turbine, 1 shaft. 40,000 shp = 12/41 knots
ENDURANCE: 50 days
ARMAMENT: 6 x 533mm torpedo tubes (bow), total 18 torpedoes or antisubmarine missiles
COMPLEMENT: 29
NOTES: The design for this class was revolutionary. It combined a streamlined titanium hull (for great strength, small size, and deep diving) with a powerful liquid metal–cooled reactor and extensive automation (to reduce crew size), resulting in the Project 705 type's becoming the fastest and deepest-diving class of submarines yet developed: it is capable of close to 45 knots on trials, and of diving to 2000 feet. Nevertheless, the type encountered many problems. The reactor coolant required constant heating to prevent it from solidifying, necessitating either running the reactor at all times or connecting the boat to an external heat source. The type's sensors were unique and difficult to maintain in service. Some of the auxiliary machinery also proved unreliable and difficult to service.

Two boats were modified under Project 671 with pressurized water reactors and used for trials. The prototype, the *K-377*, was stricken in 1974 after its reactor coolant solidified; the others were stricken by 1993.

## SOVIET UNION: PROJECT 671RT [NATO VICTOR II] (1972)
*(Courtesy of Art-Tech)*

*K-387* (2 September 1972), *K-371* (1974), *K-476* (1975), *K-488, K-495* (1976), *K-513, K-517* (1977)

BUILDER: Admiralty

DISPLACEMENT: 4245 tons (surfaced), 5700 tons (submerged)

DIMENSIONS: 328'0" x 34'9" x 23'7"

MACHINERY: 2 VM-5P pressurized water reactors, 1 geared steam turbine, 1 shaft. 31,000 shp = 18/30 knots

ENDURANCE: 60 days

ARMAMENT: 4 x 533mm torpedo tubes, 2 x 650mm torpedo tubes (all bow), total 18 plus 6 torpedoes or 36 mines

COMPLEMENT: 100

NOTES: Two elements drove this development of the original Project 671 design: accommodating the heavier Type 65–76 torpedo and substantially reducing noise. The machinery was mounted on a shock-absorbing "raft" to isolate it from the hull and limit noise emission. In addition, these boats carried the appreciably improved Skat sonar system. All seven submarines were decommissioned in 1995–1996.

## PROJECT 670M [NATO CHARLIE II] (1973)

*K-452 Berkut* (1973), *K-458* (1975), *K-479* (1977), *K-503* (1978), *K-508* (1979), *K-209* (1980)

BUILDER: Gorkiy

DISPLACEMENT: 4250 tons (surfaced), 5270 tons (submerged)

DIMENSIONS: 344'1" x 32'6" x 26'7"

MACHINERY: 1 VM-4 pressurized water reactors, 1 geared steam turbine, 1 shaft. 18,800 shp = 12/24 knots

ENDURANCE: 50 days

ARMAMENT: 8 x P-120 antiship missiles, 4 x 533mm torpedo tubes, 2 x 400mm torpedo tubes (all bow), total 12 plus 4 torpedoes

COMPLEMENT: 90

NOTES: The original Project 670 design was enlarged to accommodate longer-range P-120 Malachite solid-fuel antiship missiles, Skat-M sonar, and improved fire control systems. All these submarines were decommissioned by 1994.

## PROJECT 671RTM [NATO VICTOR III] (1977)

*K-138* (August 1977), *K-218* (1978), *K-244* (1979), *K-254*, *K-292* (1980), *K-298*, *K-299* (1981), *K-255* (July 1982), *K-324*, *K-398 Murmanskiy Komsomolets* (1982), *K-388* (July 1983), *K-414* (1984), *K-448* (1985), *K-502* (June 1988), *K-524* (August 1989), *K-527* (October 1991)

BUILDER: Admiralty

*K-242 50 Let Komsomolsk-na-Amur* (1978), *K-247*, *K-251* (1979), *K-264* (1980), *K-305* (1981), *K-355* (1982), *K-360* (1983), *K-412* (June 1984), *K-492* (1987), *K-507* (August 1989)

BUILDER: Komsomolsk

DISPLACEMENT: 4750 tons (surfaced), 5980 tons (submerged)

DIMENSIONS: 351'4" x 34'9" x 26'3"

MACHINERY: 2 VM-5P pressurized water reactors, 1 geared steam turbine, 1 shaft. 31,000 shp = 18/31 knots

ENDURANCE: 80 days

ARMAMENT: 4 x 533mm torpedo tubes, 2 x 650mm torpedo tubes (all bow), total 18 plus 6 torpedoes or antiship missiles

COMPLEMENT: 82

NOTES: This class featured still further advances in weaponry and sensors over its precursors. It was equipped to launch the RPK-55 Granat cruise missile through its torpedo tubes in addition to wire-guided torpedoes and mines. In addition to the improved Skat-K sonar in the bow, it carried a Pithon towed array sonar launched from a pod atop the stern fin. The additional compartment forward of the sail accommodated improved electronics, navigation systems, and radio and satellite communication systems. Quieting was enhanced by installing tandem four-bladed propellers in place of the single five-bladed units of the previous boats.

The final five submarines of this group were built to Project 671RTMK.

These boats were the first in the Soviet fleet to incorporate a fully integrated submarine combat direction and fire control command system. They also received the new Koloss nonacoustic sensor system.

## SOVIET UNION: PROJECT 877 [NATO KILO] (1980)

*(Courtesy of Art-Tech)*

*B-177, B-187, B-190, B-219, B-224, B-227, B-229, B-248, B-260, B-345, B-356, B-394 Komsomolets Tadjikistana, B-401, B-402, B-404 Tyumenskiy Komsomolets, B-405, B-425, B-437 Magnitogorskiy Komsomolets, B-439, B-445, B-459, B-464, B-468, B-470, B-471, B-494, B-800, B-806, B-871, B-880 Delfin* (1982–1994)

BUILDER: Gorkiy and Komsomolsk

[Romania]—*Delfinul* (1986), [Poland]—*Orzel* (1986), [India]—*Sindhugosh* (1986), *Sindhudvaj* (1987), *Sindhuraj* (1987), *Sindhuvir* (1988), *Sindhuratna* (1988), *Sindhukesari* (1989), *Sindhukirti* (1990), *Sindhuvijay* (1991), *Sindhurak-shak* (1997), *Sindhushastra* (2000), [Algeria]—*Rajs Hadi Mubarek* (1987), *El Hadi Slimani* (1988), [Iran]—*Tareq* (1991), *Noor* (1992), *Yunes* (1993), [China]—*364* (1994), *365* (1995)

BUILDER: Sudomekh

DISPLACEMENT: 2300 tons (surfaced), 3036 tons (submerged)

DIMENSIONS: 238'1" x 32'6" x 20'4"

MACHINERY: 2 1000-KW diesel generators, 1 electric motor, 1 shaft. 5500 shp = 10/17 knots

RANGE: 6000 nm at 7 knots snorkeling, 400 nm at 3 knots submerged

ARMAMENT: 6 x 533mm torpedo tubes (bow), total 18 torpedoes, 8 Strela–3 or Igla missiles

COMPLEMENT: 52

NOTES: The Project 877 type was designed as an antisubmarine warfare platform with good patrol and reconnaissance characteristics. It was the first Soviet conventionally powered type to use a teardrop hull form. Great attention was paid to noise reduction through rafting machinery, eliminating flooding ports, locating the dive planes further aft, and providing an anechoic coating for the hull. Careful design and choice of materials also drastically reduced the type's magnetic signature. These boats also introduced extensive automation of both ship and fire control to reduce crew size and improve safety. Later boats incorporated improved fire control systems and the capability to launch wire-guided torpedoes.

Large numbers of this type were built for export, usually with a slightly less capable sensor outfit. Most of the Russian boats went into reserve around 2000, but the export boats are still very active.

## PROJECT 949 [NATO OSCAR I] (1980)

*K-525 Arkhangelsk* (April 1980), *K-206 Murmansk* (December 1982)

BUILDER: Severodvinsk

DISPLACEMENT: 12,500 tons (surfaced), 22,500 tons (submerged)

DIMENSIONS: 472'4" x 59'8" x 30'2"

MACHINERY: 2 OK-650b pressurized water reactors, 2 geared steam turbines, 2 shafts. 100,000 shp = 15/30 knots

ENDURANCE: 50 days

ARMAMENT: 24 x P-700 antiship missiles, 4 x 533mm torpedo tubes, 4 x 650mm torpedo tubes (all bow), total 28 torpedoes

COMPLEMENT: 107

NOTES: Missile attack operations against U.S. carrier groups were the principal roles for these boats. The design featured a double-hull with about 10 feet between the two skins. The missile tubes, angled at about 40 degrees, were fitted between the two hulls, and the remainder of the space was filled largely with sound-deadening material to reduce noise emission. Rafted machinery and an anechoic coating also served to reduce the type's acoustic signature. Missile targeting data was acquired from an overhead satellite system or transmitted via a towed very-low-frequency buoy array. These two boats were decommissioned in 1996.

## PROJECT 945A [NATO SIERRA I] (1983)

K-239 *Tula* (29 July 1983), K-276 *Krab* (June 1986)
BUILDER: Gorkiy
DISPLACEMENT: 6300 tons (surfaced), 8300 tons (submerged)
DIMENSIONS: 351'0" x 40'0" x 31'2"
MACHINERY: 1 OK-650a pressurized water cooled reactor, 1 geared steam turbine, 1 shaft. 50,000 shp = 18/35 knots
ENDURANCE: 50 days
ARMAMENT: 4 x 533mm torpedo tubes, 2 x 650mm torpedo tubes (all bow), total 28 plus 12 torpedoes or missiles
COMPLEMENT: 59
NOTES: Project 945 generated a very successful attack submarine for the Soviet fleet. The titanium double hull was carefully streamlined and covered with an anechoic tile coating, which, combined with the use of machinery rafting and a sophisticated propeller design, dramatically reduced the type's noise and magnetic signatures. Automation for ship and fire control was expanded, a sophisticated sensor and countermeasure suite was incorporated, and the larger torpedo tubes could also be used to launch S-10 Granit cruise missiles.

The *Tula* collided with the U.S. submarine *Baton Rouge* on 11 February 1992 off the Kola peninsular. Both these boats were decommissioned in 1997 and placed in reserve.

## PROJECT 971 [NATO AKULA I] (1984)

K-263 *Delfin* (15 July 1984), K-284 *Puma* (30 December 1984), K-322 *Kashalot* (July 1987), K-391 *Kit* (April 1989), K-331 *Narval* (June 1990), K-419 *Morzh* (May 1992), K-267 *Drakon* (4 August 1994)
BUILDER: Komsomolsk
K-480 *Bars* (May 1988), K-317 *Pantera* (May 1990), K-461 *Volk* (June 1991), K-328 *Leopard* (6 October 1992), K-157 *Tigr* (10 July 1993)
BUILDER: Severodvinsk
DISPLACEMENT: 8140 tons (surfaced), 10,700 tons (submerged)
DIMENSIONS: 361'9" x 44'7" x 31'9"
MACHINERY: 2 OK-650b pressurized water reactors, 1 OK-7 geared steam turbine, 2 OK-2 turbo-generators, 1 shaft. 50,000 shp = 13/33 knots
ENDURANCE: 80 days
ARMAMENT: 4 x 533mm torpedo tubes, 4 x 650mm torpedo tubes (all bow), total 28 plus 12 torpedoes or missiles
COMPLEMENT: 73
NOTES: This class was developed as a cheaper alternative to the sophisticated and expensive Project 945 type. In place of titanium, the pressure hull used high-tensile, low-magnetism steel, cutting both the cost of materials and of the labor and specialized facilities required to weld titanium. To limit the type's acoustic signature, it features machinery rafting, an anechoic coating on the outer hull, careful attention to streamlining, spring-loaded covers for all limber holes, a sophisticated propeller design, and active noise suppression. The weapons load matches that of the Type 945, with the same capability for launching S-10 Granit cruise missiles from the larger torpedo tubes.

The *Puma* was stricken in 1995, and the remainder of this group went into reserve in 1999.

## SOVIET UNION: PROJECT 949A [NATO OSCAR II] (1985), *K-119 VORONEZH*
*(Courtesy of Art-Tech)*

*K-148 Orenburg* (August 1985), *K-132 Irkutsk* (March 1986), *K-119 Voronezh* (December 1987), *K-173 Krasnoyarsk* (January 1989), *K-410 Smolensk* (December 1989), *K-442 Chelyabinsk* (January 1990), *K-456 Viliuczinsk* (December 1991), *K-266 Orel* (22 May 1992), *K-186 Omsk* (8 May 1993), *K-141 Kursk* (May 1994), *K-512 Tomsk* (18 July 1995), *K-530 Belgorod* (May 1998)

BUILDER: Severodvinsk

DISPLACEMENT: 14,700 tons (surfaced), 24,000 tons (submerged)

DIMENSIONS: 505'3" x 59'8" x 30'2"

MACHINERY: 2 OK-650b pressurized water reactors, 2 geared steam turbines, 2 shafts. 100,000 shp = 15/30 knots

ENDURANCE: 50 days

ARMAMENT: 24 x P-700 antiship missiles, 4 x 533mm torpedo tubes, 4 x 650mm torpedo tubes (all bow), total 28 torpedoes

COMPLEMENT: 107

NOTES: These boats were slightly longer than the earlier Project 949 submarines, to allow more extensive rafting of machinery in order to reduce their acoustic signature. Three additional boats were not completed.

The *Kursk* sank after an accident on 12 August 2000 about 100 miles from Murmansk. By 2006 about six of the class remained in active service, with the remainder laid up in reserve.

## SOVIET UNION: PROJECT 945B [NATO SIERRA II] (1988)

*(Courtesy of Art-Tech)*

*K-534 Pskov* (May 1990), *K-338 Nizhniy Novgorod* (June 1992), *K-123 Mars* (July 1992)

BUILDER: Gorkiy

DISPLACEMENT: 6300 tons (surfaced), 8300 tons (submerged)

DIMENSIONS: 351′0″ x 40′0″ x 31′2″

MACHINERY: 1 OK-650a pressurized water reactor, 1 geared steam turbine, 1 shaft. 50,000 shp = 18/35 knots

ENDURANCE: 50 days

ARMAMENT: 4 x 533mm torpedo tubes, 4 x 650mm torpedo tubes (all bow), total 28 plus 12 torpedoes or missiles

COMPLEMENT: 59

NOTES: These boats featured a longer hull incorporating improved machinery noise reduction measures. It is not certain that the *Mars* was ever completed, and it seems certain that two other units were broken up before launching. The first two boats were still operational in 2006.

## RUSSIA
## PROJECT 971M [NATO AKULA II] (1994)

*Vepr* (10 December 1994), *Gepard* (1998), *Kuguar* (1999), *Rys* (2000)

BUILDER: Severodvinsk

DISPLACEMENT: 8140 tons (surfaced), 10,700 tons (submerged)

DIMENSIONS: 361'9" x 44'7" x 31'9"

MACHINERY: 2 OK-650b pressurized water reactors, 1 OK-7 geared steam turbine, 2 OK-2 turbo-generators, 1 shaft. 50,000 shp = 13/33 knots

ENDURANCE: 80 days

ARMAMENT: 4 x 533mm torpedo tubes, 4 x 650mm torpedo tubes (all bow), total 28 plus 12 torpedoes or missiles

COMPLEMENT: 73

NOTES: These boats were longer than the Project 971 boats, in order to accommodate a slow-speed transmission to reduce propeller noise. In addition, they received an additional anechoic coating on the inner face of the hull, more elaborate insulation of the machinery raft, and upgraded sensors.

## PROJECT 636 (NATO KILO) (1996)

[China]—366 (24 April 1997), 367 (17 June 1998), 368 (4 April 2001) plus 6 unknown (2003–2005) plus 1 building

BUILDER: Sudomekh

DISPLACEMENT: 2350 tons (surfaced), 3126 tons (submerged)

DIMENSIONS: 242'1" x 32'6" x 20'4"

MACHINERY: 2 1000-KW diesel generators, 1 electric motor, 1 shaft. 6800 shp = 11/19 knots

RANGE: 7500 nm at 7 knots snorkeling, 400 nm at 3 knots submerged

ARMAMENT: 6 x 533mm torpedo tubes (bow), total 18 torpedoes, 8 Strela–3 or Igla missiles

COMPLEMENT: 52

NOTES: The Project 636 type is an improvement on the earlier Project 877. The extra length was used to accommodate more powerful machinery mounted on improved rafts and running at half the speed of the previous installation, driving a seven-bladed skewed propeller, thus substantially reducing noise and increasing range. All orders for the type so far have come from China.

## PROJECT 677 *LADA* CLASS (2003)

*B-100 Sankt Petersburg* (November 2003)
2+ boats
BUILDER: Admiralty
DISPLACEMENT: 1675 tons (surfaced),
2800 tons (submerged)
DIMENSIONS: 219'10" x 23'7" x 14'5"
MACHINERY: 2 diesel generators, 1 electric
motor, 1 shaft. 2700 shp = 11/22 knots
RANGE: 6000 nm at 7 knots snorkeling,
650 nm at 3 knots submerged
ARMAMENT: 6 x 533mm torpedo tubes
(bow), total 18 torpedoes or missiles
COMPLEMENT: 41
NOTES: The Project 677 type is one of a
family of designs developed by the Rubin
design bureau for advanced conventionally powered submarines in a range of
sizes from 550 to 1850 tons surfaced. It
uses machinery arrangements and hull
features very similar to those of the
Project 636 to minimize acoustic and
magnetic signatures. It is designed to incorporate an air-independent propulsion
system at a later date, should that become necessary. The designers have high
hopes of export success with this design,
though as of 2006 the only customer has
been the Russian fleet.

# SWEDEN
## *HAJEN* CLASS (1954)

*Hajen* (11 December 1954), *Sälen* (2 Octo-
ber 1955), *Bävern* (3 February 1958), *Ut-
tern* (14 November 1958)
BUILDER: Kockums
*Valen* (21 May 1955), *Illern* (14 November
1957)
BUILDER: Karlskrona
DISPLACEMENT: 785 tons (surfaced), 900
tons (submerged)
DIMENSIONS: 216'6" x 16'6" x 16'5"
MACHINERY: 2 Pielstick diesel engines, 1
ASEA electric motors, 2 shafts. 1660
bhp/2200 shp = 16/20 knots
ARMAMENT: 6 x 533mm torpedo tubes
(bow), total 8 torpedoes
COMPLEMENT: 64
NOTES: The design for these boats was de-
veloped from extensive study of a salved
German Type XXI submarine, the *U-
3503*. They were stricken in 1980.

## *DRAKEN* CLASS (1960)

*Draken* (1 April 1960), *Vargen* (20 May 1960), *Nordkampen* (8 March 1961), *Springaren* (30 August 1961)
BUILDER: Kockums
*Gripen* (31 May 1960), *Delfinen* (7 March 1962)
BUILDER: Karlskrona
DISPLACEMENT: 835 tons (surfaced), 950 tons (submerged)
DIMENSIONS: 226'6" x 16'9" x 17'5"
MACHINERY: 2 Pielstick diesel engines, 2 ASEA electric motors, 1 shaft. 1600 bhp/2150 shp = 17/22 knots
ARMAMENT: 4 x 533mm torpedo tubes (bow), total 12 torpedoes
COMPLEMENT: 36
NOTES: These boats were very similar to the previous *Hajen* type but featured an extended stern to accommodate a gearbox driving a single five-bladed propeller for reduced noise and higher speed. They were modernized in 1970–1971, receiving new sensors.

The *Draken* and the *Gripen* were stricken in 1981. The other boats received an extensive upgrade, including new sails, sensors, and noise reduction, and were taken out of service in 1988.

## *SJÖORMEN* CLASS (1967)

*Sjöormen* (25 January 1967), *Sjölejonet* (29 June 1967), *Sjöhunden* (21 March 1968)
BUILDER: Kockums
*Sjöbjornet* (9 January 1968), *Sjöhästen* (6 August 1968)
BUILDER: Karlskrona
DISPLACEMENT: 835 tons (surfaced), 950 tons (submerged)
DIMENSIONS: 165'7" x 20'0" x 19'0"
MACHINERY: 2 Pielstick diesel engines, 1 ASEA electric motor, 1 shaft. 2200 bhp/1700 shp = 15/20 knots
ARMAMENT: 4 x 533mm torpedo tubes, 2 x 400mm torpedo tubes (all bow)
COMPLEMENT: 23
NOTES: This design introduced a teardrop hull, X-tail, and sail mounted planes for improved submerged maneuverability and performance. They received a new sonar suite and fire control system in 1984–1985. The *Sjölejonet* and the *Sjöhunden* were again upgraded between 1992 and 1994, acquiring new electronics and a towed sonar array. Singapore purchased all five boats in 1995, the *Sjöbjornet* being cannibalized for spares and the *Sjöormen* and the *Sjöhästen* being upgraded to match the *Sjölejonet* and the *Sjöhunden*. They were renamed the *Centurion*, the *Challenger*, the *Conqueror*, and the *Chieftain*, and all commissioned by 2004.

## *NÄCKEN* CLASS (1978)

*Näcken* (17 April 1978), *Neptun* (6 December 1978), *Najad* (13 August 1979)
BUILDER: Kockums and Karlskrona
DISPLACEMENT: 980 tons (surfaced), 1150 tons (submerged)
DIMENSIONS: 162'5" x 18'8" x 18'0"
MACHINERY: 1 MTU diesel engine, 1 Jeumont-Schneider electric motor, 1 shaft. 2100 bhp/1540 shp = 20/25 knots
ARMAMENT: 6 x 533mm torpedo tubes, 2 x 400mm torpedo tubes (all bow), total 12 torpedoes
COMPLEMENT: 19
NOTES: This class was a smaller version of the previous group, with a single diesel engine and highly automated machinery and tactical control. The *Näcken* was lengthened to 188'8" in 1987–1988 to accommodate two Stirling air-independent propulsion units, allowing it to operate submerged for up to 14 days without snorkeling; it also received an anechoic covering for the hull.

The *Neptun* and the *Najad* were placed in storage reserve in 1998–1999. The *Näcken* was leased to Denmark as the *Kronborg* in 2001 and returned to Sweden in 2004.

## SWEDEN: *VÄSTERGÖTLAND* CLASS (1986), *SÖDERMANLAND* (1988)
(*Courtesy of Art-Tech*)

*Västergötland* (17 September 1986), *Häls-ingland* (31 August 1987), *Södermanland* (12 April 1988), *Östergötland* (9 December 1988)

BUILDER: Kockums and Karlskrona

DISPLACEMENT: 1070 tons (surfaced), 1143 tons (submerged)

DIMENSIONS: 159′1″ x 19′11″ x 18′4″

MACHINERY: 2 Hedemora diesel engines, 1 electric motor, 1 shaft. 2160 bhp/1800 shp = 11/20 knots

ARMAMENT: 6 x 533mm torpedo tubes, 4 x 400mm torpedo tubes (all bow), total 18 torpedoes, 22 mines

COMPLEMENT: 20

NOTES: This Kockums design introduced advanced flank array sensors in addition to the large bow sonar and towed array.

They incorporate a high degree of noise reduction, including an anechoic hull coating. The mines are carried in external canisters. These boats were built jointly by Kockums and Karlskrona, with the former constructing the midsection and the latter the bow and stern sections.

The *Södermanland* and the *Östergötland* were lengthened to 191′10″ between 2001 and 2004 to accommodate 2 Stirling air-independent propulsion units, allowing them to operate submerged for up to 14 days withoutsnorkeling. They also received new thermal imaging and enhanced imaging non-hull penetrating periscopes. The two older boats were retired to storage reserve in 2005.

## [AUSTRALIA]—TYPE 471, *COLLINS* (1993)
*(Courtesy of Art-Tech)*

[Australia]—*Collins* (28 August 1993), *Farncomb* (15 December 1995), *Waller* (14 March 1997), *Dechaineux* (12 March 1998), *Sheean* (1 May 1999), *Rankin* (26 November 2001)

BUILDER: ASC

DISPLACEMENT: 2500 tons (surfaced), 3298 tons (submerged)

DIMENSIONS: 254'0" x 25'7" x 23'0"

MACHINERY: 3 Hedemora diesel engines, 1 Jeumont-Schneider electric motor, 1 shaft. 4700 shp = 20/20 knots

RANGE: 9000 nm at 10 knots snorkeling, 480 nm at 4 knots submerged

ARMAMENT: 6 x 21" torpedo tubes, total 23 torpedoes or Sub-Harpoon missiles

COMPLEMENT: 42

NOTES: These submarines are claimed to be the quietest and most shock resistant in the world. The design is an expansion of the *Västergötland* type, with more sophisticated sensors and improved automation. Kockums and the Australian government set up the Australian Submarine Corporation as a joint operation to build these boats, whose bow and stern sections were constructed in Sweden. It is proposed to add the capability of launching Tomahawk missiles to these boats, but plans to incorporate air-independent propulsion have been dropped: these boats are considered to have excellent submerged endurance and very low acoustic signatures in their present state.

## SWEDEN: *GOTLAND* CLASS (1995)
(*Courtesy of Art-Tech*)

*Gotland* (2 February 1995), *Uppland* (9 February 1996), *Halland* (27 September 1996)

BUILDER: Kockums

DISPLACEMENT: 1240 tons (surfaced), 1490 tons (submerged)

DIMENSIONS: 196'10" x 19'11" x 18'4"

MACHINERY: 2 Hedemora diesel engines, 2 Stirling air-independent generator sets, 1 electric motor, 1 shaft. 3600 bhp/1800 shp = 11/20 knots

ARMAMENT: 4 x 533mm torpedo tubes, 2 x 400mm torpedo tubes (all bow), total 16 torpedoes

COMPLEMENT: 20

NOTES: These boats essentially are modified versions of the *Västergötland* class to incorporate air-independent propulsion.

They have very highly automated machinery and combat systems and were upgraded to operate the Tp62 torpedo, whose onboard sonar links to the submarine's fire control system. Unlike the earlier boats, they do not carry a towed sonar array but are fitted with an active mine-avoidance system.

Between 2001 and 2003 these boats received upgraded air-conditioning and communications systems to suit them for operations outside the Baltic. In June 2005 the *Gotland* began joint operations with the U.S. Navy so that U.S. antisubmarine forces could gain real-time experience against air-independent conventional submarines.

## UNITED KINGDOM
### *PORPOISE* CLASS (1956), *WALRUS* (1959)
*(Courtesy of Art-Tech)*

*Rorqual* (5 December 1955), *Narwhal* (15 March 1956), *Porpoise* (25 April 1956)
BUILDER: Barrow
*Grampus* (30 May 1957), *Finwhale* (21 July 1959), *Sealion* (31 December 1959)
BUILDER: Cammell Laird
*Cachalot* (18 September 1956), *Walrus* (22 September 1959)
BUILDER: Scott
DISPLACEMENT: 1975 tons (surfaced), 2303 tons (submerged)
DIMENSIONS: 290'3" x 26'6" x 18'3"
MACHINERY: 2 ASR diesel engines, 2 English Electric electric motors, 2 shafts. 3680 bhp/6000 shp = 12/17 knots

ARMAMENT: 8 x 21" torpedo tubes (6 bow, 2 stern), total 30 torpedoes
COMPLEMENT: 71
NOTES: The design for these boats brought together British experience with S, T, and A class high-speed submarines and information from German Type XXI craft examined after World War II. They were very quiet long-range boats and very successful. All were withdrawn between 1987 and 1990.

## UNITED KINGDOM: *OBERON* CLASS, *ORPHEUS* (1959)
*(Courtesy of Art-Tech)*

*Oberon* (18 July 1959), *Onslaught* (24 September 1960), *Ocelot* (5 May 1962), [Canada]—*Ojibwa* (29 February 1964), *Onandaga* (25 September 1965), *Okanagan* (17 September 1966)

BUILDER: Chatham

*Orpheus* (17 November 1959), *Olympus* (14 June 1961), *Osiris* (19 November 1962), [Brazil]—*Humaita* (5 October 1971), *Toneleros* (22 November 1972), *Riachuelo* (6 September 1975)

BUILDER: Barrow

*Odin* (4 November 1960), *Oracle* (26 September 1961), *Opossum* (23 May 1963), *Onyx* (18 August 1966)

BUILDER: Cammell Laird

*Otter* (15 May 1961), *Otus* (17 October 1962), *Opportune* (14 February 1964), [Australia]—*Oxley* (24 September 1965), *Otway* (29 November 1966), *Ovens* (5 December 1967), *Onslow* (29 August 1968) [Chile]—*O'Brien* (21 December 1972), *Hyatt* (26 September 1973), [Australia]—*Orion* (16 September 1974), *Otama* (2 December 1975)

BUILDER: Scott

DISPLACEMENT: 2030 tons (surfaced), 2410 tons (submerged)

DIMENSIONS: 290'3" x 26'6" x 18'3"

MACHINERY: 2 ASR diesel engines, 2 English Electric electric motors, 2 shafts. 3680 bhp/6000 shp = 12/17 knots

ARMAMENT: 8 x 21" torpedo tubes (6 bow, 2 stern), total 30 torpedoes

COMPLEMENT: 64

NOTES: This class introduced high-tensile steel construction for deeper diving and very extensive noise reduction, including rafted machinery. All the class except the *Oberon* and the *Orpheus* featured a fiberglass casing in place of the steel casing of the *Oberon* and the aluminum casing of the *Orpheus*. Most of these boats received refits in the 1980s that upgraded their sensor outfits and fire control systems.

The British boats were withdrawn from service between 1987 and 1992, the *Olympus* going to Canada as a static training vessel, and the *Onyx* and the *Ocelot* becoming museum vessels. The Brazilian boats were stricken between 1996 and 2001, the Australian craft between 1997 and 1999, the Canadian vessels between 1998 and 2000, and the Chilean submarines in 2001–2002.

## UNITED KINGDOM: *DREADNOUGHT* (21 OCTOBER 1960)
(*Courtesy of Art-Tech*)

BUILDER: Barrow
DISPLACEMENT: 3500 tons (surfaced), 4000 tons (submerged)
DIMENSIONS: 265'9" x 32'3" x 26'0"
MACHINERY: 1 S5W pressurized water reactor, 1 steam turbine, 1 shaft. 15,000 shp = 13/28 knots
ARMAMENT: 6 x 21" torpedo tubes (bow), total 24 torpedoes
COMPLEMENT: 88
NOTES: Delays in designing a British submarine reactor led to the decision to turn to the United States for assistance. Consequently, the *Dreadnought* combined a British forward hull with an after section that essentially adapted contemporary U.S. practice to British design parameters. In form, the hull bore a strong resemblance to contemporary U.S. teardrop hulls, but the diving planes were mounted at the bow rather than on the sail.

The *Dreadnought* was decommissioned in 1980.

## UNITED KINGDOM: *VALIANT* CLASS (1963), *WARSPITE* (1965)
*(Courtesy of Art-Tech)*

*Valiant* (3 December 1963), *Warspite* (25 September 1965), *Churchill* (20 December 1968), *Courageous* (7 March 1970)
BUILDER: Barrow
*Conqueror* (28 August 1969)
BUILDER: Cammell Laird
DISPLACEMENT: 4400 tons (surfaced), 4900 tons (submerged)
DIMENSIONS: 285′0″ x 33′3″ x 27′0″
MACHINERY: 1 PWR1 pressurized water reactor, 1 geared steam turbine, 1 shaft. 15,000 shp = 20/28 knots
ARMAMENT: 6 x 21″ torpedo tubes (bow), total 26 torpedoes

COMPLEMENT: 103
NOTES: These boats were an enlarged version of the *Dreadnought* to accommodate a British-designed reactor that was rather larger than the U.S. unit. The *Courageous* received an updated sonar outfit, and the other boats were subsequently refitted to that standard. All boats were fitted to launch Sub-Harpoon missiles in the early 1980s. They were decommissioned between 1990 and 1992.

**UNITED KINGDOM: *SWIFTSURE* CLASS (1971), *SUPERB* (1974)**
*(Courtesy of Art-Tech)*

*Swiftsure* (7 August 1971), *Sovereign* (17 February 1972), *Superb* (30 November 1974), *Sceptre* (20 November 1976), *Spartan* (7 April 1978), *Splendid* (5 October 1979)

BUILDER: Barrow

DISPLACEMENT: 4400 tons (surfaced), 4900 tons (submerged)

DIMENSIONS: 272′0″ x 32′4″ x 27′0″

MACHINERY: 1 PWR1 pressurized water reactor, 2 GEC geared steam turbines, 1 Paxman diesel engine, 1 shaft. 15,000 shp plus 4000 bhp= 20/30 knots

ARMAMENT: 5 x 21″ torpedo tubes (bow), total 21 torpedoes plus 4 Sub-Harpoon missiles

COMPLEMENT: 116

NOTES: This design features an improved hull form for better submerged performance and maneuverability, a more sophisticated fire control system, and greater noise suppression measures. During the 1990s this class received a new integrated fire control and sensor outfit. The *Swiftsure* decommissioned in 1992, the *Splendid* in 2003, and the *Sovereign* in 2006. The other boats are scheduled to leave service between 2008 and 2010.

## UNITED KINGDOM: *TRAFALGAR* CLASS (1981)
*(Courtesy of Art-Tech)*

*Trafalgar* (1 July 1981), *Turbulent* (1 December 1982), *Tireless* (17 March 1984), *Torbay* (8 March 1985), *Trenchant* (3 November 1986), *Talent* (15 April 1988), *Triumph* (14 February 1991)

BUILDER: Barrow

DISPLACEMENT: 4700 tons (surfaced), 5200 tons (submerged)

DIMENSIONS: 280'2" x 32'2" x 31'3"

MACHINERY: 1 PWR1 pressurized water reactor, 2 GEC geared steam turbines, 1 Paxman diesel engine, 1 shaft. 15,000 shp plus 4000 bhp= 20/31 knots

Endurance: 85 days

ARMAMENT: 5 x 21" torpedo tubes (bow), total 21 torpedoes plus 4 Sub-Harpoon missiles

COMPLEMENT: 97

NOTES: Attention to the reduction of acoustic and magnetic signatures dominated this design. In addition to improved raft insulation, these boats received an anechoic covering, a degaussing system, and new seven-bladed propellers. In the late 1990s the class began a thorough refit that replaced the propeller with a pumpjet propulsor system in all but the *Trafalgar*. Beginning in 2001 all are receiving a new sophisticated integrated fire and tactical control system together with substantial upgrades to the sensor outfit.

# UNITED KINGDOM:
## *UPHOLDER* CLASS (1986),
## [CANADA]—*CORNER BROOK* [EX-URSULA, 1991] (1986)
*(Courtesy of Art-Tech)*

*Upholder* (2 December 1986)
BUILDER: Barrow
*Unseen* (14 November 1989), *Ursula* (28 February 1991), *Unicorn* (16 April 1992)
BUILDER: Cammell Laird
DISPLACEMENT: 2220 tons (surfaced), 2455 tons (submerged)
DIMENSIONS: 230′7″ x 25′0″ x 17′8″
MACHINERY: 2 Paxman Valenta diesel engines, 1 GEC electric motors, 1 shaft. 5400 shp = 12/20 knots
RANGE: 8000 nm at 8 knots snorkeling, 230 nm at 3 knots submerged
ARMAMENT: 6 x 21″ torpedo tubes (bow), total 14 torpedoes plus 4 Sub-Harpoon missiles

COMPLEMENT: 47
NOTES: This class introduced a teardrop hull with anechoic tile coating into the British conventional submarine force. These boats have an active/passive bow sonar, passive flank arrays, and a towed sonar array. Their design results in very low acoustic and magnetic signatures.

The Royal Navy declared this class surplus to requirements in 1994. They were transferred to Canada as the *Chicoutimi,* the *Victoria,* the *Corner Brook,* and the *Windsor* and entered service in 2004 after a major refit.

## UNITED KINGDOM: *ASTUTE* CLASS (2007)
*(Courtesy of Art-Tech)*

*Astute* (2007), *Ambush* (2008), *Artful* (2010), plus 3 boats

**BUILDER:** Barrow

**DISPLACEMENT:** 6690 tons (surfaced), 7200 tons (submerged)

**DIMENSIONS:** 318'3" x 37'0" x 32'10"

**MACHINERY:** 1 PWR2 pressurized water reactor, 2 GEC-Alstom geared steam turbines, 2 Paxman diesel engines, 1 shaft. 27,000 shp plus 4000 bhp= 20/29 knots

**ARMAMENT:** 6 x 21" torpedo tubes (bow), total 38 torpedoes or missiles

**COMPLEMENT:** 98

**NOTES:** An extensively updated version of the earlier *Trafalgar* type, this type deploys the same new reactor as the *Vanguard* class ballistic missile submarines and the pumpjet propulsor system of the modernized *Trafalgar* group. They will incorporate integrated fire and tactical control systems, Tomahawk missile launch capability, and very extensive measures to limit acoustic and magnetic signatures.

# UNITED STATES
## *BARRACUDA* CLASS (1951)

*Barracuda* (2 March 1951)
BUILDER: Electric Boat
*Bass* (2 May 1951), *Bonita* (21 June 1951)
BUILDER: Mare Island
DISPLACEMENT: 765 tons (surfaced), 1162 tons (submerged)
DIMENSIONS: 196'1" x 24'7" x 14'5"
MACHINERY: 3 diesel engines, 2 electric motors, 2 shafts. 1125 bhp/1050 shp = 13/8.5 knots
RANGE: 8580 nm at 10 knots surfaced, 358 nm at 2 knots submerged
ARMAMENT: 4 x 21" torpedo tubes (bow), total 8 torpedoes
COMPLEMENT: 37

NOTES: These small boats were designed as hunter-killer submarines featuring quiet operation, an effective passive sonar system, and low cost. They were found to be too small and slow, while budgetary restraints in the immediate postwar period made conversions of existing fleet boats more attractive as a solution for the hunter-killer requirement. Their large bow sonars were removed in 1959 and they were reclassified, the *Barracuda* becoming a training submarine and the other boats attack submarines. The latter submarines were stricken in 1967 and the *Barracuda* in 1974.

## UNITED STATES: *TANG* CLASS (1951)
*(Courtesy of Art-Tech)*

*Harder* (14 June 1951), *Trout* (21 August 1951), *Trigger* (3 December 1951)
BUILDER: Electric Boat
*Tang* (19 June 1951), *Wahoo* (16 October 1951), *Gudgeon* (11 May 1952)
BUILDER: Portsmouth
DISPLACEMENT: 1821 tons (surfaced), 2260 tons (submerged)
DIMENSIONS: 269′2″ x 27′2″ x 18′0″
MACHINERY: 3 FM diesel engines, 2 electric motors, 2 shafts. 3400 bhp/4200 shp = 15.5/18 knots
RANGE: 11,500 nm at 10 knots surfaced, 129 nm at 3 knots submerged

ARMAMENT: 8 x 21″ torpedo tubes (6 bow, 2 stern), total 26 torpedoes
COMPLEMENT: 83
NOTES: These boats incorporated lessons learned from the German Type XXI submarines. They were shorter, more streamlined, and with greater battery capacity than the wartime fleet boats. The new "pancake" radial diesel engines in the first four boats caused considerable problems in service, and they were lengthened to 278′0″ and re-engined with four conventional diesels. The final pair of boats were built to that specification from the outset.

The *Tang*, the *Wahoo*, and the *Trout* were scheduled for transfer to Iran, but the revolution there intervened. The last two were stricken between 1978 and 1980, while the *Tang* was transferred to Turkey with the *Gudgeon* in 1980 as the *Piri Reis* and the *Hizir Reis*. The latter was stricken in 2004, and the former was still operational in 2006. The *Trigger* and the *Harder* were transferred to Italy in 1973–1974 as the *Livio Piomarta* and the *Romeo Romei* and stricken in 1986 and 1988, respectively.

## [PERU]—*LOBO* CLASS (1953)

*Tiburon* (27 October 1953), *Lobo* (6 February 1954), *Atun* (5 February 1957), *Merlin* (5 February 1957)
BUILDER: Electric Boat
DISPLACEMENT: 825 tons (surfaced), 1400 tons (submerged)
DIMENSIONS: 243′0″ x 22′0″ x 14′0″
MACHINERY: 2 GM diesel engines, 2 electric motors, 2 shafts. 2400 bhp/2400 shp = 16/10 knots
RANGE: 5000 nm at 10 knots surfaced; submerged characteristics unknown
ARMAMENT: 6 x 21″ torpedo tubes (4 bow, 2 stern)

COMPLEMENT: 40
NOTES: These boats were built to an updated version of the prewar *Mackerel* design with modern sensors. They were renamed the *Abtao*, the *Dos de Mayo*, the *Angamos*, and the *Iquique* in 1957. They were refitted in 1981 with new batteries and updated sensors. The *Angamos* and the *Iquique* were stricken in 1990 and 1993. The other boats became training vessels in 1995. The *Dos de Mayo* was stricken in 2000, and the *Abtao* became a museum vessel the same year.

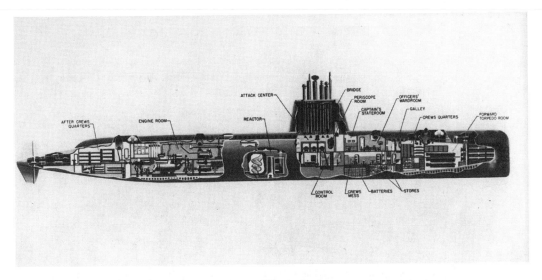

ATTACK CENTER
BRIDGE
PERISCOPE ROOM
OFFICERS' WARDROOM
CAPTAIN'S STATEROOM
GALLEY
AFTER CREWS QUARTERS
ENGINE ROOM
REACTOR
CREWS QUARTERS
FORWARD TORPEDO ROOM
CONTROL ROOM
CREWS MESS
BATTERIES
STORES

## UNITED STATES: *NAUTILUS* (21 JANUARY 1954)
*(Courtesy of Art-Tech)*

BUILDER: Electric Boat

DISPLACEMENT: 3180 tons (surfaced), 3500 tons (submerged)

DIMENSIONS: 323'9" x 27'8" x 21'9"

MACHINERY: 1 S2W pressurized water reactor, 2 geared steam turbines, 2 shafts. 13,400 shp = 22/23.25 knots

ARMAMENT: 6 x 21" torpedo tubes (bow), total 26 torpedoes

COMPLEMENT: 104

NOTES: The *Nautilus* was the world's first nuclear-powered submarine. Its hull form was similar to the German Type XXI, with a large dome faired into the forefoot to enclose passive and active sonar equipment. It had a partial double hull only, since the size of the nuclear reactor required enlarging its compartment to the outer hull. The *Nautilus* commissioned on 30 September 1954 and began trials on 17 January 1955. It demonstrated great speed, reliability, and maneuverability, but also was extremely noisy and suffered from potentially dangerous vibration at speed. The *Nautilus* decommissioned on 3 March 1980, was designated a National Historic Landmark on 20 May 1982, and is exhibited at the U.S. Navy Submarine Force Museum in Groton, Connecticut.

## UNITED STATES: *SEAWOLF* (21 JULY 1955)
*(Courtesy of Art-Tech)*

BUILDER: Electric Boat

DISPLACEMENT: 3741 tons (surfaced), 4287 tons (submerged)

DIMENSIONS: 337'6" x 27'8" x 22'0"

MACHINERY: 1 S2G liquid sodium reactor, 2 geared steam turbines, 2 shafts. 15,000 shp = 22/20 knots

ARMAMENT: 6 x 21" torpedo tubes (bow), total 26 torpedoes

COMPLEMENT: 105

NOTES: The structural design of the *Seawolf* closely matched that of the *Nautilus,* except that the bow sonar installation was modified for improved performance, and the hull was slightly larger because the liquid sodium reactor required additional shielding. Problems with this plant delayed the *Seawolf*'s commissioning until 30 March 1957, but it operated very satisfactorily thereafter. Nevertheless, in late 1958 the *Seawolf* returned to Electric Boat, where a new reactor identical to that of the *Nautilus* was installed, recommissioning on 30 September 1960. In mid-1967 the *Seawolf* was lengthened to incorporate facilities for saturation divers in an additional compartment and operated thereafter in research and intelligence-gathering roles until decommissioned in 1987.

## *SAILFISH* CLASS (1955)

*Sailfish* (7 September 1955), *Salmon* (25 February 1956)
BUILDER: Portsmouth
DISPLACEMENT: 2625 tons (surfaced), 3180 tons (submerged)
DIMENSIONS: 350'6" x 29'1" x 16'4"
MACHINERY: 4 FM diesel engines, 2 electric motor, 2 shafts. 6000 bhp/5200 shp = 19.5/10 knots

ARMAMENT: 6 x 21" torpedo tubes (bow)
COMPLEMENT: 95
NOTES: These large boats were built as radar picket submarines but were too slow to accompany the carrier force and were reclassified as attack submarines in 1961. They were upgraded with PUFFS passive fire control sonar in the early 1960s and stricken in 1977–1978.

## *DARTER* (28 MAY 1956)

BUILDER: Electric Boat
DISPLACEMENT: 1872 tons (surfaced), 2372 tons (submerged)
DIMENSIONS: 268'7" x 27'2" x 16'9"
MACHINERY: 3 FM diesel engines, 2 Elliott electric motors, 2 shafts. 3100 bhp/4500 shp = 19.5/14 knots

ARMAMENT: 8 x 21" torpedo tubes (6 bow, 2 stern)
COMPLEMENT: 83
NOTES: The *Darter* was an improved version of the *Tang* design with a console control system. It was decommissioned in 1982.

## *SKATE* CLASS (1957)

*Skate* (16 May 1957)
BUILDER: Electric Boat
*Swordfish* (27 August 1957), *Seadragon* (16 August 1958)
BUILDER: Portsmouth
*Sargo* (10 October 1957)
BUILDER: Mare Island
DISPLACEMENT: 2550 tons (surfaced), 2848 tons (submerged)
DIMENSIONS: 267'8" x 25'0" x 20'6"
MACHINERY: 1 S3W or S4W pressurized water reactor, 2 geared steam turbines, 2 shafts. 7300 shp = 15.5/18 knots

ARMAMENT: 8 x 21" torpedo tubes (6 bow, 2 stern), total 22 torpedoes
COMPLEMENT: 95
NOTES: The design for this class was based on the conventionally powered *Tang* class, enlarged to accommodate new, smaller reactors. They entered service in 1958–1959 and were stricken in 1986–1989.

## UNITED STATES: *TRITON* (1958)
*(Courtesy of Art-Tech)*

BUILDER: Electric Boat

DISPLACEMENT: 5662 tons (surfaced), 7781 tons (submerged)

DIMENSIONS: 447'6" x 36'11" x 23'6"

MACHINERY: 2 S4G liquid sodium reactors, 2 geared steam turbines, 2 shafts. 34,000 shp = 28/28 knots

ARMAMENT: 6 x 21" torpedo tubes (4 bow, 2 stern), total 12 torpedoes

COMPLEMENT: 180

NOTES: Designed as a radar picket submarine with high surface speed, the *Triton* was the largest submarine in the world when completed and the only U.S. boat built with a two-reactor plant. The double hull essentially was of an enlarged *Tang* form with a huge sail to accommodate a conning tower and the retractable (and very unreliable) air search radar. The nuclear plant proved capable of producing 45,000 shp, giving the *Triton* a speed of 30 knots. Shortly after commissioning, the *Triton* made an 84-day submerged voyage around the world. The *Triton* was reclassified as an attack submarine soon after this voyage, but it was too large and expensive to operate for this mission and was decommissioned on 3 May 1969, although not stricken from the Navy List until 1986.

## UNITED STATES: *SKIPJACK* CLASS (1958), *SCORPION* (1959)
*(Courtesy of Art-Tech)*

*Skipjack* (26 May 1958), *Scorpion* (19 December 1959)
BUILDER: Electric Boat
*Shark* (16 March 1960)
BUILDER: Newport News
*Sculpin* (31 March 1960), *Snook* (31 October 1960)
BUILDER: Ingalls
*Scamp* (8 October 1960)
BUILDER: Mare Island
DISPLACEMENT: 3070 tons (surfaced), 3500 tons (submerged)
DIMENSIONS: 252'0" x 32'0" x 25'0"
MACHINERY: 1 S5W pressurized water cooled reactor, 2 geared steam turbines, 1 shaft. 15,000 shp = 15/33 knots
ARMAMENT: 6 x 21" torpedo tubes (bow), total 24 torpedoes

COMPLEMENT: 90
NOTES: The *Skipjack* design set the basic pattern for all subsequent U.S. nuclear attack submarines. It combined the teardrop body-of-revolution hull form developed and tested in the *Albacore,* a single propeller behind the rudder and stern planes, and nuclear power. It also introduced single-hull construction to minimize wetted surface area while maximizing internal volume and large sail-mounted forward diving planes to reduce noise in the vicinity of the bow sonar. Nevertheless, these boats still generated considerable noise while operating submerged, particularly from the sail planes and the five-bladed propeller; a seven-bladed unit that rotated more

slowly was later produced, reducing the boats' top speed in the process.

The *Scorpion* was lost in the Atlantic on 22 May 1968 near the Azores after an explosion, probably attributable to one of its torpedoes. The rest of the class operated very successfully and were not withdrawn from service until between and 1986 and 1990.

## UNITED STATES: *BARBEL* CLASS (1958), *BLUEBACK* (1959)
*(Courtesy of Art-Tech)*

*Barbel* (19 July 1958)
BUILDER: Portsmouth
*Bonefish* (22 November 1958)
BUILDER: Electric Boat
*Blueback* (16 May 1959)
BUILDER: Ingalls
DISPLACEMENT: 2146 tons (surfaced), 2539 tons (submerged)
DIMENSIONS: 219'2" x 29'0" x 20'8"
MACHINERY: 3 FM diesel engines, 1 Westinghouse electric motor, 1 shaft. 4800 bhp/3150 shp = 15/21 knots
ARMAMENT: 6 x 21" torpedo tubes (bow)
COMPLEMENT: 77

NOTES: This class adopted the teardrop hull and single propeller of the experimental *Albacore*, albeit with a substantial deck casing. They introduced controls centralized in an attack center that became a standard feature in later U.S. attack submarines. The deep hull contained three levels, improving the internal layout. In the late 1960s a refit moved the diving planes from the bow to the sail.

The *Bonefish* was stricken after a serious fire in 1988, and the other boats followed in 1990.

## *TULLIBEE* (27 APRIL 1960)

BUILDER: Electric Boat

DISPLACEMENT: 2177 tons (surfaced), 2607 tons (submerged)

DIMENSIONS: 272'9" x 23'4" x 19'4"

MACHINERY: 1 S2C pressurized water reactor, 1 steam turbine, 1 turbo-alternator, 1 electric motor, 1 shaft. 2500 shp = 13/16 knots

ARMAMENT: 4 x 21" torpedo tubes (bow), total 12 torpedoes

COMPLEMENT: 36

NOTES: The *Tullibee* was a prototype for a small nuclear-powered hunter-killer submarine. Three elements were paramount in its design: quiet operation, powerful advanced sensors, and low cost. The *Tullibee* introduced a new, small reactor and turbo-electric drive that eliminated noisy gearing and provided very rapid response. Its AN/BQQ-1 sonar system was the navy's first integrated sonar system, combining powerful passive and active elements into a single large unit installed in the bow dome. This, in turn, displaced the torpedo tubes, which were mounted firing at an angle from the centerline. The goal of lower cost, however, was not sufficiently achieved: the boat's size could not be constrained, and the price for nuclear power and advanced sensors was essentially independent of hull size. The *Tullibee* was considered too slow for long ocean transits; the cost savings were insufficient; and the U.S. Navy decided to concentrate on more flexible attack submarines. It conducted mainly experimental work and was stricken on 18 June 1988.

## UNITED STATES: *THRESHER* CLASS (1960), *BARB* (1962)
*(Courtesy of Art-Tech)*

*Thresher* (9 July 1960), *Jack* (24 April 1963), *Tinosa* (9 December 1961)
BUILDER: Portsmouth
*Permit* (1 July 1961), *Plunger* (9 December 1961)
BUILDER: Mare Island
*Barb* (12 February 1962), *Dace* (18 August 1962), *Haddock* (21 May 1966)
BUILDER: Ingalls
*Pollack* (17 March 1962), *Haddo* (18 August 1962), *Guardfish* (15 May 1965)
BUILDER: New York
*Flasher* (22 June 1963), *Greenling* (4 April 1964), *Gato* (14 May 1964)
BUILDER: Electric Boat
DISPLACEMENT: 3750 tons (surfaced), 4310 tons (submerged)
DIMENSIONS: 278'6" x 31'8" x 26'0"
MACHINERY: 1 S5W pressurized water reactor, 2 geared steam turbines, 1 shaft. 15,000 shp = 15/28 knots

ARMAMENT: 4 x 21" torpedo tubes (bow), total 25 torpedoes or antisubmarine missiles
COMPLEMENT: 88
NOTES: This class represented the start of a second generation of nuclear-powered attack submarines. Great emphasis was placed on reducing noise emission, improving sensors, adding more sophisticated weapons, hardening the design against shock, and substantially increasing diving depth. Quieting was accomplished by mounting the machinery on a platform insulated from the hull (a "raft") so that noise would not radiate into the surrounding water. The raft arrangement also assisted in diminishing shock impact from explosions nearby. The large and sophisticated AN/BQQ-2 sonar, 15 feet in diameter, dominated the bow of the boat and led to the installation of torpedo

tubes farther aft that angled out from the centerline. In addition to new torpedoes, this class also could fire the new SUB-ROC rocket-propelled nuclear depth charge. Improved construction techniques and fittings endowed this class with a test depth of 1300 feet rather than the 700 feet of the previous *Skipjack* class. The *Jack* was slightly different from other members of the class in using two contra-rotating screws. The three Electric Boat submarines were lengthened to 292'3", with an additional compartment for submarine safety features (SUBSAFE) developed as a result of the *Thresher*

disaster, and also to provide space for crew and equipment for intelligence-gathering. They also had larger sails, with additional masts for the same purpose.

The *Thresher* sank on 10 April 1963 during a postoverhaul trial. The likeliest cause was the failure of a fitting or weld that caused a leak that probably short-circuited an electrical panel, leading to the machinery shutting down. Without power the submarine could not surface and sank below its crush depth. The remainder of the class were stricken in 1990–1991.

## UNITED STATES: *STURGEON* CLASS (1963), *SEAHORSE* (1968)
(*Courtesy of Art-Tech*)

*Sturgeon* (26 February 1965), *Pargo* (17 September 1966), *Bergall* (17 February 1968), *Seahorse* (15 August 1968), *Flying Fish* (17 May 1969), *Trepang* (27 August 1969), *Bluefish* (10 January 1970), *Billfish* (1 May 1970), *Archerfish* (16 January 1971), *Silversides* (4 June 1971), *Batfish* (9 October 1971), *Cavalla* (19 February 1972)

BUILDER: Electric Boat

*Queenfish* (25 February 1966), *Ray* (21 June 1966), *Lapon* (16 December 1966), *Hammerhead* (14 May 1967), *Sea Devil* (5 October 1967), *Spadefish* (15 May 1968), *Finback* (7 December 1968), *L. Mendel Rivers* (2 June 1973), *Richard B. Russell* (12 January 1974)

BUILDER: Newport News

*Whale* (14 October 1966), *Sunfish* (14 October 1966),

BUILDER: Quincy

*Tautog* (14 April 1967), *Pogy* (3 June 1967), *Aspro* (29 November 1967), *Puffer* (30 March 1989), *William H. Bates* (11 December 1971), *Tunny* (10 June 1972), *Parche* (13 January 1973)

BUILDER: Ingalls

*Gurnard* (20 May 1967), *Guittaro* (27 July 1968), *Hawkbill* (12 April 1969), *Pintado* (18 August 1969), *Drum* (25 May 1970)

BUILDER: Mare Island

*Grayling* (22 June 1967), *Sand Lance* (11 November 1969)

BUILDER: Portsmouth

DISPLACEMENT: 4250 tons (surfaced), 4780 tons (submerged)

DIMENSIONS: 282'0" x 31'8" x 28'10"

MACHINERY: 1 S5W pressurized water reactor, 2 geared steam turbines, 1 shaft. 15,000 shp = 15/27 knots

ARMAMENT: 4 x 21" torpedo tubes (bow), total 25 torpedoes or antisubmarine missiles

COMPLEMENT: 99

NOTES: This class was essentially a modification of the previous *Thresher* type. It added a larger sail and diving planes that could rotate vertically to allow penetration through Arctic ice. The final ten boats were 10 feet longer, the extra compartment providing additional space for crew and equipment for intelligence-gathering. The *Parche* was modified for special deep sea search and recovery missions between 1987 and 1991, lengthening the boat by 100 feet. The *Parche* was stricken in 2003, while the other boats in the class were stricken between 1991 and 2000.

## *NARWHAL* (9 SEPTEMBER 1968)

BUILDER: Electric Boat

DISPLACEMENT: 4450 tons (surfaced), 5350 tons (submerged)

DIMENSIONS: 314'0" x 31'8" x 26'0"

MACHINERY: 1 S5G natural circulation pressurized water reactor, 2 direct-drive steam turbines, 1 shaft. 15,000 shp = 15/26 knots

ARMAMENT: 4 x 21" torpedo tubes (bow), total 25 torpedoes or antisubmarine missiles

COMPLEMENT: 99

NOTES: The *Narwhal* was a lengthened version of the *Sturgeon* design. Its reactor plant was changed to use natural circulation via convection in place of pumps to move the pressurized water, greatly reducing machinery noise. In addition it also used slow-speed, direct drive turbines in place of the geared turbines of earlier boats, again to reduce noise. This installation, although requiring more space, proved so successful that it was adopted as standard in all later boats. The *Narwhal* was stricken on 1 July 1999.

## [THE NETHERLANDS]—ZWAARDVIS CLASS (1970), [TAIWAN—*HAI LUNG* (1986)

(*Courtesy of Art-Tech*)

[Netherlands]—*Zwaardvis* (2 July 1970), *Tijgerhaaj* (25 May 1971)

BUILDER: Rotterdamse

[Taiwan]—*Hai Lung* (4 October 1986), *Hai Hu* (20 December 1986)

BUILDER: Fijenoord

DISPLACEMENT: 2408 tons (surfaced), 2640 tons (submerged)

DIMENSIONS: 219'0" x 28'0" x 23'0"

MACHINERY: 3 Werkspoor diesel engines, 1 Holec electric motor, 1 shaft. 4200 bhp/5100 shp = 13/20 knots

ARMAMENT: 6 x 533mm torpedo tubes (bow), total 20 torpedoes

COMPLEMENT: 67

NOTES: The design for these boats derived from the Barbel type, with European sensors. The Dutch boats were upgraded in the late 1980s with improved sensors, including a towed sonar array, and equipped to launch Mk.48 torpedoes. They were decommissioned in 1989–1995 and offered for sale. An arrangement for Malaysia to purchase them fell through after they were shipped there in 2000; they are to be scrapped in Malaysia in 2006.

Taiwan planned to obtain 6 boats from The Netherlands to an improved design with updated sensors, greater automation, and stowage for up to 28 torpedoes. Protests from China led the Dutch government to block construction of all but the first two boats. Taiwan plans to upgrade these submarines to launch missiles through their torpedo tubes.

## *GLENARD P. LIPSCOMB* (4 AUGUST 1973)

BUILDER: Electric Boat

DISPLACEMENT: 4450 tons (surfaced), 5350 tons (submerged)

DIMENSIONS: 314'0" x 31'8" x 26'0"

MACHINERY: 1 S5Wa pressurized water reactor, 2 steam turbines, 2 turbo-alternators, 1 electric motor, 1 shaft. 14,000 shp = 15/23 knots

ARMAMENT: 4 x 21" torpedo tubes (bow), total 25 torpedoes or antisubmarine missiles

COMPLEMENT: 99

NOTES: This submarine was a lengthened version of the *Sturgeon* type. It used a modified reactor plant that drove turbo-alternators to provide direct current for electric drive at all times. The boat underwent extensive trials. The inefficiencies of the system reduced total power output compared with the standard system, and the use of direct current led to serious overheating problems. The *Glenard P. Lipscomb* was stricken on 11 July 1990.

## UNITED STATES: *LOS ANGELES* CLASS (1974)
(*Courtesy of Art-Tech*)

*Los Angeles* (6 April 1974), *Baton Rouge* (26 April 1976), *Memphis* (3 April 1976), *Cincinnati* (19 February 1977), *Birmingham* (29 October 1977), *San Francisco* (27 October 1979), *Atlanta* (16 August 1980), *Houston* (21 March 1981), *Norfolk* (21 October 1981), *Buffalo* (8 May 1982), *Salt Lake City* (16 October 1982), *Olympia* (30 April 1983), *Honolulu* (24 September 1983), *Chicago* (13 October 1984), *Key West* (20 July 1985), *Oklahoma City* (2 November 1985), *Newport News* (15 March 1986), *Albany* (13 June 1987), *Scranton* (3 July 1988), *Asheville* (28 October 1989), *Jefferson City* (17 August 1990), *Boise* (23 March 1991), *Montpelier* (23 August 1991), *Hampton* (3 April 1992), *Charlotte* (3 October 1992), *Toledo* (28 August 1993), *Tucson* (19 March 1994), *Greenville* (17 September 1994), *Cheyenne* (18 April 1995)

BUILDER: Newport News

*Philadelphia* (19 October 1974), *Groton* (9 October 1976), *New York City* (18 June 1977), *Indianapolis* (30 July 1977), *Omaha* (21 February 1978), *Bremerton* (22 July 1978), *Jacksonville* (19 November 1978), *Dallas* (28 April 1979), *La Jolla* (11 August 1979), *Phoenix* (8 December 1979), *Boston* (19 April 1980), *Baltimore* (13 December 1980), *City of Corpus Christi* (25 April 1981), *Albuquerque* (13 March 1982), Portsmouth (18 September 1982), *Minneapolis-St Paul* (18 December 1982), *Hyman G. Rickover* (27 August 1983), *Augusta* (21 January 1984), *Providence* (4 August 1984), *Pittsburgh* (8 December 1984), *Louisville*

(14 December 1985), *Helena* (28 June 1986), *San Juan* (6 December 1986), *Pasadena* (12 September 1987), *Topeka* (23 January 1988), *Miami* (12 November 1988), *Alexandria* (23 June 1990), *Annapolis* (19 May 1991), *Springfield* (4 January 1992), *Columbus* (1 August 1992), *Santa Fe* (12 December 1992), *Hartford* (4 December 1993), *Columbia* (24 September 1994)

BUILDER: Electric Boat

DISPLACEMENT: 6080 tons (surfaced), 6927 tons (submerged)

DIMENSIONS: 362′0″ x 33′0″ x 32′0″

MACHINERY: 1 S6G pressurized water reactor, 2 steam turbines, 1 shaft. 30,000 shp = 33 knots submerged

ARMAMENT: 4 x 21″ torpedo tubes (bow), total 25 torpedoes or antisubmarine missiles

COMPLEMENT: 141

NOTES: The design for the *Los Angeles* class represented a huge increase in size (close to 50 percent) over the previous *Sturgeon*-type attack submarines. The motivation for this increase was a desire to return to the speed of the *Skipjack* class while maintaining or improving on the *Sturgeon* class's quiet operation and powerful sonar array. This required a great increase in power output from the reactor, achieved by adapting a surface warship unit for submarine use. Nevertheless, despite the increase in power

and concomitant growth in size, the *Los Angeles* class design gave up the ability to operate under ice and minelaying capabilities; its test depth was reduced to 950 feet, more than a 25 percent reduction.

Production of the *Los Angeles* class was plagued with problems, both within the political and military establishments for funding and in the yards, where delays and cost over-runs became endemic. Consequently, construction of the entire class was spread over a 20 period. During that time the design benefited from some modifications. The second 32 boats were fitted with 12 vertical launch tubes in the forward ballast tanks for Tomahawk missiles, increasing the total weapon load to 37 torpedoes or missiles. The final 23 units additionally received modifications permitting operation under ice (with bow-mounted retractable diving planes), minelaying capabilities, and improved noise suppression and quieting, being designated the Improved *Los Angeles* class.

Eleven boats (the *Baton Rouge*, the *Omaha*, the *Cincinnati*, the *Groton*, the *Birmingham*, the *New York City*, the *Indianapolis*, the *Phoenix*, the *Boston*, the *Baltimore*, and the *Atlanta*) were stricken between 1995 and 1999. The remainder of the class is still active, deployed almost evenly between the Atlantic and Pacific fleets.

## [THE NETHERLANDS]—*WALRUS* CLASS (1985)
*(Courtesy of Art-Tech)*

[The Netherlands]—*Walrus* (28 October 1985), *Zeeleeuw* (20 June 1987), *Dolfijn* (25 April 1990), *Bruinvis* (26 April 1992)
BUILDER: Rotterdamse
DISPLACEMENT: 2450 tons (surfaced), 2800 tons (submerged)
DIMENSIONS: 222'0" x 28'0" x 23'0"
MACHINERY: 3 SEMT-Pielstick diesel engines, 1 Holec electric motor, 1 shaft. 6300 bhp/6910 shp = 13/20 knots
RANGE: 10,000 nm at 9 knots snorkeling
ARMAMENT: 4 x 533mm torpedo tubes (bow), total 20 torpedoes or Sub-Harpoon missiles
COMPLEMENT: 52

NOTES: The Nederlandsche Verenigde Scheepsbouw Bureaux developed this class as an improved version of the *Zwaardvis* type. It introduced an X-tail for greater maneuverability and higher tensile steel hull construction for greater diving depth. The sensor outfit introduced a passive flank array and towed sonar. These boats were equipped to launch Sub-Harpoon missiles but The Netherlands has yet to procure those weapons. This class is scheduled for an upgrade refit beginning in 2009 that may include the addition of an air-independent propulsion module.

## UNITED STATES: *SEAWOLF* CLASS (1995), *SEAWOLF*
*(Courtesy of Art-Tech)*

*Seawolf* (24 June 1995), *Connecticut* (1 September 1997), *Jimmy Carter* (13 May 2004)

BUILDER: Electric Boat

DISPLACEMENT: 7467 tons (surfaced), 9137 tons (submerged)

DIMENSIONS: 353'0" x 40'0" x 35'0"

MACHINERY: 1 S6W pressurized water reactor, 2 steam turbines, 1 shaft pump jet propulsor. 40,000 shp = 35 knots submerged

ARMAMENT: 8 x 26.5" torpedo tubes (bow), total 50 torpedoes or antisubmarine missiles

COMPLEMENT: 134

NOTES: The *Seawolf* class was the first thoroughly new submarine design for the U.S. Navy since the *Skipjack* type. Its characteristics were driven by the need to counter fast Soviet submarines, using high speed, powerful sensors, extreme quietness, and a formidable battery of weapons. These submarines generally are accepted to be the quietest and fastest deployed by the U.S. Navy and possibly in the world. They have a six-surface tail configuration and use a ducted shroud propulsor.

The development of this class was extremely prolonged and marked by very rapid and extensive cost escalation and major political infighting. Originally planned to form a class of 30 boats, eventually only 2 attack boats and a

substantially different special mission submarine, the *Jimmy Carter,* were ordered.

The *Jimmy Carter* was lengthened by 25 feet behind the sail to accommodate a reconfigurable cargo space and command center. It carries equipment to launch and interface with remotely operated vehicles, an extensive array of advanced communications devices, and can carry up to 50 SEALS.

## UNITED STATES: *VIRGINIA* CLASS (2005)
*(Courtesy of Art-Tech)*

*Virginia* (16 August 2005), *Texas* (9 April 2006), *Hawaii* (17 June 2006), *North Carolina* (2006), *New Hampshire* (2010), *New Mexico* (2010), 24 boats
BUILDER: Electric Boat and Newport News
DISPLACEMENT: 7835 tons (submerged)
DIMENSIONS: 377'0" x 34'0" x 30'6"

MACHINERY: 1 S9G pressurized water reactor, 2 steam turbines, 1 shaft pump jet propulsor. 23,000 shp = 25 knots submerged
ARMAMENT: 4 x 21" torpedo tubes (bow), 12 x vertical launch missile tubes, total 37 torpedoes or antisubmarine missiles

COMPLEMENT: 134

NOTES: This class was designed to be a slightly cheaper alternative to the *Seawolf* type, whose cost overruns had caused consternation within the navy and Congress. Principal savings were expected to arise from the greatest possible use of "off-the-shelf" electronics, but the type still proved more expensive than the *Seawolf* class. Congressional and naval concern that the United States might soon be reduced to a single yard capable of constructing submarines led to the decision to build these boats at both the Newport News and Electric Boat yards. The Newport News facility builds the stern, habitability and machinery spaces, torpedo room, sail, and bow, while Electric Boat builds the engine room and control room. The two yards alternate work on the reactor plant as well as the final assembly, test, outfit and delivery. Contracts have been let for eight boats so far, with orders anticipated for one additional boat in 2007 and 2008, and ultimate plans for building 24 submarines of this type with delivery on an annual basis.

# YUGOSLAVIA
## *SUTJESKA* CLASS (1952)

*Neretva* (1958), *Sutjeska* (28 August 1958)
BUILDER: Pula
DISPLACEMENT: 820 tons (surfaced), 945 tons (submerged)
DIMENSIONS: 196'8" x 22'0" x 15'9"
MACHINERY: 2 Sulzer diesel engines, 2 electric motors, 2 shafts. 1800 bhp/1200shp = 14/9 knots
RANGE: 4800 nm at 8 knots surfaced
ARMAMENT: 6 x 533mm torpedo tubes (4 bow, 2 stern), total 8 torpedoes
COMPLEMENT: 38
NOTES: These indigenously designed boats used Soviet weaponry and sensors. They became training vessels in the early 1980s and were stricken in 1987.

## *HEROJ* CLASS (1967)

*Heroj* (18 August 1967), *Uskok* (June 1970)
BUILDER: Pula
*Junak* (1968)
BUILDER: Split
DISPLACEMENT: 1170 tons (surfaced), 1350 tons (submerged)
DIMENSIONS: 210'0" x 23'8" x 16'4"
MACHINERY: 2 Sulzer diesel engines, 2 electric motors, 1 shaft. 1600 bhp/1560 shp = 10/16 knots
RANGE: 9700 nm at 8 knots snorkeling
ARMAMENT: 6 x 533mm torpedo tubes (bow), total 10 torpedoes or 20 mines
COMPLEMENT: 55
NOTES: This class was a more streamlined, modestly enlarged version of the *Sutjeska* type. They were laid up from 1993 because of a shortage of spare parts and stricken by 2000.

## *SAVA* CLASS (1977)

*Sava* (1977), *Drava* (1981)

BUILDER: Split

DISPLACEMENT: 830 tons (surfaced), 960 tons (submerged)

DIMENSIONS: 182′7″ x 23′6″ x 18′7″

MACHINERY: 2 Sulzer diesel engines, 2 electric motors, 1 shaft. 1600 bhp/1560 shp = 10/16 knots

RANGE: 9700 nm at 8 knots snorkeling

ARMAMENT: 6 x 533mm torpedo tubes (bow), total 10 torpedoes or 20 mines

COMPLEMENT: 27

NOTES: These smaller boats incorporate considerable automation to reduce the size of their crews. Weaponry was possibly of Swedish origin, while the Soviet Union supplied the bulk of their sensors. They were laid up from 1993 because of a shortage of spare parts, and it is not clear that they have become operational since then.

# Strategic Missile Submarines

**CHINA**
**PROJECT 092 (NATO XIA CLASS), *406* (1981)**
*(Courtesy of Art-Tech)*

406 (30 April 1981)
BUILDER: Huludao
DISPLACEMENT: 5500 tons (surfaced),
   7000 tons (submerged)

DIMENSIONS: 394′0″ x 33′0″ x 26′0″
MACHINERY: 1 pressurized water cooled
   reactor, 2 geared steam turbines, 1 shaft.
   14,400 shp = 20 knots submerged

ENDURANCE: 80 days

ARMAMENT: 12 x JL-1 ballistic missiles, 6 x 533mm torpedo tubes (bow), total 12 torpedoes

COMPLEMENT: 100

NOTES: The Project 092 uses the same basic design as China's Project 091 nuclear-powered attack boat with a missile-launching section inserted abaft the sail. Problems with the JL-1 missile's reliability delayed entry into service until 1988. The *406* underwent a major refit between 1995 and 1998 to accommodate JL-1A weapons with twice the range of the earlier missiles. It has been suggested that a second Project 092 submarine was built but lost as a result of an accident in 1985, but no reliable information exists on this topic.

## PROJECT 094 (2004)

1 boat (2004)

BUILDER: Huludao

DISPLACEMENT: 8000–9000 tons (submerged)

DIMENSIONS: N/A

MACHINERY: N/A

ENDURANCE: N/A

ARMAMENT: 16 x JL-2 ballistic missiles

NOTES: Little reliable information exists about China's second-generation ballistic missile submarines. They appear to be an enlarged version of the original Project 092 armed with sixteen 5,000-mile range JL-2 weapons with two to four MIRV warheads. Their power plant is derived from that of the Project 093 attack boats with much improved reliability and quieting. Reports indicate that the first boat was launched in July 2004 and that a total of three to four vessels are projected.

## FRANCE
### *LE RÉDOUTABLE* CLASS (1967), *L'INFLEXIBLE* (1982)
(*Courtesy of Art-Tech*)

*Le Rédoutable* (29 March 1967), *Le Terrible* (12 December 1969), *Le Foudroyant* (4 December 1971), *L'Indomptable* (17 August 1974), *Le Tonnant* (17 September 1977), *L'Inflexible* (23 June 1982)

BUILDER: Cherbourg

DISPLACEMENT: 8045 tons (surfaced), 8940 tons (submerged)

DIMENSIONS: 422'0" x 35'0" x 33'0"

MACHINERY: 1 pressurized water cooled reactor, 2 steam turbines, 2 turbo-alternators, 1 electric motor, 1 shaft. 15,000 shp = 20/25 knots

ARMAMENT: 16 x M-1 ballistic missiles, 4 x 550mm torpedo tubes (bow), total 18 torpedoes

COMPLEMENT: 135

NOTES: The French Navy had begun construction of a nuclear-powered submarine in 1956 but France's inability at the time to produce enriched uranium led to the design of a heavy-water reactor that was much too large for submarine use. The French decision to separate itself from the NATO command structure and develop its own nuclear deterrent force eliminated the possibility of assistance or cooperation from the United States in the process. Work recommenced on the incomplete nuclear submarine hull, which was transformed into a diesel-powered trials boat for the French independent ballistic missile system. The *Gymnôte* commissioned in 1966, carrying a launching system for four missiles (one quarter of the planned outfit of the operational boats), together with prototypes of the guidance and inertial navigation systems, and began full-scale trials of the weapons package in late 1968.

Construction of the operational ballistic missile submarines began before the *Gymnôte* commissioned. Unlike all other nations, France's first nuclear powered boats were its strategic missile submarines. They were considerably larger than the early American examples, primarily because the M-1 missile they embarked was comparable in size and weight to the Poseidon missile, although its range was less, at 1600 miles, and it could carry only a single warhead.

Because these boats were built over an extended period, successive examples embodied upgrades. *Le Foudroyant* and *L'Indomptable* embarked the M-2 missile with an increased range of 2000 miles. The final three boats have improved reactors with metallic rather than oxide cores. *Le Tonnant* commissioned with the M-20 missile with a warhead of twice the yield of the earlier weapons and the earlier boats were upgraded to the same standard from 1976. *L'Inflexible* incorporated even greater improvements with substantially upgraded sonar and navigation systems, a 50-percent increase in diving depth, major noise reduction measures, and the M-4 missile with a 2150-mile range carrying six independently targetable warheads. It also was equipped to launch Exocet anti-ship missiles.

*Le Rédoutable* decommissioned in 1991 (and became a museum ship at Cherbourg in 200) but its four successors were upgraded to a standard very close to that of *L'Inflexible* between 1985 and 1993. They decommissioned between 1996 and 2005, while *L'Inflexible* is scheduled to decommission in 2008 (later if *Le Terrible*'s entry into service is delayed).

# FRANCE: *LE TRIOMPHANT* CLASS (1994)
*(Courtesy of Art-Tech)*

*Le Triomphant* (26 March 1994), *Le Téméraire* (21 January 1998), *Le Vigilant* (August 2003), *Le Terrible* (2008)

BUILDER: Cherbourg

DISPLACEMENT: 12,640 tons (surfaced), 14,335 tons (submerged)

DIMENSIONS: 453'0" x 41'0" x 41'0"

MACHINERY: 1 pressurized water cooled reactor, 2 steam turbines, 2 turbo-alternators, 1 electric motor, 1 shaft pump jet propulsor. 41,500 shp = 12/25 knots

ENDURANCE: 18 x M45 ballistic missiles, 4 x 533mm torpedo tubes (bow), total 18 torpedoes or antiship missiles

COMPLEMENT: 111

NOTES: Initially there were to be five submarines in this class but budget constraints led to the elimination of the final two boats. In 1996 President Jacques Chirac reinstated the fourth boat. In addition to an additional pair of missile launch tubes, this class incorporates major advances in machinery arrangements, automation (reducing the crew size substantially), search equipment, and navigational systems. The hull dynamics are optimized for low noise emission, the machinery is carried on a very elaborate raft system to isolate it, there is a ducted pump-jet propeller in place of a conventional screw, and newly developed precision bearings replace even ball-bearings. The first three boats launch the M-45 missile with a range of 3750 miles carrying six warheads while *Le Terrible* will embark the new M-51 weapon with a similar range but much upgraded warheads and accuracy.

## SOVIET UNION
## PROJECT AV611 [NATO ZULU V] (1956)

*B-67* (30 June 1956), *B-73* (30 November 1957), *B-78* (30 November 1957), *B-79* (4 December 1957)
BUILDER: Severodvinsk
*B-89* (13 December1957)
BUILDER: Komsomolsk
DISPLACEMENT: 1890 tons (surfaced), 2450 tons (submerged)
DIMENSIONS: 314′4″ x 24′7″ x 16′9″
MACHINERY: 5 diesel engines, 3 electric motors, 3 shafts. 6000 bhp/5400 shp = 16.5/12.5 knots
ENDURANCE: 58 days
ARMAMENT: 2 x R-11FM ballistic missiles, 10 x 533mm torpedo tubes (6 bow, 4 stern)
COMPLEMENT: 83
NOTES: The Project 611 submarine *B-62* was modified while under construction to launch a single ballistic missile from a vertical tube passing through the hull in the aft end of the sail (Project 611A, NATO Zulu IV). It undertook extensive launching trials from September 1955 and made its first submerged launch in 1959. The *B-62* was converted to a sonar trials vessel in 1966 and scrapped in 1980.

The production boats carried two vertical missile-launching tubes. Their R-11FM missiles had a range of 150 miles with a single warhead. Almost immediately after completion they received additional diesel engines to improve their performance, and they were modified with the improve D-2 launch system. Four operated with the Northern Fleet, while the *B-89* went to the Pacific Fleet. They undertook deterrent patrols until withdrawn from service in the late 1980s.

## PROJECT 659 [NATO ECHO I] (1959)

*K-45* (12 May 1959), *K-59*, *K-66* (1960), *K-122*, *K-259* (1961)
BUILDER: Komsomolsk
DISPLACEMENT: 3770 tons (surfaced), 4980 tons (submerged)
DIMENSIONS: 364′9″ x 30′2″ x 23′3″
MACHINERY: 2 VM-A pressurized water cooled reactors, 2 geared steam turbines, 2 shafts. 35,000 shp = 15/26 knots
ENDURANCE: 70 days
ARMAMENT: 6 x P-5 cruise missiles, 4 x 533mm torpedo tubes (bow), 2 x 400mm torpedo tubes (bow), 2 x 400mm torpedo tubes (stern), total 4 plus 8 torpedoes
COMPLEMENT: 104
NOTES: Project 659, the Soviet Union's second nuclear-powered submarine type, reverted to a conventional hull form for greater stability on the surface while firing missiles. The missiles were carried in three pairs of canisters, elevating to 15-degrees for launch, built into the deck casing abaft the sail. The boats entered service in 1961 and operated extensively in the North Atlantic and Pacific, although they were withdrawn from the land-attack role after 1965 and converted to conventional torpedo attack boats. All boats were withdrawn from service by 1990.

## SOVIET UNION: PROJECT 629 [NATO GOLF] (1959)
*(Courtesy of Art-Tech)*

*K-36, K-72, K-79, K-83, K-88, K-91, K-93, K-96, K-102, K-107, K-110, K-113, K-118, K-142, K-153, K-167* (1959–1962)

BUILDER: Severodvinsk

*K-75, K-99, K-126, K-129, K-136, K-139, K-163* (1959–1962)

BUILDER: Komsomolsk

DISPLACEMENT: 2850 tons (surfaced), 3610 tons (submerged)

DIMENSIONS: 324'3" x 26'11" x 26'7"

MACHINERY: 3 diesel engines, 3 electric motors, 3 shafts. 6000 bhp/5400 shp = 14.5/12.5 knots

ENDURANCE: 70 days

ARMAMENT: 3 x R-13 ballistic missiles, 6 x 533mm torpedo tubes (4 bow, 2 stern)

COMPLEMENT: 83

NOTES: The design for this class was based on the Project 641 (NATO Foxtrot) type, with three vertical missile-launching tubes passing through the hull at the aft end of an extended sail. The first three boats were commissioned with the earlier R-11FM missile but later upgraded. The R-13 weapon had a range of 375 miles with a single warhead. From the outset these boats were equipped with the D-2 launch system. Initially the majority of the boats went to the Northern Fleet, but by 1963 they were almost evenly divided between the Northern and Pacific fleets.

Between 1963 and 1967 13 boats (the *K-72*, the *K-75*, the *K-79*, the *K-88*, the *K-93*, the *K-99*, the *K-110*, the *K-126*, the *K-136*, the *K-139*, the *K-142*, the *K-153*, and the *K-163*) were modified with the D-4 system to launch improved R-21 missiles with a range of 875 miles carrying a single warhead.

In 1969 the *K-118* was modified for trials launching the R-29 missile under Project 601, and the *K-102* was converted for trials of the R-27K missile under Project 605. In 1976 the *K-153* was converted as a trials launch platform for the R-39 missile under Project 619. The *K-61*, the *K-83*, and the *K-107* were converted into command posts under Project 629R in 1973. All missile and torpedo tubes were removed, and additional communications equipment and accommodations took their place. The *K-113* became a minelayer under Project 629E.

The *K-129* was lost on patrol in the north Pacific after an internal explosion on 8 March 1968. The *K-113* was stricken in 1974; the *K-36* and the *K-91* were discarded in 1980; and the remainder of the class were scrapped between 1990 and 1992.

## PROJECT 658 [NATO HOTEL] (1959)

*K-19* (8 August 1959), *K-33* (1960), *K-40*, *K-55*, *K-178* (1961), *K-16*, *K-145* (1962), *K-149 Ukrainskiy Komsomolets* (1963)

BUILDER: Severodvinsk

DISPLACEMENT: 4080 tons (surfaced), 5240 tons (submerged)

DIMENSIONS: 373'11" x 30'2" x 25'3"

MACHINERY: 2 VM-A pressurized water cooled reactors, 2 geared steam turbines, 2 shafts. 35,000 shp = 18/26 knots

ENDURANCE: 50 days

ARMAMENT: 3 x R-13 ballistic missiles, 4 x 533mm torpedo tubes (bow), 4 x 400mm torpedo tubes (2 bow, 2 stern)

COMPLEMENT: 104

NOTES: The design for this class was based on the Project 627 (NATO November) nuclear-powered attack submarine with a missile-launching compartment similar to that of the Project 629 inserted aft of the sail. Additional small diving planes were fitted together with noise quieting arrangements for all control surfaces. The entire class except the *K-145* was upgraded under Project 658M (NATO Hotel-II) between 1963 and 1967 with the D-4 launch system, which could fire missiles while submerged. The *K-145* was modified in 1969 under Project 701 (NATO Hotel-III) to launch R-29 missiles with a range of 4875 miles carrying a single warhead. Its length increased to 427 feet, with a surface displacement of 5500 tons and a submerged displacement of 6400 tons. Speed underwater fell to 22 knots.

The *K-55* and the *K-178* went to the Pacific Fleet, while all the other boats served with the Northern Fleet. All members of the class were decommissioned between 1986 and 1991.

## PROJECT 644 [NATO WHISKEY TWIN CYLINDER] (1960)

*S-44, S-46, S-69, S-80, S-158, S-162*

CONVERTED: Gorkiy

DISPLACEMENT: 1055 tons (surfaced), 1350 tons (submerged)

DIMENSIONS: 249'2" x 20'8" x 15'1"

MACHINERY: 2 diesel engines, 2 electric motors, 2 shafts. 4000 bhp/2700 shp = 18.25/13 knots

RANGE: 22,000 nm at 9 knots surfaced, 443 nm at 2 knots submerged

ARMAMENT: 2 x P-5 cruise missiles, 6 x 533mm torpedo tubes (4 bow, 2 stern), total 12 torpedoes

COMPLEMENT: 52

NOTES: The Project 613 boat *S-146* was experimentally modified to launch a single P-5 cruise missile in 1957. After successful trials from 1957 to 1959, six other Project 613 boats were converted as operational launch platforms for the weapon. Two cylindrical launchers were built into the deck casing abaft the sail. The submarine surfaced and elevated the launchers to fire its missiles astern. These boats were deployed in the Baltic and withdrawn from service in the mid-1960s.

## PROJECT 665 [NATO WHISKEY LONG BIN] (1961)

*S-61, S-64, S-142, S-152, S-155, S-164*

CONVERTED: Gorkiy and Baltic

DISPLACEMENT: 1055 tons (surfaced), 1350 tons (submerged)

DIMENSIONS: 249'2" x 20'8" x 15'1"

MACHINERY: 2 diesel engines, 2 electric motors, 2 shafts. 4000 bhp/2700 shp = 18.25/13 knots

RANGE: 22,000 nm at 9 knots surfaced, 443 nm at 2 knots submerged

ARMAMENT: 4 x P-5 cruise missiles, 6 x 533mm torpedo tubes (4 bow, 2 stern), total 12 torpedoes

COMPLEMENT: 52

NOTES: These boats featured four fixed forward-firing missile launch tubes built into the large bulbous sail at a 14-degree elevation. They served in the Baltic until the late 1960s.

## PROJECT 667A [NATO YANKEE] (1966)

*K-137 Leninets* (28 August 1966), *K-140* (1966), *K-26*, *K-32*, *K-207*, *K-216* (1967), *K-210*, *K-249*, *K-253*, *K-395 Orenberg*, *K-408* (1968), *K-411*, *K-418*, *K-420*, *K-426* (1969), *K-214*, *K-219*, *K-241*, *K-245*, *K-403*, *K-415*, *K-423* (1970), *K-228*, *K-444* (1971)

BUILDER: Severodvinsk

*K-399* (1968), *K-236*, *K-389*, *K-434* (1969), *K-252*, *K-258*, *K-446*, *K-451* (1970), *K-430*, *K-436* (1971)

BUILDER: Komsomolsk

DISPLACEMENT: 7760 tons (surfaced), 9600 tons (submerged)

DIMENSIONS: 420′0″ x 38′4″ x 26′0″

MACHINERY: 2 VM-2–4 pressurized water cooled reactors, 2 geared steam turbines, 2 shafts. 52,000 shp = 15/28 knots

ENDURANCE: 70 days

ARMAMENT: 16 x R-27 ballistic missiles, 4 x 533mm torpedo tubes, 2 x 400mm torpedo tubes (all bow), total 12 plus 8 torpedoes

COMPLEMENT: 120

NOTES: This class was the first comparable to U.S. ballistic missile submarines. The D-5 system could launch the missiles in salvoes of four weapons every 20 minutes at a depth of up to 30 feet. The R-27 weapon had a range of 1500 miles carrying a single warhead. The designers paid considerable attention to obtaining high speed underwater and to reducing noise through the use of rubber and anechoic tile coating and sound-absorbent machinery mounts. Beginning in 1972 the class was upgraded under Project 667AU to launch R-27U missiles (with a range of 1875 miles and multiple warheads).

The *K-140* was converted under Project 667AM (NATO Yankee-II) in 1977 to carry twelve R-31 solid-fuel missiles that could launch much more quickly than liquid-fueled weapons but had a range of 2250 miles carrying a single warhead, about half that of the standard R-29 missile. The provisions of strategic arms limitations treaties led to the removal of ballistic missiles from the Project 667A boats. The *K-420* was converted in 1982 under Project 667M (NATO Yankee Sidecar) to carry 12 launchers for P-750 Grom (NATO SS-N-24 Scorpion) anti-ship missiles. The length increased to 502 feet and the maximum beam to 49 feet. Seven boats (the *K-236*, the *K-395*, the *K-399*, the *K-408*, the *K-415*, the *K-418*, and the *K-423*) were converted between 1986 and 1991 under Project 667AT (NATO Yankee Notch) to launch 32 RK-55 Granit (NATO SS-N-21 Sampson) land-attack cruise missiles via eight horizontal tubes. The *K-403* was converted to a special-purposes submarine with large amounts of communications and sensor equipment replacing the missile launchers, and the *K-411* became a special operations submarine to launch midget submarines.

These boats served with the Northern Fleet. The *K-219* was scuttled at sea after a major reactor accident in the Atlantic on 3 October 1986. Most of the class were withdrawn from service by 1994, although up to four may still be operational.

## SOVIET UNION: PROJECT 667B [NATO DELTA-I] (1972)
*(Courtesy of Art-Tech)*

K-279 (January 1972), K-447, K-450 (1973), K-385, K-457, K-465 (1974), K-460, K-472, K-475 (1975), K-171 (1976)

BUILDER: Severodvinsk

K-336, K-417 (1974), K-477, K-497 (1975), K-500, K-512 50 Let VLKSM (1976), K-523, K-530 (1977)

BUILDER: Komsomolsk

DISPLACEMENT: 8900 tons (surfaced), 11,000 tons (submerged)

DIMENSIONS: 456'0" x 38'4" x 27'6"

MACHINERY: 2 VM-4B pressurized water cooled reactors, 2 geared steam turbines, 2 shafts. 52,000 shp = 15/26 knots

ENDURANCE: 80 days

ARMAMENT: 12 x R-29 ballistic missiles, 4 x 533mm torpedo tubes, 2 x 400mm torpedo tubes (all bow), total 12 plus 6 torpedoes

COMPLEMENT: 120

NOTES: These boats were designed to launch the powerful R-29 missile with a range of 4875 miles carrying a single warhead, enabling them to operate without exiting the Soviet bastion area. The D-9 system could launch the entire missile load in a single salvo. The class served with the Northern and Pacific fleets and was withdrawn from service by 1997.

## PROJECT 667BD [NATO DELTA II] (1975)

*K-92* (January 1975), *K-182 Shestidesy-atiletie Velikogo Oktyabrya* (January 1975), *K-193, K-421* (1975)
BUILDER: Severodvinsk
DISPLACEMENT: 10,500 tons (surfaced), 13,000 tons (submerged)
DIMENSIONS: 506'9" x 38'4" x 28'2"
MACHINERY: 2 VM-4B pressurized water cooled reactors, 2 geared steam turbines, 2 shafts. 52,000 shp = 15/24 knots
ENDURANCE: 80 days
ARMAMENT: 16 x R-29DD ballistic missiles, 4 x 533mm torpedo tubes, 2 x 400mm torpedo tubes (all bow), total 12 plus 6 torpedoes
COMPLEMENT: 135
NOTES: These boats were an enlarged version of the previous class to accommodate four additional missiles. The upgraded R-29DD missile had a range of 5700 miles. All boats served with the Northern Fleet and were withdrawn from service beginning in 1996.

## PROJECT 667BDR [NATO DELTA III] (1976)

*K-424, K-441 26 Zvezda KPSS, K-449* (1976), *K-455, K-487, K-490* (1977), *K-44 Ryazan, K-496* (1978), *K-211, K-223 Podolsk, K-506* (1979), *K-180, K-433 Svyatoy Giorgiy Pobedonosets* (1980), *K-129* (December 1981)
BUILDER: Severodvinsk
DISPLACEMENT: 10,600 tons (surfaced), 13,000 tons (submerged)
DIMENSIONS: 508'6" x 38'4" x 28'6"
MACHINERY: 2 VM-4S pressurized water cooled reactors, 2 geared steam turbines, 2 shafts. 60,000 shp = 14/24 knots
ENDURANCE: 80 days
ARMAMENT: 16 x R-29R ballistic missiles, 4 x 533mm torpedo tubes, 2 x 400mm torpedo tubes (all bow), total 12 plus 6 torpedoes
COMPLEMENT: 130
NOTES: The principal change in this class was the installation of the D-9R system to launch R-29R missiles with a range of up to 5000 miles with three to seven multiple warheads. The class was divided equally between the Northern and Pacific fleets. One submarine was decommissioned in 1994 but the remainder may still be operational.

## PROJECT 667BDRM [NATO DELTA IV] (1985)

*K-51 Verkhotuyre* (January 1985), *K-84 Yekaterinberg* (December 1985), *K-64* (December 1986), *K-114 Tula* (September 1987), *K-117 Bryansk* (September 1988), *K-18 Karelia* (November 1989), *K-407 Novomoskovsk* (January 1991)

BUILDER: Severodvinsk

DISPLACEMENT: 11,740 tons (surfaced), 18,200 tons (submerged)

DIMENSIONS: 547'9" x 39'4" x 28'10"

MACHINERY: 2 VM-4SG pressurized water cooled reactors, 2 geared steam turbines, 2 shafts. 60,000 shp = 14/24 knots

ENDURANCE: 80 days

ARMAMENT: 16 x R-29RM ballistic missiles, 4 x 533mm torpedo tubes, 2 x 650mm torpedo tubes (all bow), total 12 torpedoes or missiles

COMPLEMENT: 135

NOTES: This class was an enlargement of the previous group to accommodate improved communications and weapons gear, including antiship missiles fired through the torpedo tubes. The R-29RM missiles have a range of 5200 miles with four warheads. The designers paid even more attention to noise reduction measures, including anechoic tile coating, rafting machinery, and a precision five-bladed propeller. Two additional boats were canceled while under construction. All these submarines joined the Northern Fleet on completion and apparently remain in service.

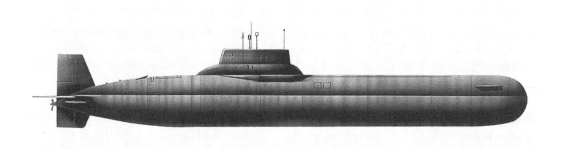

## SOVIET UNION: PROJECT 941 [NATO TYPHOON] (1980)

*(Courtesy of Art-Tech)*

*TK-208 Dmitri Donskoy* (23 September 1980), *TK-202* (26 April 1982), *TK-12 Simbirsk* (17 December 1983), *TK-13 Arkhangelsk* (21 February 1985), *TK-17* (August 1986), *TK-20 Severstal* (July 1988)

BUILDER: Severodvinsk

DISPLACEMENT: 23,200 tons (surfaced), 48,000 tons (submerged)

DIMENSIONS: 564'3" x 76'1" x 36'0"

MACHINERY: 2 OK-650 pressurized water cooled reactors, 2 geared steam turbines, 2 shafts. 100,000 shp = 12/25 knots

ENDURANCE: 120 days

ARMAMENT: 20 x R-39R ballistic missiles, 6 x 533mm torpedo tubes (bow), total 22 torpedoes or missiles

COMPLEMENT: 160

NOTES: The submarines of this class are the largest yet built anywhere in the world. The design features two parallel - full-length pressure hulls, a long missile compartment between the hulls, an attack center located beneath the sail, and a forward torpedo room. Titanium is used for the main structure, and the external casing is steel. There are very extensive sound reduction arrangements; the vessels are designed to penetrate the Arctic ice; and they have small maneuvering pods fore and aft. The R-39R missiles have a range in excess of 5000 miles and can carry up to 10 warheads. A seventh member of the class was not completed.

All boats entered the Northern Fleet on completion. Two, the *TK-202* and the *TK-17*, were decommissioned in 1997 and have been dismantled. The others remain available for service but are slated to be scrapped in the near future, since their missiles are no longer in production.

# RUSSIA
## PROJECT 955 (2006)

*Yuri Dolgorukiy* (anticipated 2006), *Aleksander Nevsky* (anticipated 2007)

BUILDER: Severodvinsk

DISPLACEMENT: 14,720 tons (surfaced), 19,400 tons (submerged)

DIMENSIONS: 557'9" x 44'4" x 28'6"

MACHINERY: 2 OK-650B pressurized water cooled reactors, 2 geared steam turbines, 2 shafts. 96,000 shp = 15/29 knots

ENDURANCE: 100 days

ARMAMENT: 12 x Bulava–30 ballistic missiles, 4 x 533mm torpedo tubes (bow), total 12 torpedoes or missiles

COMPLEMENT: 130

NOTES: This design reverted to smaller dimensions. It originally was to carry twenty improved R-39M Grom missiles, but a series of total flight failures led to the weapon's cancellation. The design was recast to accommodate 12 solid-fuel 3M14 Bulava missiles, a naval adaptation of the land-based Topol-M weapon, with a range of up to 6250 miles carrying as many as six warheads. This redesign substantially delayed progress on the new class, the first of which probably will not be complete until 2007. The Russian Navy apparently plans to commission twelve of this class by 2021, with three in service by 2010.

## UNITED KINGDOM
### *RESOLUTION* CLASS (1966)
*(Courtesy of Art-Tech)*

*Resolution* (15 September 1966), *Repulse* (4 November 1967)

BUILDER: Barrow

*Renown* (25 February 1967), *Revenge* (15 March 1968)

BUILDER: Cammell Laird

DISPLACEMENT: 7500 tons (surfaced), 8500 tons (submerged)

DIMENSIONS: 425'0" x 33'0" x 30'0"

MACHINERY: 1 PWR1 pressurized water cooled reactor, 2 steam turbines, 1 shaft. 15,000 shp = 20/25 knots

ENDURANCE: 16 x Polaris ballistic missiles, 6 x 21" torpedo tubes (bow)

COMPLEMENT: 143

NOTES: The design for the first British ballistic missile submarines essentially mated the forward and after sections of the contemporary *Valiant* class attack submarine with the missile launch compartment and control spaces of the American *Lafayette* class, supplied by the United States. Five boats were planned but construction of the fifth submarine was cancelled in 1964. From the outset these boats embarked the Polaris A-3 missile, which was upgraded in 1980 with an indigenously-developed triple independently targeted warhead as the Polaris A-3TK. These submarines decommissioned between 1992 and 1996.

## UNITED KINGDOM: *VANGUARD* CLASS (1992)
*(Courtesy of Art-Tech)*

*Vanguard* (4 March 1992), *Victorious* (29 September 1993), *Vigilant* (14 October 1995), *Vengeance* (20 September 1998)

BUILDER: Barrow

DISPLACEMENT: 14,000 tons (surfaced), 15,850 tons (submerged)

DIMENSIONS: 491'10" x 33'0" x 33'2"

MACHINERY: 1 PWR2 pressurized water cooled reactor, 2 steam turbines, 1 shaft pump jet propulsor. 27,500 shp = 18/25 knots

ENDURANCE: 16 x Trident ballistic missiles, 46 x 21" torpedo tubes (bow)

COMPLEMENT: 135

NOTES: This class was a substantial enlargement of the previous design to accommodate the larger Trident missile and a more powerful reactor. Very extensive measures were incorporated into the design to minimize noise emission while submerged. The Trident D-5 missiles were supplied by the United States under a modification to the existing Polaris sales agreement and are maintained there. The warheads are of British design, thereby eliminating American control over their use.

**UNITED STATES**
*GRAYBACK* **CLASS (1954),** *GRAYBACK*
*(Courtesy of Art-Tech)*

*Grayback* (2 July 1954), *Growler* (5 April 1957)

BUILDER: Portsmouth

DISPLACEMENT: 2287 (*Growler*—2174) tons (surfaced), 3638 (*Growler*—3387) tons (submerged)

DIMENSIONS: 322′4″ (*Growler*—317′0″) x 30′0″ x 17′4″

MACHINERY: 3 FM diesel engines, 2 Elliott electric motors, 2 shafts. 4500 bhp/5600 shp = 20/17 knots

ARMAMENT: 4 x Regulus cruise missiles, 8 x 21″torpedo tubes (6 bow, 2 stern), total 22 torpedoes

COMPLEMENT: 84

NOTES: These boats were laid down as members of the *Darter* class of attack submarines but were cut in half and lengthened on the slip to accommodate a large forward hangar for Regulus missiles and their fire control spaces. They were taken out of service as missile submarines in May 1964. The *Grayback* was converted to a transport submarine for launching special forces between 1967 and 1969, decommissioned in 1975, and stricken in 1984. A planned similar conversion to the *Growler* was canceled, apparently because of cost, and the boat laid up until it too was decommissioned in 1984.

# *HALIBUT* (9 JANUARY 1959)

BUILDER: Mare Island

DISPLACEMENT: 3846 tons (surfaced), 4995 tons (submerged)

DIMENSIONS: 350'0" x 29'6" x 20'9"

MACHINERY: 1 S3W pressurized water reactor, 2 geared steam turbines, 2 shafts. 7300 shp = 20/20 knots

ARMAMENT: 4 x Regulus cruise missiles, 6 x 21" torpedo tubes (4 bow, 2 stern), total 17 torpedoes

COMPLEMENT: 125

NOTES: The *Halibut* used the same basic design as the *Nautilus,* with the sail moved aft and a large cylindrical inclined hangar incorporated into the bow in place of the torpedo armament. The hangar was designed to accommodate four Regulus II missiles, but in practice there was space for only two Regulus II or five Regulus I weapons. The *Halibut* served with the Pacific Fleet on deterrent patrols until 1965. In 1968 it was converted to operate as a special mission submarine supporting saturation divers, oceanographic research, and intelligence operations until decommissioned in 1976 and stricken on 30 April 1986.

## UNITED STATES:
### *GEORGE WASHINGTON* CLASS (1959), *GEORGE WASHINGTON*
(*Courtesy of Art-Tech*)

*George Washington* (9 June 1959), *Patrick Henry* (22 September 1959)
BUILDER: Electric Boat
*Robert E. Lee*
BUILDER: Newport News
*Theodore Roosevelt*
BUILDER: Mare Island
*Abraham Lincoln*
BUILDER: Portsmouth
DISPLACEMENT: 5900 tons (surfaced), 6700 tons (submerged)
DIMENSIONS: 381′8″ x 33′0″ x 26′8″
MACHINERY: 1 S5W pressurized water cooled reactor, 2 geared steam turbines, 1 shaft. 15,000 shp = 16.5/22 knots
ENDURANCE: ?? days
ARMAMENT: 16 x Polaris ballistic missiles, 6 x 21″ torpedo tubes (bow), total 12 torpedoes
COMPLEMENT: 136
NOTES: The design for this class essentially inserted a missile-launching compartment into the hull of a *Skipjack*-class attack submarine. Nevertheless, contrary to much popular belief, these boats were not conversions but were laid down as ballistic missile submarines, although their construction was speeded by reallocating materials and machinery previously ordered for other attack submarines. The entire class commissioned within 1·5 months, armed with the Polaris A-1 missile (range of 1380 miles carrying a single warhead). They were refitted to operate the improved Polaris A-3 with an increased range of 2900 miles and capable of carrying up to three warheads. The *Theodore Roosevelt* and the *Abraham Lincoln* decommissioned in 1981. The *George Washington*, the *Patrick Henry*, and the *Robert E. Lee* had their missile-launching equipment removed in the early 1980s and operated as attack boats until they decommissioned between 1983 and 1985.

**UNITED STATES: *ETHAN ALLEN* CLASS (1960), *THOMAS A. EDISON* (1961)**
*(Courtesy of Art-Tech)*

*Ethan Allen* (22 November 1960), *Thomas A. Edison* (15 June 1961)
BUILDER: Electric Boat
*Sam Houston* (2 February 1961), *John Marshall* (15 July 1961), *Thomas Jefferson* (24 February 1962)
BUILDER: Newport News
DISPLACEMENT: 6900 tons (surfaced), 7900 tons (submerged)
DIMENSIONS: 419'5" x 33'0" x 27'6"
MACHINERY: 1 S5W pressurized water cooled reactor, 2 geared steam turbines, 1 shaft. 15,000 shp = 16/21 knots
ENDURANCE: more than 70 days
ARMAMENT: 16 x Polaris ballistic missiles, 4 x 21" torpedo tubes (bow), total 12 torpedoes

COMPLEMENT: 136
NOTES: This class was a more sophisticated redesign of the earlier type. They deployed with the Polaris A-2 (range 1750 miles carrying a single warhead) and refitted to launch the Polaris A-3. The *Ethan Allen, Thomas A. Edison,* and *Thomas Jefferson* decommissioned between 1983 and 1985, while the other two boats were reclassed as attack submarines and remained in service until 1991–1992.

## UNITED STATES: *LAFAYETTE* CLASS (1962), *GEORGE WASHINGTON CARVER* (1965)
*(Courtesy of Art-Tech)*

*Lafayette* (8 May 1962), *Alexander Hamilton* (18 August 1962), *Nathan Hale* (12 January 1963), *Daniel Webster* (27 April 1963), *Tecumsee* (22 June 1963), *Ulysses S. Grant* (2 November 1963), *Casimir Pulaski* (1 February 1964), *Benjamin Franklin* (5 December 1964), *George Bancroft* (5 December 1964), *James K. Polk* (22 May 1965), *Henry L. Stimson* (13 November 1965), *Francis Scott Key* (24 April 1966), *Will Rodgers* (21 July 1966)

BUILDER: Electric Boat

*James Monroe* (4 August 1962), *Henry Clay* (30 November 1962), *James Madison* (15 March 1963), *John C. Calhoun* (22 June 1963), *Von Steuben* (18 October 1963), *Sam Rayburn* (20 December 1963), *Simon Bolivar* (22 August 1964), *Lewis and Clark* (21 November 1964), *George C.*

*Marshall* (21 May 1965), *George Washington Carver* (14 August 1965)

BUILDER: Newport News

*Andrew Jackson* (15 September 1962), *Woodrow Wilson* (22 February 1963), *Daniel Boone* (22 June 1963), *Stonewall Jackson* (30 November 1963), *Kamehameha* (16 January 1965), *Mariano G. Vallejo* (23 October 1965)

BUILDER: Mare Island

*John Adams* (12 January 1963), *Nathaniel Greene* (12 May 1964)

BUILDER: Portsmouth

DISPLACEMENT: 7250 tons (surfaced), 8250 tons (submerged)

DIMENSIONS: 425′0″ x 33′0″ x 27′9″

MACHINERY: 1 S5W pressurized water cooled reactor, 2 geared steam turbines, 1 shaft. 15,000 shp = 16/21 knots

ENDURANCE: more than 70 days

ARMAMENT: 16 x Polaris ballistic missiles, 4 x 21″ torpedo tubes (bow), total 12 torpedoes

COMPLEMENT: 136

NOTES: This class represented a fully developed production version of the first generation of U.S. ballistic missile submarines. The first eight boats commissioned with the Polaris A2 missile, and all later vessels in the class deployed initially with the Polaris A-3. Beginning in 1971, the entire class was refitted to launch the Poseidon C-3 with a range of 2900 miles, carrying as many as 14 individually targeted warheads. The *Nathan Hale* was the first of the class to decommission, on 31 December 1986; the last to undertake a missile-armed patrol was the *Stonewall Jackson*, which decommissioned on 9 February 1995. Four boats, the *Sam Houston*, the *John Marshall*, the *Kamehameha*, and the *James K. Polk*, were converted into special forces transport submarines, the last of which, the *Kamehameha*, was stricken in April 2002.

**UNITED STATES: *OHIO* CLASS (1979), *PENNSYLVANIA* (1988)**
*(Courtesy of Art-Tech)*

*Ohio* (7 April 1979), *Michigan* (26 April 1980), *Florida* (14 November 1981), *Georgia* (6 November 1982), *Henry M. Jackson* (15 October 1983), *Alabama* (19 May 1984), *Alaska* (12 January 1985), *Nevada* (14 September 1985), *Tennessee*

(13 February 1986), *Pennsylvania* (23 April 1988), *West Virginia* (14 October 1989), *Kentucky* (11 August 1990), *Maryland* (10 August 1991), *Nebraska* (15 August 1992), *Rhode Island* (17 July 1993), *Maine* (16 July 1994), *Wyoming* (15 July 1995), *Louisiana* (27 July 1996)

BUILDER: Electric Boat

DISPLACEMENT: 16,764 tons (surfaced), 18,750 tons (submerged)

DIMENSIONS: 560'0" x 42'0" x 36'3"

MACHINERY: 1 S8G pressurized water cooled reactor, 2 geared steam turbines, 1 shaft. 35,000 shp = 16/25 knots

ENDURANCE: 70 days

ARMAMENT: 24 x Trident ballistic missiles, 4 x 21" torpedo tubes (bow), total 24 torpedoes

COMPLEMENT: 165

NOTES: This class was developed to take to sea a new advanced ballistic missile that materialized as the Trident. The new design incorporated much highly advanced technology for quietness, a new very powerful reactor, and a 50 percent increase in the number of its missile load. The result was the largest submarine in the world until the advent of the Soviet Project 941 in 1980. The first eight boats deployed with the Trident C-4 missile, with a range of 4600 miles and carrying up to eight warheads. The final 10 vessels took the Trident D-5 (range in excess of 4600 miles) to sea. The *Ohio,* the *Michigan,* the *Florida,* and the *Georgia* decommissioned as ballistic missile submarines between 2002 and 2004 and began conversion to guided missile boats capable of launching up to 154 Tomahawk cruise missiles and deploying special forces, a program slated to complete in 2006. The *Henry M. Jackson,* the *Alabama,* the *Alaska,* and the *Nevada* began refitting to launch the Trident D-5 in 2001, completing the operation in 2006.

# GLOSSARY

**Admiralty:** Shorthand terminology for the Royal Navy's Board of Admiralty, which heads its central administration. Unlike most such boards, it includes both the civilian political appointees and the professional heads of the fleet.

**Air Lock:** A watertight compartment through which a diver may pass between a submarine and the sea, pausing within it while the air pressure is equalized with the external environment.

**Ballast Tank:** A tank that may be filled or emptied of water to increase or decrease a boat's displacement.

**Ballast Tank, Saddle:** Ballast tank mounted outside the main structure of the hull, named by analogy with saddlebags.

**Bridge:** The ship's navigating and control station.

**Bulge:** Structures built onto a ship's side beyond the primary hull structure. Initially these were used to enhance protection against damage from a torpedo hit but they came to be employed more to enhance stability by increasing a hull's internal volume.

**Casing:** A light non-pressure-resistant structure designed to improve submarine performance and/or enhance personnel access on the surface.

**Catapult:** A device for launching aircraft into the air.

**Conseil Superieur:** The French Navy's professional leadership.

**Conning Tower:** Navigation station outside the main hull.

**Convoy:** A group of merchant vessels traveling together under escort.

**Depth Charge:** An explosive charge detonated at a preset depth.

**Diving Planes:** Horizontal control surfaces used to move a submarine in a vertical plane.

**Drop-Collar:** A mechanical arrangement suspending a torpedo that may be release remotely.

**Dynamite Gun:** A gun using compressed air as propellant for its missile, which had a dynamite explosive charge.

**General Board:** The professional leadership of the United States Navy until 1948.

**Horsepower**

**Brake Horsepower (bhp):** The measure of the power output of internal combustion engines.

**Indicated horsepower (ihp):** The measure of the power output of reciprocating steam engines.

**Shaft Horsepower (shp):** The measure of the power output of turbine engines.

**Machinery Types**

**Diesel:** Internal combustion engines using oil fuel and compression ignition.

**Triple Expansion:** Reciprocating steam engines using multiple cylinders to maximize steam usage.

**Turbine:** Engines that use the passage of steam or hot gases to rotate encased fan blade assemblies to generate power.

**Magazine:** Stowage space for munitions.

**Mine:** An underwater explosive charge.

**Monitor:** A small shallow draft vessel carrying heavy guns, primarily intended for shore bombardment.

**Pressure Hull:** The main body of a submarine that is reinforced to withstand water pressure.

**Radar:** Electronic location equipment, initially for search only but rapidly developed to provide gunnery control and missile guidance.

**Radome:** A protective enclosure for a radar antenna.

**Sail:** Streamlined superstructure containing conning stations.

**Sheer:** The shape of the top of a ship's hull as viewed from the side.

**Sonar:** Acoustic detection equipment for locating submarines.

**Spar Torpedo:** A warhead attached to a pole or spar, allowing it to project ahead of the attacking vessel.

**Submarine:** A vessel that normally operates submerged. Usually also used to describe any vessel that may operate underwater, even for a limited period.

**Submersible:** A vessel that normally operates on the surface but may be submerged controllably at will.

**Superstructure:** All a ship's structure above the hull's sheer.

**Topweight:** The component of the ship's weight that is above its center of gravity.

**Torpedo:** Self propelled underwater weapon.

**Torpedo, Acoustic:** A torpedo that that is self-guided toward the sound of a target's propellers.

**Torpedo, Homing:** A torpedo that is self-guided to its target by emissions (usually sonic).

**Torpedo, Wire-guided:** A torpedo guided to its target by an operator on the launching vessel using signals transmitted through a trailing wire.

**Torpedo Pistol, Contact:** Torpedo detonator that uses contact with its target for initiation.

**Torpedo Pistol, Magnetic:** Torpedo detonator that used its target's magnetic field for initiation.

**Torpedo Tube:** Tube for launching torpedoes, usually by the pressure of introduced compressed air, a ram, or by allowing the torpedo to exit under its own power (swim-out tube).

**Trim Tank:** Small tank used for fine adjust of a submarine's depth and inclination.

**Variable Pitch Propeller:** A propeller whose blades may be twisted to vary their angle according to power needs.

## Warship Types

**Battlecruiser:** A battleship type that trades armor protection for higher speed.

**Corvette:** A small low-speed escort vessel.

**Cruiser, Armored:** A cruising warship type used until the first quarter of the 20th century that depended on an armored belt for its main protection.

**Cruiser, Heavy:** A cruiser armed with 8-inch guns.

**Cruiser, Light:** A cruiser armed with 6-inch or smaller guns.

**Cruiser, Protected:** A cruising warship type used until the first quarter of the 20th century that depended on an armored deck for its main protection.

**Destroyer:** A relatively small, fast, multi-role warship, originally designed to defend against torpedo boats but later also used for surface torpedo attack and antiaircraft and antisubmarine defense.

**Dreadnought:** A battleship armed primarily with eight or more very large caliber guns.

**Escort Carrier:** A small aircraft carrier primarily operating antisubmarine aircraft.

**Frigate:** A more sophisticated development of a corvette.

**Pre-Dreadnought:** A battleship usually armed with four large caliber guns and a substantial secondary armament.

**Q-ship:** A commissioned warship disguised as a merchant vessel carrying concealed weapons used to attack submarines induced to surface.

**Sloop:** A sophisticated antisubmarine and antiaircraft escort vessel.

**Torpedo Boat:** A small fast vessel, originally for attack with torpedoes but later often used as a fast antisubmarine vessel.

# BIBLIOGRAPHY

Akermann, Paul, *Encyclopaedia of British Submarines 1901-1955*, Penzance: Periscope Publishing, 2002.

Alden, John D. *The Fleet Submarine in the U.S. Navy: A Design and Construction History.* Annapolis: Naval Institute Press, 1979.

Antier, Jean-Jacques. *L'Aventure Heroïque des Sous-Marins Français (1939–1945).* Paris: Editions Maritimes and d'Outre-Mer, 1984.

Bagnasco, Erminio. *I Sommergibili della Seconda Guerra Mondiale.* Parma: Ermanno Albertelli Editore, 1973.

Baker, A. D., III, ed. *The Naval Institute Guide to Combat Fleets of the World.* Annapolis: Naval Institute Press, various editions from 1976 to date (editions from 2005 edited by Eric Wertheim).

Baker, A. D., III, ed. *German Naval Vessels of World War Two: Compiled by US Naval Intelligence.* Annapolis: Naval Institute Press, 1993.

Beloff, Max. *The Foreign Policy of Soviet Russia, 1929–1941.* London: Oxford University Press, 1949.

Berman, Robert P., and John C. Baker. *Soviet Strategic Forces: Requirements and Responses.* Washington, DC: Brookings Institution, 1982.

Bethge, Hans-Georg. *Die Brandtaucher: Ein Tauchboot-Von der Idee zur Wirklichkeit.* Rostock: Hinstorff Verlag, 1968.

Blair, Clay. *Silent Victory: The U.S. Submarine War Against Japan.* New York: Bantam Books, 1976.

Blair, Clay. *Hitler's U-Boat War: The Hunters, 1939–1942.* New York: Random House, 1996.

Blair, Clay. *Hitler's U-Boat War: The Hunted, 1942–1945.* New York: Random House, 1998.

Blechman, Barry M., and Stephen S. Kaplan, eds. *Force without War: US Armed Forces as a Political Instrument.* Washington, DC: Brookings Institution, 1978.

Boyd, Carl and Akahiko Yoshida, *The Japanese Submarine Force in World War II,* Annapolis: Naval Institute Press, 1995.

Breyer, Siegfried, and Norman Polmar. *Guide to the Soviet Navy.* Annapolis: Naval Institute Press, various editions from 1970 to 1991 (later editions Norman Polmar only).

Brown, David K., ed. *Conway's History of the Ship: The Eclipse of the Big Gun: The Warship 1906–45.* Annapolis: Naval Institute Press, 1992.

Brown, David K., ed. *The Grand Fleet: Warship Design and Development 1906–1922.* Annapolis: Naval Institute Press, 1999.

Brown, David K., ed. Nelson *to* Vanguard: *Warship Design and Development 1923–1945.* Annapolis: Naval Institute Press, 2000.

Brown, David K., and George Moore, *Rebuilding the Royal Navy: Warship Design since 1945.* Annapolis: Naval Institute Press, 2003.

Busch, Harald. *U-Boats at War.* New York: Ballantine Books, 1955.

Cable, James. *Gunboat Diplomacy: Political Uses of Limited Force.* London: Macmillan, 1981.

Cable, James. *Britain's Naval Future.* Annapolis: Naval Institute Press, 1983.

Cable, James. *Navies in a Violent Peace.* London: Macmillan, 1989.

Carpenter, Dorr, and Norman Polmar. *Submarines of the Imperial Japanese Navy.* Annapolis: Naval Institute Press, 1986.

Cocchia, Aldo. *The Hunters and the Hunted.* Annapolis: Naval Institute Press, 1958.

Compton-Hall, Richard. *Submarine Warfare—Monsters & Midgets.* Poole: Blandford Press, 1985.

Compton-Hall, Richard. *Sub vs. Sub: The Tactics and Technology of Undersea Warfare.* New York: Orion Books, 1988.

Cowie, J. S. *Mines, Minelayers and Minelaying.* London: Oxford University Press, 1949.

Daniel, Donald C. *Anti-Submarine Warfare and Superpower Strategic Stability.* Urbana: University of Illinois Press, 1986.

Dönitz, Karl. *Memoirs: Ten Years and Twenty Days.* Cleveland: World Publishing, 1957.

Dull, Paul S. *A Battle History of the Imperial Japanese Navy (1941–1945).* Annapolis: Naval Institute Press, 1978.

Evans, David C. *The Japanese Navy in World War in the Words of Former Japanese Naval Officers.* Annapolis: Naval Institute Press, 1982.

Evans, David C., and Mark R. Peattie. *Kaigun: Strategy, Tactics, and Technology in the Imperial Japanese Navy, 1887–1941.* Annapolis: Naval Institute Press, 1997.

Everitt, Don. *K Boats: Steam-Powered Submarines in World War I,* London: George C. Harrap and Company, 1963.

Fayle, C. Ernest. *Official History of the Great War: Seaborne Trade.* 3 vols. plus map vol. London: John Murray, 1920–1924.

Field, Cyril. *The Story of the Submarine from the Earliest Ages to the Present Day.* London: Low, Marston and Company, 1908.

Friedman, Norman. *U.S. Naval Weapons: Every Gun, Missile, Mine and Torpedo Used by the U.S. Navy from 1883 to the Present Day.* Annapolis: Naval Institute Press, 1982.

Friedman, Norman. *Submarine Design and Development*. Annapolis: Naval Institute Press, 1984.

Friedman, Norman, ed. *U.S. Army-Navy Journal of Recognition, September 1943–February 1944, Numbers 1–6*. Annapolis: Naval Institute Press, 1990.

Friedman, Norman, ed. *Conway's History of the Ship: Navies in the Nuclear Age*. Annapolis: Naval Institute Press, 1993.

Friedman, Norman. *U.S. Submarines Since 1945: An Illustrated Design History*. Annapolis: Naval Institute Press, 1994.

Friedman, Norman. *U.S. Submarines Through 1945: An Illustrated Design History*. Annapolis: Naval Institute Press, 1998.

Fukui Shizuo. *Nihon no gunkan: waga gijutsu no hattatsu to kantei no hensen [Japanese Warships: Our Development of Ship Construction Technology and Changes over Time]*. Tokyo: Shuppan Kyodosha, 1959.

Fukui Shizuo. *Japanese Naval Vessels at the End of the War*. Old Greenwich, CT: We, 1970.

Fukui Shizuo. *Shashin Nihon kaigun zen kantei shi [A Photographic History of All the Ships in the Japanese Navy]*. 3 vols. Tokyo: Best Sellers, 1994.

Gardiner, Robert, ed. *Conway's All the World's Fighting Ships, 1922–1946*. London: Conway Maritime Press, 1980.

Gardiner, Robert, ed. *Conway's All the World's Fighting Ships, 1906–1921*. London: Conway Maritime Press, 1985.

Gardiner, Robert, ed. *Conway's All the World's Fighting Ships, 1947–1995*. London: Conway Maritime Press, 1995.

Garier, Gerard. *L'Odyssée Technique et Humaine du Sous-Marin en France*. 4 vols. Bourg en Bresse: Marines Editions, 1998–2004.

Gibson, R. H., and Maurice Prendergast. *The German Submarine War 1914–1918*. London: Constable and Company, 1931.

Grant, Robert M. *U-Boat Intelligence: Admiralty Intelligence Division and the Defeat of the U-Boats, 1914-1918*, Penzance: Periscope Publishing, 2002.

Grant, Robert M. *U-Boats Destroyed: The Effect of Antisubmarine Warfare, 1914-1918*, Penzance: Periscope Publishing, 2002.

Grant, Robert M. *U-Boat Hunters: Code Breakers, Divers and the Defeat of the U-Boats, 1914-1918*, Penzance: Periscope Publishing, 2003.

Gray, Edwyn. *The Devil's Device: Robert Whitehead and the History of the Torpedo*. Annapolis: Naval Institute Press, 1991.

Gray, Edwyn. *19th Century Torpedoes and Their Inventors*. Annapolis: Naval Institute Press, 2004.

Greger, Réné. *The Russian Fleet 1914–1917*. London: Ian Allan, 1972.

Gröner, Erich, Dieter Jung, and Martin Maass. *German Warships 1815–1945*. Vol.II: *U-Boats and Mine Warfare Vessels*. Annapolis: Naval Institute Press, 1991.

Grove, Eric. *Vanguard to Trident: British Naval Policy since World War II*. Annapolis: Naval Institute Press, 1987.

Hackmann, Willem. *Seek & Strike: Sonar, Anti-Submarine Warfare and the Royal Navy.* London: HMSO, 1984.

Halpern, Paul G. *The Naval War in the Mediterranean, 1914–1918.* Annapolis: Naval Institute Press, 1987.

Hargis, Robert, *US Submarine Crewman 1941-1945,* Oxford: Osprey Publishing, 2003.

Hashimoto, Mochitsura. *Sunk!* New York: Henry Holt and Company, 1954.

Herrick, Robert Waring. *Soviet Naval Strategy: Fifty Years of Theory and Practice.* Annapolis: Naval Institute Press, 1968.

Herrick, Robert Waring. *Soviet Naval Theory and Policy: Gorshkov's Inheritance.* Newport, RI: Naval War College, 1988.

Holmes, W. J. *Undersea Victory: The Influence of Submarine Operations on the War in the Pacific.* Garden City, NJ: Doubleday and Company, 1966.

Holmes, W. J. *Double-Edged Secrets.* Annapolis, MD: Naval Institute Press, 1979.

Hool, Jack and Keith Nutter, *Damned Un-English Machines: A History of Barrow-Built Submarines,* Stroud: Tempus Publishing, 2003.

Hovgaard, William. *Modern History of Warships.* London: E. and F. N. Spon, 1920.

Huan, Claude. *Les Sous-Marins Français 1918–1945.* Bourg en Bresse: Marines Editions, 2004.

Hurd, Archibald. *History of the Great War: The Merchant Navy.* 3 vols. London: John Murray, 1921–1927.

Huwart, Olivier. *Sous-Marins Francais, 1944–1954: La Décennie de Renouveau.* Bourg en Bresse: Marines Editions, 2003.

Ienaga, Saburo. *The Pacific War, 1931–1945.* New York: Pantheon Books, 1978.

Ireland, Bernard. *Warships of the World: Major Classes.* New York: Charles Scribner's Sons, 1976.

Ito, Masanori, with Roger Pineau. *The End of the Imperial Japanese Navy.* New York: W. W. Norton and Company, 1956.

Jane, Fred T. *The Imperial Russian Navy: Its Past, Present and Future.* London: W. Thacke, 1904.

Jentschura, HansGeorg, Dieter Jung, and Peter Mickel. *Warships of the Imperial Japanese Navy 1869–1945.* Annapolis: Naval Institute Press, 1977.

Jordan, John. *Soviet Submarines, 1945 to the Present.* London: Arms and Armour Press, 1989.

Kaplan, Stephen S., ed. *Diplomacy of Power: Soviet Armed Forces as a Political Instrument.* Washington, DC: Brookings Institution, 1981.

Kaufman, R. G. *Arms Control during the Pre-Nuclear Era: The United States and Naval Limitations between the Two World Wars.* New York: Columbia University Press, 1990.

Kemp, Paul. *The Russian Convoys 1941–45.* London: Arms and Armor Press, 1987.

Kemp, Paul. *Malta Convoys 1940–43.* London: Arms and Armor, 1988.

Kohl, Fritz and Eberhard Rössler, *The Type XXI U-Boat,* London: Conway Maritime Press, 2002.

König, Paul. *The Voyage of the* Deutschland. New York: Hearst International Library, 1916.

Konstam, Angus, *Confederate Submarines and Torpedo Vessels 1861-1865,* Oxford: Osprey Publishing, 2004.

Korzh, Viktor, *Red Star under the Baltic: A Firsthand Account of Life on Board a Soviet Submarine in World War 2.* London: Pen & Sword, 2005.

Krause, Guenther. *U-Boot und U-Jagd.* East Berlin: Military Publishing House, 1984.

Kruska, Emil and Eberhard Rössler, *Walter U-Boote,* Munich, J.F. Lehmanns Verlag, 1969.

Labayle-Couhat, Jean. *French Warships of World War II.* London: Ian Allan, 1971.

Labayle-Couhat, Jean. *French Warships of World War I.* London: Ian Allan, 1972.

Lake, Simon. *The Submarine in War and Peace: Its Development and Its Possibilities.* Philadelphia: Lippincott, 1918.

Lake, Simon. *Submarine: The Autobiography of Simon Lake.* New York: D. Appleton-Century Books, 1939.

Lambert, John, and David Hill. *The Submarine* Alliance. London: Conway Maritime Press, 1986.

Largess, Robert P., and James L. Mandelbaum. Albacore: *Forerunner of the Future.* Portsmouth, NH: Portsmouth Marine Society, 1999.

Leary, William M. *Under Ice: Waldo Lyon and the Development of the Arctic Submarine.* College Station: Texas A&M University Press, 1999.

Lehman, John F. *Command of the Seas: Building the 600 Ship Navy.* New York: Charles Scribner's Sons, Macmillan, 1988.

Le Masson, Henri. *The French Navy.* Vol. II. Garden City, NJ: Doubleday, 1969.

Le Masson, Henri. *Du* Nautilus *(1800) au* Rédoutable. Paris: Presses de la Cité, 1969.

Lenton, Henry T. *German Submarines.* Garden City, NJ: Doubleday, 1967.

Lenton Henry T., *British Submarines.* Garden City: Doubleday, 1972.

Lenton Henry T., *American Submarines.* Garden City: Doubleday, 1973.

Lenton Henry T., *German Warships of the Second World War.* London: Macdonald & Janes, 1975.

Lenton Henry T. & J.J. Colledge, [British & Commonwealth] *Warships of World War II.* London: Ian Allan, 1973.

Louzeau, B. *Les Sous-Marins Français: Les Bateaux Noirs* Paris: Editions Etai, 1999.

MacConnell, James, and Bradford Dismukes, eds. *Soviet Naval Diplomacy.* New York: Pergamon Press, 1979.

Marston, Daniel, ed. *The Pacific War Companion: From Pearl Harbor to Hiroshima.* London: Osprey Publishing, 2005.

McGwire, Michael, and John MacDonnell, eds. *Soviet Naval Influence: Domestic and Foreign Dimensions.* New York: Praeger, 1977.

Meister, Jürg. *Soviet Warships of the Second World War.* London: Macdonald and Janes, 1977.

Merrill, John, and Lionel D. Wyld. *Meeting the Submarine Challenge: A Short History of the Naval Underwater Systems Center.* Washington, DC: Government Printing Office, 1997.

Messimer, Dwight D. *The Merchant U-Boat.* Annapolis, MD: Naval Institute Press, 1988.

Messimer, Dwight D. *Find and Destroy: Antisubmarine Warfare in World War I.* Annapolis, MD: Naval Institute Press, 2001.

Messimer, Dwight D. *Verschollen: World War I U-Boat Losses.* Annapolis, MD: Naval Institute Press, 2002.

Miller, David. *U-Boats: The Illustrated History of the Raiders of the Deep.* Washington, DC: Brassey's, 2000.

Moller, Eberhard, and Werner Brack. *The Encyclopedia of U-Boats from 1904 to the Present.* London: Greenhill Books, 2004.

Moore, John E. *Warships of the Royal Navy.* Annapolis, MD: Naval Institute Press, 1979.

Naval Historical Center. *Dictionary of American Naval Fighting Ships.* 9 vols. Washington, DC: Government Printing Office, 1954–1991.

Niestlé, Axel, *German U-Boat Losses During World War II: Details of Destruction,* London: Greenhill Books, 1998.

O'Connor, Raymond. *Perilous Equilibrium: The United States and the London Naval Conference of 1930.* Lawrence: University of Kansas Press, 1962.

Orita, Zenji, with Joseph D. Harrington. *I-Boat Captain.* Canoga Park, CA: Major Books, 1976.

Paterson, Lawrence. *U-Boat War Patrol: The Hidden Photographic Diary of U-564.* London: Greenhill, 2004.

Paterson, Lawrence. *Hitler's Grey Wolves: U-Boats in the Indian Ocean.* London: Greenhill Books, 2004.

Pavlov, A. S. *Warships of the USSR and Russia, 1945–1995.* Annapolis, MD: Naval Institute Press, 1997.

Pollina, Paolo M., and Marcello Bertini. *I Sommergibili Italiani 1895–1971.* Rome: Ufficio Storico Marina Militare, 1971.

Polmar, Norman. *Atomic Submarines.* Princeton, NJ: D. Van Nostrand, 1963.

Polmar, Norman. *The Naval Institute Guide to the Ships and Aircraft of the U.S. Fleet,* 12th–18th Editions. Annapolis, MD: Naval Institute Press, 1981–2005.

Polmar, Norman. *The Death of the USS* Thresher. New York: Lyons, 2001.

Polmar, Norman, and Thomas B. Allen. *Rickover: Controversy and Genius.* New York: Random House, 1982.

Polmar, Norman, and Jurrien Noot. *Submarines of the Russian and Soviet Navies, 1718–1990*. Annapolis, MD: Naval Institute Press, 1991.

Polmar, Norman, and K. J. Moore. *Cold War Submarines: The Design and Construction of U.S. and Soviet Submarines*. Washington, DC: Brassey's, 2004.

Ring, Jim. *We Come Unseen: The Untold Story of Britain's Cold War Submarines*. London: John Murray, 2001.

Robertson, Terence. *The Golden Horseshoe: The Wartime Career of Otto Kretschmer, U-Boat Ace*. London: Greenhill Books, 2006.

Rohwer, Jürgen, *Allied Submarine Attacks of World War II: European Theatre of Operations, 1939-1945*, London: Greenhill Books, 1997.

Rohwer, Jürgen. *Axis Submarine Successes of World War Two: German, Italian and Japanese Submarine Successes, 1939–1945*. London: Greenhill Books, 1999.

Roland, Alex. *Underwater Warfare in the Age of Sail*. Bloomington: University of Indiana Press, 1978.

Roskill, Stephen W. *The War at Sea, 1939–1945*. 3 vols. in 4. London: Her Majesty's Stationery Office, 1956–1961.

Roskill, Stephen W. *Naval Policy between the Wars*. 2 vols. in 1. New York: Walker, 1968.

Rössler, Eberhard. *The U-Boat: The Evolution and Technical History of German Submarines*. Annapolis, MD: Naval Institute Press, 1981.

Rössler, Eberhard. *Die Torpedos der Deutschen U-Boote*. Herford: Koehlers Verlagsgesellchaft, 1984.

Rössler, Eberhard. *Die Unterseebootee der Kaiserlichen Marine,* Munich: Bernard & Graefe, 1997.

Ruge, Friedrich. *Der Seekrieg: The German Navy's Story 1939–1945*. Annapolis, MD: Naval Institute Press, 1957.

Sapolsky, Harvey M. *The Polaris System Development*. Cambridge: Harvard University Press, 1972.

Showell, Jak P. Mallmann. *U-Boats under the Swastika*. London: Ian Allen, 1973.

Silverstone, Paul H. *U.S. Warships of World War II*. London: Ian Allan, 1965.

Silverstone, Paul H. *U.S. Warships of World War I*. London: Ian Allan, 1970.

Silverstone, Paul H. *U.S. Warships since 1945*. Annapolis, MD: Naval Institute Press, 1987.

Sleeman, C. W. *Torpedoes and Torpedo Warfare: Containing a Complete and Concise Account of the Rise and Progress of Submarine Warfare also a Detailed Description of All Matters Appertaining Thereto, including the Latest Improvements*. Portsmouth, NH: Griffin and Co., 1880.

Smith, Gaddis. *Britain's Clandestine Submarines, 1914–1915*. New Haven: Yale University Press, 1964.

Society of Naval Architects of Japan. *Plans of Ships of the Imperial Japanese Navy: History of Shipbuilding in the Showa Era.* Tokyo: Hara Shobo Company, 1975.

Spinardi, Graham. *From Polaris to Trident: The Development of US Fleet Ballistic Missile Technology.* New York: Cambridge University Press, 1994.

Stefanick, Tom. *Strategic Antisubmarine Warfare and Naval Strategy.* Lexington, MA: D.C. Heath, 1987.

Stumpf, David K. *Regulus: The Forgotten Weapon.* Paducah, KY: Turner Publishing, 1996.

Tomitch, V. M. *Warships of the Imperial Russian Navy.* San Francisco: B. T. Publishers, 1968.

Treadwell, Terry C. *Submarines with Wings: The Past, Present and Future of Aircraft-Carrying Submarines.* London: Conway Maritime Press, 1985.

Tritten, James John. *Soviet Naval Forces and Nuclear Warfare.* Boulder, CO: Westview Press, 1986.

U.S. Navy. *Historic Ship Exhibits in the United States.* Washington, DC: Government Printing Office, 1969.

U.S. Strategic Bombing Survey. *The Campaigns of the Pacific War.* Washington, DC: Government Printing Office, 1946.

Vego, Milan. *The Soviet Navy Today.* London: Arms and Armour Press, 1986.

Watson, Bruce W. *Red Navy at Sea: Soviet Naval Operations on the High Seas, 1956–1980.* Boulder, CO: Westview, 1982.

Watson, Bruce W., and Peter M. Dunn, eds. *The Future of the Soviet Navy.* Boulder, CO: Westview, 1986.

Watts, A. J., and B. G. Gordon. *The Imperial Japanese Navy.* London: Macdonald, 1971.

Weir, Gary E. *Forged in War.* Washington, DC: Naval Historical Center, 1993.

White, John F. *U-Boat Tankers 1941–1945: Submarine Suppliers to Atlantic Wolf Packs.* Annapolis, MD: Naval Institute Press, 1998.

Williamson, Gordon, *Grey Wolf: U-Boat Crewman of World War II,* Oxford: Osprey Publishing, 2001.

Wilson, Michael. *Baltic Assignment: British Submarines in Russia, 1914–1919.* London: Leo Cooper, 1985.

Wynn, Kenneth. *U-Boat Operations of the Second World War.* 2 vols. London: Chatham Publishing, 1997.

# WEBSITES

BritSub: www.britsub.net

Dutch Submarines: www.dutchsubmarines.com

Federation of American Scientists: www.fas.org

(French Submarines) Sous-Marins Français:
   http://perso.orange.fr/sous-marin.france

GlobalSecurity.org: www.globalsecurity.org/military/index.html

Haze Gray & Under Way (U.S. Navy Submarines): www.hazegray.org

Imperial Japanese Navy Page: www.combinedfleet.com/kaigun.htm

Israeli Submarines: www.dolphin.org.il

The Italian Navy's official site:
   www.marina.difesa.it/sommergibili/index.htm

Italian submarines in World War II:
   www.regiamarina.net/subs/index.htm

Italian submarines from World War II to the present:
   www.sommergibili.com/indexen.htm

Jan-Erik Thoft's Submarines (Swedish Submarines): www.submarines.nu

John Philip Holland and His Submarines: http://www.geocities.com/
   Pentagon/Barracks/1401/index.html

Naval Historical Center: www.history.navy.mil

Norwegian Submarine History: http://home.c2i.net/geisaksen/history.htm

Simon Lake Website: www.simonlake.com

Spanish Submarine Navy history: www.submarinos.net

Submarine Heritage Center, Barrow-in-Furness:
   www.submarineheritage.com

Submariners Association, Barrow-in-Furness: www.submariners.co.uk

Turkish Submarine History:
   http://geocities.com/Pentagon/Bunker/7704/battle.html

Ubåtsvapnet 100 År (Swedish Submarines): www.ubatsvapnet100.com

U-Boat Net: www.uboat.net

Unterseeboote der Kaiserlichen Marine (Austro-Hungarian Submarines):
   www.u-boot-net.de

# INDEX

# ABOUT THE AUTHOR

PAUL E. FONTENOY, Ph.D., is curator of maritime research and technology at the North Carolina Maritime Museum in Beaufort, NC, and a visiting assistant professor in the maritime studies program at East Carolina University, Greenville, NC. His published works include *The Sloops of the Hudson River, Aircraft Carriers: An Illustrated History of Their Impact,* and more than 100 articles on naval and maritime history topics.